EMILE DURKHEIM:
Contributions to
L'Année Sociologique

EMILE DURKHEIM:
Contributions to
L'Année Sociologique

Edited with an Introduction by
YASH NANDAN

Translated by John French, Andrew P. Lyons,
Yash Nandan, John Sweeney, Kennerly Woody

THE FREE PRESS
A Division of Macmillan Publishing Co., Inc.
NEW YORK

Collier Macmillan Publishers
LONDON

THE FREE PRESS
A Division of Macmillan Publishing Co., Inc.
866 Third Avenue, New York, N. Y. 10022

Collier Macmillan Canada, Ltd.

Library of Congress Catalog Card Number: 79-54670

Printed in the United States of America

printing number
1 2 3 4 5 6 7 8 9 10

Library of Congress Cataloging in Publication Data
Durkheim, Emile, 1858-1917.
    Emile Durkheim, contributions to L'Année sociologique.

    Includes bibliographical references and indexes.
    1. Sociology. 2. Sociology--Book reviews.
3. Année sociologique. I. Nandan, Yash.
II. Année sociologique, III. Title. IV. Title:
Contributions to L'Année sociologique.
HM55.D848   1980   301   79-54670
ISBN 0-02-907980-2

To the late Talcott Parsons

a "scholarch" in his own right
a respected teacher
a genuine humanist
a true friend and follower of Durkheim
whose enthusiasm, support, and encouragement
prompted us in this undertaking and made possible
this presentation to English-speaking scholars

L'Année sociologique is taking up all my time.

—*Durkheim in a letter to Lucien Lévy-Bruhl*
7 *April 1900*

Do not pity me for the little time that I devote to *L'Année sociologique*. Since I have the evidence that everybody has been attached to *L'Année sociologique* and that the group thus formed has not been without homogeneity and solidarity, I find that the best thing I can do for it is to give it all the time I can spare from my professional obligations. In fact, you must understand that this is the first group of its kind which is organized, where there is a division of work and true cooperation. Therefore if we are able to hold out, we will be setting a good example. It is also the best way of stimulating sociological activity. Let each of us contribute little by little and it will produce results. Furthermore, there is no doubt that without our realizing it, the moral condition of sociology is going to be changed in France. Soon a decision will be made involving the opinion between good workers and otherwise. And we will have contributed something, a great deal toward this result.

—*Durkheim in a letter to Célestin Bouglé*
13 *June 1900*

First of all, I am very much indebted to you for this act of solidarity, moral effect of which, I hope, will be considerable. All the services that we are able to render most seriously show that in sociology there are workers who are mostly preoccupied in their unity to cooperate. By distinguishing themselves they are manifesting their originality.

—*Durkheim in a letter to Célestin Bouglé*
13 *August 1901*

M. Durkheim, who continues to take up the largest part of the work, is known to have gathered around him some hardworking and eminent workers, whom he inspires, or better said, who are inspired by him. In a way *L'Année sociologique* is the organ of an authentic school whose orientations are well defined, especially with respect to methods. These orientations are manifested either in the *Mémoires originaux,* in the joint criticisms posited in the reviews of books, or in the "introductions" placed at the top of certain divisions of the bibliography.

—*Edmond Goblot in a review of*
L'Année sociologique

If *L'Année sociologique* could make its contribution, however slight, by turning good minds in this direction, we would feel no remorse over our difficulties.

—*Durkheim in a preface to*
L'Année Sociologique

Contents

About the Contributors   *xii*

Periodicals Used by Durkheim as Sources of
Reviews in L'Année   *xiii*

Preface   *xv*

Editor's Introduction   1
    L'Année Sociologique and the Durkheimian
    School: Toward a Systematic Theory of
    Doctrinal Schools   1
    Durkheim as "Scholarch"   5
    The Essence of Durkheim's Doctrines   13
    Disciples and Followers: Formation, Growth, and
    Consolidation of the Durkheimian School   21
    Disseminating Doctrines: *L'Année Sociologique* 34
    Organization and Scope of This Edition   42

DURKHEIM'S CONTRIBUTIONS

Prefaces to *L'Année Sociologique*   47

Section One: General Sociology*   59
    General Conceptions and Methodological Issues:
    Philosophical, Historical, and Psychological   64
    Social Theories   93
    Social Psychology   102
    Sociological Conditions of Knowledge   106

Section Two: Religious Sociology (not included)

Section Three: Juridic and Moral Sociology   111
    General Conceptions, Theories, and
    Methodological Issues   119

* Sections and their numerical order suggested here conform to *L'Année* organization.

Juridic and Moral Systems   162

Domestic Organization   163

    The Family   163   Marriage   234   Sexual
    Morality   299

Social Organization   305

Political Organization   341

International and Moral Law: Laws and Customs of
Different Societies   359

Penal Law, Responsibility, and Procedure   362

Property Law   379

Contract and Obligation   391

Section Four: Criminal Sociology and Statistics
          on Morals   399

  General Concepts   403

  Statistics on Morals   411

    Domestic and Conjugal Life: Marriage
    and Divorce   411   Suicide   434
  Criminal Sociology   440

    Social Factors in Crime and Immorality   440

    Special Forms of Crime   441   Crime Accord-
    ing to Countries   444   Juvenile Crime   466

Section Five: Economic Sociology   447

  Regimes of Production   447

Section Six: Social Morphology (not included)

Section Seven: Miscellaneous   449

  Aesthetic Sociology   450

  Education   451

Editor's and Translators' Notes   455

List of Durkheim's Contributions Included   491

Appendix A: History of the Durkheimian School as
           Revealed through Publications of
           Periodicals (in Chronological Order)   499

Appendix B: Members of the Durkheimian School and
Their Contributions to *L'Année*   501

Appendix C: Classification of the Members of the
Durkheimian School   504

Name Index   507

Subject Index   511

About the Contributors

John French, after receiving his A.B. and M.A. from Williams College and Teachers College (Columbia University) in 1931 and 1932 respectively, went to Paris, where he studied at the Sorbonne and received a certificate in teaching French as a foreign language. After receiving his Ph. D. in romance languages (French belles-lettres) from Princeton University in 1961, he became assistant professor and eventually professor at Rider College, where he has been professor emeritus since 1971.

Andrew P. Lyons received his B.A. in law from Oxford University in 1966 and his D. Phil. in social anthropology in 1974. His interests include the history of anthropology and the anthropology of religion. He is assistant professor of anthropology at Wilfrid Laurier University, Waterloo, Ontario.

Yash Nandan, assistant professor of sociology at Rider College, studied under Raymond Aron and received his doctorate at the Sorbonne in 1974. Professor Nandan specializes in sociological theory and the history of sociology; his publications include *L'Ecole durkheimienne et son opus* (C.N.R.S., Paris); *The Durkheimian School: A Systematic and Comprehensive Bibliography* (Greenwood Press), and *Emile Durkheim's Letters* (General Hall, forthcoming). Presently he is working on a study entitled *The Durkheimian School, 1880–1940.*

John Sweeney, assistant dean at Atlantic Community College, received his M.A. from The Catholic University of America and his doctorate from L'Institut Supérieur de Philosophie, Université de Louvain.

Kennerly Woody, a former Fulbright scholar, received his master's degree and doctorate from Columbia University for his dissertation on a topic in medieval church history. After teaching for several years at Columbia University and several other colleges, Professor Woody joined Princeton University in 1970 as a bibliographer of history and religion. Professor Woody's publications include (with Professor J. H. Mundy) a book entitled *Council of Constance* (New York: Columbia University Press, 1961) and several articles in a number of scholarly journals.

Periodicals Used by Durkheim as Sources of Reviews in *L'Année*

American Journal of Sociology
Annales de l'Institut International de
   Sociologie
Annales des sciences politiques
Annales internationales d'histoire
Annals of the American Academy of
   Political and Social Science
Antropologia criminale e scienze penali
Archives d'anthropologie criminelle
Beiträge zur alten Geschichte
Bulletin de l'Académie Royale de Bel-
   gique. Classe des Lettres
Bulletin de l'Institut Général Psycholo-
   gique
Folklore
Giornale degli economisti
Globus
Jahrbuch der internationale Vereinigung
   für vergleichende
   Rechtswissenschaft und volkswirt-
   schaftslehre
Jahrbuch für Gesetzgebung, Verwaltung
   und Volkswirtschaftslehre (also called
   Schmollers Jahrbuch)
Jahrbucher für klassische Philologie
Journal de la Société de Statistique de
   Paris
Journal of the American Oriental Society

Die Neue Zeit
Nouvelle Revue historique de droit fran-
   çais et étranger
Recueil de travaux relatifs à la philo-
   logie et à l'archéologie égyptiennes
   et assyriennes
La Révolution française: revue d'histoire
   contemporaine
Revue de métaphysique et de morale
Revue générale du droit, de la législation
   et de la jurisprudence
Revue historique
Revue philosophique
Revue trimestrielle de droit civil
Rivista di diritto penale e sociologia
   criminale
Rivista italiana di sociologia
Rivista scientifica del diritto
Rivista sperimentale di freniatria e medi-
   cina legale delle alienazioni mentali
Sitzungsberichte der Kaiserlichen
   Akademie der Wissenschaft in Wien,
   philosophisch-historische Klasse
Vierteljahrsschrift für wissenschaftliche
   Philosophie und Soziologie
Zeitschrift für Sozialwissenschaft
Zeitschrift für vergleichende Rechtswis-
   senschaft

Preface

With the completion of *Le Suicide* in 1897, Durkheim turned his attention toward the launching of *L'Année sociologique,* a publication intended to serve as an instrument in providing the international community of social scientists with an annual picture of the progress being made in sociology. As Durkheim elaborated on the aims and scope of *L'Année* in the first two years after its inception, he realized that the emerging corps of sociologists who formed the mainstay of his following needed suggestive ideas and guidelines on which to premise their further research, drawn from the more advanced areas with which the discipline had already established some kind of nexus. The primary aim of *L'Année* was to cultivate, with the collaboration of young scholars, a new scientific sociology, and to disseminate these new theoretical paradigms through the conduit of *L'Année.*

L'Année sociologique consisted of book reviews from all fields of study: general sociology, social theories, social psychology, law, morals, and criminal sociology, to mention a few. Durkheim himself reviewed hundreds of books in *L'Année.* His collaborators added many more to this already tremendous list, bringing the total number of contributions to several thousand—these ranging from mere bibliographic references to more comprehensive and methodic reviews.

In choosing books to review in *L'Année,* Durkheim and his followers were meticulous and scrupulous. Sociologists, during the *belle époque* dominated by Durkheim and his associates, were much more oriented toward history than are contemporary sociologists. Given this proclivity to historicism and ethnology, *L'Année* embodied a formidable array of works identified as sociology. At the same time, its arcana revealed a wealth of information and discoveries in a variety of areas in sociology, especially valuable to historical sociology. There were certain fields of study deemed unsuitable for review, such as historical biographies and strictly metaphysical works, because they did not promote substantive scientific discussion. Despite these rules of thumb to guide them, the Durkheimians were not always sure and successful in adopting the right book for review that would have befitted Durkheim's characterization of sociology.

The selection process in adopting books for *L'Année* required contacts with the librarians and a thorough search of catalogues and periodical literature. By bringing to their attention and facilitating their search for recently published books, the librarian at the Ecole Normale Supérieure, Lucien Herr, rendered a yeoman's service to the Durkheimians. Durkheim himself used to receive books from the publishers and even from the authors themselves to review. Upon their arrival, Durkheim distributed them to the specialists in charge of a section or subsection, thus relegating the task of reviewing books to his *équipe*. He also brought their attention to the recently published material which merited examination. Fulfilling the responsibilities of an editor, Durkheim read almost every piece submitted to him for inclusion in *L'Année*. Should there be need for revision or deletions, he returned it to the author, or he himself performed the necessary editorial tasks.

To promote a systematic approach to sociology, and to foster a scientific sociology, Durkheim and his collaborators arranged the reviews with a distinct form of classification in mind. Since scientific sociology was still in its incipient stages of development, the system of classification Durkheim devised was essentially derived from Comtian theories of social statics—or social structure—in sociology, consisting of such well-established divisions as religion, property, family, and language. The system consisted of three major divisions: general sociology, social physiology, and social morphology. The confluence and synthesis formed by philosophy, history, and psychology provided a general frame of reference for sociology. Social physiology was a broad category like Comtian statics, defined as a corpus which included particular social sciences—e.g., religion, politics, law, and economics. Constituting a neologism, "social morphology" resulted from Durkheim's reflections on the synthesis of demography and what during his days was popularly known as "Anthropo-geographie," a Ratzellian improvisation for human geography. Today, many sociologists look askance at this representation of social reality, for it lacks the Comtian suggestive idea of social dynamics.

In the ordering of the classification, Durkheim placed religious sociology at the top of the other divisions of social physiology, thus giving religion preeminent status. Durkheim considered religion the most rudimentary and most primitive—as well as the original—source of all social institutions. Durkheim and his associates took pains in emphasizing that in the classification divised for *L'Année,* the section on religious sociology had priority over all other particular areas of the social sciences.

L'Année sociologique benefited from the progress made in the areas of social science, moral statistics, religion, history, and aesthetics; it also aimed to reciprocate in potlatch fashion in extending its benefits to them. Durkheim was successful in this exchange, for the periodical proved useful not only to specialists closely identified with sociology but also to those in academic areas remote from it, such as archaeology, aesthetics, sinology, Egyptology, and pedagogy. Still more rewarding was the exchange between history and sociology, even though practitioners of the former were methodologically more ethnocentric and to their disadvantage confined themselves to the history of particular periods and the nationalism of particular countries. *L'Année* earned its universal reputation as the most unique publication in the entire history of sociology for having been a repository of books in the major Western languages, and for devising a classification system of sociology which made a permanent impression and guided the activities of those who collaborated with Durkheim.

Before the publication of this volume, a major part of Durkheim's entire work had already been translated into English. However, Durkheim's contribution to *L'Année*—consisting of several hundred reviews, notes, and notices of books, introductions to sections and subsections, and some of his seminal articles known as *Mémoires originaux*—still remained untranslated. In addition, there still remain several articles written by Durkheim in his early life as a sociologist and some odds and ends. A few articles by Durkheim have been translated twice, perhaps thrice. This is due in part to the expedient publication program of the Durkheimian scholars and in part due to the suspicion, at times justifiable and at times unjustifiable, harbored by some of the sociologists concerning adequate and accurate translation of Durkheim. Several translations of a single piece and of a master's works are not uncommon, since each successive generation of scholars has its own criteria, standards, values, and *Weltanschauung*.

Even though sociologists are catching sight of Durkheim's early opuscules, their neglect of Durkheim's magnum opus, *l'Année*, was enough to evoke empathy from a sociologist with the master who dedicated more than fifteen years of his life to this periodical, which soon after its publication became an institution and spawned an authentic and systematic school of thought in sociology—the French school. Scholarly apathy of sociologists toward Durkheim's *Année* incited us to turn our immediate attention to this project. By editing and publishing Durkheim's contribution to *L'Année* with the collaboration of several helpful and competent colleagues with genuinely scholarly orientations and scientific concerns, we are fulfilling a deeply felt gap in the history of French sociology and responding to the need of sociologists.

The real repository of scientific sociology with its classification developed and practiced in its pristine form, and that of Durkheim's true legacy manifested in the collaborative work of the master's loyal, indefatigable, and sacrificing disciples and followers, is *L'Année*, a periodical which spawned Durkheim's school of sociology. What is known to sociologists and anthropologists is that Durkheim wrote some of the most profound and seminal articles for *L'Année;* what is perhaps, however, not known to them is that the "scholarch" of the French school also reviewed the works of some of the eminent and dominating scholars and specialists of this time: Kohler, Ratzel, Spencer and Gillen, Glotz, Tarde, Ribot, Höffding, Westermarck, Lang, Frazer, Marianne Weber (Max Weber's wife), Boas, Wundt, and Hartland. Durkheim has no parallel in reviewing the works of so many great scholars of his time. By publishing this edition of Durkheim's *L'Année*, we will be drawing attention to this monumental enterprise.

These reviews by Durkheim, now that they are available in English translation, will hopefully open new areas of research in sociology and anthropology, and will elicit new interest in Durkheimian thought. They will answer some of the questions sociologists are raising today; but different questions will be posed in the light of these translations. For example, if Durkheim knew Marianne Weber, whose work he reviewed and severely criticized on scientific grounds, what does it mean in terms of his relationship with Max Weber? Durkheim is known for his invention and cultivation of "social morphology" as an area of sociology, but what influence did Ratzel have on Durkheim's characterization of this new division of sociology? If *The Elementary Forms of Religious Life* constitutes his greatest work and manifests vividly his inspiration, how much does Durkheim owe for borrowing from Spencer and Gillen's scholarly work and ethnographic study of the Australian tribes? Perhaps this edition will open a new perspective in sociology, i.e., sociology of knowledge through reviews and references.

Professor Talcott Parsons, a true friend and a follower of Durkheim, gave us the honor of entrusting us with the delicate but important task of rendering Durkheim into English. The undertaking meant a great responsibility, including accountability to our two great masters, Durkheim and Parsons. We hope we have lived up to the great tradition of our masters and to their great expectations in terms of faithful and standard rendition of Durkheim. The encouragement we received from Charles Smith of the Free Press further accelerated the progress being made in the completion of the project.

A major part of the translation in this volume is the unremitting work of Professor John French, whose devotion to Durkheim made it possible for us to present to the English-speaking audience Durkheim's total contribution to *L'Année*. The cooperation I received from Professors Andrew Lyons, John Sweeney, and Kennerly Woody is no less significant.

Dr. Woody, who has been a constant source of inspiration in my work, read my introduction to this volume and made critical observations transcending style and touching upon the subtleties of the subject matter. Sometimes it becomes difficult to separate distinctly my personal editorial work from Dr. Woody's assistance in explaining in our notes Durkheim's esoteric terms and his cumbersome thought couched in historical erudition. Professors Lewis Coser and Harry Alpert also read the Introduction and made helpful suggestions on the substance of my arguments. Professor John Fine (Princeton) helped in clarifying some of the Greek terms used by Durkheim in the *Année* volumes.

There is no substitute for a demanding and meticulous but sympathetic and conscientious editor with whom an author is obliged to cooperate for the creation of an intellectually sound and important publication. By improving on the style and by suggesting some very valuable organizational changes, Kitty Moore has given this publication an aesthetic touch that it obviously needed.

On the home front I cannot dissociate the completion of this work—or for that matter, my other works—from my wife and best friend Jeffra, who worked in unison with me on many facets of this project. At the collegial level, her suggestions helped at every stage of the work in progress. Gita and Ravi, our two wonderful and beautiful children, helped by being themselves, cuddly, helpful, and understanding by forsaking some of their playtime and many weekends and leaving their daddy in his "yoke."

Indeed, it is a pleasure to acknowledge my previous publisher, Greenwood Press, for the permission to incorporate in this volume Appendices A to C from my previous publication, *The Durkheim School,* 1977. I also wish to thank the Centre National de la Recherche Scientifique to reprint two passages in the front matter from Durkheim's letters to Bouglé, which appeared in *Revue française de sociologie,* 17, 1976, pp. 173–74, 178. Lastly, but not the least, I would like to thank Ms. Janet Williams for her patience and for her invaluable assistance.

Editor's Introduction

L'Année Sociologique and the Durkheimian School: Toward a Systematic Theory of Doctrinal Schools

Neither Durkheim as the master of a school nor his magnum opus, *L'Année Sociologique*, has been explored fully, despite a plethora of literature in sociology analyzing Durkheim's work. Since 1975 my own work has been devoted exclusively to this neglected aspect of the great master of sociology.[1] The English edition of Durkheim's contribution to *L'Année*, presented herewith, is a byproduct of that unremitting effort to bring the unknown or less well known Durkheim to the attention of English-speaking scholars. Since my own undertaking began, increasing numbers of sociologists have been mining this rich and neglected vein of Durkheim's work.[2] *L'Année* is now in the forefront of the sociological literature on Durkheim and will occupy scholars for many years to come.

Presentation of Durkheim's *L'Année* is quite coincidental with an upsurge of literature on his most important area of work: creating and conducting an authentic school of sociology. Since *L'Année* represents that Durkheimian school, it behooves us to search for the connections between the two and to present *L'Année* as the repository of the Durkheimian school.

In order to synthesize *L'Année* with the Durkheimian school and also present the latter as a reality sui generis, I have developed a theory after reflecting upon the universal category of "doctrinal schools." This theory constitutes the most elementary form of sociological epistemology. Since the Durkheimian school is an example of that universal category, it may be examined in the light of my theory.

1

The sociology of the growth of knowledge has long been neglected by those interested in the history of science. Although the group behavior of scientists—or "community of scientists," to use Kuhn's popular terminology—has been given due attention, the sociological reality of doctrinal schools has gone almost unnoticed.

Since the theory presented here has a general character, it is hoped that its application will help us to understand the genetic growth of knowledge embedded in a myriad of "doctrinal schools," or systematic schools of thought, throughout the history of human civilization. The history of the growth of knowledge is one encompassing the flourishing and withering away of doctrinal schools and of their polemics against each other.

Systematic schools of thought may be defined either in the strict sense or in a broad sense. A school in the strict sense comprises a master who virtually conducts the school by gathering around him disciples and followers. Such a doctrinal school is a cohesively organized group whose members are united by intimate personal and professional relationships. The structural hierarchy is manifested in the recognized leadership of the master, who is either the founder of the school or a legatee of the founder, and the school often takes its name from that of the master, as in the Durkheimian school and some of the Greek philosophical schools.

A school in a broad sense is formed in the name of a doctrine, method, or concept shared by scholars from diverse geographic areas and backgrounds. In such a school there may be a conspicuous absence of personal relations among the disciples and followers. Instead, a powerful and cogent doctrine attracts individuals who derive their inspiration from it, who use it in their work, and who identify themselves with the heritage of the system of thought. Examples of such schools include Newtonian physics, Weberian sociology, Marxism, surrealism, rationalism, existentialism, and positivism. These are essentially intellectual movements; the histories of philosophy, religion, art, literature, and the natural sciences are cluttered with their names and ideas.

As shown throughout history, schools of systematic thought are phenomena of universal character and are the depositories of knowledge, having given impetus to further growth of knowledge in the form of commentaries, explications, compendia, and contentious literature. It behooves us to posit in general terms those essential postulates that characterize a school. The theory I shall propose constitutes four essential elements, two of which tend to explain the genesis of knowledge and thought, while the other two attempt to resolve those issues that concern further growth.[3] The four postulates constitute the integral part of the systematic theory that will subsequently be used to explain the establishment and growth of the Durkheimian school.

First of all, in the process of forming a doctrinal school there is, at the head, a richly endowed personality who may be referred to as the "scholarch."[4] In classical antiquity the scholarch was an enlightened individual with a high sense of moral obligation to instruct and edify his fellow citizens.

Typically, such a master had formulated a synthesis of religious, ethical, philosophical, and artistic ideas that presented a comprehensive view of the world and human experience. This synthesis elicited a characterization of the external world and took cognizance of the ethical principles upon which the society should rest.

After the founder's death, the leadership of a school is inherited by one of his disciples, who in classical times was also called a scholarch. For example, Plato, Aristotle, Zeno of Citium, and Epicurus were some of the established and recognized scholarchs who founded the Academy, the Peripatetic school, stoicism, and Epicureanism respectively. The progenitors of the Indian philosophical systems are known as *rsis* and the commentators as *acharyas*. There are similar suggestive expressions in Chinese classical philosophy: The "sage," *Hsien-jen,* takes upon himself the role of a "master," *Hsien-sheng,* and of a "teacher," *fu-tzu.*⁵

The masters of uncanny abilities, dubbed scholarchs, were possessed of a profound capacity to comprehend other synchronous systems. But they were far from accepting systems other than their own, let alone seeking a syncretism of conflicting doctrines. Socrates was familiar with the doctrines of nature of his time, but he did not accept them as realistic schemas for explaining the universe. Aristotle referred to his predecessors and their doctrines only to refute them. The scholarchs built their doctrines on the ashes of older doctrines, by refuting and contradicting them. Through their polemics, they created new trends in art, literature, philosophy, and science. In support of this claim, Karl Pearson said that the founding of a new science, or even a new branch of one, "must be done by someone who, by force of knowledge, of method and of enthusiasm, hews out, in rough outline it may be, but decisively, a new block, and creates a school to carve out its outlines."⁶

The second constituent element of the theory of doctrinal schools is the doctrine itself. A doctrine may exist independently or as a result of the master who invented it. Although the boundary between an independent doctrine and one created by a scholarch may appear hazy, the distinction is important. For example, it would be a mistake to claim that Max Weber created the school of rational doctrine or that Karl Marx gathered around him disciples who adhered to Marxism. Although such a school of thought derives its name from its creator, it cannot be characterized as a school in the strict sense, despite the fact that the doctrines it propagates perform the same functions in the history of thought—providing an articulation of a coherent system, constructing a sort of formula to explain the whole or part of reality.

From a doctrinal point of view the institutionalization of a school depends upon three salient factors: the extensive use of doctrine in the personal works of its founder, disciples, and followers to evince its explicative powers; the extensive use of the doctrine by adversaries of the school to refute and reject the claims made about it by its proponents; and the tenacity of the doctrine.

Doctrine in itself is a very significant element because it induces a vast literature in the form of commentaries, explications, expositions, reinterpretations, and refutations. The actual content of a doctrine comes to be expressed in a particular vocabulary and style of writing. Particular forms of expression are especially prominent in schools of art and literature, but jargon is also characteristic of certain schools of science, philosophy, and social science.

The third constituent of the theory of doctrinal schools is the formation of a corps of followers and adherents. What motivates disciples, followers, and collaborators to rally around a master? For some, it is a genuine albeit naive belief of a seeker whose search for truth brings him in personal contact with an accomplished master. A disciple derives psychological as well as spiritual gratification by identifying himself with a movement of historical significance: e.g., a doctrinal school of philosophy, a system of thought in science, a religious crusade, or a political ideology based on a doctrine. One's ideological predisposition also plays a great role in identification with a particular doctrine even though it may not offer any immediate material rewards. Sometimes the talismanic powers presumably possessed by a doctrine may be inculcated in one's mind even before one acquires full consciousness of one's actions.

In some schools discipline of one kind or another is as much observed as in a religious order or in modern political parties. Independence of followers' conduct may be admitted, but also some severe limitations may be imposed upon their behavior. In any case, no one enjoys unlimited privilege to violate the decorum of sharing certain fundamental principles. Faced with the constraint of the "collective conscience," some adherents may voluntarily withdraw and others may be forced out. Some continue their nominal association with the school and express their token allegiance to the master and his doctrines, but they do not conceal their reservations about them. The so-called crypto-partisans of the school prefer to follow the master independently and privately. If the doctrine is possessed of strong powers to explicate reality, the school continues to attract the talents of successive generations, suggesting its full growth. In this process of renovation and regeneration, the school discards any undesirable members—heretics, apostates, dissenters, deviants, and those who are ambivalent.

Despite the fact that there may be many disciples desirous of inheriting the master's mantle, only one disciple is in fact the heir. In Greek philosophic tradition the scholarch decreed in his will the name of his successor. In all probability, the disciple who is personally closest to the master and spiritually closest to his doctrines inherits the leadership. In some cases, when the school is deprived of a leader, an ad hoc committee takes up the responsibility for its operations; or the system that has survived so far begins to crumble.

The strength of a doctrine is its ability to explicate reality. The master, his disciples, his followers, and his collaborators are suggestive elements of a formal structure that can be arranged in a hierarchic order. Beyond this, there is a physical structure, representing institutions that serve as the depository and conservatory of knowledge; it provides those necessary means through which knowledge is diffused and disseminated, and thus constitutes the fourth postulate of the theory.

The Academy, the Lyceum, the Stoa, and the Cynosarges were the principal seats of the Greek sects and schools. During those ancient times the means of disseminating doctrines were personal and face-to-face. The scholarchs indulged in discourses, dialogues, debates, and discussions. Writing as a means of preserving and disseminating knowledge was in its most primitive stage. To overcome this disadvantage the Indian philosophers made use of a few concise words and posited their "wisdom" in aphorisms. This device was useful as a mnemonic technique in passing on the doctrines to the next generation. Since those primitive times, humanity has made gigantic strides in science and technology, which have radically transformed the institutional character of our contemporary civilization. Whereas earlier the Academy, the Lyceum, the Stoa, and the Cynosarges used to be places from which the scholarchs delivered their discourses and promulgated their doctrines, now we have an established and intricate network of universities, institutes, laboratories, and foundations. The enormous increase in the number and membership of professional societies and associations, whose origin may be traced back to the British Royal Society and the Académie des Sciences, is unprecedented. They are, nonetheless, structured after their ancient Greek prototypes.

The development and expansion of printing has completely revolutionized the circulation of ideas. Publishing houses and periodical literature have tremendously facilitated the task of a master in the diffusion of facts and theoretical knowledge. Now that the subject of physical structure has been introduced, a doctrinal school of thought may be installed in a university, a laboratory, a publishing house, or a professional society—or it may even be formed around a periodical. The master may recruit disciples, followers, and collaborators from within institutions of higher learning, but the channels through which the doctrines are disseminated are books and periodical literature.

In sum, these physical facilities and material resources that apparently function as catalysts in the growth of knowledge and the diffusion of ideas may be designated as means of the communication and propagation of doctrines.

Durkheim as "Scholarch"

The man of knowledge who creates a strong and cogent doctrine is the first desideratum in the formation of a doctrinal school. Recognized as the sire of French scientific sociology, Durkheim also clearly possessed the attributes of a master of a school. As early as 1893, when Durkheim successfully defended his doctoral thesis, the commentator on his thesis, Lucien Muhlfeld, divined in him a future *maître*.[1] With the publication of *L'Année,* Durkheim appeared incontrovertibly as the master of the French school of sociology, a fact well recognized by the academicians of Paris.

To understand Durkheim's development as a scholarch it will be useful to place his life and work in a chronological perspective so that one can see the distinct stages in his career. They are as follows:

1. Early reviews and opuscules, 1885–1890.
2. Theoretical maturation and formulation of doctrines, 1891–1897.
3. Formation, growth, and consolidation of his school, 1898–1913.
4. Period of life and work *pro patria,* 1914–1917.

The first period of Durkheim's career as a sociologist began in 1885 with an address to high school students and ended in 1890 with a critical review of Ferneuil's work, *Les Principes de 1789 et la science sociale.* In this period Durkheim produced eight book reviews, four of which were reviews of books by German authors, one of a Belgian work, and three of French works; one review article in which he examined several works by different authors; two inaugural lectures; two long articles on the German social sciences and on the subject of morals; a presentation to the French of Albert Schaeffle's economic program, which has socialistic underpinnings; and an article on suicide and natality.[2] Although many of these earlier works have gone relatively unnoticed, the germs of all Durkheim's sociological doctrines, which he would later develop in his important works, were posited within their pages.

From the very beginning of his career, Durkheim was greatly influenced by the works of German savants and scientists. He admired their accomplishments in the fields of philosophy, the social sciences, and morals. Schaeffle was the first German savant to captivate Durkheim's youthful mind.[3] His work was representative of German ideals—a moralizing spirit in philosophy, science, and ethics. Through Schaeffle's influence Durkheim seems to have become imbued with the idea of society as a superior force, an object sui generis, and a source of collective conscience and solidarity. Durkheim went so far in his zeal for the reification of society that he apotheosized it. Durkheim concluded his review of Schaeffle's work by stating that the German scholar and scientist "has strong faith in reason and in the future of humanity. In addition, he is calm and serene in his analysis, nothing disturbs him. One does not experience those fears, those vague anxieties, which are so familiar to our time. Today his optimism, even in France, is rarely seen. We have begun to realize that not everything is clear and that reason has not cured all the illnesses"[4] of society.

The same theme from Schaeffle's work and the same didactic lesson for sociology that he had learned from the German scientist were repeated in a review of Fouillée's work, *La Propriété sociale et la démocratie.*[5] In his review of Gumplowicz's introductory work in sociology, Durkheim maintained the same attitude but lamented that sociology, originally a French invention and of French origin, had become an émigré in Germany.[6]

After Durkheim had spent a leave of absence in Germany, from 1885 to 1886, he wrote two articles which are the most important and revealing of this period. In these articles he made an excellent presentation of the philosophical systems, social sciences, and ethics flourishing in the German universities at that time. He found that the German social sciences, philosophy, and ethics manifested two distinct directions: scholars working either independently or as dogmatists who attracted disciples and followers of their own. With regard to French philosophy and social sciences, he found it deplorable that the "different philosophers who teach in the university system have almost nothing in common, neither in doctrines nor"—and this he found very serious—"in method." [7] His admiration for the German style of scholarship is evident in this statement: "However, it is hardly contestable that the thing which we most urgently need at this moment is to awaken in us the taste for the collective life." [8] In his second article on the status of the German social sciences and ethics, Durkheim seemed to be captivated by the philosophy of social realism and a notion of morals that could be applied to the social sciences. [9] From Durkheim the philosopher emerges Durkheim the moralist. He went so far as to claim that the science of morals was an independent science with an existence of its own.

After his sojourn in Germany, Durkheim returned to France with the ideas of general economics as it was being practiced and professed by the "socialists of the chair." [10] At this early stage of his life, he rejected the concept of utilitarian ethics, an offshoot of the Manchester school. Instead he preferred the practice of moral ideas of the economists, who belonged to the "younger" historical school. Also reflected in this article is Durkheim's conception of the "social science" sociology that he formed through his introduction to German ideas. Wundt's influence upon Durkheim is also apparent, since he accepted the classification of sociology according to the method of Wundt's *Völkerpsychologie*. At this very incipient stage of his career, Durkheim was convinced that the ideas of *Völkerpsychologie* could be helpful in solving moral problems, in bringing about social solidarity, and in achieving a state of "collective conscience." In these two articles, we perceive the first glimmerings of Durkheim's doctrines, those that he would utilize in his lifetime and would use as major premises in later works.

In 1887, at about the same time that Durkheim's two articles on the German social sciences appeared, the position of *chargé d'un cours de science sociale*—the first in France—was created for him at Bordeaux[11] so that he could teach sociology in the guise of social science. This recognition of sociology was the result of reforms in higher education introduced by Louis Liard. Liard, one of the architects of the Third Republic and a powerful figure in the administration of higher education, was motivated by two aims: to thwart the German monopoly of the social sciences and to honor and institutionalize a science that was native to France.

At Bordeaux Durkheim assisted Alfred Espinas, a senior sociologist, and taught courses in pedagogy and the social sciences. He was known at the university for his "distinguished mind" and the "unsurpassed clarity" of his ideas. In his teaching, he referred his students to the precursors of sociology, from Aristotle to Comte. It is at this point that he appealed to his students as well as his colleagues to rally around him and help him develop the young science of sociology, whose structure he aimed to build slowly and gradually.[12] It was here, at Bordeaux, that Durkheim, with imposing authority and through personal supervision, educated and disciplined his nephew and protégé Marcel Mauss. (Mauss would later officiate in the *Année* office and act as Durkheim's alter ego.) In these surroundings, Durkheim attracted some malleable and responsive students from his vast audience and oriented them toward sociology. He recruited Lalo, Fauconnet, and some other disciples to lay the initial foundation for his school.

The appointment of Durkheim to the newly created position at Bordeaux not only ushered in a new age for the young science of sociology but was also an important step in Durkheim's development as a recognized scholarch. During the last quarter of the nineteenth century, Bordeaux enjoyed equal prestige with Paris in some of its academic disciplines—in philosophy and in other departments of the *faculté de lettres.* An appointment at Bordeaux was a necessary stepping-stone for those professors and scholars who sought status in Paris. Durkheim, if he proved worthy, could step up from this initial position to a more prestigious position in Paris.

In 1887, after his return from Germany and appointment at Bordeaux, Durkheim reviewed Guyau's book entitled *L'Irréligion de l'avenir,* which laid the foundation for his religious sociology. From Guyau, whose work contained clues to the art of polemics, Durkheim learned how to refute the ideas of others. Although the year 1912, when Durkheim published *The Elementary Forms,* * is far removed from 1887, these two dates have one thing in common: Durkheim in his opuscule in 1887 and in his opus in 1912 refuted the definitions of religion given by the English savants who were identified with either naturalism or spiritualism.

In 1888 Durkheim published two of his inaugural lectures, one of which was an introduction to the social sciences.[13] In this lecture, Durkheim announced his intention to found a science of sociology. The second inaugural lecture dealt with the sociology of the family,[14] which would remain one of his primary interests in *L'Année.*[15]

Durkheim was intrigued with the practice of dualism in sociology. In 1889 he reviewed Toennies' celebrated work, *Gemeinschaft und Gesellschaft,* agreeing with the author's dichotomy: community versus society. This dichotomy reflected the structure of contemporary society as well as its evolution. Through this eminent German sociologist, Durkheim was introduced to the practical concern of moralizing—in particular, since the German scholar em-

---

* *The Elementary Forms of Religious Life: A Study in Religious Sociology* (New York: Macmillan, 1915), translated by J. W. Swain from *Les Formes élémentaires de la vie religieuse: le système totémique en Australie* (Paris: Alcan, 1912).

phasized such concepts as *Gemeinsinn* (sense of solidarity) and *Verständnis* (consensus). In his first major work, *The Division of Labor,** Durkheim uses Toennies' dichotomous conceptualization of society; however, he reversed the order. Whereas Toennies considered "organic" solidarity to represent the "primitive" social structure of European society, Durkheim identified it with the structure of contemporary industrial society. Contrary to Toennies' terminology, Durkheim's "mechanical" solidarity represented the "primitive" society. These differences between the two great sociologists notwithstanding, Durkheim was trying to retrieve from Germany what had been taken from France and to rehabilitate the positive science of sociology in its native country. Yet the rudimentary ideas underlying the new science, as Durkheim conceived it, were posited in the German *Sozialwissenschaften* and *Völkerpsychologie.*

During this period Durkheim's view of the revolution of 1789 also became apparent. After his review of Ferneuil's *Les Principes de 1789 et la science sociale,* Durkeim provided a sociological interpretation of the French revolution and appraised its moral significance.[16] First of all, in his review of Ferneuil's work, Durkheim made scathing attacks on those moralists and philosophers who had exalted the "intransigencies" of individualism. Secondly, he felt that the revolution had a moral lesson for the scientist: society, in a state of "anomie," Durkheim admonished, required a new base in order to acquire solidarity.

This formative period in Durkheim's sociological life may be summed up in the following terms: First, Durkheim was searching for new morals for a society whose structure had been shattered. France was undergoing a period of economic growth and was converting its economic base from agrarian to industrial. Different strata of society were acquiring their own new types of consciousness. Some revolutionary movements were gaining force. Thus, in the face of revolutions in various sectors of French society—industrial, social, scientific, and so on—Durkheim the moralist wanted to heal the wounds inflicted upon the society by these "anomic" changes. His search for a new collective conscience and a new form of solidarity was not in vain, although his efforts to find moral elements to preserve the fabric of society and to reintegrate the individual into society inevitably made him a conservative sociologist.

Second, the restructuring of the moral fiber of society required a profound understanding of its institutions. The moralists and philosophers, like Comte and Durkheim, in order to solve the problems facing society, wanted to discover its laws first—those that explained its "statics and dynamics," to use Comtian terminology. The task of discovering social laws was assigned to *physique sociale,* as Comte first labeled it, or to the science of sociology, as Durkheim called it later. Scientific sociology, these thinkers felt, was alone competent to fulfill the newly imposed task of discovering the laws of society.

---

* *The Division of Labor in Society* (New York: Macmillan, 1933), translated by G. Simpson from *De la division du travail social: Etude sur l'organisation des sociétés supérieures* (Paris: Alcan, 1893; 2d ed. with new preface, 1902).

In this drive to advance the ideas of a new science and postulate a new morality, Durkheim was influenced by the German scholars, whose accomplishments in these areas had been extraordinary. Nevertheless, building a new science on their foundations would be a stupendous project. Durkheim alone would not be able to assemble the research already done in social sciences, put it together, and convert it into a comprehensive science of sociology. Therefore, he sought the collaboration of his colleagues and students. However, the germs of his major original contributions—as well as his penchant for dogmatism—were apparent during this first period.

During the second period of Durkheim's career, from 1891 to 1897, he posited his major doctrines, producing three major works: *The Division of Labor, The Rules,* * and *Suicide.*† In the eyes of many sociologists, Durkheim's fame rests on these three works and on *The Elementary Forms,* published in 1912. In addition to these important works, Durkheim also published part of his doctoral thesis in Latin, wrote three review articles on French books, and five articles on other assorted topics,[17] one of which was originally published in Italian.[18] Some portions of *Suicide* were translated and published in Italian periodicals.

The works of this period epitomize the essential doctrines of Durkheim the scholarch, including scientism, positivism, sociologism, and societism. Durkheim appeared as a master of French sociology, soon to form a school of his own. He had fulfilled the second requirement of the theory of doctrinal schools by positing his doctrines; now all that was left was the formation of a core of disciples and followers to analyze and popularize his work. It was during the third period that he attracted a group of responsive disciples and followers.

By any account, the third period in Durkheim's career stands out as the most important, rewarding, and productive of his life. It corresponds with the publication of *L'Année* (original series); and it was the period of formation, growth, and consolidation of the Durkheimian school.

In 1902 Durkheim was installed at the University of Paris. It was upon his arrival in Paris that the scope of his activities greatly increased. A vast opportunity for disseminating his doctrines was made available to him, because besides being a powerful and influential figure at the University of Paris he also taught at the Ecole Normale Supérieure.[19]

In welcoming Durkheim, the Sorbonne was opening its portals to the young science of sociology, which had once been derided by Paul Janet and some like-minded Sorbonnists. When Hubert Bourgin described Durkheim's

---

* *The Rules of Sociological Method,* edited and with an introduction by G. E. G. Catlin (Chicago: University of Chicago Press, 1938; reprint, New York: Free Press, 1950), translated by S. A. Solovay and J. H. Mueller from *Les Règles de la méthode sociologique* (Paris: Alcan, 1895; revised and enlarged edition with new preface, 1901).

† *Suicide: A Study in Sociology,* edited with an Introduction by G. Simpson (New York: Free Press, 1951), translated by J. A. Spaulding and G. Simpson from *Le Suicide: Etude de Sociologie* (Paris: Alcan, 1897).

arrival in Paris, he made it perfectly clear that a school had already been formed under Durkheim's aegis. While reminiscing about the Ecole Normale Supérieure in *De Jaurès à Léon Blum,* he said: "The sociological school, even when it consisted of only one man, was already a school. Its master, Durkheim, was not prepared to risk seeing the chit-chat of university common rooms distract him from his functions, a task, a mission which it—or rather he—held sacred."[20] Bourgin further affirmed that Durkheim the scholarch was not "a man of deviations, of deflections, of adventures and of compromises."[21]

Controversy over Durkheim's doctrines reached a peak during this period. They were the subjects of debates, discussions, and refutations by his adversaries and opponents. Attacks on the doctrines appeared in professional and scientific periodicals as well as in religious journals. To defend himself, Durkheim wrote letters to the editors, the most important of which were responses to the criticisms of Tarde[22] and Deploige.[23]

Some of the stormiest confrontations took place in the discussions of the Société Française de Philosophie (French Philosophical Society)[24] and the Union pour la Vérité (Union for Truth).[25] Durkheim and his followers defended and further elaborated his ideas in their communications to and debates at meetings of the French Philosophical Society. Three themes elicited the liveliest debates on the part of Durkheim and his chief lieutenants: the science of morals; the sociology of religion; and history as a science and its relationship to sociology. The meetings of the Union pour la Vérité were devoted to more contemporary issues and practical themes such as divorce, patriotism, internationalism, socialism, nationalism, humanitarianism, and rationalism.[26]

To Durkheim's many other activities during this period may be added his contributions to several inquiries conducted by some French periodicals.[27] The several long articles he wrote were edited and published posthumously by his disciples and constitute his two important volumes: *Sociology and Philosophy* and *Education and Sociology.*

The tirades that raged in France over the doctrines of the Durkheimian school give dramatic evidence of their popularity and notoriety. The critical attitudes adopted by some apologists, sociologists, and specialists in other social sciences indicate that in some circles the popularity and dogmatic character of Durkheimian sociology were not tolerated. Durkheim had acquired the reputation of being the "master of a school, leader of an *équipe* of collaborators," who, it was thought, "was constructing a closed system, defending it against the adversaries and the dissidents."[28] The personal attributes of Durkheim were such that he overpowered those who came into contact with him. Durkheim's students, it is remarked of him, "submitted to the influence of the master; they admired his erudition; they extolled his uprightness and genius."[29] By virtue of his personal qualities, Durkheim captivated Bouglé; seduced Richard to collaborate with him, though only for a brief while; attracted Halbwachs, Davy, and several others; incorporated Hubert in his scheme of sociology; and tantalized Worms and piqued Tarde. One of

Durkheim's students stated that Durkheim "imposed his influence upon them, whether they liked it or not. They could not resist the authority of his hollow voice and solemn tone."[30] Befitting a scholarch, he had the "air of a mystical rabbi."[31]

Once Durkheim arrived in Paris, the initially slow growth of the *Année* school began to accelerate. The publication of the sixth volume of *L'Année*, synchronous with Durkheim's arrival in Paris, marked an increase in the number of collaborators from twelve for the previous volume to eighteen. It was around the nucleus of *L'Année* that Durkehim gathered his disciples, followers, and collaborators in an undertaking that gradually resulted in a cohesive group—a doctrinal school in the real sense of the word.

Essentially, Durkheim consecrated the period 1898–1913 to cultivating and popularizing the new science of sociology. As a result of sixteen years of hard labor and dedication he was able to construct an edifice of "social science" sociology that included but was not limited to the output of *L'Année*. He wrote a few articles defining the scope of sociology, which were published in French,[32] English,[33] and Italian[34] journals, and which of course characterized the viewpoint of the Durkheimian school.

Durkheim's monumental work, *The Elementary Forms,* grew from his long and rich experience reviewing books in *L'Année*. The periodical provided Durkheim and his followers with an excellent opportunity to examine the prodigious volume of literature, especially in ethnography, that was pouring out during those years. The ethnographic studies brought forth by English, American, and German scholars were the basis of this last of Durkheim's major works.

The fourth period, spanning 1914 to 1917, in Durkheim's life—and in the lives of his disciples, followers, and collaborators—was dedicated to the defense of France. During these four short years, Durkheim did not accomplish much in the name of sociology, nor did anyone else. He did, in 1915, write for a government publication an important article entitled "La Sociologie," which aimed to ascertain the status of academic disciplines and scientific knowledge in France, a work that was intended to be displayed in the San Francisco exhibition.[35] In the same year Durkheim wrote two brochures (one in collaboration with a historian, Ernest Denis) that described the warmongering instincts of the Germans.[36] During 1916 Durkheim, along with some prominent Sorbonnists, and professors such as Lavisse, Buisson, and Meillet, issued letters to the French to uphold their morale during the painful years of the war.[37]

Durkheim's only son, André, and some of his beloved disciples were killed in the war; these tragic events hastened Durkheim's own death. In 1917 Durkheim wrote his son's obituary,[38] and he himself died the same year. After Durkheim's death, Mauss and other disciples and followers published posthumously the remaining corpus of his work, including books, articles, and lectures. They also edited some of Durkheim's earlier articles and published them in book form, in part through the efforts of Kubali,[39] a Turkish jurist, and Cuvillier,[40] a popular French philosopher and sociologist.

The Essence of Durkheim's Doctrines

Durkheim is one of those few philosophers or social scientists who never changed his fundamental ideas. Instead, as time progressed, he became increasingly sure of the validity of his theories and doctrines. His disciples and followers, even after his death, spent their lives explicating them, reaffirming them through their personal research and works, defending them when they were under attack, and retrieving them when they were threatened with oblivion. Certain illustrious figures—eminent philosophers and Durkheim's contemporaries, such as Emile Boutroux, André Lalande, Dominique Parodi, Jean Izoulet, S. Deploige, I. Meyerson, Lucien Laberthonière, C. C. J. Webb, Salomon Reinach, Georges Sorel, Léon Duguit, and Henri Berr—made literal use of the word "doctrine" when referring to the principal sociological ideas of the Durkheimian school. Ferdinand Brunetière was apprehensive about the new science of morals, whose matrix was the sociology of the Durkheimian school.[1] For Paul Janet, the young science of sociology, which had its base in positivism, was itself a doctrine, albeit an illegitimate one. One philosopher even went so far in his acclaim for a sociological doctrine, disentangled from a work by one of Durkheim's disciples, as to call the publication a "manifesto" of the Durkheimian school.[2] In short, all of this post-mortem was but further evidence of the deep and pervasive influence Durkheim's doctrines had in sociology.

Was Durkheim disposed to dogmatism while he was cultivating the science of sociology? What was his attitude, and that of his disciples and followers, when his ideas came under attack and when he was accused of being impervious to criticism, even of fostering "imperialism"? Did Durkheim's doctrines overwhelm his disciples and followers? How did other savants respond to the tenacity as well as the audacity of Durkheim's positions? Our answers to these questions, even though brief, will show the powerful appeal Durkheim's doctrines had to a wide audience.

Durkheim's rigid and dogmatic attitudes were apparent even in his early youth, when he entered the Ecole Normale Supérieure. Once, when it was charged that his ideas did not comply with the facts, he replied that the facts have a tendency to lie.[3] He was convinced, from the very beginning of his life, that scientific sociology could only be developed if he, as well as other sociologists, employed positivism as a method, and if the structure of their young science was built upon "hypostatized society." Positivism as a method—however much he adopted it and separated himself from Comtian positivism—and "hypostatized society" remained the bases of his sociological writings. He never budged an inch from these two principal concepts. Other concepts were variations of these two. The labyrinth of Durkheimian doctrines included such other shibboleths and concepts as "anomie," "collective conscience," "society as a sui generis reality," "collective representations," "social constraint," "the science of morals and customs," "social solidarity," "social consensus," and "social facts as things." Durkheim coined all these terms, making them an integral part of his sociological imagination and integrating them into his sociology. These elements of his doctrines became the objects of further analysis, examination, criticism, and refutation. Some of his adversaries called them sociological "metaphors." They still have a familiar ring that is characteristic of the French school of sociology.

A careful reading of Durkheim's works and those of his followers and disciples will reveal the following aspects of his sociology and his doctrines: (1) neo-positivism; (2) scientism; (3) comparativism; (4) societism; (5) science and the rational art of morals; and (6) sociological epistemology.

NEO-POSITIVISM

For Comte, positivism was a system; for Durkheim, it was a method.[4] Durkheim transformed Comtian positivism into a scientific methodology comparable to that of physics and chemistry. In fact, Durkheim claimed that his use of positivism was free from all metaphysical elements and abstractions. The aim of Durkheim's positivism was to convert facts into laws; to reduce the complex to the simple, the particular to the universal, and the contingent to the causally determined. Durkheim not only redefined Comtian positivism, but also gave it his personal stamp. The only way to bring the social sciences under the suzerainty of sociology, as Comte had aspired to do, was to develop the corpus of Comtian strategy in theory and practice by a method of "social facts." Durkheim incorporated all the social sciences into the corpus of his scientific sociology by treating their phenomena at the level of "social facts." This adaptation of the particular social sciences to the Durkheimian method of neo-positivism made them integral parts of scientific sociology. Thus a foundation for scientific sociology, with "imperialistic" ambitions, was laid. Durkheim's version of positivism comprised the methods of analysis and synthesis; he considered such an approach an essential component of any sociologically valid method. In addition, Durkheimian positivism also required the use of comparativism as a method. If by positivism Durkheim meant the gathering of social facts and giving them a comparative perspective, then L'Année bore final witness to this credo.

François Simiand, for his part, was unremitting in his efforts to cultivate what he called the "positive science of economics." He was an ingenious philosopher, but a lukewarm methodologist. He defined the positive method in its relationship to economic facts by refuting and undermining the theoretical premises of the traditional economists.⁵ He summed up the aims of positivism, as applied to the science of economics, in these concise words: *"to comprehend and to explicate the economic reality* [author's italics]."⁶ Such a science, which comprehends and explicates the economic reality, in the first place eliminates (according to Simiand) the final causes of the phenomena and rejects normative propensities. In the second place, it devises "conceptual and schematic hypotheses."⁷ Further, it sifts the deductive assumptions that are the result of these conjectural hypotheses. The laws of economic reality, Simiand affirmed, could only be established through external observations.

There were, however, some subtle differences between Durkheim's and Simiand's approches to positivism. Simiand fought a battle against the proponents of deductive method and mathematical abstractions in economics. He did not deny that positivism implied comparativism, but he was far from agreeing with the positivistic notion of that required scientific reductionism—explaining the complex by the simple and the compound by the elementary. For this reason he was condemned by the Durkheimians as a sociologist without a base in sociology.⁸ That also explains why economics in general and economic sociology in particular, which were the exclusive prerogatives of Simiand, have remained barren of ethnographic materials, no matter whether we examine Simiand's personal work or his reviews in *L'Année*. Nonetheless, one thing was clear to both Durkheim and Simiand: Positivism was the common bond between the two consanguineous social sciences. In any case, it was hoped that economics would ultimately, through the adoption of positivism, fuse with sociology. By this hope both flamens of positivism were inspired.

SCIENTISM

What is scientism? And did Durkheim have a doctrine of scientism? D. R. G. Owen described scientism as "omniscient, omnipotent, and the bearer of man's salvation,"⁹ a sort of "scientology." A more sophisiticated definition of the term is provided by John Wellmuth,¹⁰ who stated that the word "scientism" meant a belief in science and in "the scientific method as described by modern scientists," and claimed that it was the only "reliable method of acquiring such knowledge as may be available about whatever is real."¹¹ This definition suggests that Durkheim's methodological position of treating "social facts" as phenomena of nature was a kind of dogma.

For sociology to acquire the status of a science on a par with physics, chemistry, and biology, it must simulate the methods of the natural sciences. A sociologist, like a chemist or a biologist, will treat the social facts on a phenomenological plane; as a result he can reduce the social consciousness and individual representations to things of physical nature. For any scientific explication (even as science was practiced in Durkheim's time), causal explanation is of primary importance. Within physics and chemistry, causal relationships are established by way of experimentation and external observations. Sociology was to follow suit. Society was thought to be a concrete reality, so the social laws, which were considered intrinsic to it, could be formulated in the same way as the laws of the natural sciences. This also meant that the logic of scientific method elicited the notion of determinism. Contingent propositions could not explain social phenomena, explication of which required the existence of efficient causes. All this discussion brings us to a question: How can a social reality be explained causally? This question goes to the heart of Durkheimian scientism; it is resolved by another tenet of Durkheim—"societism." Social constraint, collective conscience, collective representations, and some other key terms conceived by Durkheim arose directly from his concept of society, a reality sui generis.

The methodological axioms of the pure sciences that Durkheim wanted to superimpose upon the new science of sociology may be designated as Durkheimian scientism. The axiomatic principles that Durkheim posited in The Rules were to be adopted as a complex of sociological methods by his disciples. Simiand made use of these rules, as presented by Durkheim, in the science of economics, further explicating them.[12] Mauss and Hubert employed them in the analysis of religious facts. Less than a decade after Durkheim had prescribed this scientific methodology in The Rules, he and his disciples became swamped by a flood of ethnographic studies; as a result, the comparative method became a part of their scientific methodology.

COMPARATIVISM

Under the influence of the ever increasing ethnological literature, Durkheim and Mauss adopted "the means of methodic comparisons" as a significant tool to discover "the causes and the laws"[13] of social phenomena. To comprehend the evolution of civilizations, they considered it necessary to compare archaic societies with the most modern ones. The Durkheimians aimed to examine the social organizations of different cultures and civilizations and to discover, if possible, a common element among them. In the eleventh volume of L'Année, the scheme of presenting a comparative analysis of the simplest and the most "primitive" forms of religious life with the most advanced and complex became clearly evident. In fact, Durkheim's use of comparativism as a method distinguished him from Comte and from Comtian positivism.[14] Durkheim asserted that Comte had made a mistake in espousing an abstract notion of civilization, which, Durkheim claimed, explained only the general and unilinear progress of humanity. But Durkheim and Mauss, in the light of new ethnographic discoveries, discerned a more logical distinction between states, nations, societies, and civilizations. Obsessed with the task of distinguishing different cultures and civilizations, and gathering facts on them, Durkheim himself, as well as his disciples, pored over a vast quantity of ethnographic studies.

The comparative method used during the latter half of the nineteenth century was characterized as a "disease emanating from comparative linguistics." Max Müller's ideas still had a strong inpact on the mind of philosophers. Durkheim and Mauss, in the background of linguistic comparativism, admitted that "all the peoples who speak one Indo-European language had a common foundation of ideas and institutions."[15] In other words, the comparative method, which the Durkheimians were practicing in *L'Année,* was, to a great extent, similar to comparative linguistics and comparative mythology. Meillet was a prominent linguist and a staunch practitioner of comparativism; he was also a member of the Durkheimian school.

The practical advantages of comparativism were most evident in the book reviews in *L'Année.* The last few volumes of *L'Année* show clearly the tendency of the members of the Durkheimian school to make use of it. Several authors were juxtaposed to give a comparative view of their works; different aspects of the same book were often discussed in different sections and subsections of *L'Année* and adapted to elicit an overall view of literature on the same theme.[16] René Worms objected to this Durkheimian practice of arbitrarily grouping the authors under one rubric and subsection, and of scattering reviews of them under different rubrics and subsections.[17] A partisan member of the Durkheimian school wanted Worms to understand their position in these terms: "We cannot attribute a great probing value to the parallelism between . . . the two groups . . . : juxtaposition is not comparison."[18] Comparativism was not a result of juxtaposing books; it elicited a perspective of parallels and contrasts of social institutions.

Durkheim and Mauss were moving in the direction of comparativism, but they had yet to perfect it. Meillet was a dauntless comparativist.[19] He explicated the doctrine,[20] practiced it himself, and advised his students and disciples to follow it. "Comparison is the only effective tool" with which to comprehend the history of languages, he once told his audience.[21] Comparison in linguistics could be used "in order to draw from [it] either universal laws or historical information."[22] Durkheim had identical views, except that he might have added that comparative analysis was also helpful in the search for causal relationships. Nevertheless, at times comparison was thought to have limited advantages; for example, Meillet stated that the method "furnishes only directions, not positive evidence."[23] No one could have been better qualified than Meillet to make such a remark.

SOCIETISM

In his works Durkheim apotheosized Society (with a capital "S") and hypostatized it as an entity that transcends God, determines morals and laws,[24] and is the fountainhead of every human activity. This doctrine is expressed in the typical phrases, quoted previously, that Durkheim himself either invented or adopted from other sociologists. The so-called sociologism of the Durkheim school was an expression that signified, among other things, the priority and supremacy that Durkheim attributed to the hypostatized concept of society. The sociologism of the Durkheim school obviously comported with the conventional doctrine of "societism," and this sociologism was the result of Durkheim's reaction to the "psychologism" of the English utilitarian economists that gave sanction to "individualism." Thus "sociologism" versus "psychologism" and "societism" versus "individualism" formed the polar extremes of two contradistinct doctrinal schools. In stating that "the cause of a social phenomenon must be sought in another social phenomenon," Durkheim made his intentions of positing a priority and superiority for society perfectly clear; and he once and for all closed the door to any further discussion that might allow for psychological explication of a sociological reality. The cause of suicide or the source of solidarity, according to Durkehim, was society and society alone. Religious ceremonies, in the performance of which an individual completely surrendered himself, characterized society in essence and in a state of effervescence. It was only when Durkheim was reflecting upon what he called *la science morale et physique des mœurs* (the science of morals and of customs) that he reified society and apotheosized it as well.[25] Durkheim argued that if the individual was a spiritual representation, then a fact higher than that, and exterior as well as superior, was the hyperspirituality of society. To be able to choose between God and Society, Durkheim presented the syllogism of his argument by stating that "the cardinal doctrine of any religion is its belief in the divinity of God. But what is divinity other than 'the society symbolically transfigured'?"[26]

As such, Durkheim established an equation: Society equals God. There is a subtle difference between the two, however, for society is a concrete reality and creates a synthesis of the individual and of his actions. The spirituality of the individual or "the cult of the individual" is, in fact, "the product of society."[27] The substance of Durkheim's argument was that it is Society that "made of man the god whose servant he is."[28]

Durkheim carried the doctrine of societism so far that it antagonized the religious thinkers and philosophers whose premises rested on individualism. In fact, Durkheim, the physician of society, after having made a thorough and penetrating diagnosis of its ills, administered such a heavy dose of medication for its recovery that the bitterness of the medicine, which he prescribed in terms of societism, is still felt by social scientists.

SCIENCE AND THE RATIONAL ART OF MORALS

For Durkheim, the edifice of scientific sociology was to be constructed on the scaffolding of social facts. As such, sociology included in its domain the social facts of all the social sciences: religion, ethics, law, linguistics, economics, and political science. And the social facts had to be analyzed as "things of nature." This, obviously, meant that the religious facts, the economic facts, and the social facts concerning morals had to be analyzed in the spirit of the positive sciences. This comprehensive method of treating social phenomena applied to the social facts of ethics, even though these lend themselves to value judgments.

Durkheim, in his zeal for the positive sciences, designated the new area of sociology as *la physique des mœurs et du droit* (the science of customs and of law). His adumbration of Comte's positivism and scientism calls for the latter's hierarchical classification of sciences. In his excessive devotion to physics, characterizing it as the *ne plus ultra* of positive sciences, Comte dubbed the science of physics as "terrestrial physics," biology as "biophysics," astronomy as "celestial physics," and, finally, sociology as "social physics." In his fondness for coining scientific terminology to designate areas of knowledge not properly belonging to the physical sciences, Durkheim appeared in every respect a Comtist and a positivist. He could have designated the newly conceived science *science des mœurs et du droit,* but he followed Comte even though they were fifty years apart. Durkheim made the same mistake as Comte when the latter initially baptized sociology as "social physics"; these errors in sociology were committed because the fathers of sociology were infatuated with the natural sciences.

Lucien Lévy-Bruhl[29] wrote a controversial manifesto for the Durkheimian school that was inspired by Durkheim's *The Rules*.[30] In it Lévy-Bruhl proposed the idea of a new science and rational arts of morals. Soon after Lévy-Bruhl's publication, this new science that the Durkheiminans were inventing became the center of controversy, and Durkheim took over responsibility for defending it himself, claiming that it was a legitimate branch of sociology. All philosophical questions and polemical disputes of the Durkheimian school with its adversaries were settled in the forums of the French Philosophical Society. Since Lévy-Bruhl was being attacked for his master stroke of contriving a new science of morals, Durkheim felt a great need to defend it and explicate its premises and subtleties. He presented the case under dispute to the French Philosophical Society for discussion.

There were four major premises on which this new science and rational art of morals were based. First of all, the facts of morals had to be extricated from philosophical, metaphysical, and religious presuppositions. A priori construction of the theories of morals was considered preposterous to those bound by the rules of the positive sciences. This sort of a priori philosophizing in the positive sciences had to be done away with. Science, it was said, examines what is; it does not indulge in what ought to be. So the second axiom of the science of morals was to study customs and norms scientifically. Durkheim and his followers held that society was the effect and the cause of all morals, including norms and customs. To prove the point, Durkheim argued at a dialectical level. Characteristics that were thought to be inherent in moral acts contained two significant elements: (1) being good, and (2) being dutiful.[31] But what could be more ethical, more desirable, or more apt to cultivate a sense of duty, Durkheim argued, than the concrete reality of society, which was superior to and outside the individual? Society itself, considered as such, was sacrosanct. It inspired deference on the part of its members. In fact, Durkheim substituted Society for God; he advocated the idea of replacing the notion of God by the notion of Society, which he assumed was a symbolic representation of human thoughts and actions. Obviously, Durkheim would care less for a science that possessed speculative elements. And thereby, the fourth principle of the rational art of morals was introduced.

Durkheim and Lévy-Bruhl insisted that such a rational art would become possible only when the science of morals had been developed, matured, and mellowed by experience. It was further suggested that the "applied aspect" of the science of morals—the "rational art," as Durkheim and Lévy-Bruhl called it—was not construed as an a priori construction of theories. Obviously, the suggested art was an application of scientific sociology to ethics and moral issues. There existed the following analogy: the ideas of the theoretical sciences have always been used for human welfare by applying them to such fields as agriculture, industry, and medicine; but the laws and causal relationships of the physical and biological sciences were already established and perfected before they were widely given concrete applications.

SOCIOLOGICAL EPISTEMOLOGY

Durkheim and his followers tried to bring about radical reforms in the areas of logic and epistemology. In some of the works by Durkheim, Mauss, and Hubert, they posited their sociological explication of the logic of categories[32]—of time, space, substance, force, causality, and so on. Antoine Bianconi was under the same influence and moving in the same direction. What was this sociological epistemology that supposedly was to replace the Kantian logic of pure reason?

According to the Durkheimians, the categories that primitive humanity devised were the first scientific classifications. The ingenuity of the primitive mind was characterized in the notion of collective representations; it formed the basis of the speculation of Western philosophers. The functional necessity of rites, feasts, and other religious activities necessitated the measurement of time and the formulation of a calendar. Man saw his first reflections in society itself. The attributes of the primitive social organization characterize man's reflections on the universe and its categories. With this background, Durkheim and Mauss insisted on viewing the Greek *phratries* as "the first genera," and clans as "the first species." At the same time they stated that "they [these institutions] were the works of science and constituted a philosophy of nature."[33] As such, the knowledge of our classifications into genera, species, and the like has no other raison d'être than society itself. The gist of their article on the primitive forms of classification was to show that the categories of "genus" and "kind" were derived from the social organization of the clan itself. From these sociological premises they made subtle attacks on the conceptualizations of logicians and psychologists.

Durkheim, in his article "Religious Sociology and the Theory of Knowledge,"[34] moved a little further from his earlier stance, although the main focus of his ideas on the subject of categories was the same as before. Now he attempted to explain the notion of space as category. By and large, he attacked and undermined the theories of the empiricists and individualists. Durkheim pointed out that "the first systems of representations that man created of the world and of himself were of religious origin."[35] He added that there "is no religion that is not a cosmology and at the same time a speculation on the divine."[36] Durkheim specialized in the category of time—"an object of collective representation" and the socially determined phenomenon that is expressed in the form of a calendar. Hubert characterized time as an object of collective representation, similar to the Durkheimians' characterization of space. Syllogism of this sort led Hubert to apply the idea of social categories and the notion of the sacred to the phenomenon of time. Conforming to the Durkheimian socio-"logical" representation of the categories of space and time, Hubert defined the calendar as a social fact that "determines the periods and gives them social meaning."[37] With respect to the distinct positions of Durkheim and Hubert, Mauss stood midway between the two.

Among all the doctrines of the Durkheimian school, the one that concerned sociological epistemology was the most effectively promulgated in the section on religious sociology of *L'Année*.

Disciples and Followers:
Formation, Growth, and Consolidation
of the Durkheimian School

Never has a doctrine or an ideology flourished without captivating and bringing into its orbit a band of faithful followers. The master and his doctrines alone do not constitute a school. Essentially, it is the undiminishing faith of the disciples that makes the master and his doctrines known far and wide and keeps his legacy alive. This is as true of the different branches of academic knowledge as it is of political ideologies and religious dogmas. The followers of a doctrine may be installed in a particular university or in one of its departments; they may work together or apart within a particular geographic area; or they may be situated in widely scattered areas. The fact remains that followers and partisans of doctrines do play a significant role, sometimes a decisive one, in society. And so long as the human mind continues to create new systems and doctrines, there are bound to be partisans and followers, who accept them as the only positive proofs of reality. A doctrinal school blossoms by virtue of its appeal to a following.

Durkheim formed a cohesive group, which consisted of disciples, followers, and collaborators of diverse backgrounds and different aptitudes. They manifested their loyalty to the group and identification with its doctrines in different ways. First we will explore the different membership groups belonging to the Durkheimian school. Then we shall consider the existence of those propitious circumstances on the fringe of which the school was formed and consolidated. We shall attempt to shed light on the social and political milieu of the France in which Durkheim's adherents were forged into a consortium of sociologists, socialists, and republicans.

The sociological school that Durkheim conducted was formed during the years of publication of the original series of L'Année (1898–1913). It was consolidated before the outbreak of the First World War, before Durkheim's death in 1917. By this time Durkheimian sociology had become fashionable. There were two primary membership groups in the Durkheimian school: those who engaged in the writing of the Analyses section of the original series of L'Année and those who did not contribute to L'Année but explicitly identified Durkheim as the source of their inspiration and expressed their unreserved identification with other members of the school

According to the first category mentioned above, most of the members of the Durkheimian school belonged to the équipe that wrote the original series of L'Année, which Durkheim himself directed, edited, and published. This classification excludes those collaborators who joined the group during the later revival periods of L'Année's publication.

Four scholars—Georg Simmel, Friedrich Ratzel, S. R. Steinmetz, and J. Charmont—who contributed articles to L'Année in the section Mémoires originaux nonetheless must be excluded from the Durkheimian school. Two reasons explain this exclusion. First, the school's activities were centered in Paris and its members were for the most part French; three of the above mentioned scholars were foreigners and did not live in Paris. Second, and most important, these scholars were not adherents of the doctrines.

Some research in the area of French intellectual history and among the ranks of contemporary men of scholarly orientation will reveal the names of Léon Duguit and Lucien Lévy-Bruhl, who might be thought of as belonging to the Durkheimian school but whose precise position in Durkheim's orbit is difficult to chart. In Duguit's case we will establish elsewhere that he should probably be excluded from the school.[1] In contrast, Lévy-Bruhl's case is less marked by obscurities and ambiguities concerning his association with Durkheim. An examination of Lévy-Bruhl's sociological works leaves no doubt in this regard. Durkheim himself[2] came to Lévy-Bruhl's defense when he was under attack by the enemies of the school, who considered him a "collaborationist" and a bit player in the grand plans of the master's scenario. Durkheim vigorously defended Lévy-Bruhl on the issue of "founding and institutionalizing" a new science of morals, which the latter had initiated.[3] Lévy-Bruhl's own intellectual itinerary reveals his progressive evolution from the history of philosophy to sociology and then to ethnology. From 1900 until 1910, when he became imbued with the notion of the *fonctions mentales* of primitive peoples, Lévy-Bruhl was a sociologist par excellence, a follower of Durkheim's doctrines, and a member of the school. The details of his precarious relationship with Durkheim, his doctrines, and his relationships with disciples and followers deserve a thorough examination, which we have presented elsewhere.[4] Here it suffices to affirm that he definitely belonged to the Durkheimian school.

We have pointed out that *L'Année*, which was the official organ of Durkheim's school, was also the principal repository of its members' works. The school flourished in its matrix. Therefore, a complete roster of its members, whom Durkheim invariably designated as his collaborators, requires a thorough search of what lies in the pages of *L'Année*.

As a rule, Durkheim listed the names of his collaborators, their professional ranks, and their educational degrees on the title page of the *L'Année*. However, some collaborators were not reported on the title page. The names of collaborators may be found at four different places within the periodical: (1) on the title page; (2) in the table of contents; (3) under the titles of sections and subsections of the main part of the analyses; and (4) at the end of each book review, where the name of the reviewer is revealed by his initials. Such distinguished savants as T. Stickney, J. Poirot, C. Fossey, A. Moret, and Isidore Lévy, who collaborated on *L'Année,* will not be noticed unless we examine its pages in detail.

F. Sigel, for instance, is listed on the front page, even though his overall contribution to *L'Année* is of no great significance. The contributions, in quality and quantity, made by Stickney, Poirot, and Isidore Lévy are no less significant than those of Sigel. Thus there is no reason for us to include one person in the list of collaborators simply because his name appears on the title page, or to exclude others because their names do not.

This method of screening the entire periodical reveals the names of forty-seven members[5] who collaborated with Durkheim—some on a regular basis, some intermittently or casually, some only once or twice. Whatever the regularity of their contributions, it is beyond doubt that some of them were savants of great stature; some were even scholarchs in their own right. The members of the school were in general philosophers and *universitaires*. Durkheim was able to lure distinguished men and specialists from diverse occupations: lawyers, jurists, paleologists, publicists, translators, and men of letters. They all participated in the collaborative work of a cohesive group whose sole aim was to cultivate scientific sociology and to perfect *L'Année*.

Up to this point we have considered the dramatis personae of the Durkheimian school in general. Now we must distinguish among "disciples," "followers," and "collaborators," even though Durkheim, as was the tradition, designated everyone who contributed to his periodical as his collaborator. That obviously befits the scientific terminology of collective work; "collaboration" is a term used to describe the public, democratic character of science in which individuals contribute as equals. In collaborative science there is a conspicuous lack of a master-disciple relationship. It is clear that such a science cannot result in the formation and growth of doctrinal schools. Durkheim's terminology, then, did not square with his practice. He trained under his imposing authority a whole generation of sociologists to be malleable and responsive disciples who believed in his doctrines. It will be noted later that the first-ranking sociologists of this era were trained and educated by him; they were his own disciples and the loyal partisans of his doctrines; the second-ranking members of the school, who were also men of great erudition and enjoyed eminent stature, were not sociologists as such but were his followers as well as collaborators. It is only the lowest-ranking members of the school—the "helots"—who qualify as mere collaborators. They were far removed from sociology and devoid of the slightest vestiges of Durkheim's doctrines. It is in this sense that we differentiate the term "collaborator" from "disciple." Durkheim had, on the whole, partisan disciples and followers, but he had collaborators too, whom we have designated as peripheral members of the school. However, the real existence and widespread reputation of the Durkheimian school rests on Durkheim's selected followers and disciples, and not on the contributions of collaborators. A doctrinal school is constituted by the existence of one master, a few apostles, some ardent partisans, and a host of collaborators.

THE SOCIOPOLITICAL MILIEU

The history of the Durkheimian school is linked to the rise and fall of the Third Republic and especially to the Republic's destiny in the period from 1870 to 1940. In fact, Durkheimian sociology and the doctrines of the school became, to a great extent, symbolic expressions of the Republic of this period. The year 1871 marked the uprising of the Paris Commune and the birth of the Third Republic. Of the Durkheimian group, only Durkheim himself, Meillet, and Lapie (born in 1858, 1866, and 1869, respectively) were born prior to these two seminal events in French history. The others were born during the next two decades—e.g., Hertz, Davy, and David in 1881, 1883, and 1885, respectively. That is, almost all the members of the Durkheimian school were born in the fourth quarter of the last century, and their education was completed during the 1890s and the first ten years of the twentieth century.

In political matters the Second Empire in the late 1860s experienced a shocking defeat through its ill-fated war with Bismarckian Prussia; after the debacle in the war with Prussia, its downfall was immediate. Prussia inflicted its first blitzkrieg upon its neighbor, thus precipitating the establishment of the Third Republic. This defeat of France at the hands of Germany, whose scientific and technological superiority[6] the French could only envy, gave French scholars and politicians a feeling of inferiority with regard to their cultural institutions. Moreover, the Prussian victory paved the way for the importation of German scientific ideas by young French scholars. The French feared German military power, but they coveted German science.

The country was plagued by anarchy. Strikes became common occurrences, and revolutionary movements had detrimental effects on the character of French institutions. The Dreyfus Affair was the last blow to a country in severe difficulties.

In sociological terms, France was in a state of "anomie." During these tormenting years of the nascent Third Republic, only a Gambetta or a Thiers could have delivered France from chaos, instability, and virtual disintegration. A kind of civil war was being waged by the republicans, the leftists, and the anticlericalists against the monarchists and Jesuits. The anticlerical elements and opponents of monarchy were united against their common enemy. The battle between these two polarized sections of society continued to the end of the first quarter of the twentieth century. In every crisis of this period, the republicans, the liberals, the leftists, and the anticlericalists emerged triumphant. The Durkheimians were always on the winning side.

Repercussions from the social and political events were felt by the political leaders as well as by the academicians, who were determined to reconstruct the moral and social fiber of society. The evils were identified with the established institutions, whether educational, religious, or political. Reform in education was considered of paramount importance. Such architects of the Republic as Louis Liard, Jules Ferry, Ferdinand Buisson, Ernest Lavisse, and Paul Lapie turned their attention to remodeling and refurbishing the entire structure of education. Such political leaders as Thiers, Poincaré, Dupuy, Briand, Clemenceau, Harriot, Jaurès, and Blum, to mention a few—most of them were *normaliens* (graduates of the Ecole Normale Supérieure) who turned to politics during these years of turbulence—were preoccupied not only with reconstruction and impending reforms but with the idea of matching the strength of the country with that of imperial Germany.

In education, reforms were concerned with the introduction of rational and positive sciences. Renovation in education required a strong emphasis on the teaching of modern languages; the teaching of classical languages and literature had to be reduced. The poignant question of "laicizing" education was also at the heart of the reforms. Durkheim, Bouglé, Lapie, and the others executed the task of secularizing education with relentless passion.

The sociopolitical situation of the Republic was not merely incidental to a *belle époque* in the history of French sociology, but was an integral part of its development. This discussion brings us to consider in more detail the educational reconstruction that was intended to imitate the German model of the natural and moral sciences.

THE SUPERIORITY AND INFLUENCE
OF THE GERMAN SCIENCES

The superiority of the German natural and moral sciences was a dominant theme of this period. The French acquired a new impetus through their contacts with their neighbor to reexamine the old structure of their institutions and bring about reform. After the debacle of 1870 it took the country almost ten years to settle the dust of devastation caused by the war. Now the country across the Rhine became a Mecca for young French scholars, who sought to identify themselves with new ideas in order to rebuild the Republic—in an attempt to overcome the French inferiority complex or perhaps even to transcend German superiority. France had a lot to learn from Germany, not only in the realms of philosophy and natural science but also in the science of morals and in the art of politics.

Throughout the 1880s and 1890s, young philosophers and scholars made pilgrimages to the German universities, particularly to those at Heidelberg, Berlin, Leipzig, and Munich. These were precisely the universities that Bouglé visited.[7] Such enthusiasts and young scholars as Lavisse, Durkheim, Charles Andler, Lucien Herr, and Charles Seignobos[8] returned from their enlightening sojourns in Germany with a desire to emulate its scientific progress. One may even be bewildered by the extent to which this demand for German ideas was carried. It went so far as to induce a Catholic savant to acclaim German superiority and to urge France to surpass her neighbor.[9] It was, in short, a period of "germanomania." The French imitated the manners and skills of the Germans to improve their primary education. Ethics had to be introduced; moreover, a rigorous program of secondary education in geography, history, sciences, civics, and gymnastics had to be inculcated upon the minds of the young students, and in higher education, some new branches of knowledge had to be cultivated. France was determined to emulate her neighbor, as is evinced by R. Didon's testimony: "I do not say let us do as the Germans; but I say let us do better than they. I do not beseech you to imitate their universities, their schools, their army, their national spirit; I urge you to act so as to transcend them."[10] The statement speaks for itself and reflects the spirit of the time. Several articles, and even some books, written during the two decades of the 1880s and 1890s by those who returned from German universities portrayed the scientific superiority of the Germans.[11] Animated by a desire to serve the Republic and to enhance the status of scientific learning in France, the young scholars whose names have already been cited, and many others supported by government funds and assurances of rewarding positions on their return, wrote accounts of their impressions of the students, professors, curricula, and even the extramural atmosphere prevailing in the German universities. The consequences of "the German question that provoked and instigated a crisis of long duration in French intellectual ideas" have been well documented and thoroughly investigated in a thesis by Digeon.[12] The so-

called German question not only made its way into the academic amphitheaters but stirred up the literary talents of the novelists. Emile Zola,
before he shouted *J'accuse!*, had admonished the Republic to emulate the
Germans in their discipline, science, and new methods of organization. He
had suggested that the science and technology possessed by the Germans were
the real source of their greater prestige and power.[13] Their institutional
superiority caused France dishonor and the French institutions discredit. Zola
advised that France should become a "scientific and naturalistic Republic."[14]

Up to the establishment of the Republic, Charles Renouvrier, Charles
Secrétan, and Jules Lachelier had been popularizing Kantian idealism. Kant's
philosophy was known to be the official doctrine of the Sorbonne; it was according to this spirit in the teaching of philosophy in the system of higher
education that the French philosophers from the academic podiums were in-
stilling the ideas of Kantian philosophy. Renouvrier, who was well known for
his doctrine of neo-criticism and for his identification with idealism and neo-
Kantian philosophy, exerted considerable influence on Durkheim, Bouglé,
Dominique Parodi, Octave Hamelin, and many other young philosophers of
this period. In 1897 A. Cresson, in his *La Morale de Kant,* showed the pervasive influence of Kant's philosophy on Secrétan and Renouvrier and affirmed that "Kantism" constituted the "base of almost all the courses of moral
philosophy taught in France, particularly. Kant's doctrine found its way into
most of the manuals on the education of children; as a result, it had an official
character."[15] Parodi—a noted philosopher, a positivist, a rationalist, and an
independent thinker—attributed the events of this period from 1870 to 1890
to the popularization of intellectualism and neo-Kantian rationalism.[16]
Bouglé's article "Spiritualism and Kantism in France" gives clear evidence of
the crusades launched by the French philosophers to "Kantize" their lectures
and seminars in the university amphitheaters. [17] In agreement with Parodi, [18]
whose work gives a brilliant analysis of the tendencies of French philosophers,
Bouglé confirmed the predominant influence of Kantian philosophy on the
minds of French intellectuals. Bouglé stated: "What still is a matter of warning to us is that the Kantian doctrine, reviewed and complemented by
Lachelier, is always alive." [19]

In spite of this general characterization of the spirit of the time, there are
some indications pointing to the revival of religious thinking known in French
philosophic thought as *néo-spiritualisme*. Revaisson and Lachelier were ingenious in their efforts to syncretize the elements of metaphysics with the logic
of science with the aim of reconciling the order of causality with the order of
finality. [20]

But Durkheim, Mauss, Simiand, and other sociologists were not in the
least interested in Kantian neo-criticism or Hegelian neo-spiritualism—or, for
that matter, in any philosophic mechanism that neglected an empirically
verifiable experience of reality and the sui generis existence of facts.
Speculating on and understanding reality through a priori method is not what

the logic of science deals with. Bouglé's and Durkheim's sojourns in Germany were marked with an otherwise serious sense of purpose. Both Durkheim and Bouglé were strongly impressed by the developments in the positive science of morals, which they observed in the works of the German economists and the reform-policy socialists. They were both strongly influenced by the monumental works of W. Wundt and by his suggestive ideas in the social sciences, which he set forth in *Völkerpsychologie*. If Durkheim and Bouglé were drawn to the works of Schaeffle, Wundt, Albert H. Post, A. H. G. Wagner, and Gustav Schmoller, it was because the practical use of their teachings was so considerable, and the scientific superiority of their works was so striking, that the two republicans could not possibly have remained unaffected.

What must be pointed out here is that Durkheim, Bouglé, Simiand, the Bourgin brothers (Georges and Hubert), and Maurice Halbwachs, as members of the Durkheimian school, appear as the French counterparts of the German *Kathedersozialisten* (literally, the "socialists of the pulpit"). Since the German *Kathedersozialisten* and the practitioners of *Völkerpsychologie* were willing to separate themselves from Kantian subjectivism and Hegelian "neospiritualism," and since they were willing to find a compromise between the ideas of absolute individualism and "the infinitely divine attributes of society," Durkheim, the moralist and sociologist, deemed it justifiable to accept their premises and implant their notions of morals and ideas of the social sciences in France.

THE ECOLE NORMALE SUPÉRIEURE AND THE WINDS OF CHANGE: EMERGENCE OF THE DURKHEIMIAN SCHOOL

Durkheim recruited his band of young Turks from the Ecole Normale Supérieure through his own efforts or through the conscientious assistance of Lucien Herr. The significance of the Ecole Normale Supérieure as a matrix of the group that espoused "Durkheimism" and "sociologism" can be understood in the light of these bare facts: In the 1890s Bouglé, Parodi, Charles Fossey, Albert Demangeon, Simiand, H. Hubert, J. Poirot, G. Bourgin, Maître, Vacher, and Halbwachs, and in the decade of the 1900s Hertz, Gernet, Antoine Bianconi, Gelly, Reynier, Maxime David, Ray, Georges Davy, Jeanmaire, and Laskine all joined the Durkheimian group. They all came from the rue d'Ulm and were children of the Ecole Normale Supérieure, and belonged to the tradition of this sanctum sanctorum of French higher learning. Paul Lapie did not enter the Ecole Normale Supérieure, failing the *concours* in the same year that Bouglé succeeded, in 1890. But the fact is that the Durkheimian school in its early stages was a *normalein* show, dominated by such graduates as C. Bouglé, Gaston Richard, Simiand, and Hubert. (The only other exceptions were Mauss and Lapie, who were not *normaliens*.) Thus it behooves us to consider the Ecole Normale Supérieure as a part of the history of the Durkheimian school. It should be included in any examination of the history of intellectual ideas in France, particularly if it concerns the history of French sociology.

Durkheim—the scholarch, the sociologist, the philosopher, the logician, the methodologist, and the moralist—recruited his original Pleiad from three major French institutions: the Ecole Normale Supérieure, the Sorbonne, and the University of Bordeaux. In addition, the Hubert-Mauss partnership was able to proselytize for Durkheim's school at the Ecole Pratique des Hautes Etudes (sixth section now called Ecole des Hautes Etudes en Sciences Sociales), the institution where they taught and directed the researches of their students. Hubert, by virtue of his distinction as an archeologist and historian of religions, was able to bring some of his colleagues at the Ecole Pratique des Hautes Etudes (Section des Sciences Religieuses) into the *Année* orbit: for instance, Alexandre Moret, Isidore Lévy, and Charles Fossey, who collaborated with him in translating Chantepie de la Saussay's *Manuel*. Durkheim, Hubert, and Mauss were well aware that the nucleus around *L'Année* could be strengthened by recruiting their own students and by attracting their own colleagues. This strategy was successful and gave the group considerable élan. *L'Année* was a laboratory where these students in particular served their first apprenticeships. Henri Beuchat, Philippe de Félice, Antoine Bianconi, Paul Fauconnet, Georges Davy, and several other more or less eminent Durkheimians were students by virtue of their formal education, but gained their professional experience of writing sociology as apprentices.

The original Pleiad of the school was already formed during the initial stage of its development, while Durkheim was still at Bordeaux. After Durkheim's arrival in Paris, the school progressively flowered in the Latin Quarter and Paris became the official center of its activities. In discussing the recruitment of members and the manner in which the Pleiad members were helpful in inducing students, colleagues, and friends to join the movement, it is worth noting that Simiand, notwithstanding his membership in the higher echelons of the Durkheimian school, and even though he was a professor at the Conservatoire Nationale des Arts et Métiers, was unable to promote the school by way of influencing his students or colleagues to join the *Année* workshop. Bouglé's assistance in this regard was limited.

The wind of change was already blowing from the Ecole Normale Supérieure. [21] At the time when Durkheim, Gaston Richard, and Jaurès entered the Ecole, and for the following few decades, the institution was a center of rational ideas, critical thinking, and empirical knowledge. Durkheim and his contemporaries entered with the hope of making new discoveries in science and philosophy. For years, Fustel de Coulanges, Boutroux, and Pasteur had inspired students through their own works and researches; the whole atmosphere of the Ecole encouraged original ideas and innovative thinking. [22] This climate has been testified to by Perrot, who claimed that the young philosophers of the rue d'Ulm at this time were less preoccupied by speculation than preceding generations. [23] The relations between professors and students were marked by their familiarity, informality, and liberalism. French philosophic "spiritualism"—metaphysical idealism—was, grudgingly, yielding to the philosophy of positivism that was autochthonous to French soil. The only opposition encountered by the new philosophy of positivism came from Brunetière, who was a staunch Catholic philosopher. He was not alone, however, in his resistance to the implantation of the German sciences on French soil; Fustel de Coulanges concurred with him in this regard. Both were opposed to the doctrine of social realism, which they thought was an alien element. Brunetière, in particular, was critical of everything that was new, whether it was the doctrine of positivism or the doctrine of materialism. Presumably his predilection for, or prejudice against, certain ideas was formed by his religious thinking and metaphysical idealism. Fustel de Coulanges, although he manifested critical thinking and favored scientific ideas, was leery of pan-Germanism, especially of German intellectualism, which he thought was being indiscriminately imported into France and becoming a "disease" of the French intellectuals.

Fustel de Coulanges officially proclaimed that the Ecole Normale Supérieure must fulfill the obligations assigned to it. He claimed it had "the duty and the right to be a great laboratory of science, of erudition, and of criticism." [24] Among the learned professors of the Ecole, Boutroux and Fustel de Coulanges can be mentioned as having exerted great influence on the intellectual formation of Durkheim and some other *normaliens*. For the noted historian, the premise of science had to be "founded on rational proofs" of which the facts must be "well established by the documents." [25] If the conclusions arrived at in a scholarly work were confirmed as substantially true, and if they could be demonstrated through the evidence of facts, then, he affirmed, "they had every right to be taught as revealed dogmas." [26] Moreover, it was the historian who inculcated in the mind of Durkheim and other students at the Ecole Normale Supérieure that they should "point out the principal theories of the contemporaries"; however, their main object should be "always to refute them." [27] Students were encouraged to criticize the works of other scholars, but it was also required of them that their allegations be supported by proofs, documentary evidence, and quotations from the works of recognized authorities. The scientific spirit of the Ecole Normale Supérieure was reflected in this statement, which reads like its motto: "Hasty specialization is fortunately prohibited at the Ecole Normale." [28] Durkheim and the *normaliens* who were the members of the Durkheimian school lived up to that adage. Durkheim, Simiand, Hubert, Mauss, and other members of the school never missed a chance when it came to criticizing others' works that they viewed as being infected by dilettantism. They frequently referred to books they reviewed as being "simplistic." It was through Fustel de Coulanges that Durkheim was sensitized to incisive criticism of others' works and to a method of examining the facts critically.

Boutroux explicated systems of philosophy; he was possessed of an ingenious ability to elucidate such philosophic terms as freedom, determination, the infinite, teleology, and so on. He insisted that his students learn to formulate original ideas; nonetheless, their new paradigms had to adapt to the contemporary trends in philosophy and the sciences. Boutroux explicitly stated that each science was possessed of its own subject matter and was quite capable of explaining its phenomena. (Under Boutroux's supervision Durkheim wrote and presented his doctoral thesis; in fact, Durkheim dedicated it to Boutroux. However, Durkheim, in his first major work, *The Division of Labor,* went so far in tendentious demonstration of his thesis that he angered his master for one reason and piqued the enemies of the new science for another.) Boutroux also affirmed the change that was evident in the institutionalization of new academic areas and emergence of new social sciences; however, he asserted that philosophy was the matrix and progenitor of what was coming about in the name of the social sciences. He stated: "The multiplicity and specificity of all the positive sciences have extended themselves to a philosophy which considers them as a model; hence one sees the formation of a psychology, a sociology, and a methodology, each having its distinct base, and consequently, its mutually exclusive existence."[29] Boutroux concluded that "instead of philosophy, one sees philosophical sciences."[30]

The first generation of eminent French sociologists, members of which were imbued with scientific ideas, issued from the Ecole Normale Supérieure. (Tarde was an exception; he graduated from the Ecole Polytechnique.) [31] The two *Grandes Ecoles,* the Ecole Normale Supérieure and the Ecole Polytechnique, are located within walking distance of each other. Both are approximately equidistant from the Pantheon and located on the edge of the famous Latin Quarter. Even such lesser known and less eminent figures in sociology as Alfred Espinas, Jean Izoulet, Marcel Bernès, and René Worms were connected with the Ecole Normale Supérieure. But they cannot be compared to Durkheim, since none of them founded a scientific sociology, nor did they prognosticate a future for it. About Worms, it may be said that he was content with the honorific titles he had earned with his three doctorates, [32] and more so with the international reputation that he had gained by organizing an international society. Also, it now becomes evident why the first generation of French sociologists originated from philosophy: their works, in part at least, manifested philosophic orientation; they were never able to extricate themselves completely from philosophy.

The political profile of the Ecole Normale Supérieure underwent marked changes during the 1890s. Before this decade the students, together with the professors, enjoyed the fruits of liberalism in education; as far as their political convictions and identification were concerned, they were truly loyal republicans. Beyond doubt, they were ardent patriots. But before 1894, or the tormenting period of the Dreyfus trials, the *normaliens* were in fact devoted exclusively to art, literature, science, and philosophy; they were filled with enthusiasm for rebuilding the foundation of the Republic. During the Dreyfus Affair itself, a whole generation of *normaliens* was converted to socialism; it was imbued with the ideal of *justitia omnibus*, including justice for Dreyfus; it fought anti-Semitism in France. These *normaliens* also waged war against the diehard forces of monarchism, the army, and the Church. One need not go so far as to accept Hubert Bourgin's satirical criticism of the Ecole Normale Supérieure as an Ivory Tower. Nor does one need to accept the claim that it had become a center of political anarchism. Yet one must at least admit that perhaps there is an iota of truth in the assertion that this institution of higher learning had become an arena of politics.

LUCIEN HERR: LINKS BETWEEN THE SOCIALIST COTERIE AND THE DURKHEIMIAN SCHOOL

The Dreyfus Affair played a significant though indirect role in the formation, growth, and consolidation of the Durkheimian school. This triggering event threw France into turmoil; individuals as well as political groups were dragged into an ugly debate in which everyone accused everybody else of wrongdoing. The Ecole Normale Supérieure, in the middle of this excruciating experience, had become a "center of conscience and of enlightened national consciousness." [33] The *normaliens* who initiated this melodrama carried it through to its finale. The cloister of philosophic erudition was transformed into a conclave of political agitation and demonstrations: It seemed that the men of science and philosophy had "prostituted" the Ecole Normale Supérieure for political profits, as Hubert Bourgin indignantly remarked. Nonetheless, the Affair produced a sense of solidarity among like-minded individuals belonging to the *cartel de gauche* and seduced the innocent *normaliens* into its orbit. From then on, and "for thirty years and afterward, Lucien Herr was the confessor, converter, and confidant of the *normaliens*. He was accepted as the director of their conscience and shaped the thinking of the univeristy elite." [34] The *normaliens* considered Herr their spiritual leader. Once they entered into his confidence, they found themselves associated with a group of *universitaires* dedicated to the discussion of socialism, the basis of which was Durkheim's positivism-rationalism-realism trilogy. By and large, Herr's followers worked hand in hand with Durkheim's followers, and not infrequently they were one and the same. During this decade of turmoil, a "Fabian" band of socialists in France was deeply under the influence of Herr's charismatic authority. Durkheim himself, however, had no sympathy with the politicizing of science. What minor intellecutal response politics induced from Durkheim was in response to Brunetière, in particular to his spiritualism and individualism. [35]

To channel the anger, anxieties, intellect, and energies of the *normaliens*, Herr created three types of variegated activities for them. Herr's acolytes and converts belonged to these groups: (1) an action group composed of the *universitaires* and socialists; (2) a circle of theoretical exponents of socialism; and (3) a group of entrepreneurs formed around the Société Nouvelle de Librairie et d'Edition, on the rue Cujas. Simiand was influential in all three facets of Herr's politico-scientific machinery. The Dreyfus Affair was a breach through which a number of *normaliens* and other intellectuals passed only to find themselves unintentionally involved with socialism or "sociologism" or both. The band of *normaliens* and *universitaires* that formed around Herr demonstrated in the streets; prepared signed petitions; joined action groups such as the League for the Defense and the Rights of Man or the Secular Circle of Moral Education; and discussed the possibility of bringing a socialist peace to the Republic. Simiand and several other members of the Durkheimian school were actively involved with Herr's groups; they came into direct or indirect contact with some of the veteran *normaliens,* staunch socialists, and politicians such as Albert Thomas, Jean Jaurès, and Léon Blum.

Those who belonged to Herr's second group consisted of *universitaires* who discussed the ideal-rational-realist ratiocination of socialism. Some of Durkheim's eminent followers used to frequent the meetings of this group. Emmanuel Lévy, a jurist and sociologist, enlightened the group about the legal aspects of creating a socialist society. Simiand, Mauss, and Fauconnet gave socialism a sociological definition, the one they had learned from their master. [36]

The third activity of Herr's group consisted of publishing and selling books. Some of the members of Herr's socialist phalanx bought Péguy's Librairie Georges Bellas and designated it as the Société Nouvelle de Librairie et d'Edition on the rue Cujas near the Pantheon. [37] It was an enterprise set up initially by a consortium consisting of Léon Blum, Hubert Bourgin, and Antoine Vacher (the latter two were members of the Durkheimian school), and was established in 1899, at the height of the Dreyfus Affair. [38] As a minor contributor, Fauconnet was an insignificant member of the consortium. Durkheim, the "sociologist of professions and organization," whose motto was "within your profession, adapt yourself to your status and function," was leery of this consortium. He declared that "it worked against the law of industrial and commercial organization, which forbids professors to manage bookshops." [39] At the time of the reorganization of the crumbling old enterprise of Peguy in 1899, four Durkheimians invested in the stock. Three of them—Bourgin, Simiand, and Vacher—made heavy financial contributions to the establishment of this enterprise, and the fourth, Fauconnet, also contributed. Three decades later, in 1929, the enterprise absorbed all of Herr's phalanx, which was formed around this group's periodical, *Notes critiques: sciences sociales;* they were also attached to *L'Année.* In addition, the enterprise included other latecomers to the Durkheimian school. [40] During the incipient stage of its development the Société Nouvelle published early works—in particular doctoral theses—by Hubert Bourgin, François Simiand, and Trumbull Stickney. (The latter was an American scholar, a classicist, Sanskritist, and poet who did his work at, and earned his doctorate from, the University of Paris.) It makes perfect sense now to conclude that the two movements of socialism and sociologism had much in common. Both movements were based on the same philosophical principles and scientific methods, e.g., rationalism-idealism-realism. Herr's phalanx and Durkheim's coterie worked together hand in hand.

When the Affair was settled and Dreyfus was exonerated of the charge of treason, and when the *normalien* youths and the university intellectuals had returned to their normal routine of teaching and learning, the new atmosphere of relative tranquillity took the edge off Herr's amateurish socialism. Professional politicians and devout socialists who were trained in the art of politics had moved into the political arena. This was a few years before the Republic again reached the threshold of war with its mighty neighbor across the Rhine. Under these more normal circumstances the group formed by Herr dissipated, but those who also belonged to the Durkheimian coterie remained with *L'Année* and with the Durkheimian school. It was not a matter of making a switch, nor did it involve a question of loyalty.

Herr's lieutenants and followers, who were essentially the theoretical exponents of a "Fabian" type of socialism, founded a social-sciences periodical and also published popular, inexpensive literature dealing with the working class and contemporary issues in a series called "Cahiers du Socialiste." [41] The periodical *Notes critiques: sciences sociales* was devoted to book reviews. The *Notes critiques* (1900–1904) and the "Cahiers du Socialiste" (1908–1914) were created in a time of delirium; both were the ephemeral scintillations of the socialist consortium consisting of Herr-Simiand-Mauss-Bourgin-Fauconnet. The *Notes critiques,* of which Simiand was editor, was a frivolous attempt in the name of the social sciences. It served the selfish motives of Simiand, who was able to scan a vast amount of literature in sociology and economics and thus keep up to date with new trends and ideas while he was still a librarian at the Ministry of Commerce. Durkheim is listed as a collaborator in this odd periodical. [42] Among the occasional contributors to the periodical, these fourteen names are worth noting: the Bourgin brothers, Chaillée, Fauconnet, Gernet, Hertz, Hubert, Emmanuel Lévy, Maître, Mauss, Roussel, Simiand, Stickney, and Vacher, all of whom also worked on *L'Année*. This points to the fact that the Durkheimian coterie had a strong hand in the operations of the socialist machinery installed on the rue Cujas.

Disseminating Doctrines: *L'Année Sociologique*

The fourth postulate of the theory of doctrinal schools refers to the existence of the various physical means that facilitate communication and propagation of doctrines. Doctrinal schools flourish in a variety of institutions: universities, university departments, and research institutes. Doctrinal schools may prosper around periodicals; they may be installed in publishing houses. These structures give such schools the opportunity for spatial growth and temporal continuity.

Our aim in the following discussion is to bring to light the character of those institutions where Durkheim and his disciples were installed, and from which they recruited most of their members; the professional organizations that were the main centers of their activities; and the manner in which the doctrine of sociology was disseminated. *L'Année* symbolizes the physical aspect of the Durkheimian school.

The first few years of Durkheim's teaching career were spent in Bordeaux. It was, however, a temporary phase in Durkheim's life; it proved to be a stepping-stone to a position of status in Paris. The Sorbonne and other institutions of higher learning in Paris were the major centers from which Durkheim and his disciples relentlessly disseminated their doctrines. The Durkheimians considered the university's precincts as the natural place to carry this out. There are references suggesting that the Nouvelle Sorbonne was dominated by the doctrines of certain distinguished masters, including Durkheim. [1]

As we have observed earlier, the Sorbonne, the Ecole Normale Supérieure, and the Ecole Pratique des Hautes Etudes contributed substantially to the Durkheimian school in terms of personnel. The members of the school, especially those belonging to the Pleiad and the secondary Pleiad, were installed in the highest-ranking professorial positions in the institutions of higher learning. It is beyond doubt that Durkheim himself covetously sought to secure positions for his acolytes. [2]

Unlike today, the Durkheimians did not have the benefits of speedy communication and transportation to help them deliver lectures, attend conferences, and communicate with other scholars. Durkheim himself never attended a conference or meeting of a professional organization outside of Paris, although he contributed his papers to professional organizations in Italy and England. [3] There is no evidence that any member of the Durkheim school even attended the founding meeting of the Gesellschaft für Soziologie (Berlin, 1910). It may be noted here incidentally that a report of this meeting appeared in the *Année*; however, one finds little therein to suggest relationships between Weber and the German sociologists, on the one hand, and Durkheim and his followers, on the other. [4]

Durkheim and his followers during the heyday of their activities never bothered to found a society or association through which they could discuss and debate sociological issues. The Institut Français de Sociologie (French Sociological Institute) and the Institut d'Ethnologie (Institute of Ethnology) were late developments in the history of the Durkheimian school, coming into existence only after the war and Durkheim's death. Bouglé's initiative in founding the Centre de Documentation to facilitate and advance further research work in sociology, [5] which was established as a part of the Ecole Normale Supérieure, was also a postwar development. However, the Durkheimians, during the nascent years of scientific sociology, were singularly dedicated to their collaborative efforts, gathering facts and developing and disseminating the doctrines of their master. They did not waste time in activities not essential to their monolithic aim of creating a scientific sociology and propagating it. They were preoccupied with the tasks of reviewing the current literature in sociology, enhancing the prestige of scientific sociology through their personal works, and debating the issues and confronting their adversaries. The first two tasks were effectuated in the laboratory of *L'Année* and in their personal published works, which were issued mainly by the Alcan publishing house. Their principal forums for discussions on the subject of sociology were the meetings of the French Philosophical Society. [6] By instinct, and by virtue of their educational formation, the Durkheimians were philosophers; they could not easily free themselves from their past indoctrination in philosophy. Not only did the Durkheimians frequently attend meetings of the French Philosophical Society, at which they defended their positions, but the more eminent among them even served as the main speakers at some of the meetings. The Society was the main artery of communication between the partisans of the Durkheimian school and their Parisian admirers and adversaries. It was not predisposed to any particular doctrine, nor did it serve as the organ of a particular group of scholars and philosophers. For this reason the Durkheimians were able to use it for their own purposes.

Worms gathered around him an eclectic "cluster" of sociologists, which attracted social scientists of all sorts and from several countries. Worms' initiatives in founding the Institut International de Sociologie (International Institute of Sociology) also inspired sociologists to found societies in their own countries. Through Worms' initiative, an eclectic group of Parisian sociologists consisting mainly of Durkheim's opponents founded the Société Sociologique de Paris (Sociological Society of Paris). However, there was practically no communication between the members of the Durkheimian school and the group formed by Worms. No Durkheimian ever became a member of the Sociological Society of Paris, or even attended the meetings. The Durkheimians had one aim and ambition: to create scientific sociology and disseminate it.

If Durkheim and his disciples did not set up such an organization, then how did they succeed in disseminating their doctrines? Durkheim, it must be admitted, was more successful than any other sociologist in his efforts to construct the edifice of scientific sociology, which he built up, brick by brick, in *L'Année*. Within his lifetime his name became known far and wide, in Germany, England, Italy, and the United States—first because of his early major works, later because of his magnum opus, *L'Année*. Worms and Tarde, it is true, were also known to some extent in these countries for their contributions to sociology; Durkheim, however, acquired international fame among sociologists which surpassed that of all his contemporaries in France. In Germany, where scholarly ethnocentrism was at its peak, a note on the launching of *L'Année* was published in a German periodical; it appeared as Durkheim had submitted it to the editor—that is, in French, [7] a very unusual achievement. In Italy, Durkheim and his followers were also well known, but it was in England that he acquired his greatest prestige among sociologists. Early English sociologists showed intense interest in the works and activities of the Durkheimian school. An article on sociology by Durkheim and Fauconnet, published in the *Sociological Papers* of the British Sociological Society, elicited debate and discussion by several eminent sociologists, who were either hypercritical or highly appreciative of Durkheim's position. [8] Durkheim was also represented in the United States at an exhibition of French books in San Francisco. [9] An emerging breed of sociologists and social scientists in the United States was critical of Durkheim's theory and method, which he was obliged to defend in a communication to the editor of the *American Journal of Sociology.* [10] Generally speaking, Durkheim was able to communicate more effectively with the English sociologists than with the Americans. During Durkheim's life some of his works were translated into English, [11] German, [12] and Russian. [13]

Three major works and some opuscules that Durkheim had published prior to his launching of *L'Année* brought him the recognition that helped him found the periodical. But the true repository of the Durkheimian school of sociology and of its collective effort was *L'Année*, which, as we have seen, created a cohesive group and attracted some eminent scholars and even scholarchs. Soon after the publication of *Suicide* in 1897, Durkheim became absorbed in finalizing the form and content of this periodical. During the last twenty years of his life Durkheim did not produce anything substantial comparable to his three early major works: *Suicide, The Division of Labor,* and *The Rules.* Those who may object to this characterization of Durkheim's sociological works by pointing to the publication of *The Elementary Forms* (1912) must bear two things in mind: (1) *The Elementary Forms* was the result of Durkheim's extensive experience reviewing books in the *Année*; and (2) sociologists have received this work with less enthusiasm than the others.

After returning from their sojourns in Germany, the young French scholars realized that the seeds of knowledge in that country were being disseminated through an ever growing number of periodicals. Lazarus and Stendhal's *Zeitschrift für Völkerpsychologie* and other German periodicals for a long time tantalized Bouglé, who, after his visit to Germany, aspired to set up similar periodicals in France to disseminate sociological knowledge. [14] One of the chief reasons that he was eager to cooperate with Durkheim in launching *L'Année* was that he was impressed by the German tradition of advancing learning through publications and seminars. Durkheim and Bouglé observed that in Germany every great master had his own periodical—edited and published under his personal authority. In fact, sometimes the periodicals were known by their founder's names—e.g., *Schmollers Jahrbuch* and *Jahrbücher für Nationalökonomie und Statistik* (popularly known as Conrads *Jahrbücher*), and so on. French sociologists, such as Worms and Durkheim, not only launched their own periodicals but also started their own series of publications in sociology.

Before Durkheim launched his *Année,* Worms had, a few years earlier, already taken the lead in this direction by founding a periodical, the *Revue internationale de sociologie.* Worms' initiative was not influenced by the German prototypes. Sociology was in the air. Its corpus was being delineated and defined. The growth of periodicals became an integral part of the whole movement of institutionalizing sociology and giving it stature as an academic discipline and a legitimate branch of knowledge. It was in this atmosphere that Durkheim founded *L'Année.*

The prefaces to the first two volumes of *L'Année* clearly indicate the purpose for which Durkheim launched the periodical. First, it would contain the results of his own researches and those of his disciples and followers. In fact (leaving aside Steinmetz, Charmont, Simmel, and Ratzel, who did not belong to the Durkheimian school anyway), no one except the members of the higher echelon got their *Mémoires originaux* published in *L'Année.* [15] Simiand, [16] on the one hand, and Mauss and Hubert, [17] on the other, soon after their articles and reviews were published in *L'Année,* collected and published them in book form. The second purpose of the *Année* was to present an annual review of sociology, showing the progress it had made during the preceding year and the tasks that lay ahead. [18] The small number of professional and dedicated sociologists not only had to be informed of what was being done in the field but also had to be given new directions through the presentation of comprehensive book reviews, notes, notices, and bibliographies. [19] Durkheim's disciples and followers provided the source materials for those who were interested in conducting further research.

At the height of *L'Année*'s activities, Durkheim himself reiterated that a *conscience collective* was being formed progressively among the collaborators that he had gathered around him by setting in motion a periodical of his own. On the eve of the appearance of the first volume of *L'Année,* he wrote to Bouglé arguing that "the time is coming when those who, for fear of dogmatism, have refused to follow us, would be ashamed of their negligence in straying away." [20] Within a few years of the periodical's publication, Durkheim declared that "the entire world was following the *Année,* and that the group thus formed was not without a cohesive representation." [21] In fact, it was the first group in the history of sociology that was "organized, and had a division of labor and a free sense of cooperation." [22] The *Année* collaborators constituted a veritable "society of mutual help" [23] for one another. But in spite of the cohesive nature of this group, Durkheim seemingly gave "independence to each editor" [24] of the sections of the periodical. The tight-knit organization of the Durkheimian *équipe* became so self-evident for the reviewers of *L'Année* and such a glaring phenomenon that Durkheim could not extricate himself from the labels "my sociologism" and "my method," [25] referring, of course, to Durkheim himself—his defense of "essentially a collective and impersonal work" [26] carried on under the banner of the Durkheimian school notwithstanding. In order to secure cooperation from his disciples, Durkheim praised them and offered his patriarchal affection; he shared with them their "joy and grief" in the course of striving for the success of *L'Année;* he counseled them in their personal problems and guided them in their studies and researches; he worked to obtain university positions for them; and above all, he inspired them with his exemplary character and awe-inspiring erudition.

The Durkheimians made special efforts to make *L'Année* a repository of a genuine nascent science. They acclaimed the merit of their collaborative efforts as superior, and they were conscious of the fact that their work would be a landmark in the history of sociology. Hubert Bourgin was tendentious in his claim on behalf of *L'Année,* whose cohesive group, he asserted, would excel Worms's "cluster"—an amorphous group lacking unity. Bourgin prophesied that Worms' group was doomed in the wake of *L'Année* and the Durkheimian school. [27] A Durkheimian who might be given credit for having made the *Année* enterprise well known to scholars was Bouglé. First, he himself brought to light the nature of the productive forces operating in the workshop [28] of *L'Année;* later, he encouraged his protégé, Marcel Déat, to investigate thoroughly the accomplishments of *L'Année* and reveal its arcana to the social scientists in a systematic and coherent work. [29] In fact, the Centre de Documentation was founded on the solid rock of the most comprehensive volumes of *L'Année.* The sociological bibliography compiled by Bouglé and Déat was meant to serve as a *vade mecum* for the generation of budding sociologists; this reference work, however, derived its source materials from *L'Année* and from the works of the Durkheimian school. When there was a need to disseminate the knowledge of sociology to the teachers of the Ecoles Normale Primaires and to the students of the Sorbonne, the Ecole Normale Supérieure, and other insitutions of higher learning in France, some of the best books that came out during this period were concocted from the recipes of *L'Année* and from other works by members of the Durkheimian school. [30]

Davy referred to *L'Année* as a "tribune" of the Durkheimian school. [31] Mauss wrote of the "schoolish"—i.e., forming a school—character of this periodical, which had spawned a "cohesive group" of sociologists and savants working in close collaboration with their master. [32] For the Durkheimians *L'Année* was a source of inspiration; and gradually the *Année* collaborators became conscious of the fact that working on the periodical was tantamount to membership in the Durkheimian school.

French periodicals dealing with philosophy and other academic disciplines saluted *L'Année* for the excellent reputation it had in scientific sociology. To introduce *L'Année* and recommend it to their readers, even such obscure periodicals as the *Année philosophique* [33] and *Revue socialiste* [34] reviewed it. Once *L'Année* had been established as an institution, Edmond Goblot, the logician and moralist, did not even consider it necessary to commend it. [35] Philosophers and scholars from other areas [36] who reviewed the status of *L'Année* unanimously recognized its encyclopedic character and its ability to stimulate further researches by providing exhaustive bibiliographies on different themes. [37] Worms' procrastination in saluting Durkheim as a scholarch and honoring *L'Année* in his periodical is something for which he cannot be exonerated in sociology. For several years an unknown sociologist, Bochard, reviewed *L'Année* for Worms's periodical. [38] Finally, when Worms's attention was attracted by the rising fortune of *L'Année,* he was moved to review the practice of sociology by Durkheim and his disciples, [39] but his review of *L'Année* was vitiated by his charge that the periodical was plagued by the "megalomania" of the social scientists who were collaborating on it. Worms' review suggests that he was tantalized by the pervasive influence the Durkheimian school exerted on the formation of French sociology.

Once *L'Année* became an established institution, Durkheim decided to reorganize its structure. During the first ten years of its publication the membership of the Durkheimian school had grown; consequently, the Durkheimians had begun to produce in great quantity the fruits of their independent researches. As a result of this productivity, Durkheim wisely separated the *Mémoires originaux* from the *Analyses* part of *L'Année;* he consolidated the former to become an independent series of publications called *Travaux de* *"l'Année."* [40] The move made by Durkheim was typical of the steps taken by influential scholars of this period to found series of their own publications, such as Worms' *Bibliothèque internationale de sociologie.* Only the faithful followers of Durkheim were able to publish their works in the *Travaux* series. The series did not last very long; nonetheless, its establishment suggests a step forward in disseminating the doctrines of the Durkheimian school.

Who preserved the vestiges of the Durkheimian school? Who gave unremitting moral and material support in publishing and disseminating the works of its members? Can the Durkheimian school be located in a publishing house? These questions point to the recognition of Félix Alcan—himself a *normalien* and a personal friend of Durkheim and his followers—as a patron of sociology of the Durkheimian school. A shrewd businessman and a congenial friend of his clients, who in large proportion were also *normaliens,* Alcan entered a publishing career at an opportune time. [41] He always welcomed the graduates of the Ecole Normale Supérieure in his publishing house, and he gladly published their works. Since Alcan was a publisher of good repute, it was considered an honor to both the *normaliens* and Alcan to develop business relations with each other. As a source of propagation of the doctrines of a school, publishing houses provide the material facilities, and some may even be identified with particular schools of thought.

Before undertaking the *Année* project, Durkheim discussed the possibility of having Alcan publish it. [42] During the time Durkheim was negotiating with Alcan, Ferdinand Pillon's *L'Année philosophique*, published by the same house, was losing its reputation and readership. To solve its problem, Alcan suggested the creation of *L'Année sociologique* as a supplement to *L'Année philosophique*, to read as *L'Année philosophique et sociologique*. Although it would have been expedient, Durkheim did not accept the offer, unwilling to compromise his journal of social scientific thought to become attached to a journal in philosophy. "The history of the Alcan House," claimed Hubert Bourgin, "forms an important part of the intellectual history of the Third Republic and of the history of the politics of the Ecole Normale Supérieure." [43] "Our philosophers, sociologists, proponents of doctrines, partisans," Bourgin stated, were looking for "a serious, honest, reputed and respectable publisher, who would publish the works of savants." [44] And their dreams materialized through Alcan. Not only the members of the Durkheimian school entered into business relations with Alcan, but also prominent historians, biologists, and medical scientists were among his regular customers. Alcan became "the center for rallying the sociological neo-positivism" [45] of Durkheim and his school. This publishing house became an unofficial rendezvous where Durkheimians of all sorts could meet and enjoy a shared camaraderie.

Some of the most distinguished periodicals in philosophy, history, and other fields were published by this house; they included *Revue philosophique*, founded by Théodule Ribot, and *Revue historique*, founded by Gabriel Monod (both in 1876). *L'Année* began to be published by Alcan in 1898. A little later, Pierre Janet (Paul Janet's nephew) and Georges Dumas also assigned the task of bringing out their periodical, *Journal de psychologie*, to Alcan. In general, those savants whose works had become part of Librairie Félix Alcan were identified as *Alcanistes,* [46] to use the French term.

All of Durkheim's and Lévy-Bruhl's works and some of Bouglé's major works were published by Alcan; Parodi and Foucault were also its clients. Durkheim's series *Travaux de "L'Année"* was issued by Alcan. The brilliant sociologists belonging to the Durkheimian school—Davy, Fauconnet, Granet, Halbwachs, Ray, and Czarnowski—graced this series of forty-five works with their doctoral theses, original researches, and other astute scholarly works.

The sociology of the Durkheimian school was ensconced in another niche of the Librairie Alcan. Félix Alcan himself founded a unique series entitled *Bibliothèque de philosophie contemporaine*. Members of the Durkheimian school, such as Mauss, Hubert, Essertier, Hertz, Lapie, Lenoir, and Lalo, made their contributions to sociology and published their works under the auspices of this series. Simiand's scientific opus on the evolution of money was published by Alcan. [47] Evidently, any research into the history of the French school of sociology and the flowering of French thought in general requires a gleaning of the files and catalogues of the Librairie Félix Alcan. [48]

Organization and Scope of This Edition

The earliest attempt ever made to reconstruct and revive Durkheim's *L'Année* was the original French edition brought out by Jean Duvignaud, entitled *Journal sociologique*. [1] Davy, one of Durkheim's loyal disciples, objected to the title, since Durkheim never wrote anything entitled *Journal*. [2] Aside from that rather insubstantive criticism by Davy, Duvignaud's French edition is marred by two serious flaws involving unity and systematics. As far as Durkheim's total contribution to the *Analyses* part of *L'Année* is concerned, Duvignaud's edited *Journal* comprises not even half of it, leaving more than half still scattered in *L'Année*. [3] Second, the French editor's use of chronological order in arranging the reviews and other contributions by Durkheim to *L'Année* gives evidence of his lack of sensitivity in faithfully reconstructing it; he did not understand the significance of the system of classification in sociology that Durkheim developed specifically for use by himself and his disciples in their arrangement of the thousands of reviews, notes, and notices that were published in *L'Année*. The *Journal* is of no help to anyone searching for clues to the methodical development of scientific sociology through a system of classification. Durkheim's reviews are not merely pieces written at random and haphazardly, as Duvignaud seems to have assumed; instead they are an integral part of a systematics of sociology established in *L'Année*. Instead of repairing the damage done by Duvignaud to Durkheim's *L'Année*, Victor Karady, by editing *Textes*, [4] has also not followed Durkheim's suggested method of classification employed in the periodical.

This English edition of Durkheim's *L'Année* is a faithful reproduction. We are not setting ourselves up as arbiter of Durkheim's systematics of sociology or creating rubrics that Durkheim never conceived of in organizing his contributions to *L'Année*. By presenting Durkheim's total contribution to *L'Année*, except his *Mémoires originaux,* in a series of publications, based on the organization of the periodical and in accordance with the nature of the subject matter, this English edition will be definitive, complete, and true to the organic unity and individuality of the subject matter.

We have justly excluded Durkheim's articles (*Mémoires originaux*) from this volume. The *Analyses* part of *L'Année* essentially contains five categories of contributions: reviews, notes, notices, bibliographic apparatus (references), and introductions to sections and subsections. [5] Durkheim himself distinguished[6] clearly the methodic reviews from the notes and notices. We did not have the courage to tamper with the formal purity of Durkheimian sociology, or even to interfere with the pristine arrangement of the *Analyses.* Without accruing any loss, we have eliminated, after much debate and hesitation, the distinction between notes and notices. In arranging Durkheim's contribution, I have placed introductions to rubrics (very few, though) and reviews first, followed by notes and notices. The reviews, on the one hand, and the notes and notices, on the other, have been arranged in chronological order under each subsection.

Although there is today a clear-cut academic distinction between sociology and anthropology, Durkheim considered the two as sides of the same coin. In fact, the scientific sociology Durkheim cultivated also spawned scientific anthropology—known as the *stade expérimental*[7]—in France. Since the output of reviews Durkheim contributed to *L'Année* is too enormous to be manageable as a publication in one volume, I have used my discreet judgment in distinguishing sociology from anthropology and have included only sociology here. In order to systematically arrange the seemingly unwieldy mass of reviews, this seemed the best possible solution. Needless to say, the works adducing the historical method, those employing statistical analysis, and the studies concerning Western industrial societies have been classified as belonging to sociology; on the other hand, the works using ethnography as source material and those which manifestly exploit to their advantage such anthropological terminology as "totemism," "exogamy," "clan," "taboo," and "kinship" have been consigned to anthropology. Sometimes the task was like walking on a tightrope with a bucketful of water. While crossing the rope both ways, we have spilled a few drops of water here and there, but on the whole, we hope to have succeeded in our mission. Sometimes, although rarely, the exigencies of publication required us to eschew these finicky criteria.

Most of the reviews in *L'Année* give clear indication of their authors; hence it is easy to identify Durkheim's contributions. The very few reviews that are in even the slightest dispute may be assumed to be Durkheim's when one senses the style Durkheim adopted, detects the number and names of collaborators in each and every rubric, follows the pattern of his special interests, and notes other ancillary factors. Often Durkheim gave cross-references in his signed reviews which are helpful in identifying his unsigned reviews, or for that matter reviews by other collaborators. For example, Durkheim's introduction to the rubric on sociological conditions of knowledge gives clear evidence of being his workmanship alone. Karady[8] has erroneously attributed this piece to Durkheim and Bouglé.

Bibliographic references in the main text appear almost exactly as they were cited by Durkheim, in places incorrect and inadequate according to modern standards and scholarly tradition. In such cases, I have not used my editorial prerogative to give them a form which they did not have to begin with. In places Durkheim translated from other languages into French the titles of works he was reviewing. In those cases alone, I have given the English rendition of the French translation. Otherwise I have not translated the titles of works from other languages into English. Throughout his reviews in *L'Année*, Durkheim conscientiously gave pagination for quotes, and also for the support of his ideas wherever necessary, from the reviewed author's original work. However, the reader should be aware that there are gaps in this regard.

Since *L'Année* did not aim to enunciate one single theme or thought, it was feasible and convenient for me to seek the collaboration of several competent, helpful, and well-disposed colleagues, to whom I assigned reviews for translation. At the end of every piece the name of the translator is cited. As befits a conscientious editor—however understanding with regard to the difficult, sometimes even ungrateful, task of translating others' ideas—I have carefully read and reread the texts of each and every contributor with an eye to accurate and standard translation rendered faithfully, and have made changes wherever I deemed it necessary, without, however, encroaching upon the individual style of a particular contributor. Except for the parts contributed by Professors Lyons and Woody, I have myself added notes to the translations, a task which I considered properly mine.

Yash Nandan

Durkheim's Contributions

Prefaces to *L'Année Sociologique*

Preface to *L'Année Sociologique*, 1898

L'Année Sociologique is not solely aimed or even chiefly intended to provide an annual index of current literature that is *properly sociological*. Thus circumscribed, the task would be too restricted and of little use, for works of this type are still too few to justify the need for special bibliographical material. But what the sociologists are urgently in need of, we believe, is to be regularly informed of the investigations being performed in the special sciences: history of law, customs, religion, moral statistics, economics, and so on, for this is where the materials are to be found with which sociology must be constructed. To answer such a need is the primary goal of the present publication.

It appeared to us that, in the present state of science, this was the best way to hasten its progress. Indeed, the types of learning a sociologist must have acquired, if he is not to indulge in a vain exercise in dialectics, are so extensive and varied, and the facts so numerous and scattered about so widely that it is difficult to find them, that we always run the risk of overlooking the essentials. It is therefore desirable that preliminary investigation put them at the disposal of those who are interested. To be sure, as sociology becomes more specialized, it will be easier for each scientist to acquire the competence and erudition for handling the particular problems to which he devotes his attention. But such an eventuality is far from being realized. There are still too many sociologists who pontificate daily about the law, ethics, and religion with haphazard information or even mere insights from natural philosophy, seemingly unaware that a considerable number of documents on such points have been assembled by historical and ethnographic schools in Germany and England. It is not a wasted effort to proceed periodically to an inventory of all such resources by indicating what profit sociology can reap in so doing. Even over and above the views and investigations they can suggest, are not such methodical analyses of works of a special nature but mutually complementary better able to give a more vivid impression and even a truer notion of collective reality than the ordinary generalizations found in treatises on social philosophy? Therefore, we hope to succeed in interesting not only professional sociologists but all the enlightened readers whom such problems preoccupy. It is important, in fact, that the public be more keenly aware of the preparation that is necessary in order to tackle these studies, so that it may become less complacent about facile constructions, and more demanding about the nature of evidence and inquiries.

Our enterprise can be useful in still another way: it can help bring closer to sociology certain special sciences that hold themselves aloof, to our mutual detriment.

It is especially history that we have in mind when speaking in that vein. Even today, historians who take an interest in the investigations of sociologists and feel that such matters concern them are rare. The overgeneralized nature and inadequate documentation of our theories cause them to be regarded as negligible; they are credited with having little more than a certain philosophical importance. And yet, history can be a science only insofar as it explains, and it can only explain when making comparisons. Otherwise, even simple description is all but impossible. The description of a unique phenomenon is defective *because our view of it is not clear*. That is why Fustel de Coulanges, in spite of his profound understanding of historical matters, was mistaken about the nature of the *gens* when he viewed it merely as a vast family of agnates, simply because he was unaware of the ethnographic analogies of this family type. The true nature of the Roman *sacer* is very difficult to perceive and understand if we do not compare it with the Polynesian *taboo*. The examples we could give are countless. It will constitute a service to the cause of history if we can induce the historian to transcend his ordinary point of view, to broaden his outlook beyond the country and period he proposes to make his special study, and to concern himself with the general problems raised by the particular phenomena he investigates.

Once subject to comparison, history does not become distinctly different from sociology. Put another way, not only is sociology unable to dispense with history, but it needs historians who are at the same time sociologists. So long as sociology is to be presented as alien to the field of history, thereby depriving it of phenomena which concern it, the contributions it can make can only be quite meager. Out of touch in unaccustomed surroundings, it is almost inevitable that there will be a failure to notice or to see clearly or perceptively enough matters that should be in its best interest to investigate closely. The historian alone is familiar enough with history to utilize it with assurance. Accordingly, far from being antagonistic, these two disciplines naturally tend to blend with each other, and every trend anticipates and calls for a merger into a common discipline wherein the elements of both disciplines will be reencountered, combined, and united. It appears likewise impossible that he whose role it is to discover the facts should be unaware of the type of comparison they invite, and that he who compares should be unaware of the method of their discovery. To create historians who know how to view historical phenomena as sociologists, or sociologists who fully grasp historical technique—such is the goal that must be sought on both sides. Under such circumstances, the explanatory formulations of science can be progressively extended to all the complexities of phenomena instead of merely reproducing them in generalized outline form, and at the same time can become meaningful, since they will be used to solve the most serious problems with which humanity is faced. Fustel de Counanges liked to repeat that true sociology is history; nothing is more indisputable, provided that history be fashioned sociologically.

In order to obtain such a result, sociologists must turn spontaneously to history, get in touch with it, show it what use can be made of the materials it accumulates, and become imbued with its spirit and penetrate it with theirs. That is what we have tried to do in the reviews that will follow. When it becomes clear that sociology in no way implies a disdain for facts, that it does not even recoil from particulars, but that phenomena are intellectually significant only when grouped according to types and to laws, we will doubtless be more conscious of the possibility and the need of a new conception whereby a sense of historical reality, in the most concrete sense, will not exclude that element of methodical search for analogies that is natural to all science. If *L'Année sociologique* could make its contribution, however slight, by turning good minds in this direction, we would feel no remorse over our difficulties. *

Our objective thus defined, the outlines of our publication will be determined accordingly.

If our main purpose is to assemble the materials essential for science, however, it appeared to us that it would be fitting to show by means of a few examples how such materials may be put to work. We have therefore reserved the first part of *L'Année* for *Mémoires originaux.* We do not require that the works we publish under this title conform to a predetermined formula; it is enough for us that they have a definite objective and that they be done methodically. While holding to this double condition, we in no way intend to exclude general sociology; we shall be able to assure ourselves of this farther on. It is a branch of sociology no less useful than the others, and, if it lends itself more readily to the abuse of generalization and to the fanciful, this is not a necessary condition of its nature. However, we admit that our efforts will tend to favor studies dealing with more restricted subjects and arising from the special branches of sociology. For, since general sociology can only be a synthesis of these particular sciences, since it can only consist of a comparison of their most general results, it is impossible for it to grow except to the extent to which they themselves have progressed. It is therefore especially necessary to apply oneself to their organization.

The second part of the work, and the most considerable, is devoted to analyses and to bibliographical notices. But since the field of sociology is still very indefinite, it behooved us, right from the start, to circumscribe the areas to which *L'Annee sociologique* intends to contribute, in order to prevent ar-

---

* All the foregoing could be applied to statistics, whether economic or moral, which are otherwise instructive only on condition of being comparative. If we speak specifically about history it is because, in the present state of affairs, it is the chief source of sociological investigation, and because, moreover, it is more resistant to the use of the comparative method.

bitrary choices and exclusions. In one sense, everything historical is sociological. In another sense, philosophical speculations on ethics, law, and religion cannot fail to be of interest to sociologists. It was therefore necessary to set these two limits.

As far as philosophy is concerned, the limit was easily determined. All doctrines concerned with customs, law, and religious beliefs interest us, provided they admit the postulate that is the essential element of all sociology—namely, the existence of laws that deliberation, logically employed, helps discover. We do not mean that we must deny every contingency in order to be sociologists; sociology, like the other positive sciences, does not have to confront this metaphysical problem. It simply assumes that social phenomena are tied in with scientific investigation pursuant to intelligible and accessible relationships; it does not have to account for systems that derive from contrary assumptions. The times have passed when to refute them could serve a useful purpose. However undeveloped our science may be, it has produced sufficient results to warrant its rights to exist.

As for history, the line of demarcation is more fluid. Even the way in which it is fixed can be merely tentative, and probably must be replaced in ways commensurate with the progress made by the science itself. However, at least one rule may be stated. The only facts we have to retain in these pages are those that appear to be scientifically compatible in the foreseeable future, that is, those that can invite comparisons. This standard practice suffices to eliminate works where the roles of historical personalities (legislators, statesmen, generals, prophets, innovators of all types) are the principal or exclusive object of research. We shall say as much for works that are uniquely concerned with retracing, in chronological order, the sequence of events that constitute the apparent history of a certain society (dynastic successions, wars, negotiations, parliamentary histories). In a word, everything that is biography, *whether of individuals or collectivities,* is of no use to the sociologist. It is in the same sense that the biologist does not pay much attention to the extraneous history of the vicissitudes that befall each individual organism in the course of its existence. No one can state that such varied peculiarities will always be scientifically intractable, but the time when it may be possible to attempt even a partial explanation of them is so remote that it is a wasted effort to apply oneself in that way. As a matter of fact, what is called a scientific phenomenon is quite simply a phenomenon that has scientifically come of age. The factors that determine this maturity vary according to whether the science is more or less developed. This is what explains why all phenomena are not of this nature at a given moment, and why the scientist is obliged to choose and to separate those that appear useful for him to observe.

With the subject matter of our reviews defined in this way, it behooved us to construct a critical procedure that might be in keeping with the goal we were seeking. We could not adhere to the current idea that makes the critic a sort of judge who passes sentence and rates talent. Posterity alone is competent to proceed with such classifications, which, besides, are of no use to science. Our role must be to extract the objective materials from the works we are studying, namely suggestive phenomena and promising views, whether they be interesting for their intrinsic value or for the discussions they elicit. The critic must become his author's collaborator, for however slight a book's substantive value, it is a corresponding gain for science. This collaborative sharing is rendered still more important and necessary by the nature of works of which we have to speak. As many among them are not explicitly sociological, we were not able to settle for making an inventory of their contents, to pass along in a crude form, as it were, the subject matter they contain; it was necessary for us to submit them, insofar as possible, to a preliminary elaboration, which would indicate to the reader what particulars emerge for the sociologist. In order that such indications might be apparent, all the analyses of works that refer to the same problem have been grouped together so as to complement each other and to provide mutual clarification. Such approximations already, in their own right, amount to comparisons that may be useful.

Such is our program. In order to carry it out, a certain number of workers have joined forces after having come to an understanding on the rules that have just been explicated. And perhaps this instinctive meeting of minds with a view to joint enterprise is a phenomenon that is not without importance. Until now, sociology has generally remained an eminently personal undertaking; doctrines depended closely on the personality of the scholar and could not be disassociated from it. Yet science, since it is objective, is essentially an impersonal matter and can develop only from collective effort. For this reason alone, and independently of the useful results that it can have, our attempt deserves, we believe, to be welcomed with interest by all those who are committed to helping sociology grow out of its philosophical phase and take its rightful place among the sciences.* (*Année sociologique,* 1, 1898, pp. i–vii; trans. J. French)

---

* A few words of explanation on the period to which the works analyzed refer. As a general rule, we go from the first of July of one year to the first of July of the following year. We have chosen this combination because, for reasons of internal order, it facilitates the work of editing and will permit us to go to press regularly at the start of each year. We reserve, moreover, the right to backtrack a bit, if there is occasion to do so, in order to remedy involuntary omissions. It appears to us, in fact, that since our goal is not to present from time to time the image of a science achieved but to assemble the materials necessary to fashion this science, the superstitious respect for dating the period exactly is without justification. The essential part is to be as complete as possible and to make known, even a year behind time, everything that is worth knowing. We have even been concerned this time, in three or four cases, to go back in time to 1895. But they are exceptions that may be self-explanatory for the first year, but will no longer have to reoccur, we hope, in the future.

We beg the reader, moreover, not to consider this first try as an indication of what we would choose to do. If the reader realizes the difficulties that such an enterprise presented, he will not be disinclined to pardon some inevitable fumbles.

Preface to *L'Année Sociologique,* 1899

We stated our program last year, so we do not feel it is necessary to repeat it. The very favorable response our attempt elicited has, moreover, proved that we were quite well understood.

There are, however, a few points about which it may be helpful to give fuller explanation.

One may feel free to reproach us either for not being complete enough, or for being too much so, and for overstepping the bounds of sociology. When, as so often happens, sociology is perceived as merely a purely philosophical discipline, a metaphysical branch of the social sciences, the very precise works we analyze may seem out of place. But our principal goal is to counter by being precise, as a way of interpreting and of practicing sociology. It is not that we mean to deny the existence of a general sociology that would be like the philosophical part of our science; we are even willing to acknowledge that sociology, in its earliest stages, was not able and not supposed to have any other characteristic. But the time has come for it to depart from such generalities and to become specialized. It will not, thereby, be mistaken for the special techniques in existence for a long time. Or, at least, it will be mistaken for them only after having changed them, for it cannot fail to introduce a sense of novelty. To begin with, it involves the notion of categories and of laws—which is still too often lacking. Indeed, many of those other disciplines are involved with literature and with erudition rather than with science; above all, they aim to relate and to describe particular events rather than to constitute types and species and to establish relationships. But what sociology brings with it is a sense that there exists a close relationship among all those phenomena of such diversity, phenomena that until now have been studied by specialists independent of one another. Not only are such studies so interdependent that they cannot be understood if isolated from one another, but they are, basically, of similar nature; they are varied manifestations of a same reality, which is social reality. That is why not only must the jurist keep up to date in his knowledge of religions, the economist up to date in his knowledge about life styles, and so on; since all these different disciplines are involved with phenomena of the same type, they must use the same method.

The basic idea behind this approach is that religious, juridical, ethical, and economic phenomena must all be treated in conformity with their nature, that is, as social phenomena. Whether for the purpose of describing or explaining them, they must be tied in with a specific social milieu, with a definite type of society. It is in the characteristics that make up this type that we must look for the determining causes of the phenomenon under consideration. Most of these sciences are still impervious to this point of view. The science of religions speaks mostly in generalities of beliefs and of religious observances as if links with any social system were nonexistent. The laws of political economy are so generalized that they are free from all considerations of time and place, growing out of all collective patterns; we view barter, production, and securities merely as a by-product of oversimplified motives, common to humanity in general. The comparative science of law is, perhaps, the only one oriented in a different direction; for example, relationships between particular institutions and particular forms of organized society have been singled out. Again, such comparisons have remained very fragmentary and have been sought out without much logic and method.

There is then a task to be attempted that is urgent and truly sociological: we must try to make out of all such special sciences a like number of branches of sociology. But to do so, it is necessary to be in close touch with them, to be involved in their life in order to reconstruct it. We must grapple with details of facts, not for the sake of making a brief survey suggestive of philosophical speculation, but in order to study them for their own sake, to try to understand them, to convert them into types and into laws that express them as adequately as possible, and in a sociological sense. In this way the sometimes very special nature of the works that we include in our analyses is accounted for and is justified. But, for the very reason that we have this objective in mind, we cannot claim to be complete in the absolute sense of the word. Special techniques habitually record the facts that concern them, without bothering to find out what typically scientific interest is involved, namely, to what extent suitable steps are taken to arrive at a general law. The investigation of specialists does not always have a bearing on matters that have the most valid meaning, precisely because interpretation is not the decisive aim of their investigation. It will, therefore, be useless and vexing to give in these pages a complete account of all the works that appear every year in these different fields; the only ones that deserve to be retained are those that seem to suggest sociological reflection. In any case, since every selection reveals regrettable omissions, we prefer, generally speaking, to extend the circle of our choices rather than restrict it unduly; since it is impossible to preserve a just limitation, it is better to search for more than enough rather than to have little or nothing to show.

Under the influence of sociology, the classification of the special sciences and their mutual relations are called upon to undergo a transformation, along with the spirit and the methodology of each one of them individually. Until now, indeed, they have been established independently of one another. Social material has not therefore been distributed among them in a methodical manner, according to a well-considered plan; rather, their reciprocal frontiers have been determined under the influence of the most casual bases, at times even the most fortuitous. As a result, there have been a number of confusions and distinctions—each one as irrational as the next. Some incongruous phenomena are often assembled under the same heading, and some phenomena of a similar nature shared with different sciences. What in Germany is designated with the untranslatable name of *Völkerkunde* comprises simultaneously studies about customs, beliefs, and religious observances, about housing, the family, and certain economic phenomena; *Kulturgeschichte* is no less comprehensive. Inversely, demography* and geography, which are so closely related to each other, are only beginning to reach a point of mutual interpenetration. It is therefore important that new divisions be substituted for those that are in use. To do that, it is necessary that all such special disciplines be compared, set side by side, so that we may perceive which are the ones that are "on speaking terms" and tend to be mutually compatible, and which are the ones that may readily remain separate. We may therefore expect that sociology will determine a new, more methodical redistribution of the phenomena that are the concern of those different studies; and this is not the least of the services our discipline is destined to render. For nothing is more at odds with scientific progress than a faulty classification of the problems it deals with. As a result of this situation there is an additional difficulty for the internal organization of *L'Année*. Since the works that we are about to take into account have not been made to fit into the framework of a rationally organized sociology, it is impossible to ascertain that their orderly arrangement will be perfectly satisfactory. We may mitigate the difficulty, not suppress it.

Heading these reviews will be those, like last year, concerning religious sociology. People were astonished at the kind of priority that we accorded these phenomena, but the fact is that they are the germ from which all the others—or at least nearly all the others—have derived. Religion holds within itself, from the very beginning, but in a muddled sort of way, all the elements that have given rise to the various manifestations of collective life by a process of separating, redefining, and combining in a thousand different ways. It is from myths and legends that science and poetry have arisen; it is from religious ornateness and cult ceremonies that the plastic arts have arrived on the scene; law and morality have arisen from ritual observances. It is impossible to understand our representation of the world, our philosophical conceptions of the soul, of immortality, of life, if one is not aware of religious beliefs that have been their formative progenitor. Family relationships started by being an essentially religious bond; punishment, contract, gift, hommage are derived from the expiatory, contractual, communal, noble sacrifice. At the very most we may ask ourselves if economic organization provides an exception and comes from a different source; although we do not think so, we grant that the question may be set aside. It is no less true that a multitude of problems are viewed in a completely new and different light once we have acknowledged their relationship with religious sociology. It is therefore to this area that our efforts must be directed. There is, moreover, no social science that is more liable to make rapid progress, for the materials assembled at this very moment are extremely abundant and ripe for sociological elaboration. That is why the two articles we are publishing deal with this particular science. It appeared to

* From the French *démologie*. ED.

us that it was useful to call the attention of the sociologists to these investigations, to give some notion of how rich the subject matter is and all the benefits we may expect from it.

It is perhaps true that the hard-pressed sociologists will find such a procedure unnecessarily complicated. In order to understand social phenomena of today to the extent necessary to direct their evolution, is it not enough to observe them as data from our contemporary experience, and is it not creating a work of vain erudition to begin by investigating their most remote sources? Rather, such a rapid method is crammed with illusions. We have no knowledge of social reality if we have merely viewed it from without and if we are unaware of its substructure. In order to know how it is created, one must know how it has been created. In other words, one must follow the history of the progressively changing nature of its composition. In order to be able, with some chance of success, to tell what the society of tomorrow will be, it is indispensable to have studied the social patterns of the most remote past. To understand the present, one must depart from it. *

But if, on this point, we were unable to defer to the observations that have been made to us, there are others that we have been glad to put to profitable use. Accordingly, we do not believe ourselves to be in error when stating that the present volume is sensibly more developed than the previous one. The number of works analyzed is more considerable. We have tried to classify them as reasonably as possible. We have even established an entirely new section (Social Morphology) and we take the liberty to call the reader's attention to its importance. Lastly, an alphabetical index of the subject matter has been added to the work and will make its handling more convenient. Other improvements will, no doubt, be possible in the future. We shall not fail to investigate them and we shall eagerly welcome suggestions about this matter from those who see fit to make them. (*Année sociologique*, 2, 1899, pp. i–vi; trans. J. French)

Preface to *L'Année Sociologique,* 1911

With this volume we inaugurate the new series of *L'Année Sociologique.* It is distinguished from the earlier series [of ten volumes] by two important

---

* But, of course, the important role we thus attribute to religious sociology in no way implies that religion must play, in contemporary societies, the same role as formerly. In one sense, the contrary conclusion would be on firmer ground. Precisely because religion is a primitive phenomenon, it ought to give way more and more to the new social structures it has engendered. To understand these new structures one must link them with their religious sources, but without mistaking them for so-called religious phenomena. Similarly, in the case of the individual, just because sensory perception exists as a primitive phenomenon from which advanced intellectual functions have resulted by way of associational procedures, it does not follow that the mind of a cultivated adult, especially today, consists merely of sensory perceptions. On the contrary, the importance of the role of sensory perception diminishes to the extent that intelligence grows.

reforms. To begin with, *L'Année* will resume publication only every three years. In addition, it will no longer include any more *Mémoires originaux.* These works will become a part of a separate collection. Three works have already been published in the *Collection des Travaux de l'Année Sociologique;* others are in preparation.

Such changes have become inevitable for several reasons.

We have had to renounce yearly publication in order to devote more time to our personal works. For ten years the collaborators on *L'Année* have been absorbed almost entirely by their work on bibliography. Certainly, they do not regret the time consumed by it. If sociology has ceased to be a purely dialectical form of literature, if historians, statisticians, and economists have learned to appreciate it, if they are beginning to realize that we are cooperating with them in the same kind of work, we believe we can say that *L'Année* has helped bring about such a result. It is no less true that the way to contribute to the advancement of a science is to deal with the problems it poses. Therefore, it has become necessary for us to set aside more time for personal research. That is what obliges us to publish *L'Année* less frequently. On the other hand, in sociology, original work lends itself more naturally to book form than to an article, for in matters where all the facts are interrelated and interdependent, and where the areas still to be explored are so considerable, it is unwise to limit investigation to narrowly conceived areas. That is why we have relegated *Mémoires originaux* to a separate publication. Such division has, moreover, the advantage of providing more space for bibliography. Since, at the same time, the size of the volume devoted to *L'Année* will be notably greater, the extent of information we shall put at the reader's disposal will not have to suffer from our new organization.

Not only will this transformation not alter the character of *L'Année,* but it will permit us to carry out a number of interesting improvements.

First, it will be easier for us to select from a greater number of the works that will be offered to us for review. We shall retain for analysis only those that have genuine value. As for the others, it will be enough for us to mention them. The reading of *L'Année* will gain in interest.

Next, the phenomena to be compared will be more numerous, more varied, and, consequently, the comparisons more instructive because we shall encompass in each volume a more extensive period. It is possible to anticipate that we shall, accordingly, be inclined to ask ourselves many questions that otherwise would have escaped us. From the beginning of this year, for example, the number of works related to the so-called primitive societies is such that we have been obliged to transfer this subject from the indeterminate state where it had remained until now. In this generally conceived area, we have distinguished certain themes. At the same time, this conceptualization has helped us to improve our classification; such distinctions, however, raise an important problem that will be found farther on (see *L'Année,* 11, 1910, pp. 286–288). *

For the same reason, it will be easier to determine certain types of civilization. Until now this notion has remained theoretical. We did not have, in a single year, the opportunity to study from a comparative point of view a sufficient number of related societies in order to induce types from the materials necessary to establish them. On the other hand, beginning with the present volume, we shall be inclined to speak of the civilization of the Bantus, the Pueblos, the North-West Americans, and so on.

We limit ourself to indicating, by means of examples, these few improvements. The future will surely permit more of them if, as we hope, our readers remain faithful and offer us their encouragement.† (*Année sociologique,* 11, 1910, pp. i–iii; trans. J. French)

---

* Translation of this piece will be incorporated in an additional volume under preparation of Durkheim's similar contributions in anthropology. ED.

† The works analyzed here are from July 1, 1906, to June 30, 1909.

Section One

General Sociology

Even though Célestin Bouglé was editor of the section on general sociology,[1] he rarely made serious efforts to sketch out the form and content of this section. One of the principal reasons for this was Bouglé's incapacity as a theoretician and an original thinker. At the time *L'Année* was being launched, Bouglé was still in his youthful years, not fully mature intellectually. Durkheim's extensive correspondence addressed to Bouglé, a total of forty-three letters [2] during the publication of *L'Année* alone, gives clear evidence of his tutoring the latter about everything concerning the periodical, including his duties as editor of the section on general sociology. Compared to the three major sections (on religion, juridic sociology, and economic sociology) of *L'Année*, the section on general sociology is weak[3] and consumes fewer pages than the others. Durkheim was not critical of Bouglé as an active collaborator and was aware of his responsibilities as editor of the section. As Bouglé's contribution to *L'Année* decreased each successive year, especially in the last two volumes, so did his interest in maintaining a high standard of publication.

From a reading of Durkheim's reviews within this section emerge some general concerns Durkheim had about the nascent science of sociology and some common themes which preoccupied him while examining certain authors. After leaving the Durkheimian school, of which he was a prominent member, around 1907, Richard at times explicitly and at times surreptitiously attacked Durkheim—with whom he was at odds for ideological and religious reasons—and his doctrines. Richard's *La Sociologie générale* obviously had these overtones of reaction against Durkheim's idea of general sociology. Now, Durkheim could hardly let its publication and its audacious defiance of his conceptualizations pass by in silence. The tenuous nature of the relationship which Durkheim had with Richard resulted from the latter's attempt, perhaps inadvertent, to misconstrue the subtleties of Durkheim's sociological thought. While reviewing this book Durkheim cautioned his former associate a second time to be aware that he was interpreting his ideas in a slipshod way. The criticism Durkheim leveled on Richard notwithstanding, both agreed on the need to distinguish the notions of general sociology from the general notions of the particular social sciences, since sociology had different aims and different methodological propositions. For Durkheim the aim of general sociology was purely conceptual and formal: to determine social laws by way of synthesizing the areas of social science and by incorporating the general notions of the disciplines of history and philosophy. For Richard the idea of general sociology had its claim on two basic concepts in sociology, namely society and community. Elsewhere in *L'Année* Richard had been criticized by other members of the Durkheimian school for his deviation from the parameters of Durkheim's scientific sociology.

A good number of reviews suggest Durkheim's dislike for dialectical method in the emergent science of sociology. Included in this group of reviews are those of sociologists and philosophers with metaphysical orientations, such as Jankelevitch, Small, and Ross, the latter two Americans. Nor did Durkheim ignore and exempt religious apologetics from his reservations concerning dialectical philosophers. Naturally, Catholic philosophers were apprehensive about positivism and scienticism, which, they thought, had ominous portents for disparaging the spiritual values of society. Durkheim, while reviewing the works of Toniolo and Belliot, was dealing with the spiritual philosophers who were growing weary of the men of science from Comte to Durkheim. Symptomatic of these reviews is Durkheim's ability to point out where the authors were remiss in their analysis of facts.

From all the reviews concerning the precarious relationships between sociology and psychology that developed while Durkheim had adapted an attitude of condescension toward psychology, the one regarding Tarde's eccentric concept of "interpsychology" is perhaps the most noteworthy, for it sheds some further light on the acrimonious personal relationships between Tarde and Durkheim. Durkheim always expressed his unqualified reservations about the conceptual instrumentality of interpsychology as a substitute, even a modest one, for sociology. By underscoring imitation, a distinctively psychological phenomenon, interpsychology (and terms associated with it) became the target of criticisms by Durkheim in his *Suicide* and elsewhere. Durkheim never ceased denouncing Tarde's sociological explication as being "tainted with ontology." Tarde, in return, labeled Durkheimian sociology as a variant of "realism" and, as a consequence, diluted with metaphysics. Durkheim reviewed the articles by Charles A. Ellwood and Adrien Naville either to show how others agreed, though independently, with his rejection of Tarde or to find an occasion to attack the "Tardean thesis," and, as usual, to distinguish the purity of his "sociologism" from Tarde's characterization of scientific sociology as an epiphenomenon of interpsychology.

Unlike Durkheim's review of some transitory themes and his reference to a score of unknown to lesser known authors dealt with in the abovementioned rubrics, in history he culled some of the prominent theoretically oriented scholars: Seignobos, Croce, Sorel, Xenopol, Berr, and Meyer. All the reviews under "Historical Sociology," or "Sociological History," manifested Durkheim's overall concern with the nature of history as a science and its nexus with social science in general and sociology in particular. The important issue of searching for the identity of the two and where they converge in their relations with each other has yet to be adequately recognized by either of the two disciplines. The Durkheimians, nonetheless, were eager and quite determined to bring history within the parameters of social science. Durkheim's personal views on the subject are eloquently expressed in his examination of Salvemini and Seignobos.

In no other section of *L'Année* have the rubrics been subjected to as many formal changes, even mutation and alteration, as in the section on general sociology. Even in the twelfth volume of *L'Année,* or after a mellowing experience of fifteen years, the overall plan of this section does not seem to be fully realized. Durkheim was too much preoccupied with other sections and Bouglé paid too little attention to the needs of his section.

The first rubric of this section, and of every other section for that matter, dealt with general conceptions and contemporary methodological issues; in the case of the section on general sociology, it presented an overview of the philosophical, psychological, and historical problems of the discipline. In different volumes of *L'Année* the title of this rubric has varied, but not the substantive discussion. Scientific sociology, which the Durkheimians were dedicated to cultivate, had to be retrieved from its misconstrued representation by philosophers, psychologists, and historians. Not only did scientific sociology have to be distinguished from philosophy, but also it had to be extricated from metaphysical adumbrations. During these years of early development, sociology maintained precarious, sometimes inimical, relations with psychology. Even some so-called sociologists mixed sociology with psychological phenomena. Some historians of this epoch, especially those who were *historiens historisants* ("historicizing historians"), either downgraded sociology or claimed that it belonged to history. Now, the Durkheimians who were fighting for sociology as a legitimate science worthy of its place in academia could hardly accept such a contemptuous attitude. The adversaries had to be fought back and the proponents had to be encouraged for their efforts, of whatever magnitude, in enhancing the prestige of the new science. With this aim in mind, Durkheim, with the cooperation of his followers, critically reviewed sociologists (such as Duprat, Richard, Sorel, Steinmetz, Waxweiller, Demolins, Pareto, Coste, Groppali, Ross, Small, and Schaeffle), and historians (such as Croce, Lamprecht, Berr, Xenopol, Lacombe, Barth, and Meyer).

The next several rubrics—on social philosophy, history of sociological doctrines, and history of sociology—appeared from time to time but separately and distinctly from the rubric on social theories. From the fifth volume of *L'Année* onward, it becomes quite clear that by adopting different rubrics in the preceding volumes, the Durkheimians, nonetheless, meant one and the same thing by social theories. In general, under the rubric of social doctrines the Durkheimians examined contemporary sociopolitical systems: anarchism, radicalism, and revolutionary ideologies. Under the rubric on the history of sociological doctrines, they gave sociological interpretation to social Darwinism and the biological school. The rubric on social philosophy was not well defined, and in the light of various other similar rubrics, the need to have it as a separate rubric seems questionable. For example, by including Lester Ward's *Dynamic Sociology* and *Outlines of Sociology,* and James Baldwin's *Social and Ethical Interpretation in Mental Development,* the Durkheimians have only added to the confusion as to the real nature of the rubric. Nuances in the discussion of various themes under these seemingly different but really identical rubrics notwithstanding, the books and authors discussed may be yoked together under the general rubric of social theories, as we have done in this edition of Durkheim's contribution to *L'Année.*

Under the rubric of social theories, the Durkheimians contributed significantly in debunking the organicist concept and biological analogy. In fact, some of the profoundest reviews and those which reflect the tenacious and tendentious dogmatism of the Durkheimian school resulted from its response to the works of Espinas, Novicow, Worms, and others, including Tarde, who adhered to organicism and the theoretical concerns of sociology *passé.* (It may be noted as well that Durkheim in his early works also followed a kind of evolutionary method.) In his analysis of Espinas and Novicow, Durkheim shows how little use the analogies have in explaining concrete and real social phenomena. Durkheim's review of Simmel's *Philosophie des Geldes* (*Philosophy of Money* [Boston: Routledge, 1978]) is exceptionally noteworthy and evocative. Like Durkheim, Simmel was a philosopher by temperament, and this work in social economics was written with logical ingenuity and sophistication. The work was divided into two parts: an analytical part which defines the essence of money and a synthetic part which transforms money into social reality. A sociological theory of money is constructed, deriving its substance from a synthesis of monetary abstraction and the concrete reality of social life. Despite the applause Durkheim accorded to Simmel for his exceedingly scholarly and analytic acumen, he did not spare him for his loss of perspicacity in indulging in illegitimate metaphysical speculation while creatively engaging himself in advancing the science of society. Phrases like the "author premises his conclusion on dialectical method," "there is too much of speculation vitiating the author's judgment," and "simplest explanation of the complex social reality" were Durkheim's strongest weapons in his insinuation that the works of others were falling short of the rigors of methodology and were incongruent with his idea of positive science and sociologism. Durkheim's ostentatious praise and then rueful characterization of Simmel's social philosophy as a travesty of sociology are typical of the criteria he adopted in upholding the distinctive marks of a scientific sociology.

Durkheim was much obsessed, rather unduly, with clearly identifying the subject matters of sociology and psychology as two distinct and separate disciplines. In the background of shared interest between sociology and psychology that became expressed in social psychology, or collective psychology, as Durkheim used to designate it, he vehemently objected to the adulteration of sociology with purely formal psychology—or individual psychology, as he used to call it. Bouglé was apprehensive of Durkheim's overly antagonistic position toward psychology, which could even discourage many others from collaborating with him, including Bouglé himself, of course. Had Durkheim at the earliest time of negotiations in launching *L'Année* not been able to convince Bouglé of his sincere intentions and propitious attitude concerning psychology,[4] he would not have succeeded in his mission. Durkheim was never able to distinguish clearly between what he designated "collective psychology" and "individual psychology." Even at the time of the last volume of *L'Année,* Durkheim still insisted on using the term "collective psychology" instead of "social psychology." (Incidentally, Durkheim had his own way of adopting certain terminology; he was rather inflexible in the use of certain terms and the adaptation of neologisms. For example, in spite of geographers' objections, Durkheim preferred the title "social morphology" for a division of sociology.) Among many other titles to designate the rubric of social psychology, including "psychological sociology," one that is frequently employed is "group mentality and collective ethology" (by the latter Durkheim meant a study of the temperament and character of a specific group in a primitive society [5]—what in modern jargon would be ethnopsychology). It is interesting to note that several studies on the primitive mind and on the psychological attributes of societies—both primitive and advanced—came out during this period. It is also to be noted that Durkheim's use of the term "ethology" is different from the biologists' use of the term in contemporary scientific literature. As far as the rubric itself is concerned, we have preferred the use of "social psychology" over others for the obvious reason that it is in popular usage and was adopted by the Durkheimians themselves.

Deposited under the rubric of social psychology are a variety of reviews, notes, and notices; but among them all Durkheim's review of Ribot's important work in sociological characterization of psychological phenomena contains the pith of Durkheimian arguments on the delicate but topical issue of the relationship between sociology and psychology. Throughout his work Ribot maintained that in some respects sociology and psychology are inseparable and indistinguishable from each other. This favorable attitude of a philosopher-psychologist toward sociology in the reigning atmosphere of acrimony between the two competing academic disciplines was a boon to the Durkheimians, who were hostile toward the dilution of the purity of Durkheimian sociologism by psychological representations. After Durkheim's death Mauss requited this debt of goodwill from a psychologist by making overtures to the proponents of psychology to forgive the past errors they attributed to Durkheim in his jealous enthusiasm for cultivating a scientific sociology. Thus an era of reconciliation and syncretism was ushered in with a formal and earnest plea by Mauss. Durkheim always hailed works which befitted his line of thought and which to any degree corroborated his doctrinaire sociology. Ribot's logical study of sentiments, even though psychological in thematic discussion, proves the Durkheimian inference that mental states, or individual representations, are derived from collective representations, and as a result are essentially sociological.

The rubric on the "sociological"—the wording is Durkheim's own, even though I believe it should read "social"—conditions of knowledge was delayed until the appearance of the eleventh volume, regardless of the fact that it was long overdue and should have been included soon after the publication of the essay "Primitive Classification" by Durkheim and Mauss. The Durkheimians had long since been practicing the sociological doctrine of epistemology as suggested by reflections on the most primitive forms of classification. Durkheim was incited by Jerusalem's article "Soziologie des Erkennens" to devise a rubric of that nature in order to accommodate the works belonging to this particular subdivision of general sociology.

General Conceptions and Methodological Issues: Philosophical, Historical, and Psychological

REVIEWS

F. Giner. *Estudios y fragmentos sobre la teoría de la persona social* (Studies on the Social Person). Madrid: Enrique Rojas, 1899, x + 433 pp.

After having studied the notion of person in general, such as it is presented in psychology, Giner applies his research to the theory of the social person, or, more precisely, to moral persons in general, including society. For him, the human being is not characterized either by its physical individuality or by impersonal reason; it consists essentially of a moral and psychic organization. This definition allows Giner to admit the reality of persons as embodiments of morals.

Opposing the theory of the social person to that of contract, he shows that every society truly worthy of that name is a rational being, a conscious organization, that it has a proper existence, distinct from that led by the [mere] union of its members. It is a personality (chapter 2, no. 1). In the light of this principle, he criticizes successively the theories of the jurists and those of the sociologists on the question. He divides the first into empiricists—who see in the collective personalities artificial combinations, beings of convention, simple aggregates of individuals—and into idealists, who, from Hegel to Lasson, base society on that which is universal in man. To these conceptions, he opposes those of the sociologists, who, after having reduced the social person to a fact of physical organization, as Spencer and Espinas have tried to do, have come little by little to recognize in society a "spiritual and moral" superorganism.

The most interesting and original part of the book is dedicated to the study of that collective personality sui generis which is called the State. The State is not an abstract entity; neither is it a part of society, nor the equivalent of the brain or the nervous system or of another organ of the human body. It is not the principle of social organization, as if society itself were only an inorganic whole. It is society itself, but a society considered in its juridical function (p. 204). It is society as legislating for itself. But the juridical life of every collective person can be manifested under two forms: One is spontaneous and continuing, adapted at each moment by itself to the necessities of existence; the other is reflective, reasoning, and consequently intermittent, and results from a personal and methodic effort. To that distinction corresponds the distinction between custom and the law. The first is a function of the entire organism; for the second, special organs are developed. The principal one is the government or the official State (p. 216). The author is thus led to speak of the constitution, of the electoral system, of the relations of the State with the other organs or collective personalities which the society contains in itself. Then he approaches the problem of the relationships of the individual with the State; he examines two opposed conceptions, individualistic democracy and authoritative statism, and he himself basically holds for a mixed solution.

The book ends with an exposition and a critique of Schaeffle's *La Quintessence du socialisme.* [6] (*Année sociologique,* 3, 1900, pp. 182–183; trans. J. Sweeney)

Charles A. Ellwood. "Prolegomena to Social Psychology." *American Journal of Sociology,* IV, March and May 1899, pp. 656–666, 807–823.

The author makes an extremely radical distinction between individual psychology and social psychology. The latter studies the substratum, and not the individual consciousness. It studies a group having its own consciousness, having a specific origin, and, equally, a specific character. But social psychology, understood in this manner, is not to be confused with sociology itself.

The author distinguishes two grand sociological sciences: social psychology, or subjective sociology, which studies social representations of all kinds; and objective sociology, which treats cosmic, ethical, and geographic facts, subject to the influence society exerts on them. The expressions thus employed are perhaps quite inappropriate, because the facts to which subjective sociology attends are, by definition, objective in relation to each individual's consciousness; they are derived from the group and need to be studied objectively—at least as objectively as those studied by individual psychology. It would be better to distinguish a functional sociology or social psychology, which studies social life, from social morphology, whose aim is to study the substratum of this life and its forms. This criticism, however, bears only on the nomenclature; it does not touch the fundamental issues.

In the second article, the author looks at the fundamental fact of social psychology as a whole and he finds it in the *group*. Social life exists only when a group is constituted, a group which has its own life. Aside from the word "group," the author also uses the word "coordination," which does not contribute substantially to the notion of a group. The one and the other, however, do not throw much light on the question. The definition given to social psychology in the earlier article tells much the same story. Also, when the author, with the help of this notion of group, undertakes to explain certain social facts, such as revolution or the role of great men, one is led to believe that he is satisfied with quite vague generalizations. On the other hand, by presenting the group as the fundamental psychological fact, he creates from a morphological phenomenon the type of functional phenomena; because the manner in which men are organized, or the form of their association, evidently belong to morphology. (*Année sociologique*, 3, 1900, pp. 183–184; trans. Y. Nandan)

Charles Seignobos. *La Méthode historique appliquée aux sciences sociales*. Paris: F. Alcan, 1901, pp. 11–322.

The purpose of this book, if we understand it correctly, is to reduce the social sciences to history, and to reduce history itself to a sort of subjective construction which can never arrive at anything more than very conjectural approximations.

In proving this the author begins by restricting the concept of the social sciences in a most unexpected way. According to him this term would apply to only three groups of studies: (1) the statistical sciences, including demography; (2) the sciences of economic life; and (3) the history of economic doctrines. In other words, the social sciences would deal only with economic and demographic phenomena. The only reason given for this restricted definition is that the term "social sciences" is not in fact ordinarily used to refer to research relating to other social phenomena (pp. 8–9).

A first reason which makes the historical method indispensable for the social sciences is the nature of the materials which they use. They do not observe directly the facts which they treat but only the documents in which these facts are reported by someone who has observed them. "The documents of demography are either elements of demographic calculation or the results of calculations. The documents of economics are either statistics or descriptions of institutions" (p. 19). Now, history is precisely the process of understanding by which one succeeds in determining facts which can only be arrived at indirectly, through the documents. "All historical knowledge is indirect" (p. 5). And the author implicitly admits as evident the converse proposition: All indirect knowledge is necessarily historical. To interpret their documents, the social sciences are therefore obliged to have recourse to the historical method.

The criticism of their material does not differ from historical criticism proper, of which the author sketches the fundamental rules (chapters 3–5).

But science is not just an inventory of facts; it groups facts and systematizes them. The historical method is equally necessary to the social sciences for their work of construction. Indeed, this construction can only be done in two ways. Either one groups simultaneous facts in order to show their relations at a given time and arrive at a description of a state of affairs or one establishes a series of successive changes within time "to arrive at the determination of an evolution." It is the old Comtian distinction between the static and the dynamic. Now, so far as grouping is concerned, the social sciences, if left to themselves, would run a great danger of not perceiving the necessity for it, or not recognizing the conditions, since "because of their special origin they have a tendency to reduce themselves to specialized studies, that is, to enclose themselves in a minute examination of a single species of abstraction" (p. 137). On the contrary, the study of the social *complexus* in its totality and of the reciprocal reactions between simultaneous phenomena is one of the objects of history. History is, above all, the science of the evolution of societies; "social science, on the contrary, is in danger of forgetting evolution because it limits itself to very short periods, where evolution is less perceptible" (p. 142).

Is it, then, a matter of interpreting documents and establishing facts? Social science must address itself to history, make itself into history; and it is also to history that it must give up its place when it comes to systematizing these same facts. We thus no longer see what remains for the social sciences as their own domain. They disappear into history and the special term by which one designates them no longer has a reason for existing. We find only one passage where the author indicates, very briefly, what could be the domain of the social sciences properly speaking: It would be that of those sciences which would operate "on the totality of societies, comparing together the evolutions of several of them" (p. 153). In any case, at present this is neither practiced nor practicable. It remains true, therefore, that at the present history and the social sciences are confounded together.

The second part of the book is devoted to the methodology of that social history which seems, in the thought of the author, to be the only social science possible at present: He understands, by that, the history of demographic and economic phenomena. We will not analyze this second part of the work, which is hardly more than the application of the principles laid down in the first part and adds nothing essential. But there is one characteristic of this history (or of this social science) which must be remarked upon: It is the imprecision, the entirely subjective and conjectural nature, which our author attributes to it and which he makes the distinctive trait of this type of research. His reasons are the following. Social life is a series and a system of representations, that is to say, of subjective states; this subjectivity must also be found in the construction of science. And indeed, since the facts consist of ideas, to establish facts, where the social sciences are concerned, means to attain these ideas through the documents which express them externally. But an internal state, which is what an idea is, cannot be observed directly; one does not see it from the outside; one can only, therefore, make conjectures about it by an act of personal imagination. In the same way, to explain an economic institution is to connect the totality of representations which have determined it, and these representations, for the same reason, can only be imagined (see pp. 111 ff. and pp. 147 ff.).

There is, in the principles on which this theory rests, something arbitrary and artificial, which we must point out simply because of the legitimate authority which the historical works of our author enjoy. First, there is the definition of the "social sciences." In fact, it is not true that this term is used only in the restricted sense given it here. Comparative law, with Post, Morgan, Steinmetz, Kohler, and many others, has become a social science, by the avowal of the scholars who devote themselves to it. The same is true of criminology, and of political geography as it is understood by Ratzel; the science of religions is more and more assuming this character and we are attempting here to orient it in that direction. What are we to say of the way in which sociology, in its totality, is put outside the circle of the social sciences? This word, the author tells us, "was invented by philosophers; it corresponded to an attempt to group together some branches of science which had remained isolated. . . . It seems to have had the same fate as that conception: After a period in which it was in fashion it seems in danger of disappearing from the language" (p. 7). In truth, this is to make very little of the work of Saint-Simon, of Comte, of Spencer, and of all their successors in all parts of the world. Such a proposition has a particularly parodoxical air at a time when one could well complain of the excessive vogue the word enjoys and of the abuse which is constantly being made of it. But furthermore, even if in current practice the term "social sciences" had only the limited signification thus attributed to it, the author would not have been justified in appropriating it from current usage without preliminary criticism. He recognizes, indeed, that the expression, so understood, designates "a disparate amalgamation" of heterogeneous researches. Now, in order to be able to determine the method of a science or of a group of sciences, it is also necessary that there be between those sciences a relationship of internal kinship which makes it possible to classify them under a single rubric and to subject them to the same treatment. But a methodological study of this sort deals with an object without unity; it necessarily lacks all determination.

The way in which sciences so grouped are reduced to history also calls for the most express reserves. No doubt, insofar as sciences use historical documents, it is necessary to apply to them the methods of historical criticism. But demography has a critical method which is its own and which is not that of history. Moreover, the social sciences, to the degree that they practice the comparative method, add new critical procedures to those which the historian has at his disposal, thanks to the comparisons they establish. But what are we to think, especially, of the prerogative accorded history as concerns systematization and explication, under the pretext that history tends naturally to synthetic views whereas the social sciences, on the contrary, are narrowly specialized? It is to the opposite reproach that we are accustomed and it seems to us, unfortunately, much more justified.

Finally, if it is incontestable that social life is made up exclusively of representations, it in no way follows that an objective science cannot be made of them. The representations of the individual are likewise internal phenomena and contemporary psychology nonetheless treats them objectively. Why should it be otherwise with collective representations? We do not think, however, that even where individual psychology is concerned the author means to relegate us to the literary fantasies of the purely introspective method. (*Année sociologique*, 5, 1902, pp. 123–127; trans. K. Woody)

Albion W. Small. "The Scope of Sociology." *American Journal of Sociology*, VI, pp. 42–66, 177–202, 324–380, 487–531.

Small's article is a continuation of the series of articles which we began reviewing here last year (vol. IV, 1901, pp. 108–109). [7] It was shown there that, for Small, sociology is a kind of philosophy with an aim to disentangle what is common to the different social sciences. Now he gives an exposition of the principles of this philosophy.

As in all science, it has postulates that it borrows from the conclusions of the antecedent sciences. There are five different kinds of them: (1) philosophical postulates, which consist of a certain conception of the world according to which it appears to be the product of an accident, a chance, an arbitrary will, or a directing prudence, and so on; (2) cosmic postulates, which are connected with the state of interdependence between man and society together with the cosmic environment; (3) individual postulates, that is to say, in sum, psychological, related to the conception of the individual; (4) postulates concerning *the association assumption,* which seem to be reduced to the assertion that man is a function of his social environment; and (5) teleological postulates, which assume that all human activity must be appreciated in its relation to some purpose. At the end, these aims have been placed under the rubric *psychological postulates.* In fact, Small believes that social objects can only consist in satisfying the individual desires that individual psychology studies. There are six of them: desire for health, for wealth, for sociability, for science, for beauty, and for morality. These are the prime movers of all social evolution.

Equipped with these principles, the author lands in the domain of proper sociology. First he undertakes to disentangle the general characteristics common to society as a whole. Here, for example, are some of those which he points up and analyzes: a diversity of individuals; a certain aptitude possessed by individuals to attract, to repel, and to exclude each other (the condition of all individuality); interdependence of the parts; existence of a certain coordination; a common conscience, [8] and so on.

Then Small undertakes a classification of societies, or rather, he indicates the principle of classification. He suggests a classification of societies according to the purpose they serve (such as pursuing health, wealth, sociability, and so on). No doubt there is no nation which does not have at least one of these activities, but there is always one of these activities which predominates over the others. It is the predominant activity which determines the type to which the state belongs. The author, in the light of this viewpoint, distinguishes four major types of state: ethnic, economic, civic, and moral. The last ones are more of a desideratum than real types.

It is obvious now that the conception of sociology results only in some vague generalizations. Let us add that this series of long articles is not based on any clearly defined fact. It is not even known what fixed types of societies conform to different social types distinguished by the author. These are all categories constructed in an entirely dialectical way. (*Année sociologique*, 5, 1902, pp. 133–134; trans. Y. Nandan)

G. Salvemini. "La storia considerata come scienza." *Rivista italiana di sociologia*, VI, no. 1, pp. 17–54.

B. Croce. "La storia considerata come scienza." Ibid., VI, nos. 2–3, pp. 173–176.

G. Sorel. "Storia e scienze sociali." Ibid., VI, nos. 2–3, pp. 212–227.

These different articles treat the same question. What is at stake is whether history is a science or an art. Salvemini holds the former thesis. However, the manner in which he expresses it does not permit him to use the ordinary proofs in demonstrating it. Generally, indeed, when one makes a science of history, one assigns as its object not the details of particular events but the institutions, the customs, the beliefs—in a word, the collective things—whose constancy and regularity one opposes to the contingency and the extreme fluidity of individual facts. Salvemini does not admit this distinction. For him, only individuals exist; social phenomena are nothing but generalized individual phenomena; as a consequence, those collective things which one would like to make the matter of history are only abstractions which one cannot study apart from the concrete forms in which they are realized.

Nonetheless, according to him, history is a science. Why, he asks, should it have this character only on the condition of bearing on a general object? Does not the science of the general presuppose, as a preliminary, the science of the particular? "The lion could not have been determined scientifically if one had not begun by observing and describing particular lions" (p. 24). Nothing is more obvious. But if all the sciences of nature begin with concrete facts, it is in order to elevate oneself to the general, to constitute types and laws; history, on the contrary, would (in the author's view) have as its function the expression of the particular as such . This is the objection Croce makes to Salvemini, and it seems to us that there is no reply to the objection. Even when science is purely descriptive, it does not describe such-and-such individuals, but a species. Doubtless history can be understood in the same way; but it then ceases to be the history of some particular people, to treat of a social species in general. It no longer has as object the web of concrete events which constitute the life of a particular society. One returns to the conception which the author puts aside. But it is especially when it is a question of explaining, of tying facts together, that history seems refractory to scientific form. For how can we choose among the enormous mass of historical facts which accompany one another and succeed one another and say that one is the cause of another? To replace experimentation, which is impossible, we would need at least comparison, and comparison presupposes that one abstracts from the particular to see only the general. The comparative method satisfies all the requirements of science, but implies that the study does not have individual phenomena as its object. Now, once this method has been rejected, nothing remains but arbitrary deduction. One ties together such-and-such events because they seem tied together logically; and, in fact, it seems that, for the author, all explanation is reduced to an ideal construction. It is true that he adds that there is need of verification, but without telling us the means. Doubtless, hypothesis plays a large part in all the natural sciences; but here, the facts which suggest the conjecture and those which verify it are different. But one does not see how this could be true in history, if it treats of events which are unique in their kind.

It is thus necessary to choose. History cannot be a science without rising above the individual; it is true that then it ceases to be itself and becomes a branch of sociology. It is confounded with dynamic sociology. It cannot remain an original discipline unless it limits itself to the study of each national individuality taken in itself and considered in the different moments of its development. But then it is no more than a narration whose object is mainly practical. Its function is to enable societies to remember their past; it is the eminent form of collective memory. After having distinguished these two conceptions of history, one should add first that, more and more, they are destined to become inseparable. There is no longer opposition between them, but only differences of degree. Scientific history or sociology cannot avoid direct observation of concrete facts, and, on the other hand, national history, history as an art, cannot but gain by being penetrated by the general principles which the sociologist arrives at. For, to make a people understand its past well, it is also necessary to make a selection out of the multitude of facts and retain only those which are particularly vital; and for this, one must have criteria which presuppose comparisons. Thus, to be able, with more security, to discover the manner in which the concrete events of a particular history are related, it is good to know the general relations of which these more particular relations are examples and, as it were, applications. Thus there are, here, not two distinct disciplines, but two different points of view, which, far from excluding each other, mutually presuppose each other. But this is not a reason to confound them and to attribute to the one what is characteristic of the other. (*Année sociologique,* 6, 1903, pp. 123–125; trans. K. Woody)

G. Tarde. "L'Interpsychologie." *Bulletin de l'Institut Général Psy-chologique,* June 1903, pp. 1–32.

At the end of his life, Tarde liked to replace the expression "collective psychology" by "interpsychology." The first expression appeared to him tainted with ontology, because it seems to imply that there is a collective psychology proper. Since, according to the author, the only reality lies in individual actions and reactions, the term "science" must have as its aim nothing other than their comprehension. It is not that all interpsychic relations are social. The impressions that the sight of other people can awaken in me have nothing social about them. Moreover, some sort of impact must be made by one mind on another mind, having the effect of awakening a state of mind. Again, all intermental impact is not social; there are some cases that are obstacles to social ties, for example, the feelings of hatred or of fear or of cannibalistic appetite. Only feelings [from the French *suggestion*] of sympathy, of confidence, of obedience would have a purely social character.

It is already clear how arbitrary and confused this notion is. First of all, if interpsychology really includes facts that are not social, it is a very bad method to confuse under the same heading two categories of facts so clearly distinct. Next, why refuse to characterize feelings like fear or hatred as manifestations of social phenomena? If hatred separates, it unites just as well; if sympathy unites, it separates as well. These two movements are correlated with each other, and how lacking in precision it is to arrange them by definition in two categories and to designate them as belonging to two different sciences!

Similarly, the author is arbitrary in dividing and compartmentalizing science. The great problems that it would have to deal with are as follows: (1) the impact of an individual on an individual; (2) that of an individual on an assembled crowd and the reverse. But in order to study an individual's impact on a crowd or of crowds on an individual, one must first of all know what a crowd is, how its mentality is formed. Does the genesis of this mentality revert to simple impact transferrals between individuals? It is a question that cannot be settled in advance, insofar as science has not made a start. Obviously the author supposes that the crowd is fashioned by a ringleader; this simplification does away with all difficulty, but cannot, however, be accepted as fact. Now, that is the problem par excellence; one wonders if Tarde had any idea of this. [9]

Let us add, in short, that these problems are singularly indeterminable and that it is far from clear how it is possible to tackle them methodically. How, by what procedures, by what experiments, does one come to grips with the study of an individual on an individual, of an individual on a crowd? Is one going to limit oneself, as was done up until now, to compiling a few freely annotated anecdotes? Is that the way to create a scientific piece of work? There are crowds of all sorts, publics of all sorts; each one has its own way of reacting. It would be necessary to set them apart, to find some way to observe objectively the way in which they behave, to note the particular situational terms under which they vary. But these special and definite investigations immediately turn one's thoughts along entirely different lines than would the vagaries of interpsychology.

One will find at the close of this article a proof of the circular direction that Tarde's thought took. According to him, as is common knowledge, all social phenomena derive "from the unilateral or mutual impact of a meeting of minds," an impact in which imitation is basic and typical. Now, the author, unaware of the vicious circle, indicates at the conclusion of his work that this impact is itself promoted or thwarted by social conditions. Expressed in another way, it presupposes what it produces. Men, for example, exert an influence upon one another in such a way as to give rise to social events only if there is between them a sufficient moral homogeneity which already represents a common way of life. One's superiors are imitated, but superiority is already a social institution, so it is true that the word "institution" is vacuous and meaningless. It is necessary to know why people imitate, and the motives that cause men to imitate each other, obey each other; they are therefore social phenomena. (*Année sociologique,* 9, 1906, pp. 133–135; trans. J. French)

A. D. Xenopol. "Sociologia e storia." *Rivista italiana di sociologia,*
    VIII, no. 4, July-Aug. 1904, pp. 405–426, and IX, nos. 3–4, pp.
    308–350.

The author distinguishes between sociology and history in the following way: Sociology sets forth the laws of the repetitions of social facts, while history sets forth the development of their succession. There are social facts which repeat themselves in an identical way; one can therefore compare them, abstract from their differences, bring out their similarities, and in this way obtain laws which are comparable to those established by the natural sciences. But, on the other hand, the sequence of facts which follow each other in history does not repeat itself; the facts are always different; here one is in the presence of a unique series which the historian reconstitutes, but without its being possible to enunciate general laws according to which that series unfolds. In a word, sociology, properly speaking, is reduced to static sociology; dynamic sociology is history, whose object is not to explain, not to reduce the particular to the general, but to connect facts, which are always different, in the order of their succession.

These remarks could apply to Comte's conceptions of dynamic sociology. If, in fact, as Comte thought, historical development is unilinear, if it is constituted by a single and unique series which begins with humanity itself and continues without end, it is evident that, since all terms of comparison are lacking, it cannot be reduced to laws. One can only put the events of the past in a series, but Mr. Xenopol seems to forget that this archaic conception now belongs to history. There is no human development [as a whole]; but each society has its own life, its own development, and similar societies, belonging to the same type, are just as comparable in their development as they are in their structure. Does one not seek the laws of biological development? Why should it be otherwise with social development? To escape this objection Xenopol maintains that only very inferior societies present marked similarities; this is an assertion which needs to be proved otherwise than by some general considerations on the role of great men in the history of superior societies. Moreover, it is hard to see how there can be static laws if societies do not resemble each other. For after all, the facts which enter into these laws are also part of the historical sequence; they exist in time as well as in space. Should the similarities which are the basis for these laws be therefore ascertained at a single and same moment of time in a single and same society? The field of possible considerations would be singularly restricted.

In his second article the author believes he verifies his thesis experimentally by demonstrating that the dynamic laws enunciated by Letourneau, Brunetière, and others are not laws in the proper sense of the word. It does not seem to us that this examination adds very much to his thesis. Even if all the dynamic laws proposed by sociologists were only untruths, how would this prove that there cannot be any such laws? (*Année sociologique*, 9, 1906, pp. 139–140; trans. K. Woody)

Giuseppe Toniolo. *L'odierno problema sociologico*. Florence: Libreria
    Editrice Fiorentina, 1905, xvii + 338 pp.

This is an application of the apologetic method begun in France by Brunetière; [10] the work might be characterized as sociologically apologetic. The manner of proceeding is always the same. The author begins by pointing out the limitations of the natural sciences; then he places in relief the spiritualistic character of certain moral or sociological theories. From this the author concludes that there is something in the social life which escapes a properly scientific investigation. Nothing remains but a short step to pass from there to faith.

It is useless to refute this way of arguing. It is very true that today there is a certain disdain for the simplistic naturalism of the past, a tendency to recognize the moral and historical role of religion, and even to treat the facts of religious life with the deference that is due to all natural facts, while the old positivist school tended to see nothing there but the product of aberrations, explainable historically, but void of any foundation. In *L'Année* more than elsewhere, religion is perceived not as a tissue of absurd fantasies but as a system of representations which express, although in an inadequate form, something real. However, from this methodological point of view, the mentality of the believer does not enter in at all. The reality which religion expresses is part of the data; it appears from observation, it is the object of science.

It is remarkable that the attempt made here to explain empirically religious phenomena while preserving their specific characteristics seems completely unknown to the author. However, our theories are examined and discussed in a number of works which he cites and upon which he depends. It is true that these investigations are singularly lacking in precision and exac-

titude. On pages 58 and 59, A. Ribot, Jannet (?),* Tarde, and Duprat are classified as students of Le Play. One might add there, perhaps with more reason, Funck-Brentano, the *celebrated* author of *La Constitution anglaise,* and director of the Ecole des Hautes Etudes Politiques et Sociales de Paris (?)†
(*Année sociologique,* 9, 1906, pp. 142–143; trans. J. Sweeney)

S. Jankelevitch. *Nature et société: Essai d'une application du point de vue finaliste aux phénomènes sociaux.* Paris: F. Alcan, 1906, 188 pp.

Here again is a book of philosopical generalizations on the nature of society, and of generalizations beyond which it is difficult to sense any very intimate and very familiar association with social reality. Nowhere does the author give the impression that he has entered into direct contact with the events he speaks of; for we do not believe that the general ideas he develops are illustrated with a single concrete example nor applied to a single definite and precise sociological problem. Whatever the dialectical and literary talents of the author may be, it is impossible to overexpose the scandal of a method that is such an affront to all our scientific habits and that is, nevertheless, still employed very frequently. We no longer admit today that one may speculate on the nature of life without being initiated beforehand into biological techniques; by what special privilege could permission be granted to the philosopher to speculate about society without becoming familiar with the details of social facts?

The object of the book is to demonstrate that the social sciences are not "sciences in the true sense of the word, that is to say, comparable to the natural sciences," and that the phenomena with which they are concerned do not fit the framework of natural phenomena, but constitute "something, if not opposite, at the very least different" (pp. 2–3). The author disavows any intention to convey thereby that society is outside of nature, "unbeholden to any law, any rule, never repeating itself and manifesting itself only through a series of chances and accidents." He is well aware that such a society is impossible; but he is, nevertheless, of the opinion that man, as a social being, has the power to oppose nature, to escape its laws, to correct them, to complete them with a view to certain goals to be realized (p. 4). It is indeed, therefore, the

---

* Durkheim leaves it with a question mark, as if Jannet were a name to be confused with the French philosopher Paul Janet. But Toniolo's work refers to Claudio Jannet as a disciple of Le Play. ED.

† Durkheim's question mark is intended to doubt the accuracy of the statement, since Funck-Brentano, even though a cofounder with Miss Dick May of Collège Libre des Sciences Sociales in 1895, taught law at the Ecole Libre des Sciences Politiques. Another private institution of similar stature was the Ecole des Hautes Etudes Sociales, where some of the distinguished scholars, including Durkheim, taught and participated in conferences. In any case, none of these institutions should be confused with one of the Grandes Ecoles, the Ecole Pratique des hautes Etudes. ED.

basic premise of Comtist sociology and, more generally, of all scientific sociology that is at issue.

As for the demonstration of the thesis, it is based in its entirety on the two following arguments, which the author repeats under different forms but without essential variation. In his exposé they are often confused; but although they are intended to provide mutual confirmation, it is, we believe, desirable to distinguish between them and to appraise them separately.

1. All things that are in nature belong to the category of being; all that can be said of them is that they are and that they are what they are. That is why natural sciences have no objective other than to inform us of *that which is;* all they do is express reality, such as it exists. But when man appears, and as a result, society (from which man cannot be separated), there also appears a new category, which is *of value.* We do not limit ourselves to knowing what things are, we *appraise* them in relation to ourselves, we declare them good, bad, indifferent, and so on, according to whether they enhance or thwart our desires or have no effect on them whatsoever. In this way we add to nature a property that is not intrinsically hers; we superimpose on the natural point of view, which is that of science, a new point of veiw that is the human point of view. Natural sciences, then, are not competent to deal with things in this second category. Now, social life alone is made up of values: religious, moral, legal, economic, artistic. Everything, in society, is viewed in relation to man. The material things of least value can have a price as far as their physical properties are concerned; they can be attributed an incomparable social prestige if human opinion makes this claim for them. It is concluded from the above discussion that social sciences cannot be compared with natural sciences.

2. Social phenomena can only be explained *historically;* they are all the result of an evolutionary process. Now, what does the idea of evolution imply? That things do not maintain the selfsame identity, that something new crops up, appears at a given moment, that was previously nonexistent; and social evolution is an uninterrupted succession of novelties of this kind. Nature, on the contrary, is that which by definition does not change, that which is forever unalterable. The subject matter of the natural sciences is the repetition of identical selves; their role is to discover laws that are always and everywhere the same, to readjust particular laws to others that are more universal, to eradicate differences and show the uniformity underlying apparent diversity. As a result, it does not seem that the natural sciences can serve as a model for the social sciences, for history never repeats itself.

From these considerations, it follows that the teleological point of view must dominate in the disciplines which deal with society. If we understand the author correctly, they ought before all else to make it their objective to set up ideal goals, to determine what one must choose, what are or rather how it is advisable to appraise the different human values. Of the method that must be followed in order to proceed in these appraisals, no indication is given us.

We are very much afraid that all this dialectical scaffolding rests upon a confused notion.

The author seems to admit as evident that there exists only one nature, namely physical nature, and that to refuse to admit a fundamental difference between the social sciences and the natural sciences is to admit ipso facto that social facts are totally reducible to the properties of matter. For him, nature is the ensemble of cosmic forces, and it is for that reason that nature and humanity are always presented to us in his book in sharply contrasting forms. Thus understood, the naturalistic thesis was easy to refute; only it should be added that thus formulated, it did not enlist the support of sociologists of any authority; and it would be very extraordinary if it should find favor, since it presumes as corollary the very negation of sociology. In any case, and since Jankelevitch does us the honor of choosing us as the contemporary representative of the thesis he attacks (p. 2), we will take this opportunity to say that our whole work is a protest against this eleatical monism. [11] If we have said that societies abide in nature, we have applied ourselves no less forcefully to show that social nature is sui generis, that it is incompatible not only with the physical nature but even with the psychic nature of the individual. To declare that societies are products of nature, that collective manifestations are subject to necessary laws, is not to maintain that there is nothing new, no diversity in the world. Nobody has tried more than we to point out that the characteristic novelties of social life are very real, and generally speaking, that the diversity of things is not in the least apparent; in so doing, moreover, we have only been following the path opened by the founder of positive sociology, Auguste Comte, who even used to go as far as admitting to a solution of fundamental continuity between the different realms of nature, and even between the different animal species. If, then—and the proof is overwhelming—it is indeed our method that the author intended to attack in his book, either he is not very familiar with it or he has misunderstood it. It is possible that we have been mistaken and that one cannot without contradiction reconcile the naturalist thesis and the principle of the specificity of social phenomena; but in another sense, in order to establish the contrary thesis, one must still not forget or overlook the fact that this reconciliation has been attempted, and by means of the very doctrine that he claims to refute.

And besides, it is not clear on what grounds the mark of distinction by means of which our author differentiates social facts should prevent their being treated in accordance with the methods of the natural sciences. To be sure, social life is fashioned from values, and the values are properties added to things by human consciences; they are in every respect the product of psychic mechanisms. But these mechanisms are facts of nature, to which science may be applied; those appraisals that opinion brings to bear on things depend on causes and conditions which can be investigated inductively. There is thus material for a whole group of sciences which, like the science of physical nature, work back from given results to the causes on which these results depend; such is the object of the social sciences. And it is only when we are better informed about what constituted in the past those creations and those classifications of values, what are the mental processes from which they result, the components of those processes, etcetera, that it will be possible to substitute more rational and thought-out methods for empirical, instinctive, self-deluding evaluations. (*Année sociologique*, 10, 1907, pp. 171–174; trans. J. French)

Adrien Naville. "La Sociologie abstraite et ses divisions." *Revue philosophique*, May 1906, pp. 457–471.

The author undertakes to define and divide sociology as if it had yet to be created in its entirety, and as if its divisions were not in the process of being formed by the real progress science has made. That is to say that the author's conceptualization has all the appearance of being arbitrary and manifestly constructed as dialectics; it is far from reality.

Here first of all is how he defines sociology: It is a science which seeks natural laws of relationships among men. These laws aim to establish relationships with "other phenomena," notably with other social relationships or with psychological, biological, or physical facts. And here is, to cite an example, one of the questions which sociology would pose to itself: "If, in a moderately rich country, the state suddenly raised taxes sharply, what would be the consequences of the change for local commerce, etcetera?"

We are absolutely surprised to see that a philosopher considers this forecast as a determination of "natural laws." If the author has, however, a concept [Durkheim's text in French reads as *définition*. ED.] I would seem to agree with, it is the identification of all natural laws by relating them to established and real facts.

From his definition, the author concludes that he must distinguish as many divisions of sociology as there are corresponding social interrelations. But to the author, the juridic, moral, political, economic, and religious relations do not seem to have "sociological character," for they have roots in man's personal desires. He proposes the following classification: collaboration, exchange, gift, spoliation, authority, and language.

The author attributes to us the view that the only social facts are those "which occur often and are frequent." We know very well that this was Tarde's thesis; it is, however, not in the least ours. (*Année sociologique*, 10, 1907, p. 176; trans. Y. Nandan)

Eduard Meyer. *Geschichte des Altertums*, 2nd ed., with preface, "Elemente der Anthropologie." Stuttgart, 1907, xii + 250 pp.

While giving us this new edition of his large and famous history of antiquity, Meyer has insisted on retaining the philosophic and sociological introduction as contained in the first edition. He has even developed it, in spite of the unsparingly critical remarks that the specialists made about it. It is also presented today in a more systematic form. In it the author proposes to set forth his conception of social history and evolution in general. He gives to this synthetic investigation the designation *anthropology*. By that he means the science that investigates the general laws governing the mind of man as it grows through history. Although, as such, historical growth is essentially collective, the word "anthropology" is nonetheless surprising. "Sociology" would appear more clearly indicated.

Meyer bases these general considerations not only on his personal experience as a historian of antiquity but also on a certain knowledge of ethnography. He is not afraid to speak of lower social orders, of clans and of phratries, of primitive forms of religion, of the family, of marriage, etcetera. In any case, it seems clear that he has no firsthand experience with ethnographical documents. Therefore, we shall leave aside the particular proposals that he sees fit to express on such matters, in order to apply ourselves to general views and methodological conceptions.

A primary idea dominates the whole work, namely, the priority of political society over the varied societies it comprises. Most often, the former is presented as a result of the latter. Social organization would have been constructed from bottom to top, so to speak. It would have started with the simplest, the most elementary, groups before rising progressively to the most complex. The first would have been shaped, under the influence of sexual instinct, by the married couple, the partnership of man and woman; the family would have resulted by means of perfectly natural expansion. Family reunions would have given rise to clans, to villages; confederations of villages or of clans, to tribes, to nations. Meyer's whole book is directed against such a conception. Very rightly he points out that in ethnography and in history, the family never appears to the observer other than in a definitely structured form—one that it is obliged to assume. However far we delve into the past, marriage consists not of a simple and free coupling of male and female but of a regulated union, subject to positive and negative conditions from which the parties concerned are not allowed to stray and involving in their case fixed obligations. Children born of such unions do not remain simply attached to their fathers and mothers by the natural feelings that the young of an animal has for its parents. They are under the compulsory supervision of either the husband or the wife, or their supervision may be assigned to either the husband's or wife's family, or even to both families at the same time. For the child such an attribution carries with it duties as well as rights: the right involving joint ownership claims on the clan's territory or the family's patrimony, the right to inherit, etcetera. In no sense do such peremptory rules derive from the general attributes of human nature, since they vary depending on time and place. There was nothing in man's organico-psychic constitution that predetermined him to sustain legal relations with his father to the exclusion of his mother, or vice-versa; nothing that predestined the oldest members to enjoy a privileged situation (seniority) in the family, since in other circumstances it is the youngest family member who excercises these same prerogatives. In other words, the family and the married couple, wherever they exist, have an organization that is imposed on them from outside by a power dominating and overruling them—the power of the state. [Here and elsewhere throughout Durkheim's writings in *L'Année, l'Etat* has a capital *E*. ED.] By "state" the author does not mean a governing agency charged with representing the political society, but it must be considered as a whole. It is characterized solely by the supreme authority it exercises over its members and by the relative autonomy it enjoys in connection with surrounding societies. In this sense it is a universal phenomenon; it exists wherever there are men. It is safe then to say, repeating the phrase of Aristotle and even what we understand by it, that political society, thus encompassed, precedes marital society, the family, and consequently the clan, the village, etcetera, and even the individual. Man does not exist (by himself) and outside the political society. It is within the confines of and under the influence of such a society that the more limited groups it encompasses have been formed. And it has also presided over the birth of these last. Here as elsewhere, it is the whole which precedes the parts and which shapes them.

The formula under which this kind of social impact exerts itself on its members is threefold—namely, law, customs, and morality. Between so-called legal prescriptions and customs, the difference is one of degree only. Both of them consist of ways of taking action involving, if need be, forcible restraint. The only difference is that the restraint is open, formal, and purposeful in the case of the law; veiled and indirect, on the other hand, when customs are involved. As for moral standards, they are, in a way, the outward aspect of that collective restraint. The individual himself is aware "that he cannot exist outside society, that he cannot possibly free himself from it, and that because of this he must submit to the demands and the commandments of the consensus, however repugnant such submission may be in particular cases" (p. 35). Morality is a whole set of acts that are inspired by such a feeling. Customs, law, and morality accordingly appear as social matters that have an existence above and beyond the individual, and it is self-evident that social rules and regulations cannot be derived from the nature of the individual. If we settle for a literal interpretation of the expressions used by the author, the preceding ideas seem to be identical with those very same ones we are constantly defending in these pages. But as a matter of fact, the agreement is only partial; it does not reach the very heart of the matter, and here already is where a grave difference of opinion begins to surface. When we say that the law expresses consensus, we mean that it is itself and in the fullest sense the result of maturation within the group, that it is fashioned by society, that it meets certain needs of the social organization from which it cannot be detached without becoming totally meaningless. For the author, on the other hand, there exists a law unto itself, a legal standard which dominates all codes and, in the case of each one by itself, every detail of the particular rules that make it up. As for this Idea of the law, each society conceives of it after its fashion, depending on the circumstances, the particular conditions within the place where it is to be found. But each is entrusted with the Idea; the latter is to be applied within the limits prescribed (pp. 38–39). (We shall soon see this primary difference of opinion lead to others.)

But however real the autonomy of each state may be, it is only relative. A society is not a sort of ideal unity closed to all outside influences, separated from the rest of the world by means of a gap in life's continuity neatly excised. Just as the human individual does not exist outside the society of his fellows, each society is related with others and lives accordingly in the intersocial surroundings that envelop it. Each is in a state of becoming, in a perpetual state of flux. From each there is a constant erosion of elements in the process of uniting with neighboring societies, and inversely each receives from its neighbors new elements which it incorporates and assimilates. There are not only exchanges of people, but exchanges of ideas, of feelings, of beliefs. Each particular state tends, as it were, to be assimilated by the others, to effect a partial merging with them in a prototype of communal living. Accordingly, this is how larger groups take shape, overriding each one of the parts and containing them; such are races, social family groups related by language, nationalities (insofar as they overflow the frontiers), the circles of civilization (*Kulturkreise*), such as the Islamic world or the Christian world (§§ 40 ff.). But, of course, however important such a trend toward mutual assimilation is, it is not the only one. There is a contrary trend which inclines societies to distinguish themselves from one another, to fashion individually a personal physiognomy for themselves. Furthermore, one encounters the two antagonistic tendencies within each society. Each individual tends in certain ways to be assimilated by his companions and in other ways to become different from them. It is in the conflict of these two tendencies that Meyer sees the dominant phenomenon throughout history (p. 89).

But where do they come from? The phenomena of assimilation can be explained by the instinct of imitation, by the natural force of dissemination we voluntarily apply to ideas. However vague, however lightly analyzed those occult properties may be, they are doubtless the reasons why Meyer credits them with different sorts of social or intersocial conformity. And if he does not raise any questions on that score, the fact is that those are matters apparently to be taken for granted, and as such they raise no questions. He does not sense the kind of scholastic and even verbal connotations inherent in this kind of explanation. But what else is there to make of the other tendency? How does it happen that each society has a definite and distinctive personality that it tends, in general, not only to maintain but to strengthen and develop?

For Ratzel, we know how the geographic factor gives nations their individuality. But Meyer rejects that theory. Even when it involves facts as general and simple as nomadic and sedentary life, the nature and configuration of the soil appear to him to have a secondary influence only. Depending on their capacity [to exploit], peoples have made total or partial use of their natural resources. They have, then, no lasting impact. Everything depends not only on the territory but on the attitudes of those who occupy it and cultivate it (§§ 30). As for these attitudes, one might seek to take them into account by following through on the way in which the society is organized, on the state of the civilization to which it fell heir, on the nature of group living that results both from that particular civilization and that particular organization. Meyer does not even stop for that kind of conjecture. At the outset, he brushes aside all factors extraneous to the individual's role. The attitudes of society revert, in his opinion, to the attitudes of the members who make it up (pp. 174–175). The individual as such would then be, in the last analysis, the sole agent of social evolution.

This is, in fact, the idea our author formulates. The individual is the creator of all things, and from him alone can everything come to pass. Only he is creative. This idea suggests the preeminent role that is, by that same reasoning, assigned to the great historical personalities. Meyer is not far from thinking that a society is worth what its great men are worth—it is what they make it. Influenced by causes that are neither foreseeable nor predictable, minds exist in which new ideas are hatched; whereupon they are spread abroad, are propagated, become common property. In the process of such propagation they cease to be mere incidents involving individual awareness in order to become social facts. But, in the process of such socialization, ideas undergo a kind of degeneracy. So long as they are states with a particular spirit, they preserve a flexibility that permits them to change direction when circumstances are favorable; once they are externalized they become fixed, fossilized, materialistic, and thus stubbornly opposed to change. Every consensus of opinion, every tradition, once established, exerts a force of inertia that resists all new growth. At each moment in history the man of genius is obliged to pierce the thick crust of the prejudices, the ready-made ideas of his time, in order to bring forth his own into the light of day. And yet he frees himself from such constraints only to become himself an instrument of oppression in the eyes of his contemporaries and his successors. By a kind of tragic necessity, liberating ideas, on becoming widespread, become oppressive in their turn. The prophets, who have revolted against the established religions, found Churches which treat each new prophet as the enemy. The most revolutionary spirits in matters of art and philosophy found schools that are opposed to the foundation of new schools (§§ 99–104).

A certain very particular way of viewing history results from this method.

Human societies can be considered in two ways. From certain vantage points they are homogeneous, comparable to each other, and by making comparisons it is possible to extract the laws that dominate them. Investigation of such laws is the aim of anthropology; we have explained earlier the reason why the author uses this expression. But states may be studied for what is inherently peculiar, specific to each. It is that study which constitutes history.

That distinction would be beyond reproach if it did not assume a very special meaning in the author's mind. We have indeed understood that it is the individual factor that makes societies different, that sets each of them apart in a very special way. Hence it follows that this factor, too, is the proper concern of history. An epoch is historic to the degree that individuals in it play a considerable role. The centuries that possess this characteristic to the fullest are those in which social conformity gives way for a while and there is a resurgence of innovative spirits who breach the bastion of the status quo. It is to misconstrue the truth of the matter to assign to history the study of collectivist states, the phenomena of the masses (*die Massenerscheinungen, Massenvorgänge*). [12] It is the personal, the singular, that are appropriate to this field of endeavor. It is, moreover, on these terms that this field can accommodate the free flow of events, since, in Meyer's opinion, the ever-changing scene is the work of single individuals (§§ 104, 106).

In another sense, since the individual is a creature of chance, he cannot be explained; he is, then, like chance itself, outside the realm of science (p. 172). As a result, history itself cannot be a science in the strict sense of the word; the propositions it establishes always remain problematical—they can transmit only the personal convictions of the historian (p. 198). Since it is to be assumed that the events it strives to link according to causal relationships do not repeat themselves because they constitute uniquely isolated cases, there is no comparative method that makes it possible to extract events acting the part of causes. It depends on the investigator's ability to ferret things out when making the selection without any chance to verify the results of such intuitions with any reliable evidence. The subjective point of view is then preponderant (§§ 113). This inevitable subjectivity is worth noting even in the way the aim of the investigation is determined. If all past events were considered equally valid as history, historical material would be boundless. A choice is necessary. In the author's opinion, those events alone should be retained that have had a marked influence on the result of subsequent events—especially those events which have contributed to make the present what it is. It is from the present that we must proceed. It is this factor which must serve as a criterion, since it is the very thing we must somehow explain. It is the links the present maintains with the past that permit us to circumscribe the areas from the past towards which our investigation of history must turn (pp. 186–187). But we are well aware—and it is, moreover, something the author himself acknowledges (§§ 112)—of everything inherently individual and a priori in these appraisals of the importance of events, the more so since these judgments precede the research instead of resulting from those events. It is notions about the period, the way in which the author conceives of it and judges it, his biases, his own temperament, etcetera, which help determine the aim of the investigation—a very far cry from enabling this investigation to be objectively determined.

We have, for several reasons, insisted on revealing in these pages Meyer's theories. To begin with, it is interesting to see a specialist of such undisputed authority acknowledge that history is not sufficient on its own terms, but calls on another type of culture that will initiate the historian into the general laws of the growth of humanity. As for this culture, Meyer calls it anthropological; but the word has little bearing on the matter at hand. Basically, it is very instructive to confirm, in this particular case, how little a historian is able to adjust to that indispensable culture himself; for it is difficult not to be aware of the fundamental inconsistency at the center of which our author's philosophy flounders. No one feels more deeply than he the incongruity existing between the individual and society. Did we not see him at the start of his work demonstrate, with a truly lavish display of examples, that social organization does not meet the needs of the individual, but fulfills requirements of a very different sort? Social institutions seemed to be so little in keeping with the inclination of our organico-psychic constitution that he made much of their power of coercion as the outstanding feature of and condition for their impact. The individual was at the time presented to us as the product of society. And the next thing we know, we are hearing him mentioned as if he were the originator of this society from which he derives his essential characteristics! It is he who would make or alter those institutions that exert compelling pressures and restraints on his person. But why such restraint if the institutions are expressions of himself, and if they express something other than himself, how can they be a derivative of himself? If it is from him that they emanate, they cannot surpass him; and inversely, if they surpass him, it is not from him that they stem. May it be said that by spreading far afield, by becoming commonplace, an individual idea becomes common property? But it does not change its nature because of that. Because of being adopted by several individuals, it does not follow that it expresses an actuality that transcends the individual. Now, such a flagrant inconsistency clearly seems to come from the fact that in Meyer's case the historian's experience is considerably overextending the resources of theoretical formulation. His experience with social matters is too intimate and too extensive for him [historian] not to feel the compelling force which they exert upon the individual and their resistance to him; and indeed, this feeling is evident throughout the entire course of the work. But, on the other hand, since the author does not suspect that there can be a reality superior to the individual, it is impossible for him to envision with clear understanding such a transcendency of social facts. And that is why it eludes him completely when he seeks to take it into account.

One will find in the book (pp. 85 ff.) a theory of religion, its origins and its evolution, about which we have said nothing because it is merely a special case of ideas that have just been revealed. Then again, taken on its own terms, it is really excessively simplistic. It is surprising that a scholar who knows how hard it is to do a history of religion has believed it possible to sketch, in some fifty pages, a sort of explanatory history of religion in general. (*Année sociologique*, 11, 1910, pp. 5–13; trans. J. French)

Gaston Richard. *La Sociologie générale et les lois sociologiques.* Paris: Doin, 1912, 296 pp.

In this book the author proposes to prove that there exists a general sociology and to determine its aim. He contrasts this thesis to the one we apparently supported. He declares, in fact, that in our view all general sociology is an impossibility (pp. 45 ff.). Such an affirmation is fundamentally erroneous. In fact, this is what we have written on the subject. After having pointed out that the analysis of social phenomena is possible only by means of separate social sciences, we added: "This is not to say, however, that there is no place for a scientific synthesis that does what it can to reassemble the general conclusions emerging from all such particular sciences. However different the various categories of social phenomena may be, they are nevertheless merely members of a single family; it is therefore fitting to investigate this *in abstracto,* and whether there are not some very general laws of which the various laws established by the special sciences are only particular forms. *Such is the aim of general sociology."* (*La Méthode dans les sciences,* p. 325 [13]; see Durkheim and Fauconnet, "Sociologie et sciences sociales," in *Revue philosophique,* 1905, I, p. 477[14]). All we did was to deny the possibility of a synthesis that would not rely on a sufficiently profound analysis.

Since the author made a mistake about our opinion, we cannot say with any certainty whether he accepts or rejects this way of understanding general sociology. Yet it seems clear that in his view it amounts to a separate science that is self-sufficient (pp. 180, 345); its aim would be to determine the two fundamental notions of *Society* and *Community.* By societies, he means the groups that depend basically on barter and other forms of trade, and that consequently rely on the division of labor and cooperation. The community exists wherever its members "can say *We* by considering themselves as a single productive and active entity" (p. 165). In the former case, the individual is in the foreground; in the latter case, it is the community. We believed, initially, that such a distinction was not unrelated to the one we established between societies that owe their unity to the division of labor and that permit the upward mobility of the individual, and those that are formed as communities in which the parts are absorbed by the whole. But the author, who is very anxious to refuse any joint responsibility for the ideas from which we draw our inspiration, applies himself to proving that such a comparison is purely apparent, not real; we confess, however, to having misunderstood his reason (pp. 238, 241, 251).

This distinction made, the task of general sociology is to establish the fundamental laws that take precedence as much in the development of society as of the community. Such laws are apparently the following: (1) "The commercial world of men (consequently society) obeys a law of expansion and acceleration" (p. 228); (2) "The history of the community is summed up in the notion of differentiation" (p. 238). It is not clear to us how such vague and indeterminate generalities can serve, as the author believes, to coordinate the investigations of particular sciences, or even what light they cast on social phenomena. The first statement is a truism, for it simply means that dealings between men—dealings in ideas or in things—become ever more active and tend to assume a worldwide character. As for the second, our understanding of the sense is very imperfect, for isn't declaring that communities continuously differentiate the same as stating that they tend to disappear, since, according to the hypothesis, they are based on the nondifferentiation of the parts of which they are composed. Besides, how is it possible to discover the supreme laws dominating all social evolution by means of an inquiry that takes up a few pages? It is not that we mean to defer every attempt at general sociology until the day when the work of analysis is terminated; such scientific phariseeism would be tantamount to postponing indefinitely the time for useful generalizations. All that is needed is that a sufficient number of particular works and of clear-cut investigations be forthcoming, that they summarize an extensive and varied scientific experiment. On the other hand, when they consist of a few summary and schematic views based on a rapid inventory of a few arbitrarily chosen facts, they cannot help losing sight of the real questions that are asked and that should be asked.

In the last three chapters, the author investigates the relationships between sociological laws and natural laws, whether in the world of physical science or the world of the mind. The preceding observations apply with particular force to this final section of the book, where, moreover, the sequence of ideas is more difficult to grasp. At last there comes a conclusion in which, once again, our so-called thesis on the impossibility of general sociology is discussed. (*Année sociologique*, 12, 1913, pp. 1–3; trans. J. French)

The First German Sociology Congress—Communications and Discussions (Publications of the .Deutsche Gesellschaft für Soziologie). Tübingen: Mohr, 1911, 335 pp.

A certain number of German professors and scholars have decided, despite the unpopularity which the word [sociology] apparently retains in Germany, to establish a sociological society, which is to undertake investigations, publish works, and organize congresses. The first of these congresses took place in Berlin in October 1910.

The papers which were published and discussed consisted for the most part of introductions and [research] programs; they delimited the fields of research and specified the links between the various social sciences.

In his opening address, "The Means and the End of Sociology," Toennies, doubtless by design, allows the task of sociology, properly so-called, to remain somewhat indeterminate. He principally insists on the need to study objectively the social events which happen around us, "as if they were happening on the moon," and to systematically avoid all "value judgments." In order to speak the truth, sociology must not restrict itself to the description of facts; by putting the mass of facts into order it will endeavor to define notions such as the State or the Church, law, customs, public opinion, and so forth. Through this "design of concepts" sociology will perform the greatest services for several disciplines—legal, economic, and political—whose materials are indispensable to it. The criterion which Toennies proposes for distinguishing the discipline from history seems rather arbitrary: The sociologist must always proceed from the present.

At the beginning of his "Concepts of Race and Society and Several Problems Connected with Them," A. Plotz opposes the viewpoint of anthropology to that of sociology. A race is a biological unit which lasts and undergoes development. A society is a group of people who help one another. Its characteristic feature is the exchange of services. Groups thus constituted can be considered as organisms of a singular sort, on whose behalf a special "hygiene" [15] should be followed, but does not this hygiene always demand behavior of a sort which would be congenial to the health of the race? Concern for the good of individuals, closely bound to the preoccupation for safeguarding the social bond, may entail more than a measure of damage to the race itself. The discussion which follows the reading of this paper proves how difficult it is to respond without having recourse to value judgments to questions which are posed in such a way.

Kantorowicz ("Law and Sociology") shows how the knowledge of social realities is indispensable to the jurist: It alone can inform him about the aims and consequences of the law which he is entrusted to apply. A "juridic sociology" should therefore find its place besides "juridic dogmatics." [16] The latter would not render the former useless, but would replenish it, give it orientation, and finally suggest to it some necessary means of adaption.

A. Voigt's communication ("Economy and Law") is most rich in usable distinctions. According to Voigt, one cannot define economic phenomena by their ends, nor by their means, nor by their motives. To say that the satisfaction of individual needs, whatever they may be, is the characteristic of economic life is to give too broad a definition. To restrict it to the satisfaction of material needs or selfish motives is to give too narrow a definition. In reality, economic activity is defined in terms of a relationship among ends, means, motives: Its specific ideal is the least possible expense, the greatest possible amount of available funds. This ideal enables us to see the difference between the economic and the legal points of view. The needs of the one do not always coincide with the needs of the other. Intervening in the name of the other's rights, the law does not always allow us to attain the economically desirable maximum with the minimum of expense and effort.

Consequently, one understands that it is inadequate to say with Stammler that law is the "form" of economic activity; it may besides, or rather first of all, be the limit of it. Certainly we are dealing here with an antithesis between rather than a subordination of points of view.

Werner Sombart, in his paper "Technology and Culture," endeavors to delineate the links not only between economic activity and judicial forms but also the links of the former with the entirety of social life, with civilization. Technology is the totality of processes and tools which facilitate activity; primary technology is what organizes economic production. According to Sombart, it is difficult to exaggerate the influence which technology in general, and primary technology in particular, exercise over all forms of culture, both objective and subjective. Not only the development of the state or the church, but also the development of science or art have as their premises certain transformations, be they of social usages, intellectual processes, or material equipment. All these transformations are strictly connected with the progress of technology. In developing these theories, the author denies that he clings too closely to historical materialism; for his part he neither believes that the economy is a function of technology nor, above all else, that culture is a function of the economy. Active or passive, negative or positive, it is the most direct operations of technology itself, operating without the intervention of the legal-economic system, which he desires to place in relief.

Troeltsch's communication ("Stoic-Christian Natural Law and the Secular Natural Law of the Modern Age") is a chapter in the history of ideas. The paper itself is held together by a general observation on the connections between natural laws and ideal laws. All civilizations, according to him, endeavor to reconcile ideal laws—moral and judicial, political and religious norms—with the positive conditions of development in societies. From this arise compromises of varied degrees and uneven flexibility, as evidenced by social groups, according to their constitution and orientation. A church, for example, will more readily accommodate itself to the times than a sect, while mysticism, in virtue of the particular form of indifference it professes vis-à-vis earthly things, will give men's minds a very special cast, which varies from extreme tolerance to total hostility towards the world.

Troeltsch follows the development of these tendencies throughout the course of history. He shows that they can be discovered, under diverse forms, among the eighteenth-century theorists of natural law. And without disregarding the differences, which are adequately explained by the difference between the times and the social questions which were put before them, he sees in the latter [the natural-law theorists]—as Espinas has not long since demonstrated in his work *La Philosophie sociale du XVIIIe siècle et la révolution* (1898)—the true inheritors of the Christian spirit.

The two other papers fall in the province of social psychology. Gothein, a pupil of Dilthey who seems also to have fallen under the influence of Simmel, delivers some ingenious remarks on the "Sociology of Panic." Panic, in a sense, isolates the individual and breaks up the entire social bond. It turns organized societies into the dust of atoms. It remains nonetheless true that the intensity of the sudden nervous shock to which individuals fall victim is increased tenfold by the pressure which they exert upon one another, the fellow-feelings which they suffer, the suggestions to which they yield. The author illustrates his arguments with numerous examples derived from all kind of panic—military, religious, political, and economic. Simmel's communication itself is dedicated to the "Sociology of Sociability." Different interests—political, economic, religious, and aesthetic—give birth to different groups. Aside from these interests, it is important to distinguish a sentiment which rejoices in social bonding in and of itself, and which in a fashion plays with this form: It is sociability. Those conditions which are required so that satisfaction of this sentiment should be at its maximum—removal of professional differences and even a weakening of personal differences, tact, the requirement of equality between individuals who are face to face, playing the game of democracy—are analyzed by Simmel with his noted suggestive finesse.

In his report, Max Weber indicates which subjects the society proposes to examine: the sociology of journals and the sociology of *Vereine*.[17] (*Année sociologique*, 12, 1913, pp. 23–26; trans. A. Lyons)

Henri Berr. *La Synthèse en histoire. Essai critique et théorique.* Paris:
    F. Alcan, 1911, xi + 272 pp.

Berr has always endeavored not to confuse the discipline which he calls *la synthèse historique* ("historical synthesis") with sociology; the latter should be merely one of the elements of the former. But since these two disciplines deal in part with the same facts, it was inevitable that there should have been much discussion of sociology in this book.

Berr distinguishes two domains in the realm of historical facts, that of contingency and that of necessity. There is in history something of the general and the permanent, which can be expressed in laws; but there is also an element of the variable and the contingent, which is unforeseeable. The origin of these contingencies is the individual in all of his forms: individuality of the person, individuality of the group, geographical individuality, etcetera. The domain of necessity is the very domain of sociology. Not only does Berr assign to that science the selfsame object of study that we do, but he recommends the selfsame method we practice here for the study of that object. He accepts the principles which inspire us in all the most essential details. Nonetheless, the historian cannot exclude the variable factor, the individual who plays a role in historical development, and the principal reproach which he addresses to us is that we deny this role. However, in a passage which Berr cites elsewhere we acknowledged that historical personages have been factors in history. But, besides the fact that we believe their influence has been greatly exaggerated, we have shown that they themselves have their reasons and these are, in part, social ones. If there is an element of necessity in the general, it must also be present in the particular, since the general is naught but the particular impoverished and simplified. The individual himself is a product of necessary causes; he has his own laws and there is no reason why science should not be made out of them. We must refrain from characterizing law by the feature of generality.

However, Berr makes another objection against us in the third part of his book; it is that we reduce the role of final causes and the role of logic. But what sort of finality are we talking about? An impersonal reason which is realized in the course of history? We have never expressed ourselves on this last philosophical question. Are we dealing solely with a need, which mankind experiences, to order and rationalize his ideas and actions? This need is a positive fact, affirmed with all the more energy the further we advance in history.

But where did this need itself arise? If, as we think, it is a function of social conditions, we do not have to go beyond sociology. As to the role which it is proper for it to play in the explanation of facts, we shall not be able to record it until we have determined it in a certain number of individual cases. This has not yet been tried. (*Année sociologique*, 12, 1913, pp. 26–27; trans. A. Lyons)

NOTES AND NOTICES

S. M. Lindsay. "The Unit of Investigation in Sociology." *Annals of the American Academy of Political and Social Science*, XII, no. 2, pp. 42–56.

In order to give unity to research in sociology, which it lacks, social fact should be considered as fundamental, the importance of which for sociology is the same as the cell for biology and as sensation for psychology. This phenomenon is the *social imperative*, the *social ought*. Its influence can be known from the fact that the individual acts differently in a group than when he is alone. This definition, even though we are not inclined to accept it in some respects, recalls much of what we ourselves have given to the social fact. So what is given to us is not fundamentally the social fact, it is only the characteristic of the social facts, whatever they may be, whether essential or secondary. The imperative character is the sign, which gives recognition to sociological phenomena, but it is not a type of phenomenon like the cell or sensation. That raises two matters which must be carefully distinguished: research on the elementary social fact and definition of social fact in general. Moreover, in this analysis, the morphological point of view is not sufficiently distinguished from the physiological point of view. (*Année sociologique*, 3, 1900, p. 160; trans. Y. Nandan)

Alessandro Chiappelli. "Sul metodo delle scienze sociali" (On the Method of the Social Sciences). *Rivista italiana di sociologia*, Sept. 1898, pp. 559–568.

The author insists on the inadequacies of the biological method; instead he proclaims the necessity of the historical method. But he concludes quite prematurely that there are no real laws of social phenomena. From the premise that society is not the same as organism, it is not to be deduced that it is out of nature. The complexity of historical phenomena is not sufficient to even partially demonstrate their irrationality. (*Année sociologique*, 3, 1900, pp. 160–161; trans. Y. Nandan)

G. Villa. "La psicologia e le scienze morali" (Psychology and the Moral Sciences). *Rivista italiana di sociologia*, Sept. 1898, pp. 600–632.

The author develops more succinctly the idea expounded by Alessandro

Chiappelli in the previous article. The principal reason for which the author is understood to have separated, more or less radically, the social sciences from the natural sciences is that the social phenomena form a synthesis in which the qualities of the total organism cannot be reduced to its elements. From that one concludes that it is impossible to foresee all that goes on in a society, even when all the circumstances are given. That kind of argument is really quite mediocre because we do not know of a synthesis in nature which, in various degrees, does not have the same character. The author concludes that the social facts in detail are not explicable by themselves. For in a manner more or less distantly removed, social facts can hardly be linked up with the psychological motives of a very general character, which, as such, interact with each other. The aim of the article is to show again that sociology can be reduced to individual psychology only by ignoring the details of facts, that is to say by denying their specificity, in order to remain content with more or less vague generalizations. Compare with the author's other article in the same review (July 1898): "L'odierno sviluppo delle scienze storiche sociali." (*Année sociologique*, 3, 1900, p. 161; trans. Y. Nandan)

Vilfredo Pareto. "I problemi della sociologia" (The Problems of Sociology). *Rivista italiana di sociologia*, March 1899, pp. 145–157.

This is an essay in justification of the old abstract and ideologically inclined method of the orthodox political economics; it aims to formulate a general method for all the social sciences. The author does not seem to doubt that if science proceeds effectively from abstractions, to be legitimate, it must comply with certain conditions that are not met by abstractions in orthodox economics. (*Année sociologique*, 3, 1900, p. 163; trans. Y. Nandan)

Lester F. Ward. "La Mécanique sociale." *Annales de l'institut international de sociologie*, VII, pp. 163–204.

The title of the article is deceiving. The term "social movement" is simply a synonym for sociology. Since social life is the result of forces, the science of society is a mechanism that is comprised of two parts. Indeed, the object of social statics is to consider social forces as they form an equilibrium among clearly defined systems. One of course studies the changes occurring in the equilibrium; thus dynamics is constructed. It is difficult for us to see what significant contribution the author makes to the old division conceived by Comte, although he does not hesitate to compare his innovations in social dynamics to the revolution brought about by Lamarck in biological philosophy (p. 191). It is a little surprising to read (p. 191) that sociology, until the present, was almost exclusively confined to statics, whereas all the work by Comte and even that by Spencer was concerned with dynamics. With regard to statics, as the author understands it, it is based upon "this substantial fact that the organization is the basis of order in the social world" (p. 189). (*Année sociologique*, 5, 1902, p. 137; trans. Y. Nandan)

Edward Alsworth Ross. "Moot Points in Sociology. I: The Scope and
Task of Sociology." *American Journal of Sociology,* VIII, no. 6,
pp. 762 ff.

The author endeavors to link all the special social sciences to sociology by
distinguishing one from the other. Sociology exercises a sort of suzerainty over
these sciences, without knowing clearly what form this suzerainty takes, nor
what kind of sociology [that he conceives] will be distinct from other special
disciplines. On the other hand, these special sciences would become pure and
simple branches of sociology. But insofar as they respond to the general
tendencies of human nature and not to social need, they would escape
sociology. The author's method is purely dialectical. (*Année sociologique,* 7,
1904, pp. 158–159; trans. Y. Nandan)

A. Andreotti. "L'induzione sociologica nello studio del diritto
penale." *Rivista di diritto penale e sociologia criminale,* V, 1904,
pp. 53 ff.
U. Matteucci. "Intorno al reconoscimento della sociologia come
scienza autonoma." Ibid., pp. 249 ff.
U. Matteucci. "L'insegnamento della sociologia." Ibid., VI, 1905,
pp. 25 ff.

We report on these articles, which are written especially as polemics and
propaganda, because they give evidence of the attempts made in Italy to
elucidate the notion of the science of sociology and the extent of its relationships with the social techniques. After reading them, it seems that their
authors have to fight against the prejudices which, generally speaking, are
without doubt analogous to those manifested in France, but which have
special characters that we do not perceive well. Andreotti shows that the penal
law must be based on criminal sociology—without the latter absorbing the
former. Matteucci, who has become co-director of the *Rivista di diritto penale,*
does not want sociology to be confused with the philosophy of law as it has
been understood in the traditional sense. Furthermore, he establishes the
necessity of an autonomous teaching of sociology. (*Année sociologique,* 9,
1906, pp. 141–142; trans. Y. Nandan)

R. P. A. Belliot. *Manuel de sociologie catholique. Histoire, théorie,
pratique.* Paris: P. Lethielleux, 690 pp.

It is impossible to present an analysis of this work, which lacks all scientific
qualifications. But it is not without advantage to point up just one example of
the way in which sociology is understood in certain intellectual circles. Spencer
is not cited in the book at all. Comte's name is mentioned only once, and here
is how the author speaks of him. The author writes that with Comte "modern
individualism has found its supreme formula. This last system gives scientific
authorization to all the excessive ambitions and to individual pretentions. . . .
In practical life the financier, the industrialist, the wealthy merchant, the hap-

py politician, all rich on their part—all these strong men view themselves as emancipated from moral constraints and they do not refuse anything when invited. More of impediments and more of restraints on passions and vices. . . ." (pp. 54–55). [Durkheim's citation of Belliot ends here. The quote reads on: Since force is on their side, and since this is what occurs most ordinarily, all the oppressive and pleasure-seeking instincts henceforth throw off restraints in the bosom of the ruling class. And that is how rationalism, extended to its utmost limits, gives origin to modern corruption.] Humanism is characterized in baneful words in the book (p. 41). These few examples are sufficient to characterize the ideological spirit of the work. (*Année sociologique*, 12, 1913, p. 14; trans. Y. Nandan)

Social Theories

REVIEWS

Jacques Novicow. "Les Castes et la sociologie biologique." *Revue philosophique*, Oct. 1900, pp. 364–373.
A. Espinas. "'Etre ou ne pas être' ou du postulat de la sociologie." Ibid., May 1901, pp. 449–480.

In an article published in the same review, called "Biological Sociology and Caste Systems," Bouglé showed how little help the organicist conception provides when it is a matter of dealing with particular and specific sociological problems like that of the castes. The two articles that we are about to discuss are replies to the foregoing.

Novicow limits himself to reviewing a certain number of social facts that have been judged to be irreconcilable with the organicist point of view, and he tries to show that these only appear to be contradictions. It is impossible to sum up here his subtle line of reasoning, in the course of which one finds the notion of the biological phenomenon either expanding in different directions or contracting, with remarkable flexibility, depending on the requirements of the argument. Besides, the author loses sight of what ought to be the fundamentals of the debate. It is not a matter of knowing whether such and such an institution may be compared, in some respects, to such and such a physiological factor, but to what extent these comparisons are useful and serve to clarify. It is their methodological utility that is disputed by pointing out that they constitute mere analogous approximations, without benefit of explanation.

With Espinas, the debate takes on a much broader scope. As a matter of fact, his discussion even transcends the issue proposed by Bouglé. His fundamental thesis is that sociology cannot exist if it is not assumed that "social phenomena constitute a separate group over and above psychological phe-

nomena, that they are concerned with observation and are subject to laws.''
We do not need to say how much this thesis is our own. With Espinas, we
believe that the contrary principle can only give rise to a vaguely philosophical
literature.

But in that case what has the organicist hypothesis to do with the point at
issue? The fact is that, for the author, social reality can be assured only if it is
bound by close ties to organic reality; it differs from it, but it goes down deep
to join it at its roots; social organization can be something real only if its
method of procedure is derived from biological organization. It is clear that we
are far removed from the analogies and the metaphors in which certain
organicists are fond of indulging. For Espinas, organicism is simply a way to
conceive of the relationships between two domains, a conception that alone,
he believes, can make the fundamental assumptions of sociology completely
sound.

But it is impossible for us to see how, in the course of his article, Espinas
has demonstrated his thesis. Why, in order to admit sui generis the reality of
society, would it be necessary to link it to the biological domain? Where does
the special privilege accorded to the latter come from? It is a salient fact that
between the world of the living and the social world, there is another one interpolated, by the author's own admission: It is the world of individual
psychology. The reply to us will be that this direct relationship is, in fact,
established through observation; that the link thus uniting the social to the
biological is visible. It is presumably the family that serves as a connecting link,
which appears, indeed, to be twofold: social inasmuch as it is an institution,
biological inasmuch as it concerns generation. Unfortunately, the family as
social institution, especially at the beginning of its evolution, is not related to
generative functions; it is, above all, an economic and religious group. The
physical factor of consanguinity is in no way a requirement for membership
therein and the relationship between the relatives in no way corresponds to
bloodline relations. We are afraid that Espinas, while speaking about the family, may be thinking especially of the various types of families that one finds in
the animal world. But the word ''family'' does not have the same meaning
when it is applied to men and to animals; for, in the case of the latter, there
are instincts and feelings, but there is no *domestic institution*. (*Année
sociologique*, 5, 1902, pp. 127–129; trans. J. French)

Georg Simmel. *Philosophie des Geldes* (Philosophy of Money). Leip-
     zig: Duncker und Humblot, 1900, xvi + 544 pp.
     The work's title could lead one to believe that it is of special interest to
economic sociology.[18] But, as a matter of fact, the issues dealt with endlessly
overflow this type of framework. There is scarcely a sociological problem that is
not touched upon; one will find here a theory of slavery, of serfdom, of traf-
ficking in women, of punishment, of seeking compromise [French *composition*], of liberty, etcetera. In sum, it is a treatise on social philosophy that is ac-

corded us, although society is chiefly considered from the point of view of money. For the author money is merely a means of indicating the bond that unites the most superficial manifestations "with the deepest currents of individual life and of history" (p. ix); it is only a starting point, a subject for subsequent expansion in such a way as to encompass, insofar as possible, the totality of existence (p. x).

By virtue of this conception, Simmel divides his book into two parts. In the first, which he qualifies as analytical, he determines the essence of money, the needs that gave rise to its use and that it meets; the object of the second, which he presents as synthetic, is to show the way in which money affects human life as a whole.

The first part, which is by far the clearer, can be summed up in this way. Things are by themselves worthless; it is man who makes them appear otherwise. And yet, in one sense, economic objects do possess an objective value. A certain quantity of a certain product corresponds to a certain quantity of a certain product of another sort, and this proportion is at each moment in time independent of individual arbitration; prices are fixed by norms that are binding on individuals. Where, then, does this objectivism come from? It is the mechanism of trade that produces it, for the worth of an object is relative to the worth of other objects; it is determined only in and by that relationship, outside of which it cannot exist. It is, thereby, disassociated from the individual and becomes an integral part of an objective system that regulates individual trade, instead of resulting from it. But this objective worth is, by itself, something essentially abstract, since it is interdependent, bound up with an infinity of other interdependent factors. It can then become really effective only by solidifying in the form of a symbol that replaces and represents it: This symbol is hard currency. Through it, trade relations are consolidated and made substantial. A common measure is established between objects, which makes them comparable and which gives an opportunity for self-expression in a mutually functional capacity.

But if money is only a symbol, an instrument of measurement, it has no need, for the accomplishment of its mission, to possess an intrinsic value of its own. And, according to Simmel, it does in fact increasingly assume a purely symbolic character expressing an abstraction. In this respect, the true nature and the worth of the material that is used in its creation would seem to become factors that are ever more insignificant in relation to the social services that they render. Today we evaluate the importance of the sums we receive without even considering the commercial value of the precious metals that go into the hard currency. This development, it is true, cannot be carried to its logical conclusion: Hard currency cannot possibly turn exclusively into something purely symbolic. The substance of which it is made must always have a minimal value, in order that governments may not cause its quantity to vary arbitrarily beyond a certain limit. But this minimum is destined to undergo a further unlimited descent.

It would seem that a pure symbol, an abstract expression of abstract relationships, is not meant by nature to exert a very profound impact on moral
life. And yet the entire second part of the work is utilized to show us the influence on individual liberty of hard currency understood as such (pp.
279–364), on the way in which personal worth is appraised (pp. 365–454)—in
short, on the rhythm and the general tone of life (pp. 455–554). Almost all
these three hundred pages defy analysis; too many different issues are examined in turn, and it is not always easy to make out the thread that binds
them into a unified whole. We must settle for the emergence of the most
general considerations.

Precisely because hard currency is a symbol, devoid of all positive content,
because it impartially represents objects of all kinds, the man whose property
consists of money does not find himself committed to a certain course of action
by the nature of his material possessions; for money, so to speak, has no
nature. Such a man's fortune does not tie him down; he can put it to use in
the most diverse ways. Accordingly he finds himself able to act more freely
than the owner of landed property, whose behavior is almost entirely predetermined by the nature of the estate he cultivates. That is why money has served
to lighten the dependency of men vis-à-vis their fellows, by helping in the
transformation, then in the suppression of the slavery and the serfdom that
purely pecuniary obligations finally replaced. Doubtless, not every dependency
disappeared; but we tend more and more to depend only on impersonal collectivities (the state, the clientele, some sort of economic society), and no longer
as in the past on a fixed group of people (a certain master, a certain lord,
etcetera). Now, this abstract subordination leaves the individual more of his
inner freedom. By reason of its formal and symbolic character, money will
always affect our moral judgments. Since it is used to measure all sorts of
things, even the humblest and the lowliest, it undergoes for that very reason a
kind of moral depreciation; as a result, we are more and more reluctant to
evaluate in terms of money the things that we are accustomed to consider
beyond compare, to which we readily attribute incomparable value—in other
words, the human being and every direct byproduct thereof. That is why we
find it a real moral scandal that a human life should be judged in terms of its
monetary value; why there is a sort of incompatibility between the notion of
certain functions (artistic, scientific, religious, etcetera) and the idea of
pecuniary remuneration. Therefore money cannot play a major role in life
without a decrease in morality resulting, and the author clearly seems to make
of this failing one of the characteristics of our age, as a result of the major
growth of the *Geldwirtschaft*.[19] In short, he applies himself to the task of giving us a demonstration of the similar workings of this abstract nature of
money, its role as a means that can lend itself to all purposes—inciting the
growth of the speculative faculties to the detriment of feeling, of spirit, of imagination, resulting in a sort of existence drained of color. At the same time
money, by making the division of work easier, also makes the production of

goods of all sorts easier; but these goods are accumulated in a thoroughly impersonal manner; they are remote from individuals who derive no profit from them, so much so that the individual culture remains rather stationary, in spite of the material and intellectual wealth that the collectivity amasses. Money would even go as far as modifying the general rhythm of the life that it would precipitate, by reason of the extreme mobility that life owes to the bare material constitution with which it is formed.

One will find in this work a number of ingenious ideas, pungent views, curious or even at times surprising comparisons, and a certain number of historical and ethnographic facts, unfortunately imprecise and unwarranted as reported. The reading of the book, though laborious, is interesting and in places suggestive. But the objective value of the views that are proposed to us is not commensurate with their ingenuity.

We do not believe that an economist can accept the theory which is basic to all these developments, for it rests on an ambiguous and confused notion. By money, Simmel means at one and the same time metallic currency that has in its own right genuine worth and paper money, the purely fiat currency. Both the one and the other are dealt with at the same time, since the fiat currency would be after a fashion the ideal limit toward which properly so-called money would tend, as an adequate expression of its essence. But these are two entirely distinct institutions that do not rest on the same principles. Paper money depends on the growth of credit, and by extension, on other factors quite apart from the monetary system. It is therefore impossible that two categories of such different facts can be incorporated, without confusion, into one and the same idea. Therefore, it is not correct to say that hard currency *turns into* more and more fiat money. The truth is that there are two countervailing types of circulation that are connected with two very different social organizations. Paper money can replace metallic currency only to the extent that economic life is socialized, and inversely, economic functions escape more fully the impact of collectivization only insofar as the role of metallic currency becomes more important. Fiat money cannot then become preponderant by a sort of spontaneous growth in the course of which the nature of money would be ever more fully realized; indeed, for that to happen it is necessary that profound transformations come about in the structure of our societies and impose a different system of circulation from the one that is presently in use.

The second part of the book would call for even more explicit reservations. Here, the ideas are more often linked to each other by ties that are more superficial than logical. Moreover, it is not hard to surmise that money cannot have such a profound moral influence on the moral and intellectual life of peoples on the sole grounds of the abstract and symbolic character that is attributed to it. Let us imagine an economic state completely socialized, where, as a result, fiat money would have replaced the money in circulation. It is readily perceivable that the manner in which its distribution will be regulated will suffice for the moral effects to be entirely different; it is for this very reason that socialism has been faulted for a certain amount of asceticism. If, then, money impinges in one way or another on the life of societies, it is not because it is more or less conventional, more or less unsullied by any essential worth; what matters is the presence or the absence of regulatory procedures by which it is controlled, and the nature of these rules and regulations.

It is true that by discussing in this fashion the author's ideas, by asking of them their claims to logic, we are applying to them a critical method that Simmel doubtless would challenge on general principles. For he considers that philosophy is not like the sciences (in the true sense of this word), subject to the usual requirements of proof; its field is undemonstrable (see Preface, p. 1). Imagination, personal sensations, would then be rightfully and freely indulged [if Simmel were right about the nature of philosophy] and vigorous demonstrations would be out of place. But, as for ourselves, we confess not to place great value on this type of bastard [20] speculation, whereby reality is expressed in necessarily subjective terms, as in art, but abstract as in science, since for this very reason it cannot give us the vital and fresh objects that the artist enlivens nor the clear notions that the scientist's inquiry seeks to define. (*Année sociologique*, 5, 1902, 140–145; trans. J. French)

S. R. Steinmetz. "Der erbliche Rassen- und Volkscharakter." *Vierteljahrsschrift für wissenschaftliche Philosophie und Soziologie,* 1902, pp. 77–126.

The author limits himself to a discussion of certain theories concerning ethnic characteristics and national attributes of heredity, without, however, giving conclusions of a very positive nature. He shows that, especially in what concerns the national characteristics, the question is not resolved and is complicated by some rules of method, which, according to him, would allow only hasty solution. Some pages of our work *Suicide,* where this sort of question is dealt with, are, incidentally, discussed by the author. We are afraid that he has read our book somewhat rapidly. He attributes to us (p. 82) the "extraordinary" opinion according to which mankind would be defined not by resemblances but by the community of origin, i.e., unity by descent. The definition is not ours, but that of Quatrefages, and we defined it likewise—according to the orginal author. Steinmetz imputes to us another theory: that the influence of heredity may only be considered as established if it presents unique factors of quality in support of the phenomena explained. We never expressed ourselves in this language, nor did we sustain this idea. We only ascertained that the influence on suicide of religious affiliation, as well as civil status, was evident throughout the statistical figures, and that it was not the same as the influence on suicide of race. We never denied that neuropathic temperament, predisposing one to suicide, was transmissible through heredity; however, we attempted to prove that this psychopathic state did not significantly affect the social rate of suicides. We have revealed these errors only to give an impression that we can not acquiesce by keeping silent. (*Année sociologique,* 6, 1903, pp. 146–147; trans. Y. Nandan)

P. Carini. "Saggio di una classificazione delle società." *Rivista italiana di sociologia,* IX, nos. 3–4, pp. 351–387.

Here is another attempt at a classification of human societies.[21] It is not of such a nature as to convince us that the problem is one of those that the sociologist can usefully approach in the present state of the science. The classification which Carini proposes does not seem to us to be more precise or solidly established than those which have preceded it, nor is it of any practical utility. It divides human societies (we are saying nothing of a classification of animal societies, which is likewise presented to us) into three fundamental classes: lower, middle, and higher societies. The first category is subdivided into two kinds: (1) classes or groups which are necessarily familial; (2) others which are constituted by the tribe. All the other categories consist of states, and these are distinguished from one another by the degree of development of the political organization—from the Sioux and the Tlinkits, who are put on the lowest level of societies which are states, up to the great European states. Each of these types thus constituted is also characterized in an intellectual and economic respect; sometimes even the consideration of the mental and economic characteristics alone serves as the basis of subdivisions.

We do not understand very well how, considering the rudimentary state of sociological investigation, one could believe it possible to attempt in a systematic manner such a vast synthesis. In order to be able to rank all human societies in determined ranks and classes, it is necessary to know them a little better than we do. Also, what about the debatable affirmations that we find being put forth? The author tells us that in familial societies there is no morality; now, we know of no society without morality. He tells us of societies limited to the clan, less than the tribe; all the clans that we know are part of tribes, which have a more or less clear understanding of themselves but which do exist. Psychology, which is nevertheless a more advanced science than sociology, still babbles when it tries to classify personalities—that is to say, characterize them. In sociology the problem is even more complex, as much because of the complexity of things as because of our consequently greater ignorance. All that it is possible to do is to schematically sketch the outlines of a possible classification—that is, trace the contours of some general classifications that only the later discoveries of science will permit us to specify and to complete progressively. (*Année sociologique,* 9, 1906, pp. 143–144; trans. J. Sweeney)

NOTES AND NOTICES

A. Schaeffle. *Bau und Leben des sozialen Körpers,* 2 vols., 2nd ed. Tübingen: Laupp'sche Buchhandlung, 1896, viii + 571, 656 pp.

This new edition is shorter than the one published in 1875.[22] The author has, however, added some explanations to the original text. He has also suppressed or published in this small text some digressions; he has divided the work in such a way that now a part of it is dedicated to general sociology and a part of it to special sociology.

In the preface to the second edition the author expresses his satisfaction, for after twenty years he has very few changes to make in his work. He informs us, however, that the part dealing with the biological analogies has been reduced in the later edition, thus proving that his essential ideas could still survive without the biological analogies. He adds that he never misunderstood the psychic character of the social organism, and he points out that the misuse of biological metaphors ever since is not his fault. (*Année socologique,* 2, 1899, p. 185; trans. Y. Nandan)

Charles A. Ellwood. "The Theory of Imitation in Social Psychology."
   American Journal of Sociology, VI, pp. 721–741.
   The article presents a quite impressive and strong criticism of the theory which explains all the social phenomena by imitation.[23] We do not imitate any one model, but we choose our models, and the instinct for imitation does not explain at all how this choice is made. How, moreover, can the instinct for imitation dominate the whole process of human societies when so many other instincts are at work in animal societies? In reality, we imitate such types of behavior as are in accord with our nature—that is to say, with all the predispositions we have acquired through heredity. Finally, there are a number of cases where imitation is scarcely apparent. The young of the animal seems to imitate the movements of his parents, but in reality does not imitate them. The proof: It is he himself who produces those movements when, in order to raise him, he is isolated from his own species. (*Année sociologique,* 5, 1902, pp. 155–156; trans. Y. Nandan)

Otto Ammon. "Der Ursprung der sozialen Triebe." *Zeitschrift für
   Sozialwissenschaft,* 1901, pp. 1–13, 101–113.
   The author's undertaking is aimed to show, contrary to Schultze[24] and Sutherland (see *L'Année,* 4, 1901, p. 312), that the domestic sentiments are never derived from the sexual sentiments, nor are the social sentiments derived from the domestic sentiments. The latter would be a product of natural selection; raising of the young cannot be prolonged without the members of the family taking more and more time for each other. As far as the social instincts are concerned, they would be the result of struggle among societies. (*Année sociologique,* 5, 1902, p. 156; trans. Y. Nandan)

Louis Wallis. "The Capitalization of Social Development." *American
   Journal of Sociology,* VII, no. 6, pp. 763–796.
   The thesis developed in the article may be described as follows: Social evolution is principally accomplished due to the progressive accumulation, in the form of capital, of the products furnished by the work of the lower class

and appropriated by a higher class, relatively smaller in number, and "the origin of which is the same as the origin of contemporary societies" (p. 268). The author verifies this proposition by a summary review of ancient and modern societies. The article ends with practical conclusions, in the light of which Wallis declares himself as agreeing in principle with the theories of Henry George. [25] (*Année sociologique*, 6, 1903, p. 147; trans. Y. Nandan)

L. Gumplowicz. "Una legge sociologica della storia." *Rivista italiana di sociologia,* V, no. 4, pp. 434–445.

This law is formulated by the author in this manner: "All central power tends to subordinate other powers, and in the case of the struggle of these powers to gain supreme domination, the central power raises itself above all the other powers, since the former is better endowed to survive in the struggle for existence." The proposition does not quite seem new to us. No doubt, according to the intellectual predisposition of the author, it results from the above premise, which illustrates his general theory explaining the great social systems as the result of conflict among the heterogeneous and antagonistic social forces. (*Année sociologique*, 6, 1903, p. 147; trans. Y. Nandan)

G. Sergi. "L'evoluzione in biologia e nell'uomo." *Rivista italiana di sociologia,* V, no. 4, pp. 413–433.

The article makes extreme generalizations. According to the author, society has its origin in the anthropological constitution of man. Sexual instinct and the attraction felt for each other by the members of a particular group are its roots. Also, at the beginning, it did not extend itself beyond the small family groups. But the family groups were united; they formed extended groups, which in turn were amalgamated among themselves. Thus emerged large human communities. But this movement of concentration and of fusion did not continue indefinitely because human beings manifest anthropological differences which cannot be erased and which show resistance to all artificial concentration. The future, therefore, holds good for a federal system which will bring unity to different collectivities by leaving to each unit its individual character, in such a way that the unit adopts organico-psychic characteristics suited to its role. But this federal character will fit only higher societies, which alone are capable of raising themselves to this lofty conception of progress. In other words, if we understand the author well, Europe and America are called upon to form a vast federal state. [26] In the face of this monstrous unity the lower parts of humanity will disappear little by little. [27] What a chasm between such an anticipation of experimental reality and [the facts of positive character] with which we are dealing. [28] (*Année sociologique*, 6, 1903, pp. 147–148; trans. Y. Nandan)

A. W. Small. "The Scope of Sociology. VIII: The Primary Concepts of Sociology." *American Journal of Sociology,* 1902, no. 2, pp. 197–254.

This is a followup on the articles of the same author that we have already analyzed before. [29] The following are the primary concepts dealt with here: physical and spatial environment; personal unity; interests; association, the group; social process—for example, the author cites the French Revolution and the American coal miners' strike; social structure, such as men acting together [with an aim to realize some sort of collective feeling] in an adjustment (p. 227); social functions; and so forth. It is useless to elongate the enumeration. What has been mentioned above is enough to give an idea of the author's treatment. (*Année sociologique*, 7, 1904, p. 185; trans. Y. Nandan)

Arthur Allin. "The Basis of Sociality." *American Journal of Sociology*, VIII, no. 1, pp. 75–84.

The idea summarily expounded in this article is exactly what we have developed in our *Division of Labor:* The division of labor is the only process which allows us to reconcile the necessities of social cohesion with the principle of individualism. [30] Since the author does not make any allusion to our work, we assume that he has not read us. We are just the same very happy to ascertain this coincidence. (*Année sociologique*, 7, 1904, p. 185; trans. Y. Nandan)

Social Psychology

REVIEWS

R. Resta de Robertis. "La psicologia collettiva della scuola." *Rivista italiana di sociologia*, V, nos. 5–6, pp. 705–730.

P. Romano. "La pedagogia nelle sue relazioni con la sociologia." Ibid., V, no. 4, pp. 446–462.

We put these two articles together because they are dominated by the same idea that education is a social phenomenon. [31] But the idea is expressed quite differently by the two authors. For Romano, education is a totality of means by which is realized, at each moment of history, the social ideals; pedagogy will be a social science in the sense that it has as its purpose the determination of these means. It will be a normative science which teaches the manner of placing the dynamics of consciousness in the perspective indicated by theoretical sociology. For Robertis, education is a social phenomenon in another sense: He claims that the school is a collectivity which intersects all sorts of collective influences. The author attempts to classify the principles of these influences: nationality; the nature of culture which is imparted in a nation (literary, scientific, or technical); pedagogic courses (methods used, such as intuitive or discursive); even the nature of the school—attending groups which enter there and the actions and reactions which are exchanged among them; the topographic situation, according to which rural and urban areas are classified; the social strata from which the school recruits its pupils; the way the classes in the school follow one another. School is, therefore, the theater of a social life which has good reasons to be studied as a phenomenon sui generis. This is precisely the purpose of the "collective psychology of education" (*psychologie collective de l'école*), a science which needs to be constructed and which has practical usefulness. This is what the author shows in conclusion. (*Année sociologique*, 6, 1903, pp. 151–152; trans. Y. Nandan)

Théodule Ribot. *La Logique des sentiments*. Paris: F. Alcan, 1905,
   x + 200 pp.

Ribot is one of the psychologists who feel most keenly about the light the study of social events can shed on psychology. It is very interesting to follow the growth of his thinking on this point throughout his successive published works. As the inferior mental functions pass on to the superior mental functions, the author feels the need to give a greater place to sociological considerations. This tendency was already very marked in his *Psychologie des sentiments*. [32] Today the issue he treats is, by his own admission, properly sociological. "This work," he says in his preface (p. x), "deals with an individual issue apparently psychological but nonetheless collective, since human groups are formed and maintained through a community of beliefs, opinions, and precedents, and it is the consistency of the feelings that serves to create them or to defend them." And that is why we could not let this important work slip by without bringing it to the attention of our readers.

The problem that is studied there is itself so sociological that we have already had occasion to tackle it in these pages. In our *De quelques formes primitives de classification,* we have applied ourselves to pointing out that beneath scientific and rational logic there is something more complex and more obscure from which the former is derived; that the notion of class, for example, has not always meant groups of beings methodically classified according to their intrinsic characteristics. However, it was formed on occasion by disparate collectivities rather than determined by obscure feelings. Obviously it was defined by objective considerations. Now, it is the same idea that has been the determining factor in Ribot's new study. The logic of sentiments is that other logic which the scientist ignores, but which nevertheless has played and still plays a considerable role in life. Most observers, while following very different paths, come to face the same question. We believe that such a problem must be noted; it is the best proof of the existence of that problem and of its importance.

Quite naturally, Ribot deals with his subject from its psychological aspect. With his usual penetration, he fragments the psychic mechanism that makes possible his line of reasoning sui generis in which feelings, emotional states, shape the web of life as it is. And there is indeed no doubt that this special logic has an essentially emotional characteristic—all of which explains the title adopted by the author. Granted, it is very obvious that this logic of sentiments would not be possible in cases where the individual conscience would not lend itself to the matter at hand, and that as a result it assumes a *method* that the psychologist is competent to study. On the other hand, it is no less certain that the states of mind which are the subject of these investigations are essentially collective. In order to be convinced of this, one has only to observe where Ribot goes in search of the facts on which to base his analysis. According to him, the most important form of emotional reasoning is the kind he calls imaginative. Now, the examples he gives of this form of reasoning comprise beliefs of a manifestly collective nature; they are beliefs, ideas, or conclusions relating to future life (p. 98), and those that are basic to divination (p. 101) and to magic (p. 107). The effect of all this is that, on this point, the psychologist cannot push his research beyond certain limits without resorting to the comparative science of religions, a science eminently sociological. In order to understand what constitutes the lines of reasoning of which these diverse states of opinion form the conclusion, one must resort to procedures other than those the psychologist ordinarily uses; one must compare the various shapes these different beliefs have taken in different societies in order to determine the causes, that is to say, the mental states that motivate them and the arrangement they make; in a word, one must create a theory of magic, of divination, etcetera. Now, we have often shown that these theories are necessarily sociological, that these mental states are collective representations and emotions and that it is their collective characteristic which explains their results. Morover, that is just what Ribot has done. In this part of his work, it is not to mental pathology that he turns to borrow his documents; it is to Tylor, to Frazer, to Bouché-Leclercq, and others that he directs his queries. He has thus demonstrated, with the authority which characterizes everything he does, that the complex forms of the individual's psychic life are unexplainable outside their social conditions—that is to say, that psychology, when it has reached a certain moment of its development, becomes inseparable from sociology; and this is not one of the least of the services rendered by his new book. [33] (*Année sociologique*, 9, 1906, pp. 156–158; trans. J. French)

R. Resta de Robertis. "L'anima delle folle." *Rivista italiana di socio-*
   logia, IX, nos. 3–4, pp. 387–396.

   The author does not admit that collective psychology can be derived from individual psychology, since, on the contrary, in the crowd the individual personality vanishes. Two principal factors appear to him to explain the way in which the crowd in essence is formed. First of all there is the contagious and imperative power of the emotions, the way in which they spread from one consciousness to another and take possession of each, the kind of singlemindedness they create; next there is the social instinct, product of the experience of the species fixed and organized within us and predisposing the *me* of individuals to interpenetrate and to merge into an undifferentiated *us*. With the author, we believe that there are differences between individual psychology and collective psychology. But it is hard for us to see in what way this makes things less problematical. To be sure, there is no doubt that psychic characteristics of the emotions play a considerable role, but the author himself recognizes that this unique cause is not enough to account for the presence of the collective factor in the phenomenon. He invokes social instinct, but it is somewhat like begging the question. That, with our temperaments socialized by education and perhaps heredity, we are better prepared for communal life is readily believable, although there are also in our case contrary tendencies, due to the same cause. But that is not a primal cause of crowds; it is perhaps simply a contributing cause. Besides, there is no way to estimate the importance of this cause without facts.

Like many others, the author offers us this opinion that the collective spirit, generally speaking, and more specifically, the spirit of crowds is a product of compulsion. We do not believe that we have written one word that justifies this interpretation of our thought. Compulsion is an *exterior symptom* whereby social factors are recognized; it is in no way an explanation. Is there, moreover, *an* explanation of social factors? (*Année sociologique*, 9, 1906, pp. 159–160; trans. J. French)

NOTES AND NOTICES

G. Tarde. "L'Esprit de groupe." *Archives d'anthropologie crimi-nelle*, Jan. 15, 1900, pp. 1–27.

The esprit de corps consists of "an intense proud collective, a very susceptible self-love, common to all the members of the group, and of a mutual and close sympathy, which evokes their group solidarity." Whether the group is periodic or permanent, the corps becomes *traditional*. But this tradition can be flexible, open to innovations, and to influence from the outside. Or it can be a routine, retiring within itself, and making itself inaccessible to external influence. Generally, it can be said that the esprit de corps develops a liberal attitude, more broad and tolerant. Each professional, ecclesiastical, and military group becomes less and less sheltered from other groups. This demonstrates the progressive disappearance of customs and ceremonial practices of all kinds. This evolution does not signify, however, that corporate feeling is destined to disappear, because it is inseparable from the association. (*Année sociologique*, 4, 1901, p. 136; trans. Y. Nandan)

Georges Palante. "L'Esprit de corps." *Revue philosophique*, Aug. 1899, pp. 135–145.

After a very sober and slightly arbitrary depiction of the spirit of solidarity, [34] Palante concludes that it is destined to disappear, for the simple reason that the social clubs in which the individual simultaneously holds membership are increasing by leaps and bounds. He does not belong to any one of them, because he belongs to them all. But even if such mutually restrictive competition between different groups is bound to prevent the hold of group solidarity from becoming too tyrannical and from too fully absorbing the individual members, it does not seem to us that competition can possibly do away with such a group entirely. Competition only corrects it, and as such prevents excesses. Perhaps the author refers to the spirit of solidarity as a form of collective conformity only when it reaches a particular degree of intensity. But in that case why combat the ideas that we have expounded elsewhere about the morally successful influence that it will have on a restructuring of the professional group? Indeed, for the very reasons that Palante gives, such a group can no longer commit the despotic and oppressive acts of the past. And that is what we have been saying. Why wouldn't the renewed corporate body benefit from the fortunate situation which allows the individual to mingle in the life of an association and become attached to it without becoming dominated by it? (*Année sociologique*, 4, 1901, p. 137; trans. J. French)

Georges Palante. "Le Mensonge de groupe: Etude sociologique."
   Revue philosophique, Aug. 1900, pp. 165–173.
   The author continues to study the process of groups in general. [35] He enumerates today the lies the group imposes on its members, such as false statements of optimism, respect for opinion, and disavowal of intellectual superiority. The author sees that these collective prejudices are, above all, aimed to regulate action and are not simply speculative expressions of reality. In order to treat them as lies, it must be shown that they are not founded in the necessity of life, that in reality they are not true. The author postulates it a little ingenuously. He even points up practical "lies," which, it may be said, are ill thought of, since they have nothing in common with true facts—for example, the obligation to resort to committees to succeed in an election. (*Année sociologique*, 5, 1902, p. 167; trans. Y. Nandan)

L. Gumplowicz. "La suggestione sociale." *Rivista italiana di sociologia*, IV, no. 5, pp. 545–555.
   The author appeals in the name of the collective action by which a society infiltrates its ways of seeing and feeling into the individual—in a word, the ways in which it socializes him. The power of this influence is affirmed and illustrated by examples, but the manner in which it operates is not analyzed. (*Année sociologique*, 5, 1902, p. 167; trans. Y. Nandan)

Sociological Conditions of Knowledge

REVIEWS

[Durkheim's Introduction]

If it is for the first time that the abovementioned rubric appears in *L'Année,* it is because the issue it raises has remained foreign to us until the present time. The topic, however, for a long time has stood in the first rank of our preoccupations. Without speaking of our study *Primitive Classification,* which appeared in these pages, and Hubert's *Etude sommaire de la représentation du temps dans la religion et dans la magie* (Paris, 1905; also included in Hubert and Mauss, *Mélanges d'histoire religieuse,* [36] Paris: Alcan, 1909, pp. 189–229), the reader will find each of these volumes* classified under the "Religious Representations of Being and of Natural Phenomena," in addition to a certain number of books and articles reviewed from this very point of view. Now, since religion is essentially a social phenomenon, in order to seek what religious factors have entered into our representation of the world, we have rigorously attempted to determine some of the sociological conditions of knowledge. Since in these works alone knowledge was studied especially in its relation to religion, we could hardly separate other works which also come under the jurisdiction of religious sociology. This year again, that very reason has obliged us to present in this very section the works of that nature, such as that by Pechuel-Loesche on the Bavili religions [37] [the two works by Pechuel-Loesche have been reviewed by Antoine Beuchat. See *L'Année,* 11, 1910, pp. 218–227, 306–307], which, however, have direct bearing on the questions of classification and categories. There was, moreover, a serious problem of corresponding interest on the part of all other works. That is why today we open a new chapter, which, we are quite sure, will not remain empty henceforth. At the very moment when we are publishing our works on the subject, some other works devoted precisely to the sociological study of knowledge have just been published or are under preparation. (*Année sociologique,* 11, 1910, pp. 41–42; trans. Y. Nandan)

Wilhelm Jerusalem. "Soziologie des Erkennens." *Die Zukunft,*
     1909, pp. 236–246.

This article is very general and very brief.[38] Nevertheless, we feel obliged to present an analysis of it, first because it is interesting and secondly because it will permit us to indicate in what terms the problem must be considered.

The author takes as his starting point the same main sources from which we draw our inspiration. He admits that society is the original source of life sui generis, which is superimposed on the individual's life and transforms it. Now, this creative power has just as much effect on the intelligence as on feeling and the will.

It is in matters of religious representations that we are made most aware of the influence of society. All those conceptions of souls, of spirits, of demons, of mysterious forces dispersed throughout nature, would have remained empty and passing fancies, and would consequently not have played any role in the history of ideas, if they had not been anything more than individual musings.

---

* Hubert's work was reviewed in *L'Année* under the rubric Durkheim refers to, but the reference to his own work creates confusion since the work was never cited under that rubric. ED.

But men have communicated their opinions and their feelings to each other, and verifying their agreement, have had their convictions mutually confirmed. By becoming collective, impressions have become fixed, consolidated, crystallized. The author calls this operation a "social condensation," *eine soziale Verdichtung.* [39] That is what gave to the world of imagination, where religious ideas hold sway, all the appearances of reality.

Our empirical conception of the universe was not formed in any other way and is of the same nature. The notion we entertain of something—as long as this notion is not formulated in accordance with rigorously scientific procedures—is essentially practical in nature; it expresses above all the automatic reactions matter provokes on our part, depending on how it affects our vital inclinations. Therefore, two phenomena that elicit similar reactions are quite naturally closely related in the mind; they "come under a same concept." Now, each of us sees how others react when faced with matters that turn up in the course of our experience; and as we mutually imitate each other, there tends to be established, by way of reciprocal borrowings, a sort of common reaction showing how the average person adapts himself to the nature of his surroundings. Notions likewise found to be byproducts of a "social condensation" correspond to such typical reactions. Language, which is itself a social institution, achieves consolidation as a result of this operation.

But, alongside the social factor, there is the matter of the individual, whose importance the author is far from denying. In every case where the issue was newly considered, the individual was sheepish in both behavior and thought; he would docilely follow the group. Now, such can be the case only insofar as personal growth is regarded. On the other hand, to the degree that the individual personality emerges from the mass of society and acquires a distinct physiognomy, it too conspires to have a mind of its own. It would seem that from this arose scientific thought, which, in the author's opinion, is true understanding (p. 243). Until then, what was considered as the truth was generally accepted as such; it was a consensus of opinion that denoted the truth. In the present case, truth is arrived at objectively as a result of the exact observation of facts. The inclination to make individual distinctions is so clearly inherent in science that if there was nothing to curb it, it would risk giving way to excesses that would make it sterile. For it is not enough that scientific truths be proclaimed to become effective, to be translated into acts; it is necessary that they be acknowledged as such collectively. If they were denied, it would be as if they did not exist; they would remain purely speculative, with no effect on behavior. It is, then, necessary that a social sense be ever-present in scientific research to prevent it from being sidetracked. But it is not so-called science that can keep alive this sentiment and curb individual excesses. That is sociology's affair.

Such is the thesis. We do not need to say that we accept it in principle. But we fear that the way it is presented and justified spoils it, or at the very least seriously weakens its scope.

In fact, if truly the role that the author attributes to society is indeed the only one that applied to it, it must be said that its influence on intellectual life, great in the past, would be destined to grow smaller and smaller. It would be responsible for consolidating mythological imaginations into obligatory dogmas, into undisputed truths. Similarly, it would formulate a crude conception of nature. But science would not be under its jurisdiction; it would be an individual creation. We would owe to society the simple, even crude, notions that would serve us day by day to direct our activities; but it would be of no use to the more refined conceptions that aim, above all, to show things such as they are objectively, with all their characteristic complexities methodically analyzed. In the last analysis, its impact would be completely normal only insofar as it was brought to bear on routine practices alone, and it would make itself felt to good purpose by our understanding only insofar as this last is involved in action, and is subordinate to it. But to the extent that needs properly speculative, cognitive, become self-sufficient, it is by other means that their requirements would be satisfied. From then on, the role of society and of social science would be limited to curbing the antisocial tendency that is inherent in pure speculation by reminding this last perpetually of the need for action.

Actually, the pursuit of science is an eminently social matter, however great a role individuals may fill. It is social because it is the product of a vast cooperative effort that extends not only through all space but through all time. It is social because it presupposes certain methods and techniques that are the creation of an authoritative tradition, comparable to the authorized rules that govern morality and law. Scientific institutions are veritable institutions that are involved with ideas, as legal or political institutions are involved with methods relevant to action. Again, science is a social phenomenon because it brings into play ideas that dominate all thought and seemingly condense—classify by categories—the whole of civilization. It is, then, far short of the truth to state that the role of society ceases at that point where pure speculation begins; for speculation rests on social grounds.

The author would not have excluded society from science in the way he does if he had not already been mistaken about the part it plays in the genesis of religious beliefs and of the empirical conception of the world. If he were to be believed, it [society] would have been limited to fixing, to crystallizing, individual conceptions. These last, on becoming collectivized, would have found more strength to resist, more authority, but as far as that goes, they would not have changed in nature. If social intervention had no other effect than to strengthen the impressions of individuals by mutually corroborating them, it would not have amounted to anything original or creative; it would not have given rise to new conceptions, different from those that the individual can elaborate under his own power. But, as a matter of fact, the impact of society is otherwise important and profound. It is the source of a life of the mind sui generis that collaborates with the individual's point of view and transforms it. Social ideas, in fact, have on the one hand a powerful and creative impact that the individual personality cannot reproduce, because it is due to the collaboration of a multiplicity of intellects and to a collaboration that is carried on even during the following generations. In another sense, society is a new reality, which enriches our understanding simply because it is revealed to our minds, and it is revealed simply because it exists, but it can exist only if it is in our thoughts. Yet since it [the social structure] is the highest form of life, it is life as a whole that is imbued with a greater sense of self-awareness in and through society.

It is, then, in the special mechanism of collective thought and in the special nature of collective reality that one must look for society's genuine contribution in giving form to our ideas. But here we touch upon an error that is still too widespread and that we regard as a sociological stumbling block. It is too often believed that what is general is social, and inversely, that the collective type is nothing other than an average type. Quite the contrary, there is an immense distance between those two types. The average consciousness is mediocre, as much from the intellectual as from the moral point of view; the collective consciousness, on the other hand, is infinitely rich since its riches come from the whole civilization. (*Année sociologique,* 11, 1910, pp. 42–45; trans. J. French)

Section Three

Juridic and Moral Sociology

Unlike the sections on general sociology, religious sociology,* criminal sociology, and economic sociology, edited by Bouglé, Hubert and Mauss, Richard (at least for the first three years), and Simiand respectively, the section on juridic and moral sociology had no permanent editor in charge, even though Durkheim alone was responsible for the rubric on domestic organization and various others, and exercised control over almost every other rubric. The lack of editorial responsibility delegated to one person was reflected in the deficiencies of the section, such as rubrics devoid of explanatory introductions. Supposedly, the subsection on moral sociology, or at least a good part of it, was to be produced under the aegis of Lapie,[1] who had little interest in explaining the rubrics by writing introductions. Even Durkheim was negligent in this regard; he was induced to present introductions to rubrics in a few cases, but only after Mauss and Hubert had created a logical system in support of their section on religious sociology.

From the fourth volume of *L'Année* onward, the order of two elements in the title of the section was reversed; the new, permanent title was "Juridic and Moral Sociology," with the subtitle "Study of Juridic and Moral Rules Considered According to Their Genesis." Durkheim's conception of *Morale* [2] embodied "all morals that present to us a system of rules of conduct."[3] The suggestive idea of moral sociology obviously referred to social customs, manners, usages, mores, and morals. Such a definition given to moral sociology, also characterized as the science of morals ac-

* Section Two on religious sociology is not included here.

111

cording to Durkheim and Lévy-Bruhl, who vainly attempted to institute it as a science next to sociology in the Comtian classification of sciences, is analogous to what Hobhouse, Sumner, and Westermarck hypothetically surmised on the subject.

The second part of the section on juridic sociology is not clearly distinguished from the complex of moral sociology. In fact, the two are confounded in the rubric on juridic systems—a sort of mélange created during the last several years of publication of *L'Année* and incarnated following a thorough examination of a myriad of ethnographic studies. The rubric—dealing with the most primitive forms of "juridic" life such as totemism and clans, as well as with national juridic and moral systems such as the Greek city-states and those of the Roman social structure—manifests in totality the individual character of the specific.[4] Thus the notion "juridic" is not what is popularly understood by it. It signifies a holistic approach to a comprehensive explication of a social system—what Mauss later defined in methodological terms as *faits sociaux totaux* ("social facts in their entirety"). The rubric is prodigiously overfilled with ethnographic studies of all sorts, and there is some discussion of historical works pertaining to the Greek and Roman societies.

The inherent ambiguity in the abovementioned rubric notwithstanding, the whole section could have been divided into three subdivisions: (1) conceptions, general theories, and methodological issues, (2) moral sociology, and (3) juridic sociology. The rubrics are arranged in the order of these themes, but the section title begins with juridic sociology. Durkheim himself was fully aware of the hypothetical character and heuristic value of the divisions and subdivisions of sociology manifested through *L'Année*'s sections and subsections.

The first rubric on general conceptions appeared regularly from the beginning to the end of *L'Année*'s publication, eliciting very lively discussion on the topical issues—in particular, on the sociological conceptualization of the science of morals, a controversial subject with strong doctrinaire dispositions that Durkheim and his associates initiated and surreptitiously meant to enliven the idea of secular morality. To defend the presumably newly founded sociological science of morals, obviously a futile creation and very vulnerable element in the entire complex of Durkheim's doctrines, from rancorous attacks, Durkheim himself reviewed at length, with a solemnity and severity suited to the complexity of the subject and subtlety of the issues involved, the works of Deploige, Fouillée, Landry, and Belot. He himself commended and reprimanded at the same time Lévy-Bruhl's disciple Albert Bayet for the latter's further explication of the newly conceived doctrine of the science of morals and for his misunderstanding of and even his slight deviation from the orthodoxy of the Durkheimian school. He himself canonized Lévy-Bruhl for the latter's most controversial doctrinaire disposition manifested in his *La Morale et la science des moeurs*.[5] Under this very rubric, Durkheim praised Westermarck for the latter's identical views on the treatment of morals and customs; and the Durkheimians criticized L. T. Hobhouse's *Morals in Evolution* (1906) but ignored a classical and influential work of similar nature by

W. G. Sumner, *Folkways* (1906).[6] When it came to defending the doctrine and premises of sociology from the rancorous attacks of adversaries, Durkheim himself and his apostles were competent in and well disposed to the art of polemics. Durkheim had a remarkable natural aptitude for disputation, but he was fully aware that a disposition for contentious arguments was unscientific and that too many polemics marked the decay of a science.[7]

After the rubric on juridic systems, a comprehensive discussion of which has been deferred to the second volume, there are rubrics—on domestic organization, social organization, and political organization—belonging to the subdivision of moral sociology. In the entire *Année,* Durkheim's greatest contribution of seminal character was made in the rubric on domestic organization. By writing comprehensive and illuminating reviews, he assiduously drew the attention of his readers to the genetic growth of sexual morals, the status of woman throughout history, and the family institution as a whole that experienced evolution throughout the ages. Essentially, he adduced the historical character of the Roman, Greek, Egyptian, Indian, and Hebraic family institution in its diverse elements. Durkheim's historical erudition, displayed through the frequent use of Greek and Latin terminology, can make the reading of this section savory in its content, though difficult, dense, and cumbersome. Other sections are not so impenetrably erudite. But then, a good part of the fault lies with us as well, since the humanistic character of our formal education has significantly declined. Nonetheless, the prolixity of these reviews on family organization makes them a rich mine of ideas about the historical information on the subject. In addition to the illuminating treatment of the family in various historical societies, the largest number of reviews under this rubric shed abundant light on the historical character of family jurisprudence: inheritance law, law of adoption, matrimonial law, and testamentary law. Obviously, the treatment of these topics creates a nexus between sociology and jurisprudence. The discussion on paternal authority and the status of women in different societies viewed in historical perspective makes these reviews a great contribution to some of the present-day academic and popular debates on sex roles and the feminist movement. Sociologists interested in the comparative analysis of the family will find Durkheim's arguments and his compiled bibliographic material a very valuable guide. Durkheim's consuming interest in the family organization while he was directing *L'Année* brought him in contact with Marianne Weber (the wife of the celebrated Max Weber) and her work on the subject, *Ehefrau und Mutter,* which he criticized for its deficiencies in method and for its lack of theoretical arguments. In light of these considerably revealing reviews, which contain original ideas on the family as an institution, Durkheim may encourage sociologists to reflect on his unknown or very little known ideas on the history of the family institution. This plausible conclusion is based on our knowledge that many modern sociologists have produced a profuse quantity of literature in sociology devoted to the family, with its structural variations and symptomatic functional characteristics.

The rubrics on social and political organization had been at different times put together by a number of collaborators working concurrently. Durkheim, Bouglé, Lapie, Gernet, and Davy were the principal authors, with assistance from a number of peripheral members of the *Année* school. Durkheim's mark as a patriarch and leading critic is quite visible in both rubrics, where he reviewed, among others, the works of such eminent historians as Sée, Bloch, Francotte, and Pirenne.

The rubric on international and moral law, with its belated appearance, meager space, and uncertain status, forms a line of demarcation between moral sociology and juridic sociology. The next three rubrics on penal law, property law, and obligation and contractual law will partly pass for what is known as criminology and historical jurisprudence. Penal law is obviously included in juridic sociology, and not criminal sociology, because of its suggestive idea of progressive genesis and its importance to historical jurisprudence. Conforming to the speciality of Fauconnet, the rubric on legal responsibility was under his direction. Durkheim had his favorite authors and historians, whom he reviewed favorably—e.g., Huvelin, Glotz, Usteri, and Dareste. The rubrics on property law and contract law were assigned to two eminent jurists, Emmanuel Lévy and Huvelin, with Durkheim aiding or substituting for them if needed. The two jurists were in agreement with Durkheim on what was required of them while reviewing works sometimes far removed from sociology. Durkheim was thrilled at his success in recruiting two jurists from Lyon, but he advised them of the need for cultivating sociology, a task which required the collaboration of many specialists, who in turn were supposed to sift sociology from their own discipline and write about it in *L'Année*. Durkheim saw nothing wrong in inviting the contributions of jurists, Assyriologists, Egyptologists, specialists in Hebraic literature, and historians, so long as their association with *L'Année* helped to cultivate scientific sociology.

Under the rubric on general conceptions Durkheim dealt with theoretical and methodological issues to elucidate what he designated as *science morale et physique des moeurs* ("science of morals and customs"). Among the French philosophers Durkheim was known for his inclination to build a complex of a new science from the premises of sociology—however unsuccessful he was in his endeavor. These reviews give a reflection of this crusade Durkheim had launched to quiet his enemies and opponents and to allay the fears of cynics who had doubts about the science of morals as a possible scion and perhaps the last descendant of the family of social sciences. Durkheim's conception of juridic sociology is reiterated in his review of Lambert's work on comparative civil law, which he distinguished from comparative history of law. With an identical operational definition and meaningful characterization of the internal relationships and genetic developments, the latter resembled *L'Année*'s conceptualization of juridic sociology. Lambert as well as Neukamp discerned law from such congenerous terms as customs, morals, and religion. (Huvelin's work on the religious origin of law, included in this section, is worth noting.) Discussion on jurisprudence by French scholars such as Saleilles, Gény, Duguit, and Hauriou, and by German scholars such as Jhelnik and Von Savigny, has often appropriated a lion's share in this section of the volumes of *L'Année*.

According to Bonucci the Greek philosophy of law considered two views: One view derived its premises from the divine—hence the natural law. Stemming from the social context and coinciding with institutional authority, the other view is congruous with the socoiological conceptualization of jurisprudence. Executed in uncompromising detail, Durkheim's examination of Lévy-Bruhl, Westermarck, Fouillée, Belot, Landry, Bayet, and Hoeffding—all moralists, philosophers, and sociologists—underscores the rich theme and deep concern of a moralist. Any condensation that we do of this aspect of his work will only do injustice to a theme that Durkheim cultivated almost all his life but elaborated in *L'Année* and in the meetings of the French Philosophical Society.

Reviews under the rubric "Juridic and Moral System's" belong to Durkheim's contributions in anthropology, which will be treated later.

Durkheim considered religion and the family the most important institutional elements of social structure. Religion had priority within the sociological classification of "social physiology." There were more reviews on the family than on any other subject in *L'Année.* One hundred-odd reviews, notes, and notices arranged in this volume under the section "Domestic Organization" were arranged by Durkheim himself under three subcategories: (1) "The Family," (2) "Marriage," and (3) "Sexual morality." Reviews on marriage and the family appearing in the section on criminal sociology and moral statistics must be distinguished from those contributed under the section on juridic sociology. Books and authors examined in the former section dealt with what in the nineteenth century was known as "moral statistics"—a branch of knowledge that defined the contemporary family as a statistical aggregate and described the aberrations in its structure involving such matters as divorce, illegitimacy, dowry, sex roles and sexual inequality, and interreligious marriages. Discussion of authors in the juridic sociology section sought to explore the comparative history of the family as an institution that had experienced genetic evolution in various societies. Because of the superabundant quantity of books and articles on the family as a historically evolving institution, works on kinship and "primitive" family structure were badly neglected in the earlier volumes of the periodical. The later volumes, however, included a large number of books—perhaps the largest—on the subject of anthropology, thus raising the comparative method not only to a parity with history but even above it.

Cunow's interpretation of the "primitive" family institution as he premised it on the economic institution strikes a chord of economic materialism. From all that we know of Durkheim as an opponent of utilitarian economics and dialectical materialism, sociologically incongruous to his approach, here in his review of Cunow he seems restrained, contrary to his image as a most trenchant defender of his methodology and doctrines. Starcke's work on the family puts forth his trite conviction that the institution is essential to the sustenance of social and moral life. Through its survey of literature on the subject, Steinmetz's research gives an orientation to the historian interested in the family. In addition to these works of general character, there are more than a dozen reviews of works which shed light on the family in different societies: Leist's work on Aryan societies; Launspach's on Roman; Engert's on Jewish; the works of Marcais and Roberts on Islamic; Jubainville's on Celtic; the works of Glasson, and Lefebvre on French; the works of Markovic, Stanischit, and Gebhard on Slavic; and Courant's on Chinese.

Perhaps the most visible aspect of the Roman family was the authority—despotic at times—vested in the father, *patria potestas* in legal parlance. Around patripotestal authority developed a complex juridic system that defined in detail the role everyone must play in his/her relationship to one another in the family and the family's obligations to and claims on the state. (As a learned man having acquired a mastery of facts concerning the Greco-Roman institutions, Durkheim made frequent use of the juridic vocabulary in Latin, which encompasses the essence of Greco-Latin influence on Western societies. Cornil, however, denied any claim of peremptory authority delegated to the father as *patria potestas*. Pro-and-con arguments on this topic make an interesting subject in jurisprudence, and they got Durkheim involved. Durkheim doubted Stockar's assumption that during the imperial era in Roman history the father's authority was absolute and impervious to outside intervention. But after the praetorian legislation the state constrained the father's authority, especially in the disposition of his property.

Historians have argued with equal vigor whether the practice of testamentary adoption was known to the Greeks first and then was diffused to the Romans or known to both at the same time. Lefas contends that the custom was widely practiced in Greece. As if he were claiming that history were synonymous with sociology, Durkheim forcefully broaches the issue of the antiquity of testaments going back to the period of the Twelve Tables—the date of this legal code being itself an object of dispute. Lambert's work suggests that essential to Roman testament was its legacy in favor of the notion of omnipotent domestic magistracy. This is in contrast to what happened to it in Germany and elsewhere in Europe during the Middle Ages as these societies interpreted testament as an exercise of the individual right. With the Church's domination of the social life of individuals, testamentary execution became an important formalistic institution. Englemann corroborates the same view that religious influence shaped the testamentary laws in Europe after the fall of the Roman Empire. With its proclivity toward abstraction and purposeful obfuscation of what can be said in simple words, Auffroy's work examines the testamentary law of the French as it was bequeathed to them by the Romans.

Discussion on marriage in *L'Année* centered around two principal themes: marriage customs in different lands and forms of marriage, and marital law. Other topics dealt with in passing or examined in lesser detail were: dowry, divorce, and the status of women. Hutchinson's discursive treatment of marriage suggests a classification of four types, and that all-inclusive classificatory statement covers the whole array of Durkheim's reviews of works by Meynial, Schulenburg, and Hermann. The studies by Loebel and Roeder are limited to an analysis of marriage customs in Turkey and among the Anglo-Saxons respectively. Nietzold's interesting treatise on Egyptian marriage during the period of Roman domination reveals three categories of valuable facts: the existence of dowry; trial marriage (what nowadays is called "cohabitation" and "common law marriage"); and authorization of incestuous marriages, considered as the most rational and the most natural. Historically speaking, the Jewish and the Catholic laws of marriage and divorce—the latter as it was influenced by the Roman juridical system—had a lot in common with but nevertheless differed in many respects from each other. Worth noting is the Jewish husband's right to renounce his wife at a time when the Roman paterfamilias enjoyed unlimited power in the family; the Roman husband, however, could not sever relations with his wife and eliminate her from his family.

This facile expediency in granting divorce to women by the Jewish husband has been extolled by Klugmann, who claims it as evidence of the superiority of women's status in Judaic religion. A brief history of the feminist movement may be read in a Spanish work by Posada. Works on women's status in society by Westermarck, Richard, and Marianne, (Max's wife, of course) Weber are indeed most helpful for their valuable insights and rigorous analysis of the subject from a historical point of view. A comprehensive historical study on the subject, in the vein of works suggested above, is needed.

The only work discussed in *L'Année* by Durkheim that places divorce in historical perspective is by Rol.

The most important issue discussed in the reviews under the category of marital law is the influence the Roman juridic system had in shaping the European laws pertaining to the family as an institution. The traditional historians and jurisconsults in general have maintained a consistent attitude that Roman jurisprudence has had a certain impact, if not an exclusive one, on European marital law. Meynial and Garufi in their respective studies examined matrimonial law during the Middle Ages as it reflected a syncretism of Roman law, barbarian law, and Church dogma. Contrary to this conventional view of the formation of European marital law, Lefebvre as a legal historian led a movement believing that Roman law was incompatible with the Church doctrine espoused by all of medieval Europe. As a result, the Roman law could not have shaped the French and the German matrimonial laws into its mold. Following this doctrinal premise, Lefebvre's students and his followers—some working independently, such as Marcou, Pidoux, Typaldo-Bassia, Saguez, Mallard, and Aubéry—took pains in advancing further the claims of their master. In agreeing with Lefebvre, Bartsch concludes that the Germanic law does not recognize the absolute power of the father as head of the family; instead, the collective rights of the family take precedence in many cases. Also, the *Sachsenspiegel* and other Germanic laws are committed to the idea of common property as a rightful basis of marriage between the two spouses, an absence of which is conspicuously felt in the Roman juridic system. Finally, a contradistinctive mark of the Germanic people's barbarism, as compared to the civilized Romans, claimed Bartsch, was their innate disposition to hold women in great esteem.

Besides the two works on the class structure of societies in Japan and

China, the rest of the entire review process in the rubric on social organization is devoted to the origin and existence of social class in Greece, Rome, and Europe during its historical evolution. What emerges from the works of Szanto and Holzapfel is that tribal organization in both Greece and Rome evolved as a consequence of national affinities, especially of consanguine character, so that the family expanded into a tribe. Symptomatic of a work by Wilbrandt is its allusion to the formation of a class structure that defined its essence as consisting of patricians and plebians. Oberziner and Bloch have employed their analytic rigor in identifying the causal relationships of the class structure in Rome. The former theorizes that the patricians were a foreign element who conquered Rome and imposed their (superior) cultural values on the (inferior) Roman aborigines, who are identified as the plebians. (A similar theory has been advanced to explain the historical origin of the caste system in India.) The same theoretical premise would be reiterated by reading Bloch, who claims that the two classes were originally two distinct peoples, known as Sabines and Latins, living side by side in the city. The works by Doniol, Sée, and Guilhiermoz complement each other, despite some subtle differences in their treatment of the European feudal society. For example, Doniol and Sée would disagree on the origin of feudalism as a social organization. The latter imputes this institutional structure to slavery, of which he sees obvious signs, even though in attenuated form, in feudalism; whereas the former discerns no causal relationship between the two. Doniol's arguement on the degree of freedom enjoyed by the serfs and their contractual relationships with their lords contradicts any derivative association of the feudal social structure with slavery. Guilhiermoz's original study on the evolution of French nobility reveals some interesting facts: that the nobles, in historical terms, were the free men who during the Middle Ages were transformed into feudal lords or into a militia that provided the *bourg* the needed protection from outside invaders. Those free men who did not upgrade themselves into the evolving ruling economic and military class were condemned to belong to the plebeians. Once the situation crystalized as the nobility was firmly established, the feudal aristocracy restricted itself to births within its ranks.

Fauconnet, Durkheim's faithful disciple and an effective and dependable acolyte of the Durkheimian school, was editor in charge of and a major contributor to the rubric on penal law, responsibility, and procedure. Durkheim's own contribution to this rubric is relatively smaller, and whatever reviews he wrote are chaotically disparate and often lacking a central theme. Also, Durkheim's reviews under the rubric on political organization in this section precluded our attempt to offer even a discursive summary. The little that comes out of a long review by Durkheim of Gunther's work is that he subscribes to a view that favors punishment to befit the crime and not necessarily the criminal—the latter view formed a doctrinal core of the Italian school of criminologists. Kohler's monumental study of penal law suggests that the Italian penal law was notably moderate compared to the Roman law, based primarily on retribution through monetary fines rather than corporal punishment. But by the end of the sixteenth century, owing to centuries of war and internal strife, the

Italian law was considerably weakened and admitted overwhelmingly the influence of Roman law. As an original thinker whose scholarly acumen transcended juridical thinking, Huvelin attributed the origin of Roman law to religious formalism. Glotz's seminal work depicts the evolution that Greek moral and legal institutions have experienced during three principal stages of development. Suggested in this work is another interesting observation: that individual responsibility has evolved from collective responsibility. It is a familiar cliché that reminds us of Durkheim's suggestive idea of organic solidarity having issued from mechanical solidarity.

General Conceptions, Theories, and Methodological Issues

REVIEWS

Ernst Neukamp. "Das Zwangsmoment im Recht in entwicklungs geschichtlicher Bedeutung" (Constraints in the Law Considered in Their Historical Development). *Jahrbuch der internationalen Vereinigung für vergleichende Rechtswissenschaft und Volkswirtschaftslehre.* Berlin: Hoffman, 1898, pp. 22–68.

Law has often been distinguished from morals and religion together by the fact that acts contrary to law can be imposed by physical coercion, while the merely moral never uses anything but moral pressure. The author easily shows that this way of distinguishing the two domains is not based on facts. There are a multitude of legal rules to which physical sanctions are not attached, such as the purely moral stigmas which sanction certain juridical precepts. The laws which allow the pronounced penalty to be indefinitely suspended, like our Berenger Law,[8] have the same character. One cannot physically constrain a debtor to pay his debts; all that can be done, indirectly, is to juridically seize his goods. Inversely, religion often has used physical means to force itself on the faithful. From this point of view, it is thus impossible to draw a line of demarcation between these different orders of facts. What distinguishes them is that in the case of law the constraint exercised on rebellious wills, whether it be physical or moral, is always organized. That organization is manifested in two ways. The precepts for which the constraint imposes respect are instituted by definite organs and under a definite form, and moreover, the whole system which the law uses to realize its precepts is regulated and organized, the author adds, even down to its last detail.

In the second part of the work, the author shows how organization of juridical coercion has gone further and further in its development; he takes as a starting point the picture which he draws of Greece, Rome, and the Germanic societies. He shows how the violent, confused, and unregulated movements which constitute the primitive vendetta were regulated and organized progressively to the extent that they were controlled further by the moderating and regulative action of the state. This first remark leads the author to make another statement. To the extent that juridical constraint is organized, it is spiritualized. Although in principle it consists of a deployment of physical force intended only to paralyze wills externally, it tries more and more to act on the interior of the criminal by modifying his mental and moral state. It tries to reform his feelings, to warn those who do wrong, etcetera. It thus becomes a teacher, an instrument of education—that is, it disappears insofar as it is coercion.

We do not have any problem in accepting the manner in which the author defines law, having ourselves proposed the same definition. "The difference which separates these two kinds of penalties, as we said (treating of moral and juridical penalties), is not their intrinsic characters but the way in which they are administered. One is applied by each and every person, the other by a definite and constituted body; one is diffuse and the other is organized!" We are very happy to note an agreement which is a guarantee of objectivity. However, this definition applies identically to a multitude of religious prescriptions as well as to juridical prescriptions. From that point of view, it is impossible to distinguish law from religion. The author himself recognizes this (p. 42) in a short parenthetic statement. But nevertheless he should not have posed the problem in the terms used and should not have announced that he was going to distinguish these two domains, since they are indistinguishable as to their form.

As to the law of progressive spiritualization of juridical coercion, it is true of penal sanctions, but we do not see at all how it applies to civil sanctions. Nevertheless, the coercive characteristic of law must not be peculiar to a particular form of law; it must apply to all forms. It is therefore not exact to say that, generally speaking, law is increasingly losing its old characteristics. (*Année sociologique*, 3, 1900, pp. 324–325; trans. J. Sweeney)

Edward Alsworth Ross. "The Genesis of Ethical Elements." *American Journal of Sociology*, V, no. 6, pp. 761–778.

By ethical elements the author means those moral ideas that are condensed in formulas the authority of which the entire world recognizes and which serve as canons for the judgment of conduct. They express a morality that is superior to the general notion of individual consciences; they are therefore whatever has been said of them—other than a simple generic image of the average moral state. But then how are they formed? According to Ross, they are the product of a kind of generalized hypocrisy that the social life imposes. In their relations with their fellow men, individuals do not dare to express ideas which would be considered as harmful to society; on the contrary, they express only those ideas which have the best chances of being accepted by others. Since the accepted ideas are generally manifested externally, they have such force and authority that other ideas, always driven back in the conscience of everyone, do not succeed in their manifestations. The great moral revolutions, however, do not take place in this manner. They are always the work of some geniuses who discover a new ideal befitting best the current state of the society, such as Moses, Muhammad, or Buddha.

It is certain that actions performed in a certain social milieu always express our slightly antimoral inclinations. but how does it happen that such views have such an influence on us? Perhaps such views in our eyes reflect a prestige *sui generis*, to which men's mind and heart surrender. The solution proposed here certainly begs the question. Shame in expressing immoral sentiments, by which we intend to explain the authority of moral ideas, is by itself a consequence and another aspect of this authority. With regard to the men of genius, how could their moral discoveries spread if the public conscience, by itself, was not ready to receive them and accept the assimilation of the new moral ideas? Certainly, the role of innovators is hardly negligible; they restore conscience and formulate aspirations that are, however, realized in part; they are never created in their entirety. However, it remains to be said that the article has merit since it draws our attention to a very much neglected subject, which is completely fundamental. (*Année sociologique*, 4, 1901, pp. 308–309; trans. Y. Nandan)

Arsène Dumont. *La Morale basée sur la démographie.* Paris: Schlei-
    cher, 1901, x + 181 pp.

In the wake of many others, Dumont records a crisis in ethics. According to him, it is due entirely to the fact that scientific method has not yet been sufficiently applied as matters stand. We decide that a certain practice is ethical because we have been reared and taught to consider it so—because, so to speak, that's the way it appears to the conscience; but such justifications cannot begin to satisfy the reason. As a result, when the mind is aroused enough to wonder about the ethical precepts in use and their rights to exist, it finds no answers. Hence the trouble, the skepticism, and the confusion that characterize our age. The only way to put an end to it is to discover an objective criterion of good and evil and to apply it methodically.

Since morality is a social phenomenon, one must rate the degree of good conduct in terms of the social validity of a practice; and this social validity is itself determined by the manner in which the practice under consideration affects society. If its effect is to raise the rate of marriages or births, to increase the population density wherever this morality is in use, to give rise to more activity, to lower the death rate, and so on, it will have to be considered a good thing. To dispute this postulate would be "to refuse to put a price on human life, to regard birth and death, and health and disease, equally" (p. 82). Since measuring the diverse manifestations of collective activity is the goal of demography, this science provides the only possible basis for all rational standards of morality. Once this premise is established, the author attempts, somewhat confusingly, one might add, to apply it to the case of alcoholism.

But how does he fail to perceive that his entire argument turns in a vicious circle? We cannot, he says, morally judge a practice solely in terms of the intuitive inner sense; it is the social consequences that it produces which must serve as a criterion for determining its moral validity. But in order that we may be able to perceive in those consequences—at least in those under consideration—the irrefutable signs of moral standards, it must be evident that we attach significance and moral validity to them. Since they are themselves the only possible criteria, by what criteria have we been able to make such attributions? Actually, since the metaphysicians and the theologians are alike being attacked, the author settles the issue in terms of his personal sentiments. He postulates as obvious that a good birthrate, a good marriage rate, a certain type of economic activity are morally good things, just as the ascetic person considers evident the moral superiority of sacrifice and of suffering. Neither the one nor the other gives his reasons, and Dumont's thesis is just as debatable as the opposing thesis. Without doubt it does happen—perhaps it is even the most frequent case—that the birth rate and the marriage rate vary like the death rate. But how many times as well do we not witness a multiple progression in the expansive growth of the economy at the same time as a considerable increase in the marriage rate, the birth rate, crime, divorces, illegitimate births, and cases of alcoholism! It is true that several of the facts do not appear to the author of very serious nature, but it is easy to find that he is quite well resigned to them.

It is curious that the minds most concerned with positivism have at times so much trouble considering social facts from a truly positivist point of view. Each type of society has its moral standards, just as each species of animal has its structure. The scientist, for whom social facts are natural, should then take as his starting point the premise that for each given social type (whether it concerns our own or not, is unimportant), these moral standards are not to be set up in their entirety simply because they exist. Yet if this morality is not everywhere what it ought to be, there as elsewhere the malady is the exception in time as in space. Consequently, there are never grounds to overturn from top to bottom something real in order to erect from scratch an entirely new edifice. And yet, Dumont admits as evident that the code of ethics by which civilized peoples have lived for centuries is nothing but a tissue of aberrations, and the Christianity, from which it is inspired, is itself probably merely an abyss of maleficent errors. Antireligious prejudice is no more scientific than religious prejudice. For the scientist, religion is a fact of life that is no loftier than the other facts, but is not some sort of unintelligible non-being, either.

Certainly, a rational code of ethics is possible, but only if it is based on more complex methods than what gratifies Dumont. (*Année sociologique*, 5, 1902, pp. 320–322; trans. J. French)

L. von Savigny. ''Das Naturrechtsproblem und die Methode seiner Lösung.'' *Jahrbuch für Gesetzgebung, Verwaltung und Volkswirtschaft*, 1901, p. 407.

R. Saleilles. "Ecole historique et droit naturel, d'après quelques ouvrages récents." *Revue trimestrielle de droit civil,* 1902, p. 80.

Through the recent books of Stammler, Gény, and Duguit a certain
tendency manifests itself to restore, in a new and above all very attentuated
form, the ancient conception of natural law. The article of L. von Savigny is inspired by the same idea. The historical school is reproached for its immobilism,
its impotence to innovate; no other recourse for this de facto sterility is seen
than a return to the notion of a justice which is immanent and unchangeable
in its essence, despite the contingency of the forms in which it is realized successively in history.

The interesting article of Saleilles aims to call attention to this tendency,
to characterize its principal manifestations, and to make a critique of it. He,
too, admits (and he demonstrates again) the impotence of the old historical
school. It is necessary for the legislator, necessary especially for the judge, to be
able to contribute actively to the evolution of law. It is thus necessary that he
not limit himself to the literal application of the legal code, but that instead
he have no fear of innovating. However (and on this point Saleilles separates
himself, fortunately, from the writers we mentioned above), his innovations
must not express simply the idea which he has personally of justice. So subjective a conception lacks authority and leaves too much room for the arbitrary. In
order to have the right to innovate he must be able to support himself by objective elements. Saleilles draws attention to three of these which should serve
to protect the judge against the exclusiveness of his individual sentiments.
They are legislative analogy (extension of existing rules by way of analogy); the
collective juridic conscience, in which the new law is in a process of formation;
and comparative law, in which it sometimes appears wholly formed.

But we do not see at all why this new law from which the judge draws his
inspiration is called "natural law" by the author. It is not more, or less,
natural than the laws of yesterday, which it replaces, or those of tomorrow, for
which it prepares the way. It corresponds to change produced in the state of
the societies where it elaborates itself, just as the law of the past corresponded
to a state which no longer exists. We see only disadvantages, and no advantages, for this term, the origin of so many confused discussions, to be put back
in usage, unless one understands it in so broad a sense as to render it useless.
(*Année sociologique,* 6, 1903, pp. 302–303; trans. K. Woody)

P. Bonfaute. "La progressiva diversificazione del diritto publico e
privato." *Rivista italiana di sociologia,* VI, no. 1, pp. 1–16.

Even though today the opposition between the public and the private law
is very marked, in Rome these two juridic forms were almost indistinct. As
proof of this the author gives the analogies that are presented by the organization of the family and that of the state. The family, like the state, has its
religion; the father is its priest; he has, at the same time, all the characteristics
of a magistrate. Now, following this established rule, the public law consists *in*

sacris, in magistratibus, in sacerdotibus.[9] The domestic patrimony is as closed to external influences as that of the state. The very ties that are formed between the individuals are contracted according to the forms that are found in the public order (the *sponsio*).[10] The dissociation of the two laws would only have been produced when Rome was united with other Latin peoples in a kind of federation and accorded them the private rights which the Roman citizens enjoyed, but not the public rights. The schism is accentuated during the invasions, the new societies having borrowed the political law from the peoples of Germany, the private law from Rome. The whole study presupposes that the distinction admitted by the jurists between the two sorts of law is well founded. But doesn't the very indistinctness that one notices even at the beginning prove the contrary? For if they were at that point different by nature, how would they have been confused? Even today, doesn't that whole section of the law called "private" which concerns the condition of persons have a public character? (*Année sociologique*, 6, 1903; pp. 304–305; trans. J. Sweeney)

Edouard Lambert. *La Fonction du droit civil comparé*. Vol. I, *Les Conceptions étroites et unilatérales*. Paris: Giard et Brière, 1903, xxiv + 927 pp.

Undertaking a great work on comparative civil law, Lambert proposed to first define its character and to determine its functions. Such is the object of the present book, which is only the first volume of the complete work, whose other parts will successively be published." [11]

Comparative civil law as it is understood by the author is not the comparative history of law. The latter is a pure science, which, by way of comparison, tries to determine the origin of juridic institutions. It is another name given to what we here call juridic sociology. Comparative law, on the contrary, is an art; its role is completely practical. It has for its object the confrontation of a certain number of juridical systems, more directly comparable by reason of their internal relations; it aims "to bring out the common basis of conceptions and of institutions which are latent there" and "in this way to gather together a treasure of maxims common to those legislative codes" (p. 916). In a word, it is concerned with doing work on the laws of different peoples analogous to that which was done by Beaumanoir [12] and so many others on the local customs of France. Instead of allowing each national code of law its actual particularity, its aim is to compare it to those with which it maintains points of affinity, in such a way as to lead them to mutually compare with each other. In this way one might obtain a new law which would rise above the particular systems and which might be considered as the collective patrimony of the international community, which would serve as material for instituting further comparisons.

As for the object of this new and more general system, it might be to assist in the development and necessary transformations of diverse national systems.

In effect, it can no longer be believed that the written and codified law is sufficient by itself; from all sides it is increasingly felt that there is a demand to give our codes that flexibility which customs provided in the past, permitting them to bend so remarkably in accordance with the diversity of circumstances and the ever-changing needs of societies. It is easily perceived that the data of comparative civil law, understood as we have just stated, will furnish useful indications for these necessary changes. Precisely because it is freer of local idiosyncrasies, the law that is established in this way by methodological comparisons cannot fail to show, on more than one point, the direction which the existing law must take.

But what are the principal agents of these changes? Lambert finds relevant the theory of Gény, [13] the usefulness of which he has amply discussed.

According to Gény (and Lambert), the law is incapable of being self-sufficient, for it is not able to foresee everything. Consequently it needs to be completed. But here is where our two authors part company. To begin with, for Gény the law has, insofar as it is not abrogated, an absolute authority. One should not try to modify it by the interpretations which one gives it; one should limit himself to applying it in the same spirit which inspired the lawmaker. It is only when the law is mute that the interpreter has the right to do positive work and to create law. Thus he can well add new dispositions to those which are legally in force; he is forbidden to alter these later. And as for the source of these legitimate additions, it is found essentially in free scientific research; it is the study of the social, economic, political, and moral organization of the country, of the average aspirations of the public spirit, of the natural balance between the diverse elements of the social life, which must furnish the directing principles from which the judge derives his inspiration. It is not that there is no other theoretically productive source of law, a source which has for a long time played an important role in juridical life: that is, custom. But today, that source is dried up. Custom, by its diffusion, by the unconscious manner through which it is elaborated, contrasts with the intelligent juridical organization of civilized peoples. Law is no longer the product of secret movements of opinion but of conscious deliberations.

It is these two propositions that Lambert does not accept. He demonstrates without difficulty that the way in which the law is applied ceaselessly modifies its meaning and that these endless variations are necessary to keep the law in harmony with the ever-changing conditions of social life. And what permits these uninterrupted changes [says Lambert] is that custom is presently far from playing the ineffective role which Gény attributes to it. It is still living and active, and if the power of its actual influence is unknown, this is because we are mistaken about what constitutes its true nature. [According to Gény] it is opposed to law as the unconscious to the conscious; custom is the anonymous and instinctive work of the crowd, fashioned in a secretive manner, while law is the product of definite organs and is elaborated in the full light of consciousness. Now, in reality [says Lambert] that opposition is artificial. Custom does not emanate from the same social organs as the law, but it emanates from organs which are no less defined. It is likewise a conscious work. It is the work, in fact, not of the unconscious multitude, but, essentially, of agents of the judicial life. The magistrates are its authors. Customary rules are born from sentences by which magistrates have resolved the cases that were submitted to them. Doubtless, it is not that they have not taken into consideration popular sentiment, but their role is never reduced to translating into norms the state of the public mind. They have created a truly original work; they have not simply discovered the law which existed in a confused manner in the collective consciousness; they have been creators; they have revealed to the people a law which the latter did not know.

Lambert verifies this interesting conception of custom by a long historical exposition showing in what way customary law was formed in England, among the Hebrews, among the Muslims, in Rome, and in the Germanic nations. The major part of the book (pp. 111–804) is devoted to that demonstration. We would not be able to reproduce it here. But one can see the conclusion at which he arrives. To say that custom is a product of judicial practice is to say that it is the fruit of jurisprudence. Now, jurisprudence still exists. It is thus false to say that the sources of customary law are dried up today. Today, just as yesterday, the tribunals are the creators of law; they are legislators in their own way. And it is to them above all that the *comparative civil law* is called to render important services; for they are in a much better position than the legislative assemblies to benefit from its information.

It is seen that this book basically treats two distinct questions; one is related to the notion of comparative civil law, the other to the notion of custom. Certainly they are not unrelated to each other, but nevertheless we believe that it would have been desirable to treat them separately, especially since the ties which unite them are rather loose. In fact, the nature of comparative civil law does not depend on the nature of custom only; the manner in which it is applied varies according to the way that one conceives customary law. In addition to the fact that it harms the unity of a book that is already too cluttered (and that renders the reader even more uneasy by the almost complete absence of chapters),* this excessively narrow interpenetration of two different problems inconveniently relegates to a secondary place what in fact constitutes the most interesting part of the work—the views of the author on custom and jurisprudence.

The book is, in fact, a useful reaction against the current conceptions that have shown how necessary it is that everything be unconscious in the formation of custom; the role of magistrates, of the lay or ecclesiastical jurisdiction in the formation of customary law has very frequently been lost from view. But on the other hand, it would not be less inaccurate to misconstrue the part played by the collectivity. Certainly this influence is difficult to analyze precisely

---

* From pages 103 to 913 there is only one chapter.

because it is unconscious, but that is no reason for denying it, and indeed the author, we believe, does not intend to contest its existence, although he tends to restrict it, perhaps excessively. Custom results from two factors whose role may indeed vary in importance according to the societies. But no methodical research has been done up to the present on the way these variations have come about. Besides, even if it is true that the agents of the judiciary life are the organs of rational reflection, it must be confessed that these are less central organs than the legislative assembly. These agents are indeed, if you will, centers of collective conscience—but secondary centers. They are not set up in a fashion to embrace the social life in its totality. They are not, as are the governmental centers, in direct or indirect relationships with all the points of the collective organism and consequently they only represent very imperfectly and very incompletely all that happens there. They are only aware of certain needs, of certain currents; and the extent of their legislative influence must be restricted because the extent of their information is restricted. That is the reason why it appears to us to remain true, to a certain extent, to the fact that in the most highly organized societies—that is to say, the most unified—the custom, even under the form of jurisprudence, can no longer be to the same extent as formerly a productive source of law.

As far as that which the author calls comparative civil law, it is better to await the following volumes of the work to appreciate the conception that he develops.[14] It is only then that it will be seen according to what method he intends to compare the juridical systems that he believes useful to discuss. It does not seem that he wishes simply to distinguish what they have in common—that is to say, to construct a sort of average model around which all the real systems oscillate. But still, how does he intend to approach it? This will only be clearly seen when he has finished his work. The idea at least merits retention. It is certain that our national laws are, in terms of mutual relationships, in the same situation as the customs of the different provinces were formerly, and a study is necessary in order to relieve them of their particularism. It remains to know what that study must be and how it must be conducted. (*Année sociologique*, 7, 1904, pp. 374-379; trans. J. Sweeney)

Lucien Lévy-Bruhl. *La Morale et la science des moeurs*.[15] Paris: F.
Alcan, 1903, 300 pp.

One will find in this work, analyzed and demonstrated with rare dialectic vigor, the very idea that is basic to everything we are doing here, namely that there is a positive science of moral acts, and that it is on this science that the moralists' practical speculations must rely.

In order to establish this proposal, the author begins by holding up to criticism the traditional conception of morality, by way of pointing out its confusion and incoherence. Usually the distinction in morality is made between two parts and two largely differentiated disciplines: on the one hand, theoretical morality, and on the other, practical morality. It is the former that is regarded as being the scientific part. Now, Lévy-Bruhl has no trouble establishing that it does not constitute a science to any degree. Indeed, its goal is not to express a reality based on fact, but to determine the general principles of *proposed actions*. It seeks what ends man *ought* to pursue, in what order these ends *ought* to be subordinated to each other. Now, the sciences, whatever they may be, have no other function than to know what is, not to prescribe and to legislate. One thought to escape the objection by calling theoretical morality a normative science, but the coupling of these two words, logically incompatible, serves merely to express, without lessening, the inherent contradiction in the conception. A science can arrive at conclusions that permit the establishment of norms; it is not normative in itself. The notion of a theoretical morality is therefore illegitimate; considerations properly scientific and theoretical are mingled with practical considerations; and finally, it is these last that are by far the preponderant ones.

This confusion of theory and practice—with its subordination of the first to the second—is not, moreover, limited to morality; it is to be found at the start of all the human sciences. Since they are the indispensable activating forces that stimulate reflection, the latter found itself directly oriented with an eye to practical ends. It is only very slowly that thought became independent and man learned to pursue purely speculative ends, to study matters with the sole purpose of knowing about them, without considering possible applications to be attained from the theoretical results. But it is especially in the study of moral acts that this progress was to be slow and difficult. For morality is stamped with a religious character that removes it from properly scientific thought, that is to say from free thought. The morality actually practiced by men has been masked in the course of time with a veneer of beliefs, of symbols that make of it a holy thing which it is not permitted to handle in accordance with the usual procedures of the positive sciences.

Well, then, if theoretical morality is not a science of moral facts, what is it? It is quite simply a way to coordinate as rationally as possible the ideas and the feelings which constitute the moral conscience of a definite period of time. Basically, the moralist legislates less than he thinks; he merely echoes the time; he simply reproduces the ethical practices of his contemporaries while putting them in order, thereby making them more readily presentable. That is why the moral speculation of the philosophers has far less often disturbed the public conscience than the discoveries of science. There are no "moral theories" that have ever created mental revolutions comparable to the one that resulted from Galileo's teaching, for example. The fact is that theoretical morality, very far from dictating laws geared to practice, merely reflects this last and translates it into a more abstract language. It is only another aspect of the moral reality. Far from its power to explain, it is, then, in part, a matter to be explained; it is the subject matter of science and not a science itself.

This coordination rests, moreover, on assumptions that are presented as evidence, whereas they are as a matter of fact untenable. In order to be able to construct a morality deductively, the moralists begin by admitting human nature as an abstract idea, always and everywhere with a selfsame identity, and sufficiently well known for one to prescribe for man the kind of behavior that is best suited to his purposes in the principal circumstances of life. Then too, since the moralists undertake to fashion a system, they suppose that normally the moral conscience possesses an inner unity, that the precepts that it decrees mutually support irreproachably logical relationships. Now, both hypotheses are belied by the facts. Human nature has varied in time; it was not yesterday what it is today. It varies in space; the Australian's nature is not ours. The notion of human nature cannot then be constructed by simple sleight of hand. As a preliminary, it would have been necessary to have constituted the different types that have appeared in the past or coexist in the present. Now, the thing that has caused this diversity is the diversity of the societies in which the human type functions; as a result, since man is a product of history, it is only by means of comparative history that he can be known. For that, all kinds of investigations are necessary that are scarcely in the preliminary stages; it is not enough, then, to borrow from current psychology the notion that it entertains of man in general. On the other hand, precisely because the moral conscience is a product of history, it is often made up of very heterogeneous elements; since all the social forms from the past have reverberations in the present.

It is, then, necessary to renounce this contradictory conception of a normative science and to be resolved to definitely disassociate science from practice. Instead of treating morality only in order to dictate duties to mankind, one must begin by studying morality—or rather the diverse moral standards that have been effectively in use in different societies—and one must do that for the sole purpose of becoming acquainted with them, of knowing of what they consist and on what factors they depend. Each social type has its moral discipline that is appropriate to it; it is made up of maxims, of customs, of beliefs that are as real as the other phenomena of nature. There are accordingly acts that are the concern of science, that can be described, and that one can endeavor to explain. The morality of a people, taken at a given moment in its history, is not to be created; it exists, it is a reality. The old conception according to which there is a natural and a sole morality—namely, the one that is grounded in the human constitution in general—is no longer tenable. All the moral institutions that are to be encountered in history are likewise natural, in this sense that they are grounded in the nature of the societies which practice them. Once given the manner in which a certain society is constituted, it is impossible for this last not to have a certain morality. It does not then receive its morality from the hands of a thinker of genius; it receives the former with its organization—that is to say, with its life. The science of moral reality considered in this way is *the science of customs* [16] that the author contrasts strongly with theoretical morality, which he started out by criticizing in his writing. Since, manifestly, the causes and the conditions on which each moral standard depends at each moment in time are social, the science of customs is a branch of sociology.

It is this science which alone can furnish a rational basis for practical applications. The more one becomes familiar with the laws of moral reality, the farther along one will be in modifying it rationally, in saying what it ought to be. But these methodological interventions will be limited, for morality is not to be constructed all in one piece. We do not have to make it a finished product; it exists and it functions and we have only to keep watch over its functioning. Doubtless, there will always be a number of cases in which science will not be in a position to furnish us the information needed to guide our action effectively, for science arrives only very slowly at results that are always partial. But there is nothing peculiar to morality in that fact. Does it not happen all the time that the clinician sets himself problems for which physiology provides no solution? What does he do in that case? He decides upon the course of action that in the present state of his knowledge appears most reasonable. Rational moral art will do likewise.

This circumspect reply will, no doubt, fail to satisfy those spirits devoted to the absolute, for whom tentative assurances, relative to science, cannot suffice. It seems to them that the art of morality is truly itself only if it decrees precepts on a note of infallibility. Alas! Every time one passes from general and theoretical propositions, in whatever way they have been established, to set practical plans, one runs, whatever one does, risks that no method can mechanically suppress; one can obtain only very uncertain approximations, and is it not the best thing to become resolutely aware of this? The abstract theories of the Kantians or the utilitarians have no advantage in this regard over the method that Lévy-Bruhl advocates; they do not show us any more surely the goals towards which one must aspire, the path that one must follow in the concrete circumstances of life. Between the categorical imperative, once admitted, and the question of knowing whether, today, we should or should not want socialism, divorce, etcetera, there is a huge gap in logic that the mind can cover only gropingly, by resorting to procedures, to operations, that are by no means foolproof. In this respect, all possible methods are equally imperfect, and as a result of this common and necessary imperfection, one is unable to take issue with any of them. (*Année sociologique,* 7, 1904, pp. 380–384; trans. J. French)

Guillaume L. Duprat. *Le Mensonge. Etude de psycho-sociologie
    pathologique et normale.* Paris: F. Alcan, 190 pp.

It is only just to recognize that Duprat has a sense for interesting ideas. We have already remarked on this right here, apropos of his work *Les Causes sociales de la folie.*[17] We can repeat it concerning his present work. It is only regrettable that the questions which he has the credit of raising are sometimes treated somewhat hastily and summarily.

The lie—that is to say, the intentional suggestion of error—is not only a phenomenon of individual psychology. It has collective forms. It even possesses veritable social institutions which are its organs, such as the press, the sects, and the life of the salon with the polite customs which it implies. On the other hand, there are social situations which foster the lie; thus the peculiar mentality of crowds is a very favorable soil for the blossoming of lies, soil which rascals are very well able to sow; the spirit of solidarity often produces the same result (the lie from esprit de corps). All currents of opinion—in political or religious or moral matters—when they reach a certain intensity, equally incline minds to alter the truth. The conflict of two civilizations of unequal worth very often obliges the representatives of the inferior culture to lie so that it can maintain itself; this is the case of the savage in the face of the European. It is also the social condition of the woman; the education which she receives explains in part the aptitude for lying for which she is often reproached.

All these topics lack neither appropriateness nor interest; but although each one demands special research and understanding, it is often treated in a few pages. Which of the facts will it be necessary to gather in order to criticize, compare, and study the lie of the savage as compared to that of the civilized man, or that of the woman? Moreover, the fundamental question is not touched upon. It would consist, we believe, in researching whence arises the tendency to the truth of which the lie is the negation. The diverse causes which the author attributes to the lie are only occasional or secondary causes. They can only produce their effect where the fundamental tendency is weak. It is above all the intrinsic power of resistance which makes the aptitude to lie more or less great. Why is it that in certain social milieux there is a respect for truth? Where this respect is strongly rooted, the collective evil sentiments remain weak. It is true that for the author ''all alterations of truth hurt the social order''—so much so that the tendency to speak the truth seems to him to be a normal fact and stands by itself. But the very unequal moral importance which has been attributed to truth according to societies and milieux proves that the problem is much more complex than the author has assumed. (*Année sociologique*, 7, 1904, pp. 512–513; trans. J. Sweeney)

Alessandro Bonucci. *La legge comune nel pensiero greco*. Perugia: Stab. Tip. Vincenzo Bartelli, 1903, 283 pp.

By νόμος κοινός (common laws) the Greeks of the classical period meant a concept which provides a synthesis of two ideas: that of a law of justice imposed on the world by nature or God; and that of a law recognized by everyone, which by universal consent gives it a superior moral value. The purpose of this work is to determine how these ideas were developed in relation to each other throughout Greek thought, and how their relationships were understood.

The originality of Greek thought since the very beginning of time becomes quite evident compared to the ideas of the Hindus, for example. The Hindus' conception involves the entire world as a whole, including man subjected to the law imposed on him by the supreme power. With Homer, on the contrary—if the metaphysical element of the idea of νόμος κοινός was still the only one present and in its initially developed stage, and if the *positive* element, that is to say, the notion of law, accepted in fact by all men, that induction could disentangle through comparison of certain legislative codes, had not been formulated yet—the universal law, the law of fate, and likewise the ethical rules were already conceived as laws. These laws were already given to man and clearly distinguished from cosmic laws. Philosophy in Greece at a later day sought to bring unity to those types of laws which Hindus did not distinguish. And according to Hesiod, the Greeks for the first time found the idea that man had an innate intelligence for justice, without doubt as a part of the divine origin, but which was completely different from the law imposed on man by the gods, and which allowed him, by a sort of inner revelation, to realize this law voluntarily, and not only to submit to this law. For Hindu thought, heteronomy was absolute. For the Greeks, on the other hand, man is autonomous; it is he himself who, through all sorts of errors, formulates the rules of supreme justice. Thus was constituted the doctrine which was considered as forming the natural or divine law, and becoming a universal and immutable part of the positive legislative codes.

With Socrates (see Xenophon's *Memorabilia, IV*), Plato (see his *Laws*), and especially with Aristotle, this positive doctrine disentangled itself, and it takes on its importance little by little as philosophical thought advanced. One generally finds among the literary men who were the translators, and especially among the orators, the popular sentiments of their co-citizens in the classical age. Bonucci has for a long time studied all these aspects; he shows what relationship the positive doctrine had with the idea of divine justice, with that of ἀγραⵁοι νόμοι (unwritten laws), and that of the common laws applied to all the Greeks, νόμοι κοινοὶ τῆς Ἑλλάδος (common laws of Greece), how it expressed itself in the belief of the sanctity of the ancient laws, and how the idea of universality or of a very large extension of the positive law was interpreted as a criterion of its moral value. It is not possible to follow it in all its details. Every writer has produced a monograph of his personal ideas full of interest for those who want to study it as historians. But the author himself has succeeded in disentangling only a small number of ideas concerning nature, to clarify the evolution of the notion which he set out to study.

Aristotle accomplished the task of elaborating on the concept of natural law by creating a harmonious fusion of two elements: metaphysical and positive. In the philosophical ideas developed subsequently, the synthetic conception remained less perfect; but some of the distinct ideas still continued to make progress. Stoics, the author notes, integrated the supreme law of justice with the rational principle, which moves the world. They developed a theory of knowledge which explains the universal aptitude of man to realize this supreme law by his own forces. Finally, Stoics reflected on cosmopolitanism and egalitarianism, which alone renders the notion of humanity possible and permits us to understand that a unique society submits to a unique law of its own. He [the author] asks whether a criterion of truth and a prominent idea favorable to the positive conception of natural law can be disengaged from a general consensus of opinions, however manifesting a general tendency of syncretism. In addition to a classical theory of a very comprehensive nature, Philo [Philo Judaeus, C·20B·C–50A·D] identified the Mosaic law with the common law of the world, which everybody in the world observes—without knowing it, however. Finally, the author remarks that the Catholic fathers retained the pagan idea of νόμος χοινός, which they considered, especially from a subjective point of view, as inscribed in the heart of man. Instead of criticizing the existence of the observed universal laws, the Catholic fathers were attached to the idea that every man has the intuition of Justice,

The subject that the author treats certainly has a lively interest for us. The study of various customs of which the *conscience collective* is a subjective representation of justice—and, in a more general way, of obligation—belongs to the domain of sociology. Unfortunately, our author treats the subject very exclusively from the point of view of a historian of philosophy. One especially sees it in a method by which he generalizes the results thus obtained and explains the development of the conception that he studies. The author argues that three forces have essentially determined it. One, which acts on all the people, from the very beginning of their civilization, is the tendency to know the authority of facts, and to assign the greatest value to a large number of facts thus collected and admitted. The other two, which are typical of Greek genius, characterize: on the one hand, a tendency to arrive at universality and a state of permanence from chaotic diversity and inconstancy; on the other hand, a tendency to glorify all that is human, to believe that man has the faculty to realize the ideals of truth, beauty, and justice. We would have liked to find in this book the most positive explanations, which would have created a nexus between the formation of a theory of natural law with the determined social conditions. Such an explanation would have rendered it possible to form a comparison of the elaboration of the natural law in Greece and in other societies, for example in Rome, and in modern Europe as well. What we find in this methodical arrangement of ideas by Bonucci amounts to very little: a brief and inadequate comparison between the Greek philosophical doctrine and the system of ideas in the works of Roman jurisprudents; a few remarks on the state of legislative anarchy in Athens, which must have constrained the Greek mind to penetrate beyond the formal legal terminology to a rational foundation for essential rules of justice and also to attribute a sacred and immutable character to very ancient laws that were never abrogated; some information about the favorable conditions for the growth of the doctrine that constituted the organization of Greece, made up of city states each having its own body of laws but all being aware of belonging to a higher social order. Lastly mention is made of certain facts that played a similar role in nature. For example, the author might have pointed out: the growing nature of relationships between Greeks and foreigners from the beginning of the fifth century; the institution of a special magistrature for the protection of foreigners and the regulation of business which concerned them; consequently, the study of foreign laws and the influence which they exerted on the law of the city in Greece; and also the formation of an international law among the Greek cities related to each other by virtue of political and religious associations. (*Année sociologique*, 8, 1905, pp. 378–381; trans. Y. Nandan)

Maurice Pellisson. "La Sécularisation de la morale au XVIIIe siècle."
   La Révolution française, Nov. 1903, pp. 385–408.

The author proposes to examine how our moral ideas became little by little free of all religious influence. It was the Renaissance which might have opened the way. But soon afterward, from the seventeenth century on, an effort must have been made for humanity to follow religious ideas. All the preachers of the time presented morals as inseparable from religious faith. The modern preachers do not hold a different view. It is therefore admitted that the proof that can be cited in this regard is less demonstrative. The author himself recognizes that the rationalist and secular conception of morals happens to be that of Descartes as well. That conception could be equally attributed to La Rochefoucauld [18] and Spinoza. It is therefore too simple an exaggeration to speak of a pure and simple reaction, especially since a certain idea of God is not totally absent from the moral ideas of Rabelais. The evolution of the idea is more complex than what the author appears to believe. If the Renaissance upset religious traditionalism, it did not replace it by any other organized system. The seventeenth century began to create this system with Cartesianism; but science, such as Descartes conceived it, was applied only to the physical universe. The role of the eighteenth century was to extend the work of rationalism that Descartes had undertaken to the moral world. There is, then, the explanation as to why in this era the moral ideas became secular.

It is surprising to note that the author imputes the idea of retrogression to Rousseau (I do not know what he means by this). No doubt there was, during the Revolution, an upsurge of religious aspirations. But they were born of the Revolution itself; they were not taken from the theories of the vicar of Savoy. [19] The effervescence, the collective enthusiasm, which characterizes the creative era must have, by reason of its intensity, taken essentially a religious character. It was, then, not a reaction, but a natural consequence of a given social state, of which Rousseau was innocent. (*Année sociologique*, 8, 1905, pp. 381–382; trans. Y. Nandan)

Harald Höffding. "On the Relation Between Sociology and Ethics."
   American Journal of Sociology, g. 1905, pp. 672–685.

The author feels very keenly about the existence of the social in the ethical ideal. He recognizes that ethics is closely related to the nature of societies and varies like the latter. Yet he believes that a discipline entirely distinct from sociology ought to be created from it. The sociologist, he says, records and explains the ethical reality of the past; he shows what was the historical nature of the different ideals men have followed, and how they are linked together; but in order to know what ideal is worth choosing at a given moment and what means make possible its realization, a different science would be necessary. It would be ethics.

But how to proceed to these value judgments? By applying the comparative method. Biology, by comparing living beings, shows that some types are superior to others. Sociology can proceed in like manner; it can establish a hierarchy of social types. A society is of a higher type insofar as it succeeds more completely in realizing two seemingly contradictory goals: full development of the individual and the most perfect possible unity of social life. In a word, the perfect society is the one in which unity and multiplicity are best reconciled. Accordingly, one would have a criterion for choosing between different possible ideals.

But it is not at all clear what justifies the choice of this criterion. Science, as such, does not establish for the beings it studies and classifies any superiority or hierarchy; at the very least, when it makes use of these terms, it does not give them any significance which implies an appraisal of the worth of things. For its purpose, all being have worth. Where, then does the unequal worth that the author attributes to them come from? What right has one to say that in a society where unity is perfectly achieved multiplicity is the ideal? The anarchist will prefer pure diversity; the authoritarian, absolute unity. Rousseau used to prefer small societies in which a strong moral homogeneity prevented individual dissentions; by what reasoning convince him that he was mistaken? To be sure, we do believe that sociology alone, or rather the branch of sociology that deals with ethical factors, can help us resolve these practical problems; but it is not by providing us with so generalized a criterion, a formula, for the universal moral ideal. Each ethical institution needs to be studied separately, in its genesis and in its functioning, in its relations with the surroundings; and it is in terms of its past that we can conjecture its future.

The same wavering is encountered in the author's thought when he indicates the individual's and society's role in ethics. Even while making ethics an eminently social matter, he nevertheless makes of it a matter of inner conscience. And doubtless, it is certain that ethical reality has two aspects, but it is not very clear what, according to Höffding, causes their unity. (*Année sociologique*, 9, 1906, pp. 323–324; trans. J. French)

Albert Bayet. *La Morale scientifique. Essai sur les applications morales des sciences sociologiques.* Paris: F. Alcan, 1905, 180 pp.

Bayet [20] clearly wishes to present his book as a practical application of the principles by which we are inspired here. He has read us, not only with attention, but with a sympathy which he expresses in such terms that we can only be grateful to him. Truth, nevertheless, obliges us to declare that on many essential points we cannot accept the interpretation that he seems to give to our thought and the consequences that he believes he is able to deduce from that interpretation.

Along with us and with Lévy-Bruhl, Bayet admits the necessity of clearly separating speculation from moral phenomena, science, and the practical applications [of moral values] that may be attributed to the former. He likewise thinks that "the role of science in the moral domain consists of studying the moral reality—that is to say, the moral facts and their laws. Sentiments, ideas, customs, mores, must be considered as things and studied as such" (pp. 4–5). Once that principle is accepted, it seems that if one wishes to remain consistent with oneself, it is necessary to consider the beliefs or moral practices which one observes at all times in all kinds of societies as things, as established and normal realities. For if universality is not considered a sign of normality, where will one find that sign? If a fact which is discovered everywhere is not an objective fact, then what is it that deserves to be called by that name? However, the author does not seem to have perceived that this was an immediate corollary of his fundamental postulate.

Morals present themselves everywhere to the observer as a code of obligations. What should one conclude from this except that morals are essentially a code of that kind, that the idea of duty expresses its fundamental characteristic? And the whole role of the science of morals must be to explain that notion by making it clear how that notion is based on reality. Rather than proceeding in this manner, our author, on the contrary, admits that this idea of duty is a kind of fantasy with no objective basis. He does not see in it any object of scientific research. He has occupied himself with the art alone; he does not seem to develop the idea of duty, nor does he attempt to make it more precise, nor to reform it, but to dissipate it as though it were a kind of nightmare which for centuries has obsessed and anguished humanity. By doing so, he must equally dissipate all the ideas that are connected with the one of duty, such as the idea of responsibility, such as the principle according to which it is the intention alone which has true moral value. The only reason that might be given to justify this attitude is that the arts which correspond to the physical sciences (the art of the engineer, of the physician, and so on) produce "machines and, in abundance, engines and products—but neither the idea that there is a duty to use these machines and these products nor that there is merit in employing them or disdaining them" (pp. 35–36).

It is certain that the art of the engineer or the farmer treats of nothing which resembles duties; but it is also a fact that the phenomena of mechanics or of organic chemistry, with which the corresponding sciences deal, contain nothing which resemble a moral obligation. It results from this that the physical facts exclude any notion of duty; why must it be likewise the case with moral facts? What is it that authorizes us to construct a portion of reality on the exact model of the other, without concerning ourselves with the differences which are always possible and even a priori probable between the different orders? Suppose that the phenomena of moral life consisted essentially of duties, and the moral art, just like the science of morals, would have to treat duties—the one in order to explain them, and the other in order to concern itself with what they ought to be. Consequently, it seems to us that the author has no right to proclaim the denial of an idea of such universality. And, in truth, what is it that precludes him from considering the obligations which are imposed on us as facts just as real and definite as the facts of material nature? It is a fact that we feel ourselves obliged, and obliged in such-and-such ways. There is nothing more contrary to the scientific mind than to deny a fact.

In order to obviate the misunderstandings which, to our great surprise, were produced, it seemed necessary for us to explain ourselves clearly on this point. We add that the rest of this work shows the author's correct understanding of that which is concrete and complex in moral reality. He clearly shows the insufficiency of the very general formulas in which the moralists take such smug satisfaction. (*Année sociologique*, 9, 1906, pp. 324-326; trans. J. Sweeney)

Alfred Fouillée. *Les Eléments sociologiques de la morale.* Paris: F. Alcan, 1905, xii + 379 pp.

Gustave Belot. "En Quête d'une morale positive." *Revue de métaphysique et de morale,* Jan. 1905, pp. 39-74; July, pp. 564-588; Sept., pp. 727-763; March 1906, pp. 165-195.

Adolphe Landry. *Principles de morale rationnelle.* Paris: F. Alcan, 1906, x + 278 pp.

Ethics is the principal issue of the day. [21] We see an ever-increasing number of the widest variety of essays about what is supposedly speculation on ethical matters. To this problem, each of the authors whose names have just been cited contributes his personal solution: Each one is intent upon *founding* ethics in his fashion. We do not believe there is any point in setting forth herewith and discussing in detail these different conceptions; for, with what they have to contribute, they are of greater interest to the philosopher than to the sociologist. [22] These three writers are, in fact, philosophers [23] and it is even their objective to argue with sociology over the study of moral facts *(faits moraux)*. For this reason, they are inclined to discuss the method we are following here and the ideas from which we find inspiration. Their criticisms (which hold, moreover, an important place in their works) cannot therefore leave us indifferent; we are going to try to reproduce them as impartially as possible and to reply to them.

To put first things first, it is not without interest to note the utter formality of their character. All these authors deal with the method that we are practicing, but in a completely abstract manner, as if it were still only a project, as if it had never been applied. Nonetheless, if the science of moral facts, such as we conceive it, is still in its rudimentary stage, it does not mean that it is not yet born; and there is some exaggeration and injustice done to us by speaking of its mere possibility—which will perhaps be realized, however, in an indeterminate future. Already our *Division of Labor* has been presented as being "first and foremost an effort to deal with the facts of moral life in accordance with the method of the positive sciences" (preface to the first edition). Our book *Suicide*, all the *Mémoires* we have published here, all the analyses and discussions apropos of books concerning juridic and moral sociology that we publish each year in *L'Année*, come from the same premises. It would, therefore, have been possible to criticize our method by pointing out how in practice it gave rise to errors; for it is in the application that a method must be judged. But, for reasons we do not want to look into, the controversy remains purely dialectical and abstract. We do not even believe that our contradictors have felt even once the need to show how their objections apply or are applicable to a definite issue. They never get away from generalities.

1. Landry is the only one whose discussion is not purely methodological, even though, it is true, it is very general and philosophical. He attributes to us "a morality" [24] (we confess to being a bit mystified as to what he means by that) and he discusses its positive content (pp. 234 ff.), without, however, those criticisms relative to the underlying ideas themselves being tied in with the criticisms of method that another part of his book (pp. 31 ff.) contains. This doctrinal discussion is limited to a single unique point. Anxious to readjust to his thesis the conceptions that appear to deviate from it most widely, Landry undertakes to demonstrate that our whole doctrine is derived from utilitarian premises (p. 238), that all our "formulas have validity only insofar as they can be deduced from the premise of general utility" (p. 241). As proof of this he submits that by our own admission the generality of the most widespread organizational forms would be unaccountable if, on the whole, they were not the most advantageous.

It is certainly true, indeed, that our conception is found to give a certain place to the eudaemonic and utilitarian principles; for we believe that moral institutions, precisely because they are social institutions, have a useful purpose and have a role to play in social life as a whole. Even though the author has exaggerated in making us appear utilitarian, the fact is that it is still easier to discover the contrary principle in our writings. It can even be said that this last comes first with us. In fact we have stopped repeating that for us the essential characteristic of the moral rules was obligation in the Kantian sense of the word: in other words that singular propriety by virtue of which a rule of conduct appears to us as an obligation to be observed simply because it is the rule. And these principles, apparently conflicting, are not reconciled by an external eclecticism; their reconciliation is effortless, for all they do is express different aspects of ethical reality. On the contrary, what defines a utilitarian is that he views only one of these aspects, that he intends to reduce everything to only one of his principles and even to deduce everything from it. Now, that is a unilateral and archaic conception, which we think is useless to dwell upon today, for it is contradicted by everything that history and comparative ethnography tell us about the moral life of humanity.

Let us, then, approach the issues of pure methodology.

2. It is with a sharp feeling of surprise that we have read the pages that

Fouillée has devoted to us,* so often have we found in them grave mistakes in the interpretation of our thought. Fouillée appears to entertain a very peculiar and, in any case, very inaccurate idea of the method we practice and of the goal we pursue. We are accused of denying human thought all value judgments and all appreciation of the subject of morals; it seems to the author that we are inclined to reduce speculation on these issues to pure "descriptions" (p. 234). On what basis does the author accuse us? On this point Lévy-Bruhl has indicated that since we are inspired by the moral rules, we are hindered in founding an objective science of moral facts *(La Morale et la science des moeurs,* pp. 187–188).

We did not think, we admit, that such an obvious truth could be disputed. Is it not clear, indeed, that the study not only of moral facts but of social facts in general is made much more difficult solely because, as we already indicated thirteen years ago, "sentiment often complicates it"?† In order that we be in the proper position not only to understand moral practices scientifically but to assess them objectively, we had to manage to consider them with an entirely free mind; now, this freedom is naturally more difficult when coping with ideas or ways of acting that we hold in veneration. The very fact of dealing with them scientifically produces an effect of desecration. Does it follow from this contention that we ought to renounce judging them? Not at all. But these ready-made judgments, due to education and habit—in a word, these thoughtless prejudices—make more difficult the thoughtful, enlightened, methodical judgments that the science of moral facts such as we understand it is intended to make possible. We even wonder, in fact, how one could have thought that we would decline to assess the morals of our contemporaries at a time when the first work of some importance that we published was precisely and avowedly intended to establish an appreciation of this genre. ‡

* Notably the preface, pp. viii ff., chapter 2, pp. 159–175, and especially chapter 5, pp. 232–286. This last chapter, it is true, is not without embarrassment in our case. Its essential substance had appeared in the *Revue des deux mondes,* October 1, 1905. Fouillée made a direct attack therein on us at the same time as on Lévy-Bruhl, Bayet, and Simmel. In the book the names of Bayet and Simmel have disappeared, which is no surprise to us, for it was a mistake to confuse their theories with ours. But, in addition, there is no longer hardly any concern with us, and Lévy-Bruhl alone is his target. In spite of this change in editing, we do believe we are also implicitly attacked. First of all, the ideas attacked are indeed those that have been inspiring us for a long time. The chapter is, in fact, directed against the "objective sociologists" who choose to study normal facts sociologically. Then, too, the allusions to our works remain numerous. We do not think, therefore, to be mistaken about the author's intentions by assuming his objections are aimed at us.

† *Règles de la méthode sociologique,* p. 41.

‡ Indeed, in our *Division of Labor,* we assess the old ideal of the moral humanist and the moral ideal of the gentleman; we show how he can be regarded today as about to be outdated, how a new ideal is taking shape and is growing as a consequence of the growing specialization of social functions.

Besides, in what way would the method that we follow exclude us from the right of appraisal? To explain a rule of conduct is to show what causes it, what its function is, from what ideas and sentiments it is derived, and what needs it meets. Once these needs are known, is it not legitimate to wonder whether they are normal or not, well founded or not? Once these ideas and sentiments are determined, what prevents us from seeking to ascertain whether they express the nature of things? (We are setting aside, for the moment, the question of knowing what nature of things is involved.) And if the result of the investigation is that they are no longer anything but relics which no longer comply with any existing reality, or are a byproduct of transient and morbid disorders, is one not within one's rights to conclude that the corresponding rule of conduct either is no longer valid or ought to be corrected, completed, and replaced, and to seek, from the analogous evidence, inductions derived from historical evolution? In a word, from all the information that science puts at our disposal, what ought these corrections or necessary substitutions consist of? To be sure, the explanation of an ethical maxim does not justify it ipso facto, but the explanation points the way toward the justification, far from dispensing with or making it impossible. The objection is raised that if, as we claim, ethics [*morale*] has a reality of its own, independent of the theories that justify it, every effort to make a rational criticism it becomes useless. It seems it would be an entirely superfluous luxury. But if, in fact, it is true as verified by all the evidence that ethics has not waited for the philosophers' theories in order to become established and functional, who then would dream of disputing that deliberation, by joining forces with this automatic and unconscious functioning, is well calculated to modify it? Consciousness and scientific thought, which is simply the highest form of consciousness, do not join forces with reality as ineffective epiphenomena; rather they enable us to make changes simply because they make things clear. If, then, we attack the methods usually followed by the philosophers when they speculate on morals, it is not because they have attempted to give it some thought and because we judge these attempts of no practical use; on the contrary, it is because the best they can do is to pay lip service to an open-minded approach, while not taking the necessary precautions to cut loose from all hidebound views when faced with sentiment and prejudice.

Indeed, in order to be able to assess in a thoughtful way the worth of a rule of conduct, once again it is necessary to possess, at the outset, some considered notion of what moral life is, and the same applies especially to the rule or the group of rules of conduct under consideration, their function, their justification, etcetera. This guideline is much more indispensable, still, if (as Fouillée seems to admit along with so many others) one sees in morals a sort of legislation that each individual establishes for himself in the deepest recesses of his conscience. In order to be able to construct a moral system in this way, again one must know what this expression means, what kind of thing it is that one is called upon to construct, what it consists of. It serves no purpose to say that morality is an art of good behavior, for there are as many kinds of good behavior as there are patterns of conduct. There is a hygienic well-being, economic well-being, and scientific good, etcetera. It is a matter of knowing what good morals and the art of good moral conduct are. How can one pin down this indispensable definition if not by observing actual morality wherever it is accessible to observation, as much in the present as in the past? In other words, by trying to discover its characteristics, elements, and conditions, we end up by creating a science of morals; and it is from this science, and it alone, that must emerge fundamental notions that presuppose practical speculations about morals. Or else will it be assumed that these notions all take shape in our minds? But, without insisting on the excessive oversimplication of the assumption, it does not even serve to resolve the difficulty; for, among the different notions that we discover impressions on our minds, whether innately or otherwise, how and by what sign can we distinguish those which ought to be useful as a basis for morals? In order to recognize them and not to confuse them with others, we need a criterion. What will this criterion be? The problem is simply brushed aside.

This truism would not even be disputed if, after the fashion of the common people, the moralists readily admitted, implicity or expressly, that to know what morality is, to understand the "why" of the different duties, ought not to require so much unnecessary fuss. The real service rendered by Fouillée's criticism is to have openly admitted this surprising assumption. According to him, there is no need "for long studies of history, comparative jurisprudence, comparative religion" in order to know "why we should not kill, steal, break the law, etcetera," moral principles from which are derived the notions of "brotherly love, regard for children and for their sense of decency, faithfulness in keeping a promise" (p. 247). These are the obvious verities that immediately stand revealed to the intuition of conscience; a little individual thought suffices to bring them to mind. "Why, one exclaims, all our duties will remain unexplainable until the moment when the folklorists, philologists, archeologists, mythologists, and all the varieties of *-gists,* backed by vast erudition, have explained to us those astonishing social pressures the motivation for which is sought in vain by the individual conscience." It is with arguments of this caliber that the old psychology has, for such a long time, been raising objections to the facts that demonstrated the extreme complexity of the conscious mind and even of each of its manifestations, and as a result, the need for new methods to analyze this complex and unknown reality in order to break it down into its components and determine their relationships. But there is an alternative to contemplating the reality of moral facts at a somewhat nebulous distance. Whoever has made some effort to enter into direct contact with it, in order to find throughout history how the special manifestations that are its basis have taken shape, knows how very far they are from being lucidly clear-headed. The ideas, the sentiments, that the rules of conduct express and that appear so simple to the masses—as the "me" appears a simple matter for introspection—are in reality the resultants at times of very numerous components that accumulate and laboriously combine with one another. That is what history and ethnography methodically investigated teach us; when one scorns their teachings, one speaks of moral facts just the way someone who is completely ignorant of the discoveries of physics and chemistry might speak of physico-chemical phenomena. Does one speak of contractual agreement as self-explanatory? But, in reality, one of the most baffling problems is to know how men have managed to conceive that mere words, emanating from their own persons, could make their wishes binding. One speaks of right to property as if it were a matter of course. But the idea that some matters can be inviolable for all men except one is, when one thinks it over, far from appearing so natural—not to speak of various terms and conditions that determine at each moment in time the right to property, without which this right is only an abstraction. If Fouillée is satisfied with one or another of the explanations that are usually given for it, to tell the truth he is not hard to please.

What contributes to the defense of this oversimplified attitude is the existence of certain very general sentiments that are considered as congenital to man's nature and that, at first glance, seem sufficient to account for fundamental duties. For example, in order to explain domestic or marital behavior, one invokes filial piety, brotherly love, sexual jealousy—all feelings that are considered inherent to the human heart. One does not see that tendencies of such a general nature can explain only very general duties themselves. Now, morality, such as men really practice it at each moment of time, consists not of those schematic and abstract duties which are discussed in philosophy courses (like that of honoring our parents, or of raising our children well or of respecting the marriage vows), but of specific, particular obligations that bear the imprint of the age where they are respected and the social type who respects them. We are not simply compelled to respect our parents, but this respect ought to evince particular characteristics, to assume definite shapes that vary according to the times and the societies. One of the ideas which dominates and summarizes in part our domestic morals is the notion of paternal authority; now, paternal authority was not in Rome what it was in the Middle Ages, nor in the Middle Ages what it is today. How could instincts, ostensibly eternal, account for such a variety of functions? There are even a number of peoples among whom the children have certain quite natural sentiments for their parents although there exists no trace of so-called paternal authority. A duty that appears not to have been ignored by any small tribe is the one which forbids a man to kill one of his companions, a member of his group. But how differently has this duty been understood depending on the society! Very often the crime committed by one member of a clan upon another member of the same clan appears to be merely venial, whereas for us it is the most heinous of crimes. The fact is that the way the murderer's immorality is judged depends on a multitude of causes, notably on the idea that we have about the value of life; and this idea itself is a product of a host of other representations that are not easy to analyze. That is why the chief role of the science of customs is to discover problems at the point where the masses see obvious facts.

It may be noticed that in order to defend our point of view, we have abstained from raising the question of knowing whether the moral facts depend, above all, on social causes. The fact is that such is not essential to the debate. What is first and foremost the necessary action to take is to dissipate the prejudice according to which morality would appear to be a system of truisms; it is essential to convey the extreme complexity of the ideas and feelings of which morality is the result. At present, there is no doubt that this complexity is much more fully sensed and understood when it is recognized that moral practices are social institutions, placed under the domination of social factors; for it is made clear in that case how the manifestations on which they are based are hard to analyze, how the causes on which they depend are so difficult to come by. The fact is that they express a nature and needs of a sort other than our nature and our needs as individuals. Again, there is a good reason to have reservations about the form in which Fouillée presents this idea for the purpose of rendering judgment on it. We do not maintain "that there exists absolutely nothing moral or immoral" that does not have social origins. Such a categorical and a priori affirmation would be completely unscientific. We limit ourselves to positing a certain hypothesis which history demonstrates by and large—namely, that morality, at each moment in time, depends on the social circumstances, and we do so in a normal and legitimate fashion; relying on an experiment that is already quite longstanding, we contend that there is in that respect a survey which has not yet been tried out logically and methodically, but which promises fruitful results. But it does not follow a priori that all moral life is necessarily, entirely expressible in sociological terms. Everything points to the fact that it has individual and subjective aspects, which sociology, as a result, is not sufficiently advanced to take into account; we would not think of disavowing that fact. * We only want to assert that this individual and inner side is neither the whole nor even the essential element of ethics [*morale*] as such for the reason that moral facts present themselves to us in history as essentially social facts, varying with and corresponding to societies. † There are

---

* We have specifically acknowledged this in a communication to the French Philosophical Society (see *Bulletin*, 6th year, pp. 117 ff). [See also note 25.]

† Fouillée disputes us on the ground that logic, since it also grows within [the parameters of] society, must be regarded as a social phenomenon as well. We reply: (1) that morality does not simply grow within the society, but is a direct *function* of society; (2) that in fact logic, likewise, is an outgrowth of social circumstance, is essentially a social matter. We have shown regarding primitive classifications how the first systems of classifications express society. And it is a point of view that we hope to probe more deeply later on. Just like moral functions, logical functions vary according to what the societies are. The logic of the Algonquins or of the Australians not only is not, but cannot nor ought not to be ours, for the sole reason that present-day societies are very different from those primitive societies. Collective understanding varies like the other mental functions of the society.

not many of us who present the social characteristic to the highest degree, even though, of all beliefs, there is no case where conformity is stricter than in moral beliefs. To begin with, we must consider the social bias if we would successfully grasp the true nature of moral beliefs; and only by starting out with the impersonal and objective forms that they assume in the collective state will we be successfully able to understand how they become individualized and diversified in particular consciences. In a word, we do not support the thesis that morality among the living has no aspect that is individual, but the social aspect is the principal part, and it is with the social side that we must come to grips first and foremost if we would understand what is behind the other. It is not a question of denying one of the two points of view at the expense of the other, but of reversing the order of preponderance between them that is accepted through habit.

3. Belot's thesis is not essentially different from Fouillée's, at least in what concerns us. While acknowledging that sociology can render distinct services to moral speculation and while having a feeling for the social as inherent in the moral, he does not appear to us to practice a method perceptibly different from that which is followed by the moralists, especially those of the utilitarian school.* But his arguments are in some respects different. He does not misconstrue the interest that can claim on its own terms the science of customs such as we are trying to cultivate it; but to the extent that he thinks it possible, he sees in it only purely erudite research, incapable of affecting the practice of moral art; the passage [from the science of customs to moral art is impossible. One cannot pass from the science of customs to moral art] for the two [following] principal reasons.

To begin with, the science of customs is of no practical use because it is essentially historical. It is preoccupied above all with investigating the more or less remote origins of our contemporary ideas of conduct; now, "within an order of social technique, the origin of beliefs and of constitutions is rather unimportant to the use we shall put them to" (p. 578). The criminologist does not have to be concerned with knowing on what grounds the penalty exists; what is important for him to know is the functions it can fulfill and whether it fulfills them in actual fact. For only this knowledge can be useful to him in resolving the only practical question that he has to ask: how to use the penal sanction in such a way as to suppress, intimidate, correct, the guilty person. "That our law, our morality, our ideas about property, the family, etcetera, stem from religious ideas—all this can be interesting to know better by understanding it; but what matters to us, practically speaking, is not where these ideas have come from but where they are leading, if they produce the results we expect of them, and if the reasons that entitle us to maintain them are substantiated by the results or are illusory pretexts, unconsciously suggested

* See, in regard to the author's positive conceptions, the article "Esquisse d'une morale positive," *Revue philosophique,* April 1906.

by the need to maintain them'' (p. 579). In relation to this last point, it is true (but in relation to this point alone) that the genetic study of moral facts can have practical consequences; these retrospective investigations can, in fact, result in demonstrating that a certain behavioral practice is connected with a belief no longer in existence today, and as a result, is completely without foundation. Such investigations can therefore be of use in dissipating certain illusions and by extension discrediting the institutions that are jointly responsible for them; but the services that they can render in this capacity are all negative. There is nothing there that can inform us about positive goals that one must pursue. As for morality, the knowledge of historical origins is more like the wrecker's sledgehammer. So much the better perhaps. . . . But it's no use imagining that the foregoing gives us the wherewithal to rebuild'' (p. 582).

Thus, of all the investigations we pursue here, all those that involve the past would serve no positive moral purpose. To use the author's very own words, the only sociological knowledge that would be of practical interest, would permit laying the foundation for a moral methodology, would be ''the kind involving the *present* social system in the midst of which action arises'' (p. 739). There, then, is science reduced to its bare essentials. But that is not everything, and this analytical roster of the present state of affairs, though not without interest, cannot suffice to lay the foundation for a rational moral art.

This art would be possible, and possible through this method, if the present social organization could be regarded as fixed, accomplished, immovable—always identical with itself. In that case, indeed, it could be expressed in a system of laws equally well defined, invariable, and susceptible, in their turn, to be translated into a body of rules of action that would become binding essentially in all respects, as the only appropriate rules to every rational purpose since they alone would be related to a given situation. It is because physical nature has this immutability that physico-chemical sciences provide a basis for rational techniques whose precepts cannot be violated without absurdity. But to begin with, if social nature had this same degree of invariability, one may wonder what practical use there would be in making it a branch of knowledge. ''If society is only a phenomenon, it is reduced to being what it is; to comprehend is its only need'' (p. 746). If the knowledge that the social sciences give us cannot change it, what is the use in seeking to know about it? But in addition, this static condition is not and can never be attributed to reality. Indeed, it is possible only insofar as society should live a purely oblivious and automatic life; for then it lacks all the means of being anything but what it is. Now, this situation is nowhere fully and wholly realized, not even in the most primitive societies. In any case, we get that much farther away from it as the role of consciousness and thoughtfulness continues to increase in collective behavior—all the more, as the science of societies is more advanced and more apt; as a result, it is able to explain social action. For science is simply the preeminent matrix of the reflective consciousness. Indeed, the awareness that society gains of itself helps to modify its nature. Simply.

because it acquires self-knowledge, it is no longer what it was. For consciousness is not merely an ineffective epiphenomenon; it affects the realities that it clarifies. When one knows one is mad, one is no longer mad to the same degree, nor in the same way. If, in 1870, we had been aware of our military weakness, we would not have been the people that we were. In addition, this knowledge that we acquire of social reality is protracted most naturally by action; now, that action, still more than that knowledge, brings profound changes to the very reality on which it impinges. By acting on society we transform it, "we modify the limits of the possible and of the impossible" (p. 750). Even if we limit our efforts to keeping the status quo, we modify it, for, by digging in, we make impossible or less readily attainable other positions that are perhaps superior. Whatever we do, we do not leave matters such as they were, and that holds true even if our action should be essentially conservative. But if this is how it is, even exhaustive analysis of the present state of affairs cannot help in determining what our conduct ought to be, since such analysis necessarily results in substituting a new state of affairs different from the previous one, whose value, consequently, cannot be reckoned in connection with this last. We are obliged therefore to find some other point of reference before acting, since the former vanishes due to the very fact that we take action. From the knowledge, though adequate, of the circumstances of the action, we cannot infer what this action ought to be, since it reacts on its own circumstances and modifies them. In order to know what must be done, we must therefore proceed in a different fashion; we must seek what goal is to be preferred to the others, and do so for reasons which cannot be directly derived from studying either the present or the past. That is the moral speculation, eluding the control of reality, and consequently the door is once more left open to the usual method of the moralists. In order to realize the goals one prefers, it will be necessary, doubtless, to know the contemporary social reality, which must indeed be reckoned with, and to that extent sociology serves morality a useful purpose. But there is no social physics that can help us establish what goals deserve preference.

Such is the criticism. Let us see what its import is.

The first argument is based on a truism which it was useless to demonstrate at such length; it is indeed clear that the only surroundings that we have some practical interest in knowing are those in which we are destined to act. The question is whether there is a way of becoming familiar with the present by any means other than by the clarification which history brings. There lies the entire problem, and it is surprising that Belot has dealt with it only by preterition. To know one of today's social institutions, or better yet, the complete system of our institutions, is not to have letter-perfect knowledge of the regulations that define them, a verbal knowledge of no great interest either theoretical or practical; it is to know the ideas and the sentiments that they express and that constitute their reality. How should one go about discovering these ideas and sentiments? Is it by questioning ourselves on our own? But introspection is much less adequate in this case than it is for the subject matter of individual psychology. It is not we who have made these institutions; we have received them almost ready-made from the past, and even the partial innovations that have been introduced in the course of our lifetime are not the personal work of any one of us, but the product of a collective action in which all our contemporaries have participated. Thus we are very badly informed about what went into their creation; they are the consequences of all kinds of unknown forces that a simple self-directed glance cannot cause us to perceive. Indeed we see, and from a muddled viewpoint, the external and apparent results of this synthesis; but we are unaware of the elements that make it up—that is to say, what gives it substance. The only means we have to sort things out is by watching through history how those elements have successively been superimposed upon one another and combined with each other in such a way as to become the complex reality of which we are presently the recipients. That is why history must play in moral speculation and in the methodical art that derives from it a considerable role. Belot is astonished: "We do not see," he says, "any technique make use of a story and this very idea is senseless" (p. 577). But it is quite simply a fact that physical sciences and the corresponding techniques have at their disposal other procedures for analyzing the realities they deal with. On the other hand, to resolve into their elements those extraordinarily complicated totalities that denote social matters, we have nothing but historical analysis at our disposal.*

It is said, to be sure, that this science is of no practical use. What difference does it make where our ethical rules come from? "That can be interesting to know in order to understand them better," not to put us in a position to make better use of them. Apparently there is, then, a realm in nature where, in order to have an impact on things, it would be useless to know them, to know what they are made of, on what causes they depend! Again, apparently it is necessary to justify by rationalization the exceptional and very surprising situation the social realm thus enjoys. How, then, does an institution exert its influence if not by having a hand in the spiritual conditions which have become rooted there, in the protestations out of which it gives rise to needs and out of which it becomes operational? Now, to have an impact on them, it is not a matter of indifference to know about them. Whether it is a matter of social facts or physical facts, one cannot achieve an effect except through its cause; it is not, then, useless to know what this last is. It is said that the cause is a dead issue. Not at all; it survives in the present, namely, in the effect that it has produced and that it is able to endure only if the precedent is

---

* Another very debatable comparison. The evolutionist hypothesis, says Belot, which is a historical hypothesis, is of no practical use. Yet, if it is true that species were born of one another, it follows that one may create some of them, and what we succeed in learning about the ways in which they were born of one another may help us in transforming them artificially, which is not without practical interest.

maintained, to change only if it changes. If our penal law, such as it presently exists, expresses certain religious beliefs, one will be able to modify it or control it suitably only if one modifies those beliefs or if one can awaken them, keep them alive, have them operate in an appropriate fashion; but to do so it will clearly be of some interest to know what those beliefs are, what realities they express (for there are no beliefs that do not express a certain reality), to what social conditions they are answerable, etcetera.

The objection is raised that social institutions can be put to uses other than those that have accounted for their primitive rationale, and that as a result it is possible, for the purpose of having them serve the goals of one's choice, to take them such as they are given to the observer, without bothering to know what they are and what has made them the way they are (p. 579). This is a strange way to abuse a proposal, unassailable but misunderstood. No doubt it does happen that an institution produces useful effects that had not been researched at the source; *but it in no way follows that this can produce any effects whatsoever*, those that one wants, and consequently, in no case would it suffice for decisions to be made to assign it such a function, such a goal, for the purpose of making its fulfillment an unqualified success. It can only have the effects that it is suited to have by nature; as a result, if one would know which are those that may legitimately be expected, one must begin by knowing that nature—all of which is possible only through historical analysis. To know what are the possible effects of a given cause is a question for science, just like that of knowing what are the causes of a given effect. Belot's attitude could be logically justified only on one condition: if he admitted that social institutions are not natural, that they are what we want them to be—that is to say, finally, that the law of causality does not apply to societies, and that in the social realm any effect whatsoever can result from any cause whatsoever. In such a case, it is perfectly clear that history cannot be of any practical use. We do not know if it is the author's sentiment, as one would be led to believe by reading certain passages, while reading certain other passages, to be sure, will contradict it. If this is really his opinion, we shall not delay discussing it. It appears to us useless to demonstrate today that, faced with the social world, it is not possible to adopt the attitude of the primitive faced with the physical world and to believe that folkways, institutions, or legal or economic systems can be evoked out of a void solely by summoning the will.

Thus, in every way, the science of customs, the genetic study of moral standards, is the indispensable base of all moral art that would be rational; even though it would not be necessary to determine the goals. To realize them, it is very necessary to make use of the existing moral reality since we have no other lever in hand; now, to be able to use it, one must know it and there is no other way to know it than to go to its source. But in addition, it is not accurate that in the determination of goals the science of customs is utterly useless.

Belot's whole plan to demonstrate this impotence of our science is based on an arbitrary notion, which corresponds to nothing in reality. Without doubt, it is very true that a science is possible only when its objective is given and relatively fixed. The scientist keeps close watch on the static situation in order to be able to observe it. Something that is forever receding escapes observation and, as a result, scientific study. But the procedure by which it is fixed, however, may not go so far as to render it unnatural—as to make, for example, something dead out of something alive. To study a society, it is necessary in all essentials for us to consider it from a static point of view; but because we consider it in this way, it does not remain any less what it is: something changing, forever evolving. Consequently, even this present phase that I attempt to fix in order to be able to describe it and to analyze it is not made up of uniquely acquired characteristics, realized, definite, achieved, and immovable. Because it is forever in motion, there is found in it tendencies toward movement, germs of change, aspirations to be something other than what it is, ideals that are striving for realization—even at this moment when, for purposes of study, I immobilize it. It may very well be that the true way for a particular society to remain true to itself is to obey one of these tendencies and to change. In order to be aware of the novelties to be introduced in the society, it is in no way useless to consider the present situation, since, in this present situation, new matters, not yet taking effect, are, as it were, foreshadowed. The future is already written there for whoever can read it; and it is the only way to anticipate it rationally. For it cannot be a matter of assigning to a society goals that it would not want under any circumstances, of which it would not have the slightest notion, for which it would feel no need. One has little choice but to make clear the worth, the true significance, of the needs that it experiences; then again, how does one choose between the various tendencies which impinge upon it, how does one decide on those that are well founded or not, other than by taking as a reference point the nature of that society? It is said that there are times when it is necessary to cut corners, to feel one's way, to take risks. What could be fairer? But if one would act rationally, again one must have one's reasons to believe that this abridged, precipitous, risky evolution is called for by the nature of things. The fact is, then, that one must always return to the analysis of the given reality, whatever one does.

The importance of the discussions raised by Lévy-Bruhl's book has obliged us to explain ourselves once more on these questions of method. [26] But, to tell the truth, we cannot deny ourselves this impression that a day will come—and it is not far off—when people will be astonished that so many controversies and the expenditure of so much dialectic were necessary to gain acceptance for this very simple proposal: that to ratiocinate about ethics, it is first of all necessary to know what it is; and that, to know what it is, it is necessary to observe it. Yet it is on this truism that the method we practice is based. (*Année sociologique*, 10, 1907, pp. 352–368; trans. J. French)

Gaston Richard. "Les Lois de la solidarité morale." *Revue philosophique,* Nov. 1905, pp. 443–471.

In this article, Richard opposes a doctrine without naming its author but characterizing it as follows: It involves "that positivist conception, so highly regarded today, that identifies morality with an entirely automatic type of society" (p. 471). We confess we do not know the nature of the conception alluded to in such terms; among the sociologists and moralists whose ideas are being freely discussed, we do not know anyone who has given the above opinion his support.

There is, in fact, overwhelming evidence that the more advanced we become, the more the personal factor becomes an essential element in the pursuit of good conduct. Heedless morality, unaware of itself and of its motives, is in our view an imperfect morality at best; on this point the public conscience is expressed with a clarity that is hard to deny. Likewise, Richard has made his point ahead of time.

But certain passages seem to imply that Richard tends to conclude from this undeniable proposal that ethical standards become less and less a group matter, without, however, our being sure of having a clear idea of what he is thinking. If such is the case, we find ourselves faced with an assertion completely different from the first one, which has none of its implications whatsoever, and which, consequently, would need to supply direct evidence as proof. Now, on this point the article does not even begin to do so. Just because we ought to maintain high moral standards more conscientiously and thoughtfully, it does not follow at all that morality ceases thereby to be a social matter if it is social by nature. In a case like that, there is a question of fact against which no amount of dialectics can prevail. It can even happen (and it is indeed what is happening) that society itself calls on its members to make a more personal effort to behave. There are thus two very different issues involved, and we fear that the author has confused the problems they raise.

In the pages of the article, there are several detailed proposals about which we have certain reservations. It is hard for us to understand what motivates the categorical contention that "*all* religion exists to solve the problem of evil," or to declare as unfounded the assumption that views the taboo as a primitive and universal religious phenomenon. We confess not to know any religion in which the notion of the taboo is not to be found, and we cannot even imagine how this may be the case. (*Année sociologique*, 10, 1907, pp. 382–383; trans. J. French)

Edward Westermarck. *The Origin and Development of the Moral Ideas*, vol. I. London: Macmillan and Co., 1906, xxi + 716 pp.

This voluminous work, [27] the fruit of an enormous amount of reading, is presented as an attempt to study moral facts scientifically. Just like us, the author proposes to give the genesis of moral facts in the light of history and comparative ethnography. This agreement between his thought and ours is not the only one that we have had the pleasure to acknowledge. It will be seen, by way of the analysis about to follow, that in the case of particular problems Westermarck's conceptions are not without comparable allusions that we have had occasion to set forth here or in other works. He himself points out some of these concurrences, that we note. The author, however, is not sure in his claim to an unwarranted right of priority, which cannot be fully established. It is, rather, because these encounters are still too rare in our science not to be noted when they arise. One cannot publicize too highly anything that gives hope that sociology will finally break out of the philosophical subjectivity in which it has languished for too long. But at the same time, there are between Westermarck's method and ours some absolutely essential divergences which naturally have repercussions in the details of the theory, and the examination of which is going to permit us to deal concretely with important questions of method.

Very justly, the author postulates at the beginning of his book (p. 2) that if one is to reconstitute the way in which our moral views took shape and grew, one must encompass the moral evolution of mankind in its totality. He then has recourse to the contributions of history and ethnography in their entirety; therefore one will find an enormous mass of facts in this work, which, in this respect, cannot fail to be useful. But how are these materials elaborated?

To give the genesis of our moral views is to seek the causes that gave rise to them. We shall not stop here to reveal once again what reasons are held in the belief that these causes are essentially social; it is, moreover, a postulate that the author will, we believe, have no trouble in explaining. But in that case, in order to discover these causes, to explain the variations through which an ethical standard has passed, one must as an absolute necessity place these variations in relationship with the social milieux where the standard was elaborated and transformed. To separate a standard from its milieu is to separate it from the vital sources from which it flows and to become incapable of grasping its significance. A study like that of our author presupposes, then, that one possesses a classification, at the very least temporarily, of the principal types of societies and of their distinctive peculiarities. Doubtless, in the present-day state of science, the establishment of a perfectly methodical and systematic classification must be out of the question. But at the very least, it is necessary that out of the motley mass of societies of every kind that have succeeded each other in history, one should be able to disengage a few organizational forms sufficiently characteristic to be able to serve as points of a reference. To these forms, certain of the transformations in moral rules under consideration can be related.

Unfortunately, Westermarck has not felt this is in any way necessary. He has remained true to the method followed for such a long time both by the German school of legal anthropology and the English school of religious anthropology. While recognizing on general principles that morality is essentially a social matter (pp. 122 ff.), he believes that at bottom the propellant for this evolution must be looked for among the most general and permanent inclinations of human nature. This will be confirmed by the evidence about to follow. In order to perceive these fundamental and universal tendencies, there is no need whatsoever to distinguish between various forms which each ethical standard assumes according to the society, nor to relate each of these to the social milieu under which jurisdiction is claimed. The differences that can be brought out by this procedure cannot have more than a secondary interest. Instead of limiting and circumscribing the field of observation in such a way as to grasp what is specifically factual, one must, on the contrary, extend it as far as possible, and introduce, into vast syntheses, all the information we have at our disposal on the moral life of humanity: On each particular issue, one must question as many people as possible, however heterogeneous they may be; then too, the more heterogeneous they are, the more chance one will have to display the very general procedures that one is concerned with mastering. And it is indeed in this way that Westermarck proceeds, after the example of Post and of the entire anthropological school. Every time he enunciates a proposition for demonstration, he borrows examples from the most disparate societies. He is concerned above all to accumulate facts, not to make a solid and demonstrable choice among them. For example, in order to establish how domestic solidarity results in collective responsibility, he cites, in a rapid and tumultuous review, the Aleuts, the peoples of the Gold Coast, those of Madagascar, China, Greece, etcetera (pp. 45–46). You would say that his aim is to create an impression of bulkiness, necessarily jumbled, rather than to leave behind distinct and well-defined ideas.

This is a statement of all the inadequacies of the method, which admits only of grossly sketchy results. Science needs, above all, topical and more limited objectives. The man who handles so many facts can do no more than describe each of them in a more or less vague fashion. Even criticism of documents utilized in this way is not possible; when one receives them from so many different handlers, one is obliged to accept them such as they are presented. Doubtless this jumbled pile of ill-digested facts had, originally, its uses; Post's work, for example, served in that capacity. It was a way of exploring, of reconnoitering, for a rough approximation of the new terrain that was open to science; of making a vague perception of the area, of awakening the taste for new and more methodical explorations. But today this work is done, and it does not appear to us useful to start over again. We must set ourselves tasks more clearly defined and involving more refinement.

But in order to be better able to judge this method, the best thing is to see how it is applied by its author.

It is a general rule of method that a positive science must be supplied with factual material that can be immediately obtained; it starts with given results in order to go back to causes that are to be discovered. In morality, directly observable facts are rules of behavior—judgments which are enunciated with authority and according to which members of a particular social group must behave in different life situations. If, then, morality is a science of facts, it seems that it cannot do otherwise than to accept these rules as immediate goals of its research, subject to seeking thereafter the causes from which they derive. And one might expect the author to practice this method, inasmuch as he sees effectively, in these systems of rules that are customs and laws, an expression of moral ideas: His chapter 7 is entitled "Customs and Laws as Expressions of Moral Ideas."

And yet his procedure is entirely different. Holding the very sound opinion that morality is not a logical structure, he refuses to see truly primitive facts in the abstract concepts around which are clustered the usual debates of the moralists (concepts of good, of duty, of right, etcetera). For him, and we shall not contradict him on this point, they are generalizations of conditions both simpler and of a very different nature. Now, he makes it his immediate task to expose these original situations. The aim of the first chapter in the book ("The Emotional Origin of Moral Judgments") is to demonstrate that they are emotional in nature. The following chapters reveal what particular kind of emotion is involved. What is abnormal about this procedure is evident. Precisely because moral facts are rooted in these emotional states, observation cannot expose them in this way from the very beginning. In order to expose them, one must start with complex but apparent and visible facts, which result from and express these prime factors, in order to go back next from causes to causes, from conditions to conditions, down as far as those deepest sources of moral life. It is not with the first step of the search, in the first chapters of the book, that it is possible to determine those primal sources of our moral judgments. Here exists an ultimate question that can be tackled effectively only at the termination of the study—far from being the subject of preliminary discussion. Now, if Westermarck felt no scruple about reversing in this way the natural and logical progression of the problems, it is certainly because of the influence of the principle that we enunciated a while back: The fact is that, for him, that emotional process comes down to something very simple; nothing intrudes there but very general opinions that every man can discover within himself by introspection.

And indeed, for Westermarck this mechanism is reduced to two completely elementary emotions. The first is anger, the indignation that grips us when confronting an act of aggression of which we are the victim, the need for reprisals as a result of it; the second is kindness, the sympathy we experience for whoever has been kind to us and the need to respond to these demonstrations of sympathy by demonstrations of a similar nature. These two types of emotions, then, are two variations on a single theme: Both of them are *retributive,* but in two opposite senses. The first is translated by reprobation, the stigma or even the physical punishment that follows the immoral act; the second results in the esteem, praise, or positive rewards accruing to virtuous acts. Punishment is, then, for our author as for ourselves, an "impassioned reaction" that expresses and relieves public indignation; and this personal reaction, precisely because it is impassioned, is not determined by utilitarian considerations; its essential justification is not to intimidate the malicious or to correct them. Its real usefulness is to bring to men's attention "what they must not do in society's opinion" (p. 90). Doubtless, in proportion to one's progress in history, one sees repression assume a more thoughtful and less violently aggressive character; yet, whatever is done, its nature can not change.

These ideas are very similar to those we have revealed in our *Division of Labor* and elsewhere on the same subject. But this theory of punishment is juxtaposed, in the case of Westermarck, with another which diverges from the first on an essential point.

According to our author, the indignation raised by the criminal act would be directed especially at the agent and would be chiefly aimed at causing suffering to his sensitive feelings. The punishment would essentially be to inflict suffering on a sentient being as a reprisal for the suffering for which he himself is responsible. Now, if moral indignation is essentially determined by the immoral act, if it has no utilitarian purposes, it appears unlikely that the agent is unanswerable to such a degree. There are as such two conceptions that do not readily jibe. But most of all a multiplicity of facts prove that, in a multitude of cases, it is anything but the agent that arouses public indignation. To be sure, repression always involves some act of violent destruction; but very often it is considered a matter of total indifference whether the victim of this destruction is guilty—in the sense that we presently give the word—or innocent. Westermarck tries to reconcile these facts, which he knows as well as we do, with his thesis. But it is impossible for us to see how he manages to do so. In order to explain such numerous cases of collective responsibility in which the condemned man being punished is innocent and recognized as such, he invokes domestic solidarity; but precisely the fact that members of the same group can be considered jointly responsible to one another in the matter of mistakes or crimes implies that social prosecution is not necessarily brought to bear on the agent. Religious criminality provides still more examples along the same lines. Westermarck replies that religious impurity is, by its nature, essentially contagious. But it is still answering the question by another question; it is a question of knowing precisely how reprobation can be extended in this way by contagion. The fact is, then, that it is not brought to bear on the person of the agent as exclusively as is claimed.

However that may be, it is clear how extreme is the generality of feelings from which moral life supposedly proceeds; they are not even peculiar to humanity, but are likewise to be found in the case of animals; for the animal, too, knows about vengeance and gratitude. Therefore, by themselves, these feelings are totally amoral; reprisals inflicted for utterly selfish ends have nothing morally admirable. In order for them to play a moral role, they must, then, be endowed with particular characteristics. Retributive emotions, to use the author's wording, are not specifically moral; in order to deserve this qualification, they must, in addition, be disinterested and apparently impartial. The author means that if indeed they are partial, this partiality should, at least, not be consciously sensed as such. And since a disinterested emotion can be experienced by everyone, the moral emotion has, in the final analysis, as criterion a certain *saveur de généralité*" ("flavor of generality"). It is the Kantian criterion extended to the affective forms of moral life.

Inasmuch as the emotions, generative forces of moral life, are characterized in this way, one must explain how it is that they present those distinctive characteristics—that is, how it comes about that the appropriately moral emotions are found to be disinterested, impartial, etcetera. As the author replies, the fact is that "society is the birthplace of moral awareness and that the first moral judgments have expressed, not the private emotions of isolated individuals, but emotions felt by society as a whole. Tribal custom was the first 'canonical duty roster' " (p. 118). Two or three pages are used to illustrate this proposal with certain facts. The evidence will be deemed somewhat slight. To be sure, we have no right to dispute a premise that is our own; but by reason of its gravity, we would have wished to find it a little more seriously demonstrated. That is where the very nub of the issue lies, or rather the issues that are raised by the scientific study of moral facts. There and there alone, according to the avowal of Westermarck himself, one can find the explanation of the distinctive properties of the moral rules. We are therefore astonished to see him resolve in a few words a problem of such importance, as if the solution was a matter of course or was of only secondary interest.

However that may be, once he has determined these emotions, the author believes he has reached the deep source from which all the essential moral ideas flow. The assertion is not a little surprising; it is not easy to see how it is possible to discover the source of moral precepts as long as nothing is known about their content, for this matter has not been under consideration up until now. The general conclusions of the analysis which we have just summed up have clearly informed us that there are acts which the moral conscience rejects and others which it praises in a positive manner; but we do not know what these acts are, the ideas they express, and as a result it appears very hard to accept the fact that we are here and now in a position to tell where these ideas come from. To tell the truth, this entire first part of Westermarck's work consists simply of a theory of moral sanctions. There are repressive and reproachful sanctions, and also laudatory ones; that is certainly a fact. The author ties them in with certain emotional states. But a theory of sanctions is not a theory of moral ideas. The sanctions only serve to express the way in which consciences react in the presence of the moral or immoral act but do not interpret directly this act itself and the state of affairs from which it derives. And besides, this theory of sanctions has been constructed in a somewhat sketchy manner; for the author did not begin by observing, describing, and classifying the different kinds of sanctions that are applied to rules of morality, in order to go back methodically afterwards to the emotional states from which they result; but right at the start it is those states that he claimed to come upon. He thought he could reveal the causes without beginning with a descriptive study of the effects.

Therefore, the way he works his way up from these fundamental emotions to essential moral concepts is purely ideological; the chapter in which he deals with this question (pp. 131–157) is only a series of introspective analyses and abstract deductions, practically empty of all objective data. What Westermarck calls *the principal moral concepts* are those cardinal ideas that are thought to dominate the whole of moral life, to contain its entire essence: ideas of duty, of right, of what is just and unjust, of property, of merit, of virtue. And surely these ideas are far from being so devoid of all reality that they must be scornfully brushed aside; they express or are intended to express the most general aspects of moral reality. But for them to take their rightful place in science, it is necessary that they be organized scientifically. Since they merely serve to interpret the most general characteristics of moral life, it is from the analysis of moral facts that they must be progressively disengaged. The method followed by Westermarck prevented him from proceeding in this way, and he set himself the problem in the same terms as ordinary moralists. These notions—he does not elaborate them himself by a methodical and objective comparison of those multiple moral rules of which they express certain properties only—he accepts ready-made, such as they are purveyed to the common conscience, with the hazy inaccuracy which necessarily accompanies ideas that are formed in this way on the spur of the moment as is customary without order and without method. And with the help of a wholly dialectical analysis, he undertakes to link them to the two main categories of retributive emotions he has distinguished. Duty, rights, the idea of justice and injustice, are considered to be various manifestations and specific examples of the feeling of reproach, whereas the idea of goodness and virtue is derived from the feeling of approval.

And here is how the connection is established. The idea of duty is the idea of a certain way of acting that arouses blame when it is not carried out in accordance with prescribed standards (p. 135). One's rights are simply the subjective point of view of duties other people owe us, and justice consists in respecting such rights. As for what is "good," it is the expression used for every act that is praised in a positive way; lastly, it is a constant inclination to do the right thing. It is evident that we are in the midst of a world of abstractions, and of abstractions constructed without much method. What is more artificial than to see duty merely in the blame resulting from its violation? To be sure, it is legitimate to make use of the sanction associated with duty as a convenient external symbol for the purpose of recognizing it and for distinguishing it from the other behavioral precepts with which it might be confused; but this provides only the external symbol, not the essential one. Quite the contrary, what constitutes essentially the idea of duty is something very positive: It is the idea of the peremptory, of the mandatory, that must be analyzed if one wants to discover the origins of the concept of duty. In another sense, it is entirely arbitrary to admit of no relationship between duty and a feeling of approval. It is said that with regard to moral opinion, he who does only his duty has no claim to any retribution. That is a case of one of those current formulas of which the sense is easily distorted because they are not very clear-cut. Is it then without reason that Kant interprets this matter, as so many others of the public conscience and declares that the one truly moral good consists solely of doing one's duty? The second aphorism is seemingly no less justified than the first and bears out the fact that the issue is not simple and that duty is not irrelevant to any idea of approval—far from it. The same goes for the notion of rights. There is at the very least good reason to believe that one's rights are a positive attribute with which the moral personality is endowed, and that as a result the link by which rights are attached to the other person's duty is singularly contrived. In any case, here is a very complicated problem that cannot be thus resolved in a few words with a purely ideological analysis.

But these very general notions are once again completely formal. In order to practice the science of moral phenomena, it is necessary in the end to come to the point of studying the content of morals—that is to say, the particular precepts that direct men's relationships. It is this study that our author tackles in the second part of his book* and that he proposes to continue in the following volume. Here the defects of his method are revealed in a manner perhaps still more apparent.

Unable to study all the ways of acting, to which are applied or have been applied in the past the rules of morality, the author retains and understands in the course of his study only the following modes of behavior:

(1) Those concerning the interests of our fellows (their life, their health, their liberty, their property, their honor).
(2) Those concerning the interests of the agent itself (moral rules relating to suicide, to temperance, to asceticism, etcetera).
(3) Those concerning sexual relations (this third group, as the author admits, partly overlaps with the first two).
(4) Those relating to the lower order of animals.
(5) Those relating to the dead.
(6) Those relating to beings, real or ideal, regarded as supernatural.

Of these six groups of facts, the author, in the present volume, studies only the first, and again only partly; he deals with rules that protect man's life

---

* Between the part we have just analyzed and the one we are about to discuss are inserted a series of chapters (7–13) in which the author deals with sanctions, chiefly or even exclusively penal sanctions and the way in which they are applied to individuals, depending on whether the criminal act is intentional or not, on the part the will plays, and so on. Apropos of the notion of morals we have already raised serious questions on the notion of sanctions. It is clear that these chapters do not seem to be very well placed. They break the continuity in the development of ideas. That is why we have ignored them in our analysis, except for drawing the reader's attention to them. Interesting facts concerning the question of responsibility may be found in them.

(prohibition of homicide and of assault and battery); those that recommend working to promote material and moral well-being of others (charity, generosity, hospitality); rules of personal freedom (in this case it is a matter of the compliance of a wife towards her husband, of children towards their father, of slaves towards their master).

We shall not insist on how irrational this classification is. It is suprising that in this chart of moral relations a place is not set aside for domestic relations, for civic relations, for contractual relations; each of these groups of facts makes up a natural whole and requires study in itself and for itself. For want of proceeding in this way, one is obliged to separate connected issues and to compare others that are unrelated. The question of relationship between husband and wife has nothing in common with that involving slavery, but, on the contrary, is only a particular case involving marital morals, itself closely bound up with domestic morals.

But what is more remarkable is the spirit in which these problems are handled; it is here that the tendencies of the school are best divulged. The author is forever concerned with linking the different ethical maxims with some constitutional tendency of human nature in general. He believes he has accounted for them only when he has demonstrated that they are beholden to certain ideas, certain sentiments, except for minor differences in degree, wherever mankind is situated. For example, the prohibition of homicide is explained by a natural feeling that predisposes man to respect the life of his companions, or those of his fellows who belong to the same social group as he (pp. 328 ff.). In time, this feeling has been refined, extended, generalized, fortified; but it already existed in the most primitive societies with which we are acquainted. The same goes for feelings of charity and generosity; they are contemporary with humanity. Only the tight circle in which they were enclosed and which did not exceed the confines of the family became progressively broader (pp. 527 ff.). Similarly, that which forms the basis of family authority in the first place is its natural superiority over the children; it is the feeling of affection and respect that the young have for their elders (pp. 618 ff.). It is not as if Westermarck does not occasionally introduce less universal and less permanent causes. There are more transient ideas and feelings that are not to be ignored for the part they play in the genesis of moral ideas—whether temporarily preventing fundamental causes from being fully effective or, on the contrary, helping them by a sort of happy accident. For example, he shows us how certain superstitions (in the practice of the vendetta or of human sacrifices) or the rude necessities of primitive life have, over a long period of time, increased the number of homicides considered legitimate; how, on the other hand, certain religious beliefs stimulated the charitable impulse and reinforced paternal authority. But these influences, in whatever sense they were exercised, were never anything but secondary; they merely served to slow down or to accelerate the evolution of moral views, the general growth of which depends on more general and more constant factors.

It is now easier to understand why Westermarck does not feel the need to put various ethical systems in harmony with social systems to which they used to belong or still belong. The fact is that for him there are no qualitatively different types of morality, in harmony with equally different social surroundings. But fundamentally, he considers it obvious that there is one and the same morality, implanted within man's congenital nature, and that the moral practices with which ethnography and history acquaint us are simply progressive approximations. They are the same ideas and the same sentiments which have an impact everywhere, except that they assert themselves with an unequal clarity and force appropriate to the degree of civilization at which men have arrived.

Now, that is a very simplified notion of moral evolution! But then, what a surprising contrast between the extreme simplicity of this conception and the enormous accumulation of facts thought necessary for its justification! As a matter of fact, was it very necessary to draw so widely both from the whole of ethnography and all of history in order to rediscover the principle on which the old philosophy of natural law rested?

Thus, there is a markedly inherent contradiction between the view that Westermarck and the school to which he belongs entertain about morality and the way in which it ought to be studied. On the one hand, they sense how complex it is, and as a result they understand that in order to know it, it is necessary to observe it in its historical manifestations; that is how they consider their obligaton to consult history. But, on the other hand, just like the classical moralists, they believe it possible to readjust all this complexity down to a few very general and very elementary ideas and feelings. The result of this is that the erudition which they display appears as somewhat external and unconnected, in any case, to the very simple theoretical conclusions that are extracted from it. However, if moral reality is truly of a kind incapable of being grasped through introspection alone, it appears unlikely that one can account for it by means of explanations that introspection suffices to suggest.

If it appeared to us necessary to criticize the method followed by the author and the conception that he entertains of the science of morals, it is only fair to pay homage to his immense learning. He has at his disposal an incomparable literature. This book represents a gigantic work, and in this respect will certainly render great services. On each of the issues which are dealt with there, one will discover a veritable abundance of references and of useful information. (*Année sociologique,* 10, 1907, pp. 383–395; trans. J. French)

Simon Deploige. *Le Conflit de la morale et de la sociologie.* Louvain: Institut Supérieur de Philosophie, 1911, 424, pp.

This book is an apologetic pamphlet; [28] it involves the discrediting of our ideas, by all means possible, for the greater glory of the doctrine of Saint Thomas. Therefore there would be no reason to make room for such a work were it not for the need to denounce the polemical arguments it uses.

In order to arrive at the desired result, it was thought clever to present our conceptions as a byproduct of Germanic imports. It was hoped thereby to divert the thrust of French sociology, such as we understand it, by seeking to establish that there is not a trace of anything "French" to be found therein [29] (p. 141), that "German input is overwhelmingly preponderant" (ibid). It is useless to point out at great length the tendentious nature of such a line of reasoning. But even more, it is completely without foundation. In our case, Comte's work had a profound impact of a different sort from Schmoller's somewhat indecisive and unsubstantive thought—and especially Wagner's. And the influence of Comte had, moreover, been preceded by that of neo-criticism; it is from Renouvier that the axiom [of the priority of the whole] came to us: A whole is not equal to the sum of its parts, and this axiom is basic to what Deploige calls our social realism. Finally, it is common knowledge what a preponderant place the study of religious phenomena occupied in our investigations. Now, the science of religion is essentially English and American; it has no trace of anything German. It is making a systematically truncated "genesis" (pp. 122–151) of our thinking to neglect everything we owe to Robertson Smith and to the works of the ethnographers of England and America.

But there is more: In order to give more force to the arguments used, there was no timidity about resorting to a *conscious alteration of the texts.* One reads on page 275: "They [Lévy-Bruhl and Durkheim] have in regard to metaphysical questions—the soul, for example—ready-made opinions and fixed answers borrowed from systems that have happened to influence their thinking." And, in support of this assertion, they quote in a footnote the following passage, borrowed, they say, from our article "Représentations in-dividuelles et représentations collectives": [30] "It is not necessary to imagine a soul. All our thoughts are in the mind." *This quotation is incorrect.* Here is what we had written: "In order to recognize the mind as that limited seat of self-government which is at the bottom all that our notion of the spiritual encompasses as a certainty, it is not then necessary to imagine a soul separated from one's body and leading a fanciful and solitary existence in some ideally indefinable sphere. The soul is in the land of the living; its life is inter-mingled with material things, and one may, *if one so wishes,* say of all our thoughts that they are in the mind. Only, one must add that inside the brain, they are not rigorously localized, they are not situated at well-defined points." The readers will judge for themselves.

We shall say nothing of the question itself that the title of the work in-dicates. To begin with, it is merely a pretext to take us to task in a general way. Next, in no way does it correspond to the facts. There is not, in our view, and there cannot be any conflict between morality and sociology: We ask simply that the moral art be preceded by a science of morals, more methodical in ap-proach than the usual speculations of so-called theoretical morality. Our whole thesis can be summed up thus: In order to determine what morality ought to be at a given moment in time, one must first know what morality is, how to distinguish what is moral from what is not; and such a question cannot be answered if one has not made a preliminary study of moral phenomena in themselves and on their own terms. We cannot choose a criterion by arbitrary decision. We can only observe it and sift out the facts.

The book concludes that a return to the social philosophy of Saint Thomas is necessary. (*Année sociologique*, 12, 1913, pp. 326–328: trans. J. French)

NOTES AND NOTICES

Alfonso Asturaro. "La scienza morale e la sociologia generale" (The Science of Morals and General Sociology). *Rivista italiana di sociologia*, Jan. 1899, pp. 1–16.

This is an interesting article. Applied ethics presupposes ethics, which is really theoretical and whose exclusive task is to determine the causes of ethical rules. These causes must be searched for in the substructure of society, essentially in its economic organization. It follows from this that ethics varies from one group to another. Consequently, the practical purpose of applied ethics must itself vary from one social type to another to which it is applicable. The purpose of applied ethics will be to show by which reforms in public order the functioning of morality could be rectified—where it is necessary. It is only at the end of the article that the author ends up in a great difficulty with the problem, and the suggested solution is a little too much of a summary. What must constitute the standard according to which those rectifications are made? Could the prevailing ethics play this role? On the whole, yes. But it is never all that it should be. Therefore, on certain points, it should rectify itself. But the author does not state precisely how these points will be determined and according to which standard this rectification will be made. He is satisfied to invoke the principle of adaptation to social needs. But what constitutes normal needs? Who are those who do not have them? And what is the degree of normal intensity of normal needs? (*Année sociologique*, 3, 1900, p. 330; trans. Y. Nandan)

Edward Westermarck. "L'elemento morale nelle consuetudini e nelle leggi." *Rivista italiana di sociologia*, iv, no. 6, pp. 677–695.

For Westermarck, the only way to treat moral ideas objectively is to study them by examining the customs and the laws of societies. Custom, in fact, is essentially mandatory, and whosoever violates the entire moral act is condemned. However, there is no difference between custom and morality. There are acts which the former prescribes and which are not [in the realm of] morality, such as good manners, and [custom] regulates external conduct exclusively, whereas morality is totally concerned with the conscience. But according to the author, these differences are more apparent than real. They reveal that custom is the rule of duty, still only partially developed. The author does not tell us what constitutes the superior sphere of morality, to which custom does not give expression. With respect to law, it is fixed custom, defined by a constitutional authority. Thus it is also an expression of moral conscience. But the distinction between the legal and the moral is more striking than between the moral and custom. The morality that finds expression in law is often an outdated morality, which, in fact, is abolished by the consciousness prevailing at the time. Moreover, law depends directly on people's will and it often expresses the ideas which rule. Nonetheless, it cannot maintain itself against public opinion. If "it does not show us the moral conscience in all its purity," it corresponds very well to what the common people instinctively understand by morality. (*Année sociologique*, 5, 1902, pp. 326–327; trans. Y. Nandan)

M. Mauxion. "Les Eléments et l'évolution de la moralité." *Revue philosophique*, July–Aug. 1903.
   The article contests the ideas of the sociological school, about which the author seems to know very little. (*Année sociologique*, 8, 1905, p. 382; trans. Y. Nandan)

Juridic and Moral Systems

REVIEWS

R. Dareste. "La Loi des Homérites." *Nouvelle Revue historique de droit français et étranger*, March–April 1905, pp. 157–170.
   In the former kingdom of Saba (Sheba) the nation of the *Homérites*, or Himyarites, was located. Originally they practiced the same religion as the Arabs before Muhammad, but the multitude of foreigners who settled in this rich country brought new cults. The Jews came first; the Christians followed under Emperor Constans. Finally, in the first half of the sixth century, the Christian party won out; thanks to the cooperation of Ethiopia, a Christian king assumed power. His first concern was to draft a general law for the whole country; this is the law that Dareste translates succinctly for our benefit. He reproduces the substance of all the articles and has omitted only the prolix elaborations with which the original text is overburdened.
   What perhaps characterizes this code most particularly is the considerable space taken up by clauses relating to attacks directed against sexual morals. Not only are misdemeanors of this kind punished with a pitiless severity, but they are very numerous. For adultery, incest, sodomy, or bestiality, the death penalty is exacted. Whoever commits an act of prostitution receives a hundred lashes, has the left ear cut off, and witnesses the confiscation of his goods. The procurer has the tongue cut in half. The widow is obliged to marry again or

retire to a monastery, and if she becomes a widow a second time, close confinement is obligatory, for it is not allowed to marry three times. In this multiplicity of restraints by which the containment of sexual instinct is attempted, in the cruelty with which deviations are repressed, one recognizes the influence of the Church and the distrust, the aversion, it has always experienced for the feelings that underlie sexual intercourse. Hence these extravagant precautions and excessive severity.

Other traces of this same influence are found in the limitations applied to paternal authority. The law intervenes in family relationhips. It does not limit itself to restraining the right of correction; it obliges the father to provide for his children's marriage or else be penalized with a fine and banishment. In certain situations it allows children to marry without the consent of their parents. Important restrictions are imposed on the power to draw up a will: "Those near death who leave large fortunes are not to confide them to executors of wills engaged outside of our authority. *Above all it is necessary that payment of the pious legacies be made in full* to the people to whom they are due." Thus the tendencies of the Church are even now what they will be much later in everything concerning domestic morality; the fact is, then, that they adhere to the essential characteristics of its moral constitution.

It is proper to tie in with the same influence a certain number of humanitarian tendencies banning the mistreatment of slaves, children, and even beasts of burden, or instituting almshouses for the aged, but forbidding begging. The very nature of penalties bears the stamp of the spirit of Christianity. Imprisonment at forced labor plays an unknown role in classic Roman law; the use of reprimand attests that punishment of the guilty one is imposed with a view to changing him for the better. The cruelty of the penalties (mutilation is given considerable space within this body of penal law) contrasts, it is true, with these tendencies; Dareste attributes this fact to the influence of Byzantine law.

This code thus allows us a glimpse of the nature of society which, it would seem, received from the Church its legal and moral organization. (*Année sociologique,* 9, 1906, pp. 340–342; trans. J. French)

Domestic Organization

THE FAMILY

REVIEWS

B. W. Leist. *Alt-Arisches Jus Civile* (Primitive Civil Law Among the Aryan Societies). Jena: Fischer, 1896, 414 pp.
  Through a series of works carried out with perseverance, Leist has under-

taken to determine the primitive law of the different Aryan societies. He began by comparing in this way the Greeks and the Italians, and this in turn gave rise to the book entitled *Greco-italische Rechtsgeschichte.* * Then he compared the laws of India with those of Greece and Italy. He took as his point of departure the idea that legal rules, common to all the peoples of the Aryan race, must have existed prior to their dispersal. This led him to believe that he could arrive at the initial character of European law by having recourse to methodical comparisons. Such is the object of his *Alt-Arisches Jus Gentium.* † We need not point out all the dubious factors within an assumption of this kind. But it is not necessary to discuss them in order to examine the conclusions of the work that is to be analyzed. Whatever the origin of this common source, it exists, it has everywhere the same distinctive characteristics, and it represents a predetermined phase in the history of these societies. It corresponds to the era when they did not yet make up city-states or nations, but formed vast aggregates of clans, without well-defined contours, and governed by religious custom; it is, in fact, a characteristic feature of this remote law that it is not written and that it is sacred. It does not emanate from the state, but from the gods. Little by little, there seems to emerge from this primary base a new law, a product of the city-state and destined to serve the interests of the city-state; it is civil law. In *Alt-Arisches Jus Civile,* Leist proposes to retrace this genesis as far back as its beginnings. It is especially Rome that he has in mind; but in order to bring out clearly what is peculiar to the evolution of Roman law, he constantly holds up to view some of the changes the Roman mentality caused the original law to experience, thus eliciting the transformations that arose along parallel lines among the peoples of the same race.

In the first part of the work, published in 1892, the author limited himself to showing what special form the old religious law assumed in Rome. It is only in the second part, with which we are to concern ourselves, that the problem just enunciated is really taken up. This second part itself includes two books: One deals with domestic law, the other with procedure. It is the first only that we are going to analyze.

Marriage (pp. 106–136). According to the author, marriage, in the primitive law of the Aryan peoples, consisted of three phases, traces of which were still to be found until a very advanced era. Marriage began with the betrothal, the *sponsio* ³¹ of the Latins, the ἐγγύησις (betrothal) of the Greeks; next was the tradition of the wife in the hands of the husband (*traditio*) the Greeks called it δόσις (giving);³² finally came the introduction of the wife into her new household, a ceremony that was accompanied by shows of violence (*deductio in domum mariti*) or what the Greeks called πομπή (procession).³³

* Jena, Fischer, 1884.
† Jena, Fischer, 1889.

Of the three kinds of practices, the first two are the logical consequences of marriage by purchase. The sponsio is the understanding reached between the wife's parents and the husband or his parents over the conditions of the sale; the *traditio* consists of the husband's taking possession of the wife, asserting rights resulting from the agreement previously established between the parties. As for the *deductio,* it is a vestige of ancient marriage by abduction that survived its primary causes. Due to its public character and the attendant boisterous ceremonies, it was a convenient method to establish *coram populo*[34] the precise moment when the marriage was to start. Leist explains that it was used in this way because of the fact that the Aryan peoples made use of writing only belatedly. Ceremonial declaration of marriage could be oral only; hence the need to impart a glow that would lodge as deeply as possible in as many memories as possible. Therefore the oral characteristic remained one of the distinguishing features of the Aryan wedding, whereas among the Semites, who practiced writing much sooner, a written act became very quickly the essential matrimonial formality (letter of marriage, letter of divorce).

But there was, on that account, no well-defined organization. These three operations, not involving any legal pacts, were derived from certain juridical concepts; they were merely the principal and ordinary steps whereby, in fact, a new household was commonly established. At the time no one had even the slightest idea of marriage such as we conceive of it today—namely, as an act whose value and effects depend exclusively on its relative conformity or nonconformity with a preestablished rule. There were, says Leist, no words in those different languages to express such an idea (p. 108). The great change introduced into those customs by civil law, when it was established, was precisely to exalt one of the formalities so that it became an exclusive criterion of the matrimonial relationship. It was felt that there was a need to mark a precise moment as a starting point for the marriage; that moment was given a place to which none of the others could aspire, and it owed its importance neither to its intrinsic nature nor to the effectiveness of its role in the establishment of the new family, but simply to the fact that it was agreed to assign to it that quality. Now, the *deductio* was a token reminder of ancient marriage by abduction. It lost all justification and all significance as the habit of looking upon the spouse as an equal and a companion was increasingly cultivated. The customs that were linked to it became ever-simpler ceremonial rituals. On the other hand, those that corresponded to the marriage by purchase became preponderant. From the moment that agreement between the parties could be considered definitive, the marriage was looked upon as conclusive. Depending on the peoples, it is either to the *sponsio* or to the *traditio* that this desired effect applied. The first system is Greek, the second is Roman. The *deductio* was maintained with its ancient characteristics only to the extent that the old religious law persisted under the civil law.

The family. The family in the case of the ancient Aryans is a community that includes parents, children, slaves, and domestic animals. At its head is the father. But the father has very different rights over the slaves and the animals, on the one hand, and over the free people, on the other. Over the first, he has property rights; over the second, he has only the authority that pertains to the administration of common matters (οἰκονόμος—administrator). Such is the sense of the *potestas* of the Latins; it is the power by virtue of which the family is governed. But this government is monarchical; everyone, regardless of the diversity of their status, must equally submit to it.

Now, in this connection, civil law gave rise in Rome, and in Rome only, to a profound transformation. There the free members of the family fell to the level of slaves and of things; they became the object of an actual law. In Greece they were simply subjects μοναρχοῦνται [i.e., they were ruled by a king]; in Rome they were dependencies of the father *(sui)*. [35] If the manners preserved many of the ancient customs, the law properly speaking made a radical break with them. It is from this particular situation of the father that all the other peculiarities of the Roman family derive—notably those concerning the right to succession. In the event that the father is only the administrator of community property, he may not dispose of it freely, neither during his lifetime nor afterwards. On the other hand, if he is personally the proprietor of the family patrimony, his right to part with it, to disinherit his children, becomes entirely natural.

As for the explanation that Leist gives of this original character of the Roman family, it is the simplest one. The fact is that the Romans occupied Latium as conquerors; the land was then shared between them *viritim*, [36] and the chief of each family community received a portion. Accordingly they made up an aristocracy; and as they all were *patres,* the class they formed took the name of *patricii.* But, like all armies, they lacked women; they therefore had to go fetch some from within the families of the subject peoples. Naturally those women found themselves in relation to their husbands in a situation of inferiority and dependency, akin to that occupied by slaves; and the same subordination fell to the lot of the children born of those women. This, it seems, had been the chief source of the *patria potestas,* such as the Roman jurists conceived of it. [37]

The origins of civil law. From the family there issued, by way of spontaneous extension, the *gens* of the Romans, the phratry or the *curia,* finally the tribe. These different groups, while being established with a view to warfare and while having for that reason a military character, were above all based on consanguinity and kinship. Only, kinship was looser and more indeterminate to the degree that the circle of association was more extensive; that is why it was at its lowest point in the tribe. Among the ancient Aryans, social organization went no farther. Different tribes lived side by side without having between them any durable bonds, except when the need to struggle against a common enemy obliged them to confederate. As long as societies remained in that condition, the law remained in its original primitive state.

But, little by little, under the influence of different causes of which the principal one was doubtless war, the relationships between neighboring tribes became more regular; the confederations assumed a more stable character. In a word, new societies came into being that swallowed several earlier societies and integrated them as their elementary parts; the new powers that were established and superimposed in this way on those who headed the isolated tribes became the source of new legal institutions. This transformation is not peculiar to Aryan societies; there is no people that did not take shape in this manner. But this is how that change was peculiar to the Aryans: The fact is that the ancient social divisions were not absorbed by the new organization. They were maintained more or less intact, whereas elsewhere (in Egypt, for example) they disappeared completely. In Rome, in Greece, and in Germania,[38] the society remained divided into tribes, phratries, *curiae,* or similar groups. Now, these groups were nothing more than enlarged families, organized on the model of the family itself. The result was that the state reproduced the same model; the political constitution was a reflection of the domestic constitution.

That explains the new characteristics of the law appearing at the time. The father of a family, among the Aryans, was not a sacred being, invested with a religious authority that raised him infinitely above the other members. He was a mere representative of the community. He was not a god, but simply a respected master; moreover, he could not make any important decision without the cooperation of the family that he headed. The same, therefore, was to apply to the heads of the nascent state. And indeed, everywhere, their authority was limited by that of an aristocracy more or less widespread or even by the people as a whole. Nowhere did they have that sacrosanct character that oriental monarchies attributed to their kings. As a result, the new powers that appeared at that moment could not fail to be secular, as well as the law they established. That law was civil law.

Thus civil law apparently was not an outgrowth, by way of development, of common and religious law; rather, it seems to have been derived from different sources, each of which must have had its special agencies. Archaic law had as its terrain the tribe, with its divisions into phratries, *gentes,* and families; civil law must have been created by the coalescence of several tribes into larger societies, and it must have emanated from new social forces that emerged from this coalescence. These two forms of collective life are even presented in a state of antagonism existing everywhere. Therefore, the same goes for the two corresponding kinds of law. Civil law *(jus)* is not a prolongation of religious law *(fas);* [39] rather, the first superimposed itself on the second, caused it to regress little by little, and finally almost totally covered it up; for the new law was not applied solely to the new relations determined by the new state of affairs, but it encroached upon the ancient versions, suppressing more and more the law which had operated for centuries. It is especially in Rome that the antithesis between these two legal conceptions is evident, since in place of the ancient organization of kinship, so directly based on the nature of the family, there was substituted another that was totally different and entirely created by the state—that is, by the city-state and for the needs of the city-state.

Such are the conclusions of this book; they obviously belong to an original mind which has sought to fashion a pathway in the history of law on its own personal terms. We do not think, however, that they can be directly put to much use by sociology. The author tackles these problems in too formalistic a spirit: He is too inclined to view law as a reality in itself, not as something issuing from the entrails of society but as its dominant factor, one that is separated from the other manifestations of collective life by an abyss. As a result, it is impossible for him to perceive the causes that have determined the evolution of law. It has been noted how simplistic his explanations are. But since he has spent his life on intimate terms with Roman law, he has a very keen feeling for the distinctive characteristics of law in general and of Roman law in particular; and he does his utmost to communicate with his readers, even though too unwary of the risk of tedious repetitions. (*Année sociologique*, 1, 1898, pp. 333–338; trans. J. French)

I. von Ačimovic. "Übersicht des serbischen Erbrechts, im Hinblick auf eine Reform desselben" (Summary of the Serb Inheritance Law as Reflected by the Introduction of a Reform). *Jahrbuch der internationalen Vereinigung für vergleichende Rechtswissenschaft und Volkswirtschaftslehre*, 1897, pp. 106–135.

The Serbian legislature in 1844 undertook to codify the domestic law by adapting it to the new conditions of social life. But it is based on wrong principles, for the legislature has considered *zadruga* and *inòkosna* [40] as two absolutely distinct forms of family organization; and this distinction has become the basis of inheritance law established by this legislation. In fact, these two types of family are similar. Both of them are based on domestic communism. They differ only in size. The *zadruga* family consists of all the collateral relatives, even those who are far removed, so long as they live together; whereas the *inòkosna* family includes only the father, the mother, and the children. But in neither of the two family organizations is the father the owner of the common property. He cannot dispose of it without the consent of his children. He is not even its legal administrator. He can be dispossessed of his functions and can be replaced. This has already been established by Bogišić in his work *De la Forme dite inòkosna de la famille rurale chez les Serbes et les Croates* (Paris, 1884). Having misunderstood this fundamental identity, the Serbian legislator has instituted two different laws of inheritance, whose application, as a result, gives rise to insoluble conflicts. The only way to eliminate the conflicts is to place the legislation in harmony with the real state of things.

The reader may as well make a note of the method followed in this article. The practical reforms suggested by the author are not dialectically deduced from the juridic principles, but are based on an objective study of morals (*moeurs*) and popular customs. (*Année sociologique*, 1, 1898, p. 339; trans. Y. Nandan)

Heinrich Cunow. "Die ökonomischen Grundlagen der Mutterherr-schaft" (Economic Bases of Matriarchy). *Die Neue Zeit,* vol. xvi, no. 1, 1897–98.

The object of this work is to verify, on the basis of a particular case, the general principle of economic materialism: Economic causes have probably given rise to the matriarchal family.

The motivating factor for this explanation may be found in an assumption set forth by Cunow in the pages of an earlier work (*Die Verwand-schaftsorganisationen der Australneger*), according to which the principle of uterine filiation was probably established only at a relatively advanced period in history. Among the most primitive societies that we are familiar with (Australian tribes), the social structure assumes one or another of the following three forms: (1) the rudimentary segment, which is repetitive, constitutes the sum total, is a purely territorial group, and acknowledges lineal descent through the male only; (2) there is, at the same time, a totemic group—in other words all the inhabitants of the same district are, in addition, bearers of a common totem, and in this case the totem is transmitted through the male line; (3) there are two groups, one territorial and the other totemic, which do not coincide; the same district includes individuals who bear different totems, and in this case the totem is transmitted on the female side whereas the district is organized according to the male line of descent. But, according to Cunow, it is the territorial grouping which probably represents the primitive factor; the totem probably appeared only subsequently and it presumably adhered to the female line only later on. The author even rates this unilateral transmission as of no importance whatsoever. As for Curr, [41] he sees in it merely a way to prevent incestuous unions between relatives on the maternal side; such usage, therefore, would have no significance from the point of view of family organization, and accordingly, it should not be concluded that there was at this moment a maternal or matriarchal family.

The latter was probably not instituted until much later. It is discovered, but only in its infancy, in New Britain, in New Ireland, and in the Solomon Islands; but it is only among the Indians of North America, and especially among the Hurons and the Iroquois, that it has been highly developed. There under the same roof lived extensive groups of relatives, all descended through the women from a common ancestral female. The household possessions and chattels were inherited from the maternal line. It was to the women that the running of the household was entrusted, and they even exerted great influence on the course of public affairs. Now, the Hurons and the Iroquois are much more advanced people than the Australian tribes. The matriarchy, therefore, was doubtless a sign of progress. Most likely it had its origins in the advent of agriculture. When agriculture begins to make its appearance, it is attended to by women. The man hunts, fishes, does battle more or less at a distance from the household. The woman stays home by herself, busy with the cultivation of the land. She thus acquires more economic importance, and as a result, more social value. So then the father insists on keeping his daughters on his premises; he parts with them as brides only for a very high price that not everybody can pay. Under such conditions, the man is obliged to approach his wife in order that the union of the sexes may be possible. It is in the wife's house that the children are born, and for that reason they very naturally follow their mother's social example; that is how the situation of the feminine sex, generally speaking, finally becomes preponderant. But when agriculture goes beyond this inferior stage, men's cooperation becomes necessary; it is the men themselves who take the upper hand. Then the matriarchy is succeeded by the patriarchy.

Cunow would have been less facile about ending with this explanation if he had not completely misunderstood the importance of the totem and of the totemic group. Far from being a conventional sign only, the totem is the symbol of religious life; and religion knows no bounds when extending its sway. As a result, the transmission of the totem through the female line is of capital importance for the constitution of the primitive family; wherever it occurs, it testifies to the existence of uterine clans. And since it is much more frequent among the most primitive societies of Australia, everything combines to prove that it is the primitive factor, that originally the clan was organized exclusively according to the female line of descent. So then, if long before the advent of agriculture the child followed his mother in everything concerning the most essential social relations, the uterine line of descent is not due exclusively to agricultural civilization. What is true is that, in the case of the American Indians, the source of this line of descent is, as it were, reinforced. It is not observed any more frequently than in Australia, but whenever it is observed, it is less contaminated by any compromise with the contrary source. As for the Australians, even if the child adopts the maternal totem, it is with his father and under the domination of his father that he lives. In America, he stays with his mother, within the family where the latter was born. Jurisdictional ties with the father do not exist or become secondary in importance. Within these limits, Cunow's remark is justified. Now, how does this reinforcement come about? Is it to be attributed to the greater economic value that the woman may have assumed? But among the American Indians as in Australia, war and hunting remain the most important occupations, so it cannot then be a question of a kind of decadence in the male. Then too, marriage by way of exchange (the husband giving his sister in exchange for his wife), so widely practiced in Australia, would have easily permitted each family to keep intact the rate of turnover in its female population. Isn't it more likely that the reason for the phenomenon must be sought in a strengthening of the very causes that produced it, but in a less prominent form, with the inception of the uterine clan? From this moment on, the clan of the young woman tends to keep her, and very frequently even lets her leave only under duress. Now, the family groups that we find among the American Indians, and where the characteristics of the maternal family are so marked, have a much sharper sense of their unity, of their individuality, than the Australian clans. Could not this be the reason why they are more energetically opposed to a rift which presents a constant threat of becoming permanent? (*Année sociologique,* 2, 1899, pp. 315–318; trans. J. French)

Maksim Kovalevski. "L'organizzazione del clan nel Daghestan" (The Organization of the Clan of Daghestan). *Rivista italiana di Sociologia,* May 1898, pp. 279–301.

The tribes of Daghestan reveal the greatest diversity as much from an ethnic as from a linguistic point of view; yet the juridic organization is everywhere the same, further proof of which inheres in the fact that it is independent of the anthropological factor. The basis of this organization is the clan (*tukhum*), or at least so the author calls it; we will have certain reservations to propose concerning this word.

The clan is a group of agnate relatives; the duties and the rights which link its members (vengeance for blood brothers, collective responsibility) do not extend to uterine relatives. The group thus formed constitutes a collective individuality, very jealous of itself; possessions and individuals which become part of it can no longer have an easy way out. The property cannot be sold to strangers; the individuals cannot simply, at their own pleasure, change clans. Therefore, marriages are concluded as a general rule between members of the same clan (pp. 284, 287). Most often, all relatives ad infinitum are members of the clan; at times, however, kinship relations beyond a certain degree cease to have this effect.

The organization is democratic; the chief is a *primus inter pares* whose sole right is little more than the right to admonish. He can do nothing without the cooperation of the assembly, whose resolutions must be agreed upon unanimously in order to be valid. This is notably the case for adoptions—which are frequent and which at times even involve entire families—and disbarments. The author gives us a description of the ceremonies which take place in these two sets of circumstances (pp. 295 ff). For adoptions, reference is made to the usage of a communal banquet, which shows the primitive religious character of the operation.

The main duties and rights are: the vendetta, contractual safeguards, and the obligation to serve as supportive witnesses for one another in court. In case of war, the members of the same clan march together (p. 298). But economic life has ceased to be communal. Even the duty of assistance is purely optional (p. 297).

However interesting these facts may be, we fear that they do not relate to an organization which can, without distortion, be called a clan. Indeed, the clan is not any fairly widespread group of relatives. Quite the contrary, to be a participant in one, consanguinity (actual or by adoption) is not necessary. What is essential is the name (*nomen gentilicium*). [42] The name symbolizes the entire organization of the clan; it is a sacred factor. Now, it does not seem in this case that it was all that important. Moreover, when the clan loses its family character, it does so in order to become a village. We therefore wonder if the clan in Daghestan does not survive rather in the form of the village, as elsewhere, whereas the *tukhum* could be an aggregation of families that are related but locally distinct; the author himself points out certain communal characteristics in the organization of the villages (pp. 297 and 299 ff). The *tukhum* could therefore be, instead, an agnate family, like the Slavic *zadruga*, which no longer had its former material unity but which kept the memory of that unity. It probably broke up into several families, economically independant, but which had not forgotten their former solidarity. Now, it is common knowledge that the clan and the family of the *zadruga* type are very different institutions, although frequently confused. (*Année sociologique*, 2, 1899, pp. 318–320; trans. J. French)

Jean Smirnov and Paul Boyer. *Les Populations finnoises des bassins de la Volga et de la Kama* (vol. ix), *Etudes d'ethnographie historique*. Paris: Leroux, 1898, 486 pp.

We have analyzed above the parts of this book that have to do with religion;[43] herewith are matters relating to the family.

In the case of these two societies there is evidence in equal measure of traces of collective kinship—that is, of a family situation in which the relatives were distributed over wide generational levels. In fact, for each sex, a single identical word designates practically the entire group of older relatives (aside from the father, the mother, and a few others of this sort), and another such word designates all the younger relatives without distinction (pp. 114 and 336). According to the author, this terminology reverts to a period when the father could be wedded to his daughters-in-law; in actual fact, it simply serves to express the organization of the relationship peculiar to the clans (see *L'Année*, I, p. 313). [44] Indeed, the clan has left among these people memories that are still very vivid: The last political unit in the successive forms these societies took is likewise a religious community which reunites at banquets, holds assemblies, and contributes to family functions, notably in the event of marriage (pp. 128–130 and 353–356).

From these large family groups, others that are more limited have emerged little by little. Probably at a given moment the line of descent was uterine. This fact would seem to be proved by both the great freedom in sexual practices and the legal prerogatives, relatively favorable, which are granted to the woman. As for the signs that Smirnov believes he detects of a primitive hetairism, they seem to us to be inconclusive. One can conclude nothing from the fact that the same word designates the man in general and the husband (p.

116), the woman in general and the married woman. Doesn't our language offer the same peculiarity?

We are equally skeptical about the so-called tolerance with which incest was supposedly regarded over a long period of time (pp. 118 and 337–338). The author himself provides us with a fact which contradicts his thesis. He reports that the people who, on the wedding day, as stand-ins for the father and mother of the fiancée, brought her to the home of the husband, etcetera, felt themselves by that very fact joined to the girl by such close family ties that all marriages between their children and the children of the young couple were banned (p. 121). The fact is, then, that kinship provided an obstacle to marriage. Besides, the presence of symbolic abduction and of the purchase during the wedding ceremonies proves that as a rule the wife's family was different from the husband's. It is true that unions between brothers and sisters were apparently not unknown; but the way in which they were negotiated makes clear to us how these facts, seemingly contradictory, were reconciled, and they become more instructive. In order to permit a brother to marry his sister, the parents had recourse to the following expedient. The girl was sent forth to spend some time away from the house; upon her return, she was received like an outsider, and it was then that the marriage took place (p. 338). This practice simply proves that kinship, for the Mordvinians, was based on the factor of cohabitation under the same roof much more than on consanguinity. With cohabitation at an end, kinship disappeared and marriage became lawful. But incest, marriage between relatives, was not for that reason authorized. Kinship simply used to be conceived of differently from what it is today. (*Année sociologique*, 2, 1899, pp. 320–321; trans. J. French)

Stanislas Ciszewski. "Künstliche Verwandtschaft bei den Südslaven"
  (Artificial Kinship among Southern Slavs). Diss. Leipzig: 1897, 114
  pp.

This is an introduction to a book which will eventually be published[45] on the topic of artificial kinship in general. The priority thus accorded by the author to what concerns the Southern Slavs is justified by the fact that the Balkan region is a classic place for this sort of kinship.

Among these peoples, artificial kinship is achieved in three different ways.

(1) It arises without having been expressly willed by those whom it unites, by the sole effect of natural circumstances, even though purely accidental. Thus all those who are encountered in the same pilgrimage, all children who have been baptized in the same water (p. 6), those who have been nourished by the same wet-nurse, the best man and maid of honor in the same marriages are bound ipso facto by a very strict fraternity. In certain circumstances a simple material contact suffices to communicate kinship from one subject to another (p. 5).

(2) It is elective. Two people of the same sex or of different sexes agree to

take each other mutually as brothers or as brother and sister. At present, this kinship is contracted by way of a religious ceremony: They go to a church, hear a prayer, and receive a blessing from a priest. But this procedure is of recent origin; it is superimposed on ancient practices, which in the beginning were the only ones used. The proof that the church was not originally the agent by which the bond was formed is that the church fought against these customs. It was forced to give them a religious character, but they were born without its consent. Besides, they are found in a number of societies which are not Christian. It is thus beneath this superficial guise that one must search for the original formalities, and they are found still persisting today: a meal taken in common, wine drunk from the same glass, an exchange of presents, physical contracts (by way of kisses or otherwise) between the two people who are united. But there is above all one procedure which is particularly meaningful: the mingling of blood. For example, each of the two subjects allows some drops of blood to fall into one and the same glass of wine, which they drink afterwards. This is thus a form of *blood covenant*. The usage is so inveterate that on many points the church had to give its blessing.

Another equally important fact is that these kinds of ties are contracted, preferably, at certain periods of the year. These are the following: the fourth day of Lent among the Czechs; after Easter in Poland, in Little Russia, and in Serbia; the eve or the day of Saint John on the Croatian coast, in Bulgaria, and in Italy (pp. 41–60). All these dates coincide with the beginning of spring or the moment of the solstice.

To the same group of facts can be added a kind of artificial kinship which results, not from a real contract but from a species of quasi-contract. Whoever is in danger or simply in difficulty has only to appeal in these words to the first person he sees: "In the name of God, help me and I will take you for a brother." This is enough to establish fraternity. This usage seems, however, little known among the Slavs; but it is met with in a great number of societies, where it is often employed as a way of disarming the anger of an enemy under whose blows one is in danger of falling (p. 75).

(3) Finally, kinship can be concluded by the command of God or of a supernatural being. Two spouses whose family has been particularly tested, who have successively lost their children, or who have had twins repeatedly, consider these misfortunes as signs of the divine will and change their conjugal bonds into fraternal bonds. Of the same kind are the relationships of kinship contracted after a dream.

Under its different forms, the institution is waning today. But formerly, artificial fraternity was a stricter kinship than natural fraternity (p. 88). Two people who were bound in that manner owed mutual assistance and dedication without limits all their lives. They mourned for each other, they were bound to each other for the obligation of the vendetta; if they were of different sexes, not only were they forbidden to marry, but the prohibition extended to their own kin up to a degree more or less distant (p. 94). The author even speaks of a right of inheritance; but that fact seems to us unsubstantiated and we do not see clearly in what that right would consist, given the domestic communism of the Slavs.

This question of artificial kinship, very improperly called, is of the greatest importance. Its considerable development in inferior societies, which is shown in the fact that it is placed by opinion on the same level as natural kinship, testifies that, originally at least, kinship is not simply a result of the physical fact of consanguinity. If, on the other hand, one notices the religious character of the ceremonies by which artificial kinship is contracted, the religious nature of the feast in the course of which it is preferably contracted, or sometimes even that it is established spontaneously, one has the right to wonder if, by itself and in a general way, kinship is not an essentially religious thing, of which consanguinity may be the ordinary condition, secondary but not essential. (*Année sociologique*, 2, 1898, pp. 321–323; trans. J. Sweeney)

W. Marcais. *Des Parents et des alliés successibles en droit musulman.*
Rennes: 1898, ix + 198 pp.

The author first of all investigates the nature of the successional customs of the tribes of the Hidjaz before the promulgation of *sura* 4 (*"Ennisa"*) of the Koran, which made new rulings on the subject. This study is made especially with the information that the very numerous commentators on the sacred text have transmitted to us.

Contrary to what Wilcken has held, the old law declared women unable to claim succession. Again today, several close relatives of the deceased are deprived of any sharing of the inheritance (granddaughter, daughter of the daughter, nieces, aunts) (p. 15). As for the wife, she remained in the husband's family as an outsider; legally, she continued to belong to the family of her birth (p. 16). The possibility of her inheriting was therefore out of the question. Only the mother perhaps enjoyed in this respect a privileged situation (p. 21); her exclusion appears more doubtful. Finally, not only women but the relatives—whatever their sex—as well through their affinal relations with women, were affected by the same exclusion (p. 24). The only eligibles were then the male agnates called *asibs* or *akila*.[46] The adoptive brothers were assimilated by the *asibs*; the author gives us some interesting details on this conventional relationship (p. 27). This right, then, corresponds to a family organization resting on agnation alone. Even if, as Marcais believes, the transmission of goods to the group of agnates taken as a unit, without preferential treatment granted to the closest living relative, was a current practice, it should be conceded that the agnate family generally lived as coproprietors who take after the *zadruga* (p. 32).

It is this law that the Koran's body of laws modified. Women and certain relations through women were admitted among the heirs. They were entitled to a fixed portion (or *fard*), subject to change according to the relationship, and deductible before the apportionment between the other heirs. They were called accordingly heirs by *fard*. In any case, the ancient exclusive right of the *asibs* did not entirely disappear; it is still recognized in the important privileges that are assured to them. First of all, many women continued to be excluded (a daughter's daughter, nieces, aunts) (p. 15), and, among those related through wives, two only have become successional, uterine brothers and sisters and the maternal grandmother (p. 25). Once the heirs by *fard* have received their portion, the last of the *asibs* collect what is left. Moreoever, the very close *asibs* (in the line of descent through the father) exclude all the more distant heirs by *fard* (uterine sisters and brothers). Finally, when there is conflict between the two sexes, the male takes a greater portion by half (p. 37). Nevertheless an important reform has been accomplished.

To what influence must it be attributed? It cannot possibly be entirely the work of the prophet; "the individual rarely draws from his own resources the principle of reform itself" (p. 39). The explanation for this revolution is that the successional right in favor of the agnates applied to Medina and to the warring tribes, at a time when Muhammad was living in Mecca. Now, in Mecca, the family organization was very different. Traces of the matriarchal regime persisted very late, and for that reason the legal position of the women was very superior to what it was in Medina (p. 39). These ideas were introduced by Muhammad into the old law of Medina and in this way the new law was born. Under the sentimental influence due to the uterine organization of the family, the narrowly agnate organization receded.

The fact remains that the Muslim law of succession is made up of two superimposed layers; the law of the *asibs*, which is the most ancient, and the law of the heirs by *fard*, which is overlaid: since these two systems are of very different origin, they have had some trouble joining and merging with each other. Hence, there are all kinds of complications, the details of which come to light in the rest of the work.

The work is fashioned in accordance with the texts, and the author makes use of certain works on comparative law that were effectively used to shed a little light on the issues under discussion. (*Année sociologique*, 2, 1899, pp. 324–325; trans. J. French)

Alexandre Lefas. "L'Adoption testamentaire à Rome." *Nouvelle Revue historique de droit français et étranger*, 1897, no. 6.

Testamentary adoption is adoption by means of a will: The testator adopts as his son the heir he designates. This practice was very widespread in Greece. Lefas has no trouble establishing that it was not unknown to the Romans, even though the contrary thesis has been upheld by certain historians. It is indeed certain that texts speak of an *adoptio testamentaria*,[47] and in a certain number of cases it has been established that this *adoptio* created a genuine affiliation (pp. 730 ff). But, at the same time, there is no doubt that this adoption was in a full state of decline as early as the end of the eighth century. The factor that made it useless was to begin with the admission of heredity as a purely testamentary matter. From the moment that the title of son was no longer indispensable in order to legalize the transmission of personal identity with and on behalf of the cult of the family, one was content to designate an heir without adopting him. It is true that the beneficiary of the will did not bear the name of the deceased and thus the pure and simple designation did not fulfill all the objectives of the *adoptio testamentaria*, which had the advantage of assuring the perpetuation of the *nomen*. But this drawback was circumvented by the practice of the *conditio nominis ferendi:*[48] The testator could make his last provisions valid on condition that the designated heir should bear his name. Therefore testamentary adoption disappeared because it was frittered away into those two institutions that complemented each other: the *conditio nominis ferendi* and testamentary heredity.

The last part of the study brings out the analogies that are present in the *adoptio testamentaria* and adrogation. Adrogation was the form used for adoption when the one adopted was *sui juris*. It could only transpire *lege curiata;*[49] the desire alone of the parties concerned was not sufficient. Now, the same applied to the last case of testamentary adoption and the most famous one known to us: that of Octavius by Caesar.

This work's sociological interest is as follows. If testamentary adoption disappeared to the degree that pure and simple testamentary inheritance was practiced more freely, it is then a fact that the first institution preceded the second. Adoption is the primitive fact, the legacy the derivative act: In order to establish itself, it first took the form of an adoption. Being unable to designate an heir, one adopted a son through post-mortem provisions. Testamentary adoption and testamentary inheritance were the probable evolutionary phases in the course of which the right to make a will was established. And this is also the evolution from which came the authority of the family's father; for the right to make a will is one of the principal points involving the *patria potestas*. In fact, it is certain that in Athens testamentary adoption clearly had this derivation; it stood in place of the designation of the heir (see Hermann, *Lehrbuch de Grieche, Antiq*, II, Part 2, pp. 63 ff.). The comparison between the *adoptio testamentaria* and the *adrogatio* [50] confirms these views, if, as we believe, the *adrogatio* is the primitive form of the *adoptio*[51] for the most part. (*Année Sociologique*, 2, 1899, pp. 325–327; trans. J. French)

George Cornil. "Contribution à l'étude de la *patria potestas.*" *Nouvelle Revue historique de droit français et étranger*, 1897, pp. 417–485.

The object of this article is to demonstrate that the *patria potestas* of the Romans was not that despotic and harsh authority for which Roman law has been held, at times, to be criminally responsible. In order to establish his thesis, the author reviews successively the chief facts which make this so-called despotism appear most obvious:

(1) *The exposure of newborn infants*. This practice was much more fre-

quent in Greece than in Rome. Moreover, it did not stem from paternal power; it involved, on the contrary the refusal of the genitor to receive the newly born infant into his family and, as a result, to acquire over him the *patria potestas*. The exposures did not take place arbitrarily, but for serious reasons, such as congenital debility and religious reasons. What is more, the exposed child was not, even on that account, doomed to die; charitable people would at times give it a home. The author, however, acknowledges that these unfortunate children also fell into the hands of unscrupulous and wretched people. Lastly, the exercise of this law was very soon regulated, subjected to inspection, and finally banned; but the ban never did succeed in radically suppressing such an inveterate practice.

(2) *The sale of children.* It likewise existed in Greece. Besides, texts show that it generally took place only in the case of abject poverty. The child sold off did not become a slave; such at least was the rule during the Imperial Age. The author admits that it was likewise the case under civil law, when the sale had not taken place *Trans Tiberium*,[52] that is, in foreign lands.

(3) *The power of life and death.* This right applied only if the child had committed a crime against the state or against family honor. Never did the father have the option arbitrarily to kill the persons subject to his authority. Public opinion surveyed attentively the way in which this right was carried out, and if need be, the censor would intervene. Lastly, the father could condemn only after having consulted a tribunal made up of parents and of close relations (*consilium necessariorum* or *propinquorum*).[53]

From this discussion the author concludes that "the dominant trait of paternal authority in Rome was, in reality, indulgence and solicitude" (p. 467). From the start the father had obligations that were purely moral, not legal (p. 474). The author perceives, moreover, that the revolution that gave them a legal character effectuated more of a relaxation than improvement in morals (p. 475).

Although relying on texts, the study has the serious flaw of being more apologetical than historical. It is a question of combating those who are systematically disparaging Roman law (p. 416); the result is that the tone smacks a little too much of special pleading. To be sure, paternal authority was a powerful counterweight in matters of morals; Ihering proved this a long time ago. But it has nonetheless specific characteristics that bring diversity to our notion of morality, so much so that it is as vain to attack it as it is to defend it. It is enough to understand it and to see what justifies it in the social context where it is to be found. Its most characteristic and also most considerable qualities are, besides, entirely omitted in this work—namely, the right to receive into the family and to maintain there only whomsoever the father wishes. All the family relations have their primary source in the will of the *paterfamilias*. Let him refuse *tollere liberum*,[54] and the child is not the brother of his brothers, and agnate of his agnates; and at all ages, emancipation had the same results. There we have a peculiarity that may be observed in a small number of societies only and that attains in Rome its greatest growth. No doubt it is possible to believe that fathers did not use this authority lightly, but it existed nonetheless. Now, it was that quality which truly distinguished the *patria potestas*. (*Année socioligique*, 2, 1899, pp. 327–328; trans. J. French)

William I. Thomas. "The Relation of Sex to Primitive Social Control." *American Journal of Sociology*, May 1898, pp. 754–776.

All familial evolution may be placed under the dependence of two organic factors which act in inverse directions and are combined in different proportions: the physical ties which unite the child to the mother and the physical and mental superiority of the man which renders him more fit for functions of relationship. Where the first is dominant, it tends to make the wife the center of the family because it is around her that the children gather. The second, on the contrary, has the effect of placing the power in the hands of the husband; but he only has influence in the measure in which the functions of relationship play an important role in individual and social life. Now, in inferior societies, where private or collective activity is languishing, these functions are secondary. The result is that the natural supremacy of the husband is partially held in check; from this arose the principle of uterine filiation and the matriarchate. But the situation reverses itself to the extent that the development of society, in necessitating a stronger governmental organization and a more active life, opens to the characteristic qualities of the husband a field of action which is extended indefinitely.

The author is perfectly right in completely separating the question of uterine filiation and that of promiscuity in the sense intended by Bachofen. It is likewise very certain that it is the development of societies which determines the institution of filiation in the paternal line. Now, are the causes of that revolution as simple as Thomas believes? It is sufficient to notice that one finds the principle of paternal filiation established in very inferior tribes of Australia. The author, in an effort to explain this fact, is obliged to admit that in these societies, no domestic organization has yet succeeded in establishing itself; this would hinder the wives from acquiring the prestige which they have in the uterine family. But this hypothesis is gratuitous. Thomas has likewise very inaccurate ideas of totemism: He claims it is "one of the means men may have used to escape from the tyranny of a maternal system" (p. 774)—even though, in the beginning, the totem was transmitted by the women. (*Année sociologique*, 2, 1899, pp. 328–329; trans. J. Sweeney)

Carl N. Starcke. *La Famille dans les différentes sociétés*. Paris: Giard et Brière, 1899, ii + 273 pp.

The title of this book badly defines its contents. It is not a matter of a comparative study of family-type organization in different societies. The author's objective is rather to show the justifications for our present-day domestic morals, as well as the way in which they appear destined to develop in the future. But he supports, if need be, his explanations and his forecasts with facts taken from history or ethnography of the family.

The entire work is dominated by the following idea: The family is the proper place of the individual. Insofar as he lives outside and mingles with his fellow citizens, man is subjected to a code of ethics according to which the unique objective is to safeguard society's interest. But "inside his house, he lives as he pleases; the tribe or the state does not demand anything of him or regulate his behavior." Domestic morals "always reflect the individual will." It does not follow, however, that customs must necessarily vary radically from one home to another; the facts show that a certain homogeneity is generally accepted, especially in the beginning. But this does not come about because each family complies with a rule that is external; the cause lies simply in the similarity of everyone's needs and circumstances and in the force which the society exerts at the primitive level. Not only is this individualism supposedly characteristic of the family of all times, but it presumably is more pronounced today than formerly. No doubt the family can be considered from another viewpoint. On the one hand, for the very reason that it involves a communal life among several people, each of its members is obliged to take into account the others and the requirements of the little consortium that is formed in this way. In another sense, the state has never lost all interest in domestic relations; the family has always been, in varying degrees, an institution subordinated to political necessities. But this dependence of the individual on the family group, or of the group on something superior to and higher than itself, tends to lessen and disappear progressively. More and more, the organization of the family becomes "a private affair determined by the individuals themselves, merely protected by and not required to conform to the authority of the state" (p. 7). There are moral needs and other interests of the individuals constituting the family. They alone determine and ought to determine its normal constitution. One should not, then, start with the family by considering it as a rounded whole, but should examine, successively, each of its elements and consider what is implicit in each one of them.

From this point of view, the people who should be taken into consideration before all the others are the ones who found the family—that is to say, the husband and wife. Now, their relationship may be formed in two different ways: marriage or free union. Where does the legal and moral priority that the first union enjoys with regard to the second come from?

On the basis of the assumption the author has made, the reason for this preference can only be found in the different nature of the feelings that the two sexes have for each other according to the way in which they have become united. A free union, contracted without mutual commitments, is motivated uniquely or chiefly by sexual desire. The man, in this case, desires in the woman only what can satisfy his senses; but he does not desire her character, everything that has to do with her spirit, with her will, etcetera. For if he loved her wholeheartedly, he would unite with her wholeheartedly, he would make her his lifelong companion, his wife. As a result, in this type of union the woman is considered in one aspect only, and her secondary aspect at that. In this way she lowers her dignity, and she cannot accept this disrespect, which is an outrage, without failing in her duties towards herself, without abdicating her sense of dignity. Marriage is therefore the only form of sexual union to which the woman can give her consent without debasement; for it is only in marriage that she plays out her role as a human being, in her complete fulfillment. But it is not only the moral superiority of marriage that may be justified in this way; by the same token, its distinguishing characteristics are explained. Indeed, it excludes the very idea of infidelity, since this last implies a free union and since these unions are immoral. For the same reason, monogamy is the only form that suits its purpose.

If such is the justification of marriage, the legal formalism that presently envelops the wedding ceremony and that determines its validity becomes, it would seem, rather difficult to explain. All that matters is that the newlyweds make their intention known in a manner that expresses their complete lifetime unity and is manifested through lawful commitments. Thus they give authentic expressions to their intentions. But why is it necessary that they should be obliged to express their consent in a form determined by the state? Starcke manages, however, by a devious route to find some justification for the obligatory ceremonies. They are the best way to forestall any confusion between the free union and the other kind. Now, the law is authorized to establish as a principle that whoever enters into matrimony with firm intent owes it to the other party to do everything possible to make sure that no doubt will arise about the nature of the union formed (p. 98). The author is inspired by the same eclectic spirit when offering a solution to the problem of divorce. Since marriage is based solely on the inclinations of the parties, one must anticipate the occasion when these inclinations would be altered to such a point that the *consortium totius vitae*⁵⁵ would cease to exist in fact. But, in another sense, "since the marriage vow is inherently irrevocable by its very nature" (p. 103), the legitimacy of divorce "has its limitations: The sanctity of marriage itself must not be violated by giving too much leeway to the individual caprice" (p. 116).

After having dealt in this way with marriage, the author passes on to the relationship of the wedded couple in the course of their married life. He points out that the legal inferiority of the wife is no more than an outmoded survival of ideas that are disappearing. Moral equality of the two sexes must be sanctioned by law. The unity of the family will not be compromised because of that, just as the unity of the state has not been undermined by substituting democratic liberalism for monarchical autocracy. Since the wishes of the married couple are supposed as a rule to be conciliatory, it is not necessary to organize all domestic society with a view to eventual discord. Consider, for example, the particular degree of intensity of feeling in the lover, due to the difference that exists between the two sexes, from the mental as well as from the physical point of view; a weakened relationship cannot be the result simply because such spouses become partners; for this equality would in no way exclude a sharing and a differentiation, even a marked one, in family functions. As for the economic relationship between the spouses, the author's thought does not emerge with perfect clarity. He compares the regime involving joint holdings and the regime of separate ownership; the first is of Germanic origin, whereas the second applies more particularly to the Romanic countries. His preference evidently favors the community, and by that he means a common administration and common property. But he realizes that, practically speaking, such a common administration can run into difficulties.

It is only in the forth and last part of the work that children and their relationship with parents come under consideration. If relations of this kind are thus relegated to the background, it is because they actually have today only a secondary importance in home life. It is the married couple that has become the center of the family. The children, whose role was formerly preponderant, are now nothing more than a happy addition to and natural complement of marriage. The husband and wife unite in order to unite, and not in order to procreate. Put differently, it follows that the children are not there for the parents, but for themselves. That is why former conceptions according to which the parents would be invested with a sort of proprietary right, with an inborn authority, over their children no longer apply to the present way of life. The father is no longer for his family the sacrosanct personification of the impersonal and eternal patriarch; he is no longer anything but a human being confronting other human beings who are younger than he. There is therefore no room for anything more than a feeling of mutual affection. It is this affection that tends, more and more, to determine the way in which they ought to behave towards one another, and no longer that indefinable reverential fear for what used to be called the majesty of the father of a family. Such liberalism would necessarily seem to entail the disapproval of the legacy *ab intestat*[56] and especially of the binding type of inheritance. For if there are between members of the family no other ties than the ones that derive from their mutual affection, how can they be under obligation towards each other in spite of their feelings? It is truly amazing to see that Starcke piles clever dodges of fine distinctions in order to escape this natural consequence of his premises.

If we have deemed it useful to give a few details about the content of this work, it is not because we saw in it a scientific theory of the contemporary family. As a matter of fact, the arguments alleged to support the conceptions that are revealed to us are generally devoid of objective validity; facts are scarce and examined without method. This entire dialectic, which often degenerates into some slight subtlety, clearly seems to be there only in order to justify aspirations stated *a posteriori*. But since these aspirations are certainly not personal to the author, for they are to be found among a goodly number of our contemporaries, it is important to know about them; and simply by attempting to put them to some sort of tests, one cannot help becoming more fully aware of them and expressing them with greater clarity. That is what makes this book interesting; it is a document that shows us the way in which the cultivated minds of our time conceive of the family and its role in society.

In any event, there is a proposition basic to this entire system the inaccuracy of which must be brought to our attention. It is not true that the family is the only domain of the individual. There is no family outside the law, without domestic moral standards, and this law and these standards are imposed on the family group by the social surroundings. Each type of family is interconnected with a definite social type; the fact, then, is that it expresses something other than individual needs. And the more one advances in history, the more one sees the state intervening in the details of family life: the importance of its role, in this respect, is different from the way it was in Rome. It is true that at the same time, domestic moral standards are becoming less progressive for individuals; but it is the same with civic moral standards or with professional moral standards. The fact remains that in all spheres of social life individualism increases with statism. For to hark back to Rome, is it not the state which freed the son of the family from the authority, so burdensome at the start, of the *paterfamilias*? (*Année sociologique*, 3, 1900, pp. 365–370; trans. J. French)

Maurice Courant. "Les Associations en Chine." *Annales des sciences politiques*, 1899, no. 1, pp. 68–94.

In the course of an article on social groups [French: *associations*] in China, on which he spoke above from another point of view,[57] Courant gives us some information on familial organization in the same country.

It resembles the Roman organization. The children enter into the family either by legitimate filiation *accepted by the father* or by adoption. But the adoption applies only to males. The father has the right of sale over his children (p. 88). He has in his hands the patrimony; the adult sons possess nothing of their own, not even their salary, even though, by a singular anomaly, the slaves keep their earnings, a system that is respected by their masters. What establishes the comparison with the Roman family is that each family is a church and celebrates a special cult. This cult is only transmitted *per masculos;*[58] the wife plays a completely secondary role in the ceremonies. But here is what distinguishes the Roman *paterfamilias* from the Chinese: the father's right to administer and to dispose of what belongs to him as a head of the community more than as an owner. It is the collectivity of the family that owns the property; ordinarily, the father administers it in concert with the adult sons. Their signature is even required on the acts which concern the domestic patrimony (p. 89). The rights of the father are limited not only by those of his sons, but even by those of the paternal kinsmen. If he adopts someone, it is from among the paternal kinsmen and from them alone that the adopted person must be taken. Consequently, the property does not risk leaving the agnatic family. It is known that in Rome the powers of the father in that regard were not subject to this restriction. These facts are very interesting, for they permit us to determine exactly the phase of familial development at which the Chinese family is supposed to have arrived. It corresponds to a moment where the little group formed by the father and his descendants begins to separate itself from the agnatic community, without having yet completely succeeded, since the rights of the paternal kinsmen to the patrimony remain considerable; and where the power of the father is beginning to establish itself and to throw off the yoke of ancient family communism, but without that emancipation being complete, since the corporate rights of the sons are still recognized.

With regard to marriage, there are two kinds. One is a ritual which is only used for the spouse of the first rank; it places the wife in the hands of the husband as long as he has not repudiated her. The dowry enters into the patrimony. As for the other spouses, there is no ritual marriage; they are simply bought. (*Année sociologique,* 3, 1900, pp. 380–381; trans. J. Sweeney)

S. R. Steinmetz. "Die neueren Forschungen zur Geschichte der Familie" (Recent Researches on the History of the Family). *Zeitschrift für Sozialwissenschaft,* 1899, no. 10, pp. 685–695; no. 11, pp. 809–826.

It is the method used in this work that hinders research on the family. Up until now, the scholars who have concerned themselves with the question have been students of either folklore or ethnography. The former have sought primarily to rediscover the primitive forms of family life through the vestigial remnants that have survived in customs or latter-day legends. This is the method followed by Bachofen; without disputing its usefulness, the author has no qualms about warning against its abuses and the whimsical use to which it has been put.

Another procedure from the same school is the interpretation of parental nomenclatures; Steinmetz defends its legitimacy against Westermarck's criticism, actually very superficial. As for the ethnographic method, it is the one employed by Post, Wilcken, Letourneau, Bastian, Westermarck, and others. Its fundamental flaw lies in the assembling of facts from all sources pertaining to the social milieux of the most diversified civilizations, and in putting all these disparate data in the same category. The line of reasoning implies that all so-called savage or primitive peoples constituted one and the same social type.

The only method that can make real headway in dealing with the question is the sociological method. What distinguishes it is that it seeks to determine the relationship of the forms of family life and marriage customs with the other concomitant social conditions. Naturally we have no objections to this premise, which is the very one we have been defending for a long time. But we must make clear our distinct reservations about a secondary procedure that the author recommends, after having, moreover, put it to use himself, and to which he attaches great importance. He asks that each time one expresses a hypothesis, one should make a free and impartial exposition of the facts contrary as well as favorable to the law under consideration; on this point, of course, we can only share this feeling. But he claims the right, moreover, to make an exact enumeration of both points of view and to give true logical precedence to whichever of the two groups is found to be numerically superior. This mathematical precision is scientific in appearance only. It is essential to assemble, not lots of facts, but facts that are at one and the same time *typical* and *well* examined. One must not enlarge the field of comparison indiscriminately (which makes it necessary to settle for unfounded facts), but must limit it with discernment and method. The numbers game is too coarse a criterion to play the decisive role that is attributed to it.

In the second article the author discusses, in the light of the preceding principles, a certain number of recent theories about the following three questions: primitive promiscuity or collective marriage, exogamy, the maternal or matriarchal family. The discussion is summary, and the solutions toward which the author inclines are extremely sketchy. He appears to support the hypothesis of collective marriage, while declaring that the evidence that has been given as proof is insufficient; exogamy, according to him, can be explained chiefly by the advantages that it holds for the race and the internal order of society, a fact which will be reluctantly accepted by those who know to what point that institution, like everything that concerns the contract involving the sexes, is stamped with a deeply religious character. On the question of uterine filiation, the thought remains even more inscrutable. (*Année sociologique*, 4, 1900, pp. 340–342; trans. J. French)

Albert Cahuzac. *Essai sur les institutions et le droit malgaches,* vol. i.
   Paris: Chevalier-Marescq, 1900, 506 pp.
   The author, a counselor at the Court of Tananarive, has studied Malagasy law, less for the knowledge to be gained from it than to make the colony easier to handle under French justice.[59] Therefore, he is attempting to translate the legal concepts. Now, this translation, unavoidably inaccurate, often prevents the facts from emerging in their truest original sense, while at the same time these inaccuracies are bound to have a prejudicial effect on the observances of the law. Cahuzac seems, moreover, to be almost entirely out of touch with comparative law; he often singles out as uniquely peculiar to Madagascar certain institutions that are known to exist in many other countries (pp. 220, 249). The information he gives us needs, therefore, to be interpreted and searched for flaws; but it is informative, these reservations notwithstanding.

It is the study of the family that fills the greater part of the work. The domestic organization of the Malagasy people brings to mind in its essential features that of the Romans. Paternal power lasts during the child's lifetime, unless he has been authorized by the father to leave the house for the purpose of founding a new family (p. 46). It is the father who has the right to dispose freely of the family possessions. Yet the children can have possessions of their own over which the father has no rights (p. 50). How is this fact to be reconciled with the limitless duration of paternal power? The author gives us no explanation.

As in Rome, adoption is widely practiced. Choice in adoption is itself almost unrestricted. Children can adopt their parents, brothers can adopt their sisters, the husband his wife, etcetera. However adoption does not give rise to as many side effects as it did in Rome: the ancestral possessions of the adopter cannot be passed along to the adoptee (p. 223); the adoptee does not leave his natural family (p. 235); the parental tie thus contracted stops with the adopter and does not extend to the latter's relatives (p. 223). In line with this limitation of the effectiveness attributed to adoption, we are aware of the pockets of resistance from the old family-type communism that the introduction of the right of adoption always brings about to a certain extent; for the group naturally resists the fact that one of its members, of his own volition, is able to modify the common statute. But at the same time, this extreme facility of adoption shows to what degree parental kinship is distinct from consanguinity. The bond of parental kinship can, moreover, be broken in the same way that it can be contracted: Again, as it was in Rome, the father can throw out of the family the unworthy son, and when the father has died, the assembled family can exercise the same right (pp. 251 ff.).

Finally, the credit for achieving the reconciliation with the *patria potestas,* considered even at the time of its greatest power, lies with the father's absolute power as testator, at least in principle. In practice, a Malagasy does not use this power to disinherit his children, but to establish a principal beneficiary, to whom is willed a lion's share, to whom the other beneficiaries owe submission and respect, and who is himself charged with apportioning the succession at a time and in a way that best suits his convenience. The will, therefore, is not used to satisfy individual feelings, but to safeguard the noble character of the family, to prevent the patrimony from being dispersed or from falling into incompetent hands; it is a feeling for the closeness of the family that inspires the testator. Besides, as a matter of fact, for a very long period of time the family exercised a direct influence over the clauses of a will; for, in its primitive form, the will was made public. The whole family was privy to it, and even the village (p. 350). What is more, other indirect restrictions were brought to bear on the rights of the testator. There were possessions that belonged to the family jointly, even though the will was administered by one of its members; therefore they could not be transmitted by will (pp. 307 ff.). There were other restrictions whereby what was bequeathed was restricted to a member of the community or to a member of the tribe (pp. 378, 387). The fact remains that there is hardly any society outside of Rome where the testator's power has been as considerable—since the most ancient times (p. 337). This, therefore, serves as proof that the will makes its appearance when it is found to be necessary because of social conditions, without presupposing at the start an erudite juridical culture.

The conjugal society generally has the same degree of stability and cohesion as the family. The bond uniting parents is always in keeping with the bond uniting parents and children. Yet marital relations in Madagascar seem, in some respects, to be quite lax. Each spouse freely adminsters his or her possessions. The wife can dispose of her fortune without any authorization from her husband; she can make her will by law, bring actions of all kinds, etcetera (p. 185). Such a degree of independence is hard to reconcile, at first glance, with a very strongly unified domestic society. On the other hand, the wife remains an integral part of her native family and returns to it, once a widow, unless she marries one of her brothers-in-law (p. 225). Her ties with her husband's family seem, therefore, to be only loosely secured. But the way in which adoption is practiced is what resolves the contradiction. Very frequently the husband adopts his wife, who thus finds herself subject to his authority and becomes a member of the family circle within which marriage has assured her a place. One can see analogies with the Roman institution of the *justae nuptiae cum manu.*[60]

The Malagasy family is, then, to be found at that phase of domestic evolution where the small group formed by the oldest male ancestor and his descendants breaks away from the rest of the relatives, forms a separate entity, and identifies with the person of its chief. Without a doubt, the rights of a more remote kinship, the memories of a family-type communism, have not disappeared—but they are fading. In any case, in order to understand clearly the position in which one observes this organization today, it is befitting to add that most likely its form today has deteriorated from what it once was. Adoption is no longer simply a means of assuring the noble character of the family; it is made to serve in the settling of a simple matter of interested parties (p. 227). Despite the resources that this same adoption law provided, the bonds of matrimony appear to have become extremely fragile; marriage seems to have become "an absolutely temporary relationship" (p. 207). The fact is, no doubt, that the adoption of the wife is an outcome of old customs. Accordingly, it turns out that in Rome the *manus* ceased more and more to be superimposed upon the legitimate wedding; and the result was the licentious marriages that are a matter of common knowledge. Perhaps it is also this decadence of the family organization that explains the right of children to hold property of their own during the lifetime of the father, just as in Rome the son of the family's "nest egg" appears on the scene when the *patria potestas* starts to be undermined.

Outside the family, properly so-called, the author studies another group, which he calls the caste (pp. 50, 150). But we believe that the expression is used here in a most inappropriate way. Each one of these so-called castes quite simply, in accordance with the definition that is given to us, constitutes "a reunion of a certain number of families descended from a common forbear" (p. 51). Social functions are in no way distributed among the different castes, although such distribution is characteristic of the caste system. Custom requires even that very elevated functions (army chiefs, prime ministers) be recruited from those group members who most typify the common people (pp. 53–54). Then again, marriage between individuals of different castes is not always forbidden; the prohibition of marrying outside one's class is rather the exception (p. 150). It is, therefore, probably a simple matter either of clans or of a few groupings that are ethnic and political at one and the same time. There is confirmation of this fact in that each so-called caste has its territorial domain and is under a chief (p. 52). Now, among these clans there was introduced a kind of hierarchy, though the information the author gives us about it is very defective (pp. 53 ff.). (*Année sociologique*, 4, 1901, pp. 342–345; trans. J. French)

Arnold Escher. *Der Einfluss des Geschlechtsunterschiedes der Descen-denten im schweizerischen Erbrecht* (Influence of the Sex of the Descendant in the Swiss Inheritance Law). Zurich: Fried. Schulthess, 1900, 114 pp.

It is generally known that in barbarian laws the importance of successional rights varies according to the sex of the children: Sons have the advantage, especially in matters that concern patrimonial lands. This inequality disappeared quite rapidly in our French law, except for feudal fiefs. On the other hand, it has been maintained up until today among the majority in Switzerland. It is not that the successional right of women on general principle was not recognized very early, but for economic reasons attempts were made to restrict it to certain limits. It is quite hard to know what was done in this respect until the thirteenth century; sources have very meager information on this point. It is even very possible that in certain regions sharing as equals was permitted. But the beginning of the fifteenth century marks the start of a movement that grew continuously until the seventeenth, when it reached its apogee, and its aim was to favor the male sex. It was above all a matter of preventing the partitioning of family communities that were basic to the cultivation of farms; now, if the daughter, once married, had been able to inherit like the son, and especially inherit landed property, partitioning would have been inevitable for each generation. Therefore, the restrictive legislation of which we are going to speak was above all rural; towns very early showed themselves to be much more liberal (p. 31). As for the causes responsible for the fact that this movement hardly began until the fifteenth century, the author believes they are to be found in the exclusive character of the corporate organization, which barred the inhabitants of the countryside from trading and manufacturing by closing to them all openings other than farming, and thus piled them into villages, forcing them into extreme overcrowding in order to be able to live (p. 33).

This last procedure led naturally to a third that substituted the law's action for private arrangements. The law officially acknowledged certain advantages for sons. If they wanted to, they could claim bequests of land, except for the indemnity owed to their sisters; but the indemnity they owed them was calculated in such a way as to remain inferior to the real value of things (pp. 57 ff.). At times even, in the bequest as a whole, the rights of the sons were superior to those of the daughters; for example, in Lucerne the former received three-fifths of the whole. But in general they enjoyed this privileged situation only in the case of the paternal bequest, although on certain points the rule was extended to cover the mother's bequest (p. 67). In certain cases, the youngest son was especially favored: The *minorat* was for the people of the countryside what the right of primogeniture was for the nobility. Besides, even in the rural population, the *majorat* was in evidence; but at least in Switzerland, it was more rarely observed. Generally, the privilege of the youngest was to inherit from the paternal household (p. 79). This practice was explained by the rather frequent habit the father had of sharing in his lifetime the patrimony with his sons, except for the house, which he reserved for himself, and where he ended his days in the company of the youngest son (p. 80).

Sex had a different, more secondary impact on the law of succession: The furnishings that pertained more particularly to the person of the father—weapons, clothings, signet rings, library—were passed on to the sons; the mother's clothes and jewels went to the daughters (p. 86).

Not only are these various provisions, under different forms, still the law in the majority of the cantons, but it is probable that the principle will be preserved by the code that is in the process of being elaborated for the entire country. The author is of the opinion that it is indispensable for a flourishing agriculture. We have here an example of the influence that the state of the economy can have on the law. (*Année sociologique*, 4, 1901, pp. 345–347; trans. J. French)

Henri Auffroy. *Evolution du testament en France*. Paris: Arthur Rousseau, 1899, 770 pp.

This work, perhaps somewhat dense and diffuse, is rich in the carefully analyzed subject matter that throws some light on the nature, the origins, and the social function of the testamentary institution.

Very rightly, the author begins by defining what he proposes to study. He defines testaments as "the act by which the rights are created, transmitted, or abolished at the will of the deceased" (p. 6). Since it is axiomatic that man's abilities do not extend beyond the grave, it is conceivable that the idea behind such a deed made an appearance only belatedly. In fact, it calls for the realization of at least three fundamental conditions.

(1) Mankind must have arrived at a point where individual wishes are regarded with a certain respect in order for them to take effect even when the subject from whom they emanate no longer exists.

(2) Since the purpose of the will has generally been to dispose of certain matters in traditional ways, it is imperative that traditional connections established between the property of the deceased and certain fixed individuals

(related to a greater or lesser degree) be sufficiently weakened to permit the right to sever these connections voluntarily and to create others.

(3) Even though the right to make a will may be considered to be legitimate in principle and in theory, this is not enough for a society to establish such a right; it is also imperative that a sense of the need for it be sufficiently felt in general—that is to say, that there be a tendency to dispose of property in ways other than those habitually prescribed as traditional. Today, for example, to understand why the law concerning the making of a will has been freed by the last restrictions imposed on it by our code, it must be recognized that such restrictions were felt as inconvenient. In other words, a sufficiently large number of citizens should be able to fulfill their desire to leave their wealth to beneficiaries other than their children.

Among the ancient Germans none of these conditions was realized. Not only were the legal conceptions too crude to permit acceptance of a deed so complex and so exceptionally effective, but also the principle of joint family ownership proved to be radically exclusive. Tradition reigned supreme. Family claims on the patrimony permitted no one to arbitrarily dispose of it. Therefore, the making of a will was entirely unknown to the ancient Germans. The situation was practically the same under the regime of barbarian laws. This time the institution did not need to be invented, since the barbarians saw it at work under their very eyes within that Roman populace with whom they mixed. But it was still faced with the same obstacle in domestic law. To be sure, one finds among the *leges* [61] a few expedients that to a certain extent replaced the will, namely, the Frankish *affatomie* and the *thinx* of the Lombards. But in the first place, they were authorized only in cases where there were no children, or else if the surviving child had been justifiably disinherited. They included a kind of adoption, *adoptio in hereditate.* [62] Furthermore, they were, in fact, ''live''[63] transactions; the beneficiary came into possession of certain rights even during the donor's lifetime. Therefore they do not present the characteristic features of the will.

It is only under the Merovingians and the Carolingians that the need for new institutions made itself felt. The changes that had arisen in ideas and customs gave rise to this development. To begin with, a keener sense of justice and a more personal type of family relations helped mitigate in certain respects the rigidity of traditional arrangements that prompted a unique or almost unique concern for the domestic order *in abstracto*. Thus, it [no longer seemed] fair that owing to a nonexistent right to be represented, the grandson was left out of his grandfather's will when the former had to compete with surviving uncles. Nor did it seem right that the wife, so closely associated with her husband all her life, should be deprived of all claims to the succession; that the sons should, whatever the circumstances, be treated just alike, however unequal their merits. And in all such cases the aggrieved went out of their way in an attempt to evade the prescribed rules of succession (pp. 186–191). But a special inducement to do the smart thing to gain their ends motivated the faithful devotees to make liberal donations to the poor or to the religious establishments in order to assure their salvation in the event of death. This practice, appearing at the start of the third century, became widespread very quickly. It finally became an indispensable accompaniment to the performance of the last rites; as a general rule, the only exceptions were those who died without having confessed their sins (p. 377). Moreover, religious and civil sanctions made the practice holy; death without a bequest to charity often resulted in denial of Christian burial or partial confiscation of property, notably involving furnishings (pp. 379, 555). It is absolutely certain that such religiously inspired largesse was by far the most frequent and the most important type of its kind. And it would be a mistake to believe that donations were extorted from the dying person through violence or trickery; the faithful were deeply anxious to acquit themselves of their duty. The Christian conception of death and of riches inclined them naturally in that direction.

Given the fact that the Roman will had been well known for a long time and that it had been the means of satisfying those new aspirations, one expects to see it introduced into legislation from that time on. Now, as a matter of fact, it was accepted for this purpose after it lost its most distinguished attributes, fused with proper Germanic institutions, and became, as a result of such blending and alterations, something entirely new in nature. As a result, there arose a feeling of antagonism that was opposed to this altered amalgam which became acclimatized on our soil: The old principle of joint-family ownership, and the beliefs in the right of the parents, who vivaciously held on to the old moral customs, were side by side with the new moral beliefs. Consequently, the wishes of the donor always risked being held in check by the traditional claims of the surviving members of the family. When they were disappointed in their expectations, they would have no scruples about taking what was not theirs. Monastic archives abound in accounts of this kind of plunder (pp. 298 ff.). The disorganized state in which society found itself facilitated such acts of violence (p. 290). Under such circumstances, the testamentary institution could not exist, since it presupposes above all an absolute respect for the sovereign will of the testator; and the two opposing forces that thus found themselves coming to grips were to initiate new arrangements appropriate to this special situation.

It took shape in two ways. In the first place, provisions made for the eventuality of death took the form of provisions made in the midst of life. Through various procedures the beneficiary was, during the donor's lifetime, granted definite rights, with the understanding that he could not enjoy any of them until the donor died (pp. 279, 436). In this way these rights became, at the moment the donor died, an accomplished fact. Furthermore, in order to confirm that these rights were passed on to the living persons, it was customary to involve relatives and even friends, who gave their approval of the largest granted them. It seems clear that with time the tendency was to broaden more and more the cirle of these *laudatores*[64] (p. 468). It was thus arranged that the largesse of the deceased be vouched for by the family itself. The other procedure consisted of holding friends responsible for carrying out the terms stipulated and recorded at the time of death. In this way, the system of *testamentary executors* had its beginnings (pp. 307, 412). But here again, everything was enacted among the living persons. During the donor's lifetime the executor acquired [the responsibility] that would be his to exercise later, and it is he who, after the donor's death, would pass [largesse] along to the beneficiary.

It is only very slowly that people saw fit to admit that largesse could be granted or an executor created by a writ which would take effect only after the author's death, that is by a so-called last will and testament (pp. 422–436). Only after the eleventh century did such a renaissance of the testamentary principle appear on the scene. What made it possible was the ever more overriding influence that ecclesiastical courts assumed in judging issues raised by acts involving death. Since it was Mother Church that profited most often from these matters, and since it was she who settled the disputes which such largesse might have caused, she used her authority to her own advantage, to cultivate respect for the wishes of the deceased. The latter, now well assured against opposition by the legitimate heirs, no longer needed to surround themselves with the same protective formalities. And yet an attitude of defiance remained very much in evidence; for even in the thirteenth century, "live" operations involving bequests were still in frequent use (p. 594). In any case, one standard practice persisted to the very last: The will, [even] reconstituted, could not be used to establish an heir; the institution of providing an heir [in a will] definitely did not exist. It was originated in order to facilitate certain legacies; it had to be used for that set purpose only (pp. 566, 591).

The proof of this genesis of the testamentary principle in France is that despite the identical names, the institution never meant for us what it meant for Rome. Here are two entirely different legal realities. In Rome the purpose of the will was, in essence, to designate the heir—that is to say, the one who would continue the family line, who would succeed the testator in the magistrate's office that he was filling; it was a question not of making a gift but of assuring the perpetuation and prosperity of the family group. Incidental legacies could only fill a role that was completely secondary to the established practice of securing an heir. Here in France the former type of legacy is all-important; the will is a donation. Therefore the moral forces that govern its effectiveness are very different in the two cases. In Rome it is the legislative act that derives its authority from the impersonal sovereignty with which the *pater familias* is endowed. If the testator's will is respected, it is because he is the embodiment of the family and because what he wishes the family wishes. On the contrary, the French will is an individual act for the purpose of securing certain benefits for the testator (the salvation of the soul); and as a result the respect that is directed at his person stems from a reputable symbol recognized ever since then according to the will of the individual as such. The right to part with property that is acknowledged during his lifetime is simply extended beyond the grave. That is why, however confining this right of alienating the property may be, as much in this life as in the life hereafter, it attests to an individualism that is much more fully developed than the Romans' absolute testamentary law. (*Année sociologique,* 4, 1901, pp. 348-352; trans. J. French)

Edouard Lambert. *La Tradition romaine sur la succession des formes du testament devant l'histoire comparative.* Paris: Giard et Brière, 1901, 105 pp.

It is known that according to the tradition of the Roman jurisconsults the institution of the testament and of the freedom to make a testament went back to the period of the Twelve Tables. Many historians have already felt that this date is much too early, and recently Pais, in his *Storia de Roma (History of Rome),* proposed to make the date a century and a half later. Lambert reviews the question again. According to him, it does not suffice to modify the traditional date. No matter at what period the maxim (*Uti legassit . . . ita jus esto)*[65] attributed to the Twelve Tables was written, it is necessary to deny to the act envisaged the true nature of a testament.

His reasons are borrowed from comparative history. The testament could not have existed in the fifth or fourth century B.C. because it is never encountered in peoples who have not passed beyond the level of culture to which Rome had then attained. Two causes make this impossible. First, an act performed because of a death presupposes juridical concepts that are concepts too advanced—which societies have arrived at only very late. What takes the place of testaments in societies where civilization is not very advanced are acts between the living which produce definitive results immediately, and before the death of the alienator, as in the Frankish *affatomie* or the Lombard *thinx.* Secondly, the principle of the joint proprietary rights of the family is opposed to any one member of the family's being able to dispose arbitrarily of the patrimony. This liberty is permitted at most when the close relations, those who are regarded most directly as coproprietors, are nonexistent.

For these reasons, Lambert believes that the juridical act which the Roman jurisconsults regarded as the initial form of Roman testament—that is, the so-called comitial testament—did not in reality deserve this name. It was, he believes, an act which created immediate rights for the benefit of the recipient, rights which the donor could not later resolve at will because they had been consecrated by a legislative sanction. As for the rights of disposition, they were certainly limited, since otherwise the intervention of the *comitia* would not have been necessary. Now, it was, Lambert thinks, to this juridical operation that the *Uti legassit* precept applied; he believes it to have had the effect of simplifying the comitial testament by suppressing the inquiry of the pontiffs and the actual vote of the *comitia*. According to this view, from then on a simple declaration of the donor before the assembled people was sufficient; the intervention of the *comitia* was limited to a sort of registration. But this declaration, he thinks, continued to confer rights immediately on the designated heir. It was thus not yet, properly speaking, a testament. On the other hand, the liberty of disposal, although greater than before, was not complete except for goods belonging personally to the donor. Lambert interprets, indeed, the phrase *Uti legassit super pecunia* as if *pecunia* signified only movable goods situated outside the family patrimony. The latter, he believes, remained the necessary heritage of the legitimate descendants. It was only much later, according to Lambert, that complete testamentary liberty was established. Following the same method, the author attempts to reconstitute the rest of this evolution.

One must draw attention, first of all, as an interesting symptom, to this use of the comparative method to resolve a problem of Roman history. One must also give due regard to the conscientiousness and rich erudition with which Lambert has conducted his demonstration. As concerns his thesis itself, while it is very probable that in Rome, as elsewhere, the testament must have been preceded by juridical operations of a different nature, the reasons given to lower the date do not seem decisive to us.

In comparing the testamentary right of the Romans and that of medieval societies, we fear that one is comparing incomparable things. Our modern testamentary right was a victory over the old family communism, an extension of individualism; this is why it could not appear until the last memories of familial property held in common were sufficiently effaced. But in Rome the testament had a much different origin and signification. It does not respond to a sort of precocious desire which individuals may have had to distribute their fortune according to their personal sympathies rather than according to the abstract rules of family law; what gave rise to it was the necessity in which the Roman family found itself constituted as a unit. The Roman family concentrated itself entirely in the person of the *pater familias*, absorbed itself in him, and this is why the goods, rather than remaining the individual property of a group, became concentrated in the person of this sovereign personality. The testament was considered in Rome, not as the right of an individual, but as one of the attributes of the omnipotent domestic magistracy. In our societies the testament has been the result of a breaking up of the family; in Rome, it had as cause a concentration of the family of which there has not been the like in history. These two institutions, although designated by the same word, are thus in reality very different; they do not correspond to the same state of civilization and as a result one can not infer the history of one from the other. These remarks apply to the comparisons which have often been made between the Roman family and the Germanic family. They belong to two different types. (*Année sociologique*, 5, 1902, pp. 373–376; trans. K. Woody)

J. du Plessis de Grenédan. *Histoire de l'autorité paternelle et de la société familiale en France avant 1789.* Paris: Arthur Rousseau, 1900, ix + 625 pp.

The object of this book is to show how the French family was constituted, such as we find it on the eve of the Revolution.

Four elements, according to our author, served to form it: Gallic customs, the law of Germanic societies, Roman law, and especially Christian ideas. The first three, it would seem, are essentially of similar nature or distinguishable from each other only in differences of degree. Du Plessis de Grenédan believes—in fact, he rediscovers in Gaul and in Germania [66]—the same family organization as in Rome, that is to say, the patriarchal family. As for the Celts, he relies upon a text of Caesar according to which the father had *jus vitae necisque* [67] over his children and over his wife. One may find that the demonstration is somewhat short; but it is more dense in matters concerning Germania. The *mundium*[68] is presented to us as analogous to the *manus* [69]. As in Rome, the father can through death or through exposure, refuse to receive the newborn infant into the fmaily; he "opens and closes at will the door of the family house" (p. 83). His authority has the same absolute character as in the city-state; "he can dispose of everything that belongs to the family, persons and things" (p. 88).

Yet, in spite of their initial resemblances, the *mundium* and the *patria potestas* have played a role of very unequal importance in our family evolution. The fact is that in the long run these two institutions have become differentiated. The *patria potestas,* in the course of its development ended by exaggerating its original characteristics. It became exaggerated to the point of absorbing the entire life of the family into the sovereign personality of the father (p. 183). It became accordingly a rigid and accomplished institution, and consequently, not easily perfectible. The *mundium,* on the contrary, remained in Germania what it was originally—without essential changes. Thus it kept the resiliency that young institutions always have. Therefore, when Germanic societies came into contact with Christian ideas, it was able, thanks to this plasticity, to let itself be penetrated by the new spirit and to be spiritualized. At first it was only a rather brutal force; by itself it had nothing kindly to offer the weak to whom it was applied; the latter were protected only indirectly, in their capacity as subordinates. But Christian morality developed this element of protection. It taught the father that he had duties, that his children had rights, and it limited his authority. By teaching that woman is the equal of man, the equality of the mother in her relations with the father and of the sister in her relations with the brother diminished—and thus a new domestic law was established. The *mundium,* therefore, was presumably the germ that, made fruitful by Christian ideas, gave birth to our whole domestic organization. From this historical conception the author draws practical conclusions, which are not logically implied in it but which indicate the book's spirit. For

him, the ideal of the modern family is to remain true to its origins; and the entire movement which since the Renaissance resulted in transforming our family
institution, in replacing the massive and communal constitution of days gone
by with a more flexible association of free personalities, strikes the author as
being a long and deplorable decadence.

If we have delayed somewhat in analyzing this work, it is not that we
would want to exaggerate its importance; if the work is quite dense, the
author's thought is obviously inundated by the material he tries to encompass.
But, especially if it is compared with certain others that are infused with the
same spirit, it appears to us to establish an interesting trend. Up until recent
times, historians would sift evidence in order to know if our family law arose
from Germanic law rather than from Roman law or inversely. They are now
beginning to teach that it is Christian ideas that have played the preponderant
role. Already last year, we found this trend in Lefebvre's book.[70] Du Plessis
does not go as far as the professor of the Paris Faculty of Law.[71] He does not say
that the entire essence of our domestic law comes to us from Christianity; he
recognizes in the *mundium* and even in the *patria potestas* a double historical
antecedent of great importance. But finally, it is most likely that the contemporary family would normally owe all the distinction and novelty it possesses to
the Christian religion.

Now, it is impossible for us to see how this assertion is to be considered
justified. Doubtless, it may be granted a priori that the ideas of humanity
which Christianity brought with it must have had their repercussions within
the family, or better yet, that the same causes which gave rise to these ideas
have also been effective in softening and humanizing domestic relations. But
we do not see in the family institution the great changes that may be imputed
to it. It has not established any of the great fundamental notions, it has found
them ready-made; and the modifications that it has contributed to introduce
do not seem dominated by a new conception of domestic life, but by preoccupations of an entirely different kind. Especially in matters concerning the
relationships of children with parents, the intervention of the Church seems to
have been for the purpose of better serving its own interests. Accordingly the
fact is that it is to be seen placing its authority at the service of the most contradictory causes, without any unity of plan. For temporal reasons, it was interested in seeing that a certain extension in making a will should be
acknowledged by the father of a family; it tried therefore to make the use of
bequests widespread. It thereby increased the head of the family's authority.
Similarly, and for analagous reasons, it acknowledged to parents the right to
give their children to the Church at an early age and declared irrevocable the
offering thus made (p. 220). But inversely, when there was at issue the interest
of the faith—when it was a question, for example, of monastic vows, of conversion—the Church took no account of the wishes of the parents (pp. 216,
220, 375). Yet it is for this reason that, led by these principles, it tended not to
make paternal consent a necessary condition for the validity of marriages (p.

402). Its influence, therefore, was exercised in the most contradictory directions, and as a result, was not of a nature to leave a very definite imprint on the domestic institution. It probably had a greater impact on marriage; for on the subject of the sexes and on the relationships of the sexes it had a definite system of ideas which could not fail to affect marital regulations. As a matter of fact, moreover, it was over a long period of time that it fell to the lot of the ecclesiastical tribunals to settle once and for all the legal questions concerning the validity of marriage.

Still, one of the most essential characteristics of modern marriage is its entirely secular origin: the publicity and the regularity of the forms according to which it must be contracted. The Church long remained indulgent towards clandestine marriages, and the state triumphed over this complacency only with great difficulty. (*Année sociologique*, 5, 1902, pp. 376–379; trans. J. French)

Félix Dupré la Tour. *De la Recherche de la paternité en droit comparé et principalement en Suisse, en Angleterre et en Allemagne.* Paris: Arthur Rousseau, 1900, 186 pp.

The situation of our law in matters concerning illegitimate children is almost unique in history. From the moment when the legal distinction of the illegitimate child and the legitimate child appears, institutions are everywhere founded in order to protect to some extent the first and by some sort of link to attach him securely to society. Rome had concubinage that canon law began by preserving; even the *vulgo concepti* [72] found, by selling himself, a way to place himself under the *potestas* of a master. The Middle Ages had the law of bastardy, which made the lord the protector and the master of bastards; however harsh this system may appear, at least it had the advantage of assuring an existence for the waifs and strays, of making a place for them in society. When the law of bastardy was abolished, paternity investigations made their appearance under different circumstances. They were generally upheld by legislative acts in the Old World and the New. A mere fifteen governments, of which only nine are European, take exception and have banned paternity investigations on general principles. Among these there is only one big state outside of France; it is Italy. The others are Holland; the Ionian islands; Serbia; the cantons of Ticino, Neuchâtel, and Vaud; Rumania; Monaco; Haiti; Costa Rica; Bolivia; Uruguay, and Venezuela. Lastly, one must add that it is France which took the initiative. The writers of the Civil Code are the ones who first recorded as law the interdiction ruling.

The latter appears in observance, then, as an anomaly, and this suffices to render suspect the reasons whereby one tries to justify it. Even when presented with the near-unanimity with which the other peoples have made known their support of the contrary principle, one wonders with astonishment what could have given rise to this peculiarity in our law.

According to Dupré la Tour, the principal cause of this surprising innovation is presumably the overly complete assimilation of illegitimate with legitimate children (law of 12 Brumaire, year 11) that the revolutionary legislator allowed. It had been declared that there "could not be two kinds of paternity." But then, precisely because the illegitimate quality of the child was becoming more advantageous, it was believed that more precautions ought to be taken against the invasion of the family by strangers, and the law recognized illegitimate paternity only when it was acknowledged by the father. The principle of absolute equality, proclaimed in theory, would then have resulted in sanctioning the most revolting of inequalities.

But without wanting to deny that these considerations may have had some influence, we are wondering if a more deep-seated cause did not intervene. First of all, if the Brumaire legislator did not approve of paternity investigation, he acknowledged the right to request maintenance for children who were able to prove their relationship in writing or as state property. The writer of the Civil Code showed himself far more pitiless. And to be sure, this greater severity arose at a time when complete assimilation of illegitimate children with the legitimate ones was revoked. The fact then is that this assimilation was not the unique cause of the evil. The latter must have originated mainly in a state of mind, common to the members of the imperial State Council and to the members of the Convention, but more pronounced in the first case than in the second. And this state of mind is very clearly brought out in the very arguments that have been given repeatedly for a century in order to justify the ban. They say that paternity investigations would disturb domestic order. But how does it happen that this fear came alive at the end of the last century and that it was unknown in the fifteenth, sixteenth, and seventeenth centuries? Could it not be that the family appeared at the time as something more intangible than in the past? In fact, it is readily self-explanatory that in the midst of the shakeup of so many institutions, others made them appear more respectable and that they were thus prompted to proscribe everything that could diminish their authority. Now, the best way to put the family in a class by itself was to separate it radically from everything that negated what it stood for, to close it off radically from irregular elements. It has been made sacrosanct ever since the Revolution and has been one of the bases of social order; from then on, it was understood that everything that might alter the purity, compromise the sanctity, of the family appeared to be intolerable and was banned, despite the possible cost in suffering to individuals. It would seem that the latter were more than compensated by a social good of which they were a necessary condition.

But we do not intend to settle once and for all and for that reason the matter of knowing if this feeling is founded on factual reality, or if it is not due simply to an excessive timidity, to an overly conservative frame of mind that put behind it the great calamitous upheavals. We are of the opinion, on the contrary, that the facts assembled by the author (pp. 151 ff.) render a disservice to the principle of interdiction. (*Année sociologique*, 5, 1902, pp. 379–381; trans. J. French)

S. Rundstein. "Die vergleichende Methode in ihrer Anwendung auf die slawische Rechtsgeschichte" (A Comparative Application of Slavic Law to History). *Zeitschrift für vergleichende Rechtswissenschaft*, XV, pp. 210–219.

This is a summary of an article by Balzer which appeared in the *Studien zur polnishcen Rechtsgeschichte* (I, no. 5, Lemberg, 1900) on the comparative history of Slavic laws. According to the author, the principal use of the comparative method as applied to the law and customs of different Slavic peoples would be to succeed in reconstructing what that law was when the different branches of the race were not yet separated. We have often pointed out here all the dangers of such a comparison. The similarities that are recorded among peoples of the same race are not necessarily assignable to their identical ethnic background. They can be due not to the pure and simple transmission of the same primitive law, but to the similarity in the conditions of existence in which different peoples have found themselves placed after their separation. The Roman city and the Greek city are certainly comparable phenomena, and nevertheless the urban form of government is not of Aryan origin, since it is not found either among the Germans or the Slavs. Doubtless, when one institution is absolutely general throughout the whole extent of a race, the chances are much greater that it may be of primitive origin; it follows from this that these chances equal certitude. Moreover, in order for an institution to present that universality, it is still necessary that it find everywhere the conditions of existence which had given rise to it and which explain it; because in order to endure, it is not sufficient that it has existed. Thus it is still necessary to return to the consideration of the conditions of existence, and the true role of the comparative method is to assist in determining them.

Regardless of the question of methodology, here are the results that Balzer has arrived at in employing comparison to discover the original forms of Slavic law.

(1) One finds among the Slavs, as a means of preventing the vendetta and of stopping it, a kind of ceremonial expiation called *pokora*, in which the guilty one makes a supplication and humiliates himself. It was believed that this was a recent practice and that it stemmed from Christian influence. Balzer establishes that it is primitive and results from the same ideas which are the basis of real expiation.

(2) In the apportionment of property of the *zadruga*, two systems are concurrently employed: the apportionment by heads [of families] and the apportionment by lineage. Which is primitive? According to the same author, the second would be employed when "the property was received by inheritance of the founders of the *zadruga*, the first when it has been acquired by recent

generations." This amounts to saying, we think, that the apportionment by lineage applies to the family patrimony, and just as, for a long time, the wealth in the latter case belongs to all, it is believable that the system of apportionment is the most ancient.

(3) On the preexistence of a maternal right in the family, Balzer thinks that it is impossible to express his opinion. He points out the facts which seem to him self-contradictory (p. 217).

(4) Private property may have been constituted by the apportionment of the common property of the *zadruga* and the distribution of different lots by chance. The author supports his position with the fact that among the Russian and the Southern Slavs private property is designated by the word *sors*. Is the proof very demonstrative? In any case, the role of chance would have been very secondary in the phenomenon. What is otherwise important is the very dismemberment of the *zadruga.*

(5) Among the Slavs, there exist territorial associations comprising many local groups who have a political life and a common administration and who are collectively responsible for the crimes committed on their territory. One has often seen institutions created artificially by the state; here they presumably were constituted spontaneously well before the state existed. (*Année sociologique*, 6, 1903, pp. 343–345; trans. J. Sweeney)

R. Caillemer. *Origines et développement de l'exécution testamentaire (Epoque franque et Moyen Age).* Lyon: A. Rey, 1901, 740 pp.

Testamentary execution, which no longer occupies, in the Civil Code, more than a very small place, enjoyed a considerable role throughout the Middle Ages. Caillemer set himself the task of determining what needs gave rise to this institution, on what ideas it was based, and how it evolved. The elements of his study are not borrowed from the history of French law alone; since testamentary execution presents the same essential features in all the countries of the West, he is careful to compare the prescriptions of our law on this point with those which were in usage in Germany, England, Italy, and Spain.

Testamentary execution appears as early as the eighth century. At that time it had as its principal and almost exclusive function the furnishing of a juridical means permitting the realization of certain very special dispositions in case of death: These are the gifts *pro anima* [for the soul]. One gave this name to pious donations made by the dying person *in extremis* with a view toward assuring the salvation of his soul. In fact, if not in law, these donations had become obligatory, and the priests had developed the habit of requiring them as the condition for absolution. But under what juridical form were they to be realized? The testamentary principle had maintained itself only in the Visigothic areas; everywhere else, either it remained unknown (this was the case in Germany) or else, where it had penetrated as a result of the Roman conquest, it had fallen into disuse and disappeared. One sole means thus subsisted to effect posthumous generosity: an act between living persons, a donation *post mortem* [after death], containing all the necessary reservations for the benefit of the donor, but having as effect the immediate and definitive passing of the donation into the possession of the person to whom it was given. Now, this procedure was very often impracticable, or difficult to apply, besides the fact that it only responded very imperfectly to the needs which it was a question of satisfying. Indeed, these donations usually involved real estate and the transfer of real estate could not be done without complicated formalities which the dying person could not perform easily. It is true that these donations could have been made before the last moment; but they were believed to have more religious efficacy when they were made, not just at the moment of death, but on the day of the funeral.* Moreover, once made, they were not revocable at the will of the donor. It was thus that the need was felt to insert between the donor and the recipient an intermediary whose role would be to transfer the donation made by the donor to the recipient once the time had come: This was the testamentary executor. Doubtless, once the executor was invested with his powers, the latter could no longer be revoked without his consent. But since he was not an interested party in the operation, this consent would not be difficult to obtain. He had no reason for not conforming to the wishes of the donor, even if those wishes changed. It would not have been the same if the ownership of the goods bequeathed had been transferred directly to the monastery which benefited from it.

The execution thus appears as a means intended to make possible bequests in the absence of a testament. It was a substitute for the institution of the testament, towards which, at the same time, it opened the way. It thus seems that one ought to see it regress and disappear as soon as the testament made its reappearance, that is, in the thirteenth century. At that time, indeed, it was no longer necessary in order to give effect juridically to revocable dispositions, since the testament itself was revocable. But nevertheless, not only did the executor retain his old functions, but his role was extended and enlarged. The donation *pro anima,* or *pro sepultura* [for burial], never involved more than certain goods, such-and-such a piece of real estate; the testament, on the contrary, had a more general application; it applies to the whole of the disposable patrimony, to the totality of goods, debts, and credits left by the legator. For this totality a liquidator was needed; this was the testamentary executor.† He is henceforth the protector and the defender of the testament; he interprets, if necessary, clauses which are obscure, and can even on occasion

---

* The author justly remarks that these beliefs are probably of pre-Christian origin. The ancient Germans had the slaves, the horses, etcetera, of the dead man burned on his funeral pyre. The Church only diverted these ancient customs from their original signification. The friends of the dead man, instead of destroying objects which had belonged to him, gave them to the Church. But, in conformity with the old ideas, these donations continued to be made on the day of the funeral.

† It is only from this point on that he can truly be called "testamentary"; for it was only from this point on that he could be designated by a testament.

modify them (p. 77); sometimes he oversees the manner in which the legatees use the sums bequeathed to them; local customs go so far as to attribute to him the guardianship of the widow and children of the legator (p. 97). He thus has key role in the settling of the estate, and this role recalls in all respects that of the heir instituted in Roman law.

This is because these customs remained refractory to the institution of a universal heir, even after the reappearance of the testament. Most of the time, one only named heirs *ex re certa* [from a certain thing], who, as a consequence, had hardly more rights than simple legatees. They did not constitute juridical continuators of the personality of the dead man. It was, however, necessary to assure continuity between the testator and those whom he called to his heritage; it was by the executor that this was realized. Thus, after having been originally a substitute for a testament, he became, once the testament was reestablished, the substitute for an instituted heir;[73] he took his place and performed his essential function, which was to represent a person who no longer existed, until the juridical rearrangements necessitated by the will of the dead man had become accomplished fact. But also, from the moment when the institution of universal heir entered further into usage and was generalized, testamentary execution no longer had a reason for existing; this time, it was condemned to disappear. And in fact one sees it recoil progressively in proportion as the new institution developed.

Such being the functions of the executor, what were his powers, his rights, over the goods he was charged with transmitting? This question is perhaps the most interesting one treated in the book, for it touches on the notion of the right of property which was current in the Frankish period and even in the Middle Ages.

It has often been said that the executor was no more than an agent of the dead man. In this case, he would have had no real right over the goods for which he was executor; in transmitting them, in alienating them, he would not have acted in his own, personal name, but in the name of the donor, of whom he was only the representative. But the author shows very strongly that this was not his juridic situation. If, at the death of the donor, the ownership of his goods does not pass to the executor, it necessarily passes to his natural heirs. It is they, then, who represent the property in question vis-à-vis third parties. But how are we to conceive that this power could coexist with the power, equal in all respects, which the executor enjoyed at the same time, over the same things? One of these rights excludes the other, and as a consequence the second, which is certain, makes the first impossible. One could believe, it is true, that the executor did not act himself, that it was the dead man who gave or ceded through him. But apart from the juridical difficulties of such a conception, in fact the executors always present themselves as the true alienators; in innumerable acts of disposition they describe themselves, and themselves alone, as donors, as sellers, etcetera (pp. 149 ff.). They declare that they possess the property which they transfer, that they have it in their *dominium* [ownership], under their *potestas* [power], etcetera (p. 153), and this word *potestas* is used to designate both the seisin of the proprietor and that of the usufructuary (p. 155). This position of the executor is perhaps still more clearly revealed after the resurrection of the testament, since he then takes the place of heir. He is the true successor and acts by virtue of his own right, which he derives from this position. Even when it occurs that the heir intervenes, this is not in his own name, but in the name of the executor (p. 215).

The latter thus had a real right over the goods for which he was executor. But one must not attempt to classify this right in some specific juridic category. For, where Germanic societies were concerned, there was only one real right; this was the right of ownership. A person who had power over a thing in some respects was regarded as its owner. Thus, from this point of view, "the usufructuary does not have title to a *jus in re aliena*,[74] but is an owner *ad tempus*.[75] The holder of a mortgage is not the holder of real rights over the thing belonging to the debtor; he is the momentary owner of the thing given as mortgage, etcetera. All these persons have the owenrship of the things; what distinguishes them is the more or less long duration of the right" (p. 339). To speak precisely, it does not appear that all the possible ways of exercising the right of ownership are only distinguished from each other by their unequal duration; the power of use is not equally extensive in all cases. But what does seem well established is that these different juridical relations were not regarded as distinct entities, but as various aspects of a single fundamental right, the right of property, which was sometimes broader, sometimes more restricted, but which always remained the same so far as what was truly essential was concerned. It is in this sense that it is possible to say that the executor was owner of the goods confided to him; but his right of property was, depending on the circumstances, either very extended or very narrowly limited.

This very flexible notion of a right of ownership susceptible to being extended or contracted indefinitely without ceasing to be itself is, we believe, fundamental to medieval organization. It would be interesting to inquire what the state of collective mentality was which made it possible. We cannot ask ourselves the question here. But what one can easily catch a glimpse of is the way in which it responded to the necessities of the time. The insecurity of relations caused a situation in which numbers of individuals did not have a social force sufficient to defend the rights themselves of ownership with which they were invested; hence the necessity of intermediaries, of warrantors, to whom this right of ownership was entrusted, but more or less limited; these limitations retained for the original holder of the right the reality of use, if not in totality at least in large part, while the authority of the new holder of the right gave to this right what it needed to be respected. At bottom, the testamentary executor must have usually been a powerful person whose position guaranteed for the donor respect for his desires; and, after all, is it not on this same principle that feudal organization rests, insofar as what is most essential to it is concerned? Also, we have difficulty understanding the sort of hesitation with which the author answers the question of whether the origins of testamentary execution are Germanic or Roman. It is quite evident that it has for roots a whole complex of Germanic ideas. (*Année sociologique*, 6, 1903, pp. 345–350; trans. K. Woody)

Milan Markovic. *Die serbische Hauskommunion (Zadruga) und ihre Bedeutung in der Vergangenheit und Gegenwart* (The Domestic Community of the Serbs). Leipzig: Duncker und Humblot, 1903, xi + 87 pp.

After a rather well documented description of Serbia's economic state, the author recalls the principal features of the organization of the *zadruga*. The picture he traces for us adds nothing essential to what is known. A communal society, consisting of several related families and outsiders who have joined up by way of adoption, the *zadruga*, which comprises at times more than thirty members, is administered by a chief, either elected or accepted by common agreement. Nevertheless, the relative individuality of each household is evident in the morphological aspect of the society. Indeed, each household has its little house and all these particular habitations are grouped around the principal establishment, which is reserved for the oldest and which is the center of communal life—this is where meals are taken and assemblies are held. Outside the so-called *zadruga* there are, it is true, families among the Serbs that include only the father and his descendants. [But although it is smaller,] this domestic society is organized on the same basis as the *zadruga*, and this last has been wrongly compared with the Roman or with our family. As a matter of fact, the father wields only a very restricted part of the authority which the *zadruga* chief has at his disposal. As soon as his sons reach their majority, they become his equals. His hands are tied without their consent and they can even depose him. Indeed we believe that such is the characteristic feature of this family type, much more than the dimension it can attain. What distinguishes it is the absence of a strongly constituted central authority. It is a homogeneous society, all of whose male members, once they are adults, have unmistakably equal standing. It is this lack of differentiation that permits the family to grow until it comprises a multiplicity of heads. But the expansion it can thus acquire is an aftereffect and amounts to a secondary characteristic only.

The author next reveals and criticizes the different theories that have been set forth on the origins of the *zadruga:* which makes domestic communism into a derived and attenuated form of tribal communism, and those writers with contrasting ideas, whom Hildebrandt and Peisker have supported. At odds with Laveleye, these last authors point out that nowhere in Serbia is there to be found the slightest trace of tribal communism. When the Serbs appeared in the Balkans, they were divided into tribes *(pleme),* themselves grouped into phratries *(bratstwo:* "fraternity"). The tribe owned forests and pasturelands common to all the phratries that comprised it, and it was the same with each phratry in relation to the particular families of which it was composed. But nowhere does it involve collective ownership of the land. Such ownership arises only when a certain family takes over at a fixed post on limited territory and cultivates it. It was by turning the soil into an asset that the basis of the right to property was originally formed. If we rightly understand the author, before this cultivation of the land, the question of identifying its owner did not even arise. Except for matters concerning pasturelands and forests, material relationships between the soil and men were not clearly defined. They were determined only when farming activity began, and such activity was never the tribe's business nor even the village's, but rather family business.

Hildebrandt, in sharp disagreement, has maintained that individual ownership was the initial factor; collective ownership, or rather joint ownership, was apparently established only because of the difficulties that arose in parceling out the land. Each person having a claim presumably felt in such a case that it was better to pool his share. But our author objects that the facts demonstrate how easily the land is divided when one wants to divide it. Besides, a theory which claims that joint family ownership is the result of a legacy without taking it into account that the legacy is an attenuated form of family communism obviously is opposed to, in our opinion, every tenet of comparative law. Peisker's theory, which also makes out the *zadruga* to be a belated phenomenon, is documented more thoroughly. According to Peisker, it would be the financial considerations that, from the Byzantine Empire on, obliged families of relatives to group themselves into two or three households in such a way as to form a single establishment only. Markovic discusses the texts on which Peisker relies and shows that their significance is very different. His conclusion is that domestic communism among the Serbs is simply the economic consequence of the cohesive strength the family had in their midst. Let us add that it is truly extraordinary that the very ancient existence of domestic collectivism is still disputed today, even though it has been recorded in a most unequivocal way among such a large number of societies.

Markovic's short treatise terminates with two chapters on the present state of the *zadruga* in law and in economic life. (*Année sociologique*, 7, 1904, pp. 425–427; trans. J. French)

Hans Stockar. *Über den Entzug der väterlichen Gewalt im römischen Recht* (The Suppression of Paternal Power in Roman Law). Zurich: Fried. Schulthess, 1903, 68 pp.

The question as to how the state has encroached upon the internal life of the family group is one of the most interesting ones raised in the sociology of the family. It is quite certain that these infringements had already started in Rome, even though there was no family which was as hermetically closed to external influences as the Roman. It has even been quite generally admitted that in some cases the state enjoyed the legal right to break up the strongest and the most intangible family bonds that have ever existed, i.e., those which issued from the patripotestal authority *(patria potestas)* and which placed the child under the domination of the father. The magistrate presumably had the power to withdraw authority from the father in order to emancipate that father's child. It is against this opinion that our author protests. According to him, paternal authority was always protected by the action of the state.

We believe there is a reason to distinguish one from the other [the state and the family] according to different time periods. During the imperial era, the state was forbidden in all cases to meddle with the patripotestal authority. This seems to us difficult to reconcile with the texts. To defend his opinion, Stockar was obliged to resort to a very ingenious exegesis of the texts. He has specified that Trajan forced a father to emancipate his son. It is possible that this sort of intervention was rare; it was not impossible either. It is also true that the emperor did not proclaim the emancipation himself; but whatever legal procedures were adopted, it is nonetheless significant that the emancipation took place on the initiative of the emperor. In other cases, forfeiture of the paternal authority is manifestly proclaimed by virtue of punishment. In order to fit his theory with the texts, the author was obliged to maintain that this decline was the consequence of *deminutio capitis*,[76] which resulted from the principal punishment, such as exile and condemnation to work in the mines. But apart from the spirit of the formulas thus invented, that hardly fits with this interpretation; one now sees indirectly that at the very least the law could strip the father of his power. Moreover, if one recalls how, since praetorian law, the state limited the authority of the *pater familias* in everything that concerned the disposition of his property, one finds nothing extraordinary about that which it protected: not only the economic interests of the child but also his existence against the abuses of the patripotestal authority.

Indeed, in the beginning of the republic this intervention was probably not allowed. Against this opinion the jurists have cited the text of the Twelve Tables, which declares in definitive terms the release from the family of the son who has been abandoned three times. It is said that this emancipation was, in fact, a deposition pronounced by the law virtually to inflict punishment on the father who was considered guilty of having abused his power in betraying his son three times. But the author refuses to admit this interpretation; he sees, on the contrary, in this disposition of the Twelve Tables an extension, and not a restriction, of the paternal authority. Following him, at the beginning, only once abandoning the son [mancipation] would have been sufficient to invoke emancipation; afterward, when patripotestal authority was more solidly constituted, it appeared that only one betrayal of the son was not sufficient to break such a strong familial bond. Surely, when something is dearly held by a person who possesses it, the ordinary procedures are not sufficient to break this exceptionally strong juridic bond. This is, in fact, what constituted the family patrimony, on which was premised the latent rights of the family, quite ready to enter anew into an act long after the betrayal. It is not surprising that in Rome it was the same regarding the son in relation to the father. (*Année sociologique*, 7, 1904, pp. 427–428; trans. Y. Nandan)

Ernest D. Glasson. *Histoire du droit et des institutions de la France.*
Vol. VIII, *Epoque monarchique.* Paris: F. Pichon, 1902,
lv + 546 pp.

It is with Charles VII that Glasson places the end of the feudal era and the
beginning of the monarchical era. In fact, at this moment, an important
novelty was created in legal evolution, a sign of new times: Local customs of
the Middle Ages were recorded and were unified; royal decisions began to
figure among the sources of French law, and precisely because they emanated
from the central authority, they immediately evinced a marked tendency
towards legislative unity in nearly all the branches of the law. There were some
[royal decisions] that were already codes of some sort. The codification movement, which was reproached at the time of the Revolution and the Empire,
does not therefore date from this belated era; in reality, it was already in the
process of a long-drawn-out preparation. It is the end product of our entire
history. Therefore it is vain to regret it, as some of our historians have done. It
was necessary.

The book is divided into three parts. the first deals with the sources of law.
The sociologist who would like to study the nature of common law—the way in
which it functions, in which it is determined and unified—will find in this
chapter certain useful information, even though a bit summary. What emerges
from this analysis is the fact that the unification of customs was the product of
two factors: royal authority, on the one hand, and legal expertise, on the
other. If, as Lambert says in a work analyzed above,[77] the men of the legal profession were, in part, the authors of common law, it is also through them that
it was transformed. They have played in the development of law a considerable
role involving its nature, the extent of which we understand only very vaguely.

The second part deals with the condition of the individual, and the third
with the family. The former heading is in current usage in works about law,
but in reality it amounts to a very artificial classification in terms of the laws.
One gathers from this idea that the individual, as such, enjoys certain rights
because a person is what he or she is—of a certain sex, a certain age (in terms of
majority, minority, etcetera), because a person represents a certain mental state
(prodigal, crazy, etcetera), because a person has a certain social standing
(noble, freeman, slave, etcetera). It seems, then, that all the rules which determine these various rights find their unity in the fact that they express different
attributes recognized by this same reality, i.e., the individual personality. That
is why one thinks it possible to classify them under the same label. But as a
matter of fact, that label has only a surface and apparent unity. The rules
which are ranked under that title depend on very heterogeneous causes and
have between them no inner connection. They belong to very different spheres
of collective living. Those that determine the rights and obligations of the
noble, the bourgeois, the serf, the slave, derive from the nature of the corresponding social classes, from their relations, and from their place in society as a
whole. Rules which concern the condition of the woman, the minor, the

liberated, the prodigal, etcetera, are closely intertwined with domestic organization. It is understandable how inconvenient it is to reassemble in this way such diverse practices by separating them from the social milieux to which they relate and which explain them. That classification by the writers of legal opinions therefore appears to us hard to apply to a study of history. No doubt, it is this rather summary and meager characterization which traces the development of the clergy, the nobles, the bourgeois, the serfs, etcetera (pp. 217–264). The fact is that basically these issues become totally valid and interesting only when they are properly placed—that is, tied in with everything concerning the social organization as a whole.

The most interesting parts of this chapter are those that deal with the family (in terms of minority, majority, situation of women, etcetera). We shall couple the analysis with that of the following chapter, which deals with domestic law and from which the abovementioned topics are inseparable. Paternal authority and majority, marriage and women's status, are matters too closely related to be severed.

In this era a great change takes place in marriage: It becomes more and more an act, both civil and public at the same time. In the Middle Ages, it consisted in its entirety of a private act of which the Church alone had cognizance. It was exclusively formulated by the consent of the parties; and this consent was not compelled to manifest itself in obligatory solemnities, of a kind to leave no doubt about the wishes of these under contract. Doubtless, it was the rule that the wedding be blessed by the priests; but this blessing was not indispensable, and furthermore, it was very generally used for simple betrothals, which as a result were hardly discernible from regular marriage. It is true that when consummation was established the distinction was easy, but then it is from concubinage that marriage was hard to distinguish. Every effort of royal authority tended to prevent these confusions that were obviously contrary to social order, and it was in this course of action only feebly seconded by the Church, which still was rather complacent about clandestine marriages. It was under pressure from the king's ambassadors and not without resistance that the Council of Trent demanded, under penalty of nullification, the presence of the parish priest as solemn witness to the marriage. The king consecrated and sanctioned the provisions of the Council of Trent on this point. This intervention of temporal authority in the organization of the wedding constituted a still more important novelty than the one before. For, owing to the very fact that he appropriated to his use certain resolutions of the Council, the king arrogated to himself the right to regulate the wedding, which up until then had been uniquely under ecclesiastical jurisdiction. This is the seed of the secular wedding.

Once this seed was planted, it was the business of the legal experts and parliamentarians to nourish it and to foster its growth. Little by little a theory was formed by virtue of which a double character for the marriage was acknowledged. It was said that it was both a contract and a sacrament, united indissolubly, the contract serving as material for the sacrament. As a result, the temporal authority had the right to regulate the conditions, the form, and the results of the marriage contract, whereas it belonged to the spiritual authority to agree to or to refuse sacramental sanctification of the marriage tie. As a consequence of this doctrine, the role of the Church in the marriage ceremony was limited in effect to the simple delegation of secular authority. From then on, the latter had power to create preventive annulments and the priest was constrained to observe the royal orders on marriage as well as the provisions of cannon law.

Paralleling this transformation in the nuptials, another was created in the condition of the wife, which, according to the author's just remark, may appear contradictory at first glance. On the one hand, the influence of women on civilization, on customs, became more and more considerable. From the sixteenth century on, the woman made it her duty to acquire a culture equal or superior to that of men of the same class; she was the object of an ever-growing deference; the role of women in the salons is well known. But at the same time, in singular contrast, from the viewpoint of civil and political rights, the condition of wives appears to have grown increasingly worse. The determining factor in this aggravated tendency was the establishment of the wife's civil incompetence. This incompetence was at first established in the exclusive interest of the husband; accordingly, if she started an action involving civil or legal settlement without the husband's authorization, only the latter had the right to call for its nullification. But little by little, this incompetence changed in nature; admittedly it had its origins, not in the nature of marriage, in the rights of the spouse, but in the weakness of the feminine sex. A way to protect the wife against herself was worked out. That is why she herself could call for the nullification of the actions she had started without authorization and could resort to legal authority when her husband refused his consent without a legitimate reason.

Besides, this contradiction is a surprise in appearance only. The moral importance of the wife's role increased to the degree that domestic life had a greater place in the context of life in general; the conjugal association became more strongly organized. For the family is unexcelled as a territory for feminine activity. But, in another sense, it is inevitable that, at least at a given moment in history, the matrimonial bond cannot become tightly constricting and the family cannot hold together without a resulting legal subordination of the wife to her husband. For this subordination is the necessary condition of family unity. Not that domestic society cannot possess a rather complex unity in order to allow each of the spouses his [or her] legal individuality, but it is easily understandable that such a well-cultivated organization can only be a later development. We are still in the process of seeking it out.

Family law has varied less in the course of our history than conjugal law. Doubtless, paternal authority did not remain entirely as it used to be in the countries of unwritten law (where it was very much toned down), nor as it used to be in the countries of written law, where Roman tradition maintained its mastery for so long. Those two conceptions interpenetrated, and it is from that mutual penetration that our modern conception resulted. But, in the final analysis, the changes that were thus created remained secondary. The great novelty that arose in our family law involves the conjugal association in particular; it consists of the progressive secularization of the marriage ceremony and the closer union established between the spouses, and it is this factor that deserves special mention. Ordinarily, changes in the matrimonial pattern are simply the consequences of changes that occurred in domestic organization; here, in certain ways, the former are self-created. The fact is that the characteristics of the modern family are found precisely in the preponderant position that wedlock and the conjugal association assumed. This last, which was at first only a consequence and a reflection of domestic society, becomes its essential element, the very first and foremost. And doubtless that is why this element was the one which underwent the first and the most profound transformations. (*Année sociologique*, 7, 1904, pp. 429–433; trans. J. French)

Fusamaro Tsugaru. *Die Lehre von der japanischen Adoption* (The Theory of Adoption in Japan). Berlin: Mayer und Müller, 1903, xxiv + 228 pp.

Adoption is an auxiliary relationship designed to supply the normal relationship when this is impeded from fulfilling the functions which are its raison d'être. The study of adoption, at a given moment and in a specific society, is thus a good way to determine what are, at that moment and in that society, the essential functions of relationship. It is from that point of view that it is befitting to question the book of Tsugaru on adoption in Japan.

Many diverse forms of adoption have developed in history and in certain regards still coexist, but they can be reduced to three principal types.

(1) At the head of a clan *(Uji)*, a group formed by a plurality of collateral families associated in the same industry *(Ko)*, there is a chief whose powers are extensive. The chief of the group can adopt someone as a successor. Such an adoption does not have as its immediate purpose to create between the one adopted and the adopter a relation of father and son, but simply to confer on the adoptee the capacity to take charge of the group after the death of the present chief. Without a doubt, because he is the designated heir, the adoptee consequently finds himself assimilated as a son of the adopter. But he only acquires that characteristic in an indirect and mediated way, because it is logically implied in being the eventual successor in the government of the family. The family relationship results from the domestic function to which the adoptee is called by the adoption. Thus understood, adoption plays the same role as the institution of the heir in Roman law.

(2) The father of a family, who is not the chief of a group, can adopt someone as son. This is adoption in the sense that we habitually use the word.

(3) Finally, adoption serves to create all sorts of familial or quasi-familial relationships. One can adopt, or at least one could have adopted at a certain period, someone as a brother, as a sister (p. 10), or as a nephew (p. 9); likewise adoption could serve for allowing a stranger into the house as a servant, a teacher, etcetera (pp. 10–11).

One institution which deserves to be mentioned separately is the adoption of a son-in-law. A man who only has daughters adopts a stranger to whom he gives a daughter in marriage. The sons born of that union are considered as the heirs of the grandfather. The adopted son-in-law plays only an intermediary role; he only assures the continuity of generation. Thus he has an unenviable situation in the family.

Of all the types of adoption, the most ancient and the most important seems to have been the first. Primitively, in effect, the Japanese society was composed of a certain number of agnatic clans, analogous to the Roman *gentes.* At the head of each clan, or *Uji,* there was a chief whose primordial function was to watch over the cult of the ancestors. That dignity belonged to one of the families who composed the *Uji* and it was transferable from father to son. Thus if the chief did not have a son, he adopted a male child. Such may have been the origin of the institution.

But towards the seventh century A.D., at the time when the Chinese civilization and Buddhism were introduced to Japan, the family organization, and consequently the system of adoption, passed through an important transformation. The *Uji* little by little lost its original strength, and a more restricted family, analogous to the *zadruga* of the Slavs, came to the forefront. It is this which, afterwards under the name of *Ko,* constituted the domestic society par excellence. Henceforth, it was to assure the continuity of the *Ko* that adoption had as its purpose the designation of *Ko*'s chief. Now, the *Ko* was no longer a partly political group like the *Uji*; it was a private association whose nature was essentially economic. While the chief of the *Uji* was charged with public functions, the chief of the *Ko* had only domestic powers. Adoption itself consequently took on a private and economic character (pp. 40–41). Doubtless, it continued to have as its principal purpose the assurance of a priest for the cult of the ancestors and an administrator for the family. But it began henceforth to produce consequences of a whole other nature. At that time, in effect, private property appeared. The chief no longer needed only to transmit his dignity but also his goods; the adoptee acquired the rights not only over the power of the adoptive father but over his fortune. Here, in reality, is a new form of adoption which was born as a consequence and under the influence of the first. What clearly shows this duality is that what concerns the transmission of the function of the chief and what concerns the transmission of his property do not submit to the same rules. In fact, the adoptee is alone called upon to exercise authority when his adoptive father is dead; he excludes all the other members of the family, even sons who could have been born after the adoption. On the contrary, as far as the fortune is concerned, only half of the share falls to a son of a concubine (pp. 64–73).

With the feudal regime, which lasted up to the middle of the nineteenth century, domestic life and political life, at least in the class of military nobles, coincided very intimately once more: In fact, the fief being transmissible from male to male by order of primogeniture, adoption was naturally employed for the transmission in the absence of a natural heir. There was, then, hardly any further point to another adoption; for the right, recognized previously, of the other members of the family to receive their share of the common fortune disappeared, and the heir of the fief became the sole heir of the entire property (pp. 81 ff.). It is true that it was otherwise in the ordinary classes; but the author does not inform us exactly about the rules which were in usage (p. 80).

It is only in the second half of the nineteenth century, after the fall of the feudal system and the restoration of the imperial power, that adoption as a way of establishing the chief and the continuator of the family in advance ceased to be the unique or principal form of the practice. This was finally conceived of as being able, by itself, to establish the relation of father and child. Furthermore, the institution was oriented in completely new ways; it no longer had for its unique purpose the perpetuation of a collective impersonal function, but offered to the private, intimate feelings of individuals a way of manifesting themselves. Between these two kinds of adoption lies all the difference that there is between the Roman will—whose role was above all to establish an heir, that is, a continuator of the religious and economic life of the family—and our modern will, which is designed above all to permit us to dispose, at least in part, of our fortune according to our personal relations. Likewise, just as a woman can be the object of these individual feelings, and also experience them, so can she adopt as well as be adopted (pp. 127, 128).

Thus the nature of adoption has regularly varied as the role which law and custom assigns to normal kinship has also varied. But Tsugaru's book provides the occasion for another observation: the great resistance which normal kinship seemed to have opposed to the encroachments of adoptive kinship. Up to recent times, the adoptee had to be chosen from among the kin of the adopter and not beyond the fourth degree. In another respect, the adoptive kinship was not completely assimilated to natural kinship. We have already seen that the adoptive son had only very limited rights to his father's property; likewise the mourning obligations were not the same for him as for the true sons (p. 61). What is more demonstrative still is that the adoptive kinship was not an obstacle to marriage (p. 99). The author believes that he can explain certain of these peculiarities by the considerable importance of the role that the cult of ancestors played in the Japanese family; it must have appeared natural, it is said, that the obligation owed to their ancestors should be rendered by someone who was joined to them by blood, and since it is participation in the cult which established the kinship, the adoptive kinship could only have been an inferior one. But in Rome, the domestic religion held no less a place and nevertheless adoption produced all the effects of natural kinship and was free from the conditions to which it had to submit in Japan. The cause of that situation thus has to be sought elsewhere. We believe it stems from the fact that in Japan the authority of the domestic chief was not as great as in Rome, but it was still strictly limited by the impersonal rights of the family. Now, the family naturally resists that intrusion of foreign elements which adoption implies; above all it is opposed to the fact that one of its members can arbitrarily modify the composition of the group. It should not be necessary to overassimilate the chief of the *Uji* or of the *Ko* and the Roman *paterfamilias*. However, it is certain that there are resemblances between them which could perhaps serve to clarify a little the origin and the nature of the *patria potestas*. (*Année Sociologique*, 8, 1905, pp. 409–413; trans. J Sweeney)

Jean Engelmann. *Les Testaments coutumiers au XVe siècle*. Paris: 1903, 286 pp.

We all know that in our European societies the testament originated under the influence of religious ideas. As a result of death, it was a way of making generous gifts to the Church and the poor. The testament even terminated by becoming a complementary rite of the *confessio in extremis*.[78] From the beginning of the tenth century, the intestate death led to serious penalties both for the deceased and the family, such as the deprivation of [Christian] burial and the levy of seignorial taxes. At the same time and for the same reason as well, the matter of contesting the testament, and of who was competent in this regard, was left to the church.

The main purpose of the book by Engelmann is to show that during the fifteenth century the testament, although conserving its religious character, started to become secular. At the head of all the testaments of this period one finds preambles of religious inspiration, in which the testator invokes God and saints and commends his soul to them; these preambulatory formulas became stylized. Likewise, the basic orientations, which had a religious purpose, remained important; but the purely profane clauses, which were originally very rare, multiplied (pp. 104 ff.). Finally, the competent civil tribunals, without however excluding the ecclesiastic tribunals which continued to exist, became more and more preponderant. The testament, freed from religious forms, now adapted itself to its new ends; for that reason alone it became complicated and diversified. The author analyzes and classifies the principal dispositions which are found in the testament, such as the institutions of heritage and regulations concerning debts, substitutions, and execution of the testament.

In substance, from this moment the essential characteristics of the modern testament were constituted. The double principle of the Legitimate and of the Reserve customary law was proclaimed (pp. 255–263), and the tendency to assure a possibly equal treatment of different children was already very much accepted, even though in practice different propositions allowed the disregard of the rule. (*Année sociologique*, 8, 1905, pp. 413–414; trans. Y. Nandan)

H. d'Arbois de Jubainville. *La Famille celtique. Etude de droit comparé*. Paris: Emile Bouillon, 1905, xx + 221 pp.

As indicated by the subtitle, this work is presented as a study in comparative law. The author's object is not to describe, overall, the organization of
the Celtic family, to point out its peculiarities and how they can be explained,
but to show the respects in which it appears to bring to mind the domestic
organization of the Romans, of the Greeks, of the Germans—in a word, of the
peoples who are properly designated as Indo-Europeans. And, if we understand it correctly, his book is above all a contribution to the study of this law.
He extends even further the field of his comparisons. Hammurabi's law
manifestly holds a considerable place among his preoccupations; he reverts to
it constantly and applies himself to showing that on many points it conforms
with Celtic law. .

These conformations, according to him, could be explained by the fact
that the Celts, like the other Indo-Europeans, probably had been "formerly in
touch with the empires which, before the conquest of the Persians, were dominant in the part of Asia nearest to Europe" (p. v).

These kinds of comparisons do not appear to us very instructive. Such
comparisons, always somewhat summary, of institutions that resemble each
other in some respects and differ in others leave us with a slightly blurred impression, an impression that is all the more blurred because of the disjointed
way D'Arbois states the case. Different aspects of the organization of Irish
family life are successively passed in review, but without any apparent order,
without it even being very clear why certain aspects have been examined rather
than others. No doubt, the author's principal aim is less to characterize the
domestic Irish code of law than to impart in a general way the feeling that
there exists an Indo-Europeans code of family law. But the method followed
by the author makes this demonstration more difficult. In order for it to be
conclusive, it would have been necessary to display only the essential characteristics of the domestic law that are common and special to the Indo-European
peoples. But the comparisons involve every type of attribute, even secondary,
in the organization of the family; certain similarities pointed out could be
likewise recorded in the case of peoples of all types who have nothing in common with the Indo-European institutions (marriage by purchase, dowry, the
daughter as heir apparent, etcetera). Indeed there is an institution, an essential
one, that the author believes exhibits a distinctive characteristic of
family life in the case of the Celts "as with the other Indo-European peoples"
in the West—namely, monogamy (p. vi). And indeed it is undeniable that
there existed in Rome, even in Greece, a tendency in this direction; but there
is no evidence that this tendency existed precisely everywhere to the same
degree. It is not at all certain that polygamy was unknown to the Greeks or
especially to the Germanic societies.*

---

* Another characteristic of that Indo-European law seems to be that the married woman leaves her
father's family (p. 63). We find such an assertion not a little surprising; it appears to us to apply
only to certain Roman marriages, those that were accompanied by the *manus*.

Besides, can one truly speak of an Indo-Germanic law? The word has one sense when it is a question of language. When one compares the languages spoken by those different peoples, one sees emerging certain verbal and grammatical forms that are common to them. But if one proceeds similarly with law, we believe that one obtains by this means only a sketchy pattern without consistency. The fact is that language is something less narrowly personal in a definite society than a legal system. Although it depends on social conditions, as demonstrated by Meillet,[79] a language expresses less than the law a definite collective personality; it is communicated much more easily by way of contagion; it passes the frontiers and assumes, if circumstances prove to be propitious, an international character. There are peoples or portions of peoples who are bilingual, and one can very easily envisage all the peoples of Europe speaking a same language without any one of them having thereby abdicated its personality. As a result, it is not hard to conceive that the different peoples who are reunited under a designation such as Indo-Europeans might have kept from their common origin a common linguistic background, which, while differentiating to the degree in which those people themselves were becoming diversified, has nevertheless continued to exist and perhaps been newly discovered and reconstituted through comparative grammar. But law possesses something less communicable; it is more immediately linked to the structure of the society, and it cannot become detached from it.

Two states can have systems of laws that resemble each other; they cannot have a common system of laws, whereas they can speak one and the same language. Consequently, the legal ideas that the Indo-European peoples were able to possess in common before their separation must, in the course of historical evolution, have undergone growth and transformation in the most divergent ways, like those people themselves. As a result, it may be anticipated before any analysis that what was able to survive from the common original background must necessarily be limited to a few very imprecise, very rough likenesses—insufficient to provide grounds for speaking of an Indo-European law, as one would of a legal, concrete, and living reality.

The interesting thing about this book is not, then, the comparisons which are vague and inconclusive; it is the information to be discovered there on Irish law. We shall point out as particularly noteworthy the way in which the Irish used to organize family relationships *(fine)*.[80] Relationships were set up in four circles. The first consisted of a living ancestor with the four generations of his descendants *(gelfine)*; the second, the father and brothers of this ancestor with the descendants of these brothers as far as the second generation *(derbfine)*; the third was formed by the grandfather and the paternal uncles of this same ancestor with the descendants likewise as far as the second generation *(iarfine)*; finally, the fourth consisted of the great-grandfather, and the great-uncles with their descendants, still as far as the second generation *(indfine)*. Each of these groups of relatives was collectively responsible for the crimes committed [by its members]. If the criminal was a member of the *gelfine,* it was on the *gelfine* that the responsibility fell; if he was a member of the *derbfine,* the latter group was held responsible and the *gelfine* intervened only if the *derbfine* was unsuccessful (p. 23). It is evident that the rules of conduct of this organization are very special; it is even regrettable that D'Arbois merely gives a somewhat summary statement of the case and one that is not always clear.

The organization of marriage is likewise very curious. Several kinds of marriage were possible, and the nature of the marriage contract depended not on the formalities employed or the intentions of the spouses but on their respective financial situation. The marriage had different effects according to whether the spouses had equal resources, or whether the man was wealthier than the wife, or whether the husband was, on the contrary, in straitened circumstances. In the second case, when the wife contributed only her person, the marriage was generally contracted for one year only, from May 1 to May 1 (p.153); in such a case the husband could have, beside this legitimate temporary wife, a spouse in superior circumstances, which goes to show that monogamy was by no means so essential a part of Irish domestic law. When the fortune belonged to the wife and the husband had nothing, the situation of the latter was identical to that of the wife when it was the husband who was rich (p. 163). In short, apart from those regular marriages, there were different forms of legal free unions (book 2, chapter 7).

D'Arbois de Jubainville is not content to describe; he strives at times to explain the facts that he describes. Judging from the few explanations he proposes, he does not appear to have a very vital sense of the complexity of social facts. The causes he ascribes to the facts are notably simple. Thus it is that he feels able to explain the existence of polygamy among the Jews and the Muslims simply with the fact that every year more women are born than men (p. 93). (*Année Sociologique*, 10, 1907, pp. 424–427; trans. J. French)

Thad. Engert. *Ehe und Familienrecht der Hebräer.* Munich: Lentner'sche Buchhandlung, 1905, vii + 108 pp.

We shall not follow the author in the hypotheses he formulates about the prehistorical forms of family life and marriage among the Hebrews. It is not that we were considering disputing the uterine family or the uterine clan, of which traces appear in certain traditions and practices that are still remembered in our own day. Everything points to the supposition that there was a time when the maternal family relations enjoyed a truly privileged position above the agnatic bloodline. But Engert goes still further; he admits a relationship between this mode of lineage and some sort of promiscuity *(Unkeuscheit)* that is sacred in character, as though there were a relationship between this promiscuity and the practice of polyandry (pp. 9 ff.). Now, these conjectures appear to us not only rash but without any justification that we know of. Polyandry agrees very well and even coexists most often with the principle of consanguinity in the paternal line, and we do not see further why the uterine organization of the family would be linked to a kind of religious hetairism.

But these reconstructive hypotheses relate only to the Hebrew people's nomadic period. From the time it became sedentary, the family became patriarchal. We would accept the word quite willingly if it were meant to designate a family whose father is the center. But in point of fact, the expression is given a much more extensive meaning. The word thus designates a family in which the father is endowed with a true sovereignty comparable to the *patria potestas* of the Romans. And in fact, it is in the guise of the Roman *paterfamilias* that the Hebrew family father is depicted for us. The children are represented to us as entirely subjected to the authority of the father, who would seem to have over them the power of life and death (p. 66); it is he who decides with sovereign authority on their marriage; he may even sell his daughters. Similarly, the wife would appear to have been like an object over which he presumably exercised an almost absolute right of ownership.

But this conception of the Hebraic—a conception that Stade, notably, has already defended—in no way tallies with the facts. Grüneisen *(Der Ahnenkultus und die Urreligion Israels,* pp. 202 ff.) has very justly shown the serious differences that separate these two kinds of domestic organization. Whereas in Rome the son of the family is subject to paternal authority all his life, in Israel he is emancipated through marriage. Whereas Roman law allows the father to introduce into the family by way of adoption anyone he wants, among the Hebrews, on the contrary, adoption is practically unknown. The same goes for the will, which is one of the essential prerogatives of the *patria potestas.* A multitude of practices testify to the fact that in the case of the Hebrews the fortune remains, to a great extent, a collective family matter, as understood even in the broad sense. Every sort of precaution is taken in order to prevent the property from leaving the family circle. In another sense, when the father is, in a manner as exclusive as in Rome, the cornerstone of the family, the agnatic bloodline either is the only one recognized by law or, at the very least, relegates the other to the background. On the contrary in Israel, the maternal bloodline is the object of great consideration.

It is, then, inaccurate thus to equate the domestic law of the Hebrews with that of the Romans. The first brings to mind rather that of Germanic societies. There are thus two very different types. It is too readily admitted that all families where the father exercises authority of a certain scope are of the same type and may be ranked under the same heading. As a matter of fact, depending on the nature of this authority, the family organization may be very diversified.

Under the influence of a similar notion, the author finds in marriage only a narrowly and dryly legalistic relation. The wife is bought by the husband and it is this purchase that forms the basis of marriage rights and all marital ethics. However, in certain places Engert appears to have felt that there was something else in marriage: He expressly points out its religious character. He stresses the close relationships uniting the marriage and the initiation, the taboos of those engaged, etcetera (pp. 43–47). From this angle, marriage is presented to us under an aspect entirely different from that of a sales contract. (*Année sociologique*, 10, 1907, pp. 427–429; trans. J. French)

Charles Lefebvre. *Cours de doctorat sur l'histoire matrimoniale française.* Vol. I, *Le Droit des gens mariés.* Paris: Larose et Tenin, 1906, xii + 291 pp.

In his *Introduction générale à l'histoire du matrimonial français,* analyzed here[81] in vol. IV, pp. 358 ff., Lefebvre revealed his general conception of our marriage law. He now undertakes to apply this view in detail to our marital institutions. In the present work, it is especially the economic aspect of marriage that is studied.

Two institutions appear to the author to be characteristic of our organization of marriage: conjugal authority and the system of joint property holdings. In his opinion, they are jointly responsible for each other. Conjugal authority, indeed, such as it is revealed in our customs, in no way consists of a sort of guardianship that the husband seemingly exercises over the wife by reason of an intellectual and moral inferiority that is attributed to her as a consequence of her sex. The wife in medieval society is nowhere treated [in France] with the scorn with which she was viewed elsewhere; she is not branded with any legal incapacity. On the contrary, she is everywhere found stepping in as her husband's associate and collaborator. The authority of the latter comes not from natural supremacy but from the fact that the community he forms by his association with his wife is in need of a chief and he is that designated chief. Because the economic interests of the two spouses are merged by the regime of joint ownership, it is necessary that the indivisible society thus formed have one head. There results from this a certain subordination of the wife, but only insofar as this subordination is needed for good conjugal discipline and for the shared interest of the household.

That said, it is a question of knowing where this double institution comes from.

The preceding work by the author permits us to anticipate his response. He declines to consider Roman law as the source of this organization. Rome knew paternal authority, but not marital authority, which is very different; as for jointly held property, the very idea is excluded by the Roman conception of marriage and the family. In the case of Germanic origins, the author's denials are less categorical. He feels strongly that among the Germans economic association between the husband and wife did not proceed without a certain intimacy. But he considers this to be a far cry from the notion of commonly held social property that was to become the characteristic feature of marriage in Christian societies. Besides, the *mundium*[82] to which the German woman was subjected was in no way a case of marital authority, since it was an authority that definitely did not arise out of the marriage, but rather accounted for the wife's submission by reason of her sex and whatever her civil status was; the conjugal *mundium* was simply the paternal *mundium* transferred to the husband. These two explanations rejected, there is only one left: The fact is that marital control and communalism are essentially due to the influence of Christian ideas. It is Christianity that has proclaimed that man and wife, by joining together, form a particularly close and even indissoluble moral society, in which the wife is the husband's associate. Is this not the very essence of our marriage law? Consequently, the latter is, it seems, simply the application of those aphorisms of the Old and New Testament, *erunt duo incarne una*[83] and *vir caput mulieris*,[84] which already contained the germ of joint property holdings and of conjugal authority.

We fear that this line of reasoning rests on a misapprehension. Within Christian societies, the conjugal society has attained a high degree of moral intimacy—a fact that nobody would dream of denying. But the communal regime is an economic regime. It is an association of goods, not of people. From the fact that public consciousness conceives of the bond that unites the persons of the spouses as very strong, it does not follow at all that at the same moment the same relationship is admissible between things. The best proof of this is in the organization of the Roman family, in which conjugal intimacy was already very great; marriage was considered as a *societas totius vitae*,[85] as creating between the spouses an entire commuity of existence, *individua vitae consuetudo*.[86] And yet Rome was the classic land for the separation of property; nowhere else were the fortune of husband and wife more carefully distinguished. The fact is that the causes which tend to join or to separate patrimonies differ from those which tend to join or to separate fortunes. Indeed it is an old principle on which family organization rests—a principle that still survives today in the form of the legacy—that an individual's property is under the jurisdiction of the family circle to which it belongs and from which it cannot be severed. The result of this is that wherever families form systems closed off from one another, without mutual penetration, it is very natural that the fortunes of the two spouses (who by definition are members of two different families) should be separated from each other by watertight barriers that prevent possible communications. In this case, the regime of separation is binding as the only one in conformity with the nature of things. Doubtless, that is why it was a basic factor in Roman matrimonial law. Nowhere, in fact, has the family lived in a more complete state of seclusion than in Rome; nowhere has each family been separated by a more sharply defined line of demarcation. The family ended at the point where agnation finished; as a result, the mother, not being the agnate of her children, was legally an outsider to their family and to that of her husband. But the same no longer holds in the case where a uterine relationship has gained recognition alongside the agnatic relationship. From then on, the mother becomes legally related to her children, and thereby she belongs to the same domestic society as her husband. Under these circumstances, the barrier that separated the property of the two spouses is let down; the communal regime becomes possible.

Now, in Germanic law, kinship did not have the strictly unilateral

characteristic which the Romans never managed fully to get rid of. It was communicated by women as by men. The terrain was thus being prepared for the
fusion, at least partially, of the two economic domains and for the establishment of community.

To be sure, the former family requirements did not cease totally to make
themselves felt. There were certain possessions that by their nature seemed
more specially to be family matters—such as dwellings, and especially dwellings that were part of the hereditary patrimony. In the case of such possessions,
one continued to judge that they could not leave the family, and as a result, to
exclude them from the entire community. But it is no less true that the great
obstacle which was blocking a closer economic association between the spouses
had disappeared. From this point of view, the role of Germanic law in the constitution of our matrimonial law appears much more considerable than Lefebvre thinks. Without it, the necessary conditions for the institution of joint
property holdings would have been lacking and all the declarations of principle that are to be found in the Old or New Testament could not have taken
their place.

But if these conditions were necessary, they were probably not sufficient.
They explain how, among peoples who are descended from Germanic
societies, the communal regime has been possible, but not what caused it to be
so, nor especially how it became the characteristic feature of our matrimonial
organization. Is it then here that Christianity must be invoked? But how about
Christianity's failure to have the same effect everywhere? Moreover, just as we
pointed out a while ago, it appears unlikely that the Christian ideal of marriage has had so direct and so decisive an influence on the economic regime of
conjugal society. Such an arrangement must have been instigated, not by entirely sentimental aspirations, but by social, perhaps even economic needs.
There must have been in the structure of society something that prodded the
spouses to become partners in this way. And indeed, at the same moment, the
same tendency towards community organization is seen to appear, not only in
marriage, but in domestic society. It is from these that the tacit[87] communities
come into being and give rise to analogies with joint property holdings between spouses—we can not deny it easily. Doubtless, it does not follow that
the latter are only an extension, a particular form of the former; but it is at
least proof that there was at the time a general state of society that disposed
men to group themselves in this manner. It is this need which asserted itself on
the conjugal group as on the others.

Might it not be the same sort of reasoning that would help explain directly
the formation of marital authority? Take the fact that the husband is often
called *his wife's baron*. Doesn't this provide the idea that there exist certain
connections between the causes that gave rise to the feudal system and those
that are responsible for the conjugal society at the same period? In any case,
that is one way to explain the peculiarities of the family structure in the Middle
Ages that appears to us more sociological than proceeding in the belief they

can be logically derived from a few texts in the holy Scriptures. (*Année sociologique*, 10, 1907, pp. 429–433; trans. J. French)

Albert de Dainville. *Des Pactes successoraux dans l'ancien droit français*. Paris: Larose et Tenin, 1905, 188 pp.

It might seem right at the start that the law of succession, on the one hand, and the law of bequest, on the other, suffice to assure in all cases the transmission of properties from one generation to the next and meet all possible needs. Indeed, the law of succession prevents disregarding the general and permanent interests in the family organization, and the law of bequest permits taking into account, at least to a certain extent, the particular and variable circumstances in which individuals and families may be situated. And yet it is possible to believe that there is every reason to arrange now, before the death *de cujus*, [88] for the procedure through which his property will be transmitted, and by an irrevocable act at that. Such arrangements obviously consist of derogations from the ordinary law of succession that cannot give satisfaction in this matter; nor can the will be any more useful to this end, for it is, by definition, a revocable act which is never binding on its author. In order to meet these particular needs, another institution may therefore be found necessary: It concerns the pacts about future successions. This type of arrangement necessarily assumes the contractual form; for in order to be able to derogate in this fashion from the regular order of succession, a person other than the donor—namely, an eventual heir, who either declares to someone a waiver of his rights or else, on the contrary, receives from the donor some exceptional favor—must intervene. Since it is especially at the time of the children's marriage that there is good reason to make arrangements of this nature, the pacts of succession generally make up a part of the marriage contract and it often happens that the pacts cannot be contracted except on this occasion.

De Dainville's work proposes to give the history of these pacts in our former laws. Our old domestic law was, on general principles, favorable towards equality of sharing between children. On the contrary, feudalism, with its rights of primogeniture, called for inequality. The pacts of succession offered the means of legally satisfying this need. Hence the waiver of daughters' rights to the paternal inheritance, in return for a dowry, and sometimes even without a dowry; hence the contractual institutions for heirs, etcetera. Besides, the commoners themselves had recourse to the same procedures in order to assure patrimonial unity.

Pacts of succession were, then, above all destined to favor inequality of treatment between the children; and even though, on the way, they had to leave room for egalitarian views in proportion to the progress made, they kept this characteristic up until the end. It is self-explanatory that under these circumstances they were viewed with disfavor by the drafters of the Civil Code, which, on general principles, banned the pacts of succession. (*Année sociologique*, 10, 1907, pp. 433–434; trans J. French)

Henri Guigon. *La Succession des bâtards dans l'ancienne Bourgogne.*
    Dijon: J. Nourry, 1905, 123 pp.

It is a question of interest to us to understand what were the social facts which gave rise to the moral blemish with which bastards have been afflicted for such a long time as well as the judicial inferiority which has been the result of it. Unhappily the criterion which the author has employed in order to ascertain the moral situation of bastards at different moments in history has not perhaps been the most suited to this object.

It is the importance of their incapacities in respect to inheritance which serves as a landmark for him; but the law of inheritance is, by its very nature, subject to variation for purely economic reasons. The changes which develop do not therefore reflect corresponding changes in moral notions.

What emerges from the picture he draws for us is, first of all, that the moral taint with which bastards were marked did not go back any further than the Carolingian epoch. Up until then, the family had not been sufficiently strongly established and organized for irregularity of birth to have a great effect on the public conscience. Even under the Merovingians, bastardy did not entail any forfeitures of rights, except when the matter was complicated by an unevenness of match. But after Charlemagne, under the influence of the Church, it grew into a blemish. The bastard was no longer able to inherit in the absence of a will, not to mention other incapacities which were inflicted upon him at the same time. Nonetheless, the emotion of reprobation exercised its full effects only on bastards of the lower orders. As far as bastards of noble birth were concerned, feudal prestige in part protected them from the severities of the law; they were less harshly treated. They could receive bounties and transmit them to their heirs, and they retained noble privilege when their quality was acknowledged.

Under the influence of custom, a double change took place. The privileges of bastards born of noble fathers tended to disappear; at the same time, the situation of the common bastard recovered by degrees. When the *ancien régime* ended, the latter was free to dispose of his goods, his children could inherit from him in the absence of a will, and he could inherit the things essential to life from his parents' patrimony. But, as we remarked at the beginning of this analysis, the most important of the capacities which the bastard thus acquired seems to have been due to causes of an economic nature. The children of common bastards, along with their father, formed part of the same community who shared ownership of property subject to mortmain;[89] in view of this capacity they possessed a right equal to their father's over property which had been commonly acquired. It was the right of the associate which was recognized rather than that of the heir strictly so-called. For his part, the duke had every interest in preserving the community of property subject to mortmain, and consequently in permitting his legitimate child to succeed him.

We know how the legislation of the Revolution undertook to give bastards legal relief up to the point of making them the equals of other children, and how, on the contrary, after the Revolution a reaction occurred in the opposite direction, the excesses of which we have, for some years past, merely sought to correct. (*Année sociologique*, 10, 1907, pp. 435–436; trans. A. Lyons)

Alexa Stanischitsch. *Über den Ursprung der Zadruga: Eine soziologische Untersuchung.* Bern: Buchdruckerei Scheitlin, Spring und Cie., 1907, 72 pp.

For a long time, there was unanimous agreement that the *zadruga* of the Slavs was a relatively primitive form of family organization. The very dimensions of this grouping (which generally consists of several collateral branches), the perfect state of communism in which its members live, seem proofs of its archaic character. One saw here the almost pure type of what Sumner Maine has called the *joint family*. But in 1899 Peisker undertook to demonstrate that this classic conception was devoid of all historical foundation.* According to him the *zadruga*, very far from being the result of a natural and spontaneous formation, seems to be, on the contrary, a governmental and fiscal construction of recent date. It is only toward the middle of the sixteenth century that it would have begun to make its appearance. In the Middle Ages the population was not able to live in restricted family units, reduced to one household only, for a farm under cultivation must be of a certain size in order to be sufficiently productive. But, on the other hand, the state could not allow families to grow too big, because taxes were paid according to the number of households and the treasury's interests would have been undermined. The state therefore was opposed to permitting the same family community to consist of more than two households. When this number was exceeded, the individuals who were in excess were compelled to leave the house and found another home. Such is the organization that was the most widespread until the end of the sixteenth century. It is at this moment that the Turks conquered Byzantium. [Durkheim committed a factual error since Byzantium was conquered in 1453 and not in the sixteenth century. ED.] The political and financial indolence of the new regime brought an end to firm enforcement of the rule of the *Doppelfamilie*. As a result, in order to escape taxation, family groups were made as extensive as possible everywhere that the condition of the land permitted. It was apparently in this way that the *zadruga* belatedly got its start.

This theory has been introduced to extend and reinforce Fustel de Coulange's ideas on the village community. In fact, it is well known that Fustel applied himself with dialectical vigor to demonstrate that there existed no historical traces of an age when the land was jointly owned by local groups. But if Peisker's thesis is fundamental, it is no longer simply village communism but also family communism that ceases to appear as a natural phase, a necessary and primal factor in an evolving society, since, in one of those cases

---

* "Die serbische Zadruga," *Zeitschrift für Sozial und Wirtschaftsgeschichte*, 1899. The article had appeared previously in *Pastrenks Narodo pisny Sbornik Ceskoslovansky*, Prague, 1899.

when it was thought to have been observed in the best and most convincing lights, it was, as it seems, due exclusively to a combination of local, fortuitous, and recent circumstances. Thus it is not hard to gather the full importance of the question at issue. From the answer that is given, historical growth is apparently understood in an entirely different light.

Stanischitsch's treatment is a critical examination of Peisker's theory. As for the institutions that have prompted belief in the discovery of the survival of an ancient village communism (the Russian *mir* and the *Allmende* of Switzerland, etcetera), he agrees that they were formed at a later date. But he upholds, on the other hand, the view characterizing the *zadruga* as natural and primal.

He points out, to begin with, how unlikely it is that the government, through purely fiscal measures, could also have had such a profound impact on the organization of the family as to substitute one family life-style for another and to impose a new domestic moral standard. It is certain that underlying Peisker's hyothesis there is an artifical notion of society that could be considered definitely discredited.

The close ties uniting the *zadruga* to certain religious beliefs and especially the primitive character of those beliefs are enough to prove that the *zadruga* cannot have originated at the recent date ascribed to it. Each *zadruga*, in fact, has its domestic form of worship. It has, under the name of *Slawa*, its god or its guardian spirit. The *slawa* is the *zadruga* personified. Therefore two individuals who have the same *slawa* consider themselves related, even though one of them could be living on the shores of the Adriatic and the other on the banks of the Danube. As with the extended kin, if they are of different sex, they are forbidden to marry. *Slawa* worship and family patrimony are so closely interdependent that one cannot claim an inheritance from the second without similarly benefiting from the first. When different families live under the same roof, they must have one and the same *slawa*. Although the Church has tried to give a Christian coloration to these practices, it is evident that they hark back to a very remote epoch. In any case, it is impossible to suppose that a religious organization so deeply rooted in tradition has been vitalized by fiscal measures (p. 45).

Peisker's theory rests, moreover, on a contradiction. It admits, in fact, that the family could maintain itself only by extending itself sufficiently. And indeed, historians of comparative law are well aware of this need, which is binding on men in slightly advanced societies. But that is like saying that beginning with the time when farming was just starting to expand, a family organization such as the *zadruga* was conjured up by the very forces of circumstance. It is not clear, therefore, why those needs were obliged to wait until the sixteenth century to be fulfilled. The cooperation of a strong and well-organized government was in no way necessary in order to obtain that effect which was brought about on its own, by a natural growth. Above all, it is in cases where the state is still rudimentary that those great family conglomerations are indispensable. For since political authority is not in that case equipped to protect individuals and their rights, it is necessary that particular groups, namely families, be responsible for that concern; and they can make it work only if they have an effective force that commands respect.

But the author is not satisfied just to show how implausible and contradictory the theory is [in its conceptualization]. He establishes the fact that the historical data on which he relies do not have the significance that Peisker has given them.

According to the latter, the *zadruga* would have been impossible in Serbia during the Middle Ages, because, according to a text by Procope, the population was at the time nomadic and dispersed in scattered rural areas. But if this dispersal is perhaps a sign that the village was nonexistent at the time among the Serbs, it makes no case whatsoever for writing off the *zadruga* (p. 42). As for nomadic mobility, the author disputes its existence. Doubtless, the population had a certain mobility. The peasants used to move from place to place quite freely in order to escape the crushing burdens which certain lords imposed on them and in order to respond to the lives which others prepared for them; but, as a rule, they lived a sedentary life (p. 55).

The remaining texts are invoked by Peisker to demonstrate that the group formed from the *Doppelfamilie* was at a given moment imposed by the state. In a discussion it is impossible for us to reproduce, the author attempts to prove that the sense the texts convey is not like the one that has been ascribed to them. When a man lived in isolation, the monastery to which he belonged was obliged to provide him with a companion as a partner for certain menial tasks. But it was a gracious move, destined to lighten the burdens and to distribute them more equitably; it was a protection for the peasant, not a privileged concession made to his masters. In any case, it is in no way a matter of obligatory cohabitation, and consequently there is nothing in those provisions that could have cleared the way for the *zadruga* (pp. 62 ff.). Furthermore, many facts establish that the *zadruga* was already in existence at that time. The truth is that during the Middle Ages it underwent, at least in certain regions, a temporary regression. Since the state was very strong and since it was the adversary of those large groups that it tended, in any case, to render useless, the vast family communities gave way to families more restricted in size. This result was particularly marked in cases where governmental impact could make itself felt more directly—that is to say, around points serving as state centers. But, with the Turkish conquest, the central authority was weakened; naturally, as a consequence the *zadruga* immediately regained a portion of the terrain it had lost. But it was far from being born at that moment.

This little book does us the favor of putting within our grasp a certain number of facts that are not readily accessible to the Western reader. The line of reasoning against Peisker's thesis appears well directed. Perhaps the author has too easily accepted the village's recent origin. From the fact that the Russian *mir,* in its present form, is not ancient, it does not follow that at the start there was not another, more widespread community over and above the domestic community—of course, family-oriented by nature. Here as elsewhere, we tend to think that the whole precedes the part, or at the very least is its contemporary. (*Année sociologique,* 11, 1910, pp. 343–347; trans. J. French)

C. W. L. Launspach. *State and Family in Early Rome.* London: George Bell and Sons, 1908, xx + 288 pp.

This work is a new interpretation of the classic theory about the origins of the Roman state and the Roman family. At the basis of the Roman family is the *gens,* a large composite family segment, essentially religious by nature, having at its head a chief, a patriarch, armed from the beginning with extensive powers which will constitute the *patria potestas* of the classic epoch. These powers are explained in terms of physical ascendancy (p. 202) and in terms of ideas involved with and kept alive by ancestor worship. The confederation of *gentes* presumably gave rise to the state. As for the constitution of the family, as it is considered in Rome from its earliest history, it presumably came about very simply from a division of the *gens* into groups smaller in size but organized according to the same principles.

The author does not seem to suspect the difficulties raised by this conclusion, apparently so simple. Just as Eduard Meyer has shown in the book that we analyze above,[90] political society, in Rome as elsewhere, if it did not precede the family, is its contemporary and is not the result of a coalition of family groupings—as too many historians have been repeating.

In another sense, it is entirely arbitrary to credit the *gens* with an organization comparable to that represented at a later date by the little group made up of the *paterfamilias* and his *sui.* Nothing warrants our crediting the chief of the *gens* with powers analogous to those later enjoyed by the properly so-called family father. The *gens* is a sort of clan, and in a general way the clan is rather more democratically organized; its chief is a *primus inter pares* rather than a sovereign. The big and difficult problem is to find out precisely how it comes about that the *patria potestas* was constituted directly in proportion to the further emergence of the small *familia* from the *gens*—thereby freeing itself to shape its own increasingly autonomous and personal existence.

Now, for the author, this problem does not exist. Its nonexistence is all the more pronounced since he does not seem to take into exact account the nature and the real dimensions of the family group within which the *patria potestas* was born. He calls it the agnatic family. "The state's civil units," he says, "was the agnatic family or group of related individuals, subject to the authority of a common living ancestor" (p. 203, cf. p. 205). But, in reality, there are only certain agnates who are subject to the *patria potestas,* namely the *sui,* and, to be exact, one would have to explain why it was applied only to such a restricted circle.

The author shows a knowledge of classic works on the subject matter, and he knows how to make discerning use of them, but without adding anything important. (*Année sociologique*, 11, 1910, pp.347–348; trans J. French)

Alfred Obrist. *Essai sur les origines du testament romain*. Lausanne: Viret–Genton, 1906, 172 pp.

It is common knowledge that a certain number of historians tend to push forward the date when authorization to make a will presumably made its appearance in the history of Roman law. This is also the thesis Obrist supports in the work[91] we are about to analyze. The testamentary institution appears to him too complex to have arisen prior to a relatively recent date. Beyond the fact that it presupposes an already very refined legal culture, it was to run up against the principle of family communism—a principle it negated.

It is in connection with adoption procedures that the making of a deed in case of death would have arisen in Rome. In order to prevent the breakup of a household, the father of a family would adopt as his son, and consequently his successor, either a distant relative or even an outsider. Such a deed already had one of the characteristics of a will, since it altered the legal order of succession. But it was not yet a will properly speaking; for it was contract that presupposed the assent of the beneficiary, whereas the will is made final solely by the wish of the testator. Furthermore and for the same reason, the adoption contract, once formulated, became irrevocable, whereas the provisions in a will are subject to change up to the very moment of death.

After the contract of adoption there followed the *testamentum calatis comitiis:*[92] After obtaining the consent of the college of pontiffs, a man would publicly designate another as his successor in the presence of the assembled committee, who, according to our author, had the power either to accept or to refuse this departure from the customary law of succession. This innovation amounted to an important step forward in the *adoptio in hereditatem:*[93] The one adopted was able to succeed only when leaving his natural family for his adoptive family, whose name he took, whereas the heir designated before the committee preserved his *status familiae*. Thus identity with the will became closer; yet, according to our author, that word cannot be properly applied to such a very archaic institution. The *testamentum calatis comitiis* was irrevocable and the author estimates that it did not amount to a unilateral type of deed, but involved the heir's consent. Furthermore, the aim of this deed would have been less to pass along property rights than to give the *de cujus* a successor who would continue his name and the cult of the family, and would discharge the ritual duties in tribute to the deceased. The principle of the family co-ownership would have remained intact. The donor would have had only the right to designate the administrator of the patrimony.

It is to the deed drawn up in committee thus understood that the famous formula of the Law of the Twelve Tables would have applied: *Uti legassit. . . ita jus esto.*[94] The latter, therefore, would not have aimed to proclaim, as has been stated, entire testamentary freedom, but would have merely simplified the drawn-up will by ridding it of bothersome formalities. Until the

Twelve Tables, the family father could choose a successor only after ratification by the college of pontiffs and the committee; this double-check system was suppressed. The committee no longer played any role except that of witness. But the *paterfamilias* had no longer the right to dispose freely of the patrimony: his power was forever confined to determining the person who, at his hearth, would administer the *domus familiaque* [95] and preside over the family sacrifices. Only with this determination could he proceed more independently than formerly; and it is not hard to believe that public opinion prevented him from using this freedom without legitimate motives.

The unlimited right to make a will would not, then, date from the Twelve Tables; it would have appeared only much more belatedly with the growth of the *testamentum per aes et libram,* [96] which was the first provision for death as a contributing factor with the direct and simple goal of transmitting property rights.

We have trouble understanding how the comitial act was able to preserve intact the old family communism. Since the successor thus designated replaced the person of the deceased, he had all the rights; consequently when he himself was dying, if he was intestate at the time, it was his own *sui,* [97] his own children, who would inherit the patrimony that he had received by bequest, and consequently the agnates of the first testator would find themselves dispossessed. Under such circumstances, what would become of family co-ownership? It is therefore very arbitrarily that our author tries to limit the rights conferred by the will made before the electoral meetings. Already and on its own it involved a new type of family regime.

But it is useless to discuss this hypothesis at length. If the author saw fit to resort to it, it is because he holds a point of view about Roman wills which, though held in common with a number of jurists, is open to question nonetheless.

This idea arises from the premise that freedom to make a will is possible only in a society where individual ownership has become known. On the other hand, it would be a historical miracle that Rome should have known about individual ownership in so primitive an age as that of the Twelve Tables; hence we conclude that the absolute right to make a will must necessarily be later than the fourth century. But actually, the institution of will making in Rome had a significance entirely unlike the one it assumed in our time. This does not mean that from that moment old-type family communism was shattering and in retreat before the thrust to acknowledge the rights of the individual, but simply that it was transformed. Instead of remaining overextended, it became organized. Influenced by causes we need not investigate here, the family was induced to incorporate within the person of the *paterfamilias,* to relinquish into his hands, the powers it held at the start. Accordingly, the father came to be invested with almost limitless power. It was not by virtue of the respect that individual personality would have inspired from then on; the fact is that he was, literally, the family personified. He was their agent. His authority stemmed from that of the family group and was entrusted to him, as it were, by delegation. Very far from resting on the principle of individual ownership, the *patria potestas* negated the idea, since all the possessions the family members acquired belonged to the father, just as previously they had belonged to the family. The institution of family co-ownership permeated the entire organization authorized by the father. In a word, freedom to make a will and all the other interlocking rights stemmed uniquely from the fact that the Roman family was predisposed to give itself a monarchical constitution. Now, the causes that made it necessary for it to organize itself in this way are of a sort that were capable of influence well before the idea of individual ownership arose. Consequently, the resulting right to make a will can, without any anachronism, be maintained at the relatively remote date that the texts assign to it. (*Année sociologique*, 11, 1910, pp. 352–355; trans. J. French)

Robert Roberts. *Das Familien-Sklaven-und Erbrecht im Qorân*. Leipzig: Hinrichs, 1908, 56 pp.

The aim of this work is to present an overall view of the principal provisions in the Koran as they relate to domestic law so as to bring out both what they have in common with Hebraic law and what distinctive characteristics they possess. From the sociological point of view, the last-mentioned peculiarities are the most interesting. As for the rest, the provisions that are available in the Pentateuch perform a double duty—the more so since, for the most part, the Koran entries are borrowed directly from it. Therefore, such borrowings do not very effectively enrich our knowledge. Because of this, we shall lay special stress on our analysis of whatever originality Islamic law possesses. Unfortunately, such originality is rather limited.

The laws of marriage are distinguished by the great ease with which marriage ties are broken. The husband may repudiate his wife at will, without having to justify the reasons for so doing; and although abuse of this right appears reprehensible in the eyes of the public, mention is made of countries where a man contracts, in the space of ten years, twenty or thirty marriages (p. 18).

And yet, at the same time, it seems clear that these same marital bonds have a religious character that renders them respectable, virtually holy. When a wife is repudiated a first and even a second time, the husband may go back on his decision and resume relations with her. But if there have been three successive repudiations, the husband may no longer marry her again, unless in the interval she has contracted with a third party a fourth marriage that a fourth divorce or a death has managed to dissolve. The fact is, then, that this triple repudiation has a well-defined character, like the triple emancipation of the Romans, and that it is considered as amounting to a kind of sacrilege that puts a barrier between husband and wife—an interdict, a taboo. Marriage with a new husband lifts this taboo, no doubt by effacing the memories left by the first union. The moment the marks left by the latter have disappeared, the husband again finds himself, when faced with his first wife, in the same situation as before their marriage. She has approached him again like a newcomer, and as such, there is consequently no further reason for her not to marry him (pp. 20–22).

This curious provision has been all the more surprising to commentators and historians since it contrasts with a very different provision in Hebrew law. According to the Pentateuch, if a repudiated wife marries again, it is forbidden for her first husband to remarry her, even if she becomes free again (Deuteronomy 24:1).

But the contradiction is only apparent. In one case as in the other, it is considered that the definite rupture of the marriage bonds gives rise to a taboo between husband and wife. However, among the Hebrews the new marriage is looked upon as the consummation of such a rupture; according to the law in the Koran, the rupture is consummated by a divorce thrice repeated. The principle is the same in both cases. We think it likely that this principle has to do with the religious character which is so often given to sexual dealings. On its own merits, it gives rise to bonds sui generis which cannot be broken without blaspheming; the blasphemy that violates a taboo re-creates more taboos in its turn. What makes this hypothesis plausible is that in the case of Muslims, the two sexes live strictly separated. Now, wherever such separate status is on record, it tends to indicate sexual relations of a mysterious and consequently mystical character.

As for family morality, perhaps its chief characteristic is the subordination of properly domestic duties to religious duties. The lack of filial piety is, as a rule, a very grievous sin; but the son is supposed to disobey his parents if they ask him to betray the faith. Children are looked upon as something to treasure, but at the same time as dangerously seductive, like wealth itself, for they can cause one to forget God (pp. 36–37).

This superiority of confessional ties over parental ties was even indicated originally in certain provisions of the law of succession (p. 50). On this score, Islamic law contrasts with Roman law, which recognizes in family concerns a kind of supremacy over all the others. Would it be to such influential religious ideas that one should attribute the very lofty conception the Muslims have of guardianship? Whereas in Rome this last appears to be set up in large part to suit the needs of the guardian; according to the Koran the guardian is, above all, duty-bound to watch over both the person and interests of his ward (p. 35).

In a general sense, the law of succession shows singular disparities by which it may be distinguished from Roman law (pp. 51–52). (*Année sociologique*, 11, 1910, pp. 355–357; trans. J. French).

Richard Gebhard. *Russisches Familien-und Erbrecht*. Berlin: Guttentag, 1910, 122 pp.

In Russia, the laws that govern marriage and the family were assembled and codified in 1833. Although in the course of such codification a few borrowings were made from Western legislation, the fundamental principles preserve an archaic character. This is what the author of this little work, who is from Strasbourg, brings out.

To begin with, marriage is essentially a religious matter; civil marriage does not exist. It is even forbidden to marry a "pagan", such is the designation given to anyone who is neither a Christian nor a Jew nor a Muslim. The variety of persuasions acknowledged results in the diversity of marriage laws that are applied to each case. Thus, orthodox Catholicism, while admitting the principle of divorce, is far from favoring its practice; legitimate causes for divorce are very rare. On the other hand, the Lutherans acknowledge as many as ten causes, including simple antipathy.

As for possessions, the normal matrimonial system is that of separate maintenance—joint holdings are unknown in Russia. The wife has the right to dispose freely of everything she owns; the husband has no powers over his wife's fortune other than those which the wife chooses to delegate to him. Husband and wife can even arrange to be in each other's debt. The furnishings themselves are not considered to be common property; it is a rule that each of the household items belongs to one of the spouses, and to one only (pp. 72 ff.). The author considers this type of matrimonial regime superior to the joint-holdings type. Such a preference is very debatable. The conjugal association always becomes more powerful and cohesive as history advances. It is unlikely that this greater moral unity is not reflected in economic life, and it seems unlikely that it can come to terms with a radical separation of property. It is true that for the author joint holdings imply expanded marital authority, but these two institutions are not interconnected. The former comes to us from Germanic law; the latter, from Roman law.

But in spite of this distinction, each of the spouses has the right to inherit from the other. This right is applied to a quarter of the furniture and a seventh of the landed property. Such a right even extends to the bequests that are opened after the death of the deceased spouse and from which the latter would have benefited if he (or she) had been living at that moment. For example, a wife may inherit, in the prescribed proportion, from her father-in-law, if the latter survives his son. On this point, then, Russian law surpassed our French law for a long time.

But on the other hand, the provisions related to women's rights of succession are symptomatic of a backward civilization. It is a matter of principle that men inherit just about everything. The daughter's share is only an eighth of the movable wealth and a quarter of the landed property of her parents. Furthermore, if there are several daughters, the sum of the portions that thus fall to their lot may in no case exceed the sons' portion; the former can be very inferior to the latter, but not be superior to it. The same rule is applied to the bequest involving collateral heirs. It is obviously a survival from the time when the woman did not inherit. Destined to prevent the family patrimony from passing into a family of outsiders, this exclusion derived from the old-type family communism. Since the traces of such communism are still perceptible in Russia, it might by expected that the right to make a will was very limited—in reality, it is just about limitless. Presumably it was introduced and developed in order to correct what was outdated in the laws of succession.

According to our author, another characteristic of Russian law is the excessive extent to which paternal power is carried. As evidence he submits that the father can be stripped of his powers in a very limited number of cases only; the crimes he has committed must be of a particularly serious nature. Furthermore, the father's right to punish is almost without limit. But such provisions are perhaps to be imputed to a certain primitive life-style more than to a Roman conception of paternal authority. Clear evidence to the effect that the father is definitely not a kind of absolute sovereign is the number of rules relating to guardianship. There exists a court, adaptable to the various social classes, which is charged with inspecting the way in which the guardian, including the father, performs his duties (pp. 48–51). Besides, the father does not inherit his children's possessions, even when the latter die without leaving any descendants; his only claim involves the usufruct (p. 101).

Not only is investigation of paternity permitted, but the father need only provide the material upkeep of his children in order to have important claims on the latter: the right to see them regularly, even to supervise and direct their upbringing. In case there is a disagreement with the mother, the court confers on the father the powers of guardianship (pp. 54–55). (*Année sociologique*, 12, 1913, pp. 424–426; trans J. French)

NOTES AND NOTICES

A. Moret. *La Condition des féaux en Egypte, dans la famille, dans la société, dans la vie d'outre-tombe* (Vol. IX), Recueil des travaux relatifs à la philologie égyptienne et assyrienne, Paris: Bouillon.

The author shows how in Egypt the feudal relationships were the model for family and political relationships in this world and in the other. (*Année sociologique*, 1, 1898, p. 338; trans. Y. Nandan)

Ernest Miller. *Die Hauskommunion der Südslaven* (Domestic Community of the Southern Slavs). *Jahrbuch der internationale Vereinigung für vergleichende Rechtswissenschaft und Volkswirtschaftslehre*, 1897, pp. 106–135.

The author gives a quick history of the *zadruga*, in different Slavic countries of the south, by emphasizing especially the most recent legislation. What emerges from this account is that the legislators, after having attempted to fight against the *zadruga*, seem to have progressively abandoned the struggle.

Experience has shown that the destruction of this old family organization would have disastrous effects on the agriculture of these peoples. It is especially evident in Croatia and Slavonia.

The author points out the existence of the *zadruga* nobles, who today have submitted themselves to a special legal system, but who in the past did not distinguish themselves from others. The formation of this country nobility does not go far beyond the sixteenth and seventeenth centuries. The study of this feudal system, as well as of that which we also observe among the Slavs of the north, will singularly help to understand the Western feudal system. (*Année sociologique*, 1, 1898, pp. 339–340; trans. Y. Nandan)

N. Tamassia. "L'allevamento dei figli nell'antico diritto irlandese" (The Education of Boys Under the Ancient Irish Law). *Rivista italiana di sociologia*, May 1899, pp. 294–302.

The article deals with the frequent practice (called *altrum*) of raising boys outside of their families. The *altrum* created durable relations between the young man, his real father, and the foreign father who raised him. There used to be among them the exchange of rights and duties. The author attempts to give an explanation of this practice. It resulted from the fact that certain members of a clan, being kept outside of the territory or being deprived of their domestic occupations, could not raise their sons. The sentiments of solidarity befitting the clan made it seem natural that their boys' education be accomplished by other fathers of the family. The author's explanation is quite simplistic. In reality, it concerns without doubt one of those innumerable cases of so-called artificial kinship which shed so much light on the nature of family relations. (*Année sociologique*, 3, 1900, p. 382; trans. Y. Nandan)

Lucien Marchand. "Les Gard'orphènes à Lille." *Nouvelle Revue historique de droit français et étranger*, 1902, no. 3, pp. 268–299.

Here is a curious case of intervention by the commune in domestic life. The custodians of the orphans were municipal officers, who in Lille and in many northern cities were commissioned to safeguard the interests of the minors. They appointed tutors in case there was a need; they controlled the behavior of the tutors thus engaged; and so on. The author describes this interesting institution and its function. (*Année sociologique*, 6, 1903, p. 345; trans. Y. Nandan)

H. A. Rose. "Unlucky Children." *Folk-lore*, 1902, XIII, pp. 63–67.

The article throws light on the condition of children in the family according to their age. (*Année sociologique*, 6, 1903, p. 351; trans. Y. Nandan)

Ernest Cartier. *Le Célibat à Rome*. Paris: Plon et Nourrit, 1902, 159 pp.

With scientific pretensions, the work manifests an elegant humanism. (*Année sociologique*, 6, 1903, p. 351; trans. Y. Nandan)

F. Carli. "La religione naturale e la famiglia. *Rivista italiana di sociologia*, VII, nos. 1–2, 1903, pp. 135–150.

The article presents a summary treatment of evolution of the family as discussed in the works of secondary character. (*Année sociologique*, 7, 1904, p. 433; trans. Y. Nandan)

Ottorino Clerici. *Sul diritto successorio dell XII tavole. Indagini storiche di diritto Romano*. Torino: Tip. Baravalle e Falconieri, 1903, 45 pp.

The law of the Twelve Tables presumably proclaimed only the freedom to make a will for nonpatrimonial property. (*Année sociologique*, 8, 1905, p. 414; trans. Y. Nandan)

Louis Germain Lévy. *La Famille dans l'antiquité israélite*. Paris: F. Alcan, 1905, 296 pp.

One finds in this book a collection of major texts which refer to the subject of marriage and the family among the ancient Hebrews. But the method in which the texts are interpreted does not always conform to what the critical mind requires. The author, defending his conclusions, often does so after a vast summary examination. He even concludes that there does not exist any relationship between affirmations contained in the body of the work and the texts to which the notes refer. (*Année sociologique*, 9, 1906, pp. 372–373; trans. Y. Nandan)

MARRIAGE

REVIEWS

E. Meynial. "Le Mariage après les invasions." *Nouvelle Revue historique de droit français et étranger*, 1896, nos. 4, 6; 1897, no. 2.

The author proposes to investigate how matrimonial law in the Middle Ages was constituted.

This law was shaped under a triple influence: Roman law such as it appeared at the end of the Empire, barbarian laws, and the Church. It constitutes the first part in a series of three articles dedicated to examining matrimonial law in the Middle Ages.

The forms of marriage. Although on the surface the institution of marriage remained in the late Roman Empire what it was at the end of the Republic, a profound transformation took place. In the beginning, as Leist has shown us above,[98] the *justa nuptia*[99] comprised three phases: (1) the betrothal, a simple preliminary that did not yet partake of the nature nor of the results of marriage; (2) the *traditio*, [100] and (3) the *deductio*. [101] It is the last two ceremonies that truly constituted lawful marriage customs. Now, little by little, they fell into disuse. They had significance only because they were bound up with the cult of ancestors; they vanished with this last. They doubtless survived for a long time, but as far as their practical usage was concerned, they served no useful purpose under law. The generating factors in marriage became not ritual formality but consent of the parties. Now, this consent was a result of voluntary and prolonged cohabitation; consequently, cohabitation, if it was never a necessary condition for marriage *(nuptias non concubitus, sed consensus facit)*, [102] became a sufficient condition for it inasmuch as it was symptomatic of the *consensus*. But then lawful marital practices became, from this point of view, indistinct from concubinage, which is likewise simply cohabitation by consent. At first, it is true, the concubine was distinguished from the wife not only through the absence of matrimonial formalities but because she was and could only be a person of inferior position. But when the day came that one could take as concubines women whom one could also take as wives and vice versa, this distinction itself disappeared.

A single difference continued to exist: the act of betrothal. That is why, though this act was separate from marriage at the start, the betrothal became more and more its essential element. A full-fledged procedure was developed, the result of which was to raise it to the dignity of the so-called marriage. All the rules that were being applied to marriage were extended to the betrothal. It involved similar terms regarding age and consent; it was subject to similar prohibitions, gave rise to similar obligations. It was marriage during a trial period, but the period alone was left up to the free choice of the parties concerned. Since the betrothal plays an equally preponderant role in the Germanic marriage, it is clear that, by itself, the Roman marriage tended to converge with this last; this spontaneous rapprochement was naturally destined to facilitate their fusion.

The terms of marriage. In earliest times, the right to marriage was an exclusive prerogative of paternal authority; from this it follows that a person *sui juris*[103] did not need any consent. It is true that women, even when they were not subject to the authority of a *pater familias,* were still under the agnates' protection. But it is not known if this protection conferred the right to consent to the marriage; in any case, it disappeared under Claudius. But under the Late Empire, a return to the ancient legislation is a matter of record; the woman, even *sui juris,* was once more subjected to a more rigorous control; only the people who exercised it were no longer the same. Those whom the ancient law used to exclude were now on call to perform this duty: to begin with, the mother; then the *propinqui*. [104] Although this expression is nowhere defined, it is very probable that it designated the cognates as well as the agnates, perhaps even the neighbors and members of the same social class. Finally, when there was disagreement between the woman and her mother and the *propinqui,* it was the emperor, or the judge, or his delegate, who settled the dispute and chose the husband. In this way the imperial power obtained a foothold within the family, and there was even acknowledgement of his right to act as deputy in giving consent not only for the parents but for the spouses, and to enforce the marriage. These facts prove that there arose at the time a new concentration of the family; during the same period, it was one of the shapes that the awakening of the corporate spirit took as attested in the records. In order to avoid being crushed, individuals were obliged to group themselves and to form groups that were as strong as possible. But it is evident that this concentration of the family group came about on grounds very different from those which had formerly been the case.

Another novelty, no less important, is the addition of the *contubernium*[105] to the number of regular and regulated unions. In earliest times, the law did not take a hand in it; it did not produce any legal result, did not engender any so-called kinship. Little by little, at least in certain cases, it assumed the character of a marriage—inferior no doubt, but recognizable. Thus, at the same time that concubinage became comparable to lawful marriage practices, the *contubernium* came to resemble concubinage. It will be seen that these uncertain unions are to be encountered frequently in the period of barbarism, and that they played an important role in that period.

The results of marriage. The great change that came about in this respect is that marriage tended more and more to become a special institution, distinct from the family and serving as its base.

Originally, in Rome, the keystone of the family was not marriage but the *patria potestas.* Marriage did not necessarily result in founding a new family, but simply in giving a new member access to the husband's family. By himself, the husband was nothing or almost nothing; it was the *pater familias* who was everything. It was not towards her husband that the wife was submissive, but towards her husband's *pater familias.* It was only as *pater familias* of his wife that the husband could chastise conjugal infidelity, etcetera. Marital authority was only one aspect of paternal authority. But to the degree that the second declined, the first emerged and established itself independently and more strongly. The husband had rights in his capacity as husband, notably to punish the adulterer or press for its repression. The married couple, at first lost in the crowded family, detached itself, became a group sui generis that had its own physiognomy and its special set of rules. It was especially from the monetary point of view that this transformation was notable. Originally, the wife's dowry used to go into the patrimony of the husband's *pater familias,* and if there was restitution it could only be brought about by the wife's *pater familias* and it was acted upon to his advantage. Little by little, matters changed. The dowry went into the husband's *peculium,*[106] then was declared completely independent of the family patrimony. At the same time, the wife's consent became necessary in order that there might be restitution, and all kinds of conservative measures were introduced in order to safeguard the dowry fund's proper nature. Accordingly there was established, over and above the husband's family patrimony and that of the wife, a marital patrimony, which the practice of the *donatio ante nuptias*[107] served further to swell. Thus the matrimonial society found itself on an economic footing that was solely its own.

Under the influence of this new action center, the ancient family grouping was transformed. Linked to the core formed by the two spouses, thus isolated, there were of course the children. Very quickly they were acknowledged to possess special rights to this conjugal patrimony, and consequently from that time on they maintained with their parents relations unknown until then, since they were independent of all *patria potestas*. In a word, under the ancient family, based entirely on that authority sui generis of the *pater familias*, there was gradually taking shape another entirely new unit based on marriage and blood ties.

At this present point in our writing, this interesting study now comes to a halt. In a sequel promised by him, the author will present the corresponding provisions to be found in barbarian lawmaking as opposed to the status of Roman legislation. (*Année sociologique*, 1, 1898, pp. 340–343; trans. J. French)

Karl Friederichs. "Familienstufen und Eheformen" (Types of Family and Forms of Marriage). *Zeitschrift für vergleichende Rechtswissenschaft*, XI, 1897, pp. 458 ff.

The object of this article is to show that the same type of family can very well be accommodated to a different matrimonial form. Such facts abound. In the Slavic *zadruga,* such as it still existed a short while ago, monogamy was strictly enforced. In Tibet, one encounters the same domestic organization, but marriage is collective; all the brothers marry the same woman. Under the maternal family regime, it is considered very good form for a group of sisters to marry a group of brothers, or to marry one and the same man (a sort of polygyny of a particular kind), or for each one to marry a different husband, etcetera, etcetera.

But the proposition, to be exact, needs to be qualified; it is true only of that portion of the marriage regulations which concerns the number of spouses who fit in with conjugal logic. Up until the time when monogamy becomes legally obligatory, the approach of the matrimonial society is not well-defined; the parties concerned fix it as they choose, according to circumstances. At the very most, there are customs generally followed in the same country, precisely because the conditions of existence are generally the same for everybody. And again one finds at times very marked differences. Consequently, :he most varied combinations can take place, even though the type of family is the same. But it is not the same for the formalities of marriage—they are much less variable. One does not find marriage by purchase until a certain moment in the evolutionary process, and one no longer finds it, except in an outmoded state, once that phase of history has passed by.

But even qualified in this way, the law is important. Several inferences may be derived from it:

(1) The family cannot be defined by the nature of the conjugal society; one must therefore renounce making a distinction between families that are polyandric, polygynic, etcetera. Characteristic family traits must be investigated, moreover.

(2) A corollary of the preceding is that marriage does not explain the family, since a single family includes very different kinds of marriage. One must not, then, explain uterine kinship or Morgan's nomenclatures by speculating about collective marriage, any more than one should explain agnatic kinship by the circumstances under which lawful weddings take place and the presumptive evidence they support.

(3) In a more general sense, it is clear how erroneous it is to view as common sense that opinion which considers marriage the foundation of the family, since the latter is so feebly affected by marriage practices. (*Année sociologique*, 1, 1898, pp. 343–344; trans. J. French)

C. A. Garufi. *Richerche sugli usi nuziali nel medio evo in Sicilia, con documenti inediti* (Researches on Nuptial Usages in Sicily During the Middle Ages, with Unpublished Documents). Palermo: Alberto Reber, 1897, 103 pp.

Sicily is one of the countries in Europe where the greatest number and variety of races and civilizations have been found living together. Greeks, Latins, and Jews were very numerous during the Middle Ages; Arabs and Normans have rubbed elbows at any given moment. From this mixture a composite civilization has resulted. Each of these peoples has marked Sicilian law with its imprint, which is consequently very different from that which was practiced on the peninsula. It has a physiognomy that is peculiar to it. This is what Garufi has set out to establish with respect to nuptial practices.

What makes it peculiar in this regard is, to begin with, the fact that ceremonial customs were nowhere so numerous, precisely because the Sicilians borrowed a little from everybody. In the fourteenth century the complete marriage consisted of three layers of superimposed formalities. In the first place, there was the ancient betrothal *(sponsalia)*, to which the Eastern Church had given a religious character; secondly, the couple went to church to render thanks to God and to receive the priest's blessing; finally, between these two practices a third one was inserted, brought about without doubt by peoples of Germanic origin. This was a transformation in the ceremony whereby the husband acquired the *mundium*[108] over his wife. And these three formalities were essential to the validity of the marriage.

Not only were ceremonies numerous, but they were carried out with a lavish display of festivities and adornments of which there is no example to be found in the West. Banquets, theater performances, torchlight promenades kept following each other for several days. This sumptuous extravagance became so extreme that the Norman kings tried to impose restraints, as proven by the great number of sumptuary laws in all the towns of the island. The same prohibitions may be found in several *fueros*[109] in Spain, from which it follows that nuptial ceremonies had the same characteristics in Spain. Would it not appear that this exceptional glitter is an Arab importation? (*Année sociologique*, 1, 1898, p. 345; trans. J. French)

Emil Schulenburg. "Die Spuren des Brautraubes, Brautkaufes und ähnlicher Verhältnisse in den französischen Epen des Mittelalters" (Traces of Marriage by Abduction, of Marriage by Purchase, and of Analogous Practices in the French Epics of the Middle Ages). *Zeitschrift für vergleichende Rechtswissenschaft*, XII, pp. 128–140, 161–186.

In the epic poems of the Middle Ages, a knight very frequently abducts either by force or by ruse the woman he loves; now, it is considered that abduction constitutes, on behalf of the abductor, a genuine right to marry the person abducted. In other cases the knight is obliged, in order to merit the hand of a girl, to undergo real trials—to evince his courage by some brave deed or even to render a signal service to the parents of his beloved. Schulenbug sees in the first of these usages a remnant of marriage by abduction, and in the second a survival of marriage by purchase.

If, by these customs—marriage by purchase and marriage by abduction—is meant the symbolic abduction and the regular purchase of a fiancée such as those are practiced among relatively advanced societies (Slavs, Greeks, Hebrews, etcetera), the comparison is arbitrary. These two ceremonies are, in fact, defined procedures, having a determined juridical meaning. They accompany the transformation from the maternal family to the agnatic family and they result from it. They are intended to allow the husband to incorporate into his own family the children born of his marriage. There is therefore nothing in common between these valid institutions and those deeds of force and skill that were so much honored during the Middle Ages. The tolerance which they enjoyed at that time shows only that the society was in the process of organizing itself; consequently, many acts escaped collective regulation, which was still weak and inconsistent, and many situations were resolved by violence, which consequently played an important role. This is what happens: Under different forms, whenever the social forces have not yet reached a sufficient state of equilibrium or have lost it, marriage by abduction and marriage by purchase have been wrongly confused. In that case, the practices of which we have just spoken are not without analogy with certain facts that have been noted in societies completely inferior, such as the Australian tribes. With these peoples, it happens that either the young man abducts the woman without the consent of the parents or that he buys their consent. But there is nothing in this of juridical acts intended to produce certain legal effects. A man takes a woman by force, or to avoid a vendetta, buys off the parents; these are private arrangements, more or less frequent, but without value and without social sanction. There is nothing in all of this which affects the structure of the family. The analogy with what is observed in the Middle Ages is striking enough, and it could be explained by the fact that these two kinds of societies were, mutatis mutandis, in a corresponding state of disorganization, chronic in the one case and temporary in the other. There is nothing in it [the medieval practices] of a survival, except that the superior societies begin to pass through phases that bring to mind certain traits of inferior societies—with this difference: they do not stop there. (*Année socioligique*, 1, 1898, pp. 346–347; trans. J. Sweeney)

H. N. Hutchinson. *Marriage Customs in Many Lands,* vol. VII. London: Seeley, 1897, 348 pp.

A good study of nuptial formalities would be of very great interest when studying marriage itself. For these solemnities do not involve, as it might seem, a superficial procedure—outside matrimonial and domestic relations. On the contrary, they sustain with these relations an intimate connection. The form the marriage takes varies according to what the marriage is and what the family is—so much so that from the nature of nuptial practices one can infer the essential features of the organization of the family.

It is not this type of study that Hutchinson gives us; he has simply assembled the materials that are necessary to make it. He passes in review the different countries, and in connection with each one describes the customs which are practiced not only on the wedding day but also during the entire period of time that elapses from the moment the first negotiations are entered into between the young people or their families. Since many of these practices are repeated almost identically in very different societies, the reading of the book leaves a certain feeling of unrelieved monotony, while at the same time the essential analogies are not set forth distinctly. The overall impression remains murky. The author generally fails to give his references; all this precludes either criticism of his sources of verification of his assertions. However, he does seem to be quite responsibly informed. Also, even though his work does not contain a methodical classification, the simple material proximity of the facts provokes and facilitates comparisons; they fall quite naturally into four main groups.

(1) There are, first of all, societies where there are no nuptial formalities whatsoever. Such are the tribes in Australia (pp. 148 ff.). A man takes a wife either by carrying off the one he desires, with or without the consent of the women, or by giving the girl's relatives one of his own relatives in exchange or a sum of money. The second procedure has the advantage of forestalling any feuding; it is a real compromise as expected. But all methods are valid, and

each uses the one he wants and in the way he chooses. Marriage, moreover, cannot be confined to predetermined forms for the excellent reason that there is no marriage properly speaking. The woman stays with the same man only if some other abductor does not come along to take her from her first proprietor. If she is beautiful, she passes from hand to hand (p. 149). It does not appear that there are more clearly defined ceremonials among the Indians of North America. The nature of the uterine family, which is very widely spread, hardly calls for them.

(2) Formal patterns appear with the family types which are based on the principle of the paternal line of descent. They are of two sorts: the simulated abduction of a minor or the redemption of the rights of the family into which the young woman was born by means of a certain sum paid out by the young man. These practices must not be confused with the somewhat similar deeds that are encountered in Australia. In the last-named country, abduction or payoff to avoid the anticipated vendetta are arrangements to which the participants may resort as it suits their pleasure and meets their purpose; solemn rites are not the means by which orderly marriage is distinguished from unruly union. It is not necessary to explain why the purchase ceremony (engagement) and the simulated and symbolic abduction are generally two connected formalities, the first issuing from the second.

Sometimes marriage is made up solely of these two operations, more or less developed. Yet it is quite apparent that most often these are encompassed with religious and magic rites of varying importance. A worthy study of such rites would, we believe, cast a great deal of light on the nature of marriage and of certain nuptial practices still in use today. The most essential are the following: Purification by means of baths or holy water liberally sprinkled over the young woman [Armenia (p. 18), Bulgaria (p. 187), Russia (p. 199)]; blood sacrifice of a beast or even a bloodletting sacrifice practiced on the spouse [Borneo (p. 28), Arabs (p. 73), Kafirs from the Bay of Delagoa (p. 125), Araucania[110] (p. 147)], in which the blood is very often sprinkled upon the threshold of the husband's house; meals and libations in common; gifts to each other from the spouses; gifts from the families to the spouses; and lastly, magic rites of all kinds in order to exorcise the activities of evil spirits or to assure the household's prosperity.

Doubtless the object of purification is, as for all lustrations, to wipe out or to attenuate the taboos aimed at the young woman and intended to isolate her from all sexual intercourse. As for sacrifices, meals, and libations in common, they serve as religious adjuncts to every contract of any importance; it is by bloodletting or joint banqueting that the knot is tied. It is entirely possible that the practice of mutual gift-giving is a substitute for the preceding, just as the sacrifice in the form of giving homage or donations to the gods is a procedure derived from the sacrificial communion. Along the same line of reasoning, there would be grounds for investigating what are the factors, probably religious in nature, causing marriages to be celebrated during a well-defined time of year, from preference or to the exclusion of any other. As nearly as can be determined from the somewhat confusing mass of facts in this book, it seems that the dates chosen fall on great feast-days when diverse forms of religious communion are employed and predispose the spirits to all sorts of ef-fusions (see pp. 9, 176, 192, 213).

(3) In all the above cases, the religious rite is merely the adjunct of the wedding ceremony, without playing an essential role. But little by little, for-malities of abduction and remuneration fade into the middle ground; religious ceremonies gain in stature and come to the fore. Their object is no longer to sanctify a contract settled without them or to ward off bad influences; it is through them that the conjugal knot is tied. In this guise, they begin by possessing a domestic and private character; they are destined to initiate the young woman into her husband's life-style of worship within the family. Mar-riage of a type that was practiced in Rome is recognizable. Since our author does not study the historic forms of marriage, but only those that contem-porary observation can encompass, he does not cite this example; but he points out these same practices in China (p. 43), in Melanesia (p. 161), and in Tahiti.

(4) Religious ceremonies within the family are replaced by religious ceremonies in public (marriage in *conspectu Ecclesiae*),[111] and the latter in turn give way to celebration under the solemn auspices of the secular power.

It is evident that these four types of marriage correspond to important stages in moral evolution. (*Année sociologique*, 2, 1899, pp. 331–334; trans. J. French)

D. Theophil Loebel. *Hochzeitsbräuche in der Türkei* (Marriage Customs in Turkey). Amsterdam: J. J. de Bussy, xv + 298 pp.

Although the author has occasionally penetrated authentic [written] sources, his book is written notably with the help of personal observations. Having passed long years in the Balkan peninsula, he has managed to penetrate to the core of the Turkish family, witnessing its function at close range; and it is because of this that his description is valuable and interesting.

Since Turkey contains populations of different cultures, consequently widely varying marriage procedures are to be found there. The author has classified them according to the ethnic groups who practice them: Muslim Turks, Arabs, Cherkess (Circassians),[112] Kurds, Armenians, etcetera. This classification was the most convenient, not the most instructive nor even perhaps the most natural. For different ethnic groups often have the same marriage customs, and inversely, within the same group there are found at times quite marked differences.

Among the Muslim Turks, the respective situation of the spouses is quite similar to what it used to be among the ancient Germans. The woman has no dowry; she must herself be dowered by the husband. The latter is compelled to defray all the expenses; moreover, he pays out to his wife a sum which, de-pending on the fortunes involved, varies between 500 and 50,000 piasters (1 piaster = 22½ centimes).[113] This sum stays with the wife in case of divorce or widowhood. The wedding is celebrated at the home of the fiancée, behind closed doors, before an audience which consists only of married couples and the priest *(imam)*. The latter records the event in a special ledger and in so doing gives the wedding religious sanction. In a general sense, these wedding ceremonies are distinguished for their aura of quiet calm; they have none of that noisy clamor that is encountered elsewhere, notably among Christian populations within the same empire. But the absence of the bride and groom is what makes the ceremonies most exceptional. They are represented by two people, friends or relatives, who bring the wedding to its conclusion in their name (pp. 26–38).

This marriage procedure is the most outstanding to be found in Turkey, aside from the fact that in places where European customs have made their influence felt, notably among certain Armenians, the custom of the dowry is beginning to take hold (p. 87). On the other hand, almost all the inferior types of procedures are found there. If the settlement of the widow's dower is, perhaps, a substitute for the marriage by means of purchase price, it is at least a transformation which frees that practice of its primitive meaning. But there are Turkish populations among whom the purchase of the fiancée is practiced literally (see pp. 129, 159, etcetera). Elsewhere, violent use of force suffices to confirm the marriage, such as in some parts of Albania (pp. 166 ff.). Elsewhere, indeed, elopement is connived at by the young man and the young woman (pp. 226 ff.).

But there is a marital peculiarity which is well highlighted by this study, because it is very frequent in Turkey, although most certainly it is found elsewhere; it is the kind of mutual avoidance which the betrothal brings about on the part of the two young people, who, nevertheless, are about to unite for life. Very often, from the moment their marriage is decided, they must exercise the greatest care to avoid each other. If they happen to meet each other, they must look away and act as if they had not seen each other (pp. 86, 183–184). Elsewhere, during the wedding festival, which very often lasts a week, the young woman is confined to a special room (p. 153). Occasionally, even at the time when the marriage is consummated, the newlyweds are not permitted to show themselves in public; their union remains clandestine for several weeks. One would think that it were barely tolerated. If they happen to be surprised by some stranger, they hurriedly leave each other; people have seen the young man jump from a high window in order to conform to the customs (p. 70). Thus everything transpires as if the couple managed to get together only by triumphing over some mysterious antagonistic forces that tended to separate them; as if this event that was being celebrated joyously were something to be ashamed of. It is hard to ignore the connection between these customs and the special taboo by virtue of which, in so many different societies, every kind of relationship is suspended between the son-in-law and his mother-in-law. These similar acts are perhaps of a nature to be mutually revealing and to make more understandable the nature of marriage and the moral forces that it sets in motion.

Another matter for the study of which this book provides an important number of examples is one which might be called that of the kinship contrivance with regard to marriage. Very often the leading roles are not performed by the parents of spouses, but by their (ad hoc) sponsors, sort of godparents of a very special kind. These godparents are venerated like true male parents (see notably p. 232). Likewise, the designation as best man gives rise to a brotherly relationship. How, then, does it come about that marriage is thus privileged to create close family ties? We have seen above that it is not unique in producing this effect (p. 171). In order to understand the reason for this peculiarity, it should then be of interest to compare marriage with other social practices which have the same result. In addition, what gives rise to this substitution of strangers or of distant relations for those who are properly called close relatives?

Equally remarkable is the self-effacing attitude of the spouses. They are present at their wedding; but the main acts are carried out through the instrumentality of their representatives, the best men and the matrons of honor (pp. 130, 166). At times they appear mute and motionless while attending all the ceremonies which transpire in front of them and at which they are, nevertheless, the heroes (p. 173). Among the Muslims of Turkey, they must not be present and the marriage takes place by proxy (p. 26). These diverse customs are not contingent oddities, but must draw attention if one would achieve deeper insight into the nature of conjugal society. And it is in this way that books like the one we have just analyzed can be of service. (*Année sociologique*, 2, 1899, pp. 334–336; trans. J. French)

David Werner Amram. *The Jewish Law of Divorce According to Bible and Talmud.* London: Nutt, 1897, 224 pp.

Three great monuments record the principal stages of judicial evolution in Jewish society; they are the Pentateuch, the Mishnah, and the Gemara.

The Mishnah is the oral law, as opposed to the Pentateuch, which is the written law. According to tradition, the two codes could be strictly contemporary; at any rate, the Mishnah is certainly very old. It is a collection of commentaries on the Pentateuch and of rabbinical jurisprudence: moreover, it was fashioned, refashioned, and transformed by the rabbis who applied it. In the end the Mishnah itself became the basis of a new commentary, known as the Gemara. The object of Amram's book is to show how the law of divorce developed in the course of this evolution.

At the very beginning—that is to say, according to the Pentateuch—the husband had the right to renounce his wife at will without having to justify his decision. This fact alone, it may be said in passing, serves to make us distinguish between the Jewish and Roman families, although both are sometimes characterized as patriarchal. In Rome, at the time the *patria potestas* was at its zenith, divorce did not exist even as the husband's privilege. Moreoever, according to the Pentateuch, it is the husband and not the patriarch, the oldest ascendant male, who is qualified to renounce [the wife]. This right is, accordingly, not a corollary of a very extensive paternal power.

Whatever the case may be, the whole course of history shows us that the husband's original power was subjected to more and more numerous restrictions. To begin with, Deuteronomy withdrew it from him in two cases, on pain of penalty (pp. 28, 29). The Mishnah went much further; it forbade divorce to the husband in all cases where the situation of the wife aroused a special degree of pity (states of madness, captivity, minority, etcetera).

The obligation to pay a settlement to the repudiated wife, an obligation which was doubtless ancient in origin but was extended and reinforced by the rabbis, naturally worked in the same way. Furthermore, the rabbis were in all ways opposed to the husband's arbitrary exercise of his right; finally, from A.D. 1025 onwards, divorce was no longer possible except when there were reasons in law or when the wife acquiesced (p. 52).

At the same time, the wife herself was acknowledged to possess a sort of right to request divorce. To put it accurately, the wife could never obtain divorce against her husband's wishes; the tribunal could never officially pronounce dissolution of marriage on the wife's complaint. It was merely that the rabbinical tribunals obliged the husband to renounce the wife in certain cases, on the latter's complaint, afflicting him with a penalty in the event of his refusal. The seeds of this new right already existed in the Bible (Exodus 21:7–11), but the cases where it was applied, at first very rare, became in the end very numerous (chapter 6).

Divorce rendered the wife *sui juris*. She could remarry without asking for her father's consent; she could acquire and possess in her personal capacity. Her husband had to pay her a fixed amount as settlement.

The origin of this practice was as follows. In early days, the husband paid a fixed sum to the young girl's father at the time of the betrothal. Little by little, this sum was considered as being vested in the young girl herself. Accordingly her husband, instead of remitting the sum to her father, kept it as part of his patrimony, but in the event of divorce he had to pay it out, supplying it to his wife in the form of liquid cash. She became the absolute owner of the money. In the beginning, it must be borne in mind, no dishonor fell on the character of the divorcee, because her husband could renounce her out of pure caprice. But a certain disfavor became attached to this situation once divorce without mutual consent was forbidden except in cases where the wife had committed some fault. (chapter 8, p. 104).

The divorce was definitely completed only when the husband had delivered to his wife a letter of repudiation, which had been drawn up before two witnesses. This practice seems to have been peculiar to the Jews. It does not seem to have existed among their neighbors; certainly it was unknown to Western peoples. In what lies its origin? According to Leist, it could have arisen out of the fact that the use of writing spread most rapidly among the Semitic peoples. But, on the contrary, far from this procedure's being utilized because it was convenient, it presented a difficulty for the majority of the people, who were ignorant of writing and were obliged to have recourse to an intermediary. One could even question whether or not this difficulty was not the raison d'être for this custom, in that it would have been a way of restraining the originally limitless rights of the husband. Indeed, it did contribute to this result, by permitting the rabbis to apply a moderating action to the exercise of this right.

Apart from these immediate findings, this book serves to prove that Jewish justice, although apparently immobilized by the letter of the sacred law, has nevertheless evolved until it has become completely transformed, thanks to the supple jurisprudence of the rabbis. (*Année sociologique*, 2, 1899, pp. 336–338; trans. A. Lyons)

J. Schnitzer. *Katholisches Eherecht, mit Berücksichtigung der im Deutschen Reich, in Österreich, der Schweiz, und im Gebiete des Code civil geltenden staatlichen Bestimmungen* (Canon Law Concerning Marriage, with Comparison of Present Laws in Effect in the German Empire, Austria, Switzerland, and Countries with a Civil Code), vol. IX. Fribourg-im-Breisgau: Herder, ix + 681 pp.

This is a new edition, completely revised, of the book by J. Weber, *Die canonischen Ehehindernisse: Nach dem geltenden gemeinen Kirchenrechte*, 1872. Weber's work was only a practical treatise on canon law; Schnitzer has given it a more scientific and historical character, and moreover, instead of just restricting himself only to the question of matrimonial obstacles, as Weber has done, he has treated the entire scope of the subject of marriage according to canon law.

What is interesting about canon law on this subject is that the entire system of nuptial formalities that are at the moment in effect are derived from it, as are our moral conceptions of the conjugal bonds—except that the economic system of marriage is of either Roman or Germanic origin. For that which concerns formalities, the custom of banns *(banni nuptiales)*[114] and that of public celebrations *(in facie Ecclesiae)*[115] have come to us from the Church. It is, therefore, by virtue of the Church that marriage has ceased to be a private (even though it is still more or less solemn) contract. When it became a public act, the authorities started participating in it from the moment it was barely conceived as a proposal until the time it was definitely accomplished.

This external organization conforms to the idea that the Church sealed the conjugal bonds. It saw in them something of a sacred nature; and this is what was expressed in the proclamation that marriage is a sacrament. It is true that marriage already had a religious character in Rome, Greece, and India, as Fustel de Coulanges has shown us. But this religiosity was extrinsic to it; it was a part of the consequences of marriage and was not attached to the marriage itself. Since the young woman could not enter the house without participating in the family worship, her participation in the rites was necessary to initiate her into the house. By a kind of Communion, she became a member of the religious society to which her husband belonged. But the fact of her being married, by itself, did not have sacred virtue. On the contrary, for Christianity marriage is a sacrament by itself and independent of its consequences, such as all the events that follow it. It is, in fact, an error to believe that according to the dogma it appropriates this status by the fact of religious celebration. In principle, the priest's function is not necessary to give marriage this character. The efficacy of the divine grace that is attached to the marriage is complete, since the spouses have agreed to mutually accept each other as husband and wife. Since the contract is formed among the two parties, the sacrament is received to the same effect (see pp. 31–39). No doubt, after the Council of Trent the Church required the valid marriage to be celebrated within its boundaries *(in conspectu Ecclesiae)*. But the priest who presided over the ceremony was only a principal witness present at the time—*testis spectabilis, autorizabilis*[116] (p. 190). His function was not to dispense the sacrament inherent in the state of marriage.

Perhaps there is a sort of contradiction between this notion of marriage and the moral superiority that the Church attributes to the state of virginity. But in reality these two conceptions complement and mutually confirm each other. It is because sexual relations are impure in themselves that a special institution was necessary to allow the loyal to submit to the law governing sexual relations without being defiled by this impurity. It is exactly this grace that is attached to the matrimonial sacrament. If it is true that the theory is exempt from all logical contradictions, it is because in the first place it seems to have only pure theological interest, without possible use outside of it. But in fact it must be understood that the concepts formulated by theologies result from their vain dialectics. They are formed under the impression of being real, and if they express this reality in the guise of their authority, they do not succeed in giving such impression and they do not manifest their true nature. It is enough to know how to interpret symbols which they express in order to discover, in the myth and the allegory, the social sentiments which are the source of their origin. In terms of space, what this Christian doctrine of marriage shows is that for European societies from the very beginning the conjugal bond had a value and a dignity which it did not have for the ancient societies, becasue it constitutes, by itself and without external intervention, a religious act. In the second place, this character of marriage evidently suggests the establishment of intercourse between two spouses—quite other than sexual intercourse. If public conscience represents marriage as a source of morality, so to speak as a sacrament, it is because the spouses conceive in their minds the formation of a moral unity [*société morale*] of exceptional significance, and not simply a physical identity. Sociologists, therefore, must hasten to reject these speculations of theology as deprived of all sociological qualifications. These speculations constitute very instructive social facts. All knowledge is useful by using it.

The matrimonial law of the Church presents another peculiarity which must draw the attention of sociologists: the enormous sentiment of conscience concerning prohibitions that developed in the guise of marriage to prevent incest. There was a time when marriage was forbidden among relatives seven times removed (p. 385). Presently the interdiction is still extended to relatives four times removed (p. 387). Kinship by marriage was assimilated by the natural parents. A man could not marry the parents of his wife (and reciprocally), nor the relatives by marriage of the latter. The children from the second marriage could not marry the relatives of the deceased spouse (p. 402). Even engaged couples were considered as having formed a kinship by marriage, a sufficient reason to prevent marriage among relatives (p. 414). The entirely spiritual relationship with the godfather and the godmother had the same consequences. The author naturally gives only theological reasons to justify this regulation, but evidently the causes of this prohibition were social. Even if one approaches the question with extreme latitude, allowing that among certain peoples of all races and creeds there are formed artifical kinships which have, especially from the point of view of marriage, the same effects as natural kinship, one comes to conclude that there are some socially determined conditions under the influence of which the kinship extends well beyond what generally passes as its normal sphere of action. Moreover, as in the case of Christianity, it is manifestly a religious state of mind that has produced this expansion. One can see now that in this fact lies more proof to support the hypothesis that we have earlier indicated and according to which this curious phenomenon would be placed under the immediate subordination of religious causes. (*Année sociologique*, 2, 1899, pp. 339–341; trans. Y. Nandan)

E. Meynial. "Le Mariage après les invasions." *Nouvelle Revue historique de droit français et étranger*, 1898, no. 2.

This is the sequel to articles that we have analyzed here (*Année sociologique*, 1, pp. 340 ff.).[117] After describing what marriage became at the end of the Roman Empire, the author reveals its nature in the body of Germanic laws and customs. He does not study them in the light of barbarian laws, since he considers them too brief and too inadequate—besides they have undergone the alterations of Roman editing—but bases his work on the *Germania*[118] of Tacitus and on scattered allusions in ancient epics.

In this way he believes he can establish two propositions that appear to him contradictory, although undeniable in both cases. At the outset, he states that the woman enjoys in marriage a large measure of independence. Marital authority is very limited—in no way resembling the *manus*[119] of the Latins. On marrying, the woman continues to be of consequence in her native family, and she comes back there to live in case she becomes a widow—all of which shows clearly the almost privileged situation that she occupies; the fact is that the woman with family ties enjoys a real moral, and at times legal, superiority. On the other hand, in spite of this independence, the strictures involving marital behavior are very severe: Adultery, almost unknown, is harshly punished, and polygamy is very rare. This rigor appears to the author irreconcilable with the prerogatives the wife enjoys, for this type of feminine supremacy seems to imply a martriarchal family organization. The matriarchate "is a regime of female promiscuity" (p. 191); it is encountered only in an age "when sexual relations have not yet been subject to any kind of regulation," when man is still "very close to the animal." But in that case, how explain why under a regime so favorable to sexual lewdness marriage customs could have acquired such a degree of purity? This would be a curious and insoluble paradox. The Germans, the article concludes, have practiced certain rules of conduct hardly commensurate, in sociological parlance, with the social order they have attained. And it is this contradictory state of affairs which has apparently served as a starting point for the evolution the author intends to describe in forthcoming articles.

But the contradiction comes solely from the fact that the author has too easily accepted conceptions that are outmoded today, at least if they are taken literally, from Bachofen and from Giraud-Teulon. The uterine relationship in no way implies a confusion of sexual relations and promiscuity. It is encountered at a relatively advanced evolutionary stage, within the confines of families already representing a very well defined organization. Therefore, when patrilineal relationships were established, the marital fidelity thus implied on the part of the wife did not have any difficulty being maintained. In another sense, the memories left by the preceding family type, preserving for the woman some part of her former prestige, temporarily prevented the man from abusing to his advantage the ascendancy that he had recently acquired. That is, no doubt, the reason for the apparently idyllic character of the matrimonial situation in primitive Germania. (*Année sociologique*, 2, 1899, pp. 341–342; trans. J. French)

Heinrich Gürgens. *Die Lehre von der ehelichen Gütergemeinschaft nach livländischem Stadtrecht* (The Theory of Common Ownership Among Spouses Under the Law of the Cities of Livonia). Riga: Jonck und Poliewsky, 1899, 190 pp.

The work is divided into two parts. In the first, one is exposed to the historical record of the regime of joint property holdings in the cities of Livonia[120] and the fundamental principles on which this regime rests; the second is devoted to detailing their applications. But since the application, in subject matter such as this, is indispensible for the understanding of the theory, we will make no distinction between them in our analysis.

In order to understand clearly the genesis of this law, one must go back to the old Saxon law (*Sachsenspiegel*[121] and the Magdeburg Law), which provided for the first court sessions. With that as a starting point, one can easily follow the entire sequence of legal evolution that came into being, thanks to a set of successive codifications. The most recent is from 1864. Now, this entire development follows a very well defined course; it goes from the regime involving separate maintenance to that of common sharing. The author establishes the point by retracing the successive stages of this transformation, but we shall now follow him in his investigation of it.

The codification of 1864 definitely sanctions the community regime. It constitutes a formal declaration that the property of both spouses forms an indivisible whole "in which neither of them has a fixed share as long as the marriage lasts" (p. 31). The husband administers but does not own. This co-ownership is especially remarkable in the case of nondivision that occurs by law between the surviving spouse and his (or her) children. It surely suggests one of the most curious details in Livonian law. The child who thus has everything in common with his father or his mother owns, as rightful beneficiary, an ideal share of the indivisible property. According to common law, when he dies, this share should pass along to his heirs; now, this transference comes about only when his heirs are direct lineal descendants; if they are of collateral descents, the deceased child's share goes back to the indivisible total estate (pp. 136–139). The fact is that the direct lineal descendants form a part of the community that continues to live in this way even after the death of one of the parents; the collaterals, on the other hand, are excluded. There is, then, a special kind of inheritance that applies to the special nature of this community.

Generally speaking, the joint property holdings of spouses are nevertheless a source of confusion for jurists. They have some trouble making them fit in with one or another of the current notions. It is not a question of co-ownership in the Roman sense of the word *(condominium)*; for, in an association of this kind, each associate owns a specific share of the total estate and can part with this share at will. Such is not the case with spouses. It should be added that the association is a community of mortmain.[122] Here, in fact, there is no longer a division of the material, even ideally, between the members of the community. It is theirs to enjoy so long as they are on hand; but this right to its enjoyment does not belong to them personally. They cannot dispose of it. If one of them dies, his share is not passed along to his heirs, but goes as increment to the others associated with him. According to the author, joint property holdings of spouses would be of this last type. The usual regime of mortmain would be modified on certain points only, by reason of the special characteristics of the conjugal society. Certain privileges of the husband would be explained in this way: They would pertain to the special role the husband plays in the household, to the duty he has to protect and to direct the wife—in a word, to the overall rights and obligations which make up marital prerogatives (pp. 35–63).

This discussion appears to us quite vain. An institution is not made to be subsumed under a legally defined category; there is, then, nothing very interesting about the attempt to define the technical notion from which it could be logically deduced. For every association, the regime involving property is a reflection of the people involved and vice versa. The property held in common by spouses pertains, then, to the special character of the conjugal society; and since this society is sui generis, the regime involving possessions that relates to it must have the same specifications. It cannot be arbitrarily realigned with another nor with a combination of several others.

Clear-cut evidence of the appearance and the development of the principle of community comes with the tightening of matrimonial bonds, the progressive consolidation of the society formed by both husband and wife. How did this consolidation take shape? The author does not give us much information on this point. Scarcely a page is devoted to the question, and the cause invoked is purely economic (p. 24). There was, it seems, a need for credit, grown greater as a result of industrial and commercial development, that presumably brought about the establishment of institutionalized rulings by virtue of which both husband and wife answered collectively for the debts contracted while administering the household. This is how the merger of both fortunes would have been brought in. The author would not have been content with this consideration alone if he had noticed that among the Germanic peoples the tendency towards community was apparent long before economic progress. It existed at all times, at least ever since there was *morgengabe*.[123] The *morgengabe* is in fact the property of the wife, and yet, for the duration of the marriage, it is included with the husband's property. Thus there is already, in this instance, no distinction. Generally speaking, the orientation of countries that have known the *morgengabe* has been community-directed; in case of separation their peoples have preferred the practice of the Roman dowry system. Where does this divergence come from? The fact is that the dowry and the *morgengabe* apply to different family types who were not able to adjust to the same matrimonial regime. (*Année sociologique*, 3, 1900, pp. 386–388; trans. J. French)

N. Klugmann. *Vergleichende Studien zur Stellung der Frau im Altertum*. Vol. I, *Die Frau im Talmud* (Comparative Studies on the Condition of Women in Antiquity: Women in the Talmud). Frankfurt: Kauffman, 1898.

This is, rather, a study of the condition of Jewish women in general; the Bible is cited just as much as the Talmud. The author even seems to consider the two sources as equivalent, and he puts them almost on the same plane, as if the spirit of Jewish law had not changed between the Bible and the Talmud, notably in matters which concerned the condition of women. The general bent of this work is, moreover, more apologetic than historical and critical. We feel that there is too much preoccupation with demonstrating the superiority of Jewish morality. It is for this reason that the author believes he must extol the facility with which Jewish law permits divorce or, rather, repudiation by the man; whereas this indicates, on the contrary, a considerable weakness in the conjugal bond. The author forgets that the priests had to observe mourning for their parents-in-law but not for their wives (Leviticus 21:1; Ezekiel 44:25). Not a word is said of the *mohar*,[124] a custom which implies that at least at the beginning the young girl was purchased by the husband and consequently was the possession of the father.

It nonetheless remains incontestable that the condition of women in Judaea was much superior to that which they enjoyed under most oriental legal systems. The woman was not excluded from the ceremonies of the cult; she could even be instructed in the law. Just like the man, she carried inside her the image of God (Genesis 1:27). All of this permits one to believe that her inclinations were heeded at the time of marriage (p. 22). The widow and the divorcée were *sui juris*. The sexes enjoyed a great deal of freedom in their relations (p. 61). There were even seven prophetesses in Israel. This situation was countenanced to such a degree that we are inclined to explain it in terms of the memories and usages which were the remnants of the uterine family in Judaea. The latter certainly existed there for a long enough time to make its imprint on ideas and customs (see the facts in support of this argument in Buhl, *Die Sozialen Verhältnisse der Israeliten,* p. 28); and it naturally tended to establish a certain measure of equality between the sexes, a trace of which remains, even though the organization of the family has changed. The relative weakness in the conjugal bond is another fact which confirms this hypothesis. (*Année sociologique,* 3, 1900, pp. 388–389; trans. A. Lyons)

A. Posada. *Feminismo* (Feminism). Madrid: Fernando Fé, 1899, 296 pp.

The three studies which are included in the work (I, ''Doctrines and Problems of Feminism''; II, ''The Progress of Feminism''; III, ''The Juridic Status of the Spanish Woman'') have already been published in various issues of *La España Moderna.* However, by their collection into a volume, the author has made significant revisions by updating the feminist movement.

The second part of the work contains an exposition of doctrines and facts concerning the status of women, which in most cases are very well known. The author studies, one after another, facts that are antecedent to the modern feminist movement: the span from Plato to J. Stuart Mill forming chapter 1; the origin and character of feminist movements in different countries forming chapters 2–9; the relationship of feminism to socialism and anarchism forming chapter 10. And finally, the author arrives at certain conclusions: Concessions which the adversaries of the feminist movement must make are discussed in chapter 12; suggested modifications either in public opinion or in legislation concerning the civil, economic, and political status of women are dealt with in chapters 13–15.

In the third part, the author does not limit himself to enumerating legislative provisions; he has also examined the state of public opinion, which, he thinks (not without reason), is a more important factor in the determination of the juridic status of the woman than the articles of the codes.

It is only in the first part that the author has given his personal ideas, especially in chapter 6. He maintains that the physiological inferiority of the woman and her lack of intellectual aptitude are not attributes given to her by all scholars. In spite of the prejudices which hold her back, there is not a single branch of human activity in which the woman has not excelled. However, the author rarely goes beyond generalities. He has not examined or discussed in detail the reasons why certain thinkers—among them some women, like Mrs. Laura Marholm—have argued against the feminist movement. What makes this work useful and interesting is that it gives an excellent idea of the feminist movement among different peoples; and it is this aim which the author seems especially to have set for himself. (*Année sociologique,* 3, 1900, p. 391; trans. Y. Nandan)

Fritz Roeder. *Die Familie bei den Anglesachsen. Erster Hauptteil: Mann und Frau* (The Family among the Anglo-Saxons, Part 1, Husband and Wife). Halle: Max Niemeyer, 1899, 183 pp.

With the help of literary texts even more than with legal texts, the author undertakes to reconstitute the inner life of the family among Anglo-Saxons. The present volume of the work is especially devoted to marital relations; the sequel, which is announced as forthcoming, will deal with relationships between parents and children.

Marital relations are studied from their early stages, that is, from the first step before the engagement. Personal tastes, especially the girl's, played no part in them. She did not even show herself for the duration of the negotiations that were brought to a close by the parent under whose power she was placed. The father's authority was so broad that he could even compel her to enter into a marriage which she did not like, so long as she was no more than fifteen years old (p. 24). Just as the preliminary negotiations consisted essentially of a contractual settlement, the engagement had all the earmarks of a deal (p. 32); it was concluded by an exchange of down-payments (p. 33), by a handshake, etcetera. But although the engagement was the most clear-cut of all the nuptial ceremonies, it was not enough to constitute marriage ipso facto. The proof of this is that the laws anticipated and provided for the annulment of the engagement contract in case the fiancé refused to uphold it—in other words, refused to marry. Such a refusal was, moreover, considered the most mortal of insults; the girl was forever dishonored if some shattering vengeance was not dealt out to the offender (p. 36).

Marriage was definitely valid only through the tradition of matrimonial union *(die Trauung).*[125] As for that ceremony, the author teaches us nothing that is not already known. Beginning with the conversion to Christianity, the religious blessing was customary, but it was not obligatory and it in no way constituted the marriage bond (pp. 58–61).

The legal relationship between the spouses is compared by the author to the one which was formed between each person of importance and his clients,[126] and which gave rise to the institution of the peculiar type known as the *Gefolgschaft* (the *comitatus*[127] of which Tacitus speaks). The analogies are, in fact, remarkable: The formula by which the wife placed herself in her husband's hands was exactly the one the client used in order to place himself under the authority of his master (pp. 25, 83–85). It was, then, a relationship implying supremacy and protection on one side and submission and self-sacrifice on the other—without, however, anything degrading being attached to this subordination. Besides, however great the husband's authority might be, it was held in check by the assistance the wife found on occasion from her parents. For, and this is an important fact to keep in mind, marriage did not require her to leave her native family; she continued being a part of it and could return to it in case of widowhood, if she had no child. A fact that clearly shows the persistance of these ties is that the *wergeld* was estimated not on the basis of the husband's circumstances but on those of the brothers (pp. 88–89, 141). One must therefore guard against comparing, as has sometimes been done, the acquisition of the *mundium* by the husband and the acquisition of the *manus* by means of *coemptio*[128] in Rome.

As for the social position occupied by women, it is presented from two entirely opposite viewpoints, according to whether it is a question of the upper classes or the lower classes. The noblewoman enjoyed the greatest respect: It was she who presided over parties, who received her husband's clients, who distributed presents to them, and who excited their warmth and sensibilities (pp. 100 ff.). On the other hand, in the countryside she appears at times to have lived in a truly abject and demoralized condition (pp. 128–129). It is doubtful that this contrast was encountered to the same degree in ancient societies; therefore it throws some light on the causes that enhanced the social condition of women in societies of the Middle Ages, and more generally, among modern peoples. The woman owes this respect of which she has become the object to the absolutely special position she has assumed in the life of luxury, of art, of the imagination. Now, this sort of life can only be developed in comfortable surroundings. That, no doubt, is why the enhancement of feminine dignity began in the upper classes of society and spread to the others only later on and very slowly. (*Année sociologique*, 4, 1901, pp. 357–358; trans. J. French)

Charles Lefebvre. *Leçons d'instruction générale à l'histoire du droit matrimonial français*. Paris: Larose et Tenin, 1900, 497 pp.

The object of the work is to determine what fundamental elements went into the shaping of our marriage laws. The author comes to the conclusion that Roman law did not have and could not have any part in it; that the Germanic customs have, to a certain extent, prepared the ground, but that the decisive influence was that of Christianity.

In order to establish his first proposition, the author acutally puts to test the family organization of the Romans. On several occasions he declares it was contrary to nature. Its keystone was the institution of the *patria potestas*. Family members were all those who submitted to the absolute sovereignty of the *pater familias*—and only those, from which it followed that one could not belong to two family groups at one and the same time. The woman, upon marrying, could therefore enter her husband's family only on condition of leaving her own family; or if she kept her place in her family, she remained in many respects a stranger to her husband and her children. The two combinations were used by the Romans: These are the *justae nuptiae cum manu* and the *justae nuptiae sine manu*.[129] But each of the systems had grave drawbacks. The first had the advantage of making a close union between husband and wife, but attained it thanks only to an unnatural expedient (the wife entering the connubial household *loco filiae*[130] and losing this status within her native family circle). The other was somewhat more humane; therefore it became more general once customs had lost their harsh primitive character. But it was the negation of the whole society by those united in wedlock, since the married couple was not under the jurisdiction of one and the same household. Under these circumstances, the marriage ties could not possibly be anything but very weak, and as a result were to be most easily broken. Lefebvre does not hesitate to impute to that vicious legal conception the increasing multiplicity of divorces starting with the end of the Republic and the resulting breakdown of domestic morality. On that account there was nothing, therefore, that could be used as a model for family organization in Christian societies. Doubtless, under the Empire, Roman law began to take remedial action against these dissolute excesses, but the fact is that the Christian religion was already beginning to make itself felt.

With Germanic customs, Lefebvre is far less severe. He recognizes that on certain points they were closer to modern law and preparing it for future innovation. The bonds of wedlock were more secure, especially with regard to property. The dowry that the husband was obliged to settle on his wife, bringing about the opening up of the two fortunes while leaving them separate, brought the married couple together and obliged them to cooperate at all times (pp. 431 ff.). Then again, the unilateral character of the Roman kinship had disappeared: The agnates were denied the enjoyment of any prior rights, and paternal and maternal lines were both on the same level. But this entire organization was at the stage of common practices of customs; it had not yet been consolidated with clear-cut and sanctioned legal precepts, and according to the author, there is a great distance between simple collective habits, more or less general, and customs sanctioned by law (pp. 305 ff.). Moreover, certain institutions characteristic of our marriage laws were still deficient, notably marital prerogatives. Lefebvre does not concede the fact that the Germanic woman was subject to the *mundium* of her husband. It is Christianity which supposedly introduced the Germans to this institution, as well as the principle of the indissoluble marriage. It is the Christian spirit that presumably developed and made specific the vague tendency of Germanic law towards a better-organized conjugal society.

The author's conclusions, like the method he uses, seem to us to invite a number of grave reservations.

To be sure, we believe with him that the new characteristics of our system of marriage are entirely incompatible with the Roman system. But this thesis can be upheld without it being necessary to downgrade unjustly the Roman organization. Now, it is unfair and more a forgetting of the facts than a case of misunderstanding to fail to recognize the worthy position the wife enjoyed in Rome, the respect *(obsequium et reverentia)*[131] that the children owed their mother, the perfect high-minded partnership that prevailed for centuries between husband and wife, and the strength with which the marriage bond held firm as a result. The hermetically closed Roman family was very much drawn in upon itself. As a result, it obviously brought together, in close unity, husband and wife acting like parents) and their children. It is, then, we believe, a mistake to impute even to the structure of the Roman family the disruptive lack of standards that are a matter of record at the end of the Republic; one must not attribute to the family constitution itself what is due solely to the general breakdown of morality. One might as well blame Christianity for the period of disarray our marriage customs are passing through at the present time. In one respect only was the Roman family a prisoner of this organization: The system of agnation necessarily resulted in a very strong tendency to prevent the mixing up of the parental patrimonies of both husband and wife, for the simple reason that they belonged to two different families. Still, it is not possible to assert that some way could not have been discovered to make it possible to mitigate the evil. The *manus* was a case in point; it may, no doubt, be deemed crude, but there is no proof that it could not have been progressively modified if the letdown in public morality had not kept people from feeling the need for it.

As for the Germanic influences, we are in agreement with the author if he means to say simply that there is perhaps not a single one of our marital institutions that is not inherited in its pure and simple form from the barbarian law. Generally speaking, when a new legal system replaces another, it does not borrow from the latter clear-cut elements that it retains just as they are, but an indeterminate body of material that it elaborates in its fashion, or rather that society elaborates and transforms in order that its inclusion may be in keeping with new requirements. One needs to know to what extent this primary material, inherited from the past, was an essential factor in shaping the new legal principles. Now, we are afraid that the author has weakened, somewhat systematically, the role that the Germanic element has played, in order to enhance so considerably the contribution of Christianity. The proof lies in the fact that wherever Christian activity exerted itself in an area that Germanic customs had not made accessible, the former remained relatively unavailing; it was only in the liberal countries that marriage was transformed. Lefebvre cites the strong resistance that was due to the scholarly organization of Roman law, but customs may be unwilling to accept any change without confining themselves to clear-cut legal formulas. Lastly, it is very doubtful that the contribution of Christianity has been presented to us in its true light. The Germans had everything they needed to formulate their own conceptions of marital authority, which are to be found fully formed in texts of obviously Germanic inspiration. It is much more likely on questions of sexual and connubial morality that Christian influence made itself felt.

But what is especially open to criticism is the author's method (p. 52): The existence of the uterine or maternal family is denied for the reason that the author could not manage to make anything out of the whole idea. From pages 354 to 384, one finds a long discussion aiming to demonstrate that marriage by purchase did not exist in Germany, a discussion that is completely beside the point. Lefebvre establishes that the wife was not sold since she could not be resold; now, the object of the sum paid out by the young man's family was, not to buy him a wife, but to buy back the rights of the wife's family to the children to be born from the marriage. This is the procedure whereby the paternal line of descent is substituted for the uterine line of descent of which there are so many traces in Germanic law. What is there to say of *pretium nuptiale* being translated as "wedding present," and of *emptio uxoris* being given the meaning "to take to wife" (p. 365)? It is with a keen sense of surprise that one sees a historian seeking in a text from Genesis, which refers to a prearchaic family organization, the basis of the modern family (p. 463). It is true that the author refuses to admit that in the moral order there are radical differences between the man of bygone times and the one living today (p. 56). But the least that can be said of this assertion is that it constitutes a rash denial of everything that has been established, in the course of this century, by history and comparative ethnography. (*Année sociologique*, 4, 1901, pp. 358–362; trans. J. French)

Otto Müller. *Untersuchungen zur Geschichte des attischen Bürger- und Eherechts* (Studies on the History of the Athenian Right of Citizenship and Matrimonial Law), 25th supplementary vol., *Jahrbücher für klassische Philologie*, pp. 663–866. Leipzig: Teubner.

We are given in this work a history of Athenian matrimonial law, considered especially in its relationships with the right of citizenship. In his exposition the author, for reasons unknown to us, has reversed the chronological order, beginning with the more recent facts and then turning progressively to the more distant ones. We will follow in our analysis the reverse order, which is much more methodical.

The first historically dated fact that we know of concerning this question is a disposition of Draco establishing (or consecrating anew), alongside legitimate marriage, which could only be contracted between Athenian citizens, a lower form of marriage, a sort of legitimate concubinage. This was the character of every union between an Athenian and a free foreign woman; the woman bore, in this case the name παλλακή (concubine, mistress). How this sort of marriage was concluded is not well known. There was probably an ἐγγύησις (betrothal) analogous to that which took place in legitimate marriage; all the difference was in the juridical quality of the woman. These unions were, like the others, protected against adultery. For a time the children even had an alimentary debt with regard to the father,[132] but they did not have the right of citizenship and were included among the metics (pp. 848, 859). They bore the name of νόθοι (bastards, baseborn children).

From this time up to the year 451, the situation of the νόθοι, despite a moment of temporary reaction, kept improving. It is true that according to the author Solon was hostile to them, but this opinion is a pure conjecture which is not based on any fact. All we know is that Solon freed the νόθοι from their alimentary debt; since they formed a true part of the state, this measure does not seem to indicate a spirit of hostility regarding them. What is certain is that they acquired the right of citizenship under the tyrants. They ceased to be listed among the metics and formed a corporation of their own, alongside the other social groups: This was the συντέλεια (company, community) of the Cynosarges.[133] But despite this, they were not assimilated with legitimate children; they remained νόθοι. They had only a very restricted portion of the paternal heritage, except in cases where there were no legitimate descendants. Finally, despite a tentative effort by Hippias to reduce them to their former condition—an effort which, notwithstanding a temporary success, failed in the end—they obtained complete assimilation from Cleisthenes. The συντέλεια of the Cynosarges was suppressed and the νόθοι were incorporated into the phratries. All distinctions between them and the legitimate children (γνήσιοι) disappeared.

This complete equality lasted nearly sixty years. We thus arrive at the time of Pericles. During this period, a turnabout took place in Athenian ideas and policies. There was a tendency to restrict the number of citizens. Thus, in 451 Pericles decided that in the future only the children born of parents having Athenian citizenship would enjoy the right of citizenship. The children of a marriage between an Athenian citizen and an alien no longer had rights of citizenship or rights of inheritance. They resumed their place among the metics. And this principle remained as the basis of Athenian matrimonial legislation, except for a short period from 411 to 403. This was the period following the Sicilian catastrophes. Athens had a shortage of citizens; for this reason, it opened itself up to those who were closest to having the right of citizenship, that is, to those born of an Athenian citizen and an alien. But this exception lasted only as long as it was needed. As early as 411[134] exclusion became the rule. From this the author concludes that even the old legitimate concubinage disappeared, although one cannot see the reasons for this very well.

What seems to emerge clearly from this picture is that the νόθοι owed the progressive amelioration of their condition to the popular party. It is Cleisthenes who conferred on them complete equality with the γνήσιοι; and on several occasions one finds them seeking support among the partisans of democracy. The author, nevertheless, supports the opposite thesis. According to him, when the Athenian constitution was a pure aristocracy, marriage between Athenian eupatrids and aliens of the same class was perfectly legitimate, the children enjoyed all the rights of citizenship and of the family, and this liberalism did not come to an end until the entrance of the plebs into the city. But besides the fact that this hypothesis is not based on any well-established fact, it is hard to see why the plebians should have shown themselves more anxious to preserve the purity of Athenian blood than the aristocratic caste. It is true that after 451, restrictive measures were adopted. But this is because it was at this moment that Athens arrived at the summit of grandeur and exerted a hegemony over Greece; as a consequence she had an opinion of herself and of her dignity which led her quite naturally to close herself to foreign elements.

Müller seems to us, moreover, to have confused two very different questions in this work; that of legal concubinage and that of marriage between Athenians and aliens. For him, indeed, these two institutions are the same. Legal concubinage, according to him, was nothing else than marriage with an alien insofar as it conferred on the child certain civil or family rights without conferring all of them. From this it follows that it would naturally disappear every time the νόθοι were assimilated to the γνήσιοι, or else, on the contrary, would be totally excluded from the city; for, in the first case, it would have been confounded with marriage proper; in the second case, with free unions without legal standing. But this identification of two very different institutions is arbitrary. It is altogether excessive to say that the παλλακή (concubine) was always a ξένη (alien). As a matter of fact, and the author knows this, there were Athenians who married Athenian citizens "by the left hand." There was a sort of ἐγγύησις (betrothal), perhaps without the payment of the dowry.

The notion of concubinage is thus artificially restricted [by the author]. Moreover, one is in no way justified in concluding that the law of 451 must necessarily have had as a consequence the disappearance of this matrimonial institution. Doubtless, after this children born to an alien woman no longer had the right of citizenship. But morganatic unions with Athenian women were still possible; moreover, from the fact that marriage with a non-Athenian woman no longer conferred the same rights as formerly, it does not at all follow that it was deprived of all legal standing. It is nowhere said that the law of Draco protecting such unions from adultery was abolished. This alone would suffice to make of it a legal *(régulière)* union, although on an inferior level. What is more, it is far from certain that the children in this case were deprived of all rights of succession. The question is very controversial, and Müller's laborious discussions do not seem to us to have settled it.

We thus believe that concubinage always coexisted with marriage, perhaps as early as the most ancient times; it responded to much more general needs than that of regularizing unions with aliens. For the same reason, it does not seem to us at all demonstrated, even after 451, that a man could not have a legal concubine alongside his legitimate wife. Certainly, there was a time when this quasi-bigamy was permitted, since Socrates practiced it (p. 800); and we do not know that this right was, at some given moment, suppressed. (*Année sociologique*, 5, 1902, pp. 383–387; trans. K. Woody)

Edmond Marcou. *De l'Autorisation maritale au XIIIe siècle comparée à celle du code civil.* Paris: Arthur Rousseau, 178 pp.

Manifestly inspired by Lefebvre's theories,[135] the author sees in Christian ethics the original source of the sanction of marriage. We already had occasion last year (p. 361) to set forth our reservations about this doctrine.[136] In order to link in this way the establishment of the institution of marriage with Christianity, it is not enough to quote two or three expressions borrowed from the Church Fathers that appear to accept it in principle. From the book itself there emerges an argument that is turned against this thesis. Marcou does indeed establish, and very rightly, that the sanction and empowering of marriage are bound in with the regime involving joint holding of property. It is because the spouses had a common patrimony, over which each had rights, that it was necessary to organize its administration and to fix the role of each. For reasons easy to understand, the husband was placed in charge—all of which necessarily put the wife in a subordinate position in relation to him. But joint holding of property is in no way connected with Christian ideas. It is common knowledge that it is an institution of Germanic origin, connected with the *dos* and the *Morgengabe* of the German peoples. Consequently, the causes which have given rise to the sanction of marriage are also the ones that have engendered common property holding; and they are to be found, not in the prestigious influence of some sacred text or other, but in circumstances as a whole which have induced the conjugal society to assume the form it possesses at present among the Europeans. It is, in fact, characterized by the closeness of the two spouses; instead of remaining strongly committed, as formerly, to their original families, they create by their union the family group par excellence—one in which domestic life attains its maximum intensity.[137] The sanction of marriage was established because it was found to be necessary to the organization of this group.

But though such was the initial foundation of domestic life; it experienced in the course of history the influence of different principles and altered its development. Understood as a means of unifying the conjugal society, such an influence was required only to the degree and in the circumstances where it was indispensable to domestic discipline. In fact, this was just how the idea was first conceived in the thirteenth century. The married woman was not given the burden of any incapacity; she was simply subject to her husband in the running of the family. Therefore, if the husband was absent, or impeded in his functions for any reason whatsoever (madness, being too young to fulfill his duties), the wife resumed all her rights. But little by little a new idea came to light. It was implicitly admitted that the married woman was incapable from the viewpoint of general principle; she was viewed as a weak being who always needed protection, whatever the circumstances. If the husband was not able to make sure she had it, she would have to take it up with the judge. She would be in the custody of the latter whenever the custody of marriage could not be exercised. For the same reason, she herself would be able to claim the acts that she had accomplished without legal authorization. That is to say that these acts were considered to be wrongs committed against her rights as a minor, and not against her husband's authority.

How did this adventitious idea come to be introduced into our legislation on marriage? According to Marcou, it was presumably due to the influence of Roman law. It is, in fact, a matter of common knowledge that in Rome the woman, married or not, was perpetually incapable. But the author is himself obliged to acknowledge that Christian ideas about women, about their moral inferiority, have made an impact along the same lines. And he is certain they appear much more likely to produce such a result. Indeed, the Roman woman's incapacity was not linked to any unfavorable consideration of the feminine sex, generally speaking; it was above all a measure destined to prevent property owned by the woman from leaving the family. Besides, we wonder if legal provisions that one seeks to explain are necessarily an echo of such-and-such a law, and if they have not resulted in part from a natural and spontaneous growth. Since the establishment of joint holding of property involved a certain economic subordination of the wife to the husband, this relative dependence ended by being set up as a sort of absolute standard that became detached from the reasons that originally created and justified it; and on top of that came Christian ideas on the role of women which tipped legislation necessarily in the same direction.

The fact remains that as our author very rightly points out, the system of sanctioning marriage, such as it is ruled by our code, is placed at one and the same time under these two different standards: the need to assure family discipline and the so-called intellectual and moral inferiority of the woman. Now, since the second of these standards is very debatable and is no longer in keeping with our modern ideas, it is necessary to revise the institution to make it more compatible with itself. Moreover, the urgent need of this revision is acknowledged by a large number of people. (*Année sociologique*, 5, 1902, pp. 387–389; trans. J. French)

A. Esmein. "Les Coutumes primitives dans les écrits des mythologues grecs et romains." *Nouvelle Revue historique de droit français et étranger*, 1902, no. 1, pp. 5–32; no. 2, pp. 113–146.

By means of the myths of antiquity, Esmein tries to reconstruct the customs of the peoples who elaborated them. In these two articles, he is concerned especially with the family and above all marriage.

In the ancient legends of Greece we find the rudiments of the family and of marriage, which, however, seem relatively recent; they were "superimposed on an anterior state of almost complete promiscuity between the sexes, which doubtless no longer exists, but partial survivals of it are so numerous that its preceding existence cannot be called into doubt" (pp. 5–6). The earlier custom survived in the following forms: (1) the frequency of sexual relations outside of marriage and the complete indulgence which they are allowed; (2) the custom which permitted or prescribed a husband's loan to a special guest of his daughter or his wife; (3) the practice of incest; (4) the absence of any difference between legitimate filiation and natural filiation. As for an explanation of that "great promiscuity" which men apparently practiced even when they were "already united in small societies," the author thinks that he finds it in the fact that the sexual act was considered to be religious; as a proof of that characteristic, he points out sacred prostitution and the veritable rites to which, among the primitives, sexual commerce was submitted. He cites a certain number of facts which demonstrate that the sexual taboo was known as characteristic of the Greeks; many myths or stories manifestly presuppose it.

Even though the facts gathered by Esmein are somewhat interesting, the author seems to us to be very brash in perceiving these facts as vestiges of a primitive state of promiscuity. The practice of lending the wife to a guest, far from implying a complete absence of all matrimonial regulation, presupposes on the contrary that marriage has already been instituted. In fact, that custom is found among people who have already attained a certain degree of civilization. Nor is the ease with which sexual relations are engaged in a proof of it; this situation coexists very frequently with a perfectly regulated marriage. The feeling of shame and the institution of marriage are two different things. The absence of any difference between the condition of illegitimate children and legitimate children is observed among the ancient Germans and yet they had very rigid conjugal customs. As far as incest is concerned, in fact so common in the ancient legends, it is very difficult to see in it an echo of a time when incestuous relations were permitted, especially when it is realized that we have no knowledge of those primitive peoples, no matter how grotesque those primitive peoples seem in practicing this custom with such a tolerance. Everything demonstrates that from the day when societies comprised a minimum of two clans, exogamy appeared. It is contemporary with the lowest social organization that we have been able to observe directly. The great nations who came to conquer and civilize Greece had, when they arrived in that country, passed that inferior stage, doubtlessly for a long time. It is thus very unlikely that the myths which have come down to us reflect a still lower moral and social state. It remains, it is true, to explain how the popular imagination was able to impute so easily to the gods the acts which were forbidden to men.

But it is precisely because the gods are not men. In many societies where incest is forbidden to ordinary men, it is legally practiced by the aristocratic classes, the royal families, etcetera. If the opinion could have been admitted that the powerful of this world enjoyed such a privilege, it is very understandable that it did not seem in any way wrong to imagine that the divinities would likewise have been able to escape from the common rules.

The very reason which the author gives to justify his thesis seems to us to go against it. It is very true (this is a point upon which we do not cease to insist here) that the sexual act has a religious character for the primitive. But for that very reason, it must be submitted to rites; and the very idea of a ritual regulation excludes the contrary idea of promiscuity. This is not to say that we believe there would have existed as a matter of course among the primitives marriage properly so-called, analogous to the institution that we call by that name. Nevertheless, we must discover from it something that must serve as a seed of the evolution from which marriage has resulted. The true problem would be to search for what that complex and ambiguous state would have consisted of. Esmein certainly expresses a characteristic form of it when, in the second part of his work, he says that marriage was at first a relationship of fact more than a juridical relationship. But that characteristic is a little too negative and would have to be completed [by something positive]. (*Année sociologique,* 6, 1903, pp. 359–361; trans. J. Sweeney)

Charles Lefebvre. ''Le Mariage civil n'est-il qu'un contrat?'' *Nouvelle Revue historique de droit français et étranger,* 1902, no. 3, pp. 300–334.

Under the influence of practical concerns and because of the theory that defines marriage as a contract, the author was led to defend the notion of free union; however, he responds negatively to the question he posed himself. The principal thrust of his argument lies in persuading us to believe that marriage does not fit into a preliminary definition of ''contract.'' For Lefebvre, a contract is a juridic pact ''binding only in principle if one wants it to and as much as one wants it to.'' After admitting this postulate, it becomes quite clear that marriage should not be considered as a contract. But where then are the pacts which, in that case, would deserve such a designation? Every time we draw up a contract, in addition to the commitments that we want to be included, there are others that we assume without having to make them an explicit part of it. We are obliged, for example, to fulfill obligations imposed by custom; the law imposes other obligations on us. The employer and worker who are linked by a labor contract cannot assure that the former owes the latter legal indemnity in case of accident. All contracts are regulated, and, to the commitments contained in the agreement, regulations add still others, in the name of public interest, as corollaries of the first. In this respect it is not clear how civil marriage is different from contractural agreements. (*Année sociologique,* 6, 1903, pp. 365–366; trans. Y. Nandan)

William Rullkoeter. *The Legal Protection of Woman among the Ancient Germans*. Chicago: Chicago University Press, 1900, 96 pp.

It is to an inborn superiority of Germanic societies that the author ascribes the relatively better living conditions that the woman used to enjoy and that Tacitus had already noted, not without surprise. It would seem to be the genesis of that very special prestige which the woman enjoyed from the Middle Ages on. But from the very beginning, there is some partiality in the manner of representing the situation ascribed to the German woman; such a portrayal too closely resembles special pleading. If, as most barbarian laws would have it, the woman's *Wergeld* was equal and often even superior to the man's, other conditions being equal, it was certainly not due to a precocious idealism which those races were presumably privileged to possess. Rather, the fact is that the wife was acquired at a price, and that furthermore she embodied, so to speak, a multiplicity of existences. It was her fertility that gave her value; therefore such an increase in *Wergeld* generally occurred only during the period when the woman was old enough to bear children. On the other hand, unless one is prejudiced, one cannot fail to recognize the inferior position that she occupied with regard to her husband. Only adultery involving the wife was severely punished, and all the author manages to establish is that the customs of the times seem to have found adultery on the part of the husband equally reprehensible. And furthermore, such examples are relatively recent (p. 74). By the same token, the husband's right to repudiate his wife was certainly very widespread, even though more recent legislation attempted to set limits to this. Finally, according to Tacitus, farm work, namely work of a menial kind, fell to the wife. It remains no less true that she was the object of attentions that are not always granted even in societies of a higher order. Rather, she enjoys the same advantages in all societies where the uterine family has lasted long enough to have a profound effect on domestic customs and legal institutions. Now, this is certainly the case with Germanic societies. Accordingly, there is no reason to look for any other explanation. The author, not content to leave it at that, embellished far too much the German woman's situation to the point of making it, wrongly, a unique case in history. (*Année sociologique*, 6, 1903, pp. 366–367; trans. J. French)

Pierre-André Pidoux. *Histoire du mariage et du droit des gens mariés en Franche-Comté*. Dôle: Bernin, 1902, iv + 185 pp.

A student of Lefebvre, Pidoux applies himself to a special question as he examines the general ideas of his master. For the author, the matrimonial law of Franche-Comté [the Free County of Burgundy] is the result of conciliation between two opposed influences: that of the Roman law and Christianity. It is not a question of Germanic law. Yet it must be added that of the two conceptions, Christianity, presumably, finally prevailed. "The matrimonial law of Franche-Comté is an essentially Christian law, its Roman appearances notwithstanding" (p. 2), states the author. And this proves that the authors of the sixteenth and seventeenth centuries, who, however, were very anxious to give themselves the appearance of savants, did not make allusions to Germanic sources. Quite the contrary, they explicitly invoked the authority of holy books, and notably they supported the principles of community according to the famous verse of Genesis: "For this reason man will leave his father and mother, and he will be united with his wife and they will be two in one flesh" (Genesis 2:24). The argument is hardly convincing. The reason which predisposed the jurisconsults of the seventeenth century to quote their citations from one source rather than another cannot be confused with the deep causes which determined the evolution of our law. The latter was the result of obscure and remote influences. These erudite scholars could not have disentangled that law from a simple work of intellectual analysis, and the way they justified it could have been very different from the manner in which it was constituted objectively. Just because they do not make any reference to Germanic law does not mean that it has been without influence. Besides, it is obvious that they were subjective and arbitrary in their interpretations and citations of texts; they did not even hesitate to invoke the sacred texts in support of their theory. Is it possible to admit that a phrase invented out of [the Scriptures], which were edited thousands of years ago, referring itself to a prehistoric civilization, where one felt more the influence of old uterine right, could have served as the basis of the modern conception of marriage? The jurisconsults were naturally induced to depend on the holy books in their argumentation; by reason of the authority with which these books were invested, nothing was more natural to them.

It is true that the reforms of the Council of Trent were published in Franche-Comté in 1573, and the matrimonial law of the county was confused ever since then with the canon law. But it is an error to attribute to the Church the reforms put forth by the Council. It is known, on the contrary, that by adopting the dispositions which proscribed clandestine marriage, declared obligatory the presence of the priest, and emphasized the juridic distance between engagement and marriage, the Council appeared only to be ceding to the pressure of the civil power. In spite of the Church, all these results were accomplished pretty much in their own right. No one can exaggerate their importance. Now, because of both the publicity and the typical awe that accompanies it, marriage is distinguished from free union [cohabitation]. As a consequence, marriage is truly a unique institution in itself.

It is, moreover, impossible to find anything concerning the details of the matrimonial organization of Franche-Comté which justifies the fundamental thesis of the author. Pidoux considers that if the freeman was not known for enjoying the inalienable *(mainmortable)* rights by the fact of his marriage to a serf woman, it is because under the influence of religious thinking, the fewest obstacles possible were placed in the way of marriage in order to prevent concubinage. But the interest of the *seigneur* is sufficient to explain this custom. He had a truly vested interest in it: the attraction of workers to his domain.

Likewise, to Christianity is attributed the idea of communal property among spouses. It was conceived with the Christian idea of marriage as a complete and absolute association. However, in fact, the communal character of property originated with the Germanic societies. By that reason alone the husband from his property assigned to the woman the *Morgengabe* [the gifts the bridegroom gave the day after the marriage to the bride] and dowry (*dos*); the two fortunes, woman's dowry and husband's property, were partially confused.

The conflict, then, took place between German customs and Roman law; or rather, such were the two kinds of elements which furnished the material for elaboration by the new societies and for becoming the matrimonial law of medieval societies. From this point of view, the law of Franche-Comté presents interesting elements of friction among the two diverging tendencies. Thus, paternal authority over the sons, even married, lasted indefinitely—except, however, in what concerned household administration. As far as the other children were concerned, marriage emancipated the daughters. But in general, by reason of their marriage, and in exchange for their dowry, they renounced it [emancipation] to the succession of their relatives (p. 96).

We do not want to say, moreover, that Christian ideas were without influence on this marriage, but this influence was not of the preponderant significance that has been attributed to it. It has been especially felt, we believe, on sexual morals, upon which it has thus far imposed unknown purity. (*Année socioligique*, 7, 1904, pp. 436–438; trans. Y. Nandan)

Johannes Nietzold. *Die Ehe in Ägypten zur ptolemäisch-römischen Zeit nach den griechischen Heiratskontrakten und verwandten Urkunden* (Marriage in Egypt in the Roman Period during the Ptolemaic Era). Leipzig: Veit, 1903, vi + 108 pp.

At the time when the Romans arrived in Egypt, they found there with regard to marriage an old Egyptian law, at least as it revealed its fundamental principles, because, in the details, the προστάγματα (decrees) of Ptolemy had modified it and had Hellenized it in more than one respect. The specifics of this law continued to be maintained, with a remarkable degree of perseverance, even during the Roman era; thus we find them still as they were during the second century of our era.

First of all, the ἔγγραφος (written law) must be distinguished from ἄγραφος γάμος (unwritten law). What defines the first is the existence of a solemn written contract where the spouses come to an agreement on the conditions under which their union takes place. The essential part of this convention is that which determines the woman's dowry. The ἔγγραφος γάμος (written contract of marriage) was the normal type of marriage; it was this form of marriage that produced its fullest effects.

The ἄγραφος γάμος (unwritten contract of marriage) did not result in a contract; nor could they marry without a written deed. The word which defines it must not be taken literally. The essential element which characterizes the first form of marriage—i.e., the constitution of the dowry—can be excluded only if the convention thus fixed by the parties stipulates it. Moreover, the spouses in the convention give their consent not to a definitive marriage but to simple cohabitation: συμβιωσις (cohabitation). The ἄγραΦος γάμος is, in fact, a provisional form of marriage, a trial marriage, destined especially to test the fecundity of the woman. Definitely it was an inferior form of marriage, and for this reason alone it established a very fragile relationship between the spouses. The legal situation of the children from these unions also shared this inferiority. But surprisingly, what resulted from this law was that this inferiority was especially applicable to the laws which, in this case, were recognized by the father. Even though his paternity was less validly established in the ἐγγραΦοι γάμοι, his authority over the children was extensive. The son, so to speak, so long as his father lived could not inherit from other sources; he did not have the right to test a woman for her fecundity; and the married daughter was obliged to separate herself from her husband only under paternal injunction, even though, personally, it was against her wishes to divorce her husband.

Another special characteristic of the Egyptian matrimonial law is that it authorized incest. Marriages between sisters and brothers were not only tolerated but as a rule were consummated. This conjugal arrangement was considered as the most natural and the most rational. This practice can be certainly traced to the most primitive times; and it was so deep-rooted in the customs that it persevered until a very late era in the history of Egypt. Long after the Romans set their feet in Egypt, incestuous unions still constituted the majority of marriages. The fact appears surprising, especially since the very ancient Egyptians seem to have practiced totemism—and totemism generally left behind it a horror of incest. How, in this particular case, could contradictory customs have taken root? We do not think that anybody has yet attempted to answer this question (pp. 12–15).

Another fact, not less curious, is that very often filiation had all the appearance of being established in the maternal line (p. 18). In the very ancient demotic contracts, it is the mother's name that the child bears, and not that of the father. A change, however, took place at the time of Ptolemy, when a double denomination became customary; the child was designated by the names of both his father and mother. In the bilingual inscriptions, the Egyptian text mentioned the mother's name, whereas the Greek text spoke of the father's name. These usages quite certainly seem to be vestiges of the uterine family. Moreover, the woman held legally a relatively high position; she could legitimately engage in a contract without the assistance of any guardian (p. 30). Is it not then proper to explain in the same manner the fact that very often, in the marriage contracts, it was the fiancée's mother whose name was mentioned, not that of her father (p. 43)?

The principal chapter of the work that we review here is naturally devoted to the marriage contract, since it is by the nature of the contract that different kinds of marriages are distinguished. We can follow its evolution from the fifth century before Christ until the sixth century of our era. At the beginning, the dowry was unknown. The only pecuniary dispositions which were at issue were those which concerned the bridegroom's gift to the bride and the indemnity for which the husband was responsible in case he repudiated her. These protective measures often proved favorable to the woman. In the same manner, it is interesting to note that in the ancient contracts it was the woman who took the initiative and addressed herself to the husband in order to confirm her intention of marrying him; later it was the husband who played the role (pp. 44–47).

It is only at the end of the Ptolemaic era that the dowry made its appearance; it was essentially of Greek origin, however. Also, the principles of Greek law governed domestic property. The dowry was considered the property of the woman, and the husband enjoyed only its usufruct rights; [however] in the case of a breakup in the marriage she could not take it back to her father's home. In return, the dowry totally deprived the woman of paternal heritage. The fact that the dowry is of recent origin, it seems to us, has raised a problem, which the author does not seem to be concerned with. If the institution of the dowry appeared late, and if on the other hand it constituted an essential and typical element of the *engraphos gamos,* does it not follow that this form of marriage by itself is of recent origin? And therefore is this the *agraphos gamos,* which would, rather, remind us of the primitive matrimonial type?

But these orientations are not the only ones that are found in these contracts. They manifested how the two spouses would determine, in a general way, the model by which they would agree on their mutual duties. The obligations were not the same according to the marriage thus contracted; they were very loose in the case of αγραΦος γαμος (p. 48). Other agreements determined the nature of support which the husband promised to assure his wife (p. 51). Finally, what is especially interesting with respect to Egypt is the existence of a very great number of contracts and of testamentary dispositions. By marrying off their children, the parents regulated at the same time their rights of succession; this usage was, though, very ancient and survived until a very late era.

The last part of the book is devoted to a sort of inferior marriage, a legitimate concubinage which was customary for the Roman soldiers in Egypt. It provides further proof of the very great flexibility which the matrimonial institution in this country had, which allowed it to adapt itself without difficulty to a variety of circumstances and changing situations. (*Année sociologique,* 8, 1905, pp. 415–418; trans. Y. Nandan)

Roberto de Ruggiero. *Studi papirologici sul matrimonio e sul divorzio nell'egitto greco-romano.* Rome: Istituto di diritto romano, 1903, 104 pp.

The book contains three studies. In the first one, the author shows that the matrimonial contracts in the Greco-Egyptian law are contracts with a focus on the dowry. It has been held that the contracts had this character only in appearance. The dowry which the wife supplied had a purely fictive character, and in fact was concocted from the wealth belonging to the husband, of which he made a gift to his wife at the time of marriage. This was called a disguised *donatio ante nuptias*.[138] The author refutes this theory by showing, notably, that the property assets thus brought in dowry by the wife often consisted of clothes and personal objects which were already used.* Moreover, the dowry was often constituted by the mother. This intervention of the mother is irreconcilable with the role attributed to the husband.

Therefore, for this author as for the previous author [Nietzold], the dowry remains one of the characteristics of $\overset{\text{3}}{\epsilon}\gamma\gamma\rho\alpha\Phi o\varsigma \ \gamma\alpha\mu o\varsigma$ (written contract of marriage), but according to him, it was not the only one. The word $\overset{\text{3}}{\epsilon}\gamma\gamma\rho\alpha\Phi o\varsigma$ must be understood in its etymological sense, and marriages by dowry would then be distinguished from other types only in the sense that they would be accompanied by a written contract. By a somewhat subtle and brief examination of the texts, the author attempts to prove, contrary to the generally held opinion, that in the $\overset{\text{3}}{\alpha}\gamma\rho\alpha\Phi o\iota \ \gamma\alpha\mu o\iota$ there are no written agreements, or that at least, whenever there are, they do not have a matrimonial character.

The last part of the work deals with different questions concerning divorce, the mode of restituting the dowry, and so on. (*Année sociologique*, 8, 1905, pp. 418–419; trans. Y. Nandan)

M. Mielziner. *The Jewish Law of Marriage and Divorce in Ancient and Modern Times.* New York: Bloch Pub. Co., 1901, 149 pp.

The object of this book is to retrace the principal stages through which the Jewish law of marriage has passed from ancient times up until the recent endeavors of the contemporary reformist sects. The author adds little to what is known concerning Biblical and Talmudic law; he arouses our sharp interest by the information gathered in his volume concerning the results achieved by the different synods which were held during the nineteenth century with a view to modifying the traditional law. But since these modifications possess more than anything else a practical interest, insofar as they have not, after all, been hallowed by custom, but have remained, for the most part, designs, we shall not have to describe them. One easily conjectures what the sense of them is: They aim to place the old practices of Judaism in harmony with the present conditions of social life.

Admittedly in an altogether unconscious way, our author does, however, bring to light a fact which is of some theoretical interest to us—that is, the

---

* From Durkheim's interpretation the author's position can be easily misconstrued as if he were contradicting himself. But in actuality Ruggiero maintains that the dowry was a part of the marital institution as opposed to the belief held by other scholars who attribute to it only a fictive character. The theory of dowry that assumes its imaginary existence is thus refuted by the author. Ed.

magico-religious character of the conjugal tie. It is called *kiddushin* from the word *kaddesch*, which is the Hebrew word corresponding to the Latin *sacer*, and implies the idea of consecration (p. 27). The matrimonial bond is sealed by a form of consecration; the husband places a ring over the wife's finger or hands her a piece of money while pronouncing the following words: "Be thou consecrated unto me" (p. 78). The idea that marriage possesses, of itself, some element of the mystical and the religious, that it constitutes a sacrament independently of the religious blessings which may be added to it, is not therefore exclusively Christian in character. Perhaps it may even result from some very ancient conceptions. Doubtless there are some differences between the Christian and the Jewish ideas; however, there are also some resemblances which merit comment.

At the basis of both of them is this sentiment: The conjugal act (and more generally, the sexual act) is not religiously neutral, but brings into play forces which are sacred and consequently formidable. Now, we find some other manifestations of this sentiment in Jewish law and custom. If sexual intercourse is dangerous in this regard, it must be strictly prohibited, inasmuch as the rites designed to neutralize its harmful effects have not been completed [unless there is a marriage]; from this arises the quite common institution of the taboo on engaged couples. The young man and the young girl who are engaged to be married must maintain a respectful distance between each other, avoid any meeting, conversation, etcetera. This was the customary practice among the Jews. A period must elapse between the betrothal and the wedding, during which the engaged pair must abstain from any relationship which hints of intimacy. This period varied from a month to a year depending on whether the betrothed female was a young girl or a widow (p. 82).

Reading this book has furnished us with the chance to make another remark which it will not be uninteresting for us to record here. With regard to the fourteen types of marriage proscription specified in Leviticus, there are nine which refer to kinship by marriage. The overwhelming importance attributed to this inferior and secondary mode of kinship may surprise us at first glance. It dissuades us from thinking that the prohibitive consequences thus attributed to marriage may be due to a simple logical extension of the idea and sentiments awakened by direct kinship or kinship properly so-called. We may therefore inquire whether or not these prohibitions may have originated in the institution which is well known as "the taboo on in-laws." Certainly, we know that the mother-in-law taboo is merely a special case of a more general taboo, which, so far as each spouse is concerned, extends to all kin by marriage who are of the opposite sex to her/him. The husband's father is very often taboo for the wife, just as the wife's mother is taboo for the husband. Now, the prohibition of all intimate relationships necessarily entails the prohibition of marriage. Prohibitions on marriage between in-laws would therefore have a source which is sui generis—distinct, at least in its origin, from that which gave birth to the same proscriptions on blood kin. It is nevertheless allowable for us to consider that the ideas from which both prohibitions are derived are not unrelated.

In connection with this same question, the author justly remarks (p. 36) that Leviticus does not expressly prohibit marriage between father and daughter. Is it because this prohibition is self-evident, being implicit in the others? It is possible. However, this omission merits remark, especially when one recalls that there is mention in the Bible of several cases of union between father and daughter, and that it is spoken of with a certain tolerance (see the case of the daughters of Lot and Tamar). (*Année sociologique*, 8, 1905, pp. 419–421; trans. A. Lyons)

Kojiro Twasaky. *Das japanische Eherecht* (Japanese Matrimonial Law). Leipzig: Rossberg, 1904, 64 pp.

Saburo Sakamoto. *Das Ehescheidungsrecht Japans* (Divorce in Japan). Berlin: Mayer und Müller, 1903, viii + 107 pp.

Even though the Japanese law of marriage has certainly evolved in the course of history, its essential principles were fixed very early in its development. They remained until the second half of the nineteenth century approximately the same as we find them in the *Taiho* Code, which goes back to the beginning of the eighth century of our era. This codification, which took place under the emperor Mommu, corresponds to the period when the imperial power was established for the first time on the ruins of what was then the old tribal *(gentilice)* organization. After this, nothing happened until the imperial restoration of 1867; subsequently [another] great codification was undertaken. At this time, the concern to modify the Civil Code of Japan was confined to our compatriot, Boissonnade. The code which he inspired came into effect in 1893; but it did not remain enforced for a long time, and after 1898 a revision was undertaken which showed German influence and whose main purpose was to take into account the Japanese customs and traditions.

It is obviously impossible to follow in detail a long evolution. But we would like to throw light on the most general conclusions which have been arrived at in this work.

It is quite likely that at the beginning the family had been of the uterine type. We know, in reality, that according to ancient Japanese law the woman with her children remained at her parents' house. Her husband only had the right to visit her at night. The word that signified "marriage" also had the significance of "slipping at night into the house" *(se glisser la nuit dans la maison)* (p. 12). It is only from the fifteenth century onward that the husband's house became the center of family life and that marriage took the form of regular cohabitation of the spouses. Many ancient customs survived, however, such as the custom which required the marriage to be concluded by way of an intermediary; the violation of this rule was punished by a fine. This practice, certainly very old, is probably connected with the taboo of the fiancés

(p. 20). What is curious about this is that the same intervention, by an intermediary, was necessary in case of divorce.

Without doubt the persistence of the uterine family explains two matrimonial forms that are still observed in Japan. When the family has only a daughter for inheritance, the matrimonial system of the uterine family comes into effect: The husband comes to live in the house of his wife, and the children bear the name of the maternal family—this is called the *Iri-Muko* marriage. In this case, it is the woman who is charged with the duty of paying the expenses. Occasionally, as we have seen above[139] (see p. 410), the young man who thus enters the house as a son-in-law of his wife's family is, at the same time, adopted as their own son. He accumulates two domestic roles: This is called the *Muko-Ioshi* marriage. This type of marriage presents two different modalities, according to whether the adoption takes place at the same time as the marriage, of which it is a complementary effect; or whether, on the contrary, the adoption precedes the marriage.

Generally speaking, the woman seems to have enjoyed an autonomy that was not recognized in the law of the European societies. In these special marriages of which we speak here, autonomy was naturally preponderant. But even in ordinary marriages, autonomy for the woman remained important. In principle, the marriage did not diminish its juridic scope. It is true that there were exceptions, that is to say, cases where woman could legally act only with the consent of the husband. Thus, this authorization accorded to her was necessary in order that she might receive and exploit a capital investment, lend and guarantee a loan, engage in lawsuits, accept and refuse an inheritance, and so on. But she could engage in commercial activities without having an authorization, even though marital authorization was practically useful. She could, under certain conditions, act in the name of and in place of her husband (p. 41).

This autonomy of the woman did not remain unaffected by a certain degree of laxity in the conjugal relationship which was especially efficacious in the dispositions concerning property. Therefore the Japanese law did not recognize the system of community, either total or partial. The wealth of the two spouses never constituted an indivisible totality—not even postmarital acquisitions. Wealth acquired by each spouse remained distinct from that of the other. The one who had the largest part of the total wealth of both administered the whole of it (p. 47). The independence of the spouses was so great that the husband could not start a legal process concerning the wealth of the woman, either in her name or representing her. The legal system, which became applicable when the spouses could not agree due to their contradictory claims, implied an absolute separation of their wealth (pp. 49 ff.).

The Japanese marriage thus appears as an institution of extreme flexibility; it has nothing of that rigidity, that air of formality, which characterizes European societies. The Japanese marriage is contracted with the most extreme facility. The formalities are very simple. For a long time, though, the marriage was even contracted without formalities; it resulted often from a simple fulfill-ment of certain conditions (see Sakamoto, p. 64 and p. 48). Henceforth we will see that it winds up in the same manner.

There were numerous causes, in effect, that could determine the rupture of conjugal relationships.

First of all, at least under the system of the Taiho Code, divorce could have been imposed by the state. This was the case: (1) when the husband hit the parents or the paternal grand-parents of his wife, or else when he killed either the maternal grand-parents of his wife or her uncle, her aunt, her brothers, or sisters; (2) when the woman committed a misdemeanor or a crime of the same type affecting the relatives of her husband; (3) when an act of homicide was committed by the parents of one of the two spouses against the parents of the other (p. 27). On the other hand, some of the rules concerning divorce were sanctioned by public penalties. Thus the husband who divorced his wife in the absence of seven legitimate motives for divorce recognized by the law was punished by a year in prison; and the couple who had one of these seven motives but nevertheless continued to live in the state of marriage re-ceived one hundred blows with a bamboo rod (p. 30).

In the second place, divorce by mutual consent was allowed. Formerly, a simple will was sufficient to break the conjugal relationship; today the authorities demand that it also be registered. But the formalities have been reduced to a minimum. Assent of those whose consent is necessary for the validity of marriage is equally required in case of divorce; but if the spouses are no longer united in an effective marriage, they only declare their agreement before the competent authority. It is true that if one of them refuses to receive the declaration, the marriage is not considered dissolved; but this refusal is only possible when the divorce is contrary to the law.

Finally, the cases where the divorce may be brought up before the tribunals by only one of the two spouses are relatively numerous. An absence of three years constitutes a sufficient motive for the condemnation of one of the spouses to a penalty involving loss of civil rights. The usage by virtue of which a father who only has daughters can adopt a young man for his son can also be a cause for divorce. This special adoption creates, in fact, a double rela-tion: relation of father to son as adopter and adopted, relation of husband to wife as adopted and adopter's daughter. Now if, for any reason whatsoever, the first of these relations should happen to come to an end, the second ceases for the same reason; the spouses separate simply because the husband now fails to qualify as adoptive son (pp. 79–81). The same applies when both spouses are adopted together as children and if the ties of kinship thus contracted by the wife should happen to be broken off, the marriage bonds may be severed as a result. It is clear that the strength derived from such bonds is notably in-ferior to the marriage ties.

To explain this relatively fragile relation, we have not ventured to risk a hypothesis; instead, we have limited ourselves to confirming it. Another more or less valuable fact demonstrates an extremely great indulgence of the Japanese law for divorce. It is that once the declaration of divorce by mutual consent is arrived at and received in due form, it cannot be challenged anymore, even though it may be in contradiction with the prescriptions of the law (p. 70). Therefore the absence of assent by the ancestors vitiates the marriage, and not the divorce. It is, then, not an exaggeration to say that divorce enjoys a favorable treatment. (*Année sociologique*, 8, 1905, pp. 421–425; trans. by Y. Nandan).

Robert Bartsch. *Die Rechtsstellung der Frau als Gattin und Mutter. Geschichtliche Entwicklung ihrer persönlichen Stellung im Privatrecht bis in das achtzehnte Jahrhundert* (Juridic Situation of the Woman as Wife and Mother). Leipzig: Veit, 1903, vi + 186 pp.

The juridical condition of the woman depends on her situation in the family, and that situation itself varies with the nature of the family; for, according to the manner in which the family is composed and organized, the woman plays a role which is more or less important. The question dealt with by Bartsch is consequently related to a multitude of other factors which are very complex. The author has an understanding of the problem; unfortunately, the diverse problems which he is led to touch upon are raised by him simultaneously and a bit confusedly; and this tends to obscure the clarity of the impression which remains with the reader of his book.

It is Germanic law that Bartsch sees as the point of departure of the evolution that he is attempting to retrace. The state in which this law is found, from the time we begin to know it through authentic documents, seems to the author to have been closely related to that of the very ancient *jus civile* in Rome. There should be many reservations with regard to that opinion. Undoubtedly, Bartsch himself does not deny that between the two juridical systems there are some differences, which he points out (p. 67); he recognizes that the power of the father in the Germanic societies was not at all absolute, that it was limited by the collective rights of the family. But in sum, the differences which he does admit are only differences of degree. Now, we believe that these differences are more profound, especially with regard to what concerns the woman. At all times, in fact, in the Germanic customs the uterine relationship was recognized side by side with the agnatic relationship; at all times the woman seemed to have enjoyed special consideration.

Moreover, Bartsch himself is obliged to affirm that in any case, in the course of time, under the influence of Christian ideas and for economic causes, the Germanic law and the Roman law diverged. The divergence was such that at the time of the reception of Roman law, a reconciliation between these two kinds of conceptions was logically impossible. Nevertheless, it was attempted; the jurists were forced to relate the Germanic usages to the Roman concepts. But since such a reconciliation was impossible, it could be accomplished in appearance only, or merely semantically, but at least the jurists did not try to obtain it by gravely altering the fundamental ideas of German law. Likewise, generally speaking, the author does not believe that the influence of Roman law on domestic or conjugal law was either very important or very felicitous. The progress which was accomplished little by little seems to him to have been above all the result of a spontaneous development. Thanks to local particularism, the law escaped the leveling influence of Roman law. It is there, in the particular law of different countries, of different towns, that the juridical conceptions proper to Germany were conserved and developed. It is thus that the paternal power was tempered and became less and less effective, becoming a simple obligation of tutelage with rights founded on that obligation. The effect of that transformation was to diminish the distance which separated the husband and the wife and to reinstate the status and the authority of the mother in the family.

However, this local law—precisely because it was the product of a spontaneous and instinctive evolution—was not at all systematic or scientific. The Roman law had that character; it presented a beautiful logical regularity, but it could not be applied, without artifices or violence, to the juridical reality of modern Germany. From this arose a veritable antinomy; on the one hand, we have a theory which could not be related to practice, and on the other, a practice refractory to theories which were constituted outside of it. That situation lasted until a new theory originated, developed by modern law itself and not by an archaic law; this was the theory of natural law. It accepted the principles which oriented juridical evolution toward new paths, drawing from them their logical consequences. It affirmed the equality and the natural autonomy of men; it declared that rights are only rationally based when they are corollaries of reciprocal obligations. It is easily understood how these ideas should have had as an effect the modification of the situation of the wife and the mother. Undoubtedly, this school of thought could be reproached for the intrepidness of its generalizations, its simplicity, its taste for dogmatism; nevertheless it played a major role in the development of our law. It clarified it, made it conscious of itself, subjected it to criticism, and for that reason put it in a position to develop itself in its proper direction. (*Année sociologique*, 8, 1905, pp. 425–427; trans. J. Sweeney)

A. Typaldo-Bassia. *La Communauté de biens conjugale dans l'ancien droit français. Etude de droit coutumier*. Preface by Ludovic Beauchet. Paris: Chevalier-Marescq, 1903, 67 pp.

The author has a good reason for saying that ''the history of the origin and the development of the common property belonging to the spouses is one of the most interesting points in the general history of civilization.'' This matrimonial regime corresponds, in fact, with a certain conception of marriage and of the family. And since it was and still remains to a certain extent at the root of our law, it helps us to understand our domestic organization and at the same time is explained by it.

Typaldo-Bassia's thesis is that the notion of communal conjugal property arose from the customary French law. Undoubtedly he is not ignorant of the fact that the first seed of it was found in the *leges barbarorum;*[140] but according to him, this vague, rudimentary seed would only be developed in the Middle Ages, and it is only then that it would have given birth to the institution that bears this name. What seems clearly to have determined our author to adopt this opinion is, besides the examination of the texts, the idea, found throughout this book, that "the institution of community is that which is most fitting to the character of the conjugal association" (p.3). It is therefore completely natural that he should find himself inclined to attribute to such a perfect institution an origin that is relatively recent. Community,[141] he says, presupposes that "the wife is no longer the subject but the companion of the husband"—his associate and his equal. Now, he recognizes that this conception of the woman and her role in the family was not foreign to the ancient Germanic societies; however, he thinks that it was only clearly affirmed, popularized, and developed by Christianity. It is thus under the influence of Christian ideas that the institution of community would have been born. The mind of the barbarian peoples was, no doubt, a favorable terrain for the development of these ideas; but it did not draw them out of its own roots. The barbarians received these ideas from outside (p. 6).

In unison with Beauchet,[142] we believe that this theory, in which the influence of Lefebvre[143] is recognizable, is completely excessive. It is completely unwarranted to refuse to see a beginning of community in the institution that Caesar tells us he observed among the Gauls (VI.19). A woman's dowry, together with a portion of the fortune of the husband, equally corresponding to that of the dowry, formed a common property, which was administered in common *(hujus omnis pecuniae conjunctim ratio habetur)*[144] and which, enlarged with profits, returned to the surviving spouse upon the death of the other. That community was undoubtedly limited to this determined portion of the property, but within these limits it was real. Likewise, to the extent that the fortune of the two spouses was equal, the acceptance of their common rights as equal was universal. It is true that in the era of the invasions no further trace of that usage is found in Gaul. It disappeared under the influence of Roman ideas. But it proves at least that the ideas from which community originated are not at all imputable to a civilization necessarily advanced or backward. Likewise, in the laws of the Ripuarians (XXXVII, 2) and the Visigoths (IV, 2, 16) we find all the essential elements of community. To begin with, it is a question of property acquired in common by a *collaboration* and the woman has a right to a third of it. Second, the savings made in common must be shared between the spouses. Is this not the essential point of the institution?

Furthermore, Typaldo-Bassia seems to us to be mistaken about the historical meaning of this institution. It is not at all certain that it implies a very lofty conception of women and their role in the family or in society.

Above all what is presupposes is a widespread practice of familial communism and a state of domestic organization which allows different families to interpenetrate one another with sufficient ease to assimilate foreign members. That the conjugal community is interdependent with the familial community, and is in part modeled on the latter, confirms the undebatable analogies that it presents with the tacit *(taisible)*[145] communities (see pp. 32 ff.). Certainly we do not wish to say that the first institution may have been born from the second, but that each derives its origin from the same basic ideas. Community between spouses could never have been born where community between relatives was unknown. On the other hand, in order that the two spouses could be so intimately associated, it was necessary that their families were not, as they were in Rome, closed and uncommunicative with each other. Insofar as they were in a state of mutual occlusion, the idea that the husband and wife could form such a tight economic society could not have been born. In a general way, the conjugal society can only achieve cohesion and intimacy to the extent that familial despotism is relaxed—for the two spouses can only relate and belong to each other to the extent that they are not so jealously monopolized by their respective families. Now, these two conditions so favorable to the appearance of the conjugal community were realized in the Germanic societies. It is known, in fact, that domestic communism was very deeply rooted there and also that the family was not organized there on foundations so narrowly and exclusively agnatic. There the relationship in the maternal line counted as much as the other; each spouse belonged, therefore, to the family of the mother and that of the father, which proves that the families were not impenetrable to each other. (*Année sociologique*, 8, 1905, pp. 427–429; trans. J. Sweeney)

Eugène Saguez. *Etude sur le droit des gens mariés dans les coutumes d'Amiens.* Amiens: Yvert et Tellier, 1903, vi + 113 pp.

The object of this work is to study the conjugal law of Amiens—first in the thirteenth, then in the sixteenth century—in such a way as to follow its evolution from one epoch to another. The documents which serve as a basis for the first study are: (1) the great charter of Amiens granted to that city in 1117 and confirmed by Philippe Auguste in 1185; (2) two municipal customs, one drawn up around 1210 and the other around 1292. In order to determine the state of the law in the sixteenth century, the author uses the General Custom of Bailliage of Amiens, which was drawn up for the first time in 1507 and a second time in 1567. However, since it is sometimes very obscure, Saguez often resorts to commentaries on it which were given by different jurists in the middle of the seventeenth century.

What characterizes the conjugal society in the thirteenth century as very strict and very egalitarian is community[146] between the spouses which is widely practiced. The community extends to all the possessions, but that word is taken in a very extended sense; it comprehends not only the valuable property subject to taxation but also that part of the property received free of charge in the course of the marriage, with the sole exception of that property a spouse . receives by inheritance from one of his or her ancestors. Likewise, from a negative point of view, it comprehends all the debts of both spouses together, even those which are anterior to the marriage. Finally, the wife appears as the associate of the husband. She has a proper right to the property acquired which may not be dispensed without her consent.

In the sixteenth century that notion of community is no longer intact; it appears that it begins to weaken under the pressure of new ideas. The sphere of possessions remains just as extensive as in the past; but the negative character of community is more restrained. The legally unpaid debts are no longer to be discharged except from the property belonging to the delinquent spouse. In a general way, the tendency to clearly separate the property of one from the property of the other and to prevent complete fusion becomes more marked. At the same time, the community is losing its egalitarian character; the rights of the husband increase while the role of the wife diminishes. She is becoming unfit, and the precautions taken by the law to protect her against the power of the husband are only the consequences of that inferiority.

This fact seems to us to give evidence of a contradiction that the theory of Lefebvre[147] on the origins of conjugal community conceals, a theory to which our author subscribes. According to that position, the community of property between the spouses would be essentially a Christian idea. But it is likewise that these same authors attribute to that same influence the formation of the husband's power, formulation of which they believe they find in the well-known verse of Genesis. Now, it is clear that in fact the power of the husband and of the community are two institutions which seem rather to exclude each other; the one regresses while the other is developing. It is thus very difficult to see that they would have the same origin.

Another institution about which one will find very interesting information in this book is the [widow's] dower. The dower has often been regarded as a survival benefit assured by the husband to the wife so that she would not be reduced to an impoverished existence if she was widowed, and this definition is accepted by our author. However, the very facts that he cites cause us to think that this definition might well be inexact, or in any case too narrow. In fact, the dower has certainly served other functions. To begin with, in the thirteenth century the dower was constituted by the wife's own property (p. 53); in that case it was evidently no survival benefit. The advantage that the woman found in that arrangement was that the landed property included in the dower was inalienable. It could not be encumbered by any charge, rent, quitrent, or mortgage. From another point of view the dower benefited not only the wife but also the children, who, in fact, had the clear ownership of the property that their mother had received for her dower. The consent of the child heir was necessary in order that the property might be sold. If the mother died first, the father had only the right to the use of the property (p. 60). In this respect, the dower appears as a safeguard for the benefit of the mother and the children against the mismanagement of the property by the father or husband (p. 64). It seems clear, then, that inalienability is one of the characteristic traits of the dower; moreover, it is this trait which caused its disappearance in the eighteenth century. In fact, it was an obstacle to the necessary circulation of wealth. (*Année sociologique*, 8, 1905, pp. 429–431; trans. J. Sweeney)

Josef Kohler. "Zur Urgeschichte der Ehe." *Zeitschrift für vergleichende Rechtswissenschaft*, XVII, pp. 256–280.

Following Spencer and Gillen, Kohler explains in this article the matrimonial system and the kinship nomenclatures used by the Arunta and other similar tribes. The author believes to have found in this organization the proof that the institution of group marriage was originally at the basis of matrimonial relations in this society. We have often criticized this notion in these very pages[148] (see above, p. 366); this is what impelled us to return to it here again. Furthermore, we would not have reviewed the author's work again had he not attempted to make a rejoinder to the objections that we expressed about his theory[149] (see *L'Année*, 1, p. 314) and had his response not given evidence that he misunderstood the nature of our objections. He declares to have read them with a surprise. He states: "They lead him to the question: How can a child be considered a child of different mothers? If its paternity were in doubt, it would not then claim to have a mother." Our author continues: "This criticism rests on a misunderstanding. The group marriage does not imply any uncertainty as far as either the father or the mother of a child is concerned; instead, it rests on this principle that it is the group itself that is considered as having the ability to function as father or mother. Motherhood signifies, then, only the fact that the child is born of a particular mother, but he descends from such a group of women; he belongs to a group to which his own mother belongs . . . and thus the entire gamut of objections is shattered." Kohler seems to have read us in the wrong spirit. On the same page where he refers to us as having expounded this very conception, he accuses us of not having understood it, even though we discussed it. It is quite true that in order to show that group marriage cannot account for the collective character of kinship relations, we have tried to show first of all that if the child is believed to have many mothers, this does not mean that he does not know who his true mother is. Besides this remote explanation, we would like to pass on to that which Kohler proposes in the following terms: "The only reason that the marriage took place between the groups and not between the individuals would have been sufficient to produce this result (that is to say, the collective character of kinship relations). Since a fixed number of men as a whole are joined together with a fixed number of women as a whole, the child would be indistinct in his regard for all the members of the first group as his fathers and all the members of the second as his mothers." Is this not the notion that Kohler accuses us of having misunderstood? Here is, on the other hand, how we contest this notion: "Why does the author not see that such a motherhood has nothing in common with the *blood relation* that the word designates? Because this bond can be established only among clearly defined individuals. If I am descended from such-and-such a woman, I can only conceive that I maintain the same relation with other women, no more than with the group formed by their reunion. No doubt, it is the words that I use to express my relationships with this group and the manner by which I understand them; but it is impossible to conceive that they express relationships of consanguinity. *"If, then, these expressions have nothing in common with any idea of descent, they would not be explained by the nature of marriage, nor by the consequence that served to prove that marriage at that time had such-or-such form."* This is, in fact, a serious question, and this is what Kohler does not seem to have noticed. The nature of marriage cannot explain the kinship nomenclatures, even though the latter express the relations of consanguinity, since marriage can hardly determine the principles on which the question of descendance is based. Now, the manner in which the word "mother" is employed shows that it would not signify a bond by blood. That is why the nomenclature would prove nothing as far as the form of marriage is concerned. And that is all we wanted to show Kohler[150] (*Année sociologique*, 9, 1906, pp. 378–380; trans. Y. Nandan)

Edward Westermarck. "The Position of Women in Early Civilization." *American Journal of Sociology*, Nov. 1904, X, pp. 408–421.

Very justifiably, the author warns against the prejudice that makes the condition of women in primitive societies completely pitiful. As burdensome as her task sometimes may be, it must not be forgotten that that of the husband is not always without difficulty and that he cannot carry out his proper functions of defense, hunting, and so on if he is not relieved of burdens; there is, therefore, a common concern with the duties of the woman. Moreover, it frequently happens that the woman enjoys real privileges; the author establishes this by a certain number of examples.

Then he searches into what can be the causes of this relatively favorable and independent situation of the woman in at least certain societies. He sets aside, after a summary examination, the theory which attributes it to the existence of the uterine family. Nevertheless, it appears very certain that under this domestic regime the woman is less dependent on the husband because she remains strongly attached to her natural family. The author maintains that two other causes play a very important role in the explanation of the phenomenon. First, there is the importance of the economic role, which sometimes devolves on the woman and which gives her some prestige, especially among those societies which live in part on the produce of the earth; then there is the magical character which is frequently invested in the woman. This latter consideration seems to us to be particularly important. (*Année sociologique*, 9, 1906, p. 380; trans. J. Sweeney)

E. Hermann. *Zur Geschichte des Brautkaufs bei den indogermani-*
schen Völkern. Wissenschaftliche Beilage zum XXI. Programm der
Hansa-Schule zu Bergedorf bei Hamburg, 44 pp.

The purchase of a fiancée is a practice which is encountered in all the Indo-Germanic societies; must we therefore conclude that it predates the separation of these societies, that it stems back to the period when they still formed an undivided group? This is the question which is treated in this brochure.

In order to resolve it, the author begins by establishing the universality of the practice in all the societies which he successively passes in review; at the same time, he shows that none seem to have received it from a foreign society. This first fact is already a proof that the institution extends back to a very remote period. Likewise, among many of these societies, especially among the Greeks and the Germans, the most ancient traditions which tell us about it show it to be already in the process of regression, which proves that it was already ancient. But that does not suffice to prove its origin in the times when these different societies were not yet detached from their common source.

The question would be resolved if one succeeded either in finding a common word in all the Indo-Germanic languages which meant the price of the fiancée, as Schrader seems to have done (*Reallexicon*, p. 110), or in establishing that the price of the fiancée was the same among the majority of these societies. But the author successively refutes both of these hypotheses. On the first point, one can only conjecture that the common ancestors of the Greeks, the Germans, and the Slavs had a word which meant the price of the fiancée and which was related to the root *vedh*. As for the amount of the price, it is true that in India, among the Saxons, and among the Ossetians it was a hundred head of cattle. But according to the author, this agreement arises simply from the fact that the round number one hundred easily impresses itself on people's minds. It seems inadmissible that in fact that price, or any other price, would be maintained throughout the centuries.

The author ends with some considerations on the extreme prudence which must attend the solution of these problems. It is not enough that an institution be spoken of in the most ancient traditions of different societies to have a basis for admitting that all these societies have it from one and the same source. For example, we believe otherwise: that the science of comparative law tends to resolve the question in a clearly negative direction. The unmistakable vestiges of uterine filiation which the Germanic law presents on the very eve of the advent of Christian societies attests that this domestic regime was practiced there very late. Now, it excludes the purchase of the fiancée, which is related to an opposed system of filiation. This usage among the Germans does not therefore reach back to its first origins. (*Année sociologique*, 9, 1906, pp. 381–383; trans. J. Sweeney)

Ernst Behre. *Die Eigentumsverhältnisse im ehelichen Güterrecht des Sachsenspiegels und magdeburger Rechts.* Weimar: Hermann Böhlaus Nachfolger, 1904, xiii + 110 pp.

The author intends to determine what were, according to the *Sachsenspiegel*[151] and the Magdeburg Law, the respective rights of the two spouses over the common property of the household.

The common property consisted only of the chattels; for the woman did not bring landed property with her, and the landed property remained under the ownership of the husband. But among the chattels there was an important distinction to be made. On the one hand there were those which were especially intended for use in the interior life of the household: kitchen utensils, beds, tables, instruments of all kinds. They constituted a group of things which had their own characteristics and a particular juridical condition. The totality which they formed bore a special name, the *Gerade*. All the other chattels, which did not have that purpose (the animals, for example), were a different group which bore another name, the *Ungerade*.

Whatever composed the *Ungerade*, whether contributed by the woman or by the husband or acquired during the existence of the marriage, belonged completely to the husband and at his death passed to his heirs. But for those things that were a part of the *Gerade* there was a necessary distinction, according to our author, between the *Gerade* of the man and that of the woman. For the husband likewise brought a certain number of domestic chattels to the household. Those which the woman brought belonged to her; on the death of the husband she retained them not by right of inheritance but because they were hers. If it was she who died first, they reverted not to her husband but to her closest relative in the feminine line. Thus they belonged to the woman by a very strict bond and even, in general, to the feminine relations; one can suspect that here was a vestige of the uterine family. As for the *Gerade* of the husband, it naturally belonged to him; but his wife had an eventual right over these movable goods, which, throughout the whole life of the husband, was superseded by his superior right, but was affirmed as soon as the marriage was dissolved by his death. The wife could reclaim this special *Gerade* from the heirs of the husband.

It was the same kind of right that she had over her *Morgengabe* ("dowry") and over what was called the *Mussteil*.[152] The *Morgengabe* was a designation for property (natural or financial) that was transferred from the husband's personal fortune to the woman in case she became a widow; the purpose of this designation was to compensate for the loss that the woman underwent by the fact that the movable objects of her personal *Ungerade* became the property of her husband. The *Mussteil* consisted of the right of the widow over a certain share of the food provisions stocked by the household. It was a way of assuring her of her daily bread in case at the moment of widowhood she would have to or want to leave the property on which she lived with her husband.

All these dispositions show that even the *Sachsenspiegel,* the property of the two spouses—at least the movable property—was strictly united and sometimes confused; and nevertheless, in the Saxon law, the idea of the community of property holds a lesser place than in the other Germanic laws. (*Année sociologique,* 9, 1906, pp. 383–384; trans. J. Sweeney)

Auguste Rol. *L'Evolution du divorce. Jurisprudence et sociologie.*
  Paris: Arthur Rousseau, 1905, vi + 486 pp.

The word *sociology* that figures in the subtitle is scarcely justified by the work's subject matter, which contains no sociology properly speaking. It is above all a legal study that aims to bring out the present tendencies of the courts in the matter of divorce. But since these tendencies are important social facts, they should not leave the sociologists unconcerned.

The author has no trouble establishing that the courts tend more and more to reduce all the reasons for divorce to only one, namely the obvious impossibility of continuously living together. The legal nature of the grievances invoked by the parties concerned hardly matters. The only question the judges ask themselves is involved with finding out whether or not the couple is able to live together. Now, the logical corollary of such court action is, Rol very rightly states, divorce by mutual consent. The appropriate consent of the two parties concerned is, in effect, the best evidence that cohabitation has become intolerable to them. As a matter of fact, it is a matter of common knowledge that in various forms of disguise divorce by mutual consent enters increasingly into the practices of our courts.

Not only does this stretching of the divorce law appear logical to Rol by reason of the standards followed by the magistrates, but he believes it conforms to the nature of things and to the requirements of the public conscience. Two reasons appear to him to justify it. First, the religious respect that the marriage bond inspired in days gone by appears to him to result from outmoded religious beliefs. In his opinion, secular morality can look upon marriage only as a contract that no longer has any justification the moment the two parties who have formed it stop wanting it. In the second place, the growth of economic life, the promiscuities of working-class life, the rise in drinking, and the increasing number of those who have lost social position (which the author ascribes to the spread of education) are some of the many reasons that have an effect of multiplying the disagreements between husband and wife; the state of married life having thus become worse, it would seem necessary to provide an easy way for the parties concerned to leave each other.

This justification, which takes up only a few pages, is doubtless, in the opinion of the author and of Toulouse,[153] the sociological part of the book. It does not strike us as very solid. It is in no way demonstrated that the marriage bond ought to lose its former holy character simply because such sanctity ceases to exist in the mind in the form of religious symbols. The institution of marriage has in itself a moral validity and has a social function, the implications of which go beyond the concerns of the individual. In another sense, the promiscuities of the workers, drinking, etcetera, are blemishes on our civilization that the legislator ought to combat, very far from having to give them his blessing. (*Année sociologique*, 10, 1907, pp. 437–438; trans. J. French)

Henri Mallard. *Etude sur le droit des gens mariés d'après les coutumes de Berry.* Saint-Amand: Pivoteau, 1905, viii + 210 pp.

This work is directly inspired by some of the ideas developed by Lefebvre[154] in the book that has just been analyzed. It involves the verification of general theories that have been discussed concerning data derived from Berry.[155] After the examination we have made of these theories, it is useless to go over them once again. Here we shall settle for a few particular remarks the present work suggests.

After having agreed with his master[156] that the communal regime is essentially of Christian origin, Mallard applies himself to showing that if our marriage law took another direction, it is because of the predominant influence of Roman law since the sixteenth century. It is the prestigious impact of this law that one would have to credit for the characteristic alternative to the communal regime, the establishment of different regimes, and a variety of measures (chiefly the one involving separate maintenance) that aim to give the couple a free hand in the economic sphere. From here on, one is about to note that this whole evolution in our laws has something abnormal about it. And this is, we believe, the author's opinion. All such changes in our earliest constitution on marriage are, it seems, changes for the worse, the work of pedantic and clumsy jurists. And doubtless, it is very plausible that the establishment of the dowry system has had no different origins; therefore it remains sporadic and it tends to lose ground. But it is quite another matter in the case of the economic independence of both husband and wife, a move that is apparently very much in accord with our modern aspirations. In order that the wife can enjoy the autonomy that our trend towards self-sufficiency calls for in her case, she must indeed be autonomous, to some extent, in the circle of economic interests. Our conception of the marital association can no longer be what the Middle Ages has bequeathed to us, without holding Roman law responsible for the changes that have thus affected our way of thinking.

We find in the book a fact that would tend to confirm a hypothesis we were expressing above. We were saying that there is no difference in kind between the regime of tacit communities[157] and its corresponding association between married couples, and that as a result there must be at least a partial identity between the causes that gave rise to the one and the other. What seems indeed to bear out this kinship is that if one of the spouses involved in the joint ownership should happen to die, the association is continued automatically between the survivor and the children and even at times the nearest collateral kin. The marital association becomes ipso, facto a tacit community—all of which already shows how they were related to each other. Furthermore, these two kinds of societies were considered to have such neighborly ties that the jurists would hold discussions to find out whether one was different in kind from the other. We do not have to solve the problem; but the fact that it was a subject of controversy is already significant. (*Année sociologique*, 10, 1907, pp. 438–439; trans. J. French)

Marianne Weber. *Ehefrau und Mutter in der Rechtsentwicklung. Eine Einführung.* Tübingen: Mohr, 1907, xvi + 572 pp.

The aim of this book is both theoretical and practical at the same time. To begin with, the author proposes to portray the situation of women during the principal epochs of history; it is to this use that the major portion of the work is put (pp. 1–506). But in the last chapters it seeks from such historical investigations the solution to problems arising today and having to do with the present legal situation of women as much domestically as socially. Being a historical account that goes from the most primitive societies that we know to the recent reforms in German civil law, the work naturally touches on too great a number of very complex issues for the deepest kind of research to be possible. Mme. Weber,[158] more often than not, is obliged to settle for secondary sources. It is, however, only just to acknowledge that for each of the numerous societies she is induced to discuss, she has made as much of an in-depth inquiry as the breadth of the subject allowed her to encompass in her attempt. For the most part, she has managed to discover the most important works and she generally makes use of them judiciously and with a critical mind which is worthy of respect.

What is lacking in this book is a disposition to organize facts according to a methodical plan and mark out the points of convergence on which to arrive at intended conclusions. The order in which the issues are tackled is rather extraneous. The first chapter is devoted to all the *primitive* forms of sexual relationships and of marriage; in the following one are confused the Egyptians, Babylonians, Hebrews, Arabs before and after Islam, Greeks, and Romans. The third chapter deals separately with Germanic law without it being clear why it comes at this juncture, unless it is because it precedes (but no more than Roman law) medieval law and modern law, which are tackled next. Furthermore, in each of these particular studies, the author has been unable to direct her energy to a limited number of points that are clearly defined, chosen because of their importance to the general problem under consideration; but it is confusingly a question of everything that has to do with moral standards of the sexes, with marriage, with the family, with women's civil rights, etcetera. This dispersal succeeds in rendering the troubling impression that the work is difficult.

It is not as if the entire work is without a directive in the form of a dominant idea; this last is, as will shortly be seen, even quite simplified.

To begin with, the author refuses to admit that there exists a definite relation between successive economic regimes throughout history and the social situation of women. To be sure, she does not fail to recognize that women are more or less well treated depending on how important their economic role is. But as she sees it, the impact of such factors is merely secondary. Above all, she does not deny that, as certain socialists maintain, monogamous marriage and the subservience of the woman are essentially caused by the institution of private ownership. One has the feeling that Mme. Weber is constantly preoccupied with combating Engels' well-known thesis. It is permissible to find such preoccupation excessive and the place thus assigned to that theory entirely out of proportion to its scientific value.

It is chiefly domestic evolution that would have determined the way in which women's rights have grown; it is woman's place in the family that would have determined her place in society. The principle is undeniable, but the author's conception of the history of the family is so simplistic as to conceal, in part, the complexity of the problem under examination. Mme. Weber, following Grosse's lead, acknowledges only two family types, clearly distinct from each other. There is the clan (die Sippe), a vast conglomerate of individuals who are not necessarily blood relations; then there is the patriarchal family, which can be very extensive, as among the Slavs or (less so) among the Romans, or still more restricted, in cases where it includes only the descendants of a single couple, but which, in different forms, is based on the same principle and presents the same distinctive characteristics. It is made up of a group of relatives under the authority of a male head appointed on the basis of age or because of an election or his position on the family tree. Not only are a large number of different types to be found commingled in this way under the same head, but it will be further noted that the uterine, or maternal, family is not at issue. Indeed, the fact is that the author sees therein, not a predetermined family pattern, but a very casual arrangement due to certain combinations of circumstances—one that is capable of perpetuating itself under all possible regimes. When the wife's family enjoys some sort of economic advantage with regard to the husband's family, the former naturally tends to involve in its sphere of action the new household and its progeny. Therefore, it is only rarely that the uterine bloodline does not meet and converge with the opposite bloodline in the same society. It would be in a very small number of cases only that the first system would prevail almost exclusively and would be considered as the normal basis for domestic and marital relations. Then too, in our author's opinion, the direction that the bloodline takes would not affect the inner structure of the family and would not suffice to give rise to a well-defined family type.

It appears to us useless to discuss a thesis that contradicts too many known facts. Moreover, we cannot help thinking that Mme. Weber would not have accepted it so readily if Engels' theory, which she has constantly in mind, had not ascribed to the matriarchal family a primordial importance. Whatever may be the case with this particular point, that is how women's history is connected with the history of the family.

Communism was characteristic of the clan. It was an extensive group in which everything was shared by everyone alike, and the individual, consequently, had no sphere of action he could call his own; he could not be his own as a persona; he was absorbed into the collectivity. The institution of the patriarchal family corresponded to a first move in the direction of individual distinction. The vast conglomerate which made up the clan was segmented into a certain number of private, autonomous families; each one administered its particular interests as it saw fit. Thus, in place of the unified and homogenous life it once knew, there was substituted a multiplicity of heterogeneous and independently activated homes. Moreover, at the head of each of these groups there was placed an individual who, thanks to the extensive powers with which he was armed, was aware of himself as a person. To the degree that family groups continued to break into further segments and diminish in size, this movement toward individual distinction was confined simply to the point of growing and gaining strength until the moment when the family was normally composed only of the married couple and its underage children. Then each man, once he became an adult, was in a position to exercise the full rights that reverted to an exemplary person.

But this movement benefited only the male side of humanity. Heads of private families were always men. That such hegemony was necessitated by the very conditions of day-to-day living is something the author does not deny. Notably, the importance of military functions explains such social priority attributed to the stronger sex. But it has resulted in an everlasting subordination of women. For the sovereignty of men, once established, was maintained by the force of prejudices, and that is why today, although patriarchal power is no longer justified, the woman is always treated like an inferior being, and in that capacity she is prevented from freely developing her personality, as much inside the home as in public life. In a situation like that, Mme. Weber sees nothing other than an outmoded survival that one must work to do away with.

Since it is marriage which shackles the wife to the husband and puts her in a state of dependency, it has been proposed to suppress marriage as a social institution and to make it freely contracted and left entirely to the discretion of the parties concerned. Prudently conservative in outlook, the author rejects this remedy, which appears to her both ineffectual and dangerous. The formalities of a wedding appear to her indispensable as a way to record in public and with certainty the desire of a man and a woman to live together in a state of matrimony and to accept the legal consequences of that state. But since marriage seems of little use except for the purpose mentioned above, Mme. Weber could adjust very well to a regime under which the bond of marriage would be singularly loosened—marriage would no longer be anything more than a lesser marriage. In the name of personal morality, for which she appeals, she asks to make it possible for the marriage to be broken simply at the wish, confirmed and duly recorded, of the parties concerned. When one conceives of marriage in this way, one easily makes up one's mind about everything that can compromise the organic unity of the marital society and

the family. That is why the author sees fit to call for a fully equal status of husband and wife before the law. Whether it involves the overall training of the
children or decisions to be made about family matters, neither the wife nor the
husband should have prior claims over the other. *

We are far from disputing the fact that legal regulations concerning the
woman, such as they are defined in the civil law of European societies, call for
important reforms. But on the other hand, Mme. Weber's simplistic line of
reasoning and the conclusions she draws from it too often fail to recognize, we
believe, the complexity of the problem.

Her whole theory rests on the premise that the patriarchal family has
brought about the woman's complete subservence. Now, formulated so
categorically, the assertion is wide open to question. To be sure, such a
domestic regime has given rise to the woman's legal status as a minor in civil
life. But on the other hand, in this patriarchal family type, family life is much
more intense and more important than in previous types; the woman's role,
which is precisely to preside over life indoors, has also assumed more importance, and the moral scope of the wife and mother has increased. At the same
moment and for the same reason, husband and wife have become closer, more
directly and more constantly in touch, because the center of gravity in the life
of the male has ceased to be sidetracked away from the home as much as in the
past. The more family matters intervene to occupy the man's mind, the more
he falls out of the habit of regarding his wife as an inferior. This result is all the
more notable as the patriarchal family becomes more powerfully and more
solidly organized. Accordingly, in Rome the authority of the father reaches its
maximum growth, the wife is respected by those around her, she shares her
husband's position. In this relationship, Rome is oddly ahead of Athens.†

But who does not feel that whatever may contribute to the weakening of
the organic unity of the family and of marriage must inevitably dry up the
source of woman's rise to a higher status? The feelings of respect that have
directed her way and have become more and more pronounced with the further progress of history originate, in large part, in the religious respect inspired
by hearth and home. If family life should cease being regarded as something
more than a precarious cohabitation between two beings who can at any moment separate if they so desire, who for the duration of the partnership each
have their center of interests and concerns, it will be difficult for such a
religion to survive. And woman's stature will be diminished because of it. To
be sure, it is commonly held that her loss in one respect will be her gain in
another as a result of the more considerable role she will play in civil life. The
fact remains that the gains she will settle for with the acquisition of the rights

---

* In case of disagreement on how to raise the children, the author demands that the daughters be
placed under the supervision of the mother, and the sons under the father.

† The author attributes this to the institution of the *justae nuptiae sine manu* that the Roman
matron enjoyed. But this historic assertion appears to us very hard to justify.

claimed in her behalf will be offset by important losses. There is ample evidence that the problem is less simple than is commonly believed, and that is all we wish to establish. (*Année sociologique,* 11, 1910, pp. 363–369; trans. J. French)

Gaston Richard. *La Femme dans l'histoire* (Bibliothèque biologique et sociologique de la femme). Paris: Octave Doin, 1909, 465 pp.

The question that Richard raises is the same one Mme. Weber handles in the book which has just been reviewed.[159] It involves making a historical and ethnological inquiry into the past and future condition of women. In this attempt to answer this question, the two authors sensibly use the same method. Richard's survey of the various societies is in a way, like Mme. Weber's short summary. In any event, he has the advantage over his predecessor of being aware of how difficult and almost impossible the enterprise is (p. 1). He excuses himself for attempting it by pointing out that had he not done so, the series *Bibliothèque biologique et sociologique de la femme* would have been incomplete. He is too well informed not to be aware of the serious and even practical drawbacks of such premature generalizations.

Somewhat like Mme. Weber, he distinguishes three principal stages (we leave aside the intervening transitions in the history of the family. To begin with there is the maternal phase, characterized by the absorption of the individuals of both sexes into the interior of a family group restricted by uterine lineage. In this phase the woman is practically on the same footing as the man, but group law has prior claim over the rights of the individual. Next comes the patriarchy, under which group law is concentrated in the hands of the father because of primarily religious influences. Consequently, as a general rule men enjoy within the family a privileged situation, whereas the woman "is henceforth an inferior being destined to become an outsider" (p. 164). Lastly, the third period is the one we are in; Richard defines it by the individualism that forms the basis of its morality. Group responsibility is replaced by individual responsibility. From this results a tendency towards the increasingly complete assimilation of both sexes from the moral, legal, and political points of view.

On the strength of this pattern, family growth appears to be a fairly simple matter. Unfortunately, such simplicity is possible only by confounding and placing very different social forms under the same rubric. Accordingly, the rights of the mother would be observed [in the same way] among the Australians, the Melanesians, and the Indians of North America. Now, Australians do not know about the house. American Indians for the most part possess such an item, and that alone is already enough to show that organized domesticity cannot be the same in both places. We do not even know how the rights of the mother in Australia are to be discussed. Actually, it is the rule that the husband takes his wife away to his place; it is where their father is that the children are born. Therefore the wife lives among people who are strangers to her, just as in the patriarchal society. No doubt, in an important number of such societies it is through the mother that the totem is transmitted; but the legal situation of the woman is not otherwise affected. It may, it is true, be presumed that the wife and her children remain on their native territory. But it is only a hypothesis; we cannot possibly know what organized domesticity was like at the time of the matriarchate in Australia, and in any case one can be certain that it must be different from what is to be found in North America. Likewise, the patriarchal regime presumably was like that of the Romans, the Greeks, the Chinese, the Germans, the Jews, and the Japanese of primitive times (p. 171). These are, nevertheless, very different civilizations. The fact is that for Richard, agnation and patriarchy are interchangeable terms; one should never be separated from the other. Now there are, in fact, agnatic families without a father in the position of authority. The family, in the case of the Slavs, is made up of a vast group of agnates who live with the group and maintain their status intact; but group rights remain diffuse within the community and are definitely not concentrated within the hands of a single individual as was the case in Rome. There are, therefore, two family types that were supposed to be differentiated, and the rights of the woman are not the same in both cases.

The work ends with a note in which the author discusses our theory of incest. Richard states that our theory draws on kinship relations as derived from religious sentiments. He further states that our theory of exogamy is based on incest taboo combined with totemic taboo. The objection Richard makes on our account is twofold. "It is," he says, "impossible to affirm a cause-and-effect relationship between the totem and the taboo" because "the taboo is a Polynesian institution; the totem is an Amerindian institution" (p. 435). It is with the greatest surprise that we have read such a proposal. Actually, totemism is essentially Australian; in America only highly developed and altered forms of it are still to be found (pp. 75, 108 ff.). The taboo, or a system of interdictions, has nothing inherently Polynesian about it; it is universal.

In the second place, we are told, if prejudices relating to blood ties, notably to menstrual-blood ties, had rendered the woman inviolable, the fact is that every marriage would have been impossible. In these pages we have often insisted on the fact that in the lower social orders and even in others, the consummation of the marriage is regarded as a dangerous act from the religious viewpoint—one that puts the man in touch with formidable forces. Out of that there arises the betrothal taboo, the taboo of the married couple, and all sorts of practices, including ritual deflowering. (*Année sociologique,* 11, 1910, pp. 369–371; trans. J. French)

Otto Opet. *Brauttradition und Consensgespräch in mittelalterischen Trauungsritualen. Ein Beitrag zur Geschichte des deutschen Eheschliessungsrechts.* Berlin: Vahlen, 1910, 160 pp.
    This little book deals with two nuptial rites that were practiced in the Mid-

dle Ages. At a given moment during the ceremony the priest performed a traditional act involving the girl. Taking her by the hand, he gave it to the husband, or else he joined their two hands. Before this, he had questioned the couple in order to find out if they wished to take each other mutually as husband and wife. Opet's aim is to determine the origins of these two rites.

According to Sohm and Friedberg, the tradition involving the girl was apparently a secular Germanic practice which the Church inherited. After a very closely reasoned criticism of the texts, Opet rejects this hypothesis. In his opinion it is, on the contrary, the Church that introduced this practice into Germanic societies. The *dextrarum junctio*[160] was already a regular ceremony in Rome; presumably the Church simply proceeded to assimilate it.

The second rite, on the other hand, was presumably of secular and popular origin. The practice of questioning the betrothed in order to find out if they wished to marry arose naturally, beginning when the *mundium*[161] lost its primitive authority, when the girl's personality began to be free of the former guardianship to which she was subjected. The conclusion is interesting. It implies, in fact, that the marriage by mutual consent was not instituted all of a piece by the Church; it was a spontaneous byproduct of the moral evolution of Germanic societies. The Church, on this point, merely proceeded to continue a movement that was born outside its jurisdiction. (*Année sociologique,* 12, 1913, p. 433; trans. J. French)

F. K. Neubecker. *Die Mitgift in rechtsvergleichender Darstellung.*
 Leipzig: Deichert, 1909, vi + 251 pp.
 The book's title is somewhat deceiving. The author does not propose to do a history of the dowry in itself and for itself. The aim he has in mind is legal and practical. It is a matter of knowing how the dowry must be regarded today and the promise of a dowry, what is behind its compelling force, on what conditions such an obligation depends, etcetera. But the author believes he must, first of all, consult history in order to solve these legal problems. Accordingly, four chapters (pp. 8–83) are devoted to summing up relevant subject matter from the past on Greek law, Roman law, that of Germanic societies, Slavic law. Such a cursory statement is necessarily very elementary, hardly calculated to add much to what is already known worldwide. One may even discover here the enunciation of proposals that, far from being the convincing evidence they appear to be to the author, would seem to be greatly in need of justification. Accordingly the *justae nuptiae usu*[162] are represented as a survival of marriage involving abduction of a minor, the *coemptio*[163] as derived from the former marriage by purchase, the *confarreatio*[164] as a more or less belated form of marriage—in any case subsequent to the aforementioned (pp. 24–25). As for us, we estimate that Roman marriage *cum manu*[165] has nothing in common with what has been called, more or less appropriately, marriage by purchase. The *manus* of the husband over his wife is a peculiarly Roman institution linked to the full organization of the *patria potestas.*

This historical briefing is followed by a second part (pp. 83–180), in which one finds a statement on the current laws of different European societies in the matter of the dowry. Lastly, the author comes to German law and to the practical issues that we indicate above. The link between such issues and the retrospective investigations that open the volume appears to be quite lax, if indeed there is any such. (*Année sociologique*, 12, 1913, p. 434; trans. J. French)

Gaetan Aubéry. *La Communauté de biens conjugale. Origines et évolution du régime légal. Som amélioration (Etude d'histoire et de droit comparé)*. Paris: Pichon et Durand-Auzias, 1911, xx + 610 pp.

Two essential features characterize the marriage partnership. First, it is an association of common or residual holdings between spouses: It presupposes a common pooling of assets which comprises possessions in bulk or in part, and over which each spouse has coproprietary rights. Secondly, at least under our law, the husband heads such an association. Aubéry proposes to investigate the origins of this regime, how it has evolved, and finally what it appears destined to become.

Very rightly, he goes back for his primary sources to the Ripuarian law that assures for the wife, in case she is a widow, the right to share in the property acquired together with a legal marriage portion of fifty sous[166] (p. 89). But, at the bottom, this provision of the barbaric law did not yet contain anything but the first rudimentary features of the well-named partnership: Thus, what was guaranteed to the surviving spouse was simply a survival grant, nontransmissible to the wife's heirs. The latter had, therefore, no right to the property acquired during the marriage. It is only with the advent of the Carolingians that the idea of a real partnership begins to develop (pp. 111 ff.). By the thirteenth century, it is firmly established. It has become the lawful regime; it is a necessary consequence of marriage (p. 187).

As for the causes that gave rise to the institution, the author singles out two types. First, there is the already very high opinion in which Germans held the wife, an opinion that Christianity, then the tradition of chivalry in the Middle Ages, simply helped to strengthen: The wife was regarded as the husband's partner, and as a result, marriage was viewed as a partnership. In another sense, all causes that prodded men of the Middle Ages to form societies based on partnerships (for example, the tacit[167] societies) were to predetermine the marriage partnership's formation as an association involving joint property holdings (chapter 9).

Without intending to deny the reality of such influences, we tend, nevertheless, to believe that they have not played the decisive role that is attributed to them. The Romans had no less high an opinion of the wife than the Germans; never was the bond of matrimony stronger than in Rome, never was the union of man and wife more fully regarded as an inviolate partnership throughout the whole of life. And yet the system of joint property holdings has nothing Roman about it. By the same token, economic communism is basic to family organization among vast numbers of people, for example among the Slavs; but far from clearing the way to communal marriage, there are ever-present obstacles in doing so. The family, on the one hand, and the marriage partnership, on the other, are themselves two antagonists who cannot follow parallel courses of growth. If the former is strong, if it feels its unity keenly—and that is what the communal family makes clear—it is against taking the risk of having some part of the common patrimony fall into the hands of a female outsider. For the joint property settlement to be well established, it is necessary therefore that the partnership formed by the married couple, instead of remaining absorbed within the circle of relatives, should break away from it, set itself apart, and even become the focal point of family life. Now, this sort of tendency exists beginning with Germanic societies. Whereas in Rome the married sons remained under the father's authority and as a general rule did not possess any separate patrimony, and whereas in the case of the Serbs they continued to be a part of the *zadruga,* among the Germans it frequently happened that they set up an independent home-life when they married. Under such circumstances, marital sentiments ceased to be neutralized by feelings more appropriately domestic, and the possessions acquired by husband and wife in the course of their collaboration appeared most naturally as a commonplace of their association as spouses.

These sources of the joint property settlement permit a glimpse into their future. The more one advances in history, the more the association of husband and wife is featured and becomes the essential and permanent element of the family. The joint property settlement, therefore, comes increasingly to be regarded as a normal marital practice. Indeed, it tends to become increasingly widespread in the civilized countries; although the other regimes are maintained, they lose ground. If England, in 1882, adopted the separation of property, it was under the influence of political circumstances and economic conditions (pp. 381–384). The more the marriage bond tightens, the more the moral communion it implies calls for, as a natural counterpart, a community of interests.

But in the course of this development, a new factor intervened that caused it to deviate from its normal direction. In the Middle Ages, although the wife was subordinate to the husband, she was nevertheless considered to be his partner: The husband was administrator of the common property, not the master of the situation. From the moment Roman law made its influence felt, the Roman notion of marital authority was substituted for the Germanic conception of the *mainbournie:*[168] The husband became "lord and master" of community property, which he could dispose of "as he pleased and at will"; the wife, on the contrary, was branded as being radically inferior and incompetent. Now, this supremacy of the husband ran counter to the very idea of marital partnership, since common property was thus, in a sense, considered to be a concern of the husband. On the other hand, since this subordination of the wife would have left her defenseless when faced with her husband, it was necessary, for her protection, to grant her various privileges (a lawful separate property settlement, the right to waive a claim, pay benefits, legal mortgages, etcetera). But apart from the fact that such measures spring from a mutual feeling of defiance between the spouses, and consequently can only weaken the marriage ties, they are, for the most part, vexations that tie up property settlements and paralyze other transactions. All such difficulties have at times been imputed to the communal regime, whereas they are due uniquely to an unwarranted conception of marital prerogatives. The only way to remedy them is to renounce such a conception, to make the ordinary wife the equal of the husband, to increase her powers and her participation in the administration of the matters at hand. The author examines in detail the different reforms which have been proposed to this end. We shall not follow him in such an investigation, since it is enough for us to have indicated a principal source from which one would do well to draw one's inspiration. (*Année sociologique*, 12, 1913, pp. 434–437; trans. J. French)

Laurent Laborde. *La Dot dans les fors et coutumes du Béarn*. Bordeaux: Cadoret, 1909, 227 pp.

In Béarn, as in the other parts of the Pyrénées, the peculiar disposition of the dowry is worth noting. Depending on the circumstances, it is provided sometimes by the wife for the husband, sometimes by the husband for the wife. This curious practice is due to the very principles on which the entire organization of family life in this region is based.

The first of those principles is that only one heir per family was possible. All possessions were concentrated in the hands of a single individual. And yet the other children were not completely excluded from the benefits of succession: Either they were fed by the heir or else they received a lawful portion of money and notably a dowry.

The second principle is that the heir was the eldest regardless of sex. If the eldest was a daughter, it was she who became owner of the patrimony and head of the house. The younger children were called *cadets*.

These two rules explain the existence of endowed husbands. Marriage between an heir and an heiress was all but impossible; for the result of this would have been the loss of one of the two houses, which the law involving rights of succession sought, above all, to avoid. Marriages between two young children—involving one male and one female *cadet*—were extremely difficult because neither one nor the other had a house. Normally, therefore, the heir married a *cadette*,[169] and the *cadet* an heiress.

If the woman was a *cadette*, she provided her legitimate portion as a dowry; she forfeited her name in order to take her husband's. But if the husband was a *cadet* and the wife an heiress, the roles were reversed. It was the husband who provided his legitimate portion as a dowry. He entered his wife's home, as "son-in-law" took the latter's name, and put himself completely in the new family's service.

It is clear that this whole organization rests on the feeling that the patrimony is tied in with a specific family by an almost unbreakable bond. The same principle was applied to the dowry. It was passed along by the endowed husband or wife to their children, but if there were no children it was turned back to the original family. And again the children received it as a kind of tacit trust settlement and not by right of succession. A wall was thus erected between the holdings of the two spouses. Therefore the joint holding was unlawful in that region.

Another curious feature of this law is the equality of the sexes. This equality was not confined to the right of the firstborn: The *cadets* and the *cadettes* had equal rights as well. (*Année sociologique*, 12, 1913, pp. 437–438; trans. J. French)

NOTES AND NOTICES

A. Zocco-Rosa. "Sulle cerimonie nuziali dei Lusitani." *Rivista scientifica del diritto,* Aug.-Sept. 1897.

Relying on a text of Strabo (III, 4, 18), and on a passage of E. de Hinojosa (*Historia general del derecho español,* XV, pp. 73 ff.), the author points out some similarities of nuptial usages among the ancient Lusitanians, Greeks, and Romans. One finds among them, in fact, a solemn sacrifice effectuated with the help of the wife, her head covered with a veil, just as in Rome. The resemblance, moreover, is quite striking. The usage of the bridal procession, in which the bride is led to her husband's house, is too general to be characterized as a definite family type. So much can be said of the traces of purchase, which, moreover, have almost completely disappeared in Rome; because the *coemptio,*[170] which serves the purpose of bringing the woman under the *manus*[171] of the man, and not simple and pure marital rights, should not be confused with the purchase of the fiancée. (*Année sociologique*, 2, 1899, p. 343; trans. Y. Nandan)

Victor Marx. *Die Stellung der Frauen in Babylonien, gemäss den neubabylonischen Kontrakten aus der Zeit von Nebukadnezar bis Darius* (Condition of the Woman in Babylon). Leipzig: Pries, 1898.

With the help of contracts, texts of which have been preserved, the author undertakes to establish the relatively independent status of the woman in Babylon; but he has collected the materials necessary for this work rather than following them through. He cites the documents one after the other, which seem to him have the natural strength to clarify the question. He comments on each of them separately, however, without presenting the general results which emerge from the evidence. One discovers from this discussion that the woman intervenes in business contracts, without even pronouncing the name of her husband. In the marriage contracts, the sum of money the husband must pay his wife in case he sends her back home is fixed in advance—likewise the punishment he could inflict on her in case of infidelity. In the contracts of endowment, which are distinct from the marriage contracts, one often sees that the mother intervenes on the same side as the father, or even acts by herself. (*Année sociologique*, 3, 1900, pp. 389–390; trans. Y. Nandan)

Anna Lampérière. *Le Rôle social de la femme. Devoirs, droits, éducation*. Paris: F. Alcan, 1898, 174 pp.

The book is written with a generous disposition, seeking a middle solution of the problem. The thesis has been developed by way of amplification rather than demonstrated methodically. The author expounds her personal views with enthusiasm, however, without giving objective evidence. The future role of the woman can, however, only be determined by understanding her role in the past, and the functional conditions in the parameters of which that role has differed. The ideas enunciated here, moreover, are not stated with perfect precision. Woman must leave the function of production to man, and limit herself to the functions of organization and assimilation. But what is to be understood by that? For the married woman, one understands well that it is worth saying. In sum, it simply concerns the domestic functions of housekeeping. But for the spinster and for the widow without children or whose children have become adults, the explanations which the author gives us (pp. 35 ff.) are quite vague. As for the married woman, is the author sure that she must more and more confine herself to domestic affairs? Feminism, an unconscious movement, without doubt deceives itself when it formulates the details of its demands. But it is not to be implied that the movement is a short-lived vogue. Nonetheless, it is quite true that woman should seek for equality in the functions which are commensurate with her nature. (*Année sociologique*, 3, 1900, pp. 390–391; trans. Y. Nandan)

A. C. Winter. "Eine Bauernhochzeit in Russisch-Karelien" (Marriage of Peasants in Karelian Russia). *Globus*, LXXVI, no. 20, pp. 315–321.

These observations have been made for the eastern region of Finland, occupied by a special branch of the Finnish race. What is absolutely remarkable is the crying and groaning which take an enormous place in the wedding ceremonies. It is true of the mourning ceremonies as well. From the moment she is engaged, the young girl must adopt a grievous attitude, even though the event itself will bring her happiness. Her mother, as well as the friends who accompany her, must for the same reason wear their ordinary clothes. The songs that they sing are deeply woeful. On the day of marriage, the young bride has her face covered with a veil; it reminds one of a funeral. The author sees in this usage a survival of marriage by capture. The explanation, it seems to us, does not conform with the facts. This *obligatory* display of sadness must be evidently aimed to ward off certain dangers; it is a kind of anticipated expiation, the aim of which is to avert an evil that one dreads. But what is the evil? Would these be the perils to which the sexual relation is exposed, when it is not reduced to an accidental rapprochement? We are satisfied in posing this question. (*Année sociologique,* 4, 1901, pp. 362–363; trans. Y. Nandan)

Ludwig Fuld. "Die Frauen und das bürgerliche Gesetzbuch"
(Women and the Civil Code). *Zeitschrift für Sozialwissenschaft*, 1900, no. 4.

The author enumerates the new laws which the recent German Code has instituted for the woman. Principal among them are: the possibility of making contracts and of acting within justice without the husband's authorization under specific conditions; the right of the guardian mother to exercise tutelage under the same conditions as the husband; equality before the law of the adulterer and the adulteress; the ability of the unmarried young mother to obtain child support from the father. (*Année sociologique,* 4, 1901, p. 365; trans. Y. Nandan)

Raoul de la Grasserie. "Des Régimes matrimoniaux chez les peuples
germaniques et les peuples slaves." *Revue générale du droit, de la
législation et de la jurisprudence*, 1901, pp. 42ff., 136ff., 242ff.,
449ff.

The article presents a summary of the present state of legislation concerning marriage in Germany, Austria, Hungary, and Switzerland. A study will ultimately be undertaken of the Germanic and Slavic peoples. (*Année sociologique,* 5, 1902, p. 392, trans. Y. Nandan)

Henri d'Alméras. *Le Mariage chez tous les peuples*. Paris: Schleicher,
1903, 198 pp.

The article, without scientific foundation, summarily reviews all the possible forms of matrimonial relations. (*Année sociologique,* 8, 1905, p. 431; trans. Y. Nandan)

August Ebeling. *Ehescheidung, Eheschliessung und kirchliche
Trauung, nach der Schrift und der Gesetzgebung*. Gütersloh:
Bertelsmann, 1904, 82 pp.

The most interesting first part of this work contains an exegetic study of the texts of Corinthians and Gospel regarding divorce and marriage. (*Année sociologique*, 8, 1905, p. 432; trans. Y. Nandan)

Josef Vogt. *Handbuch des katholischen Eherechts*. Cologne: Heinrich
    Theissing, 1904, vii + 219 pp.
    The work contains a very useful codification of canon law on the subject of marriage. (*Année sociologique*, 9, 1906, p. 392; trans. Y. Nandan)

Heinrich Detmer. *Uber die Auffassung von der Ehe und die Durch-
    führung der Vielweiberei in Münster während der Tauferherrschaft*.
    Munster: Copperath, 1904.
    The author attributes the practice of polygamy among the Anabaptists to the personal action of John of Leyden. (*Année sociologique*, 9, 1906, p. 393; trans. Y. Nandan)

James Bryce. *Marriage and Divorce*. New York: Oxford University
    Press, 1905, 80 pp.
    The work constitutes a short history of matrimonial law from the Roman days to the present, with a view to showing how the problem of marriage is to be construed today. The author's thinking wavers to some extent. He points out that the more advanced people are, the more the wife becomes the husband's equal, and he declares that any reaction aiming to bring her around to her former subordinate status is bound to fail. But he is convinced that marriage ties are losing their former holy character; they are becoming more fragile—all of which may not go on without a serious weakening of the institution itself. His idea, indeed, appears to be that if it is right that the partnership should continue to be based on a more equal footing, it is necessary that the sense of morality in marriage should regain its former vigor. And the factor that leads him to believe such an awakening possible is that the holy character of marriage does not appear to him to be logically bound in with some sort of religious dogma, but to depend on the nature of the institution itself, on its role in society. (*Année sociologique*, 10, 1907, pp. 436–437; trans. J. French)

Charles Lefebvre. *Histoire du droit matrimonial français. Le Droit
    des gens mariés*, pt. 2. Paris: Larose et Tenin, 1908, pp. xvi and
    289–596.
    This is a follow up of a work, a general part of which we examined in the previous volume.[172] (*Année sociologique*, 11, 1910, p. 374; trans. Y. Nandan)

L. Freund. "Zur Geschichte des Ehegüterrechts bei den Semiten."
    *Sitzungsberichte der Kaiserlichen Akademie der Wissenschaft in
    Wien, philosophisch-historische Klasse*.
    It is an important publication. (*Année sociologique*, 12, 1913, p. 440; trans. Y. Nandan)

SEXUAL MORALITY

REVIEWS

Wilhelm Rudeck. *Geschichte der öffentlichen Sittlichkeit in Deutsch-land* (History of Public Morality in Germany). Jena: Costenoble, 1897, 447 pp.

If the author has an exaggerated opinion of his book (he speaks of it in the preface as of an unprecedented work), it must nevertheless be acknowledged that he has been able to assemble, around an issue rarely studied, an important number of interesting documents. By public morality, he means exclusively morals relevant to sexual relations—that is, the way in which societies view sexual feeling and regulate public manifestations of it. In brief, it is a question of showing how uneven in Germany was the line that separated the decent from the indecent. The author poses this problem successively when dealing with the different spheres of social activity, such as: (1) relations in everyday life; (2) festivals; (3) law; (4) religious life; (5) art and literature.

During the Middle Ages, tolerance for everything that has to do with sexual morality was pushed to a point we find hard to believe. Despite the bans of the Church, baths were very generally communal affairs for both sexes. In certain towns the bathers undressed at home and proceeded to the bathing premises in a more or less complete state of nakedness. People of the upper classes alone observed greater reserve. Many baths, moreover, had one room only, common to both sexes, where one could disrobe (pp. 5, 6). Very often a single bathtub with two places was occupied by two people of different sex (p. 7). A large number of drawings reproduce scenes of this nature. Service was ordinarily provided by women. And what makes this state of affairs most significant of all is the fact that the bathing establishments were very widespread and very well attended in the Middle Ages. Even the small towns possessed some of them (p. 12). They were places to enjoy, where people went to relax, to drink, to eat. On feast-days they were opened free to the public. The sexual promiscuity that was practiced was then in no way offensive to the public conscience.

The history of prostitution is no less demonstrable. Pleasure houses appeared very early in Germany; from the start they were placed under the supervision and even under the direction of the public authority. They paid dues either to the town or to the lord of the manor; and the lord was very often an abbot or a bishop who received this revenue which no one would dream of finding scandalous (pp. 26, 27). On the other hand, the licensed prostitutes enjoyed true privilege; they formed a recognized corporation that if need be intervened with the public authorities in order to have all illegal competition banned (pp. 30–32). But still more curious is the role they played in public life. They took part officially in all the festivities: They danced, sang, etcetera. Suppose a prince was arriving in a town—the way to do him honor was to take him to the pleasure establishment. At marriages, public women would come at times to present their good wishes to the couple (p. 34). Moreover, nobody concealed his visits to them (pp. 35–36).

The history of dress (pp. 44 ff.), of popular proverbs (pp. 91 ff.), etcetera, gives evidence along the same lines. Also, relations between young men and girls were very free. It was even the usual custom in the countryside to permit a boy to spend freely a night in the course of the year with the girl of his choice. The date on which those privileged nights fell was fixed by custom (pp. 146 ff.). Under these circumstances, it is not surprising that no taint of disapproval was attributed to the qualities of the illegitimate child. All we are, of course, doing is reproducing the most salient facts. One must add that all such cases reported by the author are not equally important. There are some which are of little significance or which have only an indirect bearing on the issue considered (notably chapter 3).

The fact remains that, very obviously, sexual relations did not have the character that they assumed later on with regard to the conscience of the community. They were not viewed, as they are today, as a sort of quasi-immoral act which can be tolerated only on condition of being hidden; rather, they were something perfectly natural—there was no fear of the full light of day. Towards the end of the sixteenth century a reaction began to set in against this liberalism and a new state of mind took shape. Yet it is not as if primitive ideas and habits vanished at that moment by magic. They ceased influencing customs, ways of acting. People dressed with more decency, nudity was more generally prohibited, etcetera, but the art of literature remained for a long time open to obscenity. One would think that obscenity, partially shunned as behavior, found refuge in the imagination and the works that originated with the artist. Deleted from body language, it was maintained in language proper. Indeed, the author has no difficulty in showing that at the theater and in literature in general the place taken over by sexual feeling has not diminished, except perhaps since the last century; it is only since yesterday (see p. 389) that the governments have taken measures against what is called immorality (preventive censorship, repressive provisions). The author does not note, however, that obscenity in the seventeenth and eighteenth centuries does not resemble that of the preceding centuries. Whereas the earlier type was displayed frankly, without affectation, the more recent type is shrouded in clever forms that keep it partly concealed. It holds its own solely by disguising itself; it is obliged to have recourse to artistic artifice. The fact is, then, that in spite of everything the repression it has undergone is very real and has spread to that ideal which serves as its last refuge. Even there where it persists, it is compelled to remain veiled. It is possible that in certain respects those veils with which it is enfolded have a bad effect, that they excite desire and arouse curiosity. They make it no less clear that a great change has come about in moral views concerning relations between the sexes. Because of his failure to perceive the importance of the secrecy to which even literary and aesthetic obscenity has been reduced, the author has misunderstood the ongoing process and the regularity of this development, which, viewed in its entirety, is perfectly continuous.

It seems that the causes which have given rise to the above remain to be discovered. We shall not report the explanations proposed by the author, for they appear to us of no great value. According to him, all sorts of different circumstances, unrelated to each other—some aesthetic, others political, others economic—were presumably the only factors in this evolution. But in another sense, the usual explanation that takes into account this increasing strictness because of increasing progress in moral sentiment appears to us no better; it is purely verbal. It is like explaining the quality of opium by its quality as a specific. It remains to be stated why the greatest demands of the moral conscience have been brought to bear on this point rather than on others; what is there in the dealings between the sexes that can explain this type of disapproval? And why is this disapproval of such recent date? The book we have just analyzed leaves the entire issue unsettled. (*Année sociologique*, 2, 1899, pp. 310–313; trans. J. French)

Max Bauer. *Das Geschlechtsleben in der deutschen Vergangenheit* (Sexual Life in Ancient Germany). Leipzig: Hermann Seemann, 1902, 366 pp.

One of the major problems which the history of sexual morality raises, not only in Germany but also in the whole of Europe, is to know how the sentiments of sexual modesty and mutual continence were constituted which even today dominate sexual relationships. Certainly, they are not primitive. The facts collected in Bauer's work demonstrate it more than once. Until a relatively advanced period of the Middle Ages, the two sexes, instead of forming two distinctly separate worlds, as they do today, constantly blended their existence in the most intimate acts of life. It is from this that a chapter devoted notably to the bath results (pp. 215–265). Men and women bathed together, in a state of more or less complete nudity. Afterward, naturally, the proscriptions of the Church and the civil authority strived to fight sexual promiscuity, but without much success. On this point, the medieval societies are a curious contrast with the tribes of Australia and North America where, albeit they are much more uncivilized, the separation of the sexes is ordinarily absolute, and where the boys and girls are prohibited from seeing or even speaking to one another.

One is then justified in believing that if this separation ended up by establishing itself among the European peoples, this was for other reasons than in the primitive societies. The author does not preoccupy himself in his research with looking into these causes. However, he incidentally gives us some indications which could be helpful in resolving the problem. No doubt, it is probable that the disfavor with which Christianity has always looked upon sexual intercourse has played an important role in the development of these ideas and practices. Excessive proximity and too much intimacy between persons of opposite sexes was considered as leading to sin, and as a consequence was proscribed. But it is not unlikely that certain artistic concepts were also influential. In the days of knighthood, for reasons which have never been analyzed, the woman acquired a prestige which had never been hers until then. She became an incarnation of an aesthetic and even moral ideal, representing it, par excellence, as symbol of all the refinements and elegances of civilization. Such a change could not have failed to affect the relationship between the sexes. The promiscuity of the earlier time was now incompatible with the dignity with which the woman was from now on invested. She allowed herself, therefore, to be approached less easily. Owing to the moral distance which from then on separated them, the two sexes mingled less in their lives than in the past. Now, this separation first became established in literature, in the chivalric romances; and it is from these only that it passed into real life. Seemingly, then, there was a curious reaction of the world of art and imagination upon the world of reality.

Another question, not less interesting, is how radical separation occurred between free love and love from the time of marriage. At the beginning of the Middle Ages the two types of love were only faintly differentiated. Morals were much too easy and all sorts of excesses were tolerated. What really seems to have rendered the public conscience more severe on this point was the event of the bourgeoisie taking to political life (and coming to power). It is quite certain that in order to protect their wives and daughters, the bourgeoisie felt the need to control debauchery. From there came the institution of the house of prostitution (at the end of the thirteenth century), to the history of which the author dedicates an interesting chapter (pp. 148–215). The houses constituted a truly public service. The keeper of the house was considered as a true functionary of the commune. He took an oath not only to remain loyal to the commune, but also to keep a fixed number of "clean and healthy" women (p. 152). The price was officially fixed. But in exchange for the monopoly enjoyed by the house, the keeper was forever forbidden to receive a woman or a girl from the locality in his house. The character of these establishments explains the role the prostitutes often played and the very mixed sentiments which were aimed at them. People often saw them appearing in the public ceremonies (pp. 159 ff.). They were often permitted to carry on their business in return for "good services" they had rendered to the young people. This situation lasted until the sixteenth century. It is only from this moment that the current ideas concerning official prostitution began to change.

It is to these two questions that the principal information contained in this book relates. We would like to point out, moreover, a chapter on clothes (p. 318) and another on the charms of love. (*Année sociologique*, 7, 1904, pp. 438–440; trans. Y. Nandan)

Karl Khamm. *Der Verkehr der Geschlechter unter den Slaven in seinen gegensätzlichen Erscheinungen.* (Sexual Relations Among the Slavs). *Globus*, 1902, LXXXII, pp. 103ff., 186ff., 271ff., 320ff.

The first article is written from a somewhat subjective point of view and according to Slavonic documents. The slackening of sexual morality (pp. 104–105), infatuation with scatological literature, and the cases of quasi-promiscuity will lead to the moral decomposition of the nation. The second article is a summary study of sexual interdictions, especially those concerning marriage. The taboo of the fiancé is so strong that breaking it constitutes a crime that is punished publicly (p. 187). If someone reflects on the slackening of sexual morality, he will see clearly that there is no necessary relationship between sexual morality and the rules concerning marriage and conjugal morality. In the third study the author deals with the custom of slavery, which considers the woman, for the first time, treated as a stranger. The article ends by making comparative observations on the taboos of commensality among spouses. Among the southern Slavs, the wife is nothing other than a "bride"; her real kinsman is her brother. Finally, the last article insists on two other equally contradictory practices. On the one hand, an immense hardship is imposed on the fiancée during the course of engagement in Little Russia *(Petite Russie);* and on the contrary, according to a custom in Great Russia *(Grande Russie),* the son in his early age fictitiously marries a woman, and his father administers, in effect, the marriage rites. In sum, the articles contain an interesting catalogue of facts of sexual morality, but they are very short on method. *(Année sociologique,* 7, 1904, pp. 440–441; trans. Y. Nandan)

NOTES AND NOTICES

K. Heinrich Schaible. *Die Frau im Altertum (Ein kulturgeschicht-liches Bild)* The Woman in Antiquity. Karlsruhe: Braun, 1896, 96 pp.

This is a study on the condition of women in Egypt, Greece, Rome, Asia Minor, India, Germany, and Gaul. That is to say, the book is exoteric; it is a collection of lectures delivered in London. Generally, the author seems to be well informed. But unfortunately his work is dominated by an idea that we believe wrong. His point of departure is that the degree of independence enjoyed by the woman gives her a position of rank in society. For this reason, the author thinks that the woman is more favorably treated in Egypt than in Greece (p. 12), in Sparta than in Athens, in Athens than in Rome, in ancient Rome than at the apogee of the Republic (pp. 23 ff.). Nothing seems to us more contestable than this. The independence of the wife vis-à-vis the husband often results from the loose conjugal relationship. But the latter cannot be loose without the two spouses becoming more or less strangers to each other; this is precisely the greatest obstacle in bringing about moral equality between the two sexes. This gives the Roman matron a far superior social status over the Greek woman. Some of the types of servitude to which women [in both cultures] are often subjected are, in fact, the result of this inequality rather than a claim that her status is improving. When she is admitted to the right of inheritance, a system of guardianship is instituted to prevent her from taking away the wealth she acquires from her family of orientation. This gives her the status of a minor. But this minority comes from her being an heiress—that is to say, from the fact that she has won the rights which she originally did not have. One can see how complex the question is. (*Année sociologique*, 2, 1899, pp. 313–314; trans. Y. Nandan)

Albert Reibmayr. *Inzucht und Vermischung beim Menschen* (Incest and Crossbreeding in the Human Race). Leipzig: Deuticke, 1897, 268 pp.

    The author attempts to demonstrate that incest and crossbreeding each have their place and usefulness. Crossbreeding is necessary for the purpose of rejuvenating and renewing societies and races. Incest, or at the very least endogamy—that is to say, sexual union within a group restricting or homogenizing social and physiological traits—serves to fix the characteristics acquired due to crossbreeding. There is more dialectic in the work than facts. However, some information of a historical nature is there (pp. 130, 175), but the facts have all been accepted uncritically. (*Année sociologique*, 2, 1899, p. 314; trans. Y. Nandan)

Karl Weinhold. *Die deutschen Frauen in dem Mittelalter* (German Women in the Middle Ages), 3rd ed., 2 vols. Vienna: Geroldsohn, 1897, iii + 393 pp., 358 pp.

    With satisfaction, we point to the new edition of this classic work. (*Année sociologique*, 2, 1899, p. 315; trans. Y. Nandan)

Paul von Gizicki. *Das Weib* (The Woman). Berlin: Dümmler, 1897, x + 775 pp.

    The work is almost exclusively dialectical and practical. (*Année sociologique*, 2, 1899, p. 315; trans. Y. Nandan)

Joseph Müller. *Die Keuschheitsideen in ihrer geschichtlichen Entwicklung und praktischen Bedeutung* (The Ideas of Chastity in Their Historical Development and in Their Practical Sense). Mainz: Kirchheim, 1897, iii + 196 pp.

    In the first part, the author has given a rapid history of ideas concerning chastity. But the book is written, above all, in the vein of Christian apologetics. (*Année sociologique*, 2, 1899, p. 315; trans. Y. Nandan)

Jacques Lourbet. *Le Problème des sexes*. Paris: Giard et Brière, 1900, 302 pp.

    The author shows that, at the beginning, the subjugation of woman was not without basis because physical force played a preponderant role in social life and woman was physically weak. But this inequality is not justified anymore today, since intellectual abilities have taken the place of physical strength and there is nothing in woman's constitution which predisposes her to intellectual inferiority. The conclusions are very tenuous and a little vague. The author demands an equality which results from a growing differentiation of the sexes, without quite showing of what one and the other must consist. He merely says that a woman must become a mother in the full sense of the word. The sociological part of the work is very weak. The author does not treat the following difficult question: The equality of the two sexes will be achieved only if the woman blends herself more and more into external life; but then how will the family be transformed? Some profound changes are necessary and we cannot defer those desired changes which must be anticipated. (*Année sociologique*, 4, 1901, p. 364; trans. Y. Nandan)

Havelock Ellis. *Studies in the Psychology of Sex.* Philadelphia: F. A.
    Davis, 1901, vii + 275 pp.

We are interested in a chapter of this book; it is the first one devoted to the evolution of modesty. The chapter contains a great number of ethnographic facts and an attempt to interpret them. The author's attempt to interpret the facts, however, is quite simplistic. In order to discover the origin of the sentiment of modesty, it would be better to know what has led primitive societies to form the kind of conception of sexual relations which they have. The relationship between sexes has a magico-religious character which is communicated to what concerns sex, even indirectly. (*Année sociologique*, 5, 1902, p. 392; trans. Y. Nandan)

R. Schmidt. *Liebe und Ehe im alten und modernen Indien.* Berlin:
    Barsdorf.

The work is a followup and development of the author's ideas posited in his previous book, *Beiträge zur indischen Erotik* (Contribution to Indian Eroticism.). The author has collected citations and information concerning the psychology and physiology of sexual life in India. Chapter 4 contains some information on marriage; however, it is not well classified. Chapter 6 deals with prostitution. (*Année sociologique*, 8, 1905, p. 432; trans. Y. Nandan)

Social Organization

REVIEWS

[Durkheim's Introduction]

In every state, there exist groups that are legally constituted outside the organization properly designated as political: such are castes, classes (insofar as they have at least a basis that is legal and not simply economic), and communes. On the other hand, there are societies in which the state does not exist as yet and which nevertheless are not without a certain organization: Such are tribes consisting of a variety of segments. Such an organization is different from the political organization and requires separate classification and study. Consequently, we will examine here primary social groups, although they are not constituted as states, and secondary legal groups which are properly called states.

We would expect to discover from this works relevant to the family and to economic corporations—those two kinds of groups corresponding to the aforesaid conditions. But it appeared to us befitting to devote a special chapter to the family, because of its outstanding importance, and on the other hand to link the corporations to economic sociology, because of the close relations they maintain with industrial and commercial life. (*Année sociologique,* 6, 1903, p. 316; trans. J. French)

Abel Hagelstange. *Süddeutsches Bauernleben im Mittelalter* (Life of the Peasants in Southern Germany in the Middle Ages). Leipzig: Duncker und Humblot, 1898, 268 pp.

In order to make sure we understood the German peasant of today, Meyer was obliged time and again to speak of the peasant of the old days; it is particularly the life of the latter that Hagelstange describes for us.

To begin with, the peasant's lot was very hard at the start of the Middle Ages. Apart from particular cases (p. 4) in which free communes of farmers managed to set themselves up and to maintain themselves, as a general rule their economic inferiority caused the peasants to sink to the status of slavery in their relations with the seigneur, who did not even have the means to guarantee them, in exchange, a life of material security (pp. 7–11). But the very excess of the evil gave rise to the remedy. No longer finding life in the countryside possible, these unlucky peasants emigrated to the towns, which did, moreover, everything possible to attract them (p. 12); the diminishing population that resulted from this obliged the Seigneur to tone down the regime. The Crusades had a similar impact, and that is why, from the thirteenth century on, a great change for the better began to make itself felt. The greatest part of the farming population was, from then on, composed of long-term tenant farmers (p. 13), who, while still finding themselves in a markedly dependent condition in their relation with the landowners, were no longer stripped of their total rights (p. 37). Therefore, the peasant began, from this moment on, to play a role in the literary works of the time; he became a classic type that writers took pleasure in describing in a thousand ways. Much fun was made of the luxuries in bad taste that he adopted, in contrast with his appearance and manners, which the time had not shaped. He gladly assumed the airs of a seigneur. This was the best proof of change manifested in the status of his life (pp. 38–54).

Although the author does not say so in so many words, it seems that it is especially this well-to-do peasant he has in mind in the following descriptions. To begin with, he depicts for us his domestic customs. The picture he traces is somewhat idyllic. It is not that the traits reported are inaccurate, but they should certainly be supplemented by different or contrary traits that might give us a better idea of the harsh and gross aspects that characterized the rural mentality. One fact, however, is certain—namely, the high value placed upon fidelity in marriage. That is why the penalty for certain crimes consisted of bringing dishonor to the wife of the guilty party (p. 70). The virginity of maidens was even at times protected by rather serious penalties that were applied equally to the seducer and to his victim (p. 70). A woman, moreover, was never considered to be anything but a second-rate creature. She could not bear witness; she sometimes received a very different kind of punishment than the man; she could not inherit furnishings (p. 79). She did not enjoy any real privileges except in two cases: during pregnancy and confinement. Pregnant, she could with impunity satisfy her cravings in the form of fruits, vegetables, fish, and game, even at the expense of others; and the confined had analogous rights (pp. 79 ff.). It is to be noted that from this moment on it was standard practice concerning possessions in the conjugal society to maintain separate ownership (pp. 73 ff.). In that respect there is a peculiarity in Germanic customs which has had a major influence on our law. Domestics were a part of the family and sat at the master's table, except among the great property owners. Morals and the Church intervened in order to protect them (pp. 93 ff.). The author acknowledges, however, that wages were meager—"even," he says, "if one disregards our present ideas." At the start of the Middle Ages they included only upkeep, one shirt or paltry garment a year, and a few shillings (pp. 96 ff.).

There is not much to say about economic life,* which, according to the author's remark (p. 160), has not changed very perceptibly since this era, so slow is the evolution of the industry of farming. The raising of cattle was the principal economic activity; the cultivation of grains took second place; truck-gardening, the cultivation of fruits, appeared only later. Yet agriculture was becoming markedly progressive at the end of the Middle Ages. In their two primary forms especially, farming procedures gave evidence in particular of being closely regulated by the commune. It was the commune that fixed the way in which fallow years were to alternate with growing years, the date for harvesting, for sowing, the way in which fields were to be marked with the boundaries, in which flocks were to be put to pasture, etcetera. In line with

---

* We are leaving to one side a description of the household, which does not add much to the one Meyer has given us. Worth noting, however, is the fact that each family had its coat of arms; they were marked on the agricultural instruments, on the household utensils, on the boundary markers of the property, etcetera. They were held in high esteem on all sides. They were the proof that one was a member of a certain village. Family coats of arms are, then, not a feudal and aristocratic institution. They originated in certain fundamental characteristics of domestic organization.

this communal spirit, few changeovers have been recorded at the start. During the entire first half of the Middle Ages, the peasant practiced nothing but barter (p. 126). Hard currency began to play an important role only beginning with the thirteenth century. By the fifteenth, markets were already fully developed (pp. 127 ff.).

The most interesting chapter is perhaps the one devoted to festivals and amusements. Following Mannhardt's lead, the author shows how great and popular feast days celebrated by Christians have their roots in old pagan practices. Easter *(Osterfest),* a substitute for the festival that the primitive Germans used to celebrate, at the same period of the year, was in honor of the goddess Ostara; the festival of Saint John is derived from magic ceremonies that were enacted at the moment of the solstice; the festivals of the season when it was customary to slaughter animals needed for food during winter are an echo of the religious rites with which every operation of this nature were encompassed in days gone by. The festivals of Saint Nicholas and Saint Martin, All Saints' Day, pre-Lenten festivities, all have similar origins. There are explanations of this sort, even in detail, for certain usages that have survived. For example, Easter eggs are a survival of the offerings of eggs that were carried out formerly at the beginning of spring (p. 225). A common feature of all these rejoicings is the unbridled violence with which people indulged themselves. They came to a stop only when exhausted. Meals that lasted all day, interrupted from time to time by fights that were occasionally bloody and by dances which quickly degenerated into unruly behavior of all kinds—that is what public festivals amounted to. The contrast with the plodding monotony of day-to-day existence was therefore at its *maximum.* The scope of vacillations through which social life passed depending upon whether it was holiday or workaday time proceeded to diminish with civilization.

We have passed over in silence a chapter on the legal organization of the village that breaks somewhat the unity of the book and of the picture, in spite of the interest of the information that is to be found there. *(Année sociologique,* 2, 1899, pp. 306–309; trans. J. French)

M. Wilbrandt. *Die politische und soziale Bedeutung der attischen Geschlechter vor Solon* (Political and Social Significance of Attic Clans before Solon). Leipzig: Dietrich, 1899, 96 pp.

At the close of the seventh century, the Athenian constitution already gives the appearance of a very complex system of tribes, of phratries, of classes, of political organs of all kinds. The result is that what makes up the primary foundation is hidden from view by the mass of institutions which are superimposed on it and which have therefore altered it. It is this foundation that the author proposes to penetrate by using Aristotle's Ἀθηναίων πολιτεία (constitution of the Athenians.)

It is formed by the γένη or clans; the γένος is the original home for all social life in Athens.

And first of all, in the matter of freedom of the city, the necessary and sufficient condition for this is the act of ownership of a γένος.

This is how the author undertakes to demonstrate it. Of every designated archon, the Senate asked if he observed the cult of Apollo Patroos and of Zeus Herkeios. It was an old question that went back to the time when the eupatridae alone could be archons, and it consisted, in short, of making sure that the candidate was truly a eupatrid, belonging to a γένος; for the cult of these divinities was specially characteristic of the γένος—more so even than of the phratry. Now, we know that, already before Solon, the two lower classes, that of the farm laborers and that of the artisans, were admitted to the archonate. Hence one must conclude that they were in a position to respond in the affirmative to the question relative to the cult of Apollo Patroos and of Zeus Herkeios; but as a result, it was necessary that they themselves be organized in γένη. Accordingly, the γένος was so essential to the freedom of the city that it was to spread to the plebeians when the full exercise of that freedom was accorded to them. The latter formed γένη, modeled after those that the eupatridae formed; they were rather like *gentes minores*,[173] analogous to those that were to be found in Rome but practicing the cult of Apollo and Zeus. Wilbrandt supposes that the word ὀργεῶνες that appears in texts as expressing a sense analogous (but not identical) to that of γεννῆται (clan members) designated the members of these *gentes*. There was probably, on the one hand, the ὀργεῶνες, members of the plebeian *gentes,* and on the other, the ὁμογάλακτες, members of the patrician *gentes*. But there was not any phratry reserved especially for the nobility; the phratries comprised indistinctly the *gentes* of two sorts.

From the point of view of property, the author is of the opinion that there is a close connection between landed property and the γένος. For the facts that seem to him to prove this proposal, he refers to his dissertation, *De rerum privatarum ante Solonis tempus in Attica statu* [174] (Güstrow, Opitz & Co.). He particularly stresses the nontransferability of the heritage. But this nontransferability does not necessarily imply a direct link between the γένος and the heritage. In the case of the southern Slavs, the land is nontransferable in principle and yet the rights of the clan over it are imperceptible. Nontransferability clearly implies that the true landowner is an ideal being, and not the gathering of individuals who actually occupy the land at any given moment. But it is not necessary that this ideal being represent the clan; it can be the family itself, considered as an entity sui generis, distinct from the members who comprise it at each moment of its existence. But whatever the conclusions that are drawn from this nontransferability, it proceeds to run into certain objections in matters that concern Athens. According to tradition, the Athenians could, even before Solon, sell or at least mortgage their lands, by drawing up mortgages with overly burdensome conditions the plebeians would have been ruined and the situation would have arisen which Solon tried to remedy. The author, by means of a very ingenious discussion (pp. 39–65), tries to show that there was no so-called mortgage. It was the fruit of the land, not the land itself, that was mortgaged (p. 43). It is only with Solon that property presumably became entirely transferable. The fact that freedom to make one's will dates from Solon renders this assumption very plausible.

Lastly, the γένη probably were for a long time a territorial unit; this helps explain the case with which Cleisthenes converted them into demes and how a number of demem had surnames (pp. 71–72). They were also the last units of political (pp. 78–80) and even financial (pp. 81 ff.) organization.

This work is very useful in showing how the clan was an essential element of the Athenian constitution. But the evidence remains quite remote from the matters under discussion. The clan is studied from without, and not in a way that gives it life, and one even wonders if the allegations about it the author makes in certain passages are quite accurate. He seems at times to view it as a creation of the legislator (p. 79). (*Année sociologique*, 3, 1900, pp. 352–354; trans. J. French)

Maurice Courant. "Les Associations en Chine." *Annales des sciences politiques,* 1899, no. 1, p. 68.

The Chinese state finds confronting it, not a pulverized mass of individuals, but a very complex system of secondary components. China is made up of a multitude of particular groups having a history, a strong organization, and a sort of substructure within Chinese society. The Chinese have a strong tendency to form groups. Associations are countless. One of the most curious is that of the beggars, powerful enough to oblige the public authorities to reckon with them. One cannot rid oneself of them without giving charity (p. 69).

Chief among these secondary groups are the following:

(1) *The corporation.* It has no official character and yet its influence is considerable. "It fixes the rules for transactions and makes sure they are observed; in the case of bankers, it supervises the issuing of banknotes and stops it in case of excesses." It assists its members, etcetera. Although these regulations have no legal sanction, they are strictly observed; whoever tries to get away with something is mercilessly boycotted. The authority of the corporation is such that the public authorities never intervene in the daily economical life of the people.

(2) *The provincial association.* In each locality, people from other provinces (merchants, mandarins, etcetera) form their groups in order to fight malevolent discrimination. Each of these societies forms a world of its own, a Church of its own. It may happen even that people from the province will usurp a commercial or industrial monopoly. Sometimes these associations become very powerful; they play the role of consuls and of foreign chambers of commerce in Western countries.

(3) *The commune.* Farm families remain no more isolated that those of merchants. They form groups of five or of ten (*quintenier* or *dizenier*);[175] those from the same village or from several neighboring villages take shape as com-

munes with a general manager. These are spontaneously and voluntarily formed by the interested parties. In fact, today, all inhabitants of the village are obliged to join them; whereas the outsiders, on the contrary, have a very hard time being accepted. Solidarity is very close-knit there, and everybody lives on the basis of absolute equality. One senses that morals are shored up by a foundation of communist ideas. What's more, there is no intimate home life. Just as everything is common property, what goes on at each one's abode occurs for all to see.

(4) *The clan.* This is the most ancient form of group living. It is disappearing; it reemerges only when the circumstances are favorable; it is holding out especially in the center of the country and the south. The clan is a group of related families (or those considering themselves as such), sometimes comprising thousands of people, occupying entire districts, and having as chief the head of a privileged family which is considered as constituting the elder branch.

It will be noted that except for the clan, these various associations are almost all voluntary; they take shape by themselves and without being activated by a central power. Such an aptitude can only be explained by a very intense need for these sorts of groupings. Individuals have to be strongly pushed into joining forces with the clan, and they cannot be pushed into it except through the need to protect themselves. This proves that the protection by the public authorities is inadequate. The spontaneous formation of secondary groups and their excessive development are sure signs of the absence or the weakness of the central authority. When the state does not protect the individual, the latter sets up associations which will provide that function. (*Année sociologique*, 3, 1900, pp. 354–356; trans. J. French)

Henri Doniol. *Serfs et vilains au Moyen Age.* Paris: Picard et Fils, 1900, vi + 290 pp.

In this book, Doniol has only covered again, with more precision and with new elucidation, the first part of his *Histoire des classes rurales* (History of the Rural Classes). The object of the work is to determine and distinguish two essential elements of the feudal system.

According to the author the feudal organization had a twofold origin. There was, on the one hand, the influence exerted by the great landowners over the territory surrounding them—influence which assumed a political character when the central power fell into anarchy after the decomposition of the Carolingian empire. At that time, indeed, those [in the surrounding territory] sought from the rich landowners the protection which they no longer received from the government, in such a way that the original powers of the rich were increased by political functions. The large landed estate thus became the seat of a true sovereignty, something which is typical of the feudal regime. Thus was born the seigniory of the fief. But there is another element which was constituted much differently. Under the influence of the same general disorganization the high officials, the counts, viscounts, the *judices* (judges), retained for themselves the authority which, till then, they had exercised by delegation; since they controlled jurisdiction, imposts, and military forces, they acquired, by usurpation, wealth along with power. The same phenomenon took place among their subordinates, and thus was created another series of private powers. They had as their origin, not a manorial supremacy, but rather the various political powers which the officials exercised "on every person and everything subject to the government, in other words on the taxpayers": persons or things of every social rank, the middle or small possessors, the bourgeoisie or artisans in the towns, rural tenants, or salaried persons. The powers were essentially political or fiscal. Such were the *seigneuries de justice,* as they were still to be found in the sixteenth century, after the revisions of the customaries [i.e., codes of the customary laws].

Doniol does not go so far, however, as to contend that the *fiefs* and the administration of *justice* always had distinct origins and distinct existences in the seigneurial state. He recognizes that the possessors of fiefs were able to establish by and for themselves the rights and powers characteristic of the seigniory of justice. Nonetheless, there are two different aspects of seigneurial organization that needs to be considered, for the action exerted by the seigneur on the classes who did the work of production was not the same in the two cases. Insofar as it was an essentially manorial institution, the seigniory comprised, above all, work services; for the "fief" the cultivation of the earth was "the immediate object, the natural and legitimate form of revenue" (p. 50). This was an economic association. The vassal was the associate of the seigneur, although not his equal. He was a farmer who owed his master a certain portion of the product of his labor, in exchange for certain advantages. In the administration of *justice,* on the contrary, the seigneur had, not collaborators but subjects, men under his power. They did not work for him in an enterprise in which he himself had an interest. But he could lay imposts on the products of their labor, whatever that might be—cultivation of the earth, commerce, or industry. In short, from this point of view, his subordinates were essentially taxpayers; from the other point of view, they were workers, tenants of farms, manual laborers, whose work belonged to him either in whole or in part.

It is to this twofold aspect of the system that the distinction of serf and villein would respond. The serf is the man of the fief, the servitor of the manorial seigneur, who works for his master but who is, in exchange, protected by him. The villein is the political subject, the taxpayer whose activity does not belong to the seigneur, but who serves as a source of taxes. The serf, placed very close to the seigneur, tightly bound up with his existence, is a simple dependent of the master and sometimes ends by being a mere instrument. The villein, more distant from the seigneurial authority, retains his individuality: He is free, he enjoys the court rights denied the serf. Moreover, as long as the seigniory was only manorial—and as long, consequently, as the seigniory only needed domestic services—the serfs sufficed for it; they held, in principle, the entire manor. There were, it is true, taxable freemen, but they were not very numerous and were not constituted as a class. The class of villeins appeared only when the action of the seigneur extended beyond the circle of his immediate interests, when a world having its own interests formed itself outside the manor, a world for which the seigniory acted as a government (p. 168).

One consequence of this conception is that serfdom does not derive from slavery. It is an institution peculiar to the "Gallic Occident" (p. 71). While slavery suppresses all civil individuality, serfdom, like the fief, in a general way has "as principle (though, to speak truly, a latent principle) consent, a contract." Whether it has as origin commendation, patronage, or benefice, "one cannot recognize any other point of origin than consent; consent which was more or less inevitable or imposed by violence, undoubtedly, but which was always considered to preexist" (p. 53). Even in this regard the condition of the villein is inferior to that of the serf. The rights of the seigneur over the serf (and especially the exercise of these rights) are, in fact, limited by the fundamental contract, either real or supposed, and by the reciprocal obligations which the contract implies. There is an association here, despite the fact that one of the associated parties is in an inferior position as regards the other. The fact that even the strongest needed the cooperation of the other in order to live imposed restraints. In the case of the villein, on the contrary, no original contract can be supposed. The submission of the villein to his lord is entirely political; it is a state of fact which has become a legal state by force of usage (p. 55). As a result, nothing limits the seigneurial power, which can be extended as far as the needs or demands of the master require. This is why the villein was, by definition, taxable at will. The difference of the two conditions was such that over a long period the condition of the serf was accepted as natural and justified while that of the villein early aroused violent protests; this was because nothing prevented or limited abuses of power (p. 56, cf. chapters 12 and 13, notably pp. 186–187).

Since the contrast between the serf and the villein was so marked, one can understand that the evolution of the two classes and their elevation to liberty had to take place in very different ways. The author attempts to indicate for us, as regards what is most characteristic of them, the principal phases of both evolutions. But finally, the two conditions were merged. The last part of the work, moreover, is devoted to an analysis of the social and juridical situation of the agricultural population of the Middle Ages. (*Année sociologique*, 5, 1902, pp. 336–339; trans. K. Woody)

Henri Sée. *Les Classes rurales et le régime domanial en France au Moyen Age*. Paris: Giard et Brière, 1901, xxxvii + 637 pp.

The domanial regime is, above all, an economic system, especially as it is presented to us here. What characterizes it is the existence, exclusive or preponderant, of large domains cultivated by tenant farmers for the profit of the master, who, for the very reason that he enjoys economic supremacy, exercises more or less extensive political and judicial powers over them. If we believe it our duty to speak of this book here, it is because of the relationship that the domanial regime has with the feudal organization. According to Sée (and to Fustel de Coulanges) it seems that this regime explains the formation of serf and peasant classes.

It appears that serfdom is a derivative and attenuated form of slavery. Wherever great landed property is set up, the big landowning class quickly becomes an aristocracy that monopolizes the noblest social functions (political, religious, etcetera); consequently, the master of the domain cannot cultivate by himself the land he owns. In antiquity, cultivation was carried out by slaves. But this method of cultivation was no longer adequate to the new needs that made their appearance when the Middle Ages dawned. The slaves used to live in the master's own house and cultivate the domain as a unit. But as new lands gained in importance, and consequently, as the population of farm workers increased, it became handier to quarter each worker with his family on a fixed portion of the domain in the guise of tenant farmer. In this way there arose a sort of decentralization of the primitive system, which resulted in serfdom. The slave quartered at a fixed post, burdened with land-grant fees, fixed or not in a certain way—such was the serf (pp. 51 ff.). In parallel fashion, whereas the slave rose thus to the status of tenant farmer, the sharecropper, who started out as a free tenant farmer, gradually became a subject person. Apparently it is the encounter of these two movements that gave rise to the class of serfs. From the Carolingian age on, its essential features became established (p. 63). Feudalism, then, presumably did not create serfdom, but found the latter fully established; however, the impact it had was not inconsiderable. What was the nature of this influence? It is quite difficult to disentangle the answer given to this question by the author. On the one hand, he establishes that the feudal regime had increased the overlord's exploitation through the multiple obligations that were imposed on the vassal and that had repercussions on the serfs (p. 134); that its effect was to separate the two classes more radically; that wherever it was less strongly organized, the parceling out of the noble property was more easily brought about, a phenomenon eminently favorable to the emancipation of the classes of serfs (p. 137). And at the same time, he admits that the same feudal organization was contemporaneous "with a crumbling of landed property" (p. 134). What doubtless reconciles, in his mind, these two contradictory propositions is that according to him the vexations arising from the feudal institutions presumably affected the personal condition of the serfs and effected changes for the better on the domanial regime itself. New obligations, binding on the person, presumably were added to those derived from the holdings; but the holdings in themselves more nearly approximated full ownership. However, it is hard to see how such changes in the holdings would not have resulted in freeing the people in the same proportion and how feudalism could have created a breaking up of property if this dismemberment varied inversely with the growth of feudalism.

In any case, beginning with the twelfth century, the movement for emancipation became the foremost concern. In order to keep the serfs on the domain, to prevent them from emigrating, even to attract the newcomers he needed, the lord preferred to renounce certain of his original privileges. Whereas up until then the land-grant fees were arbitrarily fixed by the landowner, they were henceforth regulated. That is what contributed to the transformation from serfdom to peasant farming. The peasant was a tenant farmer, like the serf, but having freedom; the obligations to which he was subjected were determined once and for all. Without being owner of his holding, he occupied it for life provided that he fulfilled his obligations, and these obligations were tied in, not with his person, but with the land he occupied.

Serfdom and peasant farming are thus bound up with a social, or rather economic, organization that was far more general than feudalism; for the large property is encountered, with its characteristic particularities, from Greco-Latin antiquity on and has persisted long after the fall of the feudal regime. The extremely general nature of such an explanation already gives sufficient cause to suspect its inadequacy. And indeed, it can be granted only if one misunderstands what is truly characteristic of medieval serfdom—that is to say, the close relationships that it sustains with the feudal system. Doubtless, the holding is a far cry from the fief. But there are obvious similarities between the relationships of the suzerain with his vassal and those of the lord with his serfs. Serfdom properly designated did not apply without the lord's domanial authority. The master on whom the serf depended was not simply, like him on whom the slave formerly depended, a rich and powerful landowner; he was a person invested with political authority. Notably, he had the right to dispense justice. In order to be able to reconcile his theory with the existence of this right, Sée is obliged to maintain that this judicial power was merely a direct consequence of the domanial regime; and he believes this assertion is proved by showing that justice used to be, especially for the lords, a matter of land-grant fees (p. 434). But the use they made of it, the way in which they used it, in no way detracts from the fact that they were thus fulfilling a function that ordinarily reverts to the state or to its agents. It appears, then, hard not to witness in serfdom an essential element of the feudal organization, and consequently, the causes which engendered it are the very ones that gave rise to feudalism. Now, feudalism is certainly not a product of purely economic causes, however important the role of this factor may have been. Besides, it was possible to discover, in the course of our analysis, to what a great extent the variations through which serfdom has passed are misconstrued from this point of view. One is not even fully aware of the source from which its distinctive features can have originated. Indeed, in what way did the exigencies of the domain imply that the tenant farmer was deprived of liberty? Why did not one find the sharecropping system instead of serfdom replacing former slavery, and why was the sharecropper, originally free, downgraded from his first position? This is what is hard to understand if this whole procedure actually depends solely on economic causes. (*Année sociologique*, 5, 1902, pp. 339–342; trans. J. French)

Tokuzo Fukuda. *Die gesellschaftliche und wirtschaftliche Entwicklung in Japan* (Social and Economic Evolution of Japan). Stuttgart:
Cotta, 1900.

This book offers us a picture which is succinct, but adequately clear and documented, of the principal phases through which Japanese social organization has passed during the course of its history.

These phases are three in number.

The first dates originally to A.D. 644. It begins, as does Japanese history itself, at the time when the Yamato tribe was proceeding to settle in the country, driving back or assimilating the natives.

It was the Yamato, indeed, who in the course of their development, became the actual Japanese people.

There were three tribes of this name which were united under one and the same authority. Each one of them, in its turn, was composed of groups called *Uji*, which were nothing other than clans analogous to the Roman *gentes*. The members of the same *Uji* considered themselves, in fact, to be descendants of one and the same ancestor, and they practiced the same cult, making this common ancestor its object. Each *Uji* in its turn was divided into narrower groupings called *Ko-Uji* ("'Little *Ujis*"), which were made up of families, the lowest units. But the family was not confined to a single married couple and their descendants; brothers, uncles, nephews, and others shared a common life. It was therefore a familial corporation, whose extent recalls that of the Slav *zadruga*, for example; the recruitment of the family, and consequently of the clan, took place by means of filiation in the paternal line. But whatever the author may say, through the very facts which he cites we may clearly see that filiation was originally uterine. Indeed, when a man could neither purchase his wife nor capture her, he could not bring her to his home. He could have intercourse with her only in his in-laws' house, and the children which were the issue of such a union belonged to the mother's family. Doubtless, it does not follow that the regime was *matriarchal;* indeed the matriarchal family and the uterine family are very different things—Fukuda seems to ignore this distinction.

Each clan had a chief at its head; in the same way, each subdivision of the clan (the Little *Uji* and the family) had its chief. The power of each one of these chiefs over the members of the group immediately subordinate to him was absolute (p. 20). In this description we recognize the distinctive attributes of what we call politico-familial organization, or a social organization basically of clans. The conclusive justification of this denomination is the fact that the different clans regarded themselves as being, all alike, the descendants of one and the same ancestor, who was therefore the ancestor of the entire tribe. The

Uji which was deemed to contain the direct descendants of this ancestor exercised supremacy over the others. Its chief was charged with the administration of the national cult, which was common to all of the clans, and through these functions he enjoyed prestige and some special rights. This is the original form of imperial dignity.* Each *Uji* collectively possessed the soil which it occupied. But it was the Little *Uji* which constituted the fundamental economic unit. Each of these groups had a single, fixed commercial function (fishing, hunting, agriculture, some crafts; but the latter were the monopoly of the imperial *Uji*). The occupation of each family *(Ko)* was that of the Little *Uji* to which it belonged, and there was no room for free choice. As to the way the soil was cultivated, the author supposes that it was collective (p. 25).

But in time, the clan lost its early stability. The causes of this erosion are somewhat confusingly explained by the author; the principal one appears to have been the increase in population. It is probable that as a consequence of marriages and domestic migrations, the different *Uji*s mutually intermingled and interpenetrated one another. Since they no longer possessed a sufficient degree of individuality, they could no longer continue to serve as political, economic and religious units. Accordingly, no more than two firmly established elements of the old organization remained: the imperial power, on the one hand, and the families *(Ko)* on the other. The preponderance attained by these two elements indeed characterizes the second phase of this process of social evolution (A.D. 645–930). Up until this point, the only contact between the emperor and the families was through the mediation of the chiefs of the clans and subclans; henceforth, no element of power was interposed between them and him (p. 41). Originally each *Uji* was the fully independent possessor of the land it occupied; now that the *Uji*s had disappeared, the emperor succeeded them; he was considered to be the sole and uncontested proprietor of the entire territory. But in order to ensure that the land was cultivated, he divided it up among all his subjects. Each individual male who had reached the age of five had about 16,500 square meters; the women had about two-thirds as much. Every six years, the portions which the deceased had possessed reverted to the state, which apportioned them among those who were newly entitled (p. 53). But albeit they were calculated on a per capita basis, they were not granted separately to each individual; it was the *Ko,* the family, who jointly cultivated the totality of the portions which were assigned to all its members. The *Ko,* which had played a humble role in the primitive system, thus took over the important position which the clan had lost. It was the refuge of the old communist ways practiced by the larger groups, which had disappeared. It formed an indivisible, compact mass, which was only very occa-

---

* Relying on the fact that marriages between brothers and sisters are not unknown in Japan, even in historical times, the author questions whether one does well in this context to write of clans and a family [*gentilice*] organization. But exogamy is only characteristic of the clan at one moment in its evolution (the clan with uterine filiation). Moreover, we may ask ourselves whether or not Japanese endogamy proceeds out of the development assumed by caste systems; for, due to reasons which are easy to comprehend, caste society becomes tolerant of incestuous practices.

sionally allowed to break up. It became the cornerstone of the society. Outside and beyond it, there were indeed scarcely any more secondary groupings, apart from administrative districts with artificial boundaries and no roots in custom (pp. 48 ff.).

But because of this absence of secondary groups, an organization of this type could only be ephemeral; the central power could not be omnipresent in such a way as to ensure social cohesion. Thus, in reality, the system was only applied in its entirety for a century, and it worked in a partial and irregular way for two others. The individual proprietors released themselves from the state of dependence in which they had stood vis-à-vis the emperor. The more enterprising, those who possessed a measure of power, enlarged their domain; the emperor himself aided this movement by conceding lands to certain of his functionaries by way of recompense. Little by little a class of great proprietors became established. This class, owing to the might which gave them their economic supremacy and owing to the weakness of the central authority, ended up by absorbing all political, military, and judicial powers. The Japanese Empire was thus dissolved into a multitude of territorial seigniories which preserved only loose links with the emperor. The small proprietors were obliged to make themselves the subject of the seigneurs, whose vassals (in the European sense of the word) they became. Thus a vast feudal system was created. It lasted as long as seven hundred years (up to the beginning of the seventeenth century). This was the era when towns began to appear; just as in Europe, they originated around the seigneurs' residences and under their protection (pp. 104–111). Likewise, as in Europe, along with the towns one sees the foundation of the first guilds.

An era of absolute government succeeded the feudal era (1603–1867). The natural consequence of the autonomy of all these local seigniories was interminable internecine wars, which ruined the system. Money was necessary in order that these conflicts might be sustained. The nobility was duly obliged to request it from the peasants and the towns, and it became, in many cases, the ransom of their independence (p. 121). At the same time, a change took place in ideology. Religious sects were established, and developed very rapidly. Their spirit was very different from that which had inspired the ancient cults of the country. They possessed some features of the most simple and the most popular kind (p. 122). Necessarily, a change occurred in the organization of society. The need was felt for strong centralization, in order that the heterogeneous elements of which Japanese society was composed might be firmly united. But this centralization did not take place around the person of the emperor. Without a doubt imperial dignity was sustained, but the person in whom it had been invested exercised no effective power. Withdrawn into the depths of his palace, invisible to the profane, surrounded by luxury and prestige, he could do nothing by himself (pp. 127–128). The real authority was held by a sort of functionary named the *Shogun*, who in principle was appointed by the emperor but was not in any way selected by him. This centralist organization, which established its seat in the center of the country, inaugurated an era of economic prosperity and intellectual progress, the like of which Japan had not known since; but in order that the regime might be securely maintained, it resorted to an intractably conservative political policy. Japanese society withdrew into itself; all relations with the outside were prohibited; all sorts of obstacles to the production of novelties were created. This situation lasted until the middle of the century,[176] the era when the emperor recovered the reality of power. At that time a more liberal regime came into being: Japan opened up to foreigners, parliamentary institutions were founded, etcetera. Nevertheless, without denying the importance of these transformations, the author cautions us that they possessed reality only for the upper classes, and had scarcely any effect on the vast masses of the nation.

One will note the analogy which the evolution of Japan, thus described, presents with our own social evolution. We have passed through almost the same stages. Feudalism followed the Carolingian Empire; absolute monarchy followed feudalism. One finds resemblances even in the details. In Europe, as in Japan, towns were formed in the shadow of the seigneurial power, only to turn against it afterwards. Just as the Crusades, by ruining the lords, prepared the way for communal emancipations, so in like fashion the domestic and other wars of Japan weakened the power of the warrior classes and opened the way for a new regime. Indeed, in both cases, the fall of feudalism coincided with a literary and artistic renaissance and a religious reformation. The analogy between the Japanese sects and Protestantism is striking. That is to say that both developments alike resulted from general causes and that we are here, perhaps, in the presence of an abstract type of social evolution. (*Année sociologique*, 5, 1902, pp. 342–347; trans. A. Lyons)

Emil Szanto. *Die griechischen Phylen* (The Greek Tribes). From *Sitzungsberichte der kaiserlichen Akademie der Wissenschaft in Wien, philosophisch-historische Klasse*, CXLIV. Vienna: Carl Gerold's Sohn, 1901, 74 pp.

L. Holzapfel. *Die drei ältesten römischen Tribus* (The Three Oldest Roman Tribes). *Beiträge zur alten Geschichte*, vol. I, pp. 228–255. Leipzig: Dietrich, 1901.

These two studies are related to the same question and tend to answer it in the same way. It is a question of knowing the nature of the φυλή (tribe) of the Greeks and of the *tribus* of the Romans, that higher division of the Greek and Latin city-states. Should one see in the groups thus denominated societies which, originally autonomous, coalesced to form each city? Or else, on the contrary, are they only artificial divisions introduced into already constituted societies? One can understand the interest of the problem: The manner in which one should envision the genesis and the structure of the city-state depends on the solution one adopts. Now, it is the second which is defended by our two authors, the one for the Greeks, the other for the Romans.

As for Greece, here is how Mr. Szanto proceeds to his demonstration. He believes it is possible to reduce the different systems of φιλαὶ to two original types of which the others would be only the derivatives: the Doric type and the Attic type. In the first, the city-state is divided into three tribes: the Hyleans, the Dymaneans, and the Pamphylians. Since this tripartite division, with the same terminology, is general in the Doric states, it is evident that it must have been found in the Doric nation before its dispersion into different city-states. But, on the other hand, since one never sees these tribes act as relatively autonomous collective units and since the members of two different city-states are not tied to each other by special obligations for the sole reason that they bear the name of the same tribe, all reason is lacking for admitting that these tribes began by being independent societies whose association formed the large Doric nation. From this it follows that the latter must have divided itself, at a given moment, into three parts. This organization, according to the author, was instituted voluntarily after the conquest. To facilitate the division of the land, this would have been first divided into three parts, which were given to three different parts of the nation. It was the division of the land which was the basis for the division of the people; the latter would thus have been at first purely territorial, and would not have taken on a tribal character except over a long period of time, as a result of the transmission of the same lands in the same families from generation to generation. As for the Attic type, which con-sists of four tribes and not of three, it would differ from the preceding one in that it made its appearance, not at the moment of conquest, but at a time when the different populations of Attica were already unified morally to the point where there was no distinction between conquerors and conquered. As a result, the organization into tribes at Athens included all the regular in-habitants of Attica, while among the Dorians it included only the conquerors. But in both cases it was only an artificial procedure, an administrative measure.

But the very fact that the Doric organization was general in all Doric city-states makes it difficult to conceive this theory. If the nation was not divided into three tribes until it was fixed on the land and if each tribe had begun by being only a territorial division, there would have been a time when all the area occupied by the invaders was divided into three large territories, three geographical provinces, independent or not, at the same time as there was no trace of such a division. But how are we to admit that a wholly artificial divi-sion, without roots in the consciousness of the people, should have been so religiously imitated and reproduced, down to the nomenclature adopted, by the different Doric city-states once the latter had constituted themselves in an independent way? It thus seems much more natural to suppose that the Dorians were organized in this way from the start, that is, at a time when they were only an ethnic group without a territorial base. To make this hypothesis it is not, moreover, necessary to imagine that these three tribes had originally been three distinct societies. It is enough to see in each original tribe a natural group of phratries linked to each other by special ties, in the same way as each phratry was a natural group of γένη. In this way one could explain the fact that much later, when the phratries, after being established on the soil and dispersed in villages, concentrated themselves again in such a way as to form cities, the need, and, as it were, the obligation, were felt to revive this old tripartite division, which, consecrated by long tradition joined with old beliefs and religious practices, appeared as the necessary foundation of all social organization. If this model had not had such an authority, if it had been from the beginning only a conventional arrangement, it would not have been reproduced everywhere with such faithfulness.

Thus, the tribe must be considered a natural group, in the sense that it was originally formed under the influence of natural affinities; this is the only way to explain why it is found throughout Greece and also Italy. On the other hand, the tribes such as we find them in the Greek city-states once they are organized, no longer have this character except in a partial manner. They are natural insofar as they reproduce a form of organization which was produced naturally. But the symmetry of their subdivisions into phratries and clans obviously betrays the influence of the legislators. Such as we know them through the historical documents they are no longer the product of a spontaneous formation. But they are not, on the other hand, the creatures of pure convention, created wholly by statesmen.

All these observations apply to the Roman tribes and to the work of Holzapfel. After criticizing the reasons which led certain historians, notably Mommsen, to see the original tribes of Rome as autonomous peoples, the author concludes on the basis of his examination that since they did not have this autonomy, they could not have been anything but artificial constructions. We have just seen that another solution is possible. The author himself, moreover, furnishes us with reasons which support our thesis. All the first part of his work has as its object the demonstration of how the division in three tribes profoundly affected the whole structure of the Roman city-state. In all the details of the political, religious, and military organization one finds the number three. But it is not probable that a wholly artificial arrangement, lacking all moral basis, could have had such an influence. The author himself realizes the difficulty and he is obliged to have recourse to the mystic power which all of Latin antiquity lent to the number three. It is very difficult to admit that this magical belief was able to serve as the basis for a whole social organization. (*Année sociologique*, 6, 1903, pp. 324–327; trans. K. Woody)

Werner Wittich. *Die Frage der Freibauern. Undersuchungen über die soziale Gliederung des deutschen Volkes in altgermanischer und frühkarolingischer Zeit* (The Question of Free Peasants. Research

on the Social Organization of the German People in Germanic
and Carolingian Times). Weimar: Böhlaus Nachfolger, 1901,
111 pp.

According to a very well known opinion, landed property and social
organization in the Germanic societies may have passed through the following
three phases:

(1) Agrarian communism. The land is possessed in common, periodically
    partitioned and cultivated.
(2) Establishment of individual ownership. Each family becomes owner of
    its part and the parts are all equal. The result is an essentially
    democratic and agricultural organization. Each person is an owner, he
    himself cultivates the lot which belongs to him, and among all the
    farmers there is neither distinction of rank nor dependence of any
    kind. The society is formed by peasants free from all subjection
    (Freibauern). It is this organization that is believed to be still found in
    Germanic societies at the beginning of the Carolingian epoch. It was
    thought, in fact, that the class of free peasants continued to form the
    most important part of it and that if there were nobles who were more
    or less estranged from the agricultural life, these were only a very small
    minority. Their number, consequently, would not seem to have been
    sufficient to gravely change the democratic character of these societies.
(3) It was only afterwards that the number of freemen presumably de-
    clined and that the aristocratic class developed.

Wittich opposes this conception. His thesis, expounded in a preceding
work,[177] has raised very lively criticisms, notably on the part of Brunner and of
Heck. In the present work he takes it up again, justifying it with new
arguments and responding to the objections which were addressed to him. In a
hermetically closed discussion, whereby he gives proof of remarkable dialectical qualities, he tries to show that the class of free peasants at the beginning
of the Carolingian period had none of the preponderance which is attributed
to it.

Notably in Saxony, he finds nobles who only exceptionally cultivated the
land themselves and upon whom the peasants depended. Those who did cultivate the land were, in general, either serfs who worked directly for the master
or peasants who cultivated land that was held by the noble upon whom they
depended. Thus there may have been in that time a beginning of a feudal
organization: some landowners who alone enjoyed complete liberty, some
tenants who presumably were only half-free, some serfs attached either to the
landowners or to the tenants.

Going back to the Germans of the time of Tacitus, the author believes he
finds in the society which the Latin historian describes to us the germ of this
organization. In that period, he says, agriculture was of completely secondary
importance. Hunting, fishing, and above all war constituted the principal

social functions. Agricultural labor was considered to be servile, unworthy of freemen. Consequently, it was the slaves and the half-free men who were charged with it; but by the very reason of their rank they were not landowners. Only the fully free citizens had rights over the land and they thus constituted a nobility. And the author confirms this view by an ingenious interpretation of the famous text *Agri pro numero cultorum ab universis in vices occupantur quos mox inter se secundum dignationem partiuntur.*[178] The *secundum dignationem* might imply that a hierarchy and economic inequalities existed corresponding to these social inequalities. The author thus means that the freemen together *(universi)* divided the land, parceling it out in as many portions as there might be available workers *(cultores)* in the community. Each portion corresponded to the amount of land that a man could cultivate by his own powers. Then each freeman received a number of these lots in proportion to his rank *(secundum dignationem),* that is to say, in proportion to the number of serfs or semi-freemen that he held under his domination.

Wittich, however, only offers this interpretation of the facts as a hypothesis; he is certain, in fact, that it raises difficulties. But above all he proposes to show that the conception currently accepted is in great need of being revised. In any case, it is interesting to compare this theory to that which Fustel de Coulanges has held in France and which equally tends to push back much further than was done up to now the first origins of the feudal regime. For one and the other writer, the great landowner might not be as late a phenomenon as has been said. (*Année sociologique,* 6, 1903, pp. 331–333; trans. J. Sweeney)

P. Guilhiermoz. *Essai sur l'origine de la noblesse en France.* Paris: Picard et fils, 1902, 502 pp.

Nobility is defined by the author as "a social class, for which the law acknowledges privileges handed down through inheritance due to the single factor of birth." Three elements serve, then, to characterize it: (1) legally recognized (2) privileges connected with (3) birth alone. Hence it is to be distinguished from simple aristocracies whose privileged situation is either in no way hereditary or is hereditary in fact and not in law. The aim of the book is to investigate the evolutionary process from which French nobility has resulted. Frequent comparisons with other European societies ensure, moreover, that the conclusions in the book are not limited to our country alone.

The first question Guilhiermoz asks himself deals with determining the people from whom we have borrowed the prototype of this organization. Among the Germans on the one hand and the Romans on the other, we find two institutions. Among the Germans, the princes had an entourage of freemen whom Tacitus calls their companions *(comites);* made up of chosen warriors, they formed an elite guard who lived at the expense of the chief they were serving. In the Roman Empire from the fifth century on, the entourage of generals, governors, or emperors consisted of domestic soldiers of sorts called *buccellarii,*[179] who formed a guard called *schola.*[180] Between the Germanic *comitatus* and the praetorian *schola,* there is the great difference that the former comprised only chosen subjects, selected from the best families, whereas the *buccellarii* were mercenaries, enjoying no social status. According to the author, it is from these domestic soldiers that Frankish vassals probably derived their origin. In fact, he finds among the Visigoths, the Lombards, and in Frankish Gaul a completely analogous organization. Merovingian kings and lords were surrounded by servants whose functions were military in particular; they were called *pueri, vassi,*[181] or *antrustions.*[182] In the case of the Visigoths, they bore the same name as did the Roman *buccellarii.*

The situation of these military clients was rather demoralizingly humble. It changed for the better with the Carolingians. In one sense, among the Anglo-Saxons there is an analogous institution with the difference nevertheless that it is still closer in type to the Germanic *comitatus.*[183] The king's *thanes,* who played the same role as the continental *antrustions,* were often people of the highest rank; and it was much the same, although to a lesser degree, with the *gesith* in relation to ordinary lords. Both of these were held in high regard. Now, the founders of the Carolingian dynasty were strongly influenced by the Anglo-Saxons. It is, then, not impossible that they imitated in this respect, as in several others, Anglo-Saxon ideas and practices. Furthermore, the revolution in military tactics originating with Charles Martel contributed to the same result. In order to make a stand against the Arabs, Charles Martel had to greatly increase the number of his cavalry. To that end he developed the *antrustionat*—i.e., he sought to attach to his person the greatest number of freemen possible through the bonds of vassalage. At the same time, in order to give them an incentive to bear the heavy burdens of such service, he distributed lands to them. Territorial grants to the *vassi* had been customary for a long time. But these deals assumed a new character at this time in addition to their increase in number. Charles Martel was obliged to take the lands he needed from the Church, but he consented that the Church should remain owner of the lands thus granted. The grantor simply had the usufructs of the land. The tenure type of vassalage was thus created. Once established, it spread quite naturally even to the grants that did not involve ecclesiastical lands.

The system thus used by kings in their relations with principal lords was likewise used by the latter in their relations with people of lesser importance. The domains granted by the king were generally extensive. The beneficiary therefore granted some parts of his domains to freemen who became his vassals, just as he was the king's vassal. In this way there was established a hierarchy which underwent alterations in form depending on the times, but which became established in principle from then on. But within this hierarchy the differences in degree were based henceforth, no longer on the quality of the vassal's person, but on the quality of his fief. A great change in the institution of vassalage had thus been created along the way. Originally, the vassalage was absolutely independent of increments. Now one was a vassal only if one possessed a fief; vassalage, formerly a personal bond, became a real bond. It became feudalism.

But feudalism and nobility are and above all were originally different things. In the beginning, in fact, all free men were called *nobles,* and they enjoyed all the advantages that came with this title. There were only two classes: those who were free, whether they were vassals or not, and those who were not free. What made nobility of the first was the nobility of their functions, which were essentially military. They were called *bellatores*[184] or *milices,*[185] as opposed to the unfree, who were designated by the words *rustici* or *villani.*[186] It is not that the latter were exempt from the burdens of warfare; but the former alone fought with the complete set of armor, which characterized the *chevaliers.* Therefore one could belong to the class of noblemen or freemen only if one had oneself armed as a knight. Standards were so rigorous that a knight's son who did not take care to have himself armed fell ipso facto to the class of the *rustici.* The ceremony of *adoubement*[187] was then absolutely essential; legal consequences of the highest importance were attached to it. It meant conferring on the young man all the distinctive privileges of nobility (p. 395). The author cannot help noting how closely it resembles the ceremony of the bestowal of arms on the young German, such as Tacitus has described it to us, and he admits that one proceeds from the other. Just as the young Germans were raised in the presence of kings or of princes who then saw to their indoctrination into their *comitatus,* so too the future knight went off to live in the presence of some great lord, who, when the day came, armed him and formed with him a lasting attachment through a personal bond.

There were, then, two different systems that coexisted without exactly overlapping: the hierarchy of vassalage, or feudal system, on the one hand and chivalry on the other. One could very well be a knight without being anybody's vassal. What brought these two institutions together as a unit is the fact that vassalage ended by absorbing the whole class of freemen. In fact, with time, military burdens became very heavy; the result of this was that people could not support them without major resources. Freemen who did not possess them had therefore no alternative but to renounce the privileges of freedom and to descend to the rank of *rustici,* or to hand over their precariously held possessions to some lord who in exchange provided them with the necessary resources and whose vassals they became. Thus there was no one else around except noble vassals on the one hand and the bonded, the commoners, on the other.

In order that the nobility might become definitely established, so that birth alone provided access to it, it would suffice from then on for it to become shut away from the outside. This change was accomplished in two stages. To begin with, as a result of the progress of pacification, the lords had less need to obtain knights for themselves by all possible methods; hence "public opinion did not take long in declaring itself against admitting to knighthood anyone who was not himself a knight's son,'' and royalty legislatively consecrated this doctrine. From then on, birth was the necessary condition of entering the knighthood; but it was not enough to be born a knight's son—it was still necessary to have gone through the ceremony of dubbing. Since armor was very expensive, many young men were not prepared to have themselves armed as knights, even though they fulfilled all the conditions of birth. For their part, they formed the habit of delaying the period when that rite was to be accomplished. Little by little this first legal delay became an adjournment *sine die,* and "then the nobility found itself definitely established, that is to say on a social level to enjoy all ancient legal privileges of knighthood but accessible through the sole fact of birth."

We have strived to reproduce as faithfully as possible the sequence of ideas revealed in this book, but without being certain of having succeeded, for the link that ties together the facts and their place in the demonstration as a whole does not appear to be perfectly evident. The chief interest of this work appears to us to consist of having drawn attention once more to the importance of the military element in the establishment of feudal society, whereas in recent times one tended perhaps to accord a preponderant role to the economic factor too exclusively. But if one finds in this book a very great number of interesting views on questions of detail, it does not seem that it has advanced by much the fundamental problem it treats—namely, the problem of the origins of the nobility. The author himself establishes that vassalage is something distinct from nobility, at least in principle. Knighthood is presumably the source in which nobility found its roots. Now, it is a very remarkable fact that knighthood occupies the smallest part in the work (pp. 346–490). And in that part the issues on which there is the greatest need to be informed are more or less neglected. We do not know what determined the Germanic *comitatus* to survive under that form, from what source came the significance of such note that was attached to the ceremony of the dubbing which created the knight. There is no explanation of knighthood with its privileges, by calling attention to the situation of primitive knights as freemen, nor the military importance of cavalry, since the knight is not only a horseman, and since, in order to be a knight, it was not enough to be born free but was also necessary to have oneself armed in a ceremonial way. A ritual of such basic importance needed therefore to be studied in its own right. In short, it is above all to the study of vassalage that Guilhiermoz' book makes an important contribution. (*Année sociologique,* 6, 1903, pp. 333–337; trans. J. French)

Paul Viollet. *Les Communes françaises au moyen âge.* From *Mémoires de l'Académie des Inscriptions et Belles-lettres,* vol. XXXVI, pp. 345–502. Paris: Klincksieck, 1900, 159 pp.

"Social activity is in inverse ratio to state activity"—at the start of his work the author recalls this remark of Réveillère and puts it to his own use. He believes to have found its verification in the history of the eleventh and twelfth centuries. At that time "state activity is nil or almost nil," but marvelous activity follows "that breakdown of central power" everywhere in Europe. Communal organization seems to be a byproduct of that activity.

What, then, is the commune, at least in its essential properties? The author reduces it "to the right of an important group of inhabitants to have authorized agents or permanent representatives" (p. 14). But this representation is merely an outward symbol that attests to the fact that this group of inhabitants has progressed to the status of a constituted body. This is what the Latin expression so aptly designates by which it has so often been defined: *Incolarum urbis aut oppidi universitas.*[188] Specifically, the commune is a collective personality of a new type that emerges from the social masses, and it is self-constituted as against those that existed previously. It is the result of a movement of differentiation and of individualization of the highest importance. Whereas, up until then, the sum total of inhabitants that served to make up the communes were merely dependencies of lordly authority, they are henceforth to make up new social powers, endowed with a certain autonomy, and hence capable of taking the initiative.

Originally at the very least, the commune included all the inhabitants residing in a particular place, with the single exclusion of the floating population. Certain charters, it is true, appear to require, over and above residency, the ownership of a house or of a building site. But it is likely that in essence the two situations were one and the same, for the very simple reason that our rental system was very uncommon at the time. Whoever took up residence took a house on a permanent tax or rental basis; thus he was owner or near-owner (p. 45). Even members of the privileged classes, nobles or churchmen, were in certain respects members of the community, although the real site they occupied is often very difficult to determine (pp. 47 ff.).

All the members of the commune owed each other *fidem, auxilium consiliumque.*[189] The aim of diverse obligations was to assure security and peace. The words *pax* and *institutio pacis*[190] often served to designate the commune itself. The communal charter was often called *carta pacis.*[191] It is clear from this that the communes are tied in with the great movement that gave birth to truces and peace pacts with God. It is one of a multiplicity of means to which men of the Middle Ages had recourse in order to suppress or attenuate conflicts that were forever shaking society—that is to say, in short, in order to establish a regular social order. This peace was, moreover, rooted in a feeling of solidarity that sometimes assumed an aspect of genuine brotherhood. Accordingly, in certain communes each inhabitant had the right to intervene in every transaction made by one of his fellow citizens and to contribute his share of the bargaining (pp. 59–60).

Such being the commune, how did it get started?

According to Viollet, it was simply the organization and consolidation of a prior regime where freedom was germinating. At a time when the commune was not yet in existence, the community of inhabitants, without having regular and permanent representatives, nonetheless intervened collectively in public life. The public is often seen assembling and deliberating; it took part in the elections of bishops, who on certain matters consulted it spontaneously (pp. 23–24). It is the former who regulated all matters concerning pastureland rights, the utilization of common lands, etcetera. By growing from that seed, the commune came into being. "The communes appeared on the day when group interests, having become considerably augmented and increasingly separated from seigneurial interests, grew and took shape" (p. 28). The means by which this evolution took place were very dissimilar at different points in the country and in different countries. The social forces that assumed the direction of the movement were not everywhere the same: Here it was around former royal or seigneurial officers (city magistrates, consuls) that the people grouped themselves; there it was around powerful corporations; elsewhere the nascent commune sought the strengths it needed solely within itself. But this diversity in methods is secondary and does not alter the general aspect of the phenomenon. Everywhere it involved the coalition of mutual interests that become aware of their solidarity and of their antagonism in regard to the differing interests that had absorbed them at the start. The idea of coalition was even such an essential element in the notion of the commune that the two words *communia* and *conjuratio* are often used as synonyms (p. 16).

It is especially in the towns that these coalitions were created and that they came to an end: the author tells us somewhat briefly the reason for it. He points out on the one hand that the towns of ancient foundation were richer than the countryside in materials that were originally free. On the other hand, the newly created towns themselves enclosed a more advanced and more affluent population than the villages. The needs of both of these were "more important and more varied than in the countryside." That is why they felt more keenly "the need to organize and to administer themselves, by disengaging themselves from subservience to the secular and the ecclesiastical lords" (p. 13). The reply to such an important question [How did communes start?] is given in a terse summary. Since the communal movement was essentially urban, it is important to demonstrate precisely what factors in the urban constitution predisposed the towns to that end and what was the role of each factor. Doubtless, there were towns without communes, just as there existed rural communes. But these exceptions themselves need to be explained at the same time, so as to facilitate understanding of the general conditions of the phenomenon.

Considered in this way, the commune appears exclusively to be the result of a process of disassociation and of disintegration. From the feudal grouping, there were detached communal groups whose autonomy vis-à-vis the authorities on whom they originally depended kept on increasing. But that is only one aspect of that evolution. Alongside the process of "disintegration," there was another one of an opposite nature. At the same time that the communes freed themselves from feudal powers, they reattached themselves to royal power; they placed themselves under the king's influence in order to fight better against the lords. As a result the king, by himself, spontaneously tended to bring the communes under his sway. From the start the royal power intervened in their formation, and later on, in their organizational growth. Without saying it in so many words, Viollet seems to consider this centralizing process more or less regrettable and unsound. This is what already appeared to indicate the profession of liberal faith with which his work begins and from which we have produced the explanation. It is, however, this centralization which has made great modern societies and given to the communes, most particularly the French communes, a part of their distinctive characteristics. If while establishing themselves they had not been bound to one another by a strong governmental authority, if through the instrumentality of the state they had not acquired a feeling of moral unity and of solidarity, we would have been witness to a dispersal of medieval societies that would have made ensuing progress impossible. We would have witnessed communes being transformed into as many little autonomous republics, independent of each other, but whose intellectual and moral growth would have been confined to the limits of their own territorial size. That dispersive tendency is itself so inherent to the attributes of the commune that we have seen it become vigorously manifest each time in the course of our history that governmental action has been excessively lax. Therefore, the role of the state has been far from passive. It is the agent that has prevented social forces which were dispersed in this way from being fruitlessly isolated from one another; it is the agent that by giving them concentrated focus has given them back all their productive capacity.

Viollet discloses, in the last chapters of his thesis, the commune's inner organization. He estimates that its evolution, at least in general, was directed towards a growing oligarchy (p. 119). To tell the truth, the author himself acknowledges that from the start the democratic regime and the aristocratic regime are equally in evidence and that the diversity of types is not hard to understand in view of the fact that the communes were established in very different ways, relying here on seigneurial authority, there on rich merchants, elsewhere solely on the power of the people. If, however, the oligarchical character appears to have become preponderant subsequently, it seems to be so under the influence of a central authority. It is conceivable, in fact, that the state has been somewhat averse to popular assemblies; for their instabilities and their riotous nature turn them into agents unfit to receive and to transmit action, which should be characterized above all by a sense of method, order, and regularity. (*Année sociologique*, 6, 1903, pp. 337–341; trans. J. French)

Giovanni Oberziner. *Origine della plebe romana*. Leipzig: Brock-
  haus, and Genoa: Tipo-litog. e libreria sordomuti, 1901, 232 pp.

It has often been maintained that social classes resulted from ethnic differences in ancient history as well as in the Middle Ages. Oberziner reconsiders this idea by applying it to Roman society. According to him, the plebeians would be the former aborigines of Latium,[192] and patricians certain immigrants who, thanks to advantages that gave them a superior civilization, probably conquered the primitive inhabitants of the country and reduced them to a state of subjection. By way of proving this thesis, he relies on legends having to do with the founding of Rome and on a kind of duality that seems to him to reflect the religious and legal system of the Romans. In fact, he claims to discover in Rome two coexisting religions—one anthropomorphic, which would represent the aborigines, and the other idealized and symbolic, which would apply to the conquerors. Likewise, there probably existed, side by side, two forms of common law corresponding to two very different sorts of family structure.

We shall not discuss the arguments presented by the author for the purpose of proving that the population of Rome was formed by superimposing one very different race upon another. The problem is to ascertain if it is those two races that gave rise to the orders of plebeian and patrician. Now, the reasons calculated to prove such an identity are completely deficient. It is very arbitrary to attribute the anthropomorphic elements of Roman religion to the plebeians, as is done here. Nothing warrants such a discovery of one particular kind of racial infusion rather than another. The truth is that Roman religion represented those two characteristics simultaneously because they are inherent in every religion that has achieved a certain degree of growth. As for the differences in the legal situation, they can be explained very well by the difference in the two classes' social status. Once the plebs had set themselves apart from the patrician *gentes,* thus reduced to a mass apart and a self-contained body politic, they existed, for that very reason, outside the organized family [of *gentes*]. It is true that the author rejects Mommsen's theory that makes the class of plebs out to be an outgrowth of the patrician clientele.[193] The reason given is that if the plebians had first been such clients, they would not have become plebeians. But why should there not be clients of different kinds, some more dependent than others? (*Année sociologique,* 7, 1904, pp. 412–413; trans. J. French)

H. Munro Chadwick. *Studies on Anglo-Saxon Institutions.* Cambridge University Press, 1905, xiv + 422 pp.

It is quite difficult to sum up this work, which is made up of a series of themes. Within its pages quite a variety of issues relative to the Anglo-Saxons are considered: the monetary system, the social and administrative organization, royalty, the origin of the nobility. Besides, although the author strives to put to the uses of history his competence in philology, the philological point of view predominates over the historical point of view. Therefore the sociologist will not find the reading of this book as profitable as the title might lead one to believe.

There is, however, an issue that occupies a preponderant position in the work—the issue of classes. If Chadwick deals with the monetary system, it is in order to establish accurately the scale of *wergeld* depending on the social category of those penalized. In this way he demonstrates the existence in the majority of royal families of primitive England (Kent's excepted) of three classes clearly distinct from one another. Their *wergelds* were different, as well as the fines to which each was entitled for any breakdown of the *mund*—that is to say, of the peace which was its due. Oaths sworn as legally binding were themselves of unequal validity, depending on the class to which the one who took an oath belonged. For example, the oath of a man of the highest class was worth the word of six men in the lowest class, and very frequently the worth of the oath was even expressed in monetary units (see on this point an interesting chapter, pp. 134–154).

The author then wonders where the idea of class or of the better classes comes from—that is to say, what was the origin of the nobility within the Anglo-Saxon estates. He applies himself especially to the task of showing that class is a very ancient institution, precursor to the invasion of Britain.

On the question of the causes that have given rise to the institution of the nobility, his thinking is more tentative. It may, he says, have originated in the hereditary possession of lands, or have been a consequence of service to the king (p. 401), and he points out elsewhere (p. 376) that these two explanations are not mutually incompatible, lands being generally assigned by the king to his servants. (*Année sociologique*, 9, 1906, pp. 345–346; trans. J. French)

Julius Cramer. *Die Verfassungsgeschichte der Germanen und Kelten.*
   Ein Beitrag zur vergleichenden Altertumskunde. Berlin: Karl Sie-
   gismund, 1906, viii + 208 pp.

Claudius von Schwerin. *Die Altgermanische Hundertschaft (Unter-*
   suchungen zur deutschen Staats- und Rechtsgeschichte, hgg. von
   Otto Gierke). Breslau: H. and M. Marcus, 1907, 215 pp.

The first of these two works is a study in comparative law, while the second bears only on a very special question relative to the organization of German societies. Nonetheless, there is some interest for us in comparing them in the analysis we are about to make, for Schwerin's work, without making any particular references to that of Cramer, calls attention to certain difficulties which the latter has not perhaps adequately considered.

Cramer's book is a comprehensive portrait of the social and political constitution of the Germans, as compared with that of the Celts. Let us see what its principal characteristics may have been.

The constitution of the German people was a good example of the type of social organization that we have termed segmentary (see *The Division of Labor*, 2nd ed., pp. 149 ff.). The society was composed of a certain number of elementary groups which were similar to each other. Sometimes they were simply juxtaposed to one another; sometimes they were organized according to a more complex system. Among the Germans, this basic group possessed a double character; it was, at the same time, a family and a territorial unit. Indeed, we know that the constituent units of the army (and consequently of the people, for the army is nothing other than the armed people) were large domestic associations; these were the *familiae et propinquitates* of which Tacitus spoke. In battle each one of them protected its own individual interest. That is to say that we are talking here not of families, in the strict sense of the word, but of clans. On the other hand, as early as Caesar's time the Germans had been a sedentary group; they possessed a territorial organization. Now, the elementary district, which, we discover, was the basic unit of this organization, was likewise occupied by a group of families who were kin to one another or who considered themselves as kin; it was an established clan. This geographical division was accordingly at the same time an ethnic division: Such were the characteristics of the *mark*, [194] of the village *(vicus)*, the collective owner of the soil which the various families shared out in such a way that they might separately cultivate it. These segments, which constituted the substance of society, were organized in the following way.

A certain number of villages conjointly formed a higher-level social and political division. This was "the hundred," *die Hundertschaft*, which had a special leader called the *hunno* or *centenarius*. A certain number of hundreds, between which there existed special neighborhood links and perhaps even kinship bonds, made up the canton *(der Gau, pagus)*, at whose head was a leader of more elevated rank than the *hunno*. This man was the *princeps*. Lastly, above the canton, there was the tribe, *civitas* in Latin texts, which itself was formed out of a confederation of cantons.

Thus, there would have been four stages in the whole social organization, each one ranged above the other.

The expression hundred *(centaine)*, which is used to describe the second-order social division, has at all times intrigued historians, and has given rise to many theories, about which we shall say a word later on. Here is the explanation which our author advances.

Relying on a text from Caesar *(Gallic Wars, IV.1)*, he supposes that in the beginning the *pagus* [195] was a unit of population which furnished a thousand warriors; in all likelihood it bore a name which called to mind this characteristic trait—it was a "thousand" *(Tausendschaft)*.

Moreover, it contained ten divisions of the level which was immediately inferior to it; thence would have arisen the name hundred which is used to designate them. This military organization, arranged on a decimal base, was presumably the primary one; it was presumably Indo-European in its origin. Since the organization was wholly artificial, we may understand that each subdivision had a constant complement, and that consequently numerals were used to define it. With respect to the organization into family and territorial groups which we described first, it could not of itself be contained in such a fixed framework, and it could be of later origin. A moment must have arrived when the thousand changed in character; this is how the *pagus* could have originated; but, for reasons we are not aware of, the subdivisions of which it had been composed preserved their original name, hundred, even though from this time on it was no more than a relic of the past.

The reason why the author supposes that this tenfold division of society was the original one is that he believes we can meet with it among the most diverse European peoples: in Rome, where each tribe was composed of ten *curies* and each *curie* of ten *gentes*; in India, in ancient Russia, etcetera. From this he concludes that this system preceded the separation of these peoples, and consequently there could have been no system which was earlier.

This social formation, when it was unadulterated, implied a political organization characterized by a perfect egalitarianism. Each social segment, in fact, was similar to and consequently equal to the others; within each of them, all families and all individuals were on the same plane. There were relations of coordination rather than subordination between the different groups which made up the society. The most comprehensive divisions exercised only a limited and precarious authority over the elementary units of which they were composed. In the German societies this initial state began to alter, because the segmentary organization itself did not retain its pristine purity. There were leaders, as we have remarked, and a certain hierarchy was present among these leaders; there was a nobility, some clients, and some slaves side by side with freemen. However, this differentiation of ranks and classes, and the hierarchy which was its result, were not yet very marked. The authority of the chiefs in themselves was, in great measure, personal. This is especially true of the leader of the tribe, the *princeps civitatis,* wherever there was one; he proceeded by dint of persuasion rather than coercion (p. 79). All the *principes,* both those of the *pagus* and those of the *civitas,* were elected. It is true that the elected leader had to belong to a noble family, but it is probable that this nobility in itself was a product of election. Originally the people had chosen its leaders from its own midst; now little by little the choice fell upon a certain fixed group of families who enjoyed a special degree of esteem. Thus placed above everyone else's level, they constituted an aristocracy. But underneath this aristocratic organization, which was somewhat rudimentary, one could still perceive, quite near the surface, the democratic organization from which the former evolved.

Schwerin compares the constitution of the Celts to that of the Germans. His study deals not only with the Celts of Gaul but also with those of Galatia and Brittany.

With respect to certain of its features, this constitution recalls the one which has already been described. It was still a segmentary organization, but in contrast to what Cramer believes he observed in Germany, it permitted of only three stages. The tribe was divided into *pagi,* called *tetrarchies* by Strabo, because these divisions were four in number. The *pagus* was the basic solid foundation of society. Beneath it there were the villages, or else a great many dispersed farms. But we encounter nothing which resembles the hundred.

Now, over and above this segmentary organization, there arose another, more complex type. It tended more and more to expand and to conceal the old segmentary type. Distinctions of rank and class became more marked; the social hierarchy became consolidated. The gap between the masses and the privileged castes of nobles and druids became more considerable. A new class appeared in between the common and the slave; it was the class of clients. In an attempt to preserve their positions a great number of freemen were obliged to make themselves the clients and dependents of a noble. Economic considerations, here as well as in Greece and Rome, seem to have given rise to this hierarchal relationship. The nobles therefore were not just simply men who belonged to some of the more esteemed families: their authority rested on a stable material base, independent of opinion.

The people, however, possessed a means whereby they could resist the nobility; they organized into a faction. They established a party, charged with the protection of its members. A noble was always at its head, and this situation sometimes afforded him a considerable amount of authority. Naturally, an aristocratic faction arose in opposition to the popular faction. The history of Gallic society is, largely, the history of these internal divisions.

There is another difference, on which the author does not insist, albeit it appears to emerge strongly from the facts. It is that the concentration of the social body was perceptibly more advanced among the Celts than among the Germans. Among the former, there was generally no permanent authority at the head of the tribe. The tribe was a confederation of *pagi* which as yet possessed only a somewhat wavering sense of its unity. When it waged war it attached itself to a leader *(dux, herzog)*, but only in Tacitus do we find any mention of a stable medium of authority in peacetime, and that is merely in two passages (see p. 62). On the contrary, the Celts were not infrequently organized according to the monarchic principle, and in all cases a permanent council existed, under various names, at the head of the tribe.

On account of these similarities and differences, the author concludes that the social organization of both the Celts and the Germans rested on a common base, which had come down to them from distant times, and from which they had not become separated. It was a sign of their common origin (p. 2). Having started out from the same point, these two kinds of people seemed to have subsequently evolved with unequal speed. The Germans apparently represented a phase which was closer to their social beginnings; the Celts seemed to have attained a higher form of organization.

Presented in these terms, the conclusion of the book calls forth the most express reservations. Just because some resemblances are noted between two social systems, it in no way follows that there is a link of kinship between them. By this reckoning, one would have to say that the organization of the

Indians of North America and that of the Australians are each derived either from the other or from a common source; for betweeen them there is the same relationship as that which existed between the Celts and the Germans. Two peoples can have the same institutions without it being necessary for one group to have borrowed them from the other or for both to owe them to an identical third party. It suffices that they were both placed in similar conditions of life and that the same causes produced the same effects. Segmentary organization is extremely common. It may be found at the most different points on the globe. It corresponds to a determinate phase in social evolution. It is accordingly not surprising that one finds it among both the Celts and the Germans, as well as in so many other societies. The correspondences which have been indicated could well be the product of two independent, parallel developments.

On the other hand, the author does not attach sufficient importance to a serious difference between the two forms of organization, though he does indicate it by way of conclusion. Among the Celts, at least among the Celts of Gaul, there was a lively sentiment not merely of tribal but also of national unity, which did not exist in Germany. The Gauls formed a nation which possessed a sense of itself. Not only did they all practice the very same religion, but their religious life was administered by the very same priestly corporation, which was independent of all the separate states, and which had a single head for the nation of Gaul in its entirety. Likewise, lay assemblies were held in Gaul, albeit intermittently. To these *concilia totius galliae* [assemblies consisting of all of Gaul] each *civitas* sent its representatives, and debates took place here on affairs of common interest. Indeed, on many occasions one people or a group of peoples endeavored to unify the country politically. The idea of a Gallic empire haunted the Gallic consciousness up until Caesar's time (p. 183). This moral homogeneity and this inclination towards unity were completely remarkable in a social body which was so extensive, and was dispersed over so vast a territory, and at a time when the technology of communications was as yet so rudimentary.

We have seen that according to Cramer, German societies contained four divisions, arranged in stages and ordered in hierarchy. One of them bore the name hundred. This expression has intrigued historians at all times. We have seen the explanation which our author gave for it; on this point he follows Maurer, Brunner, and many others. The hundred was originally a division of the army, which had been organized on a decimal base. But this explanation raises the most serious difficulties, and the precise object of Schwerin's book was to expose them.

Indeed, we do know, moreover, that the army had been divided up according to family groups, *familiae et propinquitates*.[196] Now, it is difficult to see how this clan [gentilice] organization could be confused with the last-mentioned form. All clans did not contain the identical number of persons; the effective strength of each one of them was liable to vary according to time and circumstance. How could divisions so unequal in size and so changeable in nature have possibly coincided with numbered divisions, which of necessity were equal to one another in size and immutable?

Cramer responds that the numerical organization is the original one, that it is a legacy of the Indo-European epoch, and that the organization based on the family only subsequently supervened. It would thus have utilized names which had not been coined for it out of respect for tradition.

However, Schwerin very justly objects that this hypothesis is contrary to all probability and contradicts all the teachings of comparative law. The family organization is the earliest and most natural form. We find it at the beginning of history, and it subsequently disappears. The other form, wholly conventional and artificial, already presupposes a culture of a certain refinement. It is therefore impossible that it could have preceded the first type. The fact that it could be found in Rome and in India by no means proves that it dates back to the very origins of Indo-European civilization, for it became established among these various peoples at a relatively late time. It was an administrative organization, established by deliberate design when the old family organization began to disappear. Moreover, we know that these resemblances do not in any way possess the meaning in retrospect which some people have occasionally wished to attribute to them.

According to some other historians, the hundred could have been a geographical district, comprising a hundred estates or villas, which at the time the Germans became a sedentary group might have been granted to a group of a hundred family heads. However, since this theory failed to explain why the number one hundred was chosen in preference to any other, its partisans, among whom was Vaitz, have been obliged to suppose that the division into hundreds was at the beginning the basis of the military organization; tradition would subsequently have imposed the same framework on the territorial organization. This new hypothesis therefore implies what we have just discussed; consequently it is exposed to the same objections, and it is also subject to its own particular objections, because the number of family heads grouped together in such a fashion must necessarily vary from one generation to another. Moreover, one is hard-put to see by what miracle the country could submit itself to such a mathematical division. The villas, which existed beforehand, were not in any case grouped in hundreds (p. 34).

From this critical examination, Schwerin concludes that if one gives the word a strictly numerical significance, the problem of the hundred is insoluble, because it would seem impossible that any group, be it familial or territorial, could have been defined once and for all time by a fixed number. Accordingly he endeavors to establish that the radical *hund*, which forms part of the relatively recent word *Hundertschaft*, originally had an entirely different acceptation. *Hund* would simply have meant "many," a plurality of things or individuals. This expression would have been employed to designate the elementary groups of indeterminate strength which formed the units of the army. When the Germans ceased to be nomads, their land was divided among groups which were so named, and which were at the same time composed of kindred families. The territorial districts, which thus originated, very naturally retained the same name.

We do not possess the necessary competence to discuss this etymology at the moment. It continues to seem somewhat labored to us. And indeed it is not as indispensable as the author thinks; apart from the hypotheses which he has justly criticized, there is another which is at the very least possible. Assuredly, a social group, such as the hundred, could not have contained a fixed number of families and family heads if the rule was that the children of the same father were to separate, whether at the moment of death or at the moment of marriage, in order to become the heads of independent and distinct families. But it would be an entirely different matter if the family were to remain, in principle, indivisible and were to preserve its individuality through the course of generations. Under these circumstances, one could very well understand how, at a given moment in time, a fixed number of family units of this type could have been placed, by dint of an agreement, in one and the same division of society, and how their number would stay perceptibly the same for a very long time. For this arrangement to be feasible, it would suffice, for example, that the family group, which was utilized as the basis for this enumeration, consisted of a set of individuals who bore the same name, because in that case the number of families so conceived would be necessarily as invariable as the number of names by which they described themselves. Moreover, the old Roman *curies* were organized in accordance with this principle. The *gens* was established, to speak precisely, by the combination in one group of citizens who possessed the right to bear the same name. Likewise the *gentes* were distributed among the *curies* in proportion to a ratio which had been established once and for all time: Each *curie* comprised ten *gentes*. The hundred, of course, could have originated in the same way. The artificial character of this formation would thus have been easily reconciled with the fact that among the armies and peoples of Germany, men were grouped *per familias et propinquitates*. At the same time, the author questions the way in which the hundred is ordinarily understood. Schwerin also disputes the place in German social organization which is normally attributed to it.

Most frequently, the hundred is held to have been a division of the *pagus* or *gau;* this was, as we have seen, Cramer's conception of it. But Schwerin remarks that the Latin texts do not mention any subdivision of this type: In them the *civitas* is shown to be composed of *pagi;* the latter, in their turn, are broken up into *vici;* but no intermediate district becomes interposed between the canton and the village. Moreover, our author notes, we cannot see what reason there could have been for its existence. The assembly of the *mark* proved adequate for the administration of the economy; legal affairs were apportioned, according to their importance, between the cantonal and tribal assemblies. There was accordingly no space for the activity of any other [social] organ. From these facts Schwerin concludes that the structure of German societies was composed of only three compartments, nested within each other, in place of the four which Cramer distinguishes; the three were the *civitas*, the *pagus*, and the *vicus*. As to the hundred, it could merely have been another name given to the *pagus*. The hundred would be the *pagus*, but the *pagus* viewed purely as a group of people, without consideration of its geographical basis. Conversely, the *pagus*, in the strict sense of the word, would be the hundred, inasmuch as it was a territorial district. Only during the Frankish period would a more extensive administrative district have been established over and above the *pagus* or hundred. It would have comprised a fixed number of hundreds, and a count would have been placed at its head. This change would have been a consequence of modifications which had occurred in the political organization of these peoples.

We mention this point without stopping to discuss it, because, besides the fact that we can only find a very hypothetical solution for it, it does not possess any sociological interest. There have been some German societies which throughout time have only reckoned three divisions, while others have been composed of less. If this number varies in this respect, it is because it does not constitute a distinctive trait of this mode of social orgnization. (*Année sociologique*, 11, 1910, pp. 387–395; trans. A. Lyons)

G. Bloch. *La Plèbe romaine. Essai sur quelques théories récentes* (The Roman Plebs: Essay on Some Recent Theories). From *Revue historique*. Paris: 1911, 77 pp.

One will find in this opuscule a very clear exposition and a subtle and solid discussion of the principal theories concerning the origins of the Roman plebs. After an examination of the theories of Vico, of Fustel [de Coulanges], of Oberziner, and of Bernhöft, the author comes to the recent hypothesis developed by Binder in his work entitled *Die Plebs, Studien zur römischen Rechtsgeschichte* [The Plebs: Studies on the History of Roman Law]. According to Binder, the duality of plebs and patricians was due to the existence, within the city, of two towns and two peoples: one established on the Quirinal Hill, composed of Sabines; the other purely Latin, which had its principal seat on the Palatine Hill. It was the Sabines on the Quirinal Hill who, according to this theory, became the patricians; the Latin group constituted the plebs. The two classes began by being two nations. Bloch, although he shows what in this hypothesis is excessively systematic, nevertheless retains one of the facts established by Binder; this is the constant alliance which one finds, all through history, between the Latins within [the city] and the Latins outside. Both advanced at the same rate in acquiring the right of citizenship (p. 33). Now, the parallel thus ascertained seems to bring a confirmation of the old theory of Niebuhr. In this conception, the patricians were the earlier citizens, the founders of the city or the descendants of the founders. The plebs, according to this theory, were originally formed of conquered peoples, some transported to the city, others left in their original habitat. Afterwards, around this original nucleus, other elements were added, clients[197] who had left their respective *gentes* (clans), different foreigners, ecetera. This is the thesis which Bloch takes up again, contenting himself with modifying it on secondary points.

We cannot analyze here the very tight argumentation with which he supports his theory, nor discuss it in detail. But it seems to us to be exposed to this objection: It tends to make a specifically Roman phenomenon of the patriciate and the plebs. However, one finds at Athens an organization which was, no doubt, not identical, but which was comparable. The political situation was, however, not the same in these two places, and the two towns did not develop in the same way. On the other hand, there are serious reasons for thinking that at Athens the formation of the two classes was due to causes which were principally economic. May it not have been the same at Rome? This was already supposed by Eduard Meyer. As that historian justly remarks, everywhere where the role of the state is still minor, the weak inevitably fall into dependence on the strong. Bloch objects to this theory because it does not take into account the fact of the conquest. But from the fact that the conquest could have affected the development of the institution it does not follow that it was the generating cause of it. And we do not see why the prohibition of *connubium* (intermarriage) cannot be explained as well by the one hypothesis as by the other. This is not a purely "Roman" phenomenon, as our author says; one finds it everywhere where strongly constituted classes oppose each other. The whole question thus reduces itself to knowing where this opposition comes from. (*Année sociologique*, 12, 1913, pp. 441–443; trans. K. Woody)

NOTES AND NOTICES

Attilio de Marchi. *La beneficenza in Roma antica* (Charity in Ancient
   Rome). Milan: Tip. Galli e Raimondi, 1899, 68 pp.
   The book makes pleasant reading, however esoteric; it successively gives an exposition of and briefly characterizes the principal charitable institutions of ancient Rome: first, the public institutions which benefited the Roman citizens only, such as the sharing of lands, distribution of grains, and laws to defer debts, ecetera; then the private welfare operations which benefited both the foreigners and the citizens (pp. 23–61). According to the author, the spirit of humanity and of charity seemed to have been less developed in Rome than it was in Greece. (*Année sociologique*, 3, 1900, pp. 448–449; trans. Y. Nandan)

J. Rhys and D. Brynmor-Jones. *The Welsh People: Chapters on Their
   Origin, History, Laws, Language, Literature, and Characteristics.*
   London: T. F. Unwin, 1900, xxxvi + 678 pp.
   The authors of this considerable volume have participated in the work of the Royal Commission on Land in Wales and Monmouthshire; a part of the

work has already been published in the report of this commission. Here we intend to point out particularly the chapter edited by Seebohn, which treats the history of landed property in Wales, and chapter 6, which presents a summary picture of the ancient customs of Cimry—remarks on the formation of the laws of Howel, monuments preserved pertaining to these laws; political organization; different local conditions; domestic organization; change in the ancient organization through settling the land, which led to territorial organization; the dwelling place; the law of inheritance; marriage; criminal law and jurisdiction.

The other chapters treat the origin of the mixture of different ethnic elements of the Welsh population; Welsh history until conquest by the Normans; the religious movement since the Reformation; Welsh language and literature; and the modern conditions of the rural population. (*Année sociologique*, 5, 1902, pp. 334–335; trans. Y. Nandan)

E. Loncao. "La genesi sociale dei communi italiani." *Rivista italiana di sociologia*, V, nos. 5–6, pp. 639–688.

The author conceives of economic factors as the determining cause of the communal movement. The growth of population, by necessitating more abundant production, presumably obliged the proprietors of land to progressively attenuate the ancient servile system. In order to make the work more productive, the need was felt to make the worker interested in it; in order to accomplish that, the worker was given more and more liberty. The same movement occurred in the professions, which, first simply depending upon each *curtis*,[198] at the end became emancipated from it and were eventually constituted and organized as autonomous units. The liberated segment of the population thus felt a genuine need to form an organization of its own, which consequently found itself in antagonism with the feudal organization. Obviously, the professional organization could not be developed without having detrimental effects on the feudal organization. This was the character of communal organization. (*Année sociologique*, 6, 1903, pp. 341–342; trans. Y. Nandan)

Edward Jenks. *Essai sur le gouvernement local en Angleterre*. Translated into French by J. Wilhelm. Paris: Giard et Brière, 1902, xxvi + 327 pp.

Jenks's work is a useful manual. (*Année sociologique*, 6, 1903, p. 342; trans. Y. Nandan)

Joseph Calmette. "Le 'Comitatus' germanique et la vassalité, à propos d'une théorie récente." *Nouvelle Revue historique de droit français et étranger*, 1904, pp. 501–507.

The article shows; contrary to Guilhiermoz, that there are relationships between the Germanic *comitatus* and vassalage. (*Année sociologique*, 9, 1906, p. 346; trans. Y. Nandan)

Jaromir Celakovsky. "Les Origines de la constitution municipale de
Prague." *Nouvelle Revue historique de droit français et étranger,*
1905, pp. 195–212.

The article shows the origins of the city in the institution of the great
market established at the foot of the palace in Prague. Cf. *L'Almanach de
l'Académie tcheque,* vol. xiii, p. 185, and *Manuel historique du droit
Bohême,* 2nd ed., p. 386. (*Année sociologique,* 9, 1906, pp. 348–349; trans.
Y. Nandan)

Political Organization

REVIEWS

Harold E. Gorst. *China.* London: Sands and Co, 1899, 300 pp.

Although this book has a more practical than theoretical aim, since the
author proposes above all to determine the attitude that Western societies
should observe in their relations with China, it does not fail to give us interesting information on the social and political organization of China.

To judge things from the outside, China appears as an autocracy. The
authority of the emperor is theoretically unlimited: It is he who owns the land;
he has the right of life and death over his subjects; he is the one who chooses
his successor, without even taking him into his family. But in fact these powers
are limited in the first place by the numerous advisers who assist him in all his
acts. There is even one, the Board of Censors, which exercises a veritable control on the manner in which the sovereign fulfills the duties of his office.
Moreover, the right of rebellion is, in principle, recognized for the people if
the emperor carries out his functions poorly. The despot, all-powerful in appearance, can on occasion be deposed (p. 139).

This contrast between appearance and reality is found throughout the
whole extent of the administrative system. To have this hierarchy intelligently
organized, with its viceroys attached to the central government, the governors
subordinated to the viceroys, these mandarins of all kinds, one must have a
powerful centralization. In fact China is the most decentralized country in the
world. The population pays very little attention to the mandarins; all that is
demanded of them is not to interfere in local affairs, which the interested parties mean to deal with directly themselves. The mandarins are paid for their
abstention. One fact, in particular, has contributed to diminish their authority
to that point. The conquering Manchus, fearing that their local functionaries
might conspire with the natives against the foreign dynasty, believed it expedient to perpetually change their residence. The result of this is that they are
not knowledgeable about the affairs that they have to administer, and consequently they themselves refuse to be bothered with them.

Finally, the people are found to enjoy "an enormous power" (p. 82).

Nowhere is local self-government more developed than in China; it is characteristic of the Chinese organization (p. 140). Each village, each district (the smallest administrative unit), has its council, composed of the most influential men. The mayor is chosen by election. The functions of these local authorities are very extensive. They are not only charged with overseeing all that concerns municipal life; they have jurisdiction over all civil affairs, fill the role of judges in commercial disputes, and even intervene sometimes in criminal cases (p. 85).

Beneath the village and the district, there is found another local group still more jealous of its autonomy, in which the common life of the Chinese, so poor otherwise, reaches its maximum intensity: this is the family. This is the community which is the most stable in the whole social system. The attachment of the Chinese to his family surpasses all that we know. By the autonomy that it enjoys, it recalls the Roman family. The majority of the offenses (delits) are directly punished by the domestic tribunal. The organization is patriarchal; the powers of the father are very extensive. However, a clear indication that his authority is not completely that of the *paterfamilias* in Rome is that one very often sees that, after the death of the father, the brothers continue to live together under the direction of the eldest (pp. 86, 88). The daughters inherit nothing, but they have a dowry. The widow receives double the share of the child.

Finally, over and beyond the communities of the village and the family, but always outside the administrative cadres, there is formed a vast network of professional organizations. Two kinds of corporations are distinguished: One embraces all the merchants of the same province; the other is local. Their power is enormous. Their decisions are imposed with a force which permits no resistance; all opposition is broken. The government itself has more than once been obliged to lower its flag before these almighty corporations (p. 120). Moreover, this organization is far from being without its advantages. The corporative control is frequently very salutary. Each corporation is, besides, a mutual-aid society.

This book gives a very clear impression, therefore, that there are in China two social systems superimposed one upon the other. The one, official and apparent, is formed by the mandrinate and the vast administrative hierarchy. The other, hidden under the first, is, on the contrary, characterized by highly developed decentralization and great local autonomy. From the first point of view, China appears as a strictly unified society; from the second, as a federation of secondary groups, territorial or professional, very independent from one another and from the central power. And of these two Chinas, it is the second which is the true one, the only one which has profound roots in the popular mind. The administrative network which has been imposed on it only covers it superficially and has not penetrated it. It is an external garment which does not express the real life of the situation.

The duality is the same in the religious order. The general cults are not the object of any fervor; the offical priests are universally despised. But the local superstitions, the popular cults, and the cult of the dead are practiced with an ardent devotion (p. 168). From this arises that singular mixture of skepticism and superstitious credulity, one of the distinctive traits of the Chinese character. (*Année sociologique*, 4, 1901, pp. 323–325; trans. J. Sweeney)

H. Singer. "Die Karolinen" (The Caroline Islands). *Globus*, LXXXI, pp. 37–52.

Each island forms an independent political unit, and sometimes even one and the same island consists of several political units. The social organization is generally aristocratic. There is a council of chiefs who are under a supreme chief, whose powers are very limited because of those of the principal lords; underneath the latter are the remaining nobility, whose hierarchy, in Ponape, accounts for no less than twelve degrees, followed by the people of common degree and finally the slaves. Supreme dignity of position is not hereditary: The title bearer is designated by election, but generally selected from the same family. A singular practice formerly observed in Ponape is worth noting: When a chieftain died, his next-in-line vassals were entitled to pillage his house.

This relatively complicated organization is not to be found everywhere. In Ruck and in Mortlock[199] there is no central government. There are several independent states; each of them is made up of a gathering of villages, but the inhabitants of the same village do not belong to the same *Stamm*. One must no doubt infer from this that they are under the jurisdiction of different clans—implied by the system of marriage practiced.

Territorial organization and organization based on clans thus overlap each other, as happens so often in Australia (p. 45). There is a certain hierarchy among these clans: In Mortlock seven own all the land and the three others have nothing.

The wife enjoys a very special consideration. In Ponape she is the sovereign lord in the home; in Mortlock she is a woman who holds the highest power; in Ruck the husband comes to dwell at his wife's place. Out of that comes the mixture of clans within the same village. Marriage and divorce are, moreover, carried out informally. Sexual freedom is widespread except during the two or three months following puberty. At that time, the girl must shun men's glances.

Information about religion is not specific. From what we are told, we may presume a sort of totemism, quite similar to that observed by Spencer and Gillen in central Australia. Funeral rites are highly developed; on the tomb is constructed a miniature house. When the deceased is a chieftain, a mourning hut is built where the son spends one hundred days. (*Année sociologique*, 4, 1901, pp. 327–328; trans. J. French)

Félix de Rocca. *Les Zemskie Sobors. Etude historique.* Paris: Larose et Forcel, 1899, 194 pp.

When the different Russian principalities began to centralize under the authority of the czar of Moscow in the course of the fifteenth century, there appeared on the scene, besides the sovereign and his privy council, a political organ that at first glance seems incompatible with the principle of autocracy: the assemblies of the Russian land to which history has assigned the name of *Zemskie Sobors,* or Estates General. They comprised or were supposed to comprise representatives of all classes of the population. Some were designated on the basis of their public record itself or their high position (members of the privy council or of the sacred college, boyars, court dignitaries); others (Lower ranks of every sort, merchants, peasants) were designated through the election process. By themselves the deliberations of these assemblies had no executive force and always needed the sanction of the czar, but the role they played was nonetheless very important in the history of Russia.

Where does this institution come from? At the outset it may be thought that it originated in part from Russia's former democratic constitution. Before the formation of the Muscovite state and the following centralization, each commune had its popular assembly, called *Veche.* Now, this assembly survived, although under different names and different forms, the collapse of the former principalities. Under the pressure of events, in direct proportion to the increase in centralization, it even broadened its field of action and encompassed entire regions (p. 17). It is, then, natural to believe that the new state of affairs, once established, produced a new assembly that was to the country as a whole what the *Veche* was to the commune and that assured the participation of everyone in public life, which the Russians made a lasting habit.

Yet the *Sobors* were something other than a simple restoration of former customs. Lingering memories of the past effectively paved the way towards a new institution, but were not decisive in causing it to take shape. What brought it to life was, above all, a certain number of brand-new needs the Russian state experienced in the formative stages. The political growth of Russia was, in fact, very different from what one observes in occidental societies. In our case, monarchical authority when it was set up was faced by well-organized social forces against which it had to struggle; and it is even in part because of this struggle that it was constituted. Russia, on the contrary, was untouched by any political organization. As a result of the nomadic state of its populations, it was an unstable conglomerate of heterogeneous elements that no social ties united. "No corporations or castes were well established and riveted to the territory. The inhabitants moved about at whim" (pp. 24–25). It is the state itself which had to create that organization which was lacking; the constitution of social classes was its work, instead of being an obstacle, as elsewhere, to its growth. It is this last which created the nobility, as a caste created to serve its lords; it is this last which attached the inhabitants of the towns and of the countryside to their profession or to their land. Now, the state could not succeed in such an enterprise without the cooperation of the elements it was involved in organizing. It was all the more obliged to resort to such cooperation because of the scant means it had at its disposal to take proper action, its poor information about the nation's forces. Then, while determined to assure the execution of these restorative measures, it was impossible fully to rely on the boyars alone, with their rather hostile attitude toward the new order of things. Therefore, it had to call upon the support of the country. This is how a representative regime came into being (p. 26). The *Sobors* are the organ by means of which the state created in successive stages the other organs essential to Russian life.

It is clear, from this example, how variable are the circumstances under which governmental centralization can be established. In the West, the state has succeeded in superimposing itself on political orders already in existence and divided among themselves by all sorts of conflicts of interest, and it has made it its business and raison d'être to merge them and to unify them. In Russia, by way of contrast, it is unity that is more of a primary factor, and it is the state that has dispersed the population into distinct political orders; it is the former which has divided the inhabitants into categories and classes in order to give society a more solid base. The result is that these diverse classes have never been separated from each other by chasms; unlike Western societies, they are not societies within the society. Created by the state for the needs of the state, they simply represent corps of functionaries between whom there are merely differences in rank depending on the importance of the role they fill. Attachment to the service of the state dominates all social distinctions. Certainly in that fact lies one of the characteristic features of the political and moral structure of Russia.

This example can also serve to demonstrate how much political institutions, apparently similar, can actually differ. In certain respects, Russian *Sobors* bring to mind our representative assemblies; and yet their role was very different. Our assemblies have had, above all, their raison d'être in representing the interests of the nation as against the state, so to speak; hence an antagonism that in our case is traditional. Our Parliament House [legislative body] and Judiciary function especially to contain, to control, the government. In Russia, no opposition of this kind exists. The *Sobors* and the czar are collaborators in the same type of work, representatives of the same interests. Thus there are types of political assembly which, in spite of superficial resemblances, would call for distinctions to be made.

The *Sobors* disappeared when the work for which they had been born was accomplished—that is to say, when Russia was organized in a stable manner, when Russian bureaucracy, solidly established, could function on its own and automatically. (*Année sociologique*, 4, 1901, pp. 330–332; trans. J. French)

W. Liebenam. *Städteverwaltung im Römischen Kaiserreiche* (Administration of Cities under the Roman Empire). Leipzig: Duncker und Humblot, 1900, xviii + 577 pp.

The first two parts of the book are well informed, rather purely erudite. In the first part, the author establishes the nature of the receipts and the nature of the expenditures in the cities of the empire (pp. 1–73); in the second, he analyzes the various agencies charged with the financial administration of the town (pp. 174–430). The last part (pp. 431–538) is broader in scope and of greater interest. Treated there is the part played by the progressive decline of the cities in the dissolution of the Roman Empire. With the beginning of the second century, the cities have reached the culmination of their growth and signs of decadence are appearing. Municipal functions are being relinquished; the economic situation of private individuals and of the city-states is going from bad to worse; everywhere forces are being dissipated in petty internal rivalries, etcetera (pp. 476–477). For the purpose of curing the sickness, the state finds nothing better than to gradually retire autonomy from the cities by imposing on them its own officials and its will; it all ended by drawing away the underlying sources of urban life (pp. 478 ff.)

As for the causes of this decadence, the author sees them not in economic conditions, but rather in the legal organizations of the empire. Rome could never give the cities the place which was rightfully theirs and organically reintegrate them into the social system as a whole. Between them and the central power there were no intermediary groups to provide possible channels whereby they could become closely associated with the life of the state. This constitutional flaw would inevitably stunt their growth. If, notwithstanding, they did at a certain moment attain a rather high degree of prosperity, it is because the general economic situation of the empire was at the time exceptionally prosperous and accordingly was able to neutralize, for a time, the harmful effects of imperial policy. But the causes of the sickness were in existence from then on, and their impact was to be felt in the long run (p. 507).

Overshadowing this total decline in social forces, the Church shows a steady rise in power. (*Année sociologique*, 4, 1901, pp. 337–338; trans. J. French)

Louis Stouff. *Les Comtes de Bourgogne et leurs villes domaniales. Etude sur le régime communal, forme de l'exploitation seigneuriale, d'après le cartulaire de la ville d'Arbois, suivie du texte de ce cartulaire, de pièces annexes, etc.*[200] Paris: Larose, 1899, pp. 102–219.

The work calls attention to a special form of communal emancipation. The author has observed it in Burgundy, especially with respect to the city of Arbois, which he takes as a typical case. Whereas in the large city-states this emancipation ended in a veritable political revolution, with a constitution of a new social form, the cities of average size stopped halfway—they remained equidistant from the commune, which was truly free and self-controlled, and the ancient rural community. They were forever being subjected to seigneurial exploitation. They were not invested with seigneurial rights; they had neither sanction nor jurisdiction; their inhabitants were not of the bourgeois class (p. 54). All the count did was to give official recognition to the community which existed in fact, to give it a legal personality and a definite organization, to confer on it a right of administration extended to include possessions that the inhabitants had been holding for their own use since time immemorial, which were declared from then on *free and communal* (p. 65). But the community was not their owner; it was not on its own; the land was only granted for tenant-farming rights.

Of course, such tenant farming was not granted free of charge; accountability was exacted for expenses that conservation and cultivation of the domain entailed. Therefore the lord was able to profit from this arrangement, and he even saw to it that the arrangement was entirely to his advantage. For this reason, Stouff considers the liberation of these cities only a matter of a "financial operation," of "business speculation" (pp. 3, 101).[201] Such an interpretation is due, we believe, to a failure to recognize the full import of the phenomenon. If the seigneur considered it to his advantage to let the communities administer their domains themselves, it is because former administrative procedures had outlived their usefulness; the fact is that even for purely economic reasons it was useful to permit more interplay among the moving parts of the feudal machine, a greater liberty having become the precondition of a greater productivity. The historical phenomenon to which our attention is drawn is then, in its turn, a byproduct of general and profound causes that impinged upon the feudal system and that were to multiply the centers of autonomous life. But in this particular case, it is the economic aspect of this movement that is especially in evidence and that accounts for its interest. (*Année sociologique*, 4, 1901, pp. 338–339; trans. J. French)

Charles Bellange. *Le Gouvernement local en France et l'organisation du canton*. Paris: H. Didier, 1900, 465 pp.

Although in principle we do not undertake here a review of works belonging to the applied sciences, we are inclined to mention this book because of the efforts it makes to be methodical and because of its very legitimate desire to understand certain social processes. Two fundamental propositions dominate the entire work. The first is that centralization and decentralization, the powers of the state and the autonomy of local groups, far from being antagonistic as is too often believed, are on the contrary two sets of facts which are enmeshed with each other. Second, the only way to revive local life is to constitute, at the very base of the society, groups that are small enough so each individual has a strong group feeling and large enough so that public activity of a certain intensity can be developed. The partial aggregate which seems to the author to respond to this double desideratum is the canton or association of neighboring communes. Consequently, the major part of the work is devoted to setting forth the method by which the canton must be constituted in order to render services expected of it. But if we recognize the theoretical principles from which the author finds support, we must admit that he does not exaggerate the consequences of reform that he proposes. He ignores the law by virtue of which the territorial groups lose more and more of their importance; men are less and less attached to them. It would not therefore be sufficient to enlarge the geographic limits in order to revive and intensify the public life which has languished. In fact, it is groups of another category, better in harmony with its mode of existence, that modern society needs to have. (*Année sociologique,* 4, 1901, pp. 339–340; trans. Y. Nandan)

P. Milioukov. *Essais sur l'histoire de la civilisation russe.* Translated
    from Russian into French by P. Dramas and D. Soskice, preface
    by Lucien Herr. Paris: Giard et Brière, 1901, viii + 299 pp.

What is special about the social organization of Russia is that it is entirely the work of the state. Among the Western peoples of Europe, the state resulted rather from the spontaneous development of the society; the political organization was formed little by little under the influence of the economic, demographic, and moral situation of the country. The historical process developed there from bottom to top. In Russia, it took place in inverse order. The state was organized before society, which as a consequence was an organized structure developed by the state. It is the political structure which has determined the social structure.

It is the peasant class which formed the foundation of the edifice. Now, by itself, the rural population of Russia constituted a kind of homogeneous mass, which was amorphous and without coherence. It was divided into a certain number of territories; but the ties which united the inhabitants to the prince, possessor of the territory, were very personal, temporary, and almost contractual. Each subject could leave his master voluntarily to go and place himself under the protection of a neighboring prince; the population thus had no fixed character at all. In the midst of "that fluid element," the first solid knot which formed was the Muscovite state. This was the first stable and defined group which exerted its power to fix, to frame, and to organize the soft substance over which it exercised its influence.

It was the demands of external and military order which gave rise to and developed the state. To fight against the *Ulus*[202] of the Tartars, on the one hand, and against the Lithuanians, on the other, the Muscovite princes "became the military organizers in the style of the conquering Turks." This first seed, once disseminated, grew by itself. Conquests engendered conquests; for this reason the army had to be enlarged, its technique had to be improved, and it occupied governmental activity almost uniquely. However, to satisfy these needs, it was necessary not to allow the Russian population to remain in the incoherent and anarchic state in which it found itself; for a large army cannot live if the financial resources of the state are not regularly assured. Thus the czars were led to organize the country. But that organization was born only to respond to military and fiscal necessities, and consequently it bears the mark of the causes which have determined it.

Thus, it is in order to regulate the collection of taxes that the state consolidated the *mir*. The communal group was hit collectively and hence it had an interest in exercising pressure on its members to hinder them from departing and going somewhere else to settle; for the departure of one increased costs for the others. In this fashion, the population lost its mobility (pp. 170–196). More generally, the administrative districts were exclusively fiscal districts. It was in the same way that the classes were formed. The nobility was not constituted by itself; it was the state which created it (pp. 219–237) by according to subjects who owed military service certain privileges (the right of ownership over their lands and over the peasants who occupied them).

Thus the Russian state is not a product of society, but it is, on the contrary, external to it. It is from outside that it has always sought to influence it. One will notice the analogy between this situation and that which we pointed out last year in the Chinese state (see *L'Année*, 4, 1901, p. 323).[203] But then a question is raised: What was the real extent and depth of the influence exercised in Russia by the state on society? Did it penetrate into the mind of the population, or did it only succeed in modifying the external ranks of life without reaching the life itself? To that question, the interesting work which we are analyzing gives no answer. However, it seems from many signs that the work of the state is superficial and without roots. Since the political organization of the country does not express its moral constitution, it has hardly been able to affect it profoundly. In reality, there has been a simple superimposition, just as in China. There is therefore a type of state which is characterized by a kind of exteriority in relation to the underlying social life. (*Année sociologique*, 5, 1902, pp. 358–359; trans. J. Sweeney)

Henri Francotte. *Formation des villes, des Etats, des confédérations, et des ligues dans la Grèce ancienne* From Bulletins de l'Académie Royale de Belgique, *Classe des Lettres,* 1901, nos. 9–10. Paris: Emile Bouillon, 1901, 66 pp.

When the Greeks penetrated into the country that was to bear their name they formed large ethnic groupings—Arcadians, Dorians, etcetera—which included, in their turn, other groupings of the same nature but of lesser extent (Mainalians, Parrhasians, etcetera). Once they were settled on the soil, a double movement was produced: First the large original nations disintegrated and were dispersed in a multitude of small villages weakly tied to each other; then these villages concentrated themselves, integrated themselves, in such a way as to form larger groups, which, without exactly reproducing the previous ones, did not fail to resemble them. This movement of concentration took various forms. Synoecism is the simplest of these forms. It is the main one studied by Francotte; the others are only varied combinations of it.

Synoecism is a union of elemental groups which join together and absorb each other (or are absorbed) into a single state. It itself presents different varieties depending on the nature of the groups which combine, and on the results of this combination. The simplest form (although it is not the one discussed first by the author) is that in which the component elements are demes, or villages; in this case there is a distinction, depending whether this integration of villages does or does not produce a town. Sparta is an example of the former, Megalopolis (and perhaps Athens) of the latter. A more complicated form is that in which synoecism takes place between towns (πόλεις)[204] which have already been formed; in this case, as in the preceding one, there is a distinction depending on whether or not this concentration results in a new town. Once a new town is formed, the previously existing towns disappear and their population is grouped together in a new enclosure; it was thus that the town of Rhodes was formed. In the contrary case, the component towns continue to exist, but one of them becomes the seat of the state.

It can be seen from this that synoecism was a very complex social phenomenon. It presents two aspects. It is, on the one hand, a political phenomenon, since it always implies the establishment or the transformation of one or more states. It has as effect the association in the same public life of social groups which, up to then, were relatively independent of each other. But at the same time it is a morphological phenomenon. It presupposes a new distribution of the population, especially when a town is formed; for the inhabitants of the countrysides or towns which already exist leave their original habitations to establish themselves in the town which is founded. For our author, it is political unification which is the essential characteristic of all synoecism. This very broad definition has the disadvantage of confounding in a single term two realms of phenomena as different from each other as a political organization and a geographical process. The author gives as his reason the argument that synoecism usually has as its point of departure an already existing town; that only the most recent towns resulted in the establishment of others, and as a result, in morphological phenomena of some importance. This assertion is surprising; is it not true that the original towns of Greece were themselves the products of synoecism of some sort?

Whatever may be the case where this point is concerned, these transformations, whether they were political or morphological, made necessary a renewal of social frameworks; for it was necessary for the constituent groups to fuse into a single organization. Two types of groupings were possible: one purely tribal, the other purely territorial. In the first, men were grouped according to their kinship relations (whether real or imagined doesn't matter); in the second, according to their relation to the land. Neither the one nor the other principle served as the exclusive basis of the different synoecisms. We find the tribal organization everywhere in the primitive forms of the city, generally in the three forms of clans. phratries, and phylae. But it is never found there in a pure form. In itself, in fact, it does not admit of any regular form since it depends on the accidents of birth, death, adoption, and the extinction or the evolution of familial groups; it cannot therefore be enclosed in rigorously defined frameworks. Now, in Greece it always presents itself with perfect symmetry, which indicates the hand of the legislator; each phyle contains so many phratries, each phratry so many clans. We are thus in the presence of a kinship system which has been reworked by the art of politics, and as a result more or less changed, although it is not possible to perceive just what those changes consisted of. It is known how, in the sequel to the story, this kinship character, which had been stated, but in a restricted way, was progressively weakened. This organization, as it developed, became narrowly aristocratic; it was thus necessary to break it up and replace it when the day came when democracy was in a position to enforce its rights. The best way to efface the social distinctions which had thus developed was to take territorial groupings (the demes) directly as the basis for social groupings; it was thus that Cleisthenes, notably, proceeded at Athens. And nevertheless, so strong was tradition that the new social frameworks were conceived to a certain degree according to the model of the old ones. There were still phylae, phratries, etcetera; moreover, it was inheritance, a principle which is essentially one of kinship, which determined membership in a deme. "One can thus say the idea of sovereignty which is strictly territorial was never developed in Greece in a complete way" (p. 32). Under the new system the old system showed through, although it was more effaced. It never disappeared entirely, but after the appearance of towns it never existed except in a mitigated and weakened way.

This role of the kinship principle in synoecism appears inexplicable to us if we lose sight of the fact that it is just as much morphological as political. If the demes had only been grouped politically they could have entered just as they were into the new organization, which as a result would have had a territorial basis: The state would have been a confederation, more or less tight, of villages. But it could not be thus from the moment when this moral and political concentration was accompanied by a material concentration—that is to say, from the moment in which a morphological unit of a new sort, the town, was superimposed on the already existing ones (the villages). For the village could not remain the basic social framework, since the town was not a compound of villages. The only principle which was then common to the town and the countryside was thus the kinship principle, which had been the first basis of the old ethnic organizations and had never disappeared entirely; one can even believe that each village was nothing more, in the beginning, than a clan which had settled down. There was, therefore, no difficulty in restoring this principle. But precisely because it was restored in a voluntary way and adapted to a society for which it was not naturally made, it was necessary to retouch it; hence that symmetry, that regularity, which is presented by the way it was employed and which characterizes man's deliberate works.

We do not dwell upon the other forms of political concentration studied by the author. He distinguishes three: sympoly, league, and perioecism.[205] This terminology is not lacking some confusion. Strictly speaking there is already sympoly (confederation of πόλεις) in simple synoecism, wherever the latter is established between already constituted cities, for example, at Rhodes. But doubtless Francotte reserves this word for instances in which confederated cities retain their personality in a federal state of a certain extension, such as the Achaean confederation. Perioecism occurs when one of the constituent cities subordinates the other or others and reduces them to the position of demes; but this was already the case with Stiris and Medeon, the union of which, however, was considered as a form of synoecism. The league is a temporary confederation, formed for a specific purpose and placed under the hegemony of a specific state. What one should especially stress, in regard to this classification, is the proof of the Greeks' tendency to form larger and larger social groupings, which recalled, although differing from them, the original groupings.

This tendency, moreover, is not peculiar to Greece. There is not, perhaps, any ethnic group which, once dispersed, does not attempt to reconstitute its original unity, but in new ways. Pan-Latinism, Pan-Slavism, Pan-Germanism, etcetera, are only different forms of the same phenomenon. (*Année sociologique*, 6, 1903, pp. 373–376; trans. K. Woody)

V. Budanov. "L'Autorité dans la Russie ancienne." *Nouvelle Revue historique de droit français et étranger*, 1903, no. 1, pp. 35–75; no. 2, pp. 137–158.

The history of Russian law is divided into three periods: (1) the territorial or princely period, from the ninth to the thirteenth centuries; (2) the Muscovite or Lithuanian period, when all the Russian lands were grouped into two states, Muscovy and Lithuania, which lasted up to the seventeenth century; (3) the imperial period. It is authority during the first period that the author analyzes in these two articles, which are otherwise only a partial translation of his history of Russian law.

At that phase of history, society was established on a foundation which was at the same time familial or lineal and territorial. The line of descendants, established on the land, is the *zadruga* or *vervi*; the author (or the translator) designates this as the phratry, understanding by this, without doubt, a somewhat extended group of blood relations. Each of these groups has its own dwelling place. A collection of dwelling places of this kind constitutes the commune or union or neighbors. A collection of associated communes is sometimes called a province *(volosti)*—more usually *Zemliá** land. Budanov tells us that in principle the *volosti* is a portion of the *Zemliá*. Nevertheless, the difference which separates these two kinds of groups does not appear very clear throughout his analysis.

According to him, all that organization may be due to a veritable swarming. The lineage or house, in dislocating itself, would have produced the com-

---

* The Russian word *Zemliá* could mean "country, state and various kinds of territorial political units, nation, region, landholding, field, earth . . . . In the *Book of Annals, Zemliá* is used not as a geographical term but in the sense of nation or state." See S.G. Pushkarev, *Dictionary of Russian Historical Terms from the Eleventh Century to 1917*. New Haven, Conn.: Yale University Press, 1970, s.v. *Zemliá*. ED.

mune; from the commune other filial communes would equally have been derived. The original commune, by reason of its authority, would have enjoyed privileges; it would have become the capital of the group, exercising a real preponderance over all the others. We have no need to say that that genesis seems suspect to us. The state is not a development of the family; but the family is constituted in the midst of more extended social groups which have provided the state with its substance.

Still, the joining of filial communes and the metropolis to which they were subordinated formed the first seed of the Russian state; the land was thus its predominant element, whence its characteristic traits. The Russian state is not a union of classes, like the feudal society, nor of persons, like the order of knights, nor of lineage, like the *Ulus* of the Tartars; it is the union of communes. The configuration and the number of these states remained variable for a long time. But with time there were founded ten definitive political units which later developed the character of provinces in the Muscovite state and the Lithuanian state.

At the head of each state, or *Zemliă*, there was a prince; and that is why the *Zemliă* was also called the principality. Around the prince there was a court of assistants *(Drougina)*. Below this were the notables, *Startzi*, a word which signified "ancient citizens;" they were also sometimes called territorial boyars, in opposition to the members of the princely boyars.[206] Little by little the difference betweeen them disappeared. But the class of boyars in ancient Russia were never a corporate organization, nor did social privileges belong to them such as the noble classes had. The landholding character of ancient Russia was opposed to it. Each commune had its boyars, and the social importance of a boyar varied according to the importance of his commune—so much so that the whole population of the capital was boyar by comparison to the population of others. The other classes were: (1) that of the bourgeois, or the townsmen, very similar to boyars except that they did not take part in the administrative council, which will be discussed later; (2) that of the villeins, some free, attached to the glebe, some not free; (3) that of *izgoi*, formed of all the people who had lost their right to occupy their ancient social position.

Such being the structure of society, the constitutive elements of authority were three in number: the prince; the council of boyars, or *Duma;* the popular assembly, or *Veche*. [Durkheim gives different spellings at different places.] These three elements complemented and limited one another.

Primitively, the authority of the prince was unlimited. But that patriarchal unlimitedness had nothing in common with the later absolutism of the Western epoch; it had as its principal cause the absolute identity of interests between the prince and the people, who could elect the best prince and depose those with whom they were discontent. But since this spontaneous agreement, indispensable to the authority of the prince, could not be maintained everywhere and invariably, it ended by defining and delimiting more exactly the princely powers. The means used for that was first a pact concluded with the new prince. These pacts were renewed at each new accession; then, in the second half of the twelfth century, they passed into *customs.*

Otherwise, in fact, before the institution of these pacts, the authority of the prince was always limited by the two other forms of authority which we have mentioned above: the council of the boyars and the popular assembly. The first had daily meetings and the prince was obliged to consult it. That is to say, its role was considerable. As for the popular assembly, it was formed by the whole people and included the boyars. Originally, it was composed of delegates sent by the lower communes, who came to the capital to deliberate on political affairs with the citizens of that town. But from the eleventh to the twelfth centuries it included only the citizens of the capital, who later found themselves invested with important prerogatives. The rights of this assembly otherwise extended as far as those of the *Duma* and the prince. The latter could not disregard the agreement of the people, and consequently he was morally obliged to consult them every time there was an important decision to make. However, whereas the *Duma* was assembled every day by law, the popular assembly was intermittent and took place only by the convocation of the prince.

Thus we find, in the constitution of the first Russian states, three forms of political organization, one superimposed on the other and representing as many successive historical layers. First, the assembly of the people, an echo of the times when the organization was democratic, when there was not as yet any organized authority outside of that which was diffused throughout the collectivity. It is from this that both the authority of the boyars and that of the prince were separated. And because these latter were the most recent, they little by little made that which preceded them decline. However, in northwest Russia, the evolution developed in a democratic direction (p. 142), notably at Novgorod and at Plotyk; but this is an exception due to certain local peculiarities (commercial development in that region).

But as independent as were the different Russian lands, they were at all times united to one another by ties more or less strict according to the times and the circumstances. The population of all Russia was aware that it formed a whole, a moral unit. One even sees there sometimes an attempt to end the disputes of the princes, and this in the name of the common interests of the Russian land; there were even efforts with a view of establishing a political center at Kiev, "mother of the Russian lands." This fact deserves to be noted; it proves once more that the particular states are formed, by a phenomenon of differentiation, in the midst of larger societies, all of whose members feel themselves united by ties of ethnic and moral relationship. And if, after they are established and separated from one another, they feel at a later period of their development the need to be related and unified, that tendency has, in reality, its roots in the distant past. The sentiment of unity which manifests itself then is only a souvenir and an echo of an ancient sentiment which for a long time has remained invisible, without, however, ever disappearing. Pan-

Slavism has existed from the beginning of the Slav societies. One might say so much for the present Pan-Germanism, the Pan-Hellenism of the past, the unification of Italy. Here there might be the influence of a general law which deserves our attention. (*Année sociologique*, 7, 1904, pp. 447–450; trans. J. Sweeney)

H. Pirenne. *Histoire de la Belgique,* vol. 2. Brussels: Lamertin,
   1903, viii + 470 pp.
   Even though in this history and particularly in this volume, the details of events hold a considerable place, the general and impersonal evolution of institutions is not obscure, and the author, moreover, takes care to indicate, albeit quite briefly, the principal phases of their development.
   It is especially with regard to political organization that we are interested in this volume. The author has brought to our attention, first of all, the struggle launched in the fifteenth century in the Belgian cities, where two classes were present: the aristocracy and the "common man." This conflict resulted in the general defeat of the aristocracy. The urban constitutions were transformed into democratic institutions. It is very interesting to see what diverse and subtle shades they present, reflecting exactly the diversity presented in the economic conditions of various cities. Notably, the democratic movement appeared to be in inverse proportion to the development of large industry (pp. 22–69).
   At the same time, the powers enjoyed by the princes were consolidated. Each principality tended to become a true territorial sovereignty. But then another curious transformation occurred. At a time when these principalities attained their full political autonomy, they were involved in a movement to centralize everything. Against all these territorial and distinctive governments, this trend helped in sustaining a common and unitary organism which enveloped them. It was the dukes of Burgundy who achieved the unification. This centralization had the same causes and produced the same results as that which operated at the same moment in France. This was the result of the great many supervening changes in the economic conditions of the society, in the respective situation of the classes. The progressive complication of social life, the development of extensive commercial activity, the expansion of an intellectual community, and growing individualism became necessary to disintegrate the rigid groups of medieval society (p. 316). Modern egalitarianism began to manifest its first symptoms. Now the sovereign was the natural medium for this leveling process; from then on, centralization resulted in the constitution of the state of Burgundy, and as a result, in a very clearly marked tendency of political institutions toward monarchy.
   In addition, this book contains information on economic evolution in the fourteenth and fifteenth centuries. (*Année sociologique*, 7, 1904, pp. 453–454; trans. Y. Nandan)

Ferdinand Lot. *Fidèles ou vassaux? Essai sur la nature juridique du lien qui unissait les grands vassaux à la royauté depuis le milieu du IXᵉ jusqu'à la fin du XIIᵉ siècle.* Paris: Emile Bouillon, 1904, xxxiv + 286 pp.

It is known that the bond which united the vassal with his seigneur could take two forms: (1) simple homage; (2) liege homage [by which the vassal gave the promise of absolute loyalty]. The second was much stronger and tighter than the former. Simple homage involved all the seigneurs from whom a vassal had received a fief; and since it was permitted to receive fiefs from different hands, the same vassal could pay homage in equal measure to several seigneurs to whom he was bound by the same obligations. Also, when two of these seigneurs were engaged in a fight, it was impossible to know which of them their common vassal had to follow. Liege homage, on the contrary, did not allow this competition. The vassal who gave it was committed to serving his seigneur, favoring him against all others, even against other seigneurs from whom he might have received a fief. It is true that liege homage was often defined otherwise. We will not examine here these different interpretations. All that we want to retain here is that, in any case, in the opinion of everybody, a liege vassal had certain characteristics which gave origin to his obligations and to a particularly strong dependence.

The purpose of this book by Lot is to demonstrate that the great vassals of the crown—the count of Flanders, the duke of Burgundy, the duke of Aquitaine, the count of Toulouse, the count of Champagne, and the duke of Normandy—owed and paid liege homage to the king. This hypothesis is already rendered probable by the fact that except for the duke of Normandy all the great vassals were the descendants of the old Carolingian counts, dukes, and marquis; and the latter obtained their *comitatus*[207] only after having been authorized by the king and having been placed under his *mundium*.[208] Moreover, the author undertakes to establish his thesis by a minute analysis of the texts.

We cannot follow him in his demonstration of the facts; but we would like to point out the sociological interest that the author has himself indicated at the end of his work. Since the principal vassals of the crown *(grands feudataires)* became, in fact, independent of the king, one begins to wonder why they did not push their interests to the extreme end and break the relationship which attached them to royalty. Now, if they did not dare to take such a drastic action, it is because they had been for a very long time the vassals of the crown, the so-called liege men of the king; and the impression of their duty as vassals remained well marked in their minds. Even though weakened, it had too much authority to emancipate them from vassalage. The author concludes that "such a system presents to us an example of the most typical of the forces concerning psychological representation, even though now weakened and vacillating." It is this sentiment of inferiority, of subordination, which the great vassals willy-nilly experienced and which allowed the king to take advantage of the feudal system whenever the circumstances were favorable. (*Année sociologique*, 8, 1905, pp. 403–404; trans. Y. Nandan)

Joseph Hitier. *La Doctrine de l'absolutisme.* Paris: Arthur Rousseau, 1903, 228 pp.

A political system, one initiated, sets up a system of ideas on which it relies and which justifies its rationale. Then this system of ideas, in its turn, once it is carried through, reacts on the political organization to which at first it simply gave expression, and alters it. Generally it tends to exaggerate it. For the standards, the formulas, that are invented to give it a logical foundation are generally much simpler, more exclusive, than the historical causes that brought about its genesis and affected its spontaneous growth. It is this exchange of actions and reactions that Hitier has proposed to study relative to the system of government that is designated by the name of absolutism and that arrived at its peak with Louis XIV.

The author starts by searching for the characteristics of absolutism. What it essentially amounts to, he says, is the absorption of the state into the person of the prince. We gladly accept the definition, provided that by "state" is meant not only the political power but all the social forces as a whole—whatever they may be. In order for the government to be absolute, in all the force of that term, it is necessary that religion as well as the military or judicial or legislative power be made strictly subordinate to the sovereign's authority. For let a collective force of some intensity keep a certain autonomy, and it will more or less limit the governmental power, which for that very reason will cease to be absolute. This is like saying, to be sure, that absolutism is never attainable in the literal sense. For this absorption of all the social energies into the person of one man is impossible. Absolutism is only an ideal goal that the realities of history approximate more or less, but never achieve. A government is never absolute except in a relative fashion. This is what Montesquieu clearly understood, as is demonstrated in his analysis of the type of government he calls despotic.

Absolutism was of such a nature as to predetermine almost inexorably the theory by which it was justified. In order that royal power might be conceived as superior to all known powers, in order that these last might be viewed as simple emanations, it was necessary that the king's person should not derive from any earthly power. From that idea came the doctrine of divine right, which remains the only way to give absolutism an apparently logical basis in fact.

The author shows in a final section how theory thus constructed has impinged upon governmental practice; how such standards have led to the negation of the rights of the individual, of local liberties, and of rights of control that the nation exercised previously by way of parliament or the state. (*Année sociologique*, 9, 1906, pp. 353–355; trans. J. French)

NOTES AND NOTICES

John R. Commons. "A Sociological View of Sovereignty." *American Journal of Sociology*, V, nos. 1–6.

This is a completely dialectical analysis of the concept of sovereignty. The author derives it from the concept of property. The *dominium* in the abstract consists of the power to impose the will on others; when it is exercised by private individuals, it constitutes private property; when it takes the form of an attribute of certain public functions, it becomes sovereignty. But in changing the name, it takes other characteristics. What distinguishes the sovereign authority is that it is not capricious but is subject to certain rules, and its legal functions have a certain aim: to achieve morality. The last two articles are devoted to the subordinate institutions of the state: the family, the Church, and the economic institutions. (*Année sociologique*, 4, 1901, p. 333; trans. Y. Nandan)

Schupe. "Was ist der Staat?" *Jahrbuch der internationalen Vereinigung für vergleichende Rechtswissenschaft und Volkswirtschaftslehre*. Year 5, pt. 1, pp. 34–53.

This is an article of purely metaphysical character. (*Année sociologique*, 4, 1901, p. 334; trans. Y. Nandan)

Abou'l-Hassan el-Maverdi. *Traité de droit public musulman*. Translated into French and annotated according to the Arabic sources by Count Léon Ostrorog. Vol. I. Paris: Leroux, 1901, ix + 262 pp.

A jurisconsult of the tenth century, the author of this treatise is an authority on Islam. His aim is to give exposition to the Islamic conception of sovereignty. What makes this study interesting is that he shows clearly the germs of anarchy which remain at the basis of this law. Its inherent sovereign authority is conceived of as being derived from a contract between the Caliph and the people. This contract is principally formed by election. But it is in no way necessary that all legal voters be convened for the election to be valid. A few are enough; some even consider that a nomination made by only one can be valid. All of which means that it is not the number which is important, it is the principle by virtue of which the Caliph is recognized by certain signs, by certain objective qualities which define him. In essence, then, individuals capable of perceiving such qualities should proceed to an examination of his qualities, not that they should be more or less numerous since their decision is, so to say, preordained for them by the nature of things. But it is easy to understand how such an indecisive law leaves them open to factionalism. In such a case, one must add that, since Caliph's high ranking position is associated with certain personal qualities, any alteration in any of his qualities leads him to a downfall. This opens a door to controversies and conflicts. (*Année sociologique*, 5, 1902, 362–363; trans. Y. Nandan)

International and Moral Law: Laws and Customs of Different Societies

REVIEWS

Alessandro Lattes. *Il diritto consuetudinario nelle città Lombarde*
(Customary Law in Lombard Cities). Milan: Hoepli, 1899, xvi +
462 pp.

By chance, the old customary law of certain Lombard cities (Bergamo,
Brescia, Cannobio, Como, Lodi) was fixed in writing during the course of the
thirteenth century; it took its place in the statutory law, which was then
codified, but without losing its proper character. It is easily recognizable there:
The rules which, in fact, express customary prescriptions do not resemble
statutory laws, precisely because they are of a different origin *(pro con-
suetudine servatur, habet consuetudo*[209] in place of *statutum est*[210] and other
equivalent expressions). The present work is essentially an analysis of these
documents.

Customary Lombard law is not, however, very original; the Latin and German influences are very marked. Nevertheless, some very interesting
peculiarities are encountered there. Under that heading, we will notice[211] a
usage known as *vicinatico,*[212] as it was practiced at Cannobio. The *vicini* were a
certain number of privileged families, considered as the descendants of the ancient founders of the city. The whole of the *vicini* formed a strong body, a city
within a city, into which immigrants were not admitted; its members were
united by very particular ties. It was they who exercised all the legislative, executive, and judicial power; they alone had the right to possess—as inalienable
property—the real estate built within the territory of the city. They received a
share of the revenues of the commune and they enjoyed—probably along with
others—the common property (pp. 155–156). That usage casts some light on
the origins of that city. The primitive nucleus was evidently formed by a group
of families who collectively possessed the land and cultivated it; their situation
was that of the *commarcani*[213] one discovers in a great number of places in
Italy. The principle of collective responsibility is discovered even in the custom
which obliged the *vicini* to periodically aid those among them who were poor
(pp. 162–163). Related institutions are discovered in other Lombard communities (p. 163).

As for domestic organization, its characteristic trait was the intransigence
with which it understood and applied the principle of agnation. The woman
was excluded from succession as long as there were male heirs; the mother
herself was not called upon unless there was an absence of male kinsmen. It is
true that this rule was somewhat tempered by the usage that accorded the
woman the right to claim a dowry, and even sometimes a dowry in proportion
to the wealth of the parents. Exception to this rule was the landed property

belonging to the family (p. 259). Moreover, the woman was forbidden to dispose of the property that she thus received *sine notitia parentum*[214] (p. 181). The author attributes this rigor not only to domestic sentiments but to the spirit of jealousy and exclusivity that the Italian cities had in regard to one another. This explains the juridical incapacity with which women who married outside the community were saddled.

The procedure may offer some interesting facts for anyone who wishes to study the way in which execution by public authority was little by little substituted for primitive execution by private authority; for in comparing the different forms that that law took in different cities, one may uncover the principal intermediary phases through which it passed in the course of that evolution. The primitive state is still very perceivable there (pp. 117 ff.). We will mention finally a peculiar trait of feudal law: This is that the fiefs there did not have, as in France, a political or military character, but a patrimonial one (pp. 337 ff.). Thus the creditors of a vassal could very well exercise their power over the products or even the lands of the fief (p. 345). In certain cities, the fief could be alienated without the agreement of the lord (p. 344). These facts tend to show that feudalism is essentially an economic institution. (*Année sociologique*, 4, 1901, pp. 418–419; trans. J. Sweeney)

Enrico Loncao. *L'inviolabilità del domicilio nell'antico diritto germanico*. Palermo: Tip. Domenico Vena, 1901, 28 pp.

In Roman law as well as in modern law, rules protecting the inviolability of the home arise from private law; in Germanic societies they arose from public law: Violation of domestic peace was considered a violation of public peace and punished as such. From what does this difference arise? According to the author, it is probably due to the exceptionally urgent interest that still-unstable and badly organized tribal societies of Germania had in preventing internal conflicts that would make the establishment of social order impossible. Later, with the association consolidated, the inviolability of the home ceased to be of interest to the state, and this quite naturally brought about the loss of its primitive characteristics. This explanation is, to say the least, incomplete. Even if domestic peace in Germania was merely a substitute for public peace, the fact remains that the former did not yet have any existence in its own right. The home was not protected because it was sacrosanct per se; rather, it was in the interest of the state to protect it. In Rome, on the other hand, and in our day, peaceful domesticity is something special for the home and even for the individual. As a result of new opinions that have arisen, the agent acting in behalf of the right to a secure peace is no longer the same; it is no longer the state—it is the family, headed by the individual. The respect sui generis in which these last are held is what protects them—not a debt to public authority. Therefore this peace is much more complete; it defends the household against the state itself, whereas in Germania the latter's intrusion into the private dwelling place does not appear to have been subject to any well-defined rules. (*Année sociologique,* 6, 1903, pp. 413–414; trans. J. French)

G. del Vecchio. "L'evoluzione dell'ospitalità." *Rivista italiana di sociologia,* VI, nos. 2–3, pp. 234–246.

Could the article be entitled "Origins of the Private International Law?" Indeed, the author very rightly shows in the institution of hospitality the primitive form of this law such as it functions in societies of a lower order. At first the stranger is outside the law for the very reason that he is not a member of the community into which he enters. Hospitality permits his entry at least on a temporary or a partial basis; the bond that is established between the outsider and his host is very much like the one resulting from an adoption. For that very reason, the former finds himself assured of a certain protection. This protection becomes more effective when the state itself intervenes; it is careful not to allow its nationals to go unprotected; but it entrusts a particular citizen from the foreign state with this protective function. It is the institution of the πρόξενος (representatives), the first seed of our modern consulate. Later, treaties with the same purpose are contracted between the different states *(foedera hospitii);*[215] they guarantee each person mutual equality of civil rights. Law courts are formed with the special purpose of doing justice to outsiders *(the praetor peregrinus of Rome).*[216] Thus it is that little by little the gap between the legal situation of the nationals and that of the foreigners decreases.

This genesis appears plausible in its general outline. But the manner in which the primitive right of hospitality is, according to the author, probably established calls, on the contrary, for some reservations. It is pity that is inspired by an outsider—unarmed, alone, powerless—and that has inspired charitable feelings in his regard. There is something very different in the general notion that the *guest is sacred.* Such an expression attests that it is invested with a religious character. Besides, the author acknowledges, but as an afterthought, that there might well be an element of religious fear in the feelings that the stranger elicits. (*Année sociologique,* 6, 1903, p. 414; trans. J. French)

NOTES AND NOTICES

Lee Warner. *The Citizen of India.* London: Macmillan, 1897, viii + 177 pp.

This small book is informative on village organization, and especially on the cities of India, on its divisions, and on the racial composition of the population. All the information given here has an elementary character, and without excluding information of a historical nature, relates more to the present than to the past. (*Année sociologique,* 2, 1899, p. 310; trans. Y. Nandan)

Penal Law, Responsibility, and Procedure

REVIEWS

L. Gunther. *Die Idee der Wiedervergeltung in der Geschichte und Philosophie des Strafrechtes. Ein Beitrag zur universal-historischen Entwicklung desselben* (The Idea of Reprisal in the History and Philosophy of Penal Law. Contribution to the General History of the Development of This Law). Part Three, Section One. Erlangen: Blasing, 1895, 658 pp.

Although this work is dated 1895, we believe that it is useful to mention it and to indicate its general tendencies, because it must have a followup which we will have to present our readers when it will have appeared.[217]

By reprisal *(Wiedervergeltung)* the author means not only retaliation proper. If we clearly understand his thought, he means by that word all the variations and all the characteristics of punishment, which is only the reflection and automatic reproduction of the modalities and characteristics of the crime to which it is attached. Insofar as it is designed to improve the criminal or to intimidate the possible imitators, there is no reason that it should resemble either nearly or remotely the act that it represses. If one wishes that it may succeed in neutralizing the tendencies of malefactors, whether of the criminal himself or of the subjects predisposed to follow his example, it is according to the temperament of the criminal and not according to the nature of the crime that it must be fashioned. Now, very frequently it is found that it is fashioned in such a way that it is nothing but a total or partial repetition of the evil inflicted on the victim. In different degrees, all people have admitted that there is a kind of parity between the crime and the repression. It is these characteristics of punishment that Gunther attributes to the idea of reprisals—that is, the need to render evil for evil. In this regard, reprisals are not to be confused with retaliation, although retaliation may be their principal form. In effect there is no retaliation except when the penalty is the exact reproduction and essence of the crime (an eye for an eye, a tooth for a tooth). Now, it can only be a symbolic image of it; it can maintain with it certain proportions of grandeur without resembling it qualitatively; the resemblance can be reduced to an analogy, and so on and so forth.

That tendency to derive the penalty from the crime never exists in its pure state: Everywhere the penalty presents properties which arise from another origin. It never has for its sole object the satisfaction of vindicative needs; other purposes have always been assigned to it and it consequently has been understood. But that trend does not exist in the least; since it depends on causes which are special to itself, it has its own individual character and consequently it can be isolated from others and considered apart. This is what Gunther proposed to do. He has undertaken to retrace the evolution of that trend from its origins up to the present.

The first two parts of the work, one published in 1889 and the other in 1891, presented us with the development of the idea of reprisals among civilized people from antiquity and in Germanic societies up to the middle of the eighteenth century. In the third part, the first section of which will concern us, the author pursues his study up to contemporary societies. What emerges from that exposition is that the notion of penalty and reprisals tends to be effaced in the face of other conceptions, without however entirely disappearing. It still marks with its imprint many legislative dispositions. The author here reports, first of all, the prescriptions by virtue of which the promoters of violence, mortal or not, are completely or partially absolved when the incriminating act has been brought about by a previous provocation. This is in effect a late ratification of the right of reprisal, and the author confirms this interpretation by the fact that among the least advanced peoples of Europe (Montenegro, Spain), the absolution, in a similar case, is much more complete than elsewhere. The persistence of the death penalty may be likewise a survival of the ancient rule according to which blood calls for blood. The other traces of the same principle which Gunther perceives in contemporary law are the following: (1) dispositions by virtue of which the false witness or the dishonest judge are condemned to a penalty either equal or at least proportionate to that which has or could have overtaken the innocent; (2) dispositions which mete out punishment to those who assist a prisoner to escape or free him illegally, equal to the penalty that the victim himself was in the process of suffering; and finally (3) in a great number of cases, an effort by the law to act in such a way that the punishment fits the crime. Thus the crimes which are indicative of base sentiments are punished by humiliating penalties (a woman's garment thrown on cowards; the whip; the pillory); included in this category are the offenses of greed, which may be punished by fines, and so on and so forth. More generally, there is no European code which does not admit that the gravity of the punishment should be in relation to that of the crime—that is to say, that there should be a quantitative tie between the two terms.

With some justifications, this work can be blamed for the excessive ideological propensities that it manifests, and likewise for the excessive vagueness of the notions, even fundamental, which are employed. Gunther takes the idea of reprisals as clear, and nowhere does he give a precise definition, even though there is a great need for such an attempt. Is he dealing with individual reprisals or collective reprisals? Both, without a doubt. But they are very different in their causes, in their nature, and in the effect which they have had on the evolution of law. They cannot be confused under the same rubric. Furthermore, for the same reason—that is to say, because such a notion seems elementary—Gunther seems to have easily discerned in diverse repressive systems what can be imputed to this spirit of reprisals. In reality, such a distinction can be obtained only through a very complicated operation of observation and comparison. A little bit of introspection and dialectic is not enough to separate each of the factors from which a penalty results. Also, the manner in which he makes the separation is very often debatable. He considers it as self-evident that the rule of retaliation by virtue of which the penalty seems to correspond exactly to the crime has no other origin. However, by themselves, vindictive feelings are not that easily satisfied; on the contrary, they tend to exact a reparation greater than the offense. They demand death for a simple injury;[218] it is not therefore their influence alone which can explain the homogeneity of the two acts. Likewise it is very doubtful that the persistence of the death penalty is to be explained as the author would like. From the beginning, it has no resemblance with the crimes which it punishes. Why shouldn't its persistence derive from the fact that the crimes of blood make the same impression on us as the crimes against the gods made on our fathers?

On whatever grounds these criticisms should be based, it seems that punishment is in part a function of crime, and not only of the criminal, as the Italian school would like: The relationship which unites the intensity of one with the intensity of the other is the best proof of it. And since this characteristic of the penalty happens to be more or less marked in all the epochs of history, it should be believed that it is essential to it and that it cannot lose it completely without ceasing to be itself. It is this which makes the work of Gunther a useful contribution to penal sociology. The work is among other things very carefully researched and one will find in it great deal of information on penal legislation of different societies from antiquity to our own day. (*Année sociologique*, 1, 1898, pp. 347–351; trans. J. Sweeney)

J. Kohler. *Studien aus dem Strafrecht. Das Strafrecht der italienischen Statuten vom 12.–16. Jahrhundert* (Study of Penal Law. The Penal Law According to the Italian Statutes from the Twelfth to Sixteenth Century). Mannheim: Bensheimer, 1895–97, 619 pp.

This work, not yet finished, has appeared in five successive installments, of which the last appeared in 1897. Its object is to explain the development of penal law in the Italian cities from the twelfth to the sixteenth century—that is to say, from the period when the municipal law was at its peak up to the moment when the action of the jurists became preponderant. However, the study does not bear on all the towns of Italy; the author has left aside lower Italy and Sicily because the penal law was not organized under the same influences. In the north, the Lombard edicts and Roman law were the point of departure of juridical evolution; what Kohler has intended to investigate is that which has resulted from this double influence, especially since the law which has come forth from it has strongly affected modern legislation on the same subject.

The work is divided into two parts. The first part (pp. 1–317) deals with penalties and conditions of responsibility in general; the second part passes in review various crimes and offenses.

It is impossible to summarize such a book, which is above all a collection of different themes. The author has catalogued with great care the numerous codes in usage in the different towns of northern Italy; he has methodically sorted out their arrangement in a thematic order. And he has placed them in relation to corresponding prescriptions which are contained either in the edicts or in Roman law. But he is satisfied to glean these facts without trying to generalize. Perhaps this is reserved for the last part of the work, which has been announced to follow. When it appears, we will have occasion to return to it.

There is, however, one general conclusion which emerges at the present from this research. It is that the penal law of Italian towns is, from the beginning, much more moderate than the Roman law; the penalties are principally monetary, rarely corporal, and in the latter case can very often be reduced to a payment of money. Little by little things change. The repressive system becomes more merciless. The second type of punishment (corporal) is more and more frequently employed; the possibility of commutation is restricted to more and more limited conditions. Finally, between the fifteenth and sixteenth century the penal legislation becomes barbaric, which is astonishing, given what it was in the beginning.

Kohler attributes this change to a double cause: the powerful influence of the Roman law, with its indifference to individual interests; and the harshness of customs, which weakened the Italian social groups by engaging them in centuries of external war and internal fighting. But without intending to deny the importance of these two causes, it appears doubtful to us that they are sufficient to explain such a moral transformation. The teaching of jurists could never be efficacious enough to modify so profoundly the system of penal law; for the penal law expresses the state of the public conscience in that which it is the most fundamental; and the juridic reasoning would not thus change the moral sentiments of the people. It acts only on the most refined and therefore most superficial parts of the national mind. As for wars, even civil, it has not been proven that they would have the effects on the penal law that are attributed to them. The law of the Germans seems to have been relatively moderate even though the state of war was chronic among them.

The fact pointed out by Kohler seems to us to have a more general significance. Steinmetz, in a book about which we will have occasion to speak,[219] has well established that in very primitive societies the crimes committed by the nationals themselves, and not by the foreigners, are treated with relative indulgence. The group does not always intervene, or only intervenes with moderation. The collective discipline is somewhat paternalistic. Du Boys has equally remarked that our penal law was relatively moderate during the first centuries of our history; it became intemperate only at a later date. Wouldn't the observation of Kohler simply confirm the preceding and wouldn't it be explained in the same way? In order for the law to be rigorous, it is necessary, it seems, for society to have reached a certain degree of concentration[220] and organization, so that the governmental organ might be constituted. The unorganized state, the democratic leveling which characterizes either the inferior peoples or even those more advanced societies at the beginning of their evolution, is reconciled, not without difficulty, with an excessively merciless repression. That is how the reduction in penalties which one notices today in all the great European nations has occurred; it can be equally observed in the epoch when they were only in the process of forming themselves.

Beyond this general conclusion, one will find in this book a number of instructive facts. In a large number of towns, there existed associations formed by free contracts and designed either to pursue the *vendetta* for the sake of the associates who found themselves injured or to pay the price of settlement, if on the contrary they were open to a legitimate vengeance; this is an example, added to many others, of the spontaneity with which social groups are formed when needed to substitute for the family, when the latter is obliged to forsake certain functions which it filled previously (p. 21). One still more curious peculiarity is the strange disposition disclosed in many statutes by virtue of which, when a crime was committed by many perpetrators, the principal penalty struck only a certain number of the guilty persons; the others were officially considered as simple accomplices and were punished less severely (p. 255). Sometimes, only one was punished. Not less remarkable is the very general principle, according to which, in the determination of monetary penalties, the situation of the condemned had to be taken into consideration (p. 285). The fine was much greater for the rich than for the poor. For the same reason, the penalties were more severe, often double, for the man than for the woman, for the *miles* or the *equester*[221] than for the *popularis*,[222] etcetera. We are only citing these facts as examples and because they seem to us of interest, especially to sociologists. (*Année sociologique*, 1, 1898, pp. 351–353; trans. J. Sweeney)

J. Kohler. *Studien aus dem Strafrecht. Das Strafrecht der italienischen Statuten vom 12.–16. Jahrhundert* (Penal Law According to the Italian Statutes from the Twelfth to the Sixteenth Century), pt. 6. Mannheim: Bensheimer.

This is the conclusion of the studies on penal law which we began to analyze in the first volume of *L'Année sociologique*.[223] The work has remained, up to the end, a collection of details without the author having attempted to disengage general characteristics from that repressive system. This last part[224] is devoted to crimes against the public peace and against the state, and to minor offenses. It finishes with some discussions which bear on points of detail. The crimes against peace and public order hold a considerable place in all these laws. The reason for this is that the turbulent societies of the Middle Ages were frequently troubled in this manner. The penalties brought against these infractions do not have, however, the relative mildness which characterized those about which the author spoke in the preceding works; these crimes result in the death penalty much more often and that severity appears much sooner than for other crimes. This is, without a doubt, because the evils produced by these disorders have led the societies in question to react much more energetically against them. The information that we are given about the law for minor offenses shows that the laws which safeguard health and public security have already reached a remarkable development. One notices in many cities the existence of sumptuary laws (p. 702).

Among the annexed essays, there is a very interesting study to be found concerning the way in which the abstract notions dealt with by jurists are formed very progressively. It deals with the notion of crimes of passion as opposed to premeditated crimes. As a starting point, the legal experts are fully aware of a group of concrete cases in which the motive plays a particularly visible role and in which the crime naturally calls for an excuse (the murder of an adulterous wife). It is only very slowly that the idea of fault *(culpa)* and the idea of rash impulsion are disengaged and distinguished from the general idea of premeditation (see pp. 704–728). (*Année sociologique*, 2, 1899, pp. 365–366; trans. J. Sweeney)

P. Huvelin. *Les Tablettes magiques et le droit romain* (The Magic Tablets and the Roman Law). From *Annales internationales d'histoire*. Macon: Protat Frères, 66 pp.

This very interesting work shows, concerning a particular case, the close ties which unify law and religion. It is a question of Roman obligations: the tie which it implies was, according to the author, of a religious nature, before becoming purely juridical, and in these general terms this proposition can hardly be doubted. Originally, says the author, it was created by special rituals called *devotiones* (consecrations).[225] *Devotio* has for effect the binding of an individual so as to put him in dependence on a particular religious force by means of particular formulas or ceremonies. A person who has been "devoted" no longer belongs to himself: he belongs to the divinity, whose actions he cannot escape. If the *devotio,* instead of being definitive, is simply employed in a conditional manner, as a possible sanction in case a certain act is not performed, an obligation in the proper sense of the word results for the *devotus* (person consecrated). If he does not do what he should do, what he has engaged himself to do, then the sanction applies; he is *damnatus* (condemned), and it is the fear of this inevitable result which constitutes the force of the engagement he has contracted, which produces the *nexum* (binding) by which wills are bound. If civil sanctions replace these religious sanctions, then a purely juridical obligation is constituted.

As for the reasons for which the divinity thus intervenes in relationships which are established between men, the author believes he has found them in the theory of Nemesis. There is a law of division, which is the law itself of fatality and by virtue of which "each being, when it is born, receives his lot, which is unchangeable in the sense that the elements composing it constitute a fixed sum" (p. 7). As a consequence, if one of the elements of the relationship varies, the others must vary at the same time. Thus, whoever has diminished the lot of another by a licit or illicit act must compensate for this diminution with an equivalent compensation. The Nemesis of the Greeks, the *numina* (divinities) of the Latins, are charged with maintaining the equilibrium "of the positive and negative elements in human existences"; and the rituals of *devotio* are precisely the means of setting these supernatural powers in motion, of obliging them to fulfill their functions when it happens that they do not fulfill them spontaneously.

But this theory, which is very intellectual, seems to us to express the exterior aspect of the mechanism rather than to explain its basis. It is assumed that there is a fixed order, willed by the gods, and that no variation can be introduced which is not counterbalanced by compensating variations in the opposite direction. But what constitutes a sufficient compensation? There is obviously no more in the past than today, no criterion which permits us to tell when two acts are equivalent, for the very simple reason that in these matters an objective equivalence is impossible. If, then, a promised act is to be performed, this is not because it is equal to another, but because it has been promised or at least because it has been promised in a certain way. In fact, we know very well that for centuries contracts have bound the parties even when they were the products of violence or deception, even when they were manifestly leonine,[226] and in consequence disturbed the order established by the gods. The magico-religious power which constitutes the constraining force of an obligation should therefore be sought, we believe, not in that abstract and philosophical conception of Nemesis, but in the forms themselves which it is held to assume in order to have the power of binding. It is the analysis of religious formalism, taken in itself, which we believe will furnish the explication which is sought.

One will find in this opuscule a number of interesting views, notably on the religious nature of *sponsio* (solemn engagement) and of *damnatio* (condemnation) (pp. 42 ff.); on the meaning of the word *nomen* (name) (p. 28); and on the relationships between *lex* (law) and magical formulas (p. 19, note 1). This last idea, although hypothetical, is particularly interesting. (*Année sociologique*, 6, 1903, pp. 388–390; trans. K. Woody)

P. Usteri. *Ächtung und Verbannung im griechischen Recht* (Proscription and Banishment in Greek Law). Berlin: Weidmann, 1903, viii + 172 pp.

This serious study is a collection of epigraphic and literary texts minutely commented; the results obtained are indicated with excessive brevity. They essentially shed light on the true difference between proscription (ἀτιμία) and exile (ἀειφυγία). It is known today that ατιμια is not, in principle, a simple *capitis deminutio*.[227] But the proscribed person was an outlaw such as was recognized by all the primitive societies (cf. Glotz, *La Solidarité de la famille dans le droit criminel en Grèce*, pp. 473 ff., especially p. 475, n. 1. Glotz's work[228] may be compared with that of J. J. Thonissen, *Droit pénal de la*

République Athénienne, 1875, p. 107). Usteri has sought to unite all the texts in which the ατιμια is pronounced by the law or is inflicted by the judgment of condemnation; these texts confirm a new interpretation of the word anyhow. The author observes that proscription was to be at all times an exceptional punishment (however, the proof that he gives of it is very weak; see p. 57). In Athens until the last third of the fifth century it struck the posterity of the condemned at the same time it struck the condemned himself. Afterward it struck only the guilty person (cf. Glotz, pp. 480–485). In addition, it always led to the confiscation of property. We can only point up the study of the synonyms of the word ατιμος (one deprived of civil rights), in its primitive sense. In the most recent law, ατιμος is not outside the law, but only *capite deminutus.*[229] He [the guilty person] is deprived of the right of citizenship but it is not true that he represents only a person and no longer enjoys the protection of the law. For example, though he cannot enter into a private action against someone, a capable citizen can render him justice by bringing a public action, if at least the offense of which he has been a victim allows it. This well-studied catalogue of facts advantageously supplements the work of Glotz, who does not seem to have knowledge of the work by Usteri.

The second part of Usteri's work is totally dedicated to the study of texts concerning the different forms of banishment; properly speaking, Usteri is concerned with the friendly or hostile attitude of foreign states toward the politically exiled, and the amnesty and return of the exiled to their country. (*Année sociologique,* 8, 1905, p. 464; trans. Y. Nandan)

Gustave Glotz. *La Solidarité de la famille dans le droit criminel en Grèce.* Paris: Fontemoing, 1904, xx + 621 pp.

The aim of this important work is to show how, in Greece, individual responsibility has little by little grown out of collective responsibility. The long evolution in the course of which this great transformation in moral and legal ideas was brought about includes three principal phases.

At the outset, the γένος (clan) incorporates preeminent social unity; it enjoys a broad autonomy, and society in its entirety is simply a confederation of γένη. To tell the truth, the author seems to have a somewhat vague notion of the nature of the γένος, and one that is not entirely exempt from contradictions. Sometimes he qualifies this organization as patriarchal and characterizes it in terms of the sovereign authority of the family father; from this point of view he seems essentially monarchical (see pp. 4, 36, 95, etcetera). Sometimes, on the other hand, he shows us how much the rights of the chief are limited by those of the γένος. It is the γένος who judges, who decides on the terms, and its chief seems very much to be only a *primus inter pares* (p. 37). This indecision is not unknown to cast some shadow on certain parts of the picture the author traces for us of the prior growth of this family group. But, in short, if Glotz does not make a firm choice, it is nevertheless quite apparent that he leans towards the second [notion of the γένος as democratic]. He feels keenly the anonymous, collective, undivided impact of the γένος, and we do indeed believe that in it lies the distinctive feature of these great domestic societies, which, generally speaking, are too vast to be organized by monarchical methods. Paternal authority appears only when the γένος, decomposing, frees the οἰκία (family in a dwelling house), in the management of which the father is the official in charge. Glotz has simply remained too faithful to the notion that Fustel de Coulanges had of the *gens*—one that it is necessary to revise.

Under these circumstances, what does penal justice entail?

The crime may be committed against the γένος of which the guilty one is a member, and in that case he is judged and suppressed without appeal by the γένος itself, whose autonomy is impervious to all outside jurisdiction. The most serious penalty is, in this case, declaring him an outlaw—expulsion which the author thinks it possible to identify with the ἀποκύρυξις (legal banishment) of a later law.

Or else, the crime is committed against an outside γένος, and it is then the family responsibility to become involved. Clearly, there are crimes of a sort for which the family can be held collectively responsible and which Glotz does not mention: they are crimes committed against the society formed by the confederation of the γένη, against the tribe, or even against that grouping of tribes which became the city-state. And yet, there is no doubt that there was very early a community life in all the associated γένη over and above the moral and religious life of each γένος. Surely, then, there were crimes against community morals or public religion, and it would have been interesting to know how the responsibility that was their concern was determined. Through a regrettable curtailment of his subject, Glotz has seen fit to touch on this issue only in his book's final section—that is to say, in regard to the third of the historical periods he studies. In the first two, he deals with family responsibility only in cases related to the crimes committed by one family against another.

In that case, suppression and at the same time atonement are shaped by vengeful bloodshed. Revenge is a duty for the family of the one wronged. It is a way of honoring the dead. One must avenge the victim in order to appease or forestall his wrath—possibly satisfactory as an explanation when the crime is homicide, but not when the reprisals are determined by a wrong done or by an aggressive act involving property. But whatever the case may be in its original form, the vendetta brings into play family solidarity on two fronts, for it is exercised by the entire γένος of the offended against the entire γένος of the offender. In any case, the author acknowledges that already by the time of Homer revenge no longer emanates from the group as a whole, in a cohesive and evenly shared manner; from then on, some relatives bear a more special burden of responsibility than others. To begin with, it is this combination of next-of-kin that forms the οἶκος (household); then the more distant collateral relatives—the relatives of maternal lineage and those united by marriage. Such a place set aside for the uterine kinfolk and for the kinfolk by marriage (that is to say, for the wife's kin) deserves, we believe, to be noted (p. 80). We tend to see here a trace of the maternal family that has left important vestiges in Greek law and customs. Finally, over and above the immediate relatives and those united by marriage, there appear on the scene as champions of the victim those who are called ἐται in the Homeric epic. The ἔται are certainly not blood relatives so far as is known (p. 85); the author believes that the word designates the phratry. But he is led to believe this hypothesis only because of his very debatable notion of the γένος. He conceives of the γένος (clan), we have seen, as a sort of extended patriarchal family, consisting of blood relations only; but in fact an Athenian was supposed to have many συγγενεῖς (kinsmen) with whom he was united by no well-defined blood ties. For it is far from true that in these great family groups everybody was related by blood. Would not such as these come under the designation ἔται?

But from the time of Homer, if revenge was a right and even a duty, it could be satisfied beforehand. Ever since then, the system of compromise was in force, and two of the most interesting chapters in the book are those in which Glotz shows us how it worked in Greece (chapters 4 and 5 in book 1).

The act whereby the victim's family reconconciled itself with the guilty family was called αἴδεσις, and αἰδέσθαι (to be reconciled) is the corresponding verb. These words are obviously akin to αἰδώς. Now, αἰδώς is the feeling of respect felt by every healthy conscience for what venerable tradition, the θέμις (Themis, a goddess of law and order, here refers to tradition), prescribes. It is then a manifestly religious feeling, analogous to the one that every holy object inspires. And in fact everything that inspires the αἰδώς is termed αἴδοις, an expression which, in a far-distant or recent era—we are leaving the issue unsettled—was applied to the divinity. This significance of the αἰδως appears clearly to demonstrate the fact that the αιδεσις was rooted in what must have been religious ideas. We are surprised that Glotz, who makes those comparisons himself, does not draw the conclusions they seem nevertheless to imply and that another fact he reports in a similar manner serves to confirm. The fact is that the supplicant is αιδοιος. He has duties to perform on his account and those duties are born of predetermined rites. For the act of supplication to be effective, for it to produce the αιδεσις, it is necessary for it to be performed with the help of time-honored gestures; "one would think they were rites which have passed down from the most distant centuries ever since the age of Homer" (p. 100). It is therefore manifest that the αιδεσις amounts to what is essentially a religious ceremony.

But it is coupled with a transaction: It is a ποινη, that is to say a compromise. The arrangement has a threefold aim: (1) It is a material recompense for the damage done; (2) it is moral atonement for the outrage; (3) it is ransom for the culprit's life. This transaction was not meant to make the family's consent to it obligatory; as a rule, the right of refusal was authorized. But very early, prevailing public opinion exerted pressure upon the victim's relatives to come to terms, and even to arrange a set rate to be paid (p. 131). But the consent, in order to be effective, was to be unanimous. It was necessary that the group as a whole agree on the terms. It remains to be seen what was the nature of this group whose unanimity was required. According to the author, it was apparently the γένος. It is possible that this was the case in pre-Homeric times. But since in the *Iliad* and the *Odyssey* we find that not all the relatives were summoned, on the same basis and to the same extent, to carry out the vendetta, it is also possible that they were not equally entitled to decide on the terms.

The religious character of this procedure was particularly evident in the final ceremony which constituted its essential element, so much so that in Athens it was sometimes called the αιδεσις itself. This final act was the one by means of which the two adversaries were reconciled, became friends (φίλοι) or resumed friendship. The author incorporates most interesting pages about the nature of the φιλότης (friendship). He shows that it is not merely a thrill of tenderness, of effusive intimacy, but it implies between the two individuals it brings together truly legal and moral ties (p. 140).

Now, these last were contracted by ritualistic means: oaths, sacrifices, communal banquets, etcetera. We do not know why the author believes to have found the prototype of these ceremonies in those that took place at the moment when two city-states, former enemies, made peace. There is nothing to warrant thinking that the φιλότης was at first an international insitution which might later be applied, by extension, to the relations of one family with another. The φιλότης seems to us to be clearly nothing other than the name given to that combination of behavioral relationships that is commonly designated by the expression—more or less felicitous—artificial kinship; and Glotz himself points out all the analogies between φιλότης and family relations (pp. 138, 139, 162).

Such is the original state of affairs. The second period is characterized by the continuous efforts made by the city-state to refrain from defining homicide as a private crime, in order to place it under the jurisdiction of the state. This alteration was apparently the byproduct of a twofold movement—religious and philosophical, on the one hand, and legal and political on the other.

With the progressive development of ideas, apparently at this moment it dawned on the Greeks for the first time that homicide amounted to a religious and moral blemish. Formulated in such a way, the idea is truly very debatable. Already in the Homeric poems it is recorded that blood spilled amounts to a stain that denies the murderer access to the altars. Glotz anticipates this in his reply (p. 229, nn. 1, 2, 3) that the purity which is exacted in this way is entirely superficial and material. It is seemingly a question of simple cleanliness, in the secular sense of the word. But this is to forget that for a very long time religious impurity and physical impurity have been inextricably mingled. One is merely an aspect of the other. We find it hard to believe that there has been a moment when the bloodstain has not been the object of magico-religious beliefs, has not been considered as a source of mysterious, more or less dreadful emanations. The truth is that this primitive notion has little by little heightened and broadened. What was at first only a blemish in regard to vague magical beliefs has assumed this very character for the gods the public worships. Accordingly, the religion of the state, and no longer that of the family, has become the avenger of voluntary manslaughter.

As for the series of legal reforms whereby homicide would have been gradually withdrawn from prosecution by the family, it is hard to follow the author step by step as he charts it for us. It seems clear, moreover, that speculation plays a major role in this very ingeniously deduced reconstitution. To cite only two examples, according to Glotz, two factors would have opened the way to social jurisdiction in the case of voluntary manslaughter: trial by combat and the conspiratorial plotting of the relatives. Now, as for trial by combat, conceived and practiced as a usual way to proceed, Glotz himself acknowledges that only very rare traces of it are to be found in Greece (p. 285). As for conspiratorial plotting, the whole line of reasoning is mainly based on a text of Aristotle, who simply says that at Kymē in Elis, if the accuser produced a certain number of witnesses ($\pi\lambda\tilde{\eta}\theta\acute{o}\varsigma\ \tau\iota\ \mu\alpha\rho\tau\acute{\upsilon}\rho\omega\nu$) the accused was declared guilty. Those witnesses, according to the author, would be conspirators; but the hypothesis is arbitrary.*

But there is a factor which certainly played a considerable role in this whole evolution—Solon's legislation. What was basic for family solidarity in the assumption of responsibility for crime is the close and solid sense of unity of the $\gamma\acute{\epsilon}\nu o\varsigma$. Now, according to our author, Solon's entire work would have amounted to weakening the $\gamma\acute{\epsilon}\nu\eta$ in their outward behavior and their inner attributes. He apparently tried hard to disrupt their association in order to suppress all intermediaries between the citizens and the state. All the acts that are traditionally associated with Solon are presented to us as so many measures with that end in view. On this point again, we fear that the author's systematic turn of mind has led him astray. It is by no means certain that the principle which allowed marriage between blood-related brothers and sisters (p. 334), that the regulation of the *epiclerat*[230] (p. 336), that the legislation relative to the $\nu\acute{o}\theta o\iota$ (p. 340), that the limitation on dowries (p. 330), have above all been measures designed to divide and to disperse the collective property of the $\gamma\acute{\epsilon}\nu\eta$; even on certain points this interpretation is hard to accept. What is true is that in a general manner Solon's reforms interpreted and hallowed certain individualistic aspirations which members of Athenian society were working for at the time (pp. 350–365). Now, the progressive thrust of individualism has necessarily resulted in the setback of domestic collectivism, and consequently of family solidarity. Out of this factor comes those great reforms going back to that era. Those reforms were aimed chiefly at abolishing the passive

---

* Glotz was taken in by this interpretation through an error in translation that has already been pointed out to him. Aristotle's text begins thus: Αν $\pi\lambda\tilde{\eta}\theta\acute{o}\varsigma\ \tau\iota\ \pi\alpha\rho\acute{a}\sigma\chi\eta\tau\alpha\iota\ \mu\alpha\rho\tau\acute{\upsilon}\rho\omega\nu\ \acute{o}\ \delta\iota\acute{\omega}\chi\omega\nu$ $\tau\grave{o}\nu\ \phi\acute{o}\nu o\nu\ \tau\tilde{\omega}\nu\ \alpha\acute{\upsilon}\rho o\nu\ \sigma\upsilon\gamma\gamma\epsilon\nu\tilde{\omega}\nu$. The author associates these last three words with $\mu\alpha\rho\tau\acute{\upsilon}\rho\omega\nu$ and translates: "if the accuser produces a certain number of witnesses taken from his $\gamma\acute{\epsilon}\nu o\varsigma$." Now, actually $\tau\tilde{\omega}\nu\ \alpha\acute{\upsilon}\tau o\tilde{\upsilon}\ \sigma o\gamma\gamma\epsilon\nu\tilde{\omega}\nu$ refers to $\tau\grave{o}\nu\ \phi\acute{o}\nu o\nu$ and must be translated: "if someone prosecuting a case of murder of a member of his $\gamma\acute{\epsilon}\nu o\varsigma$ produces a given number of witnesses."

solidarity of the family and increasing the role of the state in the settlement of transactions. Not only was the rate for making adjustments fixed, but the state began to impose a fine for crimes which gave rise to such matters (pp. 383 ff.). But group solidarity stayed entirely intact. Only the victim's relatives were charged with carrying out the suppression of the criminal act; the right to appear as the accuser was not indiscriminately granted to any citizen whatsoever.

Such were the results of the second period, the one which closes with Cleisthenes' reform—that is to say, the suppression of the old politico-family-type organization in Greece. Accordingly we have reached the third and last phase, the classic era.

Here an abrupt change arises in the plan of the work. Up until now, the author has spoken of family responsibility only in matters involving private crimes; in this last part of the book, collective responsibility in matters involving public crimes—that is to say, attacks against the state or religion—becomes the main object of research. One chapter only (2, pp. 425–443) is devoted to those responsible in cases of homicide. Indeed, the fact is that from then on there was no longer anything very interesting to say about this subject; the situation remained, throughout all the rest of Greek history, just about as we found it at the end of the preceding period—without notable progress. On the other hand, it is at this moment that responsibility involving cases of public crimes seems to have evolved in a most marked fashion. And doubtless this is the reason for the fact that from this period on such a subject has further caught the author's attention.

Now, out of the very interesting picture of this evolution that the author traces for us, a conclusion seems to us to emerge which alters somewhat the point of view of Greek law and history that he portrays. In fact, it is evident that the idea of individual responsibility has had a much harder time penetrating this part of penal law than the first. Some good minds estimate that collective penalties have never disappeared from Athenian law, wherever crimes against the state are concerned. Glotz does not accept this opinion and provides a very ingenious criticism of it. He is, however, obliged to recognize that the disappearance in question was belated—it was never even complete, since the penalty of confiscation has always survived. Furthermore, the principle of collective responsibility was "unreservedly maintained in all of Greece by religious law" (p. 556). The belief in inherited responsibility always remained very strong, and a trace of it may be discovered even in the doctrines of the philosophers (pp. 549–597).

If this is how it is, is it not somewhat exaggerated for us to imagine Athenian law as impregnated with a kind of precocious individualism, as a result of some sort of state amnesty? Belief in inherited responsibility is the very negation of individualism. Doubtless the state emancipated the individual from the γένος that first absorbed him, and this emancipation was certainly not won without a price. But the individual, freed from the family group, remained absorbed within the city-state. The regression of family responsibility in Athens was clearly due to the parallel regression of a collective tyranny; but once the omnipotence of the family was undermined, that of the political group remained intact. And besides, how easy it would be to show that the impact itself of the family always remained much more absorbing, much less indulgent towards the upsurge of the individualist movement in Athens than in Rome! And that is the reason for the fact that whatever progress it made in the direction of individualism, Athenian law never managed to free itself entirely of its origins.

But whatever may be the objections this work appears to raise, it is certain that through the issues it deals with, the inquiries assembled in it, and the solutions which are proposed, it offers the sociologists items of very great interest. It is a contribution of great importance, not only to the history of Greek law but to a comparative knowledge of the law. (*Année sociologique*, 8, 1905, pp. 465–472; trans. J. French)

R. Dareste. "Les Anciennes coutumes albanaises." *Nouvelle Revue historique de droit français et étranger*, 1903, pp. 477–496.

The customs of northern Albania have already been studied a long time ago, by Hecquart in his book *Histoire et description de la haute Albanie ou Guégarie*. This work has since been completed and clarified thanks to an on-the-spot investigation made by two parish priests of the country's Catholic party. The results of this investigation, first published in Albanian, have been translated into German, and it is a translation of that translation that Dareste gives us here.

The common-law provisions which have thus been reported to us are almost all related to criminal law, and especially to blood vendettas. Although severely regulated, the right to take revenge is very widespread. The murderer's house is torn down and burned; his movable possessions are confiscated (with the exception of weapons); he must withdraw with his whole family as soon as possible from the territory of his tribe; his land becomes the property of the person injured. For one person killed, six men from the family of the guilty one owe vengeance, and the avenger may kill each of the people included in this number. We assume that this right to kill exists only if the murderer has not been expatriated; but the texts that are turned over to us are not specific on this point. The right of vengeance may, moreover, be bought off; the ceremony which consecrates the appeasement presents some rather curious details (p. 491).

But what is particularly interesting is the way in which the duty to be hospitable impinges on the right to take revenge. In the first place the murder of a man who has placed himself under the protection of a third party and is therefore called *guest and friend* must be avenged in a more pitiless fashion than a relative. When a man who already has a debt of blood crosses a region where he is exposed to being killed by the avenger, he has himself received as *guest and friend* by a person who takes him into his house or escorts him on his way. If, under such circumstances, he is killed on the way by the legitimate avenger, the former vengeance is not wiped out, as it would be in any other case; it continues to exist, and what is more, it gives rise to a new one; for the family of the one who serves as escort avenges the killed *guest and friend* just as it would avenge one of its own members (p. 484). Even, in one of the two tribes under observation, it is not only the protégé actually escorted who is thus avenged, it is also he who, climbing a height, calls in a loud voice for another man to come to his aid. It is not necessary that this call be heard by the family to whom it was directed; it is enough if anyone heard it (p. 492). (*Année sociologique*, 8, 1905, pp. 474–475; trans. J. French)

R. Löning. *Geschichte der strafrechtlichen Zurechnungslehre* (History
   of the Theory of Penal Imputation). Vol. I, *Die Zurechnungslehre
   des Aristoteles*. Jena: Fischer, 1903, xx + 350 pp.

Löning undertakes to clarify the concepts of responsibility and imputability by a study of their doctrinal genesis; it is not with the history of penal institutions that he deals, but with that of philosophical ideas which inspire jurists more or less consciously. It is from Pufendorf that all the essential material of modern theories of penal imputability come directly;[231] and Aristotle is the most remote, even though the most important, of the sources of this doctrine. In this first volume Löning thus exposes the Aristotelian theory on what we today call imputability; the second volume will have for its object post-Aristotelian and scholastic theories; the third, Pufendorf and natural law.[232]

The author believed it necessary to devote a third of his book (chapters 1–4) to the analysis of the psychological and moral system of which the doctrine of imputability is only an element, and to give a considerable place to the discussion of the contemporary interpretations of $\phi\rho\acute{o}\nu\eta\sigma\iota\varsigma$ (practical wisdom). Whatever may be the philosophical interest of this study, we will only point it out here; we will restrict ourselves to mentioning also chapter 16, which deals with the responsibility of virtue and vice, and the appendices (pp. 333–357) on the foundation and the end of punishment and on the attempts against persons committed with the consent of the victim.

Chapters 7–19 systematically group all the ideas of Aristotle on penal responsibility. Their interest is twofold: On the one hand Löning clarifies, with a great deal of force and in a manner which seems to us to be completely satisfactory, the traditional interpretation which makes Aristotle a partisan of free will; on the other hand he discloses in him all the essential material of what modern penal law teaches on the subject of responsibility and the circumstances which exclude it. What is most striking is to see that Aristotle formulates the common principles to which, in fact, if not in theory, the codes and the jurists still refer to today; it seems that all the controversies relative to free will may have arisen merely to complicate and obscure the theory, without succeeding in modifying it, and that the ideas by which we are actually guided in our judiciary practice are reduced, if one drops all that which is related to the question of free will, to those elaborated by Aristotle. We are awaiting with impatience the conclusion of the work which will permit us to verify that opinion.

In order that the "judgment of value" provoked by an action may be applied to the agent, Aristotle demands only two conditions: it is necessary that the act be voluntary (ἑχούσιος) and accomplished with knowledge of the cause (εἰδώς)—that is to say, by an agent who knows what he is doing and is able to judge the moral value of his act. There is nothing which would allow the word *free,* in its modern sense, to be a translation of the terms which Aristotle uses to signify *voluntary;* and without this we can not count Aristotle among the determinists, since the problem of freedom was not yet posed for him. It is clear that his analysis of the will is conducive to a clearly deterministic interpretation. Undoubtedly the voluntary act is contingent (ἐνδεχέται ἄλλως ἔχειν), that is to say, it does not belong to the class of necessary things, immutable by virtue of teleological laws of nature, as does for example the movement of the stars, but to the class of things which may be or may not be, not because they may be without causes but because their very causes are themselves changing and perishable. The voluntary act is that which is according to the desire of the agent, which has its cause in us (ἐφ᾽ἡμῖν ἀρχὴ ἐν ἡμῖν). Do we not recognize here the criteria of responsibility of which in fact we make use, and the conception of a determinism sui generis on which, without admitting it, the theoreticians base their arguments rather than on the indeterminist doctrine which they pretend to respect?

The conditions of responsibility are not realized: (1) when the act is a purely corporeal phenomenon in which consciousness, i.e., that which is properly human, takes no part; (2) in case of physical constraint; or (3) a psychic [state of compulsion]; (4) when the agent knows neither the consequences of his action nor of its illegal character. Nevertheless, Aristotle did not wish to put himself in complete opposition to the positive law which punishes certain actions which are, objectively considered, infractions, even though the criminal intention was lacking in the agent. To legitimate that concession, he developed the concept of *negligence,* with the help of which he could attribute to the will an initial fault of which the imputed act was the consequence, and thus he retained, at least in appearance in that particular case, the general rule of responsibility. The passage in which Löning demonstrates the weakness of that theory of negligence and the influence it still exercises on contemporary doctrine (pp. 220–235) is one of the most interesting in the book.

Finally he adds the elements of the doctrine of Aristotle on the irresponsibility of animals, children, imbeciles, and fools, and on the imputation of misdemeanors by omission, as well as curious observations on aggravating and attenuating circumstances (pp. 327–332). (*Année sociologique*, 8, 1905, pp. 477–479; trans. J. Sweeney)

Theodor Mommsen. *Zum ältesten Strafrecht der Kulturvölker. Fragen zur Rechtsvergleichung gestellt von Theodor Mommsen, beantwortet von H. Brunner, B. Freudenthal, J. Goldziher, etc.* Leipzig: Duncker und Humblot, 1905, ix + 112 pp.

In his great work on Roman penal law, Mommsen had foresworn any comparison between Roman institutions and the institutions of other peoples. Not that he did not recognize the usefulness of the comparative method, but because of his very special expertise as a historian of Roman law he felt he was insufficiently competent[233] to speak about the law of other societies. However, once his book was completed, he had the idea of asking each of a certain number of specialists prearranged questions about penal law, his particular concern—the answers to which could then provide useful comparisons.

The questions asked concerned the following:

(1) Are crimes in their original phase exposed to two kinds of reprisals and two only: the anger of the gods and the vengeance of mankind?

(2) Do there exist in the primal phase well-defined notions and technical expressions that correspond to these three aspects of penal law: crime, punishment, repression from the bench? In Rome, there is indeed from the start the notion of a law and a court of law, but not of penal law and a criminal court.

(3) In what form does one present, when it appears, the contrast between voluntary crime and involuntary crime?

(4) Is the repression of public crimes directed against the material or moral interests of the state regarded as an expiation and not as a simple measure of defense?

(5) The way in which the state has intervened in the repression of private crimes in order to prevent individuals from coming to their own defense.

(6) A list of the main crimes.

(7) Various questions on the primitive forms of procedure (use of violent procedures like torture; magico-religious procedures; the role of the magistrate and of judicial arbitrators, respectively).

(8) A list of penalties.

The authority of the scholars who have answered this questionnaire guarantees the value and interest of the replies; but there can be no question of summing them up here. Furthermore, the questionnaire was not drafted so that a general impression might emerge from the answers submitted. To make it possible for these kinds of consultations to be productive, it is necessary that certain fundamental ideas be defined, even on a temporary basis; that certain categories be established under which the facts may emerge and fall into place; that the issues may be grouped in a logical manner, etcetera. The preceding questionnaire appears to us to satisfy these conditions only very imperfectly.

Public crimes and private crimes, whose legal situation and sociological significance are so different, are so very often compared, as well as the corresponding means of repression. Considerable problems are brushed aside, like the one concerning the connections between religious criminality and civil criminality. A questionnaire of this type would perhaps have gained by not being asked by a specialist, even a specialist of the high caliber of Mommsen. It is necessary to have had prior training in the comparative method in order to know what questions it can contribute to make things clear. (*Année sociologique*, 9, 1906, pp. 424–426; trans. J. French)

Property Law

REVIEWS

Guillaume des Marez. *Etude sur la propriété foncière dans les villes du Moyen Age.* Paris: Gand, 1898, 193 pp.

It has often been maintained that free property which is found existing in towns in the twelfth and thirteenth centuries is a form derived from the freehold of the Frankish period. The *cives*[234] and the *milites*[235] of the towns are descendants of the ancient freeholders. But this theory is contrary to the facts. The rural Frankish freehold foundered almost everywhere very early; it did not survive the end of the Carolingian period. It is therefore completely implausible that it could have maintained itself beneath the walls of a monastery or an episcopal residence—that is to say, in places where towns came into being. There, more than elsewhere, the freedom of the land disappeared rapidly (p. 28). Free urban title to property must, then, have another source. Such is the thesis of the work.

Urban title to property is a product of the very causes that have given rise to town life and have given it its precise characteristics. The source of Flemish as well as German towns can be traced back to the settlement of a group of *mercatores*[236] in a geographically favorable place (pp. 7–13). This place was sometimes part of a duty-free tract or of a great domain; sometimes it was set up directly by a justiciary seigneur, count, or viscount. The merchants who thus came to establish themselves in these propitious spots for trade were free at the time of their arrival there, and they needed freedom of movement in order to be able to put their professional abilities to good use. They then insisted and were obliged to insist that no bond tie them down to a piece of land and to a master. Accordingly, they appeared "in the social framework like a new element, sui generis, not fitting into any of the existing social classes in the large tract of land" (p. 16). As a result, the law of the domain, with its narrow obligations that kept man in bondage to the soil, could not suit their purpose. This very special legal situation was naturally mirrored in the law of property rights. And indeed, from the start, the law of urban title to property presented important innovations. The merchants who came in this way to settle on the land of a lord were, doubtless, supposed to pay him a tax in recognition of his *dominium*. But this did not imply any disruption of their freedom. A merchant could leave if he wanted. Furthermore, the exercise of rights merchants acquired for this price was in large part withdrawn from the lord's jurisdiction and was under the jurisdiction of the town magistrates. A series of continuous encroachments extended this freedom more and more; it progressively relaxed the bond that tied the inhabitant of the town to the lord in possession of the land. At times the latter spontaneously renounced his rights, at times he allowed the bourgeois to buy them back. In both cases, the town land was freed of all ties. From that day on, a new category of properties appeared—free properties beside old taxable properties. Inhabitants of towns that were so situated truly possessed a *hereditas,* holding their possessions *in allodio*[237] like the old freeholders. But this freeholder represented an entirely new kind. He was a product of town law and it was town law that guided him.

But not all the possessions owned by the bourgeois in the towns presented this characteristic. Beside the town freehold there existed a taxable property and a tenure grant. However, according to the author, this tenure grant was very different from that observed in the large domains. It was a free tenure grant. It left intact the personal status of the taxpayer and granted him the free disposal of his tenure grant (p. 118). It is true that in towns or parts of towns which were based on large domains, tenure was at first subject to the old law of domain with all the bondage it implied. But in that case also the need for a new law was not long in making itself felt under the influence of town life; the emancipation of the person and of the land came about more slowly, but was finally achieved (pp. 84 ff.).

After having shown in this way the origins of the town freeholder and town tenure, the author shows what relations this property right maintained with public town law (chapter 5). Then, in a final section, he studies town property from the point of view of private law; that is, he determines the rights and obligations of the title to property whether of freeholder or of taxpayer. We shall single out in particular the chapters on the relations of the tax to the renting of landed property (p. 254) and to rent (p. 338) which appears to be derived from the land.

The interest of this work consists in proving once again that our European civilization, insofar as its specific and original aspects are concerned, stems from essentially urban sources. Urban law and town customs are not simply derivatives of rural law and morality. A new organization was created on virgin territory—caused by the appearance and growth of sedentary merchant colonies at the heart of agricultural populations. It is in these new environments and in order to meet these new conditions of existence that urban civilization was developed. And as a result of such a background, it was, from the start, fully exposed to a liberalism that has grown with time. It is that fact which must not be overlooked if we would do justice to the import and the scope of the current that still propels a town-directed countryside. The trend is almost as old as our societies, and it is that factor which has given it a particular physiognomy. (*Année sociologique*, 3, 1900, pp. 393–395; trans. J. French)

Georg Cohn. *Gemeinderschaft und Hausgenossenschaft* (On the Domestic Community). Stuttgart: Enke, 1898, 128 pp. From *Zeitschrift für Rechtswissenschaft*.

Switzerland serves as the point of departure for this work. Indeed it stands alone and self-contained as a favorite field for the studies of comparative law, since codes of different origin coexist there.

The institution the author proposes to study is the economic partnership between members of the same family, such as it is presently organized in the cantons where the law is codified (that is fifteen out of twenty-two). It is found only among those who have adopted the French code, and those who follow the code of Zurich. But these two groups are not entirely the same in the way the partnerships are formed.

In Zurich, this partnership can be formed only between brothers and sisters; nephews are admitted to it in exceptional cases only. It never arises ipso facto, but always results from a formal and even solemn contract. It takes place every time several brothers or sisters pool all their property, or at the very least all their movable wealth. If there are no provisions to the contrary, all the possessions belong to this association. In general, this practice persists during the lifetime of the partners; there are, however, some legitimate reasons for dissolution (marriage, unexpected arrival of children, mistreatment of one partner by the others). All these features do not add up to an essential distinction between this institution and the law of modern societies. But what sets it apart and gives it a character entirely distinctive is the right of the association to inherit a portion from every partner who dies without issue (p. 12), and this is done to the exclusion of all other heirs—even those more closely related, who are not, however, members of the same association. Such a law of acquisition naturally excludes the option to make a will, except for possessions which have not fallen into the hands of the association. This exclusion shows clearly that the fundamental ideas upon which this entire organization rests are by no means modern.

Of all the cantons that have adopted the French code, Fribourg is the one where this sort of partnership is the most clearly observable; elsewhere no more than traces of it are to be found.

The fundamental difference that separates in this regard Fribourg's law from Zurich's is that the partnership no longer needs to be formed by contract. It exists "by the very fact of the ownership and enjoyment of joint holdings issuing from the father, mother, or other family ancestry." Furthermore, this state of co-ownership may be established between descendants of brothers or of sisters ad infinitum. Lastly, the law of acquisition, in case a partner dies without posterity, extends even to the possessions of the deceased which had not come within the partnership. The characteristic features of the institution are then stressed to better effect here than in Zurich.

There are perhaps no cantons where its vestiges are not detectable. Therefore everything warrants admitting that it was widespread in bygone days. The author applies himself to determine the most ancient forms it presents in history and in what way they can be distinguished from present-day forms. Partnership included relatives of all degrees, and neither death nor marriage brought about its disintegration. It was administered by a chief who was generally, but not necessarily, the eldest. Economic partnership made no progress without a truly shared existence. No one possessed anything of his own. These characteristics permit the author to link the institution to that type of family that Sumner Maine has called *joint family,* a vast accumulation formed by a multiplicity of collateral family elders living together and in a state of thoroughgoing communism.

By way of confirming this comparison, the author devotes the last part of his work to proving the widespread nature of this type of family. He shows it still existing or having existed as much among the non-Aryan peoples (China, Japan, Annam, Malabar, etcetera), as among the Aryans (Hindus, Greeks, Romans, Iranians, Armenians, Celts, northern and southern Slavs, Germans, French). It is impossible to give a résumé of this account, necessarily a summary. One will find in it useful bibliographical references and the material for a work that could be informative. It would indeed be very interesting to classify all these facts in such a way as to set forth the principal forms of this type of family, the range of subtle distinctions through which it has passed. One could accordingly better determine its place in the evolution of the family, by showing its increasingly typical tendencies as well as the types from which it keeps diverging more and more.

The book terminates with certain practical considerations on the place that can be granted this institution in the present Swiss code.* (*Année sociologique,* 3, 1900, pp. 396–398; trans. J. French)

Heinrich Schurtz. *Die Anfänge des Landbesitzes* (Beginning of Landed Property). *Zeitschrift für Sozialwissenschaft,* 1900, pp. 245–255, 352–361.

The object of these two short articles is to demonstrate: (1) that property rights at times take very different forms among primitive people living as nearest neighbors to each other; (2) that the phenomenon of property rights is one of the most complex. The most varied religious beliefs and practices tend to have their impact on economic factors, even though the latter in and of themselves give evidence of a great deal of variety. From all this the author concludes that even in closely related societies property rights have developed

* Shortly before Cohn's work had been published on the same subject, a book by Max Huber, *Die Gemeinderschaften der Schweiz auf Grundlage der Quellen dargestellt,* appeared in 1897.

in different ways and that it is impossible to derive from this development a universally valid generalization.

On the second point, the author's remarks seem to us perfectly sound. On the first, we shall gladly grant that lower social orders, even when they are of the same type and occupy neighboring habitats, often show differences in organization that, at first glance, appear quite solid. The reason for this is that these societies, just like primitive organisms, undergo very strongly the influence of the physical surroundings in which they are placed and consequently vary from place to place. But whether these variations are essential or secondary is still a delicate question, and it is not on the basis of a few facts hastily and somewhat confusedly grouped together that it is possible to decide. There are forms of individual ownership that do not exclude collective ownership or that may even derive from it. In fact, the reading of these two articles by no means left us with an impression of particularly surprising contrasts. Moreover, there are contrasts that arise from the fact that we sometimes submit as basic to primitive practices certain clearly defined and precise opinions that are irrelevant to the case in point—all of which would have us find contradictions where there aren't any. Furthermore, there is no justification in maintaining that property rights have evolved in the same way throughout all mankind. There can be a pattern of evolution which is not rectilinear. There is a great diversity of social types that are developing in the most varied directions. What we refuse to admit is that there are no types, but only individuals.

What is most interesting in these articles are the facts that demonstrate the very great role religious opinions play in the establishment of property rights (pp. 356–361); worth noting is the way in which the shedding of blood, by consecrating the land, engenders a right to property on behalf of the one whose blood has been spilled. (*Année sociologique*, 4, 1901, pp. 366–367; trans. J. French)

Eugen V. Dultzig. *Das deutsche Grunderbrecht in Vergangenheit,
    Gegenwart, und Zukunft* (The German Law of Landed Property in
    the Past, Present, and Future). Breslau: Marcus, 1899, ix + 372 pp.

Rural property has for a long time been subject, in Germany, to a particular successional law called the *Anerbenrecht*,[238] which still survives on more than one front. The principle behind it is that landed properties are handed down intact to a single heir (the *Anerbe*), who is designated according to variable rules depending on the country; he is compelled to indemnify only those of his relatives to whom custom acknowledges certain rights involving bequests. Further, these indemnities are calculated in such a way that the principal heir remains in a favorable positon.

The recent code of the empire, without consecrating this law, has left each particular state the option to maintain it or even to establish it once again. Now, this eclectic measure has been found inadequate by two opposing parties. Some want to have an institution they judge outdated abolished once and for all; others, on the contrary, ask that it be made general and become the basis for the German inheritance law in regard to rural dwellings. It is this practical question that Dultzig proposes to deal with in his book. But to resolve it, he is of the opinion, not without reason, that it is first necessary to search for the historical causes of this special right. It is on this account that his work interests us.

A certain number of theoreticians have found in this law of succession a derivative of the feudal law. Too great a partitioning of the land, by impoverishing the peasants, compromised the revenues that the master of the land drew from it, and as a result threatened his best interests. It is then he who probably imposed the provision requiring joint ownership of property and the obligation to hand down the land to a sole heir. Dultzig has no trouble refuting this theory. Not only does the *Anerbenrecht* apply to possessions that have always been free, but also it is an institution very highly general in character which is observed in countries where the feudal law has never existed—in ancient India, for example (pp. 14–15). The principle of intact status of family property, which is basic to this institution, is again much more widespread, not to mention the fact that the social organization with which it is bound up is far earlier than that of medieval Germany (pp. 16–25).

Its origins must be sought in the old conception of family community. According to this conception, the family is a group of individuals who live under the same roof and who own in common the land on which they live and which they cultivate. The father is the administrator of the community but is not the owner of the patrimony, which is collective. The author establishes easily that this family organization has existed in Germany; he shows notably how it points to the rules relating to the order in which the relatives were considered as eligible to receive an inheritance (pp. 56–80), in the manner with which the wives as well as the sons were treated outside the household (pp. 80–88). Since, then, the patrimony belonged to no one in particular but was a family matter, the idea of dividing it into sections did not even enter anyone's minds. Also, when under the influence of different contributing factors it became the general rule that each child should set up his own definite home, it was clearly necessary to assign to one of them the family property, aside from indemnifying the others to a certain extent, at the time when the children were leaving the communal house in order to settle down. Since it was the older ones who settled down first, it was the youngest who stayed behind alone with the father; that is why, very often, he was the heir. From that comes the institution of the *minorat*. As for the *majorat*, the author believes that it came into being through the associations formed, not by a father and his children, but by several brothers living together. In this last case, in fact, the eldest was supposed to take the leading role, and consequently it was to him that the inheritance reverted (pp. 108–123).

From this genesis of the *Anerbenrecht*, the author concludes that there is a need to reintroduce compulsorily the principle involved in the code of the empire; for he is of the opinion that the notion of the family community, of which this special law is the corollary; is one of the established elements of the German conscience. It seems to us that Dultzig's historical thesis implies rather more the contrary conclusion. No doubt this family organization was at one time based on the German spirit, because it was at the time in harmony with the conditions existing in Germany; but for the same reason it lacks justification today because it no longer meets the conditions of present-day existence. The progress of individualism is successively corroding the last vestiges of the old domestic communism. Consequently, the very fact that the *Anerbenrecht* possesses such a source—and we share the author's feeling on this matter—proves that henceforth it is an archaic institution, which it is impossible to revive, except artificially. (*Année sociologique*, 4, 1901, pp. 367–369; trans. J. French)

Konrad Beyerle. *Grundeigentumsverhältnisse und Bürgerrecht im mittelalterlichen Konstanz*. Volume 1, Part One *Das Salmannenrecht* (Conditions of Property in Real Estate and the Right of Citizenship in Medieval Constance. The Right of the Salmann). Heidelberg: Winter 1900, 169 pp.

The institution of the *Salmann* has long been known to us. One finds it in different forms in most of the barbarian codes.[239] The *Salmann* was the judiciary person who, in judicial transactions like that of the Frankish *affatomie* or the Lombard *thinx,* acted as intermediary between the alienator and the recipient. When a man wanted to choose an heir, he began by passing his fortune, or the part of his fortune of which he wanted to dispose, to a third person who was responsible for turning it over to the interested party. Recourse was had to the same procedure to designate a proxy in case of absence, and in some other similar circumstances. But we find at Constance, besides these classic forms of the institution, another form, which is not, moreover, peculiar to that city, the study of which is the object of the present work.

No one could possess in full liberty real property within the walls of Constance without being a citizen of that town. The title of proprietor and that of citizen implied each other mutually. But after industry was developed artisans came to establish themselves in the town who were, naturally, not citizens by birth. It was necessary, therefore, in order to attract them, to search for means of facilitating for them the acquisition of the right of property, but to take precautions that they did not acquire the right of citizenship at the same time; for the old families of the town who were the only ones who possessed this title were too proud of it to abandon it too easily to foreigners. One desired to accord them the economic advantages which they could not do without, but not admit them to the administration of the town. In order to satisfy these two conflicting needs, recourse was had to the institution of the *Salmann,* but modified in such a way as to appropriate it to this special situation.

Whenever a noncitizen wanted, for a price or for free, to acquire a piece of real property, he was obliged to associate himself with a citizen in the capacity of *Salmann*. It was this *Salmann* who acquired the right of property and who alone could exercise it as regarded third persons. But, on the other hand, he undertook to leave the free and complete possession of it to the real beneficiary. Whenever it was necessary to bring a legal action, it was the *Salmann* who intervened, and he was required not to refuse to cooperate. But the principle was saved: The alien was not considered juridically to be the proprietor. One perceives the resemblances of this institution to that which is known more generally under the same name. But the differences are no less important. The *Salmann* of Constance was also an intermediary; but he was constituted as such not by the person disposing of the property (the seller), but by the person for whom it was destined (the real acquirer). Moreover, where his role was reduced to a sort of testamentary executor, all his duties were over once the designated heir had been put in possession of his inheritance. Here, on the contrary, his function survives the moment when his principal receives from his hands the acquired property, since juridically he remains the guarantor and defender of it. Even his heirs were required to succeed him in his duty if he died.

In proportion as industry developed, and as in consequence the corporations of artisans acquired more power, they endured with more difficulty the obligation to have recourse to the intermediary *Salmann*, and the institution fell into decadence. As early as the end of the fourteenth century it no longer existed. It lasted, then, in sum, only a few centuries. But it is instructive from several points of view. First, it informs us about the way in which the right of property is susceptible to division and dismemberment. Then, it shows us that in certain German towns at least, the land was at the beginning possessed in full ownership by the citizens, and as a consequence did not belong to the domain of some lord. One sees all the consequences of this fact so far as the genesis of the towns of the Middle Ages are concerned. (*Année sociologique*, 5, 1902, pp. 393–394; trans. K. Woody)

Milan Paul Iovanovic. "Die agrarischen Rechtsverhältnisse im türkischen Reiche" (Legislation on Landed Property in the Turkish Empire). *Zeitschrift für vergleichende Rechtswissenschaft*, XV, no. 11, pp. 275–309.

In this matter, the peculiarity of Turkish law consists of a very clear distinction between two sorts of landed property. First there is full, entirely clear-titled property, which the individual holder can dispose of in perfect freedom; it is called *Mulk* in legal terminology. It consists of the house with its immediate surroundings in the narrowest sense of the word—that is to say, the courtyard and the garden, on condition that these do not exceed a predetermined surface area. In any case, belonging as an integral part to the same category are all landed properties that have been detached from state property and granted in their entirety to individuals. All remaining lands are state property. It is not that the state itself cultivates them. It very often grants them to individuals, who, however, have a limited right to the property. Right from the start, they must pay the state a tithe out of the revenues they derive from the estate; they cannot hand it over through negotiation except by consent of the authority; the latter supervises the cultivation of the land, and in the event that the individuals let the land lie fallow for a period of three years, it can withdraw their grant. In short, in matters concerning this sort of property (which is known by the name of *Mirije*), all disposal by wills is banned and hereditary legacies are governed by a special law. Whereas, when *Mulk* property is involved, all relatives, even the most distant, can be summoned for the inheritance; in this case only parents and children are legal heirs. In their absence, property was originally judged vacated, except where the nearest relatives had a preferential claim to redeem the grants (p. 277). Recently the law of common succession has been extended to include *Mirije* property rights—all of which has made it more nearly comparable to *Mulk* property rights (pp. 282–283).

One of the distinctive features of property rights, such as they are understood in the Turkish empire, is that they do not have the individualistic characteristics they had in Rome, where the preserves of an individual were narrowly closed to the outside world; no one else could gain entry there and act in the capacity of proprietor. That is why it was not permitted in Rome that one thing with something else added could have two different owners. We do not find the same exclusion in Turkey. Landed property does not extend to planted trees or constructions raised on the property. Thus in the case of *Mirije* property rights, the land belongs to the state, but the concessionaire possesses as free and clear property *(Mulk)* everything he has added to the land. If the land reverts to the public domain, it is not the same with plantings or buildings.

According to our author, this conception probably comes from the fact that in Turkey income from the land is of no economic importance, whereas human labor is highly valued (p. 285). As a result, it is work that is the real source of property rights. Accordingly, the landowner loses his right to the land he does not cultivate. By the same token, the guardian, even in bad faith, has a claim to the fruits and the seeds in the soil he has cultivated, and not the legitimate proprietor (p. 283). As for the guardian in good faith, he is still more highly favored; if his plantings and constructions are worth more than the estate itself, he becomes proprietor of the latter, reserving the right to buy off the original proprietor. But the explanation the author gives us of these various peculiarities does not appear to us very convincing. If they had really originated in the economic insignificance of income from the soil and the importance attributed to the work factor, the state would not have such extensive rights over landed property. What seems to emerge from the facts is a very clear-cut distinction between two sorts of property rights: real estate, which on general principle belongs to the state and is granted with or without reservations to individuals, and the property right to the fruits of the soil, etcetera, which is the product of labor and constitutes a distinct category. Precisely because they are not comparable, these two rights can cross over, intertwine, without there being any reason to subordinate one to the other. It would still remain to find out the origin of the bond that so directly and so tightly unites the land to the state.

The last part of the work is devoted to the origins of the institution of feudalism in Turkey (p. 297). It was essentially a creation of the state. The revenues from certain real estate owned by the state were apparently allocated to certain individuals, who in exchange were to furnish a particular force of fighting men. These benefits were not hereditary, but personal. However, in time, the system became corrupt; the beneficiaries considered themselves as owners of the lands from which revenues were being allocated to them—all of which ran entirely counter to the principle of the institution. The latter was abolished in 1839. (*Année sociologique*, 6, 1903, pp. 383–385; trans. J. French)

NOTES AND NOTICES

Franz Oppenheimer. "Die Entstehung des Grossgrundeigentums" (Formation of Large Landed Properties). *Zeitschrift für Sozialwissenschaft*, 1898, 2nd fascicle, pp. 114–126.

This is an article forming a chapter detached from a book announced on large real estate and social class. Its aim is to show that the formation of social classes has been the cause and not the result of economic inequality. It is an interesting article, although the historical facts are quite insufficient. (*Année sociologique*, 2, 1899, p. 349; trans. Y. Nandan)

Lujo Brentano. *Die Entwicklung des englischen Erbrechts in das Grundeigentum* (Evolution of English Inheritance Law Concerning Landed Property). Berlin: Simion, 1899, 31 pp.

In this very compact opuscule, which summarizes the conclusions of a book that the author has announced on the same subject, the law of inheritance is studied in its relation to the organization of property, and from the point of view of family order. Three phases in the evolution of this organization may be distinguished. Before the Norman Conquest, property was divided among all the members of the family. Therefore, there was no law of inheritance. In the case of the division of property, the last-born person remained in the house. On the arrival of William the Conqueror, the feudal system was introduced in England, and the law of primogeniture was extended to all landed property. The institution of the entail came later. By forcing the holders of feudal lands to transmit them to their legitimate inheritor, the trust institution perpetuated the power of the lord. Even the actual proprietors were reduced to mere usufructuaries. But little by little legal changes removed the difficulties. By the end of the fifteenth century, the freedom to part with property and to dispose of it through a will was complete, and it lasted until the end of the seventeenth century. But the Restoration, by giving the nobility political preponderance, brought back the institution of testament, which lasted until 1882. Along with it came the law of primogeniture and the practice of entail. It was only at this moment that through a series of measures landed property became a part of movable property; this is what concerns the law to dispose of property. (*Année sociologique*, 3, 1900, p. 398; trans. Y. Nandan)

Thorstein Veblen. "The Beginning of Ownership." *American Journal of Sociology*, Nov. 1898, pp. 352 ff.

The article has a certain ingenuity, but it is absolutely arbitrary. Property in the form of goods was presumably derived from property in the form of persons. The first objects of possession were presumably individuals taken during war, particularly women. The law concerning these kinds of subjects was supposedly extended later to the produce of their labor. The author produces no facts in support of his theory, which is much in need of proof. (*Année sociologique*, 3, 1900, 398; trans. Y. Nandan)

H. Sée. "Les Droits d'usage et les biens communaux en France au Moyen Age." *Revue internationale de sociologie*, 1898, pp. 619–650.

The author tends to refute the theory according to which collective property would have preceded individual property. Common property and the law of collective usage, far from being primitive, were presumably a product of the feudal system. But the epoch studied in the article is much too recent to allow for conclusions about the origin of property. (*Année sociologique*, 3, 1900, p. 399; trans. Y. Nandan)

Kasimir von Rakowski. *Entstehung des Grossgrundbesitzes im XV. und XVI. Jahrhundert in Polen* (Formation of the Great Landed Properties in Poland). Posen: Biedermann, 1899, 56 pp.

According to the author, the evolution of property in Poland has one and the same point of departure: the communal property. This being the primitive and simple basis of property formation, two opposed forms of property were constituted: the large and the small. Two categories of causes gave birth to the dual form: (1) the constitution of a nobility; as soon as the royal authority expanded, the chiefs of the *tribes* were transformed into the king's *councils (comités)* and the king demanded from them uncultivated land or the villages that were already settled and were administered by the councilmen as gifts. (2) The first cause, however, did not seriously change the organization of his property, because the seigneurial estates which were thus formed were not much extended. It was the economic revolution which extended its scope. During the course of the fifteenth century, the exportation of grain for food developed unexpectedly. The profits from the agricultural products thus increased; this is what induced the noblemen to devote themselves to agriculture and to replace the peasants in the exploitation of the land. With this aim in mind, they made use of their political power in expropriating little by little and thus eliminating totally or in part the small proprietors, who, as a result, disappeared. (*Année sociologique*, 4, 1901, pp. 373–374; trans. Y. Nandan)

E. D. Glasson. "Communautés taisibles et communautés coutumières depuis la rédaction des coutumes." *Nouvelle Revue historique du droit français et étranger*, 1899, no. 3, pp. 527–540.

The tacit community *(la communauté taisible)*[240] was one which resulted from the prolonged cohabitation of one year; it originated, therefore, from the free living arrangement of particular peoples. The author distinguishes it from the customary community, which existed according to some custom or was in accordance with the law. What distinguished the two organizations was that the unrecognized community implied living together in cohabitation; it presumed a limited number of individuals living under the same roof. The customary community could very well include a large number of families all constituting one population. The difference between the two is quite analogous to what separates the village community from the domestic community. (*Année sociologique*, 4, 1901, p. 374; trans. Y. Nandan)

L. Beauchet. "De la propriété familiale dans l'ancien droit suédois." *Nouvelle Revue historique de droit français et étranger*, 1900, no. 6, pp. 601–623; 1901, no. 1, pp. 1–44.

The author finds in ancient Swedish law the ordinary signs of the ancient combined-family property: obstacles in the way of freely transferring the patrimonial wealth; inheritance law; absence of testament, which in Sweden, as in France, was established above all to allow the Church to receive donations. The facts are not really new. The article is, however, interesting for its precision of exposition. Let us add that the author announces that he will eventually demonstrate that before the regime of familial co-patriarch, "ancient Sweden practiced the community system of property, under which the land belonged to the entire tribe or village, without making distinctions between the individuals or the families; the land was cultivated either as common property or was shared periodically by the tribe or the village." (*Année sociologique*, 5, 1902, p. 395; trans. Y. Nandan)

Heinrich Freiherr von Friesen. *Die Familien-Anwartschaften in ihrer geschichtlichen Entwicklung und volkswirtschaftlichen Bedeutung.* Dresden: Zahn und Jänsch, 1900, 93 pp.

The book's principal aim is essentially practical. The question of family property is a burning issue in Germany. The author belongs to those who either claim to support it or reestablish it. He is believed to justify his opinion by the long historical development of the family property. The thesis of relationship between the property and the family is often difficult to perceive. This kind of thinking is essentially backward. The author sees, par excellence, the contemporary social malaise rooted in individualism. In order to fight it, he strives to save everything which remains of the old domestic communism. (*Année sociologique*, 5, 1902, p. 396; trans. Y. Nandan)

Contract and Obligation

REVIEWS

S. R. Steinmetz. "Gli antichi scongiuri giuridici contro i debitori" (Primitive Means of Coercion Against Debtors). *Rivista italiana di sociologia*, 1889, no. 1.

The article treats the *dharna*,[241] or the Indian usage, which one finds equally in Ireland, by virtue of which the creditor, in order to force the debtor to discharge his debt, comes to the door of the latter and threatens to starve himself to death if he is not reimbursed. So that the threat will be considered serious, it is necessary, should the occasion arise, for the fasting person to go resolutely right to the end. According to Steinmetz, this custom may have had its origin in the beliefs related to the dead. The spirit of the deceased is powerful, especially if he is supposed to be angry with the survivors. The *dharna* would therefore have for its object to threaten the recalcitrant debtor with a vengeance from beyond the tomb to which one would not expose himself voluntarily; this would be a suicide for vengeance. In fact, one encounters in primitive societies a number of suicides which are real vendettas; the author cites many examples of them. The disdain that the primitive person has for existence makes the procedures of intimidation or of repression which we find so disconcerting appear very natural to him. As to the other varieties of *dharna*— a sort of fasting duel between the two parties, or the intervention of the crowd or a tribunal (whether to oppose the debtor's willingness to allow the suicide to be committed or, after the blow, to revenge the death of the creditor)—these are only secondary forms that developed subsequently.

The proofs that this practice has religious origins seem very strong to us. Perhaps the author assigns too great a role to the personal sentiments attributed to the spirit of the dead. The proof is that sometimes the creditor substitutes another victim, or even sacrifices by force the one who replaces him. It seems in this case that he would have more to fear from the hostility of the dead than his debtor, since he has caused this death. The action of the spirit was not primitively conceived under a form so humane and psychological. The souls of the dead are in part blind forces, like physical forces, which once released, produce their effects all around them indiscriminately. It should be noted equally that the sacrifice should take place either on the doorstep of the house or on the contested field. It aims above all at contaminating a place by arousing a dreadful force there. (*Année sociologique*, 2, 1899, pp. 399–400; trans. J. Sweeney)

A. Chausse. "Les Singularités de la vente romaine." *Nouvelle Revue historique du droit français et étranger*, 1899, no. 5, pp. 513–527.

In Rome, the sale contract had an unusual character in that the seller mentioned in it was obviously privileged: He was not obliged to hand over his title of ownership of the item sold, but simply to keep such vested interest in abeyance; he remained in possession as long as the price was not paid, and yet the risks involved in case of loss of the object sold were shouldered by the buyer alone. Developing an idea already expressed by Mommsen, Chausse explains that such peculiarities are due to the fact that this matter of the sale contract was probably under public jurisdiction long before deals made between private parties were permitted. It is the state that would first have put it to use in the transfer of goods in its domain. Now, it is common knowledge that the state always procures for itself a privileged situation through the court actions in which it is involved. The first sale contract that became known in Rome, therefore, gave satisfaction in behalf of the seller's exorbitant claims. Once economic growth had made such action necessary, it passed from public law into private law, although in the same form.

This theory is interesting in that it shows us how reforms of a private nature may be simply the widespread reforms of a public order. Because matters in the state's interest appear to be far more inviolate than those involving the individual, the former is much more readily freed from awkward and obsolete legal forms. The contract of the first sale is in the form of contract by mutual consent—that is to say, straightforward consent alone engenders a feeling of obligation. If the preceding explanation is admissible, it is the state that was the instigator of such a revolution; it is the state that freed itself from formalism, thus creating a new type of contract that was presumably next expanded to include types of dealings other than those for which it was first created. (*Année sociologique*, 4, 1901, pp. 376–377; trans. J. French)

G. des Marez. *La Lettre de foire à Ypres au XIIIe siècle. Contribution à l'étude des papiers de crédit*. Brussels: Lamertin, 1901, 292 pp.

Commerce, as it has developed, has caused new needs to arise, and to satisfy them has created new juridical institutions. In order for markets to expand and assume an international character it was necessary to be able to make payments otherwise than by coins, for the latter cannot be easily transported over great distances. This is what gave birth to letters of credit. The market letter which is in question here is one of the earliest papers of credit which made their appearance. The author studies it in the northern areas, for it was there that it was used most and survived for the longest time.

It is a letter by which the debtor committed himself to pay his debt to his creditor at a given fair, or else to any third party coming on the creditor's behalf or simply presenting the title to the debt, that is, the letter itself. Originally this was an entirely private act concluded between the two parties. But in time it became an authenticated act which took place in the presence of town officials. This preliminary formality had as object the facilitating of the procedure of execution. The letter, having thus passed before the officials, functioned as proof of the debt. It procured for the creditor a privileged position. It made it unnecessary for him to take an oath; it suspended for his benefit certain immunities which would have prevented him taking possession, etcetera—it was, in sum, one of the forerunners of registration (pp. 26–27, 67).

The great novelty of this letter was the clause which permitted the creditor to transfer in the future his rights to a third person *without the participation of the debtor;* this third person could, moreover, either act as the creditor's agent or else act in his own name as creditor. The transmission of the right was effected by the contracted transmission of the letter. This transmission contains the seeds of endorsement. By this means payment in paper was substituted for payment with money, since the creditor could himself pay his debts by giving to his own creditor the letter which he had received; and if it was payable at a particular fair, it was because these fairs always took place in some large commercial center which all nations used as a meeting place. One met there regularly; the visitors were almost always the same, something which made substitution easier. In sum, the medieval fairs were the prototypes of the modern stock exchanges.

In all these features the market letter resembles the bill of exchange, and it effectively filled its role. However, the identity was far from being complete. In the first place, it had purposes which were not exclusively commercial: for leases, for rentals, for sales of all sorts; all possible debts could be recognized in this manner. It was also an instrument of great adaptability and flexibility, without clearly defined functions, fit for all combinations because it was still in a process of development (p. 33). Moreover, although the clause regarding the bearer is not without relationships to the clause concerning the endorser, the idea that the simple transfer of the letter could transfer the right to the debt had not yet been accepted. In the letters of market the third party or bearer is only an agent of the initial creditor, not a true substitute for the latter. The proof of this is that he was required to give a receipt in which he bound himself to acquit the debtor with the creditor; thus the person of the latter remained in the forefront (p. 66). The Flemish commercial world did not yet have the idea of a right attached to the simple possession of a piece of writing.

Moreover, in many cases, all real transfer was impossible, even when the terms of the letter provided for it. For it happened, and often, that the stipulated payment had to be made in kind (p. 38).

The market letter is thus the product of the first tentative efforts in the course of which an attempt was made to respond to the needs of nascent credit. The manner in which it was used shows that although credit existed at that time, people were singularly fearful and suspicious of it. For the creditor surrounded himself with all sorts of guarantees. If there were several co-debtors, it was the rule that each of them be responsible for the whole debt, with the reservation that he had the right of redress by his co-debtors (pp. 40–42). The debt was, moreover, guaranteed by pledges and guarantors. To the pledge, as a third protection, was added security, and the security then produced very important juridical effects; in many cases it was the equivalent of a provisional alienation. For example, the creditor who had received a house as security could dispose of it so long as the contracted obligation to him had not been discharged (pp. 52–56). All these precautions show that the situation of the creditor remained very precarious, something which has always been a great obstacle to the development of credit.

The author points out the predilection which the northern areas have always shown for the market letter; he calls it the bill of exchange of northern Europe (p. 32). The bill of exchange proper did not, indeed, appear there until much later than in the southern areas. No reason is given, however, in explanation of this curious circumstance. (*Année sociologique*, 5, 1902, pp. 397–399; trans. K. Woody)

George Dereux. *De l'Interprétation des actes juridiques privés.* Paris: Arthur Rousseau, 491 pp.

This book is interesting as an index of the changes being made in the ideas now prevalent among expert practitioners of the law. We have already had occasion to point out in these pages the increasingly pronounced withdrawal from the old theory that once recognized as legal only the legislator's express wishes and that reduced the judge's task to a simple interpretive analysis of legal matters whose only purpose was to assess those wishes through texts that conveyed their meaning with increasing fidelity. A reaction of the same type is now taking place with regard to contracts, and more generally, private legal deeds. According to classic theory, the obligations that stem from a deed of this kind depend entirely on the intention of the authorized source or sources from which it emanates. As a result, the entire statutory problem consists of discovering such intentions beneath the formal turn of phrase. Following the lead of the German school, Dereux has no trouble showing the inconsistency and even the practical shortcomings of this idea. It is all too clear that we very frequently find ourselves under obligation by our own doing, by a show of willfulness—without, nevertheless, our having given a thought to the obligations thus contracted, so very far removed from what we wished of them. The newly insured who signs his insurance policy most often does not suspect the extent of the obligations he is incurring—as a rule he is not even equipped to understand them. The same goes for the worker who hires out his services, and who in so doing accepts being subjected to the regulations of the place of work without having known about it ahead of time. Also, the courts, in fact, disregard the intentions of the contracting parties in order that they may determine the obligations that originate in a contract. And if, nevertheless, they endeavor to draw on decisions in keeping with classic standards, it is with the help of legal stratagems that have nothing to commend them from the point of view either of logic or the best interests of legal practice.

But if the author criticizes traditional theory, he nonetheless accepts it in principle. He simply judges it too exclusive and proposes to round it out by other means. He too admits that contractual obligations have their source in the purposeful intent of the parties concerned; according to him, human will is the generative force of the law. But he asks that such intent be taken into account only in cases where it actually exists, where it leaves no room for doubt. In all cases, on the other hand, where it is a question of applying contractual rulings under circumstances which its authors did not foresee, instead of attributing to them some fictitious intent or other in a vaguely roundabout way, it seems to him more natural to invoke different standards—for example, justice or social benefit. It is in the name of the ideal of justice, in the name of social good, that the judge ought to intervene so as to round out the contract that he is charged with interpreting.

It is hard not to find this eclectic evolution rather inconsistent. To begin with, may there not be times when, in a similar situation, those different standards imply different obligations? And in such a case how to decide? Will justice win out over the good of society or vice versa? But above all, the author passes too rapidly over the issue that is fundamental to the debate. It is impossible to see how a simple decision on the part of one or several determined individuals can give rise to an obligation. Why would I be forming ties because I have wanted something or because another has shared that wish with me? Therefore we find much more logical, much more in line with historical evolution, the theory which recognizes obligations not in a show of determination but in a declaration of intent. When I have declared to another that I was making a commitment to act in a certain way, I have created in him a state of mind for which I am responsible—the more so since, in so doing, I have induced him to take steps that would become futile if I should arbitrarily withdraw my commitment. I have therefore formed ties, not because my determination is binding on me, but because by showing a changeable will I do harm to others. The objection is raised that the will nevertheless plays an important role, since there would be no obligation if the declaration had not been intentional, if the declarer had in no way taken into account its scope. Nothing could be more certain; but it is not a reason for seeing in the human will the source itself of law. If one becomes preoccupied with the intent of the declarer, it is because it is increasingly contrary to our moral standards to make a man responsible for the consequences of an act that he did not mean to perform. There are two standards at odds: one, which desires that all injury, all harm done to others, be redressed; the other, which tends to require that an act, to be imputable, should be intentional. These two contrary standards are opposed and mutually restrictive in our penal law and our civil law as well, and there is no criterion which permits determining once and for all the role of each. (*Année sociologique*, 9, 1906, pp. 418–419; trans. J. French)

NOTES AND NOTICES

D. Castelli. "Creditori e debitori nell'antica società hebraica"
(Creditors and Debtors in Ancient Hebraic Society). *Rivista italiana
di sociologia*, May 1899, pp. 302–316.

The author believes to have observed a contradiction between the prescriptions of the Pentateuch and the usages followed in practice among the creditors and debtors. On the one hand, several of the facts demonstrate that the creditors appeared very hard. They could, in case of insolvency, seize upon the debtors in person and possess them; they could even possess debtor's children, and reduce both the debtors and their children to servitude. They had almost unlimited legal rights over the debtors' property. On the other hand, the religious laws contained prescriptions inspired by a spirit of humanity—such as prohibition of loans at interest, at least among the Jews themselves; prohibition of keeping in hock more than a day the things of primary necessity; and finally and especially the institution of the sabbatical year. The author, in fact, admits that the latter implied a complete abolition of debts. The author estimates that the ideal, however, was hardly realized in practice. There seem to have been, therefore, two opposed currents of thought and action, the first that of the prophets and the other that of the common man. The first fought against the second, without completely succeeding. (*Année sociologique*, 3, 1900, pp. 403–404; trans. Y. Nandan)

Washburn Hopkins. "On the Hindu Custom of Dying to Redress a
Grievance." *Journal of the American Oriental Society*, 1901, pp.
146–159.

The article deals with suicide committed, for example, as a means to compel a debtor to pay his debt (p. 145). It is accompanied by a conditional malediction (p. 156). It is accomplished at the gate of the offender, on the sacred turf, with the simple intention to make him repent. (*Année sociologique*, 5, 1902, pp. 399–400; trans. Y. Nandan)

Georges Cornil. "L'Evolution historique de la vente consensuelle."
   Nouvelle Revue historique de droit français et étranger, 1901, no.
   2, pp. 136–161.

In Rome, the obligations of the buyer and those of the seller, once they came into existence, became independent from each other. What affected the seller's obligations did not react upon the buyer's. The author shows that the Romans never succeeded in setting themselves completely free from the principle, which formed the basis of the evolution of modern law. (*Année sociologique,* 5, 1902, p. 400; trans. Y. Nandan)

Section Four

Criminal Sociology and Statistics on Morals

The section on criminal sociology, complementing the previous section on juridic sociology, was structured to induce Richard into *L'Année* as a significant collaborator; Durkheim made him editor in charge of the section. Richard was a *normalien,* like Durkheim, and both were friends—at least they appeared to be. Richard's collaboration in *L'Année* was marked by a tenuous relation between the two, since both sociologists regarded the new science from somewhat contradistinct points of view. Richard first made attacks[1] on Durkheim's so-called metaphors posited in *Suicide* and other works; the latter squared off with him as publication of *L'Année* progressed and it became a firmly established institution. Once Durkheim gave the lead and once they sensed Richard's eventual tergiversation, Durkheim's disciples also launched a tirade of criticisms against Richard. The detrimental effect of Richard's vacillating dedication to the growth of the section notwithstanding, the significance of his total contribution, both in terms of quality and quantity, cannot be denied. Once Durkheim apprehended that Richard's collaboration in *L'Année* was capricious and unreliable, he himself moved in and rescued the section from further deterioration and deviation from the main focus. Let it be noted that Richard was editor in charge of the section on criminal sociology in the first three volumes of *L'Année,* and from the fourth volume on he is listed as a mere collaborator.

The section from the very beginning had two distinct subdivisions: criminal sociology and "moral statistics," the latter an ill-defined hybrid. The synthetic combination of the two subdivisions into one section was enough to confound it with the previous section on juridic and moral sociology. Thus a subtitle explaining the different orientations of the two was in order. Otherwise the inclusion of penal law in either of the sections might be questioned. The section on criminal sociology and moral statistics bore an explicative subtitle: "Study of Juridic and Moral Rules Considered According to Their Functions." The subtitle was adopted only after Durkheim's quite comprehensive and illuminating introduction to the section in the fourth volume of L'Année.

Whereas Durkheim in his introduction to the section was confronted with the issue of distinguishing juridic sociology from criminal sociology, Richard in the first two volumes[2] clearly defined the scope of this section consisting of criminal sociology—be it noted that Richard mistakenly deduced, at least in the rubrics of the first two volumes, the correspondence between criminal sociology and criminal anthropology—and moral statistics; and he interposed the substance of this division of sociology lying in between genetic sociology and applied sociology.[3] The two isolated residues of the criminal sociology section were equally adapted in the heading from the fourth volume on.

Durkheim, by defining sociology as the study of social facts, set the guidelines for L'Année's collaborators. Besides explaining social facts as they had evolved through dynamic historical forces, sociology was also to examine the effective functioning of moral rules and institutional norms: negatively speaking, the willful transgression of them by deviant and radical elements. Thus the synoptic themes of criminal sociology were well defined and clearly stated.

With the help of moral statistics as a methodological tool, criminal sociology aimed to study criminals in their social environment, establishing causal relationships between the infraction of legal rules and social imperatives. Criminal anthropology, as enunciated by Lombroso as the principal exponent (in collaboration with other members of the Italian positivist school, such as Ferrero, Sighele, Ferri, and Florian), had as its aim to study the biological and psychological traits of criminals, without any reference to the social substratum. Richard especially, and to some extent Durkheim too, were prone to giving a comprehensive analysis of the works of Italian criminologists, but only to criticize them for their lack of sociological orientation. Moral statistics was defined as statistical interpretation of moral and social life that included such aspects as suicide, bankruptcy, divorce, prostitution, illegitimacy, and so on and so forth. By applying comparative method to the study of variations in social rules, crime, and other deviant aspects of social life, the statistical analysis portrayed contemporary society in terms of its functioning and institutions.

After Richard's broaching of the two major divisions of criminal sociology as suggested in his prefatory introductions, Durkheim's trite claim that by introducing "moral statistics" to the title of the section and by incorporating literature on the subject matter he was perfecting the section in its form and content seems unwarranted. From the fourth volume on, Durkheim supposedly was improving the section by dealing with new substantive issues, but he failed to give it a coherent organization.

Nowhere in the entire series of *L'Année* is the area of moral statistics distinguished from criminal sociology. Whereas the title of the section reads "Criminal Sociology and Moral Statistics," the priority is assigned to the latter in arranging the rubrics—the same error Durkheim committed in the previous section on juridic sociology. By placing criminal sociology first we have attempted to put the right thing in the right place. The complex nature of the section on juridic sociology did not permit us to use the same set of rules. In the section on criminal sociology, not only are the rubrics incoherently organized, but the books belonging to this section have been frequently interspersed throughout other sections, especially social morphology. the rubrics belonging to moral statistics have been scattered, without recourse to logic. In general, the rubric on domestic and conjugal life has been arranged in sequence after the one on general conceptions and methodological issues; but a rubric on suicide, apparently a topic in moral statistics, has been placed at the end, dismembering it from the main body and completely dislocating it in relation to the rubric on domestic and conjugal life.

Criminal sociology as compared to moral statistics maintained a superior and stable position throughout *L'Année*. The rubric on criminal anthropology, a special favorite of Richard and incorporating a synoptic discussion of the entire school of Italian positivists, was eliminated under the auspices of Durkheim's dominant influence in the section. The discussion on criminal anthropology was relegated to other rubrics in the section. The popular and frequently admitted rubrics dealt with the general notions of crime, different factors determining crime and immorality, special forms of crime, juvenile crime, penitentiary systems, and crime according to other variables—age, sex, and country.

Durkheim's examination of authors under the general rubric on criminology and moral statistics suggests his role as a moralist, as is evident from the orientation of his work in sociology. Despite one's question as to whether Fouillée's work fits under this rubric, Durkheim showed no qualms in agreeing with his contemporary—whom, along with others like Fouillée, he often labeled as a dilettante sociologist—that France was, in fact, suffering from moral crisis and that its decadent institutions needed refurbishment, or rather substitution by new ones. Whereas Fouillée identified this morally degenerative process in progressive civilization, Durkheim, on the other hand, thought the French state of anomie had its roots in the Revolution of 1789 that brought discredit to the *ancien régime* along with the old sociopolitical and moral institutions. The vacuum thus created suggested the foundation of a new order, including a new morality—secular of course. Showing his discontent with the mere legislative reforms as underscored by Fouillée, Durkheim, in the vein of Comtian positivism, preferred a regenerative process at the secondary-school level whereby a new foundation of secular morality could be built. Frauenstädt's criminal statistics revealed that women's part in crime had not changed much compared to the men's rate of crime, which had doubled—thus corroborating Durkheim's thesis deduced in his *Suicide* that women share less responsibility because they participate less in collective life. By including a note on Duprat for his publication on the social causes of insanity, Durkheim intended a lecture on him in the use of a methodology similar to the one adopted in his *Suicide.*

The rubric on domestic and conjugal life incorporates a wide variety of germane and related themes in marriage and the family. A good part of the books examined under the heading have some practical significance; in other words, their discussion from the vantage point of theoretical relevance is insignificant. For example, Bertillon suggested tax cuts and budgetary favors to encourage large families and a higher birth rate. Prinzing (1902) arrived at the conclusion that in Germany the rate of marriage was on the rise. Also, the relative shortage of women accessible for marriage created a problem for men. In a series of Prinzing's articles that are quite apposite to a discussion on marriage and the family (1903), he underscored the tendency in well-to-do and wealthy families for men to delay their marriages and women to be married off promptly. Dowry is essentially an institution that has its origin and vestiges in the familial customs of the Greeks and Romans. Nigh onto the Industrial Revolution it continued its existence in the West as the European societies modeled their institutions after the prototypes of Greek and Roman ones. (I may add parenthetically that through the invasion of Islam the custom found its way to India, where it prospers as a social evil.) Depinay and Griveau in their respective investigations show that the contemporary France of their time had vestiges in only some *départements.* Illegitimacy as a social issue elicited a sympathetic response from Durkheim, who reviewed a number of books and showed a deep concern for the problem. According to Lindner, increase or decrease in illegitimacy is related to utilitarian economics, for only a prosperous and affluent society can indulge in excessive, unrestrained, and illicit sex. Durkheim had already refuted such an extrasociological and socially remote explanation in *The Division of Labor.* Confirming his theory of suicide, which implies that the rate fluctuates with the vitality of public life, Durkheim deduced that illegitimacy, as a deviant behavior like suicide, stemmed from similar causes, namely the volume and the vigor of social life. Pouzol's study of paternity and that by La Tour on an identical theme have parallels; the latter study, however, was reviewed in the section on juridic sociology and lauded for its comprehensive character. Spann brings to light another dimension of the moral development and social upbringing of illegitimate children by placing them in the context of a "stepfather family." After what has been described by the authors mentioned above, Prinzing's articles (1901 and 1902) on legitimate and illegitimate birth rates are devoid of any novelty. The moralist Durkheim was concerned about the tendency toward an increasing rate of divorce; but he did not condemn it as an anomaly of a society that sought sexual equality and freedom from maltreatment for women. The studies by Buomberger (1901) and Prinzing (1901, Berlin) allude to the strain on marriages of an interreligious character. A number of these marriages eventually end up in divorce. Being more cosmopolitan and brought up in an atmosphere of rational education, Berliners were less subjected to aggravation caused by mixed marriages; consequently, they had a lower divorce rate compared to other regions with similar marital problems. The divorce law was first introduced in France in 1884, the success of which Valensi examined in considerable detail to show its effect on French moral life during the subsequent twenty years and what reforms were needed to make it fit with contemporary thinking and changes. The theory that breakdown in the family institution was conducive to a general state of anomie in a given society guided Durkheim to agree with the author that the law and the courts should function as socially binding forces and act as controlling agents in the unrestricted access to divorces by parties soldered by the social bond of marriage.

Durkheim extolled the two germane publications by Krose as the most comprehensive and the most important study on the subject since his *Suicide,* 1897. The two reviews of Krose are the most important included under the rubric on suicide. Unfortunately very little recognition has been accorded to Krose for his important theoretical work by the contemporary scholars working on suicide. The availability of this volume will add to the factual knowledge of those who have contributed significantly in placing Durkheim's *Suicide* in historical context—such as Jack D. Douglas, through a serious and penetrating study, *The Social Meaning of Suicide*— that the French master was fully conversant with the significant work of a German writer. By reviewing Krose, Durkheim gives a comparative picture of the important works that appeared a decade apart. Even though Lasch's several articles, published in *Globus* and another German periodical, deal directly or indirectly with suicide among the "primitives" they have been included under the rubric on special forms of crime.

Under the rubric on social factors of crime and immorality, Durkheim examined the rate of crimes committed in various fields by the German Jews. Since the available statistics concerned the German Jews only, Durkheim regretted the absence of similar statistics on the French Jewish community.

General Concepts

REVIEWS

[Durkheim's Introduction][4]

When we founded *L'Année,* we thought it prudent not to adopt at once an overly systematic classification that might be hard for a badly prepared opinion to accept.[5] Besides, the subject matter that we were espousing was too vast to be organized all at once and in an a priori manner. Therefore it was necessary to await the body of information that could not fail to grow out of the experiment that we were performing jointly. But if we held back from solving the problem prematurely, we made it our duty never to lose sight of it;[6] for we are of the opinion that one of the principal tasks of *L'Année* is precisely to work progressively to determine the natural boundaries of sociology. This is, in fact, the best way to assign definite themes to be investigated, and in just that way to free our science from the vague generalizations which have delayed its progress. Then alone will one have a better sense of its unity, whereas the divisions now in use too often conceal it, precisely because they have been formulated in too empirical a fashion and in a spirit too exclusively independent of others. That is why no year has gone by without our striving to perfect our original classification.[7] Today it is in our fourth section that we are going to introduce an improvement of this kind.

Up until now, it was exclusively devoted to criminal sociology, or if it happened that moral statistics made its appearance, it was simply in the form of a subsidiary discipline of criminology: It was the statistics of crime that was under consideration. By proceding in this way, we were conforming to a tradition that makes the study of crime a sort of scientific entity, with a subject matter of its own and its own special method. But however distinct this branch of sociology may be in certain respects, it is closely related to other methods of research, and it is important to bring the former into partnership with the latter if one wants the classification of the sciences to correspond to the affinities shared in the nature of things.

If indeed crime, or more generally the immoral deed, is a sociological phenomenon, it is because it consists of a violation of moral or legal rulings. It is the social character of these rulings that influence the acts in violation of the law. But deeds carried out in conformity with these same precepts are obviously social phenomena on similar grounds and for the same reason as those just mentioned. They are therefore of the same type, or at the very most they constitute two kinds of the same type, which includes all the varied and even contradictory ways in which law and morality are practiced by societies; for to violate the rules is a way of practicing them. They are, in the final analysis, simply different expressions of one and the same reality, which is the moral condition of collectivities under consideration. This condition can just as well be reckoned from the standpoint of the number and the nature of upright actions that are accomplished from day to day as from the number and the nature of misdemeanors. Positive morality, as it may be rightfully designated, and negative morality, or criminality, are merely the two aspects of collective morality. All these factors are therefore under the jurisdiction of the same study, for they are mutually complementary and illuminating. In order to estimate conjugal morality in a given country, it is not enough to calculate the rate of adultery; one must also take into account the rate of marriage, its average duration, the respective ages of the spouses, the nature of the systems adopted in marriage, and so on. There are even acts, such as divorce, about which it is very hard to tell whether they are of positive or negative morality.

One can easily see what connections there are between this category of facts and those we previously dealt with under the title "Sociologie morale et juridique."[8] Both of these are relevant to the rules of law and of morality, but they are considered in each case from a different point of view. What was looked for in the third section was the manner in which they were progressively organized. It is their origins that we tried to examine. The study was genetic. Here the rules are assumed to be absolutely constituted, and under observation is the manner in which, once formed, they are applied. It is no longer their formation but their function that is being determined. Assuredly, there is between these two orders of investigation a close-knit solidarity. Indeed, in order to explain a rule one must know its true significance, and this significance is the result, in part, of the way in which the rule is understood and practiced. We would have a mistaken notion, for example, of what the *patria potestas* was at certain periods in Roman history if we knew only what the legal texts teach us. In another sense, the states of mind from which a moral precept resulted are discovered among the factors that determine how it is applied. It is no less true that these two sorts of studies are very different and are oriented, so to speak, in two almost opposite directions. In one, we turn towards the past and we consider the moral rule in its evolutionary process; for it is the only way to discover the elements of which it is composed. In the other, we fix it at a precise moment in time in order to measure both the amount of power it exerts, at this moment, over people's consciences and the reasons why the extent of this power varies. The research procedures are not, moreover, the same in both cases; in the one, history and comparative ethnography are used; in the other, statistics in particular.

Henceforth we shall assemble in the fourth section under the same heading everything that has to do with the functioning of legal and moral rules, whether the study of this functioning is made on the basis of decent and correct actions or on the basis of immoral acts and misdemeanors. For these different phenomena cannot be separated from each other. As a rule, each chapter of the preceding section[9] ought to have its counterpart here.[10] "Domestic Organization" has its corresponding category in statistics of domestic life (celibacy and marriage, divorces, the situation of widows and widowers, number of children raised outside the family, number of adoptions, etcetera); "Political Organization" corresponds to everything related to the intensity of public life (number of voters at elections, scope of legislative and administrative activity, etcetera); "Penal Law" to all studies concerning the way in which the rules under this law are broken. (Those studies properly belong to criminology that deal with the way penalties decreed by the code are administered by the judges; studies of the application of penalties in penitentiaries belong to penology). Since all these investigations necessarily have to do with subject matter involving deeds committed by human beings—for social institutions live and function only through the behavior of citizens, functionaries, etcetera—we had thought to call the science dealing with this subject *pragmatology,* in order to give it a definite sense of unity. But since, in another sense, any neologism that is not pretested and validated through use has little chance of succeeding, we shall limit ourselves for the time being to naming this branch of sociology after the two principal disciplines that make it up, *sociologie criminelle* and *statistique morale* (criminal sociology and moral statistics) without failing to recognize the drawbacks of this compound expression that we would be happy to see disappear.[11] (*Année sociologique*, 4, 1901, pp. 433–436; trans. J. French)

L. von Bortkewitsch. *Das Gesetz der Kleinen Zahlen* (The Law of Small Numbers). Leipzig: Teubner, 1898, vi + 52 pp.

Ordinarily, statistics does not pay much attention to the small numbers because the part played by them in the accidental causes is very much marked.[12] The author undertakes to show, by taking mathematics into consideration, that these small numbers are quite exactly consistent with the laws of random chance as the mathematicians establish them. Let us take, for example, the annual figure of suicides committed by women in a very small state like Germany; it is slightly high. In fact, from one year to another the number of female suicides quite perceptibly varies as the calculation of probabilities allows us to foresee it. This is what comprises and what the author calls the law of small numbers. At first sight, the result seems in contradiction with the facts of statistics of large numbers; the latter do not conform at all with these formulas. But the author makes us believe that the contradiction is only apparent. If, within the vast fields of observation to which these large numbers refer, one considers the most restricted circles, one will notice that the same regularity reappears. The law of small numbers, then, holds for large numbers. The author concludes that the facts accumulated by statistics are the product of certain general conditions, whose behavior is involved with that of certain accidental causes. The law of small numbers gives evidence of the influence exerted by fortuitous causes; and thus "the regularity (*Die Gesetzmässigkeit*) of the statistical data, which appears to have lost all its credibility as a consequence of Quételet's misapprehensions and those of his disciples, will regain, by virtue of this point of view, all its value." The book is presented as a further development of the works by W. Lexis, especially his *Zur Theorie der Massenerscheinungen in der menschlichen Gesellschaft* (1877) and his articles "Das Geschlechtsverhältnis der Geborenen und die Warscheinlichkeitsrechnung, 1876," and "Über die Theorie der Stabilität der Statistischen Reihen," published in Conrad's *Jahrbücher für nationalökonomie und Statistik*. (*Année sociologique*, 2, 1899, pp. 563–564; trans. Y. Nandan)

Alfred Fouillée. *La France au point de vue moral*. Paris: F. Alcan, 1900, vi + 416 pp.

This book is composed of four studies, which at first glance can appear quite independent of one another. If we understand the author correctly, it is chapter 3, on crime in France, that constitutes the central part of the work. Indeed, Fouillée proposes to study the moral crisis from which our country suffers. Now, this crisis in the spread of crime is expressed in a most forthright manner and at the same time most objectively.

Fouillée has no difficulty whatsoever in establishing that the abnormal progress of French crime in the course of this century cannot be explained either by a parallel progress of civilization, which does not result necessarily in an increase in immortality, or by the state of the economy alone. The real cause must be sought in a kind of confusion and disarray in the French moral conscience. The great revolutionary jolt brought on a general downgrading of ideas and of individuals alike, without any new order yet established. The most contrary goals incite capricious desires successively or simultaneously without any of them assuming over the others a recognizably predominant position (pp. 23 ff.). It is above all this general confusion that must be associated with "the frightful rise in juvenile crime" (p. 153). And the lay school is in no way responsible for this deplorable ascendency that began long before our recent pedagogical reforms (pp. 158 ff.).

But what are the best ways to take a stand against the evil? Fouillée proposes a fairly large number of them that should, according to him, be used concurrently: legislation against the increase in alcoholism, and against licentious behavior in the streets and theaters, etcetera, which stirs up debauchery; greater expansion of charitable institutions in order to prevent falling into the course of misery; strengthening of repressive legislation. But, unless we are mistaken, of all the remedies, the one that appears to Fouillée the most important and the most efficient is a reform in depth of education. It is by working on the young generations that one can keep corruption from spreading and from growing worse while spreading. Doubtless, that explains the important place that the question of democratic education occupies in the work; all of chapter 4 (pp. 199–389) is devoted to it.

We too are quite convinced, and we have stated it elsewhere, as Fouillée does indeed recall, that the present malaise is related essentially to a disintegration of our moral beliefs.[13] The goals to which our fathers were attached have lost their authority and their appeal, without our seeing very clearly, at least with the unanimity that would be necessary, where we should direct our steps from now on. As a result, there is a real void in our moral conscience. But we do not perceive how the remedies proposed by Fouillée are able to fill it. How could mere legal proceedings have such an effect? They would be incapable of giving us new desirable goals to be cherished. It is not clear, moreover, that the weaknesses of the magistrate or the legislator only are such that they serve to interpret the law while reinforcing the encompassing sense of bewilderment, and that one must above all put an end to the latter if one would bring the former to a halt. As far as education is concerned, without our overrating its influence we think that, properly directed, it cannot but have its effective uses. But in order that it do the good that one may expect of it, it is still necessary that the masters[14] be shown to what new ideal they are to attach themselves and to attach the hearts of the children, since therein lies the great desideratum of our moral situation. Now, we do not see how Fouillée's book helps us to discover it. The book is an effort to consolidate what can be preserved from the existing discipline rather than an attempt to determine the path on which it behooves us to set our course with firm resolve. (*Année sociologique*, 4, 1901, pp. 443–445; trans. J. French)

August Löwenstimm. "Aberglaube und Verbrechen" (Superstition
   and Crime). *Zeitschrift für Sozialwissenschaft*, 1903, pp. 209–231,
   273–286.
   This article is a supplement to the book of the same author on the same subject, a book that has been analyzed here[15] (volume 2, 1899, pp. 352–354). It involves demonstrating that crime is very often caused by a superstitious belief. On this subject the principal superstitions that are reviewed are as follows:

(1) Superstitions of pre-Christian origin: human sacrifices in order to ward off an epidemic, an extreme drought, etcetera, or on the occasion of building a house, etcetera.
(2) Christian superstitions. Beliefs in the ritual murders of the Jews, or that the red fungus that appears at times on the eucharistic host is Christ's blood itself flowing in the aftermath of a profanation.
(3) Survival of former legal practices, various ordeals ending in attacks made on the person under suspicion.
(4) Superstitions that are basic to popular medicine. Profanation of tombs and corpses whose remains are used as remedies against sickness.

The author's aim is less descriptive and theoretical than practical. It serves notice to the magistrate that crimes are sometimes motivated by ideas or feelings that are not properly criminal, that simply derive from errors of judgment for which the individual is not entirely responsible. In such a case, justice calls for considerably softening the sentence. Since he had had objections that it would be necessary to provide relevant definitions before being able to make superstition an extenuating circumstance in the crime, Löwenstimm strives to satisfy that desideratum. He terms superstitious the man who makes a causal connection between two phenomena which by their very nature can have no possible influence on each other. The formula leaves very much to be desired, since in that case scientific errors should be called superstitions. The notion of superstition is, we believe, entirely relative; it can only be defined in relation to a body of ideas and practices that is considered as the standard for what is true—at least temporarily. Pagan beliefs are superstitions for the Christian and vice versa. (*Année sociologique*, 7, 1904, p. 523; trans. J. French)

Paul Frauenstädt. *"Zwanzig Jahre Kriminalstatistik." Zeitschrift für Sozialwissenschaft,* 1905, pp. 346–359.

The Office of Criminal Statistics of the German Empire has annually published, including a report for the year 1901, a comprehensive work ever since it was created twenty years ago. Frauenstädt gives a résumé of the most general conclusions which have been disentangled from the study.

In the first place, he affirms the progressive growth in recidivism. In twenty years, the proportion of recidivists has almost doubled. He foresees a time when half of the convicts will face justice again. According to the report, the law of delay in legal proceedings, which functions in Germany as well as in France, does not seem to have produced appreciably useful results. No doubt, only one-fifth of the convicts who benefit from it commit, within three years following their conviction, a new offense, which revokes the benefit of the conditional immunity from law. But on the whole, from among the convicts of all categories the proportion of those who in the same limits of time become recidivists is rather low. It is therefore difficult to assume that the application of law in deferring the proceedings has much efficacy in stopping delinquents who are on the way to committing crime.

As for crime taken by itself, some of its aspects have perceptibly changed during these twenty years. Murder and assault and even crimes against property have lost ground. But there is one respect in which crime has increased. Minor violence has become more numerous; it is now committed twice as frequently as robbery, which exceeded it at the beginning of the period. On the other hand, astute acts of punishable character[16] have considerably increased in proportion.

Not only is the proportion of women in the entire criminal population much lower than that of men, but also it is very remarkable that the women's share is not too great in the general growth of crime we have mentioned earlier. The women's percentage of the crime rate has remained strictly the same, whereas that of men has doubled. The causes which have determined this enormous recrudescence in the male crime rate have therefore remained without similar effect on the female population. This is because the causes are social, and women, for the reasons we have elsewhere stated (see *Suicide,* p. 231), by not participating as directly as men in the collective life, submit less to its influence and experience less of its various consequences.

The German statistics give us some information on the relationship of crime with religious identification. The proportion of Catholics in the general growth of crime is considerably higher than that of Protestants. The major crimes or felonies committed by Catholics consist of violence against persons. The cause may be perhaps attributed to the fact that the countries with the most predominant Catholic population are characterized in terms of rather inferior intellectual culture. Jewish crime takes especially the form of guile. This has increased 31 percent. (*Année sociologique,* 9, 1906, p. 448–449; trans. Y. Nandan)

NOTES AND NOTICES

Rosa M. Barrett. "The Treatment of Juvenile Offenders, Together with Statistics of Their Numbers." *Journal of the Royal Statistical Society,* June 1900, pp. 183–272.

The article gives many statistical tables regarding the juvenile criminals in various countries of Europe. (*Année sociologique,* 4, 1901, p. 452; trans. Y. Nandan)

Antonio Marro. "Influence of the Puberal Development upon the Moral Character." *American Journal of Sociology,* V, no. 2, pp. 193–320.

With the help of statistics collected from the correctional and educational institutions, the author attempts to show that the appearance of puberty, by the plethora of life that accompanies it, adds to the immoral inclinations. But all that seems to have resulted from the facts which the author has gathered is that morality in children experiences deviation at the age of fourteen years. It is caused by puberty. The author confirms the fact, without further proving it. It must be remembered that this age is critical from more than one point of view. It is the time when the individual experiences two moral dispositions: that of the second part of the childhood from which he is emerging and that of the adolescence he is beginning to enter. Naturally a certain inconsistency results which characterizes the behavior. (*Année sociologique,* 4, 1901, p. 452; trans. Y. Nandan)

G. L. Duprat. *Les Causes sociales de la folie.* Paris: F. Alcan, 1900, 202 pp.

The aim of this work is to pose an important question: whether insanity, taken from a certain bias, is a social phenomenon and may be studied as such. But the method followed by the author did not lead him to any very useful results. He is satisfied in dialectically associating the general state of human incapacitation with the overexertion in work of the whole civilization that has been lured into a very intense life; he puts together a delirious feeling for ambition and the outbursts of ambitions, the religious insanity and the religion itself, the degeneration and the consanguine marriages. The only way to have really advanced in the subject would have been to look into, by means of methodic and statistical comparisons, how the rate of insanity varies from one society to another, or within the same society, according to civil status, the presence or absence of children, religious identification, and political crises, etcetera. One could determine the diversity of social status as reflected in the insanity. However, while suggesting exactly how to fight alcoholism effectively, it is not enough to make eloquent predictions. But the evil must be nipped in the bud—that is to say, in the social causes [since they are the cause as well as its effect]. (*Année sociologique,* 4, 1901, pp. 475–476; trans. Y. Nandan)

E. Fornasari di Verce. "Sul valore sociale dei pazzi" (Social Value of Insanity). Archivio di Psichiatria, *Antropologia criminale e scienze penali,* xx, no. 3.

di Verce. "Alcune osservazioni di natura economica circa l'aumento dei pazzi ricoverati in Italia." *Rivista sperimentale di freniatria,* xxv, no. 2.

These articles admit that there are relationships between insanity and genius and that insanity could have erstwhile played a positive social role in the form of prophecy. As far as modern societies are concerned, the author hardly notices a sort of decay in social organism that inevitably is the consequence of struggle for life. But the present decay has reached an abnormal proportion. (*Année sociologique,* 4, 1901, p. 476; trans. Y. Nandan)

Statistics on Morals

DOMESTIC AND CONJUGAL LIFE: MARRIAGE AND DIVORCE

REVIEWS

Paul Kollmann. "Die soziale Zusammensetzung der Bevölkerung im deutschen Reiche" (Composition of the Population in the German Empire). *Jahrbuch für Gesetzgebung, Verwaltung und Volkswirtschaft,* 1900, 2nd fascicle, pp. 59–107.

In a series of articles,[17] Kollmann tried to determine, from the results of a census in 1895, how the German population was professionally organized. Of this entire work, we concentrate on the last part, in which he attempts to study relationships of professional activity with different domestic conditions.

Celibates, spouses, and the widowed are initially classified in four categories: the first includes those who are engaged in a profession; the second, domestics; the third, individuals without a profession who are family dependents; the fourth, individuals without a profession who are independent of all family ties. Each sex behaves in a different manner. The great majority of men who have a profession are married; among those of thirty or over, the proportion comes to 80 and 85 percent; on the contrary, either spinsters or widows are numerically in the lead as career women. From thirty to forty years of age, the proportion of widows, while being higher than that of spinsters, is lower than that of married women (23 percent instead of 42 percent); but beyond fifty years of age it is the widows who take the lead over the two other categories among civilians. Inversely, the relatives who are family dependents are almost all bachelors, whereas women in that situation are almost all married. Widows themselves are much less numerous in this class than married women. The fact is that the man resigns himself to this situation only when he is prevented from founding a family himself, whereas women reach that point only through marriage.

More interesting facts turn up when, in each profession, one distinguishes between employers or heads of concerns and employees of every kind. Generally speaking, the rate of marriage among the former is at one and the same time higher than that among the latter and at an earlier age level. The gap is enormous until thirty years of age and it remains considerable thereafter. As for the women, the situation is the same during the first period; but it is reversed from thirty on. The proportion of married women comes to 53 and 55 percent for employees, and only to 27 and 13 percent for women who are at the head of a concern. Only, what these last have lost in the column of married women, they make up in the column of widows. Out of 100 women who fill in this way an independent situation, there are 44 widows from thirty to fifty years of age, and 73 thereafter, whereas among the laboring women the proportions come respectively to 13 and 28. The better marriage rate among these last from thirty on is therefore only apparently so; it stems only from the fact that in this social situation the widows remarry much more often than those in more favorable situations. The fact is worth considering. Indeed, it has often been said that the widow has only a very mediocre aptitude for making a good match the second time around. In this respect, it would probably be fitting to distinguish between the different classes of society. In the lower classes, the tendency to draw up a new marriage contract must be much more pronounced than the overall figures would have us suppose.

The type of profession also has a decided influence on these same phenomena. It is in agriculture that the proportional number of marriages is highest and marriage is earliest: Out of 100 landowners from sixteen to thirty years of age, 80 are already married. By a singular anomaly, which the author does not explain and does not even note, this figure drops to 58 percent from thirty to fifty years of age, only to rise to 84 percent subsequently. This diminution is explained in part by the considerable number of widowers between thirty and fifty years of age, which is relatively higher than the number recorded after fifty years of age. The country dweller, who is quick to marry, has little taste for a second marriage if he becomes a widower when he is still in the prime of life. The same applies to women in the same situation. Unlike the heads of concerns, the farm workers are the ones whose marital prospects are minimal, while most belated at the same time. It is in industry that those factors are the most favorable. But it is otherwise for women. Likewise it is to be noted the relatively very paltry number of widows among the women who are at the head of an industrial enterprise; one finds only 2.31, and 59 percent according to age, instead of 18.66, and 86 percent in agriculture; another proof of this fact is that widows' marriage prospects vary considerably in proportion, depending on social conditions.

The size of the enterprise is also, by itself, an important factor in marriage statistics. Among directors of large enterprises they are the weakest, as if they varied in reverse proportion with the economic situation. It is just the opposite for the worker, who marries much more often in the large enterprise than in the small one; the gap is even very considerable. The author explains these facts by purely utilitarian considerations. The phenomenon is, doubtless, much more complex and these variations in marital statistics are probably not without moral causes. (*Année sociologique*, 4, 1901, pp. 436–438; trans. J. French)

Friedrich Prinzing. "Die soziale Lage der Witwe in Deutschland" (The Social Condition of the Widow in Germany). *Zeitschrift für Sozialwissenschaft*, 1900, no. 2, pp. 96–109; no. 3, pp. 199–205.

Prinzing. "Grundzüge und Kosten eines Gesetzes über die Fürsorge für die Witwen und Waisen der Arbeiter." *Ibid.*, no. 4, pp. 262–277.

The widow's situation has always been looked upon as rather unenviable. The author lends support to this popular sentiment with the precise tools of statistics. He determines the role of widows in different professions and situations and sums up the result of his analysis with the following proposal: "In Germany as a whole, slightly more than a sixth of the widows either live only on charity, whether public or private, or else find themselves placed in the most unfavorable situation because of the precarious nature of the jobs in which they serve and the inadequacy of the remunerations, notably so in the cities" (p. 109).

After having established this deplorable condition of widowhood, the author seeks its consequences. First of all, there is an increase in the mortality rate that is observed at all ages and in all countries (p. 200); an increase in the tendency towards suicide (pp. 201–202); and finally, an increase in the crime rate, which ends only with the late years in life. This aggravated tendency has a special bearing on crimes against property (p. 203). The author's conclusion is that the state must intervene in order to improve the situation of the widow. The object of the second article, the title of which we have given above, is specifically to lay out a plan for an assistance fund for widows and orphans.

However interesting one finds the facts which are presented in this way, they appear to us to include, on more than one point, an appreciably different interpretation. The whole work is dominated by this idea that the widow's situation is much worse than the widower's. Now, if one judges both of them by the same criteria, it is the contrary conclusion that is inescapable. As for the death rate, the widower's is far worse. The same for suicide. From twenty until twenty-five years of age, the widower kills himself 1.45 times more than the married man, and 3.37 times more in the following period, whereas for the widow the coefficient comes only to 1.05 and 2.61; and the relationship is appreciably the same in the following years. Hence the loss of a spouse has a more profound effect on the man than on the woman; she can more easily do without the man than the man can do without her.[18] Moreover, we have stated what we consider to be the reasons for this difference.

There is, however, a point where the woman loses more than the man by the dissolution of a marriage; it is in matters of a moral nature. Her tendency toward crime and toward misdemeanors is, in this case, much more intensified than it is in the other sex. The aggravated tendency* is, in her case, 2.5; 2; 1.5; 1.2, depending on age; in the man's case, it is only 1.5; 1.9; 1.6; 0.6. It proves that woman's moral sense is less deeply rooted than man's, since she is less resistant to the shock of events as soon as she is subjected, by force of circumstances, to more direct involvement in the action. Put another way, woman's nature is less strongly socialized than man's, a truth which we have backed up with further proofs in our *Suicide*. (*Année sociologique*, 4, 1901, pp. 438–440; trans. J. French)

Friedrich Lindner. *Die unehelichen Geburten als Sozialphänomen*
  (Illegitimate Birth as a Social Phenomenon). Leipzig: A. Deichert,
  1900, x + 238 pp.

It is exclusively from Bavaria that the author takes the materials of his research. But though the field of his comparisons is thus limited, it is nonetheless well chosen. Bavaria, in fact, rates as the favorite terrain for illegitimate birth; in this capacity it is ahead of all the societies of Europe. Also, its percentages of illegitimate births vary widely from one province to another.

Two procedures are concurrently employed by Lindner in order to measure the intensity of the phenomenon that he is studying: one depending on the proportion of illegitimate births as a whole, the other based on the number of children that are brought into the world, in an average year, by 100 unmarried mothers from fifteen to fifty years of age. This double criterion is necessary. Too often one is obliged to settle for the first when no other is available; but it is totally inadequate. Indeed the proportion of illegitimate children in the total birthrate can be very high, not because sexual debauchery is very considerable, but because the legitimate birth rate is feeble as a result of relative marital sterility combined with a low rate of marriages. It is therefore a bad way to measure the intensity of the tendency to form irregular unions. Experience shows that we would be exposing ourselves to grave errors if we relied exclusively on this method.

As for the results of the study, they are of two sorts: certain ones positive, the others negative. These last are perhaps the most interesting. The author shows that the position of the legistature concerning natural children, as shown by the extent of the rights accorded to them as well as to the mother,

* The following figures represent what Durkheim designated as *"coefficient of aggravation"* opposed to *"coefficient of preservation"* to determine the ratio of suicide rates of two similar groups within the same age and of the same sex. For a fuller meaning of the term, see Durkheim's *Suicide*, op. cit., pp. 177–80; and for a further elaboration of it, see Whitney Pope, *Durkheim's Suicide: A Classic Analyzed* (The University of Chicago Press, 1976, pp. 77–79). ED.

does not have on the illegitimate birthrate the considerable influence that is sometimes attributed to it (pp. 74–81). Some of the countries that are under the Napoleonic Code have as high a rate as those others where the unwed mother is able to put in a claim to be helped by the supposed father. It is indeed a fact that these entirely utilitarian calculations cannot have a very profound impact on a phenomenon that depends, above all, on physical and moral conditions that are also profound. Likewise, it seems clear that city life is not as destructive of sexual morality as has been claimed. If the large cites are ill-favored in this regard, the towns, on the contrary, show a certain immunity in comparison with the countryside. It is true that one comes to a very different conclusion if one uses only the first of the two methods indicated above; but this is precisely one of the cases that show its inadequacy (pp. 81–112).

As for the positive factors in the phenomenon, the most essential are probably, according to the author, of an economic nature (pp. 50 ff.). It is incontestable, in fact, that economic crises, at a time when they are acute, are generally accompanied by a decline in the illegitimate birthrate and that a movement in reverse often arises in periods of great prosperity. But, to begin with, there are numerous exceptions (pp. 61, 62, 63); above all the relationship between the two curves is in no way consistent. There is no evidence, from one year to the next, that the illegitimate birthrate increases or decreases according to whether the cost of living rises or falls. One senses, therefore, that many other factors must intervene, and that they are purely moral. Lindner himself makes his contribution toward establishing this by pointing out the impact exerted by religious persuasions (pp. 68 ff.). The Protestants, at least in Bavaria, are less inclined towards irregular unions than the Catholics, and the Jews are almost untouched.

But furthermore, even the influence of the economic factor needs an explanation and might well depend on causes that are in no way economic. By itself, the high cost of living is no deterrent to the free union; one might rather expect it to produce the opposite effect for the very reason that, as is easily understood, it is a deterrent to marriage. The author, in order to account for the report as established, is obliged to attribute this diminution of the illegitimate birthrate to the greater number of emigrations to be observed during the years of depression. But if one considers that from one year to the next the number of natural children decreases at times by 4,000 units, or by 25 percent, one will understand the inadequacy of such an explanation. Would it not be more natural to admit that the birthrate (legitimate or not) varies with the intensity of public activity? When public vitality is enhanced, the private individual's share becomes part of this enhancement that manifests itself in all sorts of ways: one needs to feel alive and to become more active; one hungers for pleasures; so confident of the future, one plunges into adventures with a will, and as a result irregular unions, like the other kind, increase in number. What tends to confirm this interpretation is this fact, pointed out by the author himself, that periods of political agitation are likewise accompanied by a resurgence of the birthrate both legitimate and illegitimate (pp. 56, 61). It is clear that from this point of view variations in the illegitimate birthrate take on an entirely different meaning; they are symptoms of the changes that the country's mental and moral state is undergoing.

In a final chapter (pp. 179–281), Lindner attempts to determine, still by means of statistical data, what happens after birth to natural children. (*Année sociologique,* 4, 1901, pp. 441–443; trans. J. French)

J. Bertillon. "Nombre d'enfants par famille." *Journal de la Société de Statistique de Paris,* 1901, no. 4, pp. 130–145.

Two important propositions are established in this article.

(1) It has been sometimes noted that the departments in which families have the fewest children are also those with the most childless households. Since it is hard to believe that absolute sterility[19] is voluntary, the conclusion has been reached that relative sterility could indeed depend on organic factors, to a certain extent at the very least. Bertillon refutes this hypothesis. The proportion of sterile households has stayed the same since the middle of the century (16.4 per 1,000 in 1836 and 16.7 per 1,000 in 1856), whereas the number of children per family has very appreciably diminished. The above-mentioned proportion of sterile households is very similar in Paris, in Berlin, in Rio de Janeiro, whereas the birthrate among fertile families is very different in these three cities. The fact, then, is that these two sets of statistics depend on different causes. If at times they appear to vary along parallel lines, the fact is that wherever families are small in number—wherever, especially, the proportion of single children is considerable—the number of households without children must itself appear high on the day of census taking; for, in a family with a single child, the death of a child suffices to increase by a unit the category of childless families.

(2) It has often been affirmed that the number of children vary in inverse ratio to the degree of affluence, but there has never been any conclusive evidence in support of this proposition. An unpublished work carried out under the direction of the census office and at Bertillon's request permitted him to give this evidence. By means of declarations necessitated by the tax on successions, he was able to establish that the more restricted families are, the more frequently they leave a bequest. Out of 1,000 households that lasted from twenty to twenty-four years in which there was one child, an appreciable bequest was left by half of them; out of 1,000 families with two children there were no more than 359 bequests, and the proportion decreases uninterruptedly. What is still more conclusive is that the global value of declared successions decrease in proportion to the number of infants raised. The only exception to this last law is the slight superiority of the families with one child over the families with two children (11,465 francs of total average value as against 13,720). But this regularity surely comes from the fact that in households with a single child fraud more easily conceals the whole or a part of the wealth.

Another chapter in this work is devoted to the children of the families of functionaries. On this point, the conclusion is that "if the French have fewer children than the other inhabitants of Europe, French functionaries have still fewer by far." If one divides the functionaries into two classes—office workers, who live by a pen in hand, and lesser agents, for whom the pen is not the principal working instrument—the latter are the least likely to have children. Postal clerks in particular have almost no children at all.

The article is concluded with practical considerations that appear hardly in keeping with the preceding propositions.

In order to stimulate the birthrate, the author proposes tax cuts, budgetary favors granted to large families. The fact that these measures are equitable cannot be disputed. But how could they raise the birthrate if being well off tends rather to lower it? It is more readily apparent from the result of the above facts that the meager density of families is linked above all to a temperament that cannot be undermined by financial means. (*Année sociologique,* 5, 1902, pp. 435–436; trans. J. French)

Friedrich Prinzing. "Die eheliche Fruchtbarkeit in Deutschland" (The Legitimate Birthrate in Germany). *Zeitschrift für Sozialwissenschaft,* 1901, pp. 33–38, pp. 90–100, pp. 188–192.

When one makes a comparison between the different states of Germany or the different districts of the same state, the legitimate birthrate appears to fluctuate considerably at various points and even in cases where comparable localities are very close to one another. These variations certainly do not appear to be linked with the nature of the families' professions. One finds, in fact, high rates in the industrial countries as well as in essentially agricultural regions (p. 94). The phenomenon, then, seems to result above all from practices and customs—that is, in short, the ethical establishment of each milieu—and it is curious to see how much two places very close to one another can be different from this point of view. Even the influence of the state of the economy is inferior to that which the collective temper of the group under consideration exercises in this matter; and the proof of it is that districts where the material situation is equally wretched show very unequal rates (p. 93).

But if one compares in their totality the rural areas with the urban areas, legitimate procreation in the former appears to be very generally superior to that in the latter. It is evident that there are two different norms of behavior. The few exceptions that one encounters here and there cannot invalidate the general scope of the law (p. 100). The contrast appears even more marked when one knows how the legitimate birthrate has evolved in the towns and the countryside during the last third of this century. In Berlin, in twenty-three years, it has declined from 23.8 to 16.9; in the large towns of Prussia, from 26.7 to 23.5; in the towns in general, from 26.9 to 24. In the countryside, it has remained stationary. The same situation exists in Bavaria (pp. 99, 190).

The practice of reducing the family to two children is clearly becoming widespread in German towns and is beginning to penetrate certain parts of the country.

One fact that the author does not bring up, which nevertheless appears to show up clearly in the figures he quotes, is the higher birthrate in Catholic countries. Bavaria, Prussian Poland, and Rhineland Prussia have appreciably higher-than-average rates. (*Année sociologique*, 5, 1902, pp. 436–437; trans. J. French)

Abel Pouzol. *La Recherche de la paternité. Etude critique de sociologie et de législation comparée.* Paris: Giard et Brière, 1902, xii + 579 pp.

This work consists of three parts. The first reveals the history of the variations through which has passed our law relative to the investigation of paternity and the present state of foreign legislation on the same issue. This statement of the case adds nothing to the one that Dupré la Tour has already given us in his book, *La Recherche de la paternité en droit comparé* (The Investigation of Paternity in Comparative Law), analyzed here last year.[20] Let us note simply that the author is excessively simplistic when attributing to Napoleon's personal will the unjust severities of our Code. If, when banning the investigations of paternity, our law had done nothing but translate a personal feeling, however powerful it might be, the ban would not have survived its author; it would not have resisted all the attacks of which it was the target; it would not count on so many defenders to this day. Besides, this ban is not special to France; it is found in Italy, in Belgium, in Spain, in a word in most of the Catholic countries. There is no doubt, we too believe, that it constitutes an unsound phenomenon; but the causes on which this abnormal state of affairs depends are certainly more general and more profound.

The second part of the book is chiefly dialectical in character. The author establishes there, albeit deductively, the drawbacks of the French system, while at the same time discussing the objections currently being made to the opposing system. A few objective data are to be found effectively injected into the discussion, but they are reproduced, at times in identical terms, in the last part, which overlaps the earlier one, to the detriment of the composition.

The third part is the only one which has a truly sociological interest. Its aim is to determine the bad influence exercised by the prohibitory system on public morals. That is why we have included here an analysis of the work. Unfortunately, of the two hundred pages which are devoted to this study, there emerge very few items worth considering.

The author deals successively with four questions.

(1) *Influence of the prohibitory system on the rate of illegitimate births.* The author, who does nothing but reproduce on this point Bertillon's argument, strives to prove that the ban on investigating paternity results in raising the coefficient of illegitimacy. Unfortunately, the facts hardly appear to lend

themselves to this interpretation. As a matter of fact, the Germanic Empire in general, Bavaria, Saxony, Austria, Denmark, and Sweden—all countries that accept the principle of such investigation and of paternal responsibility—have an appreciably higher coefficient than France, Belgium, and Italy, which practice a contrary regime (8.57; 12.99; 13.04; 11.93; 10.69; 10.82; versus 7.26; 6.95; 7.28 in 1874). Pouzol believes he is able to account for this anomaly by attributing it to the various obstacles that the legislation or customs of these different countries bring to marriage and that naturally incite extralegal unions. But if that explanation were well founded, the occurrence of marriages would be more rare, because more difficult obstacles would cause a lower rate of marriage, a result that is easily attributed to it. We should therefore find among these people a mediocre rate of marriage; quite the contrary, it is excellent. Per 1,000 inhabitants, there are each year 8.4 marriages in Germany, 8.4 likewise in Bavaria, 9.2 in Saxony, 8.5 in Austrian Cisleithania,[21] and 10.3 in Hungary. And the precocity of the marriages is equal to their frequency. That is certainly not like saying that legislation in favor of illegitimate children necessarily increases their numbers at a great rate. Rather, what appears to stand out from the statistical information, interpreted without prejudice, is that between these two arrangements of facts there are no definite relationships. The rate of illegitimate births depends on other profound causes; at least, if those legislative provisions have some sort of influence, it is not very apparent and must have only secondary importance. This is a fact that we have already had occasion to demonstrate in *L'Année* with regard to Bavaria[22] (vol. 4, p. 441).

(2) *Influence of the prohibitory system on the mortality rate of those born illegitimate.* Here the facts appear to be quite in keeping with the conclusions. Everywhere the mortality rate is more considerable for those born illegitimate than for those born legitimate, and the coefficient of aggravation itself is higher in countries where the investigation of paternity is banned (p. 384). There is nothing surprising in this result. In view of the evidence that the rate of death at birth among the illegitimate is due to the state of misery, physical and otherwise, that is the lot of the unwed mother when she gives birth to the child, it is entirely natural that this misery is still greater and creates more disastrous results now that she has no recourse against the father.

(3) *Influence of the prohibitory system on the marriage rate.* The marriage rate is certainly better in those cases where the investigation of paternity is allowed (p. 439). What removes from this fact a little of its validity is the truth that, in these same countries, the rate of illegitimate births is at the same time very large, as we have shown above. Must one conclude that many children born in a state of illegitimacy are then legitimized by marriage?

(4) *Influence of the prohibitory system on the rate of crime in general and more specially on infantile crime.* This whole portion of the demonstration appears to us to be without any probative force. The author limits himself to pointing out that the rates of general crime and infantile crime are increasing

in France and tending to decrease in England. But from these facts there is nothing to be concluded about the issue that concerns us. It is not to the legislative situation regarding illegitimate children that this difference can be ascribed, for the English regime is not particularly in their favor. The mother can indeed bring suit against the father, but all she can ever obtain is a fixed sum of 325 francs a year until the child is sixteen. Furthermore, beyond this pecuniary aid, already so restricted, the illegitimate child has no rights; he can bear neither his father's name nor his mother's. In no case is he on call for the parental succession. Obviously it is not those 325 francs per year that can explain the better morality that England, and especially English youth, presumably enjoys. For one to be able to ascribe to legislation such a beneficent influence, one would have to assure the infant of morally decent surroundings, a family that would raise and support him; now, this kind of care is in no way a legislative concern. In another sense, it is easily understandable that whatever the circumstances, making a comparison of only two countries cannot possibly be conclusive. There are numerous countries where the rate of juvenile crime is increasing and where nevertheless the investigation of paternity is allowed.

It is clear from this example that the author is not very careful to impart a scientific character to his evidence. His book is above all a case of special pleading, in which he presents everything that can serve the thesis as testimony, if only in appearance; in which he is more preoccupied with relying on the authorities than with stating the facts, and in which all sorts of issues, borderline but separate from the one under consideration, are superficially skimmed over (questions of marriage, of the crime rate in general, of secular education and so on). To be sure, we also think that the prohibitory regime is abnormal; but we fear that such a line of reasoning does not add much weight to an opinion that we nonetheless accept in principle. (*Année sociologique*, 6, 1903, pp. 415–418; trans. J. French)

J. Depinay. *Le Régime dotal: Etude historique, critique et pratique.* Paris: Marchal et Billard, 1902, viii + 580 pp.

Paul Griveau. *Le Régime dotal en France: Ses Avantages et ses inconvénients.* Paris: Marchal et Billard, 1902, 175 pp.

The dowry is a legal phenomenon that poses a very interesting question for the sociologist. Born in Rome under the empire of fleeting pomp and circumstance, it survived for centuries the causes that apparently gave it birth, and in spite of impassioned and repeated attacks it managed to stay alive up until our own day. Where did such strong resistance come from? Was it the simple result of ingrained habits or was the dowry playing out, in spite of the critics, a role of some genuine social usefulness? In order to answer these questions, without resorting to sentimental rationalizations or a purely dialectic love of reasoning, it would first be necessary to prepare as completely as possible a geography of the dowry, to investigate if this geography has changed with the times; we would then be in a position to determine the principal conditions on which it depends and which constitute its justification.

On the first of these points one will discover some useful information in the two works of which the reader has just finished perusing the titles—works composed along identical lines, in accordance with a program set forth by the Académie des Sciences Morales et Politiques.[23] Depinay's book is the more fully documented of the two. There are the facts he has assembled, some drawn from official statistics, others from the personal and rather extensive investigation upon which he has embarked. To begin with, his conclusions indicate that the dowry no longer plays anything but a very minimal role in the legal life of the country. As a matter of fact, dowry contracts represent an eighth of the total of marriage contracts as a whole; but since, on the other hand, only 29 per 100 marriages are preceded by contractual agreements, it is clear how small a place is given to the institution of the dowry in our domestic customs.

As for geographical distribution, fifteen departments are totally without dowry practices. In thirty-eight others, there are only barely perceptible traces to be found. In the remaining departments, the proportion of dowry contracts in relation to the totality of contracts varies between 4 per 100 (Orne)[24] and 90 per 100 (Basses-Alpes and Hautes-Alpes).[25] In thirteen departments, more than half the contracts are of the dowry type. The Midi (especially Languedoc) and Normandy are the favorite terrain for this marital system. Outside of France it is preponderant in the south of Europe (Greece, Italy, Spain, Portugal). But it is totally unknown in the north. In central Europe, Austria is the only country where it exists, although in attenuated form; moreover, it is common law.

What emerges from these facts is that the dowry is linked to a certain conception of marriage. It is found, in fact, in all countries where Roman law has had a profound influence; now, for the Romans, the husband was *dominus dotis.*[26] According to Norman customs as well, the wife's personality was mingled with the husband's. Even the extent of those powers were so great that they pointed up to a need to limit them; from this came the institution of dowry. But since this conception is no longer ours, the conclusion seems likely that this marital system can no longer be justified, and indeed it is in the process of regressing. Our two authors arrive, however, at a different conclusion. They point out that if the system of the dowry in its entirety is disappearing, nevertheless partial provisions for dowry (dowry involving property acquired in common and transferability of dowry properties but with obligatory and predetermined reinvestment provisions) are being used more and more in regions which, up until now, ignored them. Therefore this mitigated system appears to have a future. But they assign to it a function very different from the one that it had originally: It would no longer by anything more than a protective measure in favor of the wife and children. However, even under this form, there exists a contradiction with the most basic ideas of what is right. As a result, all that can be said is that the law perhaps should not ban the dowry. But its sporadic character clearly shows that it can be applied to good effect only in relatively exceptional, almost abnormal cases—that is to say, in those cases where the husband's moral standards inspire justifiable feelings of mistrust. And again, even under those circumstances, its effectiveness is doubtful. (*Année sociologique*, 6, 1903, pp. 418–420; trans. J. French)

F. Buomberger. *Die schweizerische Ehegesetzgebung im Lichte der Statistik* (Swiss Legislation on Marriage in the Light of Statistics). Fribourg: B. Veith, 1901, 30 pp.

Switzerland is on the eve of codifying its civil law; a codification plan has even been filed. As for marriage, it proposes to raise the legal age from eighteen to twenty years for the man, and from sixteen to eighteen years for the woman; on the other hand, it confirms the existing legislation on divorce. Buomberger calls public attention to the danger that the proposed provisions present on these two points, and since his evidence relies on statistics, some of his observations are worth retaining.

The proposed restriction on the age of marriage would appreciably lower the marriage rate, for this restriction would not simply affect the ages at which marriage would henceforth be banned. It is known as a fact that 72 percent of the men who marry before twenty marry women older than twenty, and 52 percent of the women from sixteen to nineteen marry men of more than twenty-five. On the other hand, it would be a mistake to attribute these precocious marriages to frivolity and heedlessness. They are caused by economic necessities. In fact, they are especially frequent in the crafts that are practiced within the family, and where the man needs as soon as possible a partner who will further his interests.

But the most interesting part of the work is the one devoted to divorce. Right from the start we can see evidence of the considerable influence that legislation involving divorce has on marriage. Switzerland is excessively tolerant in matters of divorce; it permits divorce by mutual consent, for defamation of character, and even for any causes that may appear to the judge capable of disturbing the social relationship of husband and wife. The result of all this is a rate of divorce that is higher in Switzerland than in the other European countries. This influence is so marked that it makes itself felt above and beyond all others. It is a matter of common knowledge that the Catholic divorces less than the Protestant; but the Swiss Catholic divorces more often than the other European Catholics.

On the influence of religious persuasion itself, the author gives us interesting information. In Switzerland as elsewhere, the Protestant divorces more often than the Catholic; but the marriages that most easily reach the breaking point are mixed marriages. What is more remarkable is the fact that the aggravation appears to carry more weight when the husband is Catholic and the wife Protestant than the other way around. In households where the husband only is Catholic, divorce is five times more frequent than when both the spouses are Catholics; on the contrary, when only the husband is Protestant, divorce is not even twice more frequent than when both spouses are members of the Reformed Church. Given the evidence that the intensity of the trend towards divorce in a given social group depends above all on the intensity of this same trend on the part of the man of the group, the conclusion seems to be very clear. On the basis of the foregoing figures and within the area of mixed marriages, Catholicism is less effective in preserving the marriage than Protestantism. Moreover, these facts can easily be explained. Unions of this type presuppose among those who contract them a breakdown of the traditional moral equilibrium, and since most of them are incapable of finding the strength to make a new start on their own, there follows a state of insecurity that quite naturally opens the door to the divorce court. On the other hand, because Protestantism depends less on tradition and because it addresses itself more to individual initiative, it makes its followers better equipped to face up to such disturbing situations.

It is equally curious to note that the relative immunity from divorce the countryside enjoys as against the cities is disappearing in mixed households—all of which clearly proves that such a factor derives essentially from moral causes. In this case, it is the countryside itself that is taking the lead, especially when the husband is Catholic (354 divorces out of 100,000 marriages, against 303 in the town). It is new evidence of the minor preservation that Catholicism grants in this particular situation. (*Année sociologique*, 6, 1903, pp. 420–422; trans. J. French)

Friedrich Prinzing. "Die Ehescheidungen in Berlin und anderwärts" (Divorce in Berlin and Elsewhere). *Zeitschrift für Sozialwissenschaft*, 1901, no. 11, pp. 723–734.

Among the facts revealed somewhat confusingly in the course of this article, we shall note the following as the most interesting.

To begin with, we find a confirmation of the aggravation that mixed marriages create and that we have just singled out in the case of Switzerland. But it is remarkable that it is much less so in Berlin than in this last country. The Berliner can more readily than the Swiss do without the traditional culture, probably because he is the recipient of a more rational culture. Jews alone are the exception. Among them, mixed marriages have deplorable results; from a simple trend, they escalate the intensity of the tendency toward divorce three times over. Perhaps the reason for this is the overly great difference that the culture of the two spouses represents.

In Berlin as elsewhere, divorces keep on increasing. The biggest contributing factor in this increase is adultery (the cause of 112 divorces per 1,000 marriages in 1885–89 and of 154 divorces per 1,000 in 1896–98); divorces by mutual consent have risen from 64 per 1,000 to 133.9. This is conclusive evidence that the marriage bond is losing its strength, in the view of public opinion and of the courts (p. 727). The belief is even well grounded that in an important number of cases the real cause of divorce is quite simply the desire to marry again. In fact, 20 per 100 divorced spouses remarry within the year following the breakup of the marriage (p. 733); it is very hard to believe that such a prompt marriage was not provided for and anticipated in advance.

The number of divorces declared at the end of two years of marriage tends to augment in Berlin; from 1885 to 1898 it tripled. Such a reckoning bespeaks a veritable abuse. A number of divorces could be avoided if the spouses were compelled to wait longer. Proof of this lies in the relative frequency of cases where the divorced spouses marry each other again (p. 733). That is a fact which the law and the courts should take into account.

Berlin statistics confirm what was already known about the extreme fragility of precocious marriages. Out of 100 marriages where the husband is less than twenty years old, there are 68 which are dissolved through divorce. (*Année sociologique,* 6, 1903, pp. 422–423; trans. J. French)

Friedrich Prinzing. "Die Wandlungen der Heiratshäufigkeit und des mittleren Heiratsalters" (Variations in the Rate of Marriage and in the Average Age of Marriage). *Zeitschrift für Sozialwissenschaft,* 1902, pp. 656–674.

Contrary to what has often been written, the percentage rate of marriages, in spite of certain accidental and passing downward movements, is very generally on the rise among European peoples. This is particularly the case in Germany. At the same time, marriages in middle age tend to decrease. This improved rate of marriage is due almost entirely to a more emphatic leaning of bachelors toward family life; widowers apparently have nothing to do with it. In Prussia, at any rate, the proportion of widowers and the separated in the overall number of people who marry each year continues, on the contrary, to diminish. However, if the fact is correct in a general way, it is interesting to note that the two sexes do not behave similarly in this regard. In fact, since the upward move began, the number of male celibates who married increased much more than that of celibates of the opposite sex. The former augmented by 8 percent from 1876 to 1897; the latter, by 4 percent only. Thus, half the young men who came to swell the ranks of the married had to find their wives not among the unmarried girls but among the widows. When, therefore, a combination of circumstances stimulates the tendency to marry, it is mainly from among those classed as widows that the new wives are recruited. Apparently the number of marriageable girls cannot increase as readily as that of young men; apparently it is less flexible. It seems that in this sense there is a limit that is more easily reached, so much so that the new suitors are obliged to turn elsewhere in order to find the wives they need. Is this not conclusive evidence that the two sexes are not equal with respect to marriage? The woman finds it less easily accessible than the man, since the number of girls who are not summoned to the altar is somehow more irreducibly fixed. The method of choosing a mate in marriage seems therefore to be much harsher and more severe on one side than on the other. (*Année sociologique*, 7, 1904, pp. 520–521; trans. J. French)

Friedrich Prinzing. "Heiratshäufigkeit und Heiratsalter nach Stand und Beruf." *Zeitschrift für Sozialwissenschaft*, 1903, pp. 546–553.

As far as the rate of marriages is concerned, this work does not terminate with any very precise or very instructive conclusions. In respect to the marrying age, the author arrives at some more interesting conclusions. It is a general fact that in the affluent classes men marry later than in the impoverished classes, whereas for girls the reverse holds true. The richer they are, the sooner they get married. When we turn from the classes to the professions, it is a matter of record that for those in liberal careers marriage comes later in life. Sometimes, however, they are outdistanced by farm workers; in any case, the average age of the spouses is always higher than in industry. According to the author, these differences derive from economic conditions in particular; and the importance of this factor is beyond dispute. However, the fact that in the affluent classes men marry late shows clearly that other causes must intervene. According to Prinzing, if young men in such surroundings put off the date of marriage, the fact is that they need more time in order to get settled in a good job. It is, however, hard to admit that the more affluent one is, the more trouble one has earning one's living. The truth is that in wealthy circles one is content at less cost,[27] that a job which could easily suffice to maintain a family is readily regarded as insufficient in that context. Requirements increase with the degree of affluence to which one is accustomed. A moral element thus comes into the picture; it is the idea that is entertained of the type of life that must be led by an average man of the class to which one belongs. We wonder if in the matter of increase in age when marrying in the country some contributing factor of this type does not interfere. The farm worker is less in need of creating a family. Perhaps it is because the brothers live on together that the family where one was born remains more strongly and more durably compact than in town, where it is scattered even before the children's education is terminated. (*Année sociologique*, 8, 1905, pp. 487–488; trans. J. French)

Othmar Spann. "Die Stiefvaterfamilie unehelichen Ursprungs. Zugleich eine Studie zur Methodologie der Unehelichkeits-Statistik." *Zeitschrift für Sozialwissenschaft*, 1904, pp. 539–574.

Instead of confining himself to global figures that usually give statistics on the birth rate or on the death rate of the illegitimate, in addition to somewhat vague conclusions that emerge from these very general data, Spann strives to introduce some useful distinctions into this confused mass of facts in such a way as to feature the very different social conditions in which illegitimate children are to be found. For the moral environment in which an illegitimate child lives is very different depending on whether its mother remained unmarried or was married, and depending on whether she married the father of her child or a stranger. These are naturally different results, produced by those varied moral environments, that the author tries to rediscover and to calculate. He has turned his attention to illegitimate children who were called up for military duty and physically examined at Frankfurt from 1870 to 1881. They numbered 2,120, including 632 born in Frankfurt itself; the 1,488 others were immigrants.

Here are the conclusions at which he arrived:

In the first place, the number of unwed mothers who married after the birth of their child was relatively high: 42 per 100. And since this figure was established for a very special population, formed exclusively of illegitimate children who had reached the age of military service, it is certainly an inferior estimate of the real situation. For the mothers whose children had not reached that age must have found it still easier to get married.

In marriages contracted in this fashion, the husband was not the real father of the child, for if he had been the father, the child would have been legitimized in all his rights by the marriage (subject to a declaration which generally takes place the following year). Consequently, he would have been marked on the duty roster as a legitimate offspring, and not as an illegitimate one. Families that are constituted in such a way are therefore peculiar; they are different in that the child is raised by a stepfather; hence the expression *Stief- vaterfamilie* as it appears in the title of the article.

Now, according to the facts assembled by our author, the result seems to be that this kind of family, although unnatural in part, exerts a healthy influence upon the offspring in regard to physical and moral development, an influence almost equal to that which a perfectly regular family can exert. Out of 100 young men raised under such circumstances, more than half are declared fit for active service, which is roughly the proportion of legitimate children. On the other hand, out of 100 illegitimate children whose mothers have remained unmarried, the proportion is only 32 per 100.

Likewise, illegitimate children thus raised by a stepfather more readily achieve higher social standing. Hence, only illegitimate children whose mothers do not marry are exposed to physical and moral decay; they alone are illegitimate children in the full sense of the word. They alone constitute a social evil.

Another very interesting comparison made by the author contrasts illegitimate children whose unmarried mother is dead with those whose unmarried mother is still alive. In this case, it's discovered that the orphans are better off. Out of 100 illegitimate children whose unmarried mother is still living, there are only 32 fit for service, whereas for orphans in the same category the proportion is 37 per 100. Accordingly, *for illegitimate children, it is better to lose their mother if she is unmarried than to keep her.* According to Spann, what explains this distressing finding is that in cases like this it is more advantageous for the mother to be replaced by the public poorhouse.

There can be no dispute over these conclusions. Nevertheless, one must not lose sight of the fact that the grounds on which the observations were based were very narrow and that consequently they should have had needed confirmation by means of more extensive investigations. Spann is even obliged to acknowledge that certain facts which came to his attention are not in very close accord at first glance with general theory. When one considers only the illegitimate children who were born outside Frankfurt, those who were raised in a *Stiefvaterfamilie* do not seem to enjoy marked superiority, at least from the physical point of view, over the ones whose mother stayed single. The proportion of those *fit for service* is appreciably the same in both cases. The author explains this anomaly by pointing out that the immigrants must enjoy a better congenital constitution, both because they have been living in the country and because the move to immigrate, by itself, makes for a sort of selection; by and large, only very even tempered individuals immigrate to the town. The good quality of an unaffectedly natural temperament would then materialize the bad conditions in which were raised those whose family was reduced to the mother. But in that case, should not the same contributing factor also strengthen the advantage that is enjoyed by those who have had a *Stiefvaterfamilie*, that is to say a stepfather, and as a result should we not expect that the divergence between these two groups might disappear completely? A doubt, therefore, still exists, but the method is nonetheless interesting, and it is desirable that a more extensive application be made. (*Année sociologique*, 9, 1906, pp. 435–438; trans. J. French)

Alfred Valensi. *L'Application de la loi du divorce en France. Tendance générale de la jurisprudence, résultats sociaux, projets de réforme*. Paris: Larose et Tenin, 1905, 344 pp.

The law which introduced divorce in France has been functioning since 1884. Twenty years of application is a long enough time for observation in order to make it possible to assess the effect of this institution and the direction which it is destined to take. That is what Valensi has elected to do, and one can have nothing but praise for the method he has followed. Right from the start he has tried to bring out what divorce has tended to become in practice, that is to say as defined by law; then, by means of statistics, he has endeavored to determine the law's effects on society, the way in which it has affected the prinicipal manifestations of social life (birth rate, marriage rate, crime rate, etcetera); and finally, from this two-sided theoretical investigation he has drawn conclusions about the reforms the present state of divorce requires.

Beginning with legal interpretations, there is no doubt that they tend to make the avenues leading to divorce easier and more accessible. In the present state of our legislation, there exist four possible reasons for divorce. Two are peremptory, that is to say exempt from judicial arbitration; they consist of definite facts which, once established, necessarily lead to divorce—adultery and the sentencing of one of the spouses to degrading physical and civil punishment. The two others, on the contrary, are optional—that is to say, a very considerable latitude is granted to the Bench when passing sentence—excessive mistreatment and serious abuse, and separation from bed and board when such separation has lasted three years. Now, generally speaking, the judge has used the freedom thus granted him by coming out in favor of divorce. Wrongdoing has become "a general formula that has the value of offering a wide-open standard for loosely defined applications." This concept's lack of definition has allowed courts to multiply the reasons for divorce and to create others that never before occurred to the legislator. Judgments involving wrongdoing have been applied to mere convictions for minor offenses or have even involved acts considered improper or of an indelicate nature not covered by the penal code—slighting behavior, etcetera. So too, in theory the law leaves it up to the court to decide on the basis of specific cases whether or not separation from bed and board should, at the end of three years, be converted into divorce. As a matter of fact, such a conversion has become practically obligatory—it is refused in very exceptional cases only. Lastly, the Bench goes so far as to do everything in its power to cut down on the procedural obstacles that stand in the way of divorce.

Can it be then, as has been said, that judges are somehow or other animated by a spirit of anarchy? Not at all, our author answers; they are simply yielding to the pressure of events. If the law is flexible, the fact is that customs call for this greater flexibility; if divorce is made easy, the fact is that the need for divorce is growing stronger. As a matter of fact, the clever dodges of the parties involved have done even more than the artful legalities of the magistrates to create new reasons for divorce. Temperamental incompatibility is not recorded among legal reasons for divorce, and yet it is very often the real reason for divorces the judges cannot avoid approving. It is so easy for the parties involved to find some legal pretext in order to justify their request! Fictitious adulteries, planned wrongs, and so on—such are the ways that are currently practiced. How would the magistrate, feeling his powerlessness, not yield to this thrust of public opinion under such duress?

But before finding out if the legislator also must yield before this tendency and give it legal backing, one still needs to find out what the effects created by divorce are and if they are satisfactory enough to warrant the further spread of the practice. The author attempts to answer this question in the second part of his work. He has no trouble showing that divorce has not had a bad influence on the marriage rate, the birthrate, or the crime rate. At the very most there might be occasion to wonder if it is entirely certain that divorce does not encourage the rate of illegitimate births; the proportion of illegitimate births, among births as a whole, does indeed seem, at least in

France, to have abruptly become more considerable in the aftermath of the establishment of divorce. But there is a fact that Valensi does not choose to dispute: It is the obvious connection divorce has with suicide. However, our author does not want to hold divorce responsible for it. If suicide and divorce develop along parallel lines, the fact is, in his view, due to two reasons. First, many of those divorced are unbalanced, easy prey to suicide; next, divorce implies a certain trouble in the couple's material and moral way of life. This trouble would have no baneful influence on healthy individuals; but weak and irritable nervous systems do not have an easy time enduring it. Hence suicides would arise in cases where divorces are frequent; and consequently the evil would be imputable much more to the personal defects of those who are divorced than to the institution itself (p. 167).

Divorce thus being cleared of all the bad effects that have been imputed to it, the author sees no reason for the legislator to refuse to follow further the lead of public opinion and to make divorce laws still broader. Not only does Valensi ask that new reasons for divorce be acknowledged by law, but also, along with a certain number of contemporary publicists, he calls for the institution of divorce by mutual consent, and even, at least on general principle, divorce by unilateral choice.

But, however careful the author may be to proceed methodically, the facts themselves that he quotes appear to us to imply an entirely opposite conclusion. In the first place, on the tendency of the courts to facilitate divorce, there is nothing conclusive, for it is a question of finding out if this tendency is normal or not. The fact that public opinion seems to pronounce like a verdict of murder is not enough to settle the issue, for it may very well turn out that this current of public opinion is itself unsound. It is, no doubt, certain that the judge is doing nothing more than following the customs, but are the customs themselves healthy? It serves no purpose to contend that the parties involved manage quite easily to twist the law and under the cover of deceit cause the courts to acknowledge reasons for divorce that have no legal basis; this is no reason to hold up as legal a state of events which is perhaps regrettable. To be sure there are misdemeanors that are difficult in practice to track down or to suppress; one does not on that account choose to give them an official stamp of legality. Such a public admission of powerlessness would have a demoralizing effect on the conscience. Likewise, just because couples manage, thanks to successful trickery, to obtain decisions for divorce by mutual consent, it does not follow that such a divorce action must be permitted by the legislator. What is important to find out is whether or not it is justified; and if we should become convinced that it is socially harmful, then we should, on the contrary, seek in every way to arm the judge against those legal frauds; and even if it should be recognized that nothing very much can be done against those conniving people with something to gain, we should be careful not to give them official ratification which could only help encourage wrongdoing.

Is it normal that husband and wife can sever by a single willful act the marriage bond? There, then, you have the whole problem. In order to solve it, we usually are content to contrast the parents' right with the childrens' or vice versa, and we settle it in one way or the other depending on whether we are more sympathetic to one side or the other. For it is impossible to weigh objectively both the distress that divorce causes for children and the distress that keeping the marriage alive causes for parents. The issue, we believe, is of another sort. That the married couple must be allowed, under certain circumstances, to escape from their union, and that divorce is consequently a necessary institution, appears to be beyond question. But again it must not be understood in such a way that it contradicts and ruins the very principle on which the state of matrimony and the family are based. For in that case, pretending to remedy individual problems would in itself result in an impaired society.

Now, to admit that divorce can result from the sole consent of husband and wife is necessarily to admit as well that marriage itself is the byproduct solely of the wishes of the parties concerned and is nothing more than what these parties want it to be—the very negation of the institution of marriage. What characterizes marriage is the fact that the obligations to which it gives rise, even though negotiated voluntarily, once they are formulated, void the individual right to withdraw arbitrarily. The mutual duties of husband and wife, of parents towards children, do not depend on individual wishes. How, then, would individual wishes suffice to alter them as gravely as divorce does? It is said that spouses who no longer want each other are no longer in a situation that requires their union to produce those useful results that are its justification. And so, from that moment on, it is better to break away. Put in these terms, the issue is very different from the one we just examined. From that point of view, it is not because the couple no longer wants to live together that they must be separated. The fact is that their marriage runs counter to its natural purpose. The fact is that it has now produced a disrupting effect on that domestic order which should serve as a base. And it is very certain that a marriage that can no longer fulfill its function has outlived its purpose. But how is it conceivable that the feelings of the parties concerned alone suffice to establish that a marriage is in such a state? An objective fact is what is at issue, namely how their life together is working out, and this factor needs to be appraised on its own terms and objectively. Why should the manner in which each of the parties concerned views their working relationship be decisive? They see matters only from their own point of view—wholly personal and subjective. They feel the shocks, the clashes, of daily life. But as for knowing if those clashes are of such a nature as to contaminate their life together as husband and wife and prevent it from fulfilling its role in society—this is a problem that is beyond their grasp. A patient can give a good account of the aches and pains that he is experiencing; but he is not competent to appraise the nature and the gravity of his illness. Besides, if only the feelings the spouses think they have for each other were indeed like the ones they experience in reality. But it is common knowledge how frequent the errors are. It happens all the time that we love the one we think we hate, we perceive the ties that bind us to one another only at the moment when they are severed. How many couples constantly roused to mutual anger declare their life together intolerable and yet suffer cruelly once death, for example, has separated them! The idea they entertain of their relationship is therefore a very bad criterion for judging the true state of those relations. How, then, to ascribe such effective force to the simple declaration of their wishes? Only the judge is equipped to decide if an association in marriage can no longer fulfill its function. It is natural that the feelings of the couple may be, for him, a useful element of information; but what is inadmissible is that they judge such evidence sufficient to sever the bonds of matrimony.

And the demonstration of what circumspection must be brought to bear on everything concerning divorce is the fact that it cannot spread without bringing about a weakening of the marriage bond—that is what is meant, whatever one may say, by the relationship established between divorces and suicides. The explanation for it that our author gives appears to us, in fact, very difficult to uphold. According to him, as we have seen, this relation is presumably due on the one hand to the predispositions of those divorced and on the other hand to the change in the way of life that rupture of marriage ties implies. But if this were so, the abnormal excess that statistics on suicide acknowledge in countries where divorce flourished would be entirely and exclusively the work of those divorced; if there is much self-destruction it is because those who are divorced show a marked tendency to take their own lives. Now, a very simple type of reckoning shows that the impact of divorce on the rate of suicides derives from very different sources. In round numbers, there are about 20,000 divorced men in France, and perhaps a few more in the case of the opposite sex. According to observations made in Prussia, a million divorced men produce around 2,000 suicides and a million women 300. Let us accept these figures for France although they are surely too high, since there is less self-destruction in France than in Prussia. Divorced Frenchmen, then, would seem to provide 40 suicides, and women between 6 or 7. What are these 50 deaths by choice in the midst of 7,000 or 8,000 French suicides? A drop of water in the ocean. How, if the rate of divorce made itself felt in this way only, could its impact be noticed, and in a fashion so exact and so subtly distinguished from the statistics of suicide expressed in such global and enormous figures? How could this drop of water perceptibly affect the currents that furrow such an ocean? The truth is that divorce cannot advance without threatening the institution of marriage; and it is the sufferings of the individual, caused by the sickness of a social and fundamental institution, that are coming to be translated into the yearly total of suicides. That is no reason to delete divorce from our laws; for if it is necessary that controls governing marriage should not become flabby, it is further unnecessary that they become excessively rigid. But that is all the more reason to watch over its rate of growth and to contain it within justifiable limits. It is a necessity that several publicists and statesmen seem to have overlooked. (*Année sociologique*, 9, 1906, pp. 438–443; trans. J. French)

NOTES AND NOTICES

E. Fahlbeck. "Contributo allo studio demografico delle famiglie e delle generazioni umane." *Rivista italiana di sociologia*, IV, no. 1, pp. 26–34.

The object of the article is to determine, by precise statistical data, in what way the number of families in the upper class has diminshed. From generation to generation, the birthrate has decreased in a most regular manner. By the end of three generations, 83 percent of the families were extinguished. Those which survived this critical phase saw, to the contrary, their time span increased markedly. From this relatively rapid extinction results a circulation of social classes.[28] As soon as the vacuum is created in the ranks of the upper classes, some new elements coming forth from the lower classes raise themselves up and fill these gaps. There is thus a forced upward mobility which nobody can prevent. With an excessive optimism, the author attributes moralistic influence to this demographic fact, which it is not known to have. (*Année sociologique*, 4, 1901, p. 440; trans. Y. Nandan)

Clément Juglar. "Des Rapports que la statistique peut établir entre les mariages et les naissances d'un pays et sa situation économique." *Journal de la Société de Statistique de Paris*, May 10, 1900.

The author tends to show by a certain number of facts that marriages and natality decrease when economic crises are liquidated. (*Année sociologique*, 4, 1901, p. 440; trans. Y. Nandan)

Arsène Dumont. "De l'Infécondité chez certaines populations industrielles." *Journal de la Société de Statistique de Paris*, 1900, pp. 321–333, 362–369.

In the town of Condé-sur-Noireau (Somme), workers in heavy industry have only a very low birthrate, lower than the average French, instead of the relatively higher birthrate found elsewhere. The author attributes this exception to the fact that this industrial population lacks the right mental attitude. Scattered in the middle of the surrounding agricultural population, which represents the majority, they have adopted the customs of this agricultural population—that is to say, the negative moral attitude of the petite bourgeoisie and of small tradesmen. People do not steal; they are not alcoholics; instead, they are frugal, sober, and lacking all the positive energy for procreation. (*Année sociologique*, 5, 1902, p. 438; trans. Y. Nandan)

Robert Kuczynski. "Die unehelichen Kinder in Berlin." *Zeitschrift für Sozialwissenschaft*, 1900, no. 9, pp. 632–641.

The author tends to establish the characteristics of illegitimate children of different categories according to the method by which they are looked after and raised. He also shows that for some the situation is not markedly less desirable than that of legitimate children. (*Année sociologique*, 5, 1902, p. 438; trans. Y. Nandan)

Friedrich Prinzing. "Die uneheliche Fruchtbarkeit in Deutschland" (The Illegitimate Birthrate in Germany). *Zeitschrift für Sozialwissenschaft*, 1902, no. 1, pp. 37–46.

The author demonstrates by a few examples that the causes on which the illegitimate birthrate depends are not the same as those by reason of which the legitimate birthrate varies. Accordingly, the economic state of affairs does not appear to influence the first type of birthrate mentioned, whereas it certainly does have an impact on the second. Even a rise in the rate of marriage does not regularly result in a decrease of illegitimate births, as one might expect. Without denying the impact of other causes (customs, laws, etcetera), Prinzing estimates that the chief factor on which the variations of the illegitimate birthrate depend consists of the relationship between the number of male and female celibates who have reached adulthood. The more choice a man has, the easier it is for him to "marry the one and to seduce the other"; the less chance the girl has of being regularly married, the more she undergoes exposure to make herself available. The author himself is obliged to acknowledge that his law does not hold true in all cases. (*Année sociologique*, 6, 1903, p. 423; trans. J. French)

Richard Böckh. "Recherches sur les premiers, seconds, troisièmes . . . mariages considérés au moment de leur dissolution." *Xᵉ Congrès international d'hygiène et de démographie tenu à Paris en 1900.* Paris: Masson, pp. 1045–1046.

The author wants to know what statistical information must be obtained in order to calculate exactly the duration of time that a person has spent in marriage. (*Année sociologique*, 6, 1903, pp. 423–424; trans. Y. Nandan)

Clément Juglar. "Y a-t-il des périodes pour les mariages et les naissances comme pour les crises commerciales?" *Journal de la société de Statistique de Paris*, July 1902, pp. 238–247.

The author attempts to prove that the birthrate has its periods of increase and decrease which correspond to periods of prosperity and economic crises. (*Année sociologique*, 7, 1904, p. 521; trans. Y. Nandan)

SUICIDE

REVIEWS

Ivan Stchoukine. *Le Suicide collectif dans le Raskol russe.* Paris: H.
Floury, 1903, 129 pp.

What is in question here is a form of religious suicide that made its appearance in Russia in the seventeenth century and has not yet completely disappeared.

The great political and social crisis which opened Russian history in the seventeenth century, the violent acts, the vexations, the grinding poverty of all types that joined it, gave birth to a current of ascetic pessimism. The peasants fled that world of injustice and despotism. Some gained relief in freer countries; but others quite simply went off into the depths of the forests—a certain number even became hermits. Thus arose the spontaneous founding of monasteries. It is in these special surroundings that the doctrine of suicide developed. The feelings of disgust that the contemporary state of society inspired among those unfortunates extended to the priests, who by their behavior were all too often justifiably objects of scorn. And from the priests such feeling ascended aloft to religion, its rites, its sacraments. But if ritual methods are not enough, how to gain salvation? By abstinence, mortification, fasting. From that moment on, the principle of suicide, considered as the only way to salvation, was established. Voluntary death, by fasting or fire, replaced all other religious practices. With time, the doctrine was modified. The idea that the end of the world was near, that the Antichrist was about to appear, that his reign was imminent, spread abroad throughout all of Russia. Suicide was thought to be at the time a way to escape his presence. People killed themselves in order to free themselves from his persecutions. It is clear that this theoretical change simply served to express, under a slightly different form, the same feeling of weariness and of dark despair.

The epidemic was of such virulence that the number of victims is estimated at 20,000; at times there were 1,000 or 2,000 of them at one and the same time. In any case this fever did not long remain at such a pitch. From the eighteenth century on, there were no more mass autos-da-fé; during the nineteenth century, hardly twenty cases are accounted for. The act's contributing factor is always the same—alarming rumors of persecutions, new charges, new taxes, a general census, and so on. The doctrine has not varied to any extent. It is always the belief that suicide is an instrument of purification, the way to safeguard the faith of those ambushed by the Antichrist. (*Année sociologique,*
8, 1905, pp. 499–50; trans. J. French)

Hans Rost. "Der Selbstmord in den Städten" (Suicide in the Cities).
Allgemeines statistiches Archiv, VI, pp. 263–281.

Two conclusions emerge from this work. The first, negative: the fact is that if it is true that in general the cities are centers of those predisposed to suicide,[29] the rate of suicide does not increase with high population density. Berlin has only 2.75 suicides per 10,000 inhabitants; Strasbourg has only 1.95; Munich, 1.88; Cologne, 1.45, etcetera; whereas Zurich, Spandau, Kiel, Gera, and Görlitz have between 3.07 and 3.67. The second conclusion has to do with the factor upon which the differences in urban suicide rates seem especially to depend. This factor is religious persuasion. Cities of equal population account for a very unequal number of suicides depending on whether they are Protestants or Catholics.

Without claiming that such conclusions are well founded to a certain degree, they nevertheless seem to us to be considered plausible with only certain reservations. In order to be sure that the population figure is not in itself a factor in suicide, it would have been necessary to isolate its impact from a great diversity of causes that can mask it or reinforce it in particular cases. Accordingly, it would have been necessary methodically to group the cities by categories, in such a way that factors other than population cancel each other out. But it is not enough to note that certain very populous cities account for fewer suicides than other less important ones, although such a contention may not be without interest as well. (*Année sociologique*, 8, 1905, p. 502; trans. J. French)

H. A. Krose. *Der Selbstmord im 19. Jahrhundert nach seiner Verteilung auf Staaten und Verwaltungsbezirke, mit einer Karte.* Freiburg i. B.: Herder, 1906, viii + 111 pp.

The aim of this work is not to determine the reasons for suicide but to establish its method of growth in the course of the nineteenth century. The investigation of causes is postponed until the publication of a forthcoming work which is being promised us in the near future.[30]

The author proposes above all to establish the actual increase in voluntary deaths since the beginning of the nineteenth century, among European states in general, as against certain authors who had cast doubts on the matter. In Norway only is there a constant diminution in the rate of suicide. Not only is the tendency to commit suicide on the rise, but there is no good reason to anticipate that it is on the eve of a decline. Since the fact is very rarely disputed, it might perhaps be held that there is a bit of useless luxury in this ample demonstration; but along the way, and outside this issue itself, the author does make some interesting observations.

In order to be able to prove his thesis, he has very wisely divided the century into three distinct periods which themselves cannot easily be compared because the impact of the statistical data at these three periods is very unequal. Accordingly, he has been able to establish that if the growth of suicide in Europe is widespread, the way in which it grew is very different depending on the states concerned. The order in which they are classified from the point of view of their suicidal trend varies very perceptibly from one period to the other. What is striking is the enormity of the increase that is recorded in France. From 1836 to 1870, France is classified among the countries in which the frequency of suicide is only average and it ranks only eighth at that among these last (104 suicides per million). From 1870 to 1900, France passes into the category of the most severely stricken countries, even outstripping Prussia and the German Empire.

Another interesting fact pointed out by Krose is that if the progress of suicide is followed in the different regions of the same country in the course of this same century, the observation is made that the distribution is much more heterogeneous in the opening years than in the final years. There has arisen a sort of general leveling process. Furthermore, the contention has nothing surprising about it. To the degree that the channels of circulation and of communication expand, the moral differences which at first separated the provinces vanish; civilization in all its aspects becomes more homogeneous.

In this book one will find useful information on statistical sources in the different times during the century. (*Année sociologique,* 10, 1907, pp. 499–500; trans. J. French)

H. A. Krose. *Die Ursachen der Selbstmordhäufigkeit.* Freiburg
   i. B.: Herder, 1906, vii + 169 pp.

This book is the first comprehensive study that has appeared on suicide since the work we published in 1897. As so often happens with these kinds of treatises that aim to be more or less complete, the author repeats preceding works on more than one point. In our analysis we shall limit ourselves to bringing to light either the new facts or the new ideas.

The plan followed is classic. The author investigates first what may be the influence of cosmic or organic factors on the death rate by suicide. The last part of the book is devoted to social factors. Between the two are interpolated two chapters: one on individual suicidal motives, the other on suicidal methods. The place chosen for these two is nonetheless surprising. They interrupt the sequence of investigation.

As for cosmic and organic factors, the author's conclusion is practically negative: he recognizes only a very limited impact on their part. Concerning climate and temperature, he accepts the conclusions at which we arrived. If suicide increases from January until June, it is because of the fact that the length of the social day keeps on increasing during this same period. The same holds for psychopathic conditions; new documents produced by the author tend to confirm that there is no direct relation between the social rate of suicide and mental illness (pp. 40 ff.). The influence of sex and that of age are undeniable, but they are particular forms of social influences. A chart drawn up by our author (p. 22) establishes very clearly that the participation of women among suicides as a whole has been steadily on the decline from the beginning of the nineteenth century; the fact is, then, that the inclination towards suicide as a symbol of women's weakness that has been universally recognized derives from historical causes, and not organic ones. Civilization's increasing urbanization seems to have resulted in further separating the two sexes. The woman, in town, is kept more excluded from serious social life and consequently is less likely to undergo its effects. As for age, the author deals with the question of suicide among children; from the facts assembled by him, the resulting evidence shows that the number of such suicides is increasing in all the European states, except perhaps in England, where it is relatively constant. The fact is, then, that the evil is not special to France and does not depend, as has been said, on such-or-such particular causes in our social organization (pp. 33–38).

The social factors that the author tries to determine are six in number: nature of habitat and relative density of civilization, civil status, social functions and social conditions, cultivation of the mind, collective morality *(Volkssittlichkeit)*, and religious persuasion. On these different points, the author brings to bear a certain number of documents confirming results already obtained.

In our *Suicide,* we were able to measure the influence exercised by family life by means of a chart on which the impact of civil status was established for each group taken separately. The author, who reproduces this chart, is confronted with two other charts, the elements of which he has borrowed from Swiss and Swedish statistics. The first agrees with ours on the whole. From the second it follows, as from ours, that married persons enjoy a certain immunity; but this immunity, particularly in what concerns women, would be so extraordinary that it leaves us somewhat skeptical. Spinsters from 20 to 25 years of age would be 16 times more likely to kill themselves than women of the same age, and 8.5 times more likely than the latter in the following age-group. Then, abruptly, the numbers decrease; at 40 years, the coefficient of preservation would no longer be more than 1.5, and beyond 70 years it would change into a coefficient of aggravation (0.78). On the other hand, widows would be 64 times more likely to kill themselves than married women of 20 to 25 years, and 11 times more likely than those from 25 to 30 years of age. Then a still more abrupt decrease would take place, and beyond 60 years a reverse trend would be manifest. It is the widows who would be better off (73 suicides by widows as against 100 by spinsters). The situation that these statistics appear to reveal is in such disagreement with what we know from another source that we wonder if some error has not been committed. What reinforces our suspicions is that, as of 1878, Bertillon had published the results of Swedish statistics that we were able, as of 1897, to establish as inaccurate (*Suicide,* p. 179, n. 2). It is, besides, very remarkable that these two statistics disagree with each other. According to the figures that Bertillon gave us, the immunity of the husbands would keep on increasing until the extreme limits of life, and that of the wives up until 75 years of age. Then, too, women's immunity would be perceptibly lower than men's. According to Krose's chart, it is the women, on the other hand, who would have the most to gain by marrying; beyond that, the coefficient of preservation for the two sexes would diminish from 25 to 30 years and would become very weak between 40 and 50 years of age, only to decrease still more in the following years. It appears to us, then, prudent to be very circumspect about accepting information from a source of this kind.

Alcoholism has been treated as a part of collective morality. The author has no trouble showing that if excessive alcoholic comsumption may have some part in the mortality rate from suicide, its influence notwithstanding, is far from being as decisive as Prinzing has stated, for example. Between these two phenomena there are no clear-cut and reliable connections (pp. 125 ff.). This is a fact about which it is not without interest to take note in this age when people impute all the ills from which we suffer to alcoholism.

The chapter on the connections of suicide with religious identification is more extensive and rich (pp. 137–165). The relative immunity that Catholicism confers is once again demonstrated, with a great abundance of supporting evidence. In another respect, by virtue of the facts borrowed particularly from a work by Rost,[*] it seems fair to conclude that the coefficient of preservation which the Jews enjoyed tends to decrease more and more. Whereas from 1844 to 1856 a million Bavarian Jews accounted for only 105 suicides yearly, 115.8 were counted from 1870 to 1879; 185 from 1880 to 1889; and 212.4 from 1890 to 1899—that is to say, somewhat more than the Protestants (210.2). To the degree that the Jewish population is further assimilated into the surrounding population, it loses its traditional virtues, without perhaps replacing them by others. It is a special case of a very general law. A social group that has a moral culture sui generis can hardly change without running the risk of becoming demoralized. In any case, in order to be able to give the preceding figures their true significance, we must not lose sight of the fact that Jews are above all city dwellers and that urban life in itself is conducive to suicide. Though it is a fact that Jews today kill themselves as often as or more frequently than do Protestants, it does not then follow that Judaism has an impact on self-preservation that is inferior or simply equal to that of Protestantism. In order to measure exactly the influence of the religious factor, it would be necessary to eliminate the urban factor by comparing only populations from the same habitat.

On a question of detail, the author makes an observation that would not be without interest if it was confirmed. One is quite often led to believe that when a Church is reduced to minority status in a country, it has a better moral constitution and consequently [an individual adhering to it] is less inclined towards suicide. It is in fact conceivable that it may be called upon to adhere to a regime of strict discipline in order to fight against the hostile poulations in the milieux. Now, if there are truly certain facts that tend to establish the reality of this relationship concerning Protestantism, it seems, on the other hand, that Catholicism loses its prophylactic virtue when it is not the religion of the

[*] "Der Selbstmord in seiner Beziehung zur Konfession und Stadtbevölkerung in Baiern," *Historisch-politische Blätter*, CXXX, Munich, 1902.

majority. The more Catholics mingle with believers of different faiths, the more their power of resistance against suicide diminishes. One would think that the Catholic faith can retain its power on men's consciousness only on condition of not having to put up with contradiction.

The conclusion that the author draws from this comparative study is that the religious factor is the only one that makes an impact profound enough to gain conspicuous transcendency in all cases and in all combinations of circumstances. The influence of the others would be somewhat less certain and more casual (p. 138). To tell the truth, together with social religiosity and irreligiosity, there is another phenomenon the importance of which must be recognized in this respect—namely, the tendency to divorce. But the author believes that the latter depends on religion. As for this sort of religious prerogative, the author does not claim it for Catholicism alone. He estimates that every religious faith can have the same effect, provided that it proscribes suicide and believes in a future life. Everything depends on the force with which that faith is impressed on the minds of the recipients.

Such an interpretation of the phenomena appears to us entirely unacceptable. To begin with, if belief in a future life explains the impact of religion, it is incomprehensible why the Protestant faith should be so inferior to the Catholic; why a country like France, in which faith is so profoundly shaken, is not more inclined toward voluntary death than religious Germany; especially how Judaism could have for so long a time stood comparison with Catholicism, even though ideas relating to the afterlife are of relatively recent origin and are not considered to be fundamental dogma—it is on this earth that the Jew hopes for or fears divine sanctions. In order to understand to what sort of thing religion owes its beneficent authority, it must be compared with other phenomena of a similar type which have a similar impact on suicide, instead of considering it on its own terms and viewing it as a sort of unique and incomparable phenomenon. Besides religious faith, there is political faith, patriotism, which is influential in the same way and which the author is wrong not to mention. Besides the religious groups, there is the family group, whose salutary and very powerful influence he acknowledges only incidentally and completely fails to account for in his conclusion. When one compares these various factors with each other and with the religious factor, this last assumes a totally different aspect. This is what we have attempted to show elsewhere.

The simplistic radicalism of such a conclusion derives, in part, from the method the author follows. He reasons as if there were only one sort of suicide and of suicidal current. Now, actually, there are several such, as we have been striving to establish. If religion preserves from suicide, it may also exert pressure in that direction; and the suicides towards which it inclines us are very different from those it deters us from attempting. Intellectuals often kill themselves as well as subalterns; but they are two types of suicide that it is important to distinguish. It is, consequently, not hard to understand how unwarranted it is to intentionally make the mortality rate through suicide dependent on a single and unique factor. (*Année socioligique*, 11, 1919, pp. 511–515; trans. J. French)

Criminal Sociology

SOCIAL FACTORS IN CRIME AND IMMORALITY

REVIEWS

Bruno Blau. *Die Kriminalität der deutschen Juden*. Berlin: Louis Lamm, 1906, 15 pp.

Volume 146 of the *Statistics of the German Empire* (New Series) contains some very valuable information on criminality according to religious faith between the years 1882 and 1901. These twenty years have been divided into two periods of ten years (1882–1891 and 1892–1901); and we are given a mean yearly figure for each of these two periods.

Taken as a whole, Jewish criminality is perceptibly lower than that of other religious faiths. Out of 100,000 members of each group who reached the age of penal majority (not counting the military population), 784 Jews were convicted each year as opposed to 963 Protestants and 1,031 Catholics. It is true that if we compare the two periods, we ascertain that Jewish criminality has increased more than that of the other two religions. The increase has been 16.5 percent for Catholics, 18 percent for Protestants, and 32.1 percent for Jews. But this increase rests uniquely or almost so on one and the same category of delicts. These are infractions of laws concerning the labor of women and minors, sanitary laws, and the law prescribing Sunday rest. These last delicts by themselves constitute the major part of the recorded increase, which is explained by the fact that in the first period the law did not yet exist. On the other hand, if Jews have broken this law more than Christians, one must not lose sight of the fact that the Jewish population contains proportionally more subjects who are capable of breaking it. Indeed, only heads of business feel the brunt of this law; now more than half of the Jewish population fills this role, while the proportion in the population as a whole is much thinner (28.94 percent).

It is these facts which indicate the distinctive character of Jewish criminality; it is essentially professional. The crimes and delicts in which Jews play a larger role than other religious groups are above all those which are committed in industrial and commercial life; now, more than half of the Jewish population performs these sorts of occupations. Naturally, therefore, they participate in an equally high proportion of the corresponding criminal activity. However, given the actual state of our knowledge, we cannot know if this contribution is proportionally higher for Jews than it is for the other religions; this is because we do not know in what ways the various religious groups are distributed among the various professions.

On the other hand, we must observe that there are certain delicts for which the Jews show a higher propensity than the preceding cause could explain. These are insults, duels (this is attributed by Blau to the vivacity of their temperament), and certain violations of public morality (seduction and adultery); while on the contrary they fall beneath the mean for rape, sodomy, etcetera.

It is interesting to record that albeit for known reasons there are more Jewish than Christian usurers, the Jewish penchant for this delict, considered by itself, is very weak (i.e., 1.2 convictions per 100,000 inhabitants.)

How regrettable it is that French statistics do not record the necessary information for us to institute similar comparisons in our own country. (*Année sociologique*, 10, 1907, pp. 494–495; trans. A. Lyons)

NOTES AND NOTICES

Frances A. Kellor. "Psychological and Environmental Study of Women Criminals." *American Journal of Sociology*, V, no. 4, p. 527; no. 5, p. 683.

The article is based on observations made on 1,033 imprisoned women. The vital statistics on many points do not confirm the results obtained by Lombrosso. One of the most interesting remarks made in the study is the fact of mental inferiority which the women in prostitution present in relation to the women committing crime (p. 543). From the sociological point of view, the preponderance of the married women in the total female population in the prisons observed must be noted. In one of the institutions, 1,012 women out of 1,451 were married. (*Année sociologique*, 4, 1901, p. 452; trans. Y. Nandan)

SPECIAL FORMS OF CRIME

REVIEWS

Richard Lasch. "Rache als Selbstmordmotiv" (Suicide as Vengeance).
Globus, 1898, LXXIV, pp. 37 ff.

In an article examined in these pages last year[31] (*L'Année*, 2, 1899, p. 399), Steinmetz, while examining the usage of *dharna*, presented a case of suicide by vengeance. Lasch, who seems to have ignored Steinmetz's article, has gathered a great number of cases of suicide committed for this very motive. Its practice is very frequent among the primitives and among the semicivilized peoples. They believe that by killing oneself rather than the enemy, one will certainly take revenge on the enemy, because the spirit of the dead, once it is free, becomes a formidable and destructive force for the living person, who cannot escape it. The small and the humble have the means to take revenge on the powerful. In such cases suicide is committed on the property itself of that person whom one intended to take revenge on. By this, the sacrificer intended to contaminate the environment where the enemy lived. It is to be noted that in certain countries (among the Tlinkits, among the blacks of Guinea, among the Chinese, and others) the state intervened and severely punished the person who had been the cause of this suicide. On many occasions the person's house was burned and his cattle were confiscated because he had caused the sacrificer to die. In the case of homicide proper, the punishment is less severe, for it seems that the spirit of the man who commits this type of suicide becomes more formidable and more difficult to satisfy than the spirit of the assassinated person; the anger of those who serve as judge only imitates and anticipates that of the dead.

In the same volume of the *Globus* (p. 166), Rear Admiral Kühne complements the article by Lasch, by presenting the subject matter concerning Japan. (*Année sociologique*, 3, 1900, p. 481; trans. Y. Nandan)

Richard Lasch. "Die Behandlung der Leiche des Selbstmörders" (The Manner in Which the Body of a Suicide Is Treated). *Globus*, LXXVI, no. 4., pp. 63–66.

Lasch. "Die Verbleibsorte der Abgeschiedenen Seelen der Selbstmörder" (Places of Rest Attributed to the Souls of Suicides). *Ibid.*, LXXII, no. 7, pp. 110–115.

These two articles complement each other and are related to the same subject. They are concerned with an attempt to determine the manner in which primitive societies judge the act of suicide. The second article is the one which goes more to the root of the question.

The author classifies peoples into four categories according to the way they represent the life after death of the individual who has committed suicide. In the study by Lasch, one passes from one category to another without any break in the continuity. There are those who do not find any difference between the soul of the one who has committed suicide and other souls; there are those who assign to the first a privileged status and a particularly happy existence; there are those who see the suicide as a dangerous spirit, wandering restlessly, hostile to all and even to the other dead, and for that reason placed in a separate compartment in the other world. Finally there are those who see in suicide an immoral and irreligious act, punished by penalties even beyond the death. This last conception is almost exclusively Christian.

Of the four groups, the most interesting is the third, and it is principally this one which is discussed in the first article, in which the author tells us of inferior societies which submit the cadaver of the suicide to a special rite (burial apart or accompanied with particular ceremonies). These are practices corresponding to certain beliefs according to which the suicide does not pursue his existence beyond death in company with other dead people. But these practices, like the beliefs, do not have as their origin a moral reprobation directed at voluntary death; that reprobation is generally unknown in primitive ethics. It is only that the soul of the person who committed suicide, like that of all men who die a violent death, is particularly dreadful. It is presumed to have a kind of constitutional evil. It is a source of magical contamination. From this arises the precautionary measures taken against it; they are dictated by prudence and not by moral indignation.

It seems probable to us, according to the facts gathered by Lasch himself, that the same societies do not have only one, unique conception of suicide and of the posthumous existence of those who commit suicide. The ideas which he treats vary according to different cases. In fact, we see peoples who glorify suicide under certain conditions and sometimes attribute it to the influence of evil spirits; such are the Germans (LXXVI, p. 64) and the Chinese (p. 65). Above all it is the suicide committed in the moment of disgust or anger that must be dreaded and against which conjurations are employed. The sentiments in which the soul is found at the moment when it renounces its life explain the fear which it inspires. These same facts help us to understand the practice of suicides for vengeance. (*Année sociologique*, 4, 1901, pp. 462–463; trans. J. Sweeney)

NOTES AND NOTICES

Richard Lasch. "Religiöser Selbstmord und seine Beziehung zum Menschenopfer" (Religious Suicide: Its Relation to Human Sacrifice). *Globus*, 1899, LXXV, pp. 69 ff.

This is an interesting and well-documented article, having gathered the most typical facts concerning religious suicide. The part devoted to India is notably very complete. The author shows that religious suicide was first only a form of human sacrifice. It was a sacrifice in which the victim and the sacrificer were identical. The sacrificer was destined to appease a divinity. The same is true also of the usage in the moments of public agony. Religious beliefs, then, determined suicide only because they were placed in the service of the ulterior motives, more properly called morals, such as the love of country and family. It is only at a later date that suicide was practiced as a means of participating more and more completely in the joys of another life—of escaping this world and assuring oneself of a better life. Without doubt, these preoccupations were not absent from the very beginning of religious suicide. They were, however, secondary. The man who sacrificed himself committed this act, above all, to appease a divinity and thought only secondarily of the religious benefits which he could draw from the act. As time passed, the respective importances of these two orders of motives were reversed. Then came the mystic suicide.

We are willing to believe that religious suicide is related to sacrificial rites. In many cases it is merely a form of human sacrifice. But is it really true that mystic suicide itself, that is to say the act by which a man kills himself for the love of the other world, is only a transformation of these archaic practices? The fact that it is found within the context of primitive practices among the same peoples is no proof. As a result, these two sorts of practices rest on the same fundamental ideas, considered as two branches of the same trunk, the one not derived from the other. (*Année sociologique*, 3, 1900, pp. 480–481; trans. Y. Nandan)

Richard Lasch. "Der Selbstmord aus erotischen Motiven bei den
   primitiven Völkern" (Suicide for Love among the Primitives).[32]
   Zeitschrift für Sozialwissenschaft, nos. 8, 9, pp. 578–585.

This is a contribution to the study of suicide among the primitives. Alongside the religious sentiments, love seems to play a very important role in it. However, the author under this rubric has gathered facts that are quite incongruous: (1) the loathing of an existence created by the husband's ill-treatment of the woman; (2) the anticipated fear of an unhappy life if a dreaded marriage takes place; (3) sexual jealousy properly speaking. The first two motives in committing suicide have nothing to do with love. This also explains that the title of the article is thus misleading. It is a fact, however, that the woman in primitive societies is often the victim of this sort of suicide. The frequency of these suicides may be attributed to two reasons: (1) the passionate nature of the primitive, and (2) his contempt for life itself. (*Année sociologique*, 4, 1901, p. 463; trans. Y. Nandan)

CRIME ACCORDING TO COUNTRIES

REVIEWS

E. Tarnowski. "La mendicità in Russia" (Mendicancy in Russia).
   Rivista italiana di sociologia, IV, no. 2, pp. 176–190.

To judge by the official figures, mendicancy is less developed in Russia [than elsewhere in Europe]. But for various reasons that conclusion is only apparent. We only know the number of cases referred to the courts. Now, to begin with, the legislation is not the same as in the other countries of Europe, since in the village mendicancy is rarely an object of repression, because there it is considered a normal practice. It is one of the forms of common insurance against damages and setbacks of all kinds. The villagers who at the end of the winter find they do not have enough provisions take the beggar's sack and go to ask for alms from their more fortunate neighbors. Neither the beggar nor

anyone around him sees anything humiliating in this begging, which is consequently openly tolerated. As a result, the statistics show only 1,000 or 1,200
convictions, even though there are, in an average year, at least 300,000 mendicants in European Russia (pp. 176, 189).

It is the industrial centers which attract the most mendicants. However,
they are seen to gather equally around places of pilgrimage. In a general way,
religion has a marked influence on the rate of mendicancy, and in that regard
the Orthodox religion has a deplorable effect. Without any legal consequences, the Church makes a great contribution to the institution of
mendicancy.

It is not only from that point of view that mendicancy is completely different than the other legal offenses. The proportion of women is noticeably
more considerable (21 per 100 instead of 13 or 14 per 100). It is above all
widowhood which causes that situation. Out of 100 widowed of the two sexes
convicted for begging, there are 48 women. The influence of seasons is also
very different. It is in February or March that the maximum is reached; the
minimum is in July and August. The variations that the other months present
are of secondary importance. March, on the contrary, is the minimum month
for other offenses. This proves that the monthly differences in the convictions
for begging are not due exclusively to economic factors. Another cause intervenes: the moral situation that is found in Russia during the months of
February, March, and April, when the country is devoted to the fast of Lent
and is preparing for the solemn feasts of Easter. At that moment a stirring up
of religious sentiments lowers general criminality, but stimulates begging by
the exceptional rewards which are then offered to it. The relative significance
of educated people among the beggars is notable.

The end of the article is devoted to means of combatting the evil.
Everything must be done in this regard. Public assistance does not exist; prison
only creates recidivists. Moreover, it has been noted that this state of things
depends upon very profound causes—in part ideas and practices that have
their roots in the old Russian rural organization. (*Année sociologique*, 4, 1901,
pp. 460–464: trans. J. Sweeney)

NOTES AND NOTICES

Monroe N. Work. "Crime among the Negroes of Chicago." *American Journal of Sociology*, VI, pp. 204–223.

In Chicago, as in the whole of the United States, the delinquent blacks
[Durkheim uses the word *nègres*, which was common in that time] are much
more numerous than the delinquents among the white race; they are two to
eight times more numerous according to the state, and from 1872 to 1896 the
proportion has risen in an uninterrupted manner. The author attributes this
situation not to a kind of degeneration of the black race but to the state of

transition in which the blacks have found themselves since Emancipation. The blacks do not yet seem to have had the time to adapt themselves to the new conditions of their existence. This explanation, however, does not conform with the fact that black criminality is still increasing. It is to be noted, moreover, that almost all of this criminality, 80 percent, is aimed at attempts against the society, notably against the public peace. Crimes against property and people are few, however. On the other hand, 75 percent of the arrested blacks from 1872 to 1876 were without occupation. Does it not behoove us to look there for the cause of this malaise? It is to be noted that there is a high proportion of women committing the entire range of crimes against persons and crimes of theft and robbery. Women commit more such crimes than men. (*Année sociologique*, 5, 1902, p. 449; trans. Y. Nandan)

JUVENILE CRIME

REVIEWS

W. Rein. "Jugendliches Verbrechertum und seine Bekampfung" (Juvenile Crime and How to Control It). *Zeitschrift für Sozialwissenschaft*, 1900, pp. 41–57.

The increase in juvenile crime is a constant phenomenon of all civilized countries. England alone appears to be an exception; but it is only apparently so thanks to certain administrative practices that prevent crimes by minors from appearing in the statistics. The author ascribes several causes to this increase: the development of large agglomerations, which are potent solvents of domestic life and powerful stimulants for all the passions; the ruthlessness of economic competition and the resulting misery; the absence of moral guidance exercised over the young workers ever since the corporation stopped playing the role that was expected of it in the past. The proposed remedies are: laws safeguarding working conditions so as to prevent the breakup of working-class families, educational reforms, institutions of special education for young criminals, the right of the state to supervise the manner in which children are raised within the family and to withdraw them from such circumstances if they are exposed to bad influences. We fear that these palliatives will have very little effect. These various expedients are no substitute for natural social milieux that are now missing and that alone, by their continuous impact, can contain criminal tendencies. One must therefore, before all else, seek to organize them. It is not by trying to galvanize old institutions that evil will be arrested; it is by creating new ones. (*Année sociologique*, 4, 1901, pp. 451–452; trans. J. French)

Section Five

Economic Sociology

Knowing that Durkheim relegated economic sociology to a tertiary status in the hierarchy of classification and in the sectional arrangement of *L'Année,* and knowing that Simiand and his very small coterie—consisting of Halbwachs, Hubert Bourgin, and Georges Bourgin—were working in complete independence of Durkheim, one wonders why Durkheim wrote one small review of a book in this section on economic sociology, an area too far removed from his specialty and preoccupations. No doubt, Durkheim was familiar with the economic ideas of English utilitarians, with younger members of the German historical school, and with the ideas of Sismondi. But his actual contribution to economic sociology is too frivolous to be considered of any importance, notwithstanding a booklength publication in French on Durkheim's economic thought.[1] Not only did he consider religion as the source of social integration and social action, but he also rejected Marxian economic socialism and dialectical materialism as vitiated with dialectics and far removed from the pure form of scientific analysis and sociological reality. Durkheim's examination of Lasch in this section looks more like a page of *The Division of Labor* than an iota of economic sociology.

Regimes of Production

NOTES AND NOTICES

Richard Lasch. "Die Anfänge des Gewerbestandes." *Zeitschrift für Sozialwissenschaft,* 1901, no. 2, pp. 73–90.

The author looks at the occupations which are first specialized in primitive societies. There is, first of all, division of labor according to sex: certain occupations are left to women. Pottery for one is a woman's occupation, but the author recognizes that it has the distinct characteristics of a profession only in Melanesia, which is a relatively advanced society. The real primitive forms of specialized occupations are: manufacturing of arms, foundry and metal work, construction of small open boats, and at a later period construction of houses. These occupations are easily inherited and give rise to a real caste system. We wonder if the religious beliefs did not contribute to this separation which remains at the basis of all specialization, constituting the division of labor in society. It is quite certain that the manufacturing of arms and open boats is something that is invested with religious character. The aptitude to manufacture them must then involve religious or magical powers. Thus it is well explained that generally speaking these sorts of primitive artisans and their formation in castes invoke sentiments of respect. (*Année sociologique*, 5, 1902, p. 514; trans. Y. Nandan)

Section Seven

Miscellaneous

Social facts which did not fit into the major divisions of sociology or those areas of the discipline which were still in the incipient stages of their development[1] were coalesced and forced into the section entitled "Miscellaneous." But what is remarkable about these rubrics or the so-called areas of sociology is that, except for aesthetics, they are not designated as adjectives, to qualify them as areas of sociology. Whereas we note the titles "Religious Sociology," "Juridic Sociology," etcetera, in the previous sections, in this secion linguistics and education are to be seen as what they are, without subordinating them to sociology. Perhaps these areas of sociology did not exist at that time. Then was it not incumbent on Durkheim to cultivate these subdivisions as he did in the case of social morphology* and criminal sociology?

Another significant aspect of this section relates to the instability of some rubrics which have been shifted around in other sections. For example, the first volume of *L'Année,* 1898, contained three rubrics under the miscellaneous section: (1) anthroposociology, (2) sociogeography, and (3) demography. The rubric on anthroposociology, with all its manifestations of inherent and predetermined racial inequalities, was edited by Muffang during the first few years. After his dismissal or resignation from *L'Année,* the rubric under various forms and with a precarious existence was assimilated in the section on general sociology and was edited by Hubert or Mauss. The rubric on sociogeography was refurbished to become a special division of sociology and a special section of *L'Année*—social morphology. The section subsumed the rubric on demography, a topic in the miscellaneous section. With the elimination of the three rubrics men-

---

* The section on social morphology, Section Six, is not included here.

tioned above, the viable existence of this section seemed threatened unless some new forms of sociology were invented to sustain it and save other neglected areas of sociology from oblivion. With the inclusion of aesthetic sociology from 1900, and that of rubrics on technology and linguistics, which appeared regularly from 1901 and 1902 respectively, the miscellaneous section was well established and maintained a permanent structure. The rubrics on war and education appeared only once, in 1902 and 1904 respectively.

In spite of Durkheim's complaint that aesthetic sociology lacked substance, after extensive research Durkheim discovered something of interest in the area, but only from periodical literature; and the works on aesthetics that he came across were enmeshed with economic phenomena. Aside from the two brief notes on aesthetic sociology, Durkheim's contribution to the miscellaneous section consists of a comprehensive review of two articles on the sociological significance of pedagogy: his own work and that of Barth. With a complacent attitude, Durkheim first summarized the moot points of his own "Pédagogie et sociologie," and then claimed that his ideas on the subject were Barth's as well. Durkheim's review of Barth is slightly negative, but so was Barth's conception of Durkheim's economic ideas, which he refuted in his *Die Philosophie der Geschichte als Soziologie,* 1897.[2]

Aesthetic Sociology

NOTES AND NOTICES

Ugo Mazzola. "Il momento economico nell'arte." *Giornale degli economisti,* Aug. 1900.

The author shows that economic facts and aesthetic facts are not so different from each other as we have been often given to believe. Human activity has value, at least from an economic point of view, in proportion to the degree to which it becomes regulated, thus producing a rhythm of its own. Bücher has shown from where this tendency for human activity to have a rhythm comes. Rhythm is essentially an aesthetic phenomenon. On the other hand, art like industry seeks to produce the greatest possible effect with a minimum of means. These two forms of activity, then, have, in part, common principles. (*Année sociologique,* 5, 1902, p. 592; trans. Y. Nandan)

G. Sorel. "La Valeur sociale de l'art." *Revue de métaphysique et de morale,* 1901, no. 3, pp. 251–278.

The author shows that art comes very close to real life. It extends into work. Instead of making beautiful things which are useless, man has constructed beautiful machines, beautiful industrial plants and equipment, and so on and so forth. Production thus takes an attractive form which stimulates the worker and allows him to undertake without difficulty intense work that is demanded of him by the civilization. Such is the social value of art. (*Année sociologique,* 5, 1902, p. 592; trans. Y. Nandan)

Education

REVIEWS

Emile Durkheim. "Pédagogie et sociologie." *Revue de métaphysique et de Morale,* Jan. 1903, pp. 37–54.

Paul Barth. "Die Geschichte der Erziehung in soziologischer Beleuchtung" (The History of Education in the Light of Sociology). *Vierteljahrsschrift für wissenschaftliche Philosophie und Soziologie,* 1903, pp. 56–80, 209–219.

In the first of these articles, we have applied ourselves to establishing in a general way that the art of pedagogy needs the cooperation of sociology at least as much as psychology. Education is, in fact, an eminently social matter. It is social in its aim. Very far from ascertaining the individual nature of man in general, its aim varies from one society to another. To begin with, starting from the time when societies attained a certain degree of differentiation, the social unit itself is discovered re-forming into different parts according to classes and professions. Now, this specialization is dictated by the needs of society and it is responsive to the way in which the social activity is divided and organized at each moment in history. It is true that all these types of special training start diverging only at a certain point; before this point they are confused with one another.

But even this education in common is a function of the condition of society; for each society seeks to realize among its members and by way of education an ideal that suits its own purpose. Even the most advanced European societies do not escape this law. No doubt, we make it clear that we want to make men of our children, and not merely citizens in the narrow sense of the word. But the fact is, only a truly humane culture can give Europeans the citizens it needs. In societies as vast as ours the individuals are so different from each other that they have, so to speak, nothing in common with each other apart from their quality as man in general. Then again it must be added that each nation fashions for itself a conception of man that is, in part, personal to it, because it reflects the needs of its special mentality, its historical past, and so on.

In short, the purpose of education is far from merely having to develop man just as he comes out of nature's hands. The aim of education is rather to superimpose thereon an entirely new man, to create in him a new being who was not there before (except in budding formlessness), to teach us to dominate ourselves, to restrain ourselves; also to decide, as the need requires, on the amount and the nature of the knowledge that the child ought to receive. And likewise it is through education that knowledge acquired in former generations is preserved—to be transmitted as well to future generations. It is, then, this factor which fashions within us everything over and above the sphere of pure sensations; our will, like our understanding, is fashioned in its image.

But the impact of society makes itself felt even on the means used to achieve this end. Doubtless, these means will vary according to the opinion we hold of the aptitudes of children, and consequently, according to psychological data, especially child psychology. But first of all, if the ends pursued by education are social, then the means must necessarily be in the same category. And indeed, pedagogical institutions are often smaller versions of truly social institutions. For example, scholarly discipline has essentially the same characteristics as the discipline of the city-state. Furthermore, the nature of the aim predetermines the type of methodology used. Certain procedures are either taboo or highly regarded because they are or are not commensurate with the conception society forms of the ideal to be achieved. What gave rise to the Pestalozzian method, for example, is the feeling its author had for the moral aspirations in his day—much more than his knowledge of psychology.

These are the same ideas that are basic to the work of Barth. The author undertakes to demonstrate historically how, in fact, education has varied in form and in content, depending on the societies.

Here are the principal conclusions at which he arrives. In the first place, he finds no link between family organization and the nature of education; and we believe, in fact, that the place for this last is much more directly under the domination of the general social organization. An important factor would be the nature of the activity. Among peoples who hunt and fish, there would be a general lack of all educational discipline. The child is left to himself, without being compelled to curb himself and to hold back. The fact is that the occupations of those peoples are irregular, capricious; as a result, they do not feel the need to subject the children to very strict discipline. Dependability is very much greater among shepherds and farm workers; furthermore, these societies have more will to fight. They attack and they are attacked because the soil has for them a value that it did not have before. Education, then, trains the child not to give in to his passions; it exerts pressure on him to be brave, oblivious of the self, and subordinate to others. This reinforcement of discipline is again emphasized among the higher types of farm workers, such as the first Greeks used to be, or the Germans of Tacitus. As cultivation of the soil and the art of war grew more complicated, military and farming techniques, which were taught to the children, became more complicated to the same degree; at the same time, stricter discipline was exacted in domestic behavior. In short, in cases where society is organized into classes, education becomes a specialized function. In another sense, it becomes diversified depending on the milieux, varying from one class to another; and it becomes complicated by reason of the greater complexity of social life.

Such a rapid review of a multitude of different societies naturally prevented the author from using the firsthand documents, and for the same reason the conclusions at which he arrives are still very general. But this attempt to tie in education directly with the social conditions on which it depends was nonetheless worth putting in writing. (*Année sociologique,* 7, 1904, pp. 683–686; trans. J. French)

Editor's and Translators' Notes

The following abbreviations and short titles are used throughout:

PERIODICALS

AFLB	*Annales de la Faculté des Lettres de Bordeaux*
AS/ L'Année/ Année	*Année sociologique*
AAAE-ENS	*Annuaire de l'Association des Anciens Elèves de l'Ecole Normale Supérieure*
BSFP	*Bulletin de la Société Française de Philosophie*
GE	*Grande Encyclopédie*
MF	*Mercure de France*
NC	*Notes critiques: sciences sociales*
RB	*Revue bleue*
REP	*Revue d'économie politique*
RHR	*Revue d'histoire des religions*
RMM	*Revue de métaphysique et de morale*
RParis	*Revue de Paris*
RSH	*Revue de synthèse historique*
RFS	*Revue française de sociologie*
RIE	*Revue internationale d'enseignement*
RIS	*Revue internationale de sociologie*
RP	*Revue philosophique*
RU	*Revue universitaire*
RS	*La riforma sociale*

RItS	*Rivista italiana di sociologia*
SResearch	*Social Research*
SP	*Sociological Papers*

BOOKS

The Division of Labor (or *De la Division*)

Emile Durkheim, *The Division of Labor in Society* (New York: Macmillan, 1933), translated by G. Simpson from *De la Division du travail social: étude sur l'organisation des sociétés supérieures* (Paris: Alcan, 1893; 2nd ed., new Preface, 1902).

The Elementary Forms (or *Les Formes élémentaires*)

Emile Durkheim, *The Elementary Forms of Religious Life: A Study in Religious Sociology* (New York: Macmillan, 1915), translated by J. W. Swain from *Les Formes élémentaires de la vie religieuse: le système totémique en Australie* (Paris: Alcan, 1912).

The Rules (or *Les Règles*)

Emile Durkheim, *The Rules of Sociological Method*, edited with an Introduction by G. E. G. Catlin (Chicago: Univ. of Chicago Press, 1938; republished by the Free Press, 1950), translated by S. A. Solovay and J. H. Mueller from *Les Règles de la méthode sociologique* (Paris: Alcan, 1895; 2nd ed., rev. and enlarged, new Preface, 1901)

Suicide (or *Le Suicide*)

Emile Durkheim, *Suicide: A Study in Sociology,* edited with an Introduction by G. Simpson (New York: Free Press, 1951), translated by J. A. Spaulding and G. Simpson from *Le Suicide: étude de sociologie* (Paris: Alcan, 1897).

On Morality

Emile Durkheim, *On Morality and Society: Selected Writings,* edited with an Introduction by Robert N. Bellah (Chicago: Univ. of Chicago Press, 1973).

Textes

Emile Durkheim, *Textes,* presented by V. Karady, 3 vols. 1. *Elément d'une théorie sociale.* 2. *Religion, morale, anomie.* 3. *Fonctions sociales et institutions* (Paris: Minuit, 1975).

La Morale	Lucien Lévy-Bruhl, *La Morale et science des moeurs* (Paris: Alcan, 1903), translated by E. Lee (London: Constable, 1915)
Oeuvres	Marcel Mauss, *Oeuvres,* 3 vols. 1. *Les Fonctions du sacré.* 2. *Représentations collectives et diversité de civilisations.* 3. *Cohésions sociales et divisions de la sociologie* (Paris: Minuit, 1968)
The Durkheimian School, 1977	Yash Nandan, *The Durkheimian School: A Systematic and Comprehensive Bibliography* (Westport, Conn.: Greenwood Press, 1977)
L'Ecole durkheimienne et son opus	Yash Nandan, *L'Ecole durkheimienne et son opus: une étude empirique et analytique de ''l'Année sociologique,''* 1898–1913 (Paris: C.N.R.S., 1975, in microedition)
Encyclopedic Dictionary	Adolf Berger, *Encyclopedic Dictionary of Roman Law* (Philadelphia: The Philosophical Society, 1953)
Catalog	*The National Union Catalog,* pre-1956 imprints

Introduction

L'ANNEE SOCIOLOGIQUE AND THE DURKHEIMIAN SCHOOL: TOWARD A SYSTEMATIC THEORY OF DOCTRINAL SCHOOLS

1. See Yash Nandan, *L'Ecole durkheimienne et son opus;* ''A Theory of Doctrinal Schools and its Application to the Durkheimian School,'' *Sociological Research Symposium,* VI, 1976, pp. 2–7; ''Durkheim as Scholarch,'' paper presented at Columbia University Seminar in Content and Methods of the Social Sciences, 21 April 1976; ''A Theoretical Introduction to the Durkheimian School,'' in Nandan, *The Durkheimian School,* 1977; and finally a study in preparation, *The Durkheimian School 1885-1940: Theoretical Synthesis Based on Systematics.*

2. For scores of bibliographic references to Durkheim and his school, see currently published *Etudes durkheimiennes: bulletin d'information.* A Belgian group of sociologists has started publishing *Cahiers durkheimiens. Revue française de sociologie* has already dedicated a special issue, XVII (2), (1976), to Durkheim. Another special issue (XX, 2nd issue, 1979) on the Durkheimians has recently appeared. Time will provide an opportunity to review these special issues and other

current literature on Durkheim and his school in the near future. Professor Edward A. Tiryakian is editing *The Durkheimian School on Sociology and Social Issues,* a publication of the University of Chicago Press. The incoming literature on the Durkheimian school is enormous and will most probably continue to absorb the attention of many sociologists with theoretical orientations.

3. Soon I intend to undertake what here is suggested as "a generic and genetic theory of the growth of knowledge."

4. See A. Francke (ed.), *Dictionnaire des sciences philosophiques* (Paris: Hachette, 1875, pp. 647–57); and James Baldwin (ed.), *Dictionary of Philosophy and Psychology* (vol. II, New York: Macmillan, 1902, pp. 495–98).

5. A. Forke, *Geschichte der alten chinesischen Philosophie* (Hamburg: Kommissionsverlag L. Friederischen, 1927, p. 1).

6. Pearson quoted by V. Branford, "Notes on the History of Sociology in Reply to Professor Karl Pearson," *SP,* I, 1905, p. 25.

DURKHEIM AS "SCHOLARCH"

1. L. Muhlfeld, "Rev. of: E. Durkheim, *De la Division,*" *RU,* 1893, pp. 440–43.

2. See Nandan, *The Durkheimian School,* 1977, op. cit. See Section VII of this bibliography.

3. E. Durkheim, "Rev. of: A. Schaeffle, *Bau und Leben des sozialen Körpers,* Vol. I," *RP,* 29, 1885, pp. 84–101. Cf. his "Le Programme économique de M. Schaeffle," *REP,* 2, 1888, pp. 3–7.

4. Durkheim, "Review of Schaeffle," 1885, op. cit., pp. 100–101.

5. *RP,* 29, 1885, pp. 446–53.

6. E. Durkheim "Rev. of: L. Gumplowicz, *Grundriss der Soziologie,*" *RP,* 20, 1885, pp. 627–34.

7. "La Philosophie dans les universités allemandes," *RIE,* 13, 1887, p. 437.

8. Ibid., p. 437.

9. E. Durkheim, "La Science positive de la morale en Allemagne," *RP,* 22, 1887, pp. 33–58, 113–42, 275–84.

10. B. Lacroix and B. Landerer, in a perceptive article, examine Durkheim's relationship with the German socialists of the chair; see "Durkheim, Sismondi, et les sociologistes de la chaire," *AS* (3rd series), 1972, pp. 159–204.

11. The title as such, however, is no longer in popular use in the university system.

12. René Lacroze, "Emile Durkheim à Bordeaux," *Actes de l'Académie Nationale des Sciences, Belles-Lettres et Arts de Bordeaux* (4th series), 17, 1960, p. 63.

13. E. Durkheim, "Cours de science sociale: leçon d'ouverture," *RIE,* 15, 1888, 23–48.

14. E. Durkheim, "Introduction à la sociologie de la famille," *AFLB,* 1888, pp. 257–81. It constitutes inaugural lecture for 1888–89 and for the course entitled "La famille: origines, types principaux."

15. Durkheim throughout the *Année* edited the subsection "Domestic Organization," consisting of two rubrics: (1) the family, and (2) marriage, sexual

morality, and the condition of women. Under the auspices of this rubric, Durkheim reviewed Marianne Weber's (Max Weber's wife) *Ehefrau und Mutter in der Rechtsentwickelung* and criticized it on scientific grounds. See pp. 285–89. For the development of sections and subsections in the *Année,* see Nandan, *L'Ecole durkheimienne et son opus,* op. cit., pp. 52–109.

16. *RIE,* 19, 1890, pp. 450–56. Translated by M. Traugott in E. Durkheim, *On Morality and Society: Selected Writings,* edited with an Introduction by R. N. Bellah, Univ. of Chicago Press, 1973, pp. 34–42.

17. Detailed bibliographic information has not been included in this volume. Space does not allow reproduction of Durkheim's bibliography *in extenso.* Therefore, for Durkheim's bibliography before 1897, see Nandan, *The Durkheimian School,* 1977, op. cit.

18. E. Durkheim, "Lo stato attuale degli studi sociologici in Francia," *RS,* 3, 1895, pp. 607–22, 691–707. Among several other opuscules by Durkheim, this article remains untranslated.

19. For his courses and lectures delivered both at Bordeaux and Paris, see Steven Lukes, *Emile Durkheim: His Life and Work,* New York: Harper, 1972, pp. 617–20.

20. H. Bourgin, *De Jean Jaurès à Léon Blum: l'Ecole Normale et la politique,* Paris: Rayard, 1938, p. 215. Repr. as *L'Ecole Normale et la politique: de Jean Jaurès à Léon Blum* (Presentation and Introduction by D. Lindenberg), New York and Paris: Gordon and Breach, 1970.

21. Ibid., p. 215.

22. E. Durkheim, "Lettre au directeur," *RP,* 52, 1901, p. 704.

23. E. Durkheim, "Lettres au directeur," *Revue néo-scolastique,* 15, 1907, pp. 606–607, 612–14. The correspondence between Durkheim and S. Deploige had been reproduced by the latter in his *Le Conflit de la morale et de sociologie,* Louvain and Paris, 1911, 2nd ed. enlarged with a preface, 1912, pp. 393–413. English translation by C. C. Miltner: *The Conflict Between Ethics and Sociology,* St. Louis and London: Herder, 1938. The correspondence has not been incorporated in the English edition, however.

24. For a bibliography of this society's meetings and the contributions to them of Durkheim and his followers, see Nandan, *The Durkheimian School,* 1977, op. cit., pp. 428–33.

25. Established in 1904, its monthly proceedings were published from November to May each year in *Libres Entretiens* until 1919, when this organ ceased publication; the Union itself became the meeting place of some of the eminent scholars, politicians, and representatives from both the Catholic church and Protestant denominations, who participated in its meetings: viz. Laberthanière (Catholic church), Jean Monnier (Protestant pastor), Jaurès and Millerand (deputies elected to the legislative chamber), E. Vandervelde (member of the Chamber of Belgian Representatives and a socialist), and Aullard, Charles Seignobos, Charles Gide, Léon Brunschvicg, Gustave Belot, Paul Bureau, and Salleilles.

26. Durkheim contributed to the following discussions: "Sur la séparation des églises et de l'Etat," in *Libres Entretiens,* 1st series, 1905, pp. 369–71, 496–500; "Sur l'internationalisme: définition des termes, lutte des classes," Ibid., 2nd series (for complete pagination see Nandan, *The Durkheimian School,* 1977, op. cit.); "Sur

l'Etat, les fonctions, et le public: le fonctionnaire citoyen; syndicates de fonction-naires,'' Ibid., 4th series, 1908, pp. 137–38, 140, 142–45, 148, 150–52, 161–63, 169, 170, 176, 190, 194–97, 243, 252–56, 257–59, 261–66, 272, 279–81, 283, 292–95; ''Mariage et divorce,'' Ibid., 5th series, 1910, pp. 258–59, 261–62, 266–67, 270, 273, 283, 293.

27. Durkheim contributed to the following inquiries: ''L'Oeuvre de H. Taine,'' *Revue Blanche,* 13, 1897, pp. 287–91; ''La Guerre et le militarisme,'' *L'Humanité nouvelle,* May 1899, pp. 50–52; ''L'Introduction de la sociologie dans l'enseigne-ment secondaire,'' *RIS,* 7, 1899, p. 679; H. Dagan, *Enquête sur l'antisémitisme,* Paris: Stock, pp. 59–63; ''L'Influence allemande, II: Sociologie et économie poli-tique,'' *MF,* 44, 156, pp. 647–48; ''L'Impuissance parlementaire,'' *La Revue,* 63, 1908, pp. 396–71; ''La Sociologie,'' *Les Documents du progès,* 2, Feb. 1908, pp. 131–33.

28. R. Maublanc, ''Durkheim: professeur de philosophie,'' *Europe,* 22, 1930, p. 297.

29. René Lacroze, ''Durkheim à Bordeaux (1887–1902),'' op. cit.

30. Maublanc, op. cit., p. 297.

31. Ibid.

32. ''La Sociologie en France au XIXe siècle,'' *RB,* 4th series, 12, 1900, pp. 609–13. ''De la méthode objective en sociologie,'' *RSH,* 11, 1901, pp. 3–17 (this article was later reproduced as a preface to the 2nd edition of *Les Règles.* With P. Fauconnet, ''Sociologie et sciences sociales,'' *RP,* 55, 1903, pp. 465–97 (abridged translation in English was published in *SP,* 1, 1905, pp. 258–80). ''La Sociologie et les sciences sociales,'' *RIS,* 12, 1904, pp. 83–84 (a résumé of the conference at the Ecole des Hautes Etudes Sociales in which Durkheim and Tarde both were present and con-fronted each other in the debate on the contradistinct characters of their doctrines).

33. With P. Fauconnet, ''Sociology and the Social Sciences,'' 1905, op. cit.; ''On the Relation of Sociology to the Social Sciences and to Philosophy,'' Ibid., pp. 197–200 (the latter was presented in absentia, and read at the inaugural meeting of the Sociological Society by V. Branford, then secretary).

34. See ''Lo stato attuale degli studi sociologici in Francia,'' op. cit., ''La sociologia ed il suo dominio scientifica,'' *RItS,* 4, 1900, pp. 127–48 (French translation, ''La Sociologie et son domaine scientifique,'' trans. A. Cuvillier, in A. Cuvillier, *Où va la Sociologie française,* Paris: Rivière, 1953, pp. 177–208); ''Sociology and Its Scientific Field,'' by Kurt H. Wolff, in *Emile Durkheim, 1858–1917,* edited by Kurt H. Wolff, Ohio State Univ. Press, afterwards a paperback: Emile Durkheim et al., *Essays on Sociology and Philosophy, with Appraisal of Durkheim's Life and Thought,* New York: Harper, 1964, pp. 354–75 (pagination from the paperback edition). N.B.: Translated from the original Italian publication and not from French.

35. ''La Sociologie'' in *La Science française,* Paris: Ministère de l'Instruction Publique et des Beaux-Arts, vol. I, pp. 39–49. (The completely revised edition was published in 1933 by Larousse. The article by Durkheim was updated with a note on ''La Sociologie, en France, depuis 1914,'' by Mauss, pp. 36–37.) For English translation of the original article (excluding appendix by Mauss) see ''Sociology,'' trans. J. D. Folkman, in *Essays on Sociology and Philosophy,* 1964, op. cit., pp. 375–85 (pagination from the latter title, paperback edition). *La Science française,* pub-lished in 2 vols., contained articles written by eminent scholars and social scientists, e.g., Antoine Meillet, Lucien Lévy-Bruhl, and Albert Demangeon.

36. *L'Allemagne au-dessus de tout: la mentalité allemande et la guerre*, Paris: Colin, 1915. In English, *Germany Above All: German Mentality and the War*, Paris: Colin, 1915. With E. Denis, *Qui a voulu la Guerre? Les Origines de la guerre d'après les documents diplomatiques*, Paris: Colin, 1915. In English, *Who Wanted War?: The Origin of the War According to Diplomatic Documents*, trans. A. M. Wilson-Garnel, Paris: Colin. These two propaganda pamphlets by Durkheim have been translated into several other European languages. See "Durkheim's Works Translated into Languages Other Than English" in Nandan, *The Durkheimian School*, op. cit.

37. *Lettres à tous les français: patience, efforts, et confiance*, Paris: Comité de Publication, 1916 (Durkheim's contributions include: 1st letter, "Patience, effort, confiance," pp. 9–18; 5th letter, "Les Alliés de l'Allemagne en Orient," pp. 57–66; 10th letter, with A. Meillet, "Les Forces italiennes. La Belgique, La Serbie, le Montenegro," pp. 111–20; 11th letter, "Les Forces françaises," pp. 121–33.)

38. "Notice sur André-Armand Durkheim," *AAAE-ENS*, 1917, pp. 201–5. Durkheim's son's necrology, since he was a *normalien*, has been published in the *Annuaire* of the Ecole Normale Supérieure, and the same is true for other members of the school who were *normaliens*.

39. *Leçons de sociologie: physique des moeurs et du droit*, preface by H. N. Kubali, Introduction by Georges Davy. Istanbul: L'Université d'Istanbul, "Publications de l'Université: Faculté de Droit," no. III, and Paris: PUF. In English, *Professional Ethics and Civic Morals*, trans. C. Brookfield, London: Routledge, 1957.

40. *Pragmatisme et sociologie*, cours inédit prononcé à la Sorbonne en 1913–1914 et restitué d'après des notes d'étudiants, Preface by A. Cuvillier, Paris: Vrin, 1955. (Only first to fifth, thirteenth, and fourteenth lectures have been translated into English: See "Pragmatism and Sociology," trans. Charles Bend, in *Essays on Sociology and Philosophy*, 1964, op. cit., pp. 386–436.)

THE ESSENCE OF DURKHEIM'S DOCTRINES

1. F. Brunetière, "La Religion comme la sociologie," *Revue des deux mondes*, 15 Feb. 1913, pp. 853–77.

2. D. Parodi, *La Philosophie contemporaine en France: essai de classification des doctrines*, Paris: Alcan, 1919, p. 133. The chapter in which Parodi gives this characterization of the Durkheimian school is entitled "Emile Durkheim et l'école sociologique."

3. This aspect of Durkheim's personality and of his mental attitude was revealed by Bergson, who was rather hostile not only toward Durkheim but also toward his disciples. See J. Chevalier, *Entretiens avec Bergson*, Paris: Plon, 1959, p. 34. Durkheim, in "L'Enseignement philosophique et l'aggrégation de philosophie," *RP*, 34, 1895, p. 132, on the other hand, alluded to the anti-science tendencies of Bergson and insinuated that Bergsonism was new-mysticism, which, he claimed, "recruits its clientele from the ranks of our students, which is not without significance. Certainly, science has not yet acquired a place of honor. . . . But mysticism is a world of pleasures which rules the mind."

4. See E. Durkheim and M. Mauss, Introduction to: "Civilisations et types de civilisations," *AS*, 12, p. 48. In English, "Note on the Notion of Civilization," trans.

with an Introduction by B. Nelson, *SResearch*, 38, 1971, pp. 808–13. Our own translation of this piece will be included in a forthcoming volume of Durkheim's contributions in anthropology. Comtean positivism is distinguished from Durkheimian neo-positivism in an article by Eugène de Roberty, "Les nouveaux courants d'idées dans la sociologie contemporaine," *RP*, 77, 1914, pp. 2–3.

5. F. Simiand, "La Méthode positive en science économique," *RMM*, 16, 1908, pp. 889–904; repr. in *La Méthode positive en science économique*, Paris: Alcan, 1912. Cf. "Déduction et observation psychologique en économie sociale: remarques de méthode," *RMM*, 7, 1899, pp. 446–62; repr. in *La Méthode positive en science économique*.

6. F. Simiand, "La Méthode positive en science économique," op. cit., p. 889.

7. Ibid., p. 893.

8. Fauconnet remarked of Simiand that the latter was more of an economist than a sociologist. See P. Fauconnet's contribution to: R. Marjolin, "Rationalité ou irrationalité des mouvements économiques de longue durée (1)," *Annales Sociologiques*, series D., 3, 1938, p. 38.

9. D. R. G. Owen, *Scientism, Man and Religion*. Philadelphia: Westminister Press, 1952, p. 20.

10. John Wellmuth, *The Nature and Origin of Scientism*, Milwaukee: Marquette Univ. Press, 1944.

11. Ibid., pp. 1–2.

12. Simiand, "La Méthode positive en science économique," op. cit.

13. Durkheim and Mauss, Introduction to: "Civilisations et types de civilisations," op. cit., p. 50.

14. Ibid., p. 48.

15. Ibid., p. 47.

16. See Nandan, *L'Ecole durkheimienne et son opus*, op. cit., pp. 176–201.

17. René Worms, "Rev. of: *L'Année sociologique*," *RIS*, 20, 1912, pp. 712–15. The review literature on the *Année*, which still remains largely unnoticed by sociologists, is enormous. I have collected fifty-one references bearing directly on the *Année*. See "*L'Année* Index for Part Three," in Nandan, *The Durkheimian School*, 1977, op. cit.

18. R. Hertz, "Rev. of: G. Brown, *Melanesians and Polynesians*, 1910; P.J. Meier, *Mythen und Erzählungen der Küstenbewohner der Gazelle-Halbinsel*, 1909; P.G. Peekel, *Religion und Zauberei auf dem mittleren Neu-Mecklenburg*, 1910," *AS*, 12, 1913, p. 125.

19. See J. Vendryès, "A. Meillet: avec une bibliographie par E. Beneveniste," *Bulletin de la société de Linguistique de Paris*, 38, 1937 (also published separately under the same title, Paris, 1937, p. 13, pagination from the latter). In an international meeting of linguists, Meillet protested loudly and energetically against the reigning pessimism about comparativism: *Mais moi, je suis comparatiste*, cited by J. Vendryès, ibid., p. 14.

20. See Antoine Meillet, *La Méthode comparative en linguistique historique*, Paris: Librairie Honoré Champion, 1925; also published simultaneously in London, Cambridge (Mass.), and Oslo. In English, *The Comparative Method in Historical*

Linguistics, trans. Gordon B. Ford, Jr., Paris: Librairie Honoré; 1967. (The publication constitutes Meillet's inaugural lectures delivered at the prestigious Institut-tet for Sammenlignende Kulturforskning—Institute for the Comparative Study of Civilizations—in Kristiania (now Oslo). Marcel Granet was another Durkheimian who later delivered lectures at this Institute.

21. Ibid., p. 24 (paginations here and infra from the English edition).

22. Ibid., p. 13.

23. Ibid., p. 23.

24. Durkheim is famous—notorious as well, in the circles of his adversaries—for his overemphasis on the sui generis character of society and the constraint that *conscience collective* exerts on the individual. His work is saturated with the characterization of society as a superior and exterior force. Citing references from his work in support of this representation of Durkheimian thought would be an exercise in futility. Citation of his major works, however, should be sufficient to prove the point. See *The Division of Labor; Suicide; The Elementary Forms.* Also see *Sociologie et philosophie,* Preface by C. Bouglé, Paris: Alcan, 1923. In English, *Sociology and Philosophy,* trans. D. F. Pocock with Introduction by J. G. Peristiany, New York: Free Press, 1953.

    Durkheim's vital claim on society earned him epithets that he never contested—he paid no attention to what his opponents thought of his doctrine. For instance, Fustel de Coulanges (see Charles Seignobos, "L'Inconnu et l'inconscient en histoire," *BSFP,* 28, May, 1908, P. 229) "had a horror of Durkheim's notion of collective conscience." Andler (see "Sociologie et démocratie," *RMM,* 4, 1896, pp. 243–56) characterized Durkheimian theory of society as a "new mythology." According to Fouillée (see *Le Mouvement positiviste et la conception sociologique du monde,* Paris: Alcan, 1896, p. 248) Durkheimian societism was nothing less than "pure metaphysics."

25. E. Durkheim, "Détermination du fait moral (presentation of a thesis at the meetings of the Société Française de Philosophie, 11 Feb., 1906 and 27 March, 1906)," *BSFP,* 1906, pp. 113–212. Discussants: Elie Halévy, Jules Lachelier, André Lalande, Lucien Lévy-Bruhl, Dominique Parodi, et al. Written communications (letters) from Marcel Bernès, Maurice Blondel, Léon Brunschvicg, Chabrier, Alphonse Darlu, Egger, Edmond Goblot, B. Jacob, Leclère, Frederic Rauh, and Louis Weber. Repr. in *Sociologie et Philosophie,* op. cit.

26. Ibid., p. 75.

27. Ibid., p. 84.

28. Ibid., p. 84.

29. Lucien Lévy-Bruhl, *La Morale et la science des moeurs,* Paris: Alcan, 1903. Since then the book has experienced a record publication of fifteen editions in French.

30. Ibid., p. 14.

31. Durkheim, "Détermination du fait moral," op. cit., p. 51 (pagination from *Sociologie et philosophie*).

32. See Durkheim, "Sociologie religieuse et théorie de la connaissance," *RMM,* 7, 1909, pp. 733–58. Adopted as Introduction to *Les Formes élémentaires,* excluding pp. 754–58 of the article, which are omitted. Durkheim and Mauss, "De quelques formes primitives de classification," *AS,* 6, 1903. In English, *Primitive Classifica-*

tion (Chicago: University of Chicago Press, 1963. Trans. and Introduction by Rodney Needham). Mauss and Hubert, *Mélanges d'histoire des religions*, Paris: Alcan, 1909 (contains som seminal articles on the subject previously published either independently or collectively by the two colleagues). Several noteworthy review articles on the notion of categories by Mauss and Hubert are scattered throughout the volume of the *Année* and elsewhere. For Mauss's opuscules of this nature, see *Oeuvres*, vol. 2, pp. 90–105.

33. Durkheim and Mauss, "De quelques formes primitives de classification," op, cit., p. 66.

34. Durkheim, "Sociologie religieuse et théorie de la connaissance," op. cit.

35. Ibid., p. 12.

36. Ibid.

37. H. Hubert, "Rev. of: W. W. Fowler, *The Roman Festivals of the Period of the Republic: An Introduction to the Study of the Religion of the Romans*, London: Macmillan, 1899," *AS*, 4, 1901, p. 234.

DISCIPLES AND FOLLOWERS: FORMATION, GROWTH, AND CONSOLIDATION OF THE DURKHEIMIAN SCHOOL

1. Nandan, *"The Durkheimian School: Theoretical Synthesis Based on Systematics,"* (in preparation).

2. *AS*, 7, 1904, pp. 380–84; cf. *AS*, 10, 1909, pp. 352–68, and *Sociology and Philosophy*, op. cit. E. Wallwork's attempt in *Durkheim: Morality and Milieu* (Harvard University Press, 1972) is extremely poor, since it neither mentions Lévy-Bruhl's *La Morale* nor does it take into account the longstanding controversy it engendered.

3. The subject will be dealt with at great length in Nandan, *"The Durkheimian School: Theoretical Synthesis,"* op. cit.

4. A chapter is entitled "Lévy-Bruhl: A Durkheimian in Limbo" in Ibid.

5. See Appendix B.

6. The literature on German scientific and technological superiority is too abundant to be cited here in any detail. See especially G. Weill, *Histoire de l'enseignement secondaire en France*, Paris: Payot, 1921, pp. 155–56. Pasteur, *Quelques Reflexions sur la science en France*, Paris: Gauthier-Villars, 1871. Pasteur in 1868 in a letter to Napoléon III warned of "Germany which was replenished with rich and vast laboratories and everyday new ones were added to it," cited by C. Digeon, *La Crise allemande de la pensée française (1870-1914)*, Paris: PUF, 1959, p. 364. W. Rothstein, *Frankreichs Volksschullehrerschaft und Volksschullehrbuch im Spiegel der Revanchepolitik (1871-1914)*, Leipzig: Noska, 1928. Ed. Dreyfus-Brisiac, *L'Education nouvelle*, Paris: Mason, 1882. R. Blanchard, *Les Universités allemandes*, Paris: Le Progrès Médical, 1883, L. Liard, *L'Enseignement supérieure en France*, 2 vols., Paris: Colin, 1894. G. Blondel, "Notes sur l'enseignement des sciences sociales dans les universités allemandes," *RIE*, 29, 1895, pp. 133–45. G. Blondel, "De l'Enseignement du droit dans les universités allemandes," *RIE*, 10, 1885, pp.

39–56, 91–105. For a fuller and thorough discussion of the subject, see C. Digeon, op. cit., pp. 364–453. Contrary to this literature in unequivocal praise of the German sciences, cf. (author anonymous, most likely German), "Le Pauperisme dans les universités," *RIE*, 10, 1885, pp. 264–75.

7. After his return from Germany, Bouglé wrote reminiscences of his visit under the pseudonym Jean Breton and published *Note d'un étudiant français en Allemagne* (Paris: Lévy, 1895). In this memoir, Bouglé quoted Bismarck as saying: "I will be a socialist when I have time. . . . There is no good politics without *Völkerpsychologie*," ibid., p. 70. Bouglé also wrote articles, published in *RMM*, on the status of social sciences in Germany, which were incorporated in his *Les Sciences sociales en Allemagne: le conflit des méthodes*, Paris: Alcan 1896; 3rd rev. ed., 1912.

8. C. Seignobos, "L'Enseignement de l'histoire dans les universités allemandes," *RIE*, 1881, pp. 563–601. Cf. E. Lavisse, *Question d'enseignement national*, Paris: Colin, 1885. Boutroux was often chided for being drunk on too much German philosophy. So was Charles Andler. In 1887, when Andler was being examined for the *agrégation*, one of the examiners on the jury characterized Andler's excessive philosophic erudition as *encore cette philosophie d'outre-Rhin*. See, E. Tonnelat, *Charles Andler: sa vie et son oeuvre*, Paris, 1937, p. 34.

9. R. Didon, *Les Allemands*, Paris: Lévy, 1884. In appendices Didon gives testimony of the superiority of German science as evinced by French scholars.

10. Ibid., p. 7.

11. Most of these articles appeared in the *Revue internationale de l'enseignement*, the *Revue bleu*, and the *Revue des deux mondes*.

12. Digeon, *La Crise allemande*, op. cit.

13. E. Zola, *La Débâcle*, Paris: Charpentier, 1883. In English, *The Downfall*, trans. E. P. Robins, New York: Cassell, 1892.

14. E. Zola, "La Politique expérimentale," *Le Figaro*, 28 March, 1881; repr. in *Oeuvres complètes*, Vol. 14, Paris: Cercle du Livre Précieux, pp. 568–573.

15. A. Cresson, *La Morale de Kant: étude critique*, Paris: Alcan, 1897, p. 99.

16. "La Critique des catégories kantiennes chez Ch. Renouvier," *RMM*, 1934, pp. 605–20.

17. C. Bouglé, "Spiritualisme et Kantisme en France," *Paris*, 1 May, 1934, pp. 198–215.

18. See his *Du Positivisme à l'idéalisme: Philosophie d'hier et d'aujourd'hui. Etudes critiques*, Paris: Vain, 1936.

19. Bouglé, 1934, op. cit., p. 214.

20. In Boutroux's view, "whosoever applies himself to maintain the originality of philosophy, by reestablishing closer relations between science and religion, and by bringing them closer, is, to some extent, a disciple of Lachelier," *Nouvelles Etudes d'histoire de la philosophie*, Paris: Alcan, 1927, p. 31. See also G. Séailles, *La Philosophie de Jules Lachelier*, Paris: Alcan, 1920. And G. Mauchaussat, *L'Idéalisme de Lachelier*, Paris: PUF, 1961.

21. For literature on the Ecole Normale Supérieure, see H. Bourgin, *De Jean Jaurès à Léon Blum*, 1938, op. cit. J. Gautier, "L'Ecole Normale (1795–1895)," *RIE*, 30,

1895, pp. 19–38. Paul Dupuy, *L'Ecole Normale de l'an III,* Paris: Hachette, 1882. Fustel de Coulanges, "L'Ecole Normale," *Séances et Travaux de l'Académie des Sciences Morales et Politiques,* 44ᵉ année (n.s.), 1884, pp. 833–48. Paul Dupuy (ed.), *Le Centenaire de l'Ecole Normale, 1796-1895,* Paris: Hachette, 1895 (contains some very useful articles). Georges Perrot, "La Pédagogie a l'Ecole Normale Supérieure," *RIE,* 44, 1902, pp. 516–23. A. J. Ladd, *Ecole Normale Supérieure: An Historical Sketch,* Grand Forks, N. Dakota: Herald Pub. Co., 1907. C. Bouglé (ed.), *L'Ecole Normale Supérieure. D'où elle vient? Où elle va?* Paris: Hachette, 1934 (contains some useful articles written either specifically for this volume or extracted from other sources). J. Reignup, *L'Esprit de L'Ecole Normale,* Paris: Spes, 1935. P. Jeannin, *Ecole Normale Supérieure: livre d'or,* Paris, 1963 (a useful source). A. Peyrefitte, *Rue d'Ulm. Chroniques de la vie normalienne,* Paris: Flammarion, 1963. R. J. Smith, *The Ecole Normale Supérieure in the Third Republic: A Study of the Classes of 1890-1904,* Ph.D. diss., Philadelphia: Univ. of Pennsylvania, 1967.

22. Fustel de Coulanges, 1884, op. cit. G. Perrot made the same reference to this change in the Ecole Normale Supérieure in "L'Ecole Normale et son Centenaire " *Le Centenaire,* 1895, op. cit., pp. i–xlv.

23. Perrot, "L'Ecole Normale et son Centenaire," op. cit., p. xxxix. Charles Andler, *La Vie de Lucien Herr,* Paris, 1932, p. 25. Smith, *The Ecole Normale Supérieure in the Third Republic,* op. cit., p. 110.

24. Fustel de Coulanges, 1884, op. cit., p. 839.

25. P. Guiraud, "Fustel de Coulanges," in *Le Centenaire de l'Ecole Normale,* op. cit., p. 326.

26. Ibid., p. 326.

27. Ibid., p. 327.

28. Ibid., p. 845. If the eminent historian "was never vague nor was he superficial" (ibid., p. 327), this can also be said of Durkheim, whom Fustel de Coulanges inspired and whose ideas he more or less faithfully followed.

29. E. Boutroux, "La Philosophie en France depuis 1867," *RMM,* 1908; repr. in *Nouvelle Etude d'histoire de la philosophie,* Paris: Alcan, 1927, p. 142.

30. Ibid., p. 142.

31. Incidentally, it may be noted that Comte was also a student of the Ecole Polytechnique, even though he never graduated.

32. Worms is the only one in the history of the Ecole Normale Supérieure who earned three doctorates: Doctorat d'Etat (ès Lettres), Doctorat en Droit, and Doctorat en Science. This fact was brought to my attention by Professor Raymond Aron.

33. Andler, *Vie de Lucien Herr,* 1932, op. cit., p. 29.

34. Léon Blum, *Souvenirs sur l'affaire,* Paris, 1935, p. 29.

35. E. Durkheim, "L'Individualisme et les intellectuals," *RB,* 4th series, 10, 1898, pp. 7–13; repr. in E. Durkheim, *La Science sociale et l'action,* Paris: PUF, 1970, pp. 261–78. In English, "Individualism and Intellectuals," trans. S. and J. Lukes, with a note, *Political Studies,* 17, 1969, pp. 14–30. Also "Individualism and the Intellectuals," trans. Mark Traugott, in E. Durkheim, *On Morality,* op. cit.

36. Andler, 1932, op. cit., p. 163.

37. After his career as a student in the Ecole Normale Supérieure, Peguy acquired the Librairie Georges Bellais against the advice of Herr. See Smith, 1967, op. cit., p. 145. The Société Nouvelle, however, continued (Librairie Georges Bellais). See also H. Bourgin, *De Jean Jaurès à Léon Blum,* op. cit., p. 115.

38. On 10 Feb. 1929, the stockholders in the Société Nouvelle, among others, included: G. Bourgin, H. Bourgin, Demangeon, Fauconnet, Gernet, Halbwachs, Hubert, Em. Lévy, Is. Lévy, Mauss, Poirot, Ray, Roussel, Simiand, Sion, and Vacher. I cite these names only because they belong to the Durkheimian school. For a complete list of the stockholders on that date see Smith, 1967, op. cit., p. 148.

39. Bourgin, *De Jean Jaurès à Léon Blum,* op. cit., p. 117.

40. For a complete list of the stockholders on 2 Aug. 1899, and for the details of their investment in this enterprise, see Smith, 1967, op. cit., p. 147.

41. "Cahiers du Socialiste" is a type of irregular serial publication that is seldom catalogued as such by libraries. Constituting a collection of pamphlets on socialism, it is erroneously listed as a periodical in the Bibliothèque Nationale catalogue. Also, since "Cahiers du Socialiste" is italicized in some of the literature, it gives the false impression of a journal.

42. Durkheim also contributed some reviews, for instance, "Rev. of: Simmel, *Philosophie des Geldes,*" NC, 2, 1901, pp. 65–69 (also in AS, 5, 1902, pp. 140–45); "Rev. of: Demolins, *Les Grandes routes des peuples,*" NC, 2, 1901, pp. 152–53 (also in AS, 5, 1902, pp. 560–62); "Rev. of: Lambert, *La Tradition romaine sur la succession,*" NC, 2, 1901, pp. 269–70 (also in AS, 5, 1902, pp. 373–76): "Rev. of: E. Demuth, *Die wechselseitigen Verfügungen von Todes-Wegen nach alamannisch-zürcherischem Recht,*" NC, 3, 1902, pp. 77–78; "Rev. of: Bauer, *Les Classes sociales,*" NC, 3, 1902, pp. 275–78; "Rev. of: C. Letourneau, *La Condition de la femme dans les diverses races et civilisations,*" NC, 4, 1903, pp. 199–200 (also in AS, 7, 1904, pp. 425–27); and "Rev. of: E. Lambert, *La Fonction du droit civil comparé,*" NC, 5, 1904, pp. 10–13 (expanded version in AS, 7, 1904, pp. 374–79). It is easily inferred from the above that most of Durkheim's reviews were duplicated in the *Notes critiques* and the *Année.*

DISSEMINATING DOCTRINES: *L'ANNEE SOCIOLOGIQUE*

1. P. Lasserre wrote in *La Doctrine officielle de l'université* (Paris: Garnier, 1913, p. 181) that "among the chapels of university science, Durkheimian sociology is going to rise up like a cathedral, the primacy of which is known to everybody." Lasserre claimed that historians, sociologists, and a handful of literati—including Lanson, Lavisse, Seignobos, and Lacombe—had built up an empire at the Sorbonne. Seen in this light, "Lanson and his school exercise the same influence in the teaching of letters at the university and constitute an empire equivalent to that of Durkheim and his doctrine," ibid., p. 248. The second part of the book, "La barbarie en Sorbonne: la sociologie, les lettres, l'histoire," overtly and covertly points to the collusion of a few savants whose teachings and ideas loom as the official doctrine of the university. See also E. F. A. Goblet d'Alviella, "La Sociologie de M. Durkheim et l'histoire de religion," *RHR,* 67, 1913, p. 221. The issue of official doctrine of the

University of Paris has also characterized P. Leguay's *La Sorbonne,* Paris: Grasset, 1910.

2. Clark in his useful study has premised his analysis of the French social sciences of this period, including the group Durkheim formed around *L'Année,* on the "reward system" and the economic patronage (a part of the title of Clark's work reads *Patrons*) of the *universitaires* by their French masters. See T. N. Clark, *Prophets and Patrons: The French University and the Emergence of the Social Sciences,* Harvard University Press, 1973.

3. See notes 36 and 37 of "Durkheim as Scholarch."

4. The summary of this meeting published in *L'Année* ("Le Premier Congrès allemand de sociologie," 12, 1913, pp. 23–26) gives no indication of the author who contributed this report. One may assign this article either to Bouglé or to Durkheim. Based on my own judgment, I have attributed it to the latter. Jean Duvignaud in his French edition of Durkheim's *Journal sociologique* (Paris: PUF, 1969) includes this piece, thus assigning it to Durkheim; however, he does not explain why. None of the Durkheimians actually attended the meeting. The review, however, is based on the publication of the proceedings of the German Sociological Society.

5. It was created in 1920 with the assistance of the A. Kahn Foundation. Bouglé was its director. By a decree of 1925, it acquired an assistant librarian, the first being Jean Boursquet. See "Chronologie," in *L'Ecole Normale Supérieure. D'où elle vient? Où elle va?,* ed. C. Bouglé, Paris, 1931, pp. 10–18.

6. For a complete list of contributions by the Durkheimians to this Society, see Nandan, *The Durkheimian School,* 1977, op. cit., section 16.

7. "*L'Année Sociologique,*" *Zeitschrift für Sozialwissenschaft,* 1, 1898, p. 473.

8. Durkheim's paper was discussed in the meeting of the Sociological Society by Bosanquet, Bridges, Reiches, Hodgson, Hobson, Robertson, and Hobhouse. In addition, some well-known scholars from all over Europe commented through their written communications—from Germany: Barth, Tönnies; from France: Marcel Bernès (sociologist and philosopher), Lévy-Bruhl, Dareste, Fouillée, Gide, Kovalevski (historian and social scientist of Russian origin), Worms; England: Bury (historian), Chapman (economist), Crozier (author), Stuart-Glennie (author), Harley, Muirhead (philosopher), Newland (author), Russel, Sorley (philosopher), Tayler (author); Scotland: Ingram (economist), Latta (philosopher), Nicholson (economist), Pringle-Pattison (philosopher); Italy: Cosetini (editor, *La scienza sociale*), Loria; Switzerland: Stein (philosopher), Winiarski (economist); Netherlands: Steinmetz. See *SP,* 1, 1905, pp. 217–54. Durkheim neither attended the meeting nor replied to his critics. However, he wrote to Branford, then secretary of the Society: "I am glad to see, by number and importance of the answers received, the interest the question has aroused. I should have wished, in turn, to reply to some of my critics; but for that, the compilation of a considerable essay would be needed; and I cannot for the moment entertain this idea by reason of total lack of leisure," ibid., p. 257.

9. See note 35 of "Durkheim as Scholarch."

10. "Letter to the Editor," *AJS,* 3, 1898, pp. 848–49. The editor of the periodical thought it appropriate to publish the letter in its original French, lest something be

lost or misinterpreted by way of translation. He added a note to this effect, which is printed with Durkheim's letter.

11. *The Elementary Forms*, op. cit.; *Who Wanted War?*, op. cit.; *Germany above All*, op. cit.; and with P. Fauconnet, "Sociology and the Social Sciences," *SP*, op. cit.: The order in which Durkheim's works have been translated into English—or for that matter into other languages—would make an interesting analysis of the priority of scholars in this task.

12. *Die Methode der Soziologie* (translation of *Les Règles*, 1895), Leipzig: 1908. The reader may note that *Les Règles* was translated into Russian in 1899 and into German in 1908, but into English only in 1938. This points to the fact that American sociology reached puberty late. Sociology in England was still in its infancy. *Les Formes élémentaires* was rendered into English in 1915 under the impelling circumstances of its immediate interest to anthropologists in England.

13. *Metod Sotsiologii* (title transliterated; translation of *Les Règles*, op. cit.), Kiev: 1899. In *The Durkheimian School*, 1977, op. cit., pp. 229–231, I have compiled a list of translations of Durkheim's works into languages other than English. In the light of this listing, one discovers that Russian was the first foreign language into which Durkheim's complete works were translated.

14. C. Bouglé, "L'Oeuvre sociologique d'Emile Durkheim," *Europe*, 22, 1930, pp. 281–304.

15. Durkheim went so far in his claim of personal character for the *Mémoires originaux* and for the series *Travaux de L'Anneée* as to call them "our *work*, or the work of those people who are completely in agreement with us." See *Textes*, vol. 2, p. 446.

16. Simiand, *La Méthode positive en science économique*, op. cit. This is not a systematic book, as it seems to be at first. Inter alia, it includes the following comprehensive review articles from the *Année*: (1) "Rev. of: M. Bourgin, *Les Systèmes socialistes et l'évolution économique*," *AS*, 8, 1905, pp. 522–536; (2) "Rev. of: A Landry, *L'Intérêt du capital*," Ibid., pp. 572–87; (3) "Rev. of: O. Effertz, *Les Antagonismes économiques*," *AS*, 10, 1907, pp. 506–27; and (4) "Rev. of: W. Jevons, *La Théorie de l'économie politique*," *AS*, 11, 1910, pp. 516–45.

17. M. Mauss and H. Hubert, *Mélanges d'histoire des religion*, Paris: Alcan, 1909, vol. 2 of *Travaux de L'Année sociologique*. The following articles have been reproduced from the *Année*: (1) "Essai sur la nature et la fonction du sacrifice," *AS*, 2, 1899, pp. 29–138, and (2) "Esquisse d'une théorie générale de la magie," *AS*, 7, 1904, pp. 1–146. Both these articles have been translated into English, the former twice by different translators. For the former, see *The Nature and Significance of the Ceremony of Sacrifice*, translated in part by A. J. Nelson, Chicago: Open Court Pub., 1926; *Sacrifice: Its Nature and Function*, translated by W. D. Halls, Foreword by E. E. Evans-Pritchard, Univ. of Chicago Press, 1964. For the latter, see *A General Theory of Magic*, translated by R. Brown, Boston: Routledge, 1972.

18. E. Durkheim, "Preface to *L'Année sociologique*," *AS*, 1, 1898, pp. i–vii; and "Preface to *L'Année sociologique*," *AS*, 2, 1899, pp. i–vi. See pp. 47–55.

19. Except for the prefaces to the *Année* and to the sections and subsections, I have classified the *Analyses* section of the periodical into four parts in my *L'Ecole durkheimienne et son opus*, op. cit., pp. 38–46. This classification conforms very

much to Durkheim's own distinction of the various parts of the *Analyses* section. See *Textes*, vol. 2, p. 449.

20. See Durkheim's letter to Bouglé, dated 3 April, 1898, *RFS*, 17, 1976, p. 169.

21. See ibid., 13 June, 1900, In ibid., p. 173.

22. Ibid., p. 174.

23. See *Textes*, vol. 2, p. 413.

24. Ibid., p. 406.

25. Ibid., p. 465.

26. Ibid., p. 465.

27. H. Bourgin, "Rev. of: *Les Travaux de l'Institut International d. Sociolcgie*," *RSH*, 7, 1903, pp. 374–78.

28. *Qu'est-ce que la sociologie?* Paris: Alcan, 1907 (reproduces an article or the same title, *RParis*, 1 Aug. 1897, pp. 533–56). 5th edition revised and cnlarged with a preface, "Philosophie sociale et la pédagogie," and "Note sur *L'Année sociologique*," Paris: Alcan, 1925.

29. Marcel Déat, *Sociologie. Notions de sociologie*, Paris: Alcan, 1925.

30. E. Durkheim, *Choix de Textes, avec étude du système sociologique*, edited by G. Davy, Paris: Michaud, 1911; republished, Paris: Rasmussen, 1927. C. Bouglé and J. Rauffault (eds.), *Eléments de sociologie*, textes choisis et ordonnés, Paris: Alcan, 1926. C. Bouglé and M. Deat, *Guide de l'étudiant en sociologie*, Paris: Rivière, 1921.

31. G. Davy, "Emile Durkheim," *RFS*, 1, 1960, p. 4.

32. M. Mauss, "In Memoriam: L'Oeuvre inédite de Durkheim et de ses collaborateurs," *AS* (nouvelle série), 1, 1925, p. 7.

33. See *L'Année philosophique*, 9, 1899, pp. 246–48; 10, 1900, pp. 257–59; 11, 1901, pp. 246–48; 13, 1903, pp. 224–25; 14, 1904, pp. 264–66; 15, 1905, pp. 255–56; 16, 1906, pp. 240–41; 17, 1907, pp. 225–56; and 18, 1908, pp. 243–44.

34. See 27, 1898, pp. 500–501 (reviewed by Adrien Veber); 32, 1900, pp. 250–254 (reviewed by C. Rappoport); 33, 1901, pp. 756–759 (reviewed by G. Rouanet); 35, 1902, p. 762 (probably reviewed by G. Rouanet); 37, 1903, pp. 763–764 (reviewed by G. Rouanet).

35. Edmond Goblot, "Notes critiques sur *L'Année*," *RSH*, 1, 1900, pp. 265–72; 4, 1902, pp. 239–42; 6, 1903, pp. 60–68; 8, 1904, pp. 171–77.

36. For a complete list of the reviews of *L'Année sociologique* which appeared in other periodicals, see "*L'Année* Index" in Nandan, The Durkheimian School, 1977, op. cit.

37. See Nandan, *L'Ecole durkheimienne et son oeuvre*, op. cit., pp. 154–55.

38. A. Bochard, "Emile Durkheim, *L'Année sociologique*," *RIS*, 6, 1898, pp. 949–50; 7, 1899, pp. 626–28; 8, 1900, pp. 915–56; 9, 1901, pp. 945–51; 10, 1902, pp. 850–53; 11, 1903, pp. 962–65; 12, 1904, pp. 936–42; 13, 1905, pp. 919–24; 14, 1907, pp. 311–17; and 16, 1908, pp. 151–56.

39. René Worms, "Rev. of: *L'Année*," *RIS*, 20, 1912, pp. 712–15.

40. For Durkheim's justification of this bifurcation of the two and incorporation of the works of the school in a series, see "Aux Lecteurs de *L'Année sociologique*," in C.

Bouglé, *Essais sur les régimes des castes,* Paris: Alcan, 1908, pp. v-viii. In English, *Essays on the Caste System,* trans. with an Introduction by D. F. Pocock, Cambridge Univ. Press, 1971. Durkheim's "Aux Lecteurs . . . ." was reprinted in *AS,* 11, 1910, pp. i-iii; see p. 55–57. However, the idea of separating the *Mémoires originaux* from the *Analyses* struck Durkheim's mind as early as 1902. See *Textes,* vol. 2, pp. 443–44, 446–48.

41. Bourgin, *De Jean Jaurès à Léon Blum,* op. cit., p. 236.
42. See *Textes,* vol. 2, p. 392.
43. Bourgin, *De Jean Jaurès à Léon Blum,* op. cit., p. 236.
44. Ibid., p. 236.
45. Ibid., p. 236.
46. L. Lévy-Bruhl, *Félix Alcan, 18 mars 1841-18 février 1925: notice nécrologique,* Paris: Alcan, 1925, p. 2.
47. F. Simiand, *Le Salaire, l'évolution sociale et la monnaie. Essai de théorie expérimentale du salaire,* 3 vols., Paris: Alcan, 1932.
48. In a personal letter adressed to me, the editors of Les Presses Universitaires de France, the successor of the Librairie Félix Alcan from 1934 on, stated that no file or archive document pertaining to the *Année* or to Durkheim and his followers has survived or exists in their possession. The complete catalogues, however, of the Librairie Félix Alcan do exist in the Bibliothèque Nationale—and perhaps elsewhere as well.

ORGANIZATION AND SCOPE OF THIS EDITION

1. Paris: PUF, 1969.
2. See G. Davy, *L'Homme,* The Hague: Mouton, 1973, p. 298.
3. For example, Duvignaud includes only two reviews from vol. 8 of the *Année* in the *Journal,* whereas in our *Contributions* we have incorporated twenty-four in the present volume alone, not counting reviews in anthropology and social morphology set apart for publication in the near future.
4. *Textes,* op. cit.
5. See Nandan, *L'Ecole durkheimienne et son opus,* op. cit., pp. 38–47.
6. See *Textes,* vol. 2, p. 173.
7. See Louis Dumont, "Une Science de devenir," *L'Arc,* 48, 1972, pp. 8–22.
8. See *Textes,* vol. 3, p. 529.

Section One: General Sociology

1. For a thorough discussion on the development of sections and subsections of the *Année,* see *L'Ecole durkheimienne et son opus,* op. cit., pp. 52–109. Ed.

2. See "Lettres à Célestin Bouglé," in *Textes,* vol. 2, pp. 389–438; "Textes inédits ou inconnus d'Emile Durkheim: Lettres à Célestin Bouglé," *RFS,* 17, 1976, pp. 165–180. These and other letters by Durkheim will be included in *Emile Durkheim's Letters* (Bayside, N. Y.: General Hall, forthcoming). Ed.

3. "Lettres à Bouglé," *RFS,* 17, 1976, p. 172. In this letter Durkheim assured Bouglé that the section on general sociology would not be poorly furnished in the future.

4. Apropos of the fear harbored by Bouglé, Durkheim wrote to him: "Once again I would like to remind you that I never dreamed of saying that sociology could be constructed without the help of psychology, nor that sociology was anything other than psychology. All I said was that collective psychology could be directly reduced to individual psychology, for a new factor intervenes which transforms the psychic phenomenon, a factor which is the source of all differences and all the novelties, is association." *Textes,* vol. 2, p. 393. Ed.

5. *RFS,* 17, 1976, op. cit., p. 176. Ed.

6. The original German title reads *Die Quintessenz des Sozialismus;* it has been translated into French (by Paul Leroy-Beaulieu), but not into English. Let it be noted, however, that Durkheim reviewed it in *RP,* 22, 1886, pp. 61–80—along with other works, of course. In "Le Programme économique de M. Schaeffle," *REP,* 11, 1888, pp. 3–7, Durkheim made a special effort to elaborate on Schaeffle's ideas and possibly save him from undue criticism by French savants. Ed.

7. The previous article, however, is reviewed by Bouglé. Ed.

8. The identical word in French can mean either "conscience" or "consciousness." Ed.

9. Durkheim poses this question in the past perfect tense because Tarde died in 1904, leaving the controversy with him unsettled. Ed.

10. An eminent French literary critic, Ferdinand Brunetière (1849–1906) through his writings launched a strong opposition to the naturalist school. Deriving his inspiration from Bousset and Darwinism, Brunetière attempted to demonstrate that the theory of evolution was also applicable to literature. After his visit to the Vatican he championed the cause of social Christianity based on the ideas of social evolution and positivism. See Elton Hocking, *Ferdinand Brunetière: The Evolution of a Critic,* Madison, 1936. And for the relation with Durkheim see S. Lukes, *Emile Durkheim: His Life and Work,* New York: Harper, 1972, pp. 335–338.

11. The eleatic system of philosophy, founded on the notion of thesis and antithesis, became an instrument of explanation for the modern philosophers to present a view of social reality as it experiences conflict and arrives at a consensus. Monism admits only one kind of substance and ultimate reality. Durkheim here is objecting to the dialectical character and identical nature of the social and natural laws, which both are united in one single harmonius force. For a comprehensive treatment of monism as this philosophical system was conceived during Durkheim's time, see A. Worsley, *Concepts of Monism,* London, 1907.

12. Mass or crowd phenomenon, formation of the mass. Ed.

13. Durkheim's article "Sociologie et sciences sociales" was published in *De la Méthode dans les sciences,* 1st series, Paris: Alcan, 1909, pp. 259–85. But Durkheim cites page 325 in reference to his quotation, which does not exactly correspond with the pagination of the original article. Ed.

14. Once again Durkheim errs, in citing 1905 as the year of publication of his article in

collaboration with Fauconnet. The correct date is 1903; in 1905 its abridged translation was published in *SP*, pp. 258–80. The original French version has been reproduced in *Textes*, vol. 1, pp. 121–59. Ed.

15. The word "hygiène" is here used in the obsolete sense of   racial hygiene. Tr.

16. I have stayed fairly close to the French. What Durkheim is saying, if we may use modern terms, is that the sociology of law (according to Kantorowicz) should take its place besides jurisprudence.

17. Society. Tr.

18. The review by Durkheim had appeared in *NC*, 2, 1901, pp. 65–69. Several of Durkheim's reviews published in the *Année* were also published in *NC*, a frivolous scholarly attempt in the name of social sciences by the socialist coterie formed by Herr. Ed.

19. Contrary to barter, *Geldwirtschaft* is an economy based on money. Ed.

20. We have retained the literal meaning of the word *bâtard*, which could also mean "illegitimate" or "absurd." Ed.

21. Perhaps Durkheim is alluding to the methodological essay by S. R. Steinmetz, "Classification des types sociaux et catalogue des peuples," *AS*, 3, 1900, pp. 93–147. Ed.

22. Review of that original edition of Schaeffle's work constitutes Durkheim's maiden attempt in sociology, and his fascination with the German idea of social sciences and morality grew progressively. See *RP*, 19, 1885, pp. 84–101. Ed.

23. Durkheim, obviously, is alluding to Tarde's theory of imitation posited in his *Les Lois d'imitation* (Paris: Alcan, 1890). Durkeim himself in his *Suicide* refuted these premises of Tarde. Ed.

24. Who reviewed him in *L'Année* is not clear. Ed.

25. George (1839–1902) was a prominent American economist and founder of the single-tax movement. His theoretical publications, *Our Land and Land Policy*, 1871, and *Progress and Poverty*, 1879, were very influential in tax legislation in many Western industrialized societies. Ed.

26. If Sergi's conception comes even close to what NATO represents in terms of its social, political, and economic cooperation among the territorial states across the Atlantic ocean, not to speak of the defense alliance among the Western European and North American states, then he was right in his anticipation of "a vast federate state." Ed.

27. In other words, America and Europe, by forming one state, will swallow the rest of the world. Ed.

28. Obviously, Durkheim views this as symptomatic of the author's chimeric thinking. Ed.

29. Small has been reviewed often in *L'Année* by different members of the Durkheimian school. See *AS*, 4, 1901, pp. 108–109, reviewed by C. Bouglé; *AS*, 5, 1902, pp. 133–34, reviewed by Durkheim; *AS*, 7, 1904, p. 185, reviewed by Durkheim; *AS*, 12, 1913, pp. 10–11, reviewed by G. Gelly. Since Bouglé was an important member of the school and editor in charge of the section on general sociology, it would be interesting to compare the reviews of Small's work, especially of the series of articles on the same subject, by Durkheim and Bouglé. Ed.

30. Since by this time Durkheim had published his major works and had developed the

quintessence of his doctrines, it is not unusual to see him comparing others' works with his own. Obviously, Durkheim was much preoccupied with his own works and with whether other sociologists dealing with similar topics had read them or not. Ed.

31. *Chose* is translated as "phenomenon." Ed.

32. Paris: Alcan, 1896.

33. By any criterion, this constitutes one of the very positive reviews by Durkheim. Why? The question needs to be dealt with in a comprehensive manner, requiring a treatment in its own right with a view to identifying Durkheim's favorite authors and targets for attack. Ed.

34. "The spirit of solidarity" comes close to the French expression *l'esprit de corps.* Ed.

35. See the previous article by the author and review by Durkheim. This also demonstrates that the Durkheimians were prompt in their followup of certain authors and their works. Ed.

36. The title is erroneously cited: it should read *Mélange de l'histoire des religions.* Ed.

37. The two works by Pechuel-Loesche have been reviewed by Antoine Beuchat. See the *Année,* 11, 1910, pp. 218–27 and 306–307. Ed.

38. Imagine Durkheim writing a four-page review of a ten-page article! Ed.

39. The English "social condensation" is literally from the expression in French. But *Verdichtung* means concentration or consolidation. Therefore, following the German meaning of the word, it is evident from the context, that the translation should read "social consolidation" or "social cohesion." Ed.

Section Three: Juridic and Moral Sociology

1. See *Textes,* vol. 2, p. 394. Ed.

2. After much debate and careful deliberation we have decided to translate *morale* throughout our rendition of Durkheim into "morals" or "morality" wherever it fitted the context. There are a few exceptions, where we have preferred the use of "ethics" over "morals." The term *morale* in French has a wider meaning and encompasses not only ethics, but also manners, customs, folkways, and mores. Except for a few places Durkheim never used the term "ethics." He absorbed this usage of English terminology into the Latin concept of *morale.* Ed.

3. E. Durkheim, *Sociologie et philosophie,* preface by C. Bouglé, Paris: Alcan, 1924, p. 51. In English, *Sociology and Philosophy,* New York: Free Press, 1953. Ed.

4. See E. Durkheim, "Introduction to the Juridic Systems," *AS,* 11, 1910, pp. 286–88. It should be noted that Durkheim never wrote an introduction in explication of historical sociology or sociology of morals. Ed.

5. Having undergone several printings and having been reproduced in several editions, this controversial and polemical work has enjoyed unprecedented popularity— and notoriety as well. Ed.

6. The reader may note the synchronous publication of the two works by Hobhouse and Sumner. Ed.

7. *RFS*, 17, 1976, p. 180. Ed.

8. Alphonse Bérenger (1785–1866) is distinguished for his humanitarian concerns and libertarian predilections in criminal matters and correctional rehabilitation of the criminals. This liberal and humanitarian concern became reflected in the revision of the code of criminal instruction and penal code. See *GE*, s.v. Alphonse Bérenger. Ed.

9. "Of sacred things, of magistrates, of priests." Ed.

10. "The earliest form of obligation under private law assumed through an oral answer to the future creditor's question. This definition of *sponsio* was later absorbed by *stipulatio*. In a narrow sense *sponsio* denoted the obligation of a surety who equally through exchange of question and answer obligated himself to pay what another had promised." *Encyclopedic Dictionary*, p. 713. Ed.

11. According to the *Catalog* no further parts of the book were published. See *Catalog*, s.v. Edouard Lambert, *Etudes de droit commun législatif*, 1903. Ed.

12. A celebrated poet and jurist, Philippe de Beaumanoir is noted for his chef d'oeuvre on medieval law texts, *Coutume de Beauvoisis* (Customary law of the Beauvoisis Region), perhaps the work on medieval law and customs most frequently consulted by French jurists. Ed.

13. See F. Gény, *Méthode d'interpretation et sources en droit privé positif. Essai Critique*, Paris, 1899. Ed.

14. See note 11. Ed.

15. *Ethics and Moral Science*, trans. Elizabeth Lee, London: Constable, 1905. Ed.

16. This is what Sumner tried to establish in his *Folkways: A Study in the Sociological Import of Usages, Manners, Customs, Mores, and Morals*, Boston, 1906. Ed.

17. G. L. Duprat, *Les Causes sociales de la folie*, Paris: Alcan, 1900. For its review by Durkheim, see p. 410. Ed.

18. A French writer (1613–1680), La Rochefoucauld is known for his moral maxims and reflective epigrams. Ed.

19. Here the reference is to Rousseau's *La Profession de foi du vicaire savoyard*. In English, *Profession of Faith of a Savoyard Vicar*, trans. O. Schreiner, New York: Eckler, 1889. The vicar is assumed to be modeled on J. C. Gaime and J. B. Gaber. The *Vicaire Savoyard* brought Rousseau a tirade of criticisms and vehement refutations by both Catholics and Protestants for the heretic aim to profess a moral doctrine based on what he designated "natural religion." How much influence these theories had on the secularization of religion in France is beyond the scope of our prerogative in writing brief explanatory notes. Ed.

20. A student and follower of Lévy-Bruhl, Bayet attempted to enunciate and popularize through several works the science of morals and customs. For a comprehensive bibliography of his works see Nandan, *The Durkheimian School*, 1977, op. cit., pp. 341–42. Ed.

21. French sociologists and philosophers are unique in fighting battles over the question of morals—what should be its form and how it should be cultivated—from two distinctly different points of view. Durkheim's views on the subject are posited in his *Sociology and Philosophy*, op. cit. In addition to the works by Belot, Landry, and Fouillée, Deploige's work (see pp. 137–49; 159–61) is perhaps the

most critical by a Catholic savant and moralist of Durkheim's conception of morals. Other contemporary work which may be cited is that by F. Rauh, *L'Expérience morale,* Paris: Alcan, 1903. Recently E. Wallwork in his *Durkheim: Morality and Milieu,* op. cit., has supposedly attempted to bring to light Durkheim's sociological conception of morals. The work, however, is poorly accomplished as far as Durkheim's theory of morals is concerned. Ed.

22. In spite of these reservations Durkheim devotes fifteen long pages of the *Année* to reviewing these works, obviously of philosophical interest. He could not have ignored these Parisian scholars, nor could he have disposed of them in curt summaries, for they characterized a direct attack on both Lévy-Bruhl and Durkheim for their promulgation of the new science of morals. Ed.

23. I would like to correct Durkheim in this regard on his statement that Landry was a philosopher. On the contrary, Landry was an economist, his early education and his *agrégation* in philosophy notwithstanding. But then so was Simiand, Durkheim's lieutenant and a prominent member of the Durkheimian school. Fouillée was a sociologist in his own right, even though his entire work points up his philosophical orientation. Ed.

24. Since he himself was a *normalien* and a philosopher, since he and his followers moved freely in the circle of Parisian philosophers, and since, above all, he was imbued with a zest to bring reform to a society experiencing a situation of "anomie," it can be easily construed that Durkheim was a moralist. There is no denying that his contemporaries clearly saw Durkheim as a man imbued with moral ideas. See especially Bourgin, *De Jean Jaurès à Léon Blum,* op. cit., p. 218. Ed.

25. See E. Durkheim, "Détermination du fait moral," *BSFP,* 11 Feb. 1906, pp. 113–68. Discussants: Durkheim, Halévy, Lalande, Lévy-Bruhl, Parodi, and Simiand. Ed.

26. Lévy-Bruhl's work was published in 1903; subsequently Durkheim presented his thoughts on the subject and elaborated on the topical issue in two consecutive meetings of the French Philosophical Society, the complete proceedings of which have been edited and published in Durkheim's *Sociology and Philosophy,* op. cit. Ed.

27. It is interesting to note that three similar works by Westermarck, Hobhouse, and Sumner on the subject of ethics and morality appeared in the same year, 1906. Ed.

28. It is unfair of Durkheim to say that Deploige's work is a pamphlet, even though it is full of polemical remarks and perhaps lampoons on the propounders of the new science of morals. Perhaps it is Durkheim's way of disparaging a revealing work of Deploige. Perhaps Durkheim meant a propaganda pamphlet or a polemical work, which, obviously, it is. Ed.

29. In Durkheim's thought, of course. Ed.

30. Translated and reproduced in *Sociology and Philosophy,* op. cit., pp. 1–34. Ed.

31. See note 10. Ed.

32. The transfer of ownership of things through solemn rituals in which they are handed over to the transferee by the owner. See *Encyclopedic Dictionary,* s.v. *traditio.* Ed.

33. "The solemn introduction of the bride into the husband's house, accompanied by religious ceremonies. It was considered the beginning of the marriage." See Ibid., s.v. *deductio in domum.* Ed.

34. In the presence of the people. Ed.

35. "The next relatives of a person; persons living in the same household under the one head of the family." *Encyclopedic Dictionary,* p. 723. Ed.

36. To each one separately. Ed.

37. The explanation seems spurious since the class of *patricii* treated the plebeians and the slaves like "untouchables," both socially and politically. Even the marriage between the two classes was forbidden until the plebians had won in the struggle of more than two centuries against the patricians. Only with the legislation of *Lex Canulei* (445 B.C.), intermarriage between the two social classes was permitted. For more detailed discussion, see *Encyclopedic Dictionary,* s.v. *patricii;* J.A.C. Thomas, *Textbook of Roman Law* (Amsterdam: North-Holland, 1976, p. 422); R. Sohm, *The Institutes: A Textbook of the History and System of Roman Private Law* (tr. by J.C. Ledlie, Oxford University Press, 1901, pp. 40–42).

38. Durkheim meant by Germania the area inhabited by the Germanic tribes at the time of Caeser.

39. *Fas* is opposed to *jus. Fas* is "the moral law of divine origin, whereas *jus* is law created by men. The two terms appear together in the phrase *jus fasque. Fas* is what gods permit, *nefas* what they forbid. In its widest sense *fas* is what is permitted by law or custom." See *Encyclopedic Dictionary,* s.v. *fas.* Ed.

40. Also *inòkostan,* it essentially corresponds to the nuclear family type in the Western countries—however, without urban structure or industrial organization. Under the pressure of economic forces, a peasant leaves his *zadruga,* family and moves elsewhere, either alone or along with his wife and children, to settle and make a living, thus forming an *inòkosna*-type family. See *Rječnik Hrvatskoga Ili Srpskoga Jezika,* s.v. *inòkostan.* Ed.

41. See E. M. Carr, *The Australian Race: Its Origin, Languages, Customs, Places of Landing in Australia and the Routes by Which It Spread Itself over That Continent.* Melbourne: Ferres, 1886–1887. Ed.

42. The part of the name which indicated the *gens* to which a person in Roman society belonged. This common name pointed out the *gentiles* belonging to the same social unit. See *Encyclopedic Dictionary,* s.v. *gens.* Ed.

43. To maintain the integrity of the two distinct volumes, we have thought it justifiable to include the other part of the review in a forthcoming volume reserved for Durkheim's contributions to anthropology. Ed.

44. Durkheim refers to his comprehensive review of Kohler's *Zur urgeschichte der Ehe,* which will be included in the forthcoming volume indicated above. Ed.

45. On checking the *Catalog* it seems that the dissertation was never published as Durkheim had presumed. Ed.

46. "*Akila,* one of the most significant institutions of Muslim penal law as regards both the origins and the sociological evolution of that law. The term *akila* denotes, as its etymology would suggest, the group of persons upon whom devolves, as the result of natural joint responsibility with the person who has committed homicide

or inflicted bodily harm, the payment of compensation in cash or kind." See *The Encyclopaedia of Islam* (new edition), 1960, pp. 337–38. The word *asibs* should read *asaba.* "In the period before the rise of Islam, in keeping with the patriarchal system prevailing among the Arabs, the estate of a deceased tribesman went, if he died intestate, to the nearest male relative(s); the order of succession in which these relatives,—the so-called *asaba* (corresponding to *agnati*),—were called upon to inherit survives systematized in its order in the Muslim law of inheritance." *The Encyclopaedia of Islam,* 1936, s.v. *Mirath.*

47. Testamentary adoption. Ed.

48. Condition of bearing one's name. Ed.

49. "The earliest legislative assembly based upon the division of the people into *Curiae.* At the beginning of the Republic they were deprived of their legislative functions and their competence was limited to voting *lex curiata de imperio,* by which the magistrates were invested with *imperium,* and approving certain legal acts connected with the family system, as *adrogatio* and testament." *Encyclopedic Dictionary,* p. 398, s.v. *comitia curiata.* Ed.

50. Refers to the adoption of a person who himself is the head of the family, thus allowing the social and juridic fusion of two distinct families since the adopted person enters another family along with other persons subject to his authority. See Ibid., s.v. *adoptio.* Ed.

51. "Through *adoptio* a person who is under the paternal power of the head of his family comes under the *patria potestas* of another. The change of family is the characteristic feature of *adoptio.*" Ibid., p. 350. Ed.

52. Beyond the Tiber River (Latin *Tiberis*) in Italy flowing through Rome—that is to say, beyond the boundaries of the city of Rome. Ed.

53. "A family council composed of older members. Sometimes friends participated therein. According to an ancient custom the head of a family used to consult this Council before punishing a member of the family for criminal offenses, for instance his wife or daughter for adultery. But he was not bound by the opinion of the Council, which was only an advisory board to assist the head of the family in internal family matters, and had no judicial competence." *Encyclopedic Dictionary,* p. 408. Ed.

54. "To lift a child. According to an ancient custom, when a married woman bore a son, the father lifted him up from the earth, thus denoting symbolically that he was accepting him in the family as his son. The act had no legal significance." Ibid., p. 738. Ed.

55. "A community for the whole life. It is a basic element of the Roman marriage, mentioned in the definition of marriage by Modestinus. It is not affected by the possibility of divorce." Ibid., p. 409. Ed.

56. "A person who died without leaving a valid testament or whose testament, originally valid, became ineffective because the appointed heirs refused to accept the inheritance or by other reasons." Ibid., p. 515. Ed.

57. See pp. 183–84. Ed.

58. By man. Ed.

59. The Malagasy Republic, in the Indian Ocean, is a former French colony, separated

from East Africa by the Mozambique Channel. The Republic is made up of Madagascar and several small islands, with its capital in Tananarive. Ed.

60. The power of the man over the woman through legally consummated marriage, hence *patria potestas*, which also included the husband's authority over the children.

61. *Leges* mean statutes or laws passed by the competent legislative assembly. For a comprehensive definition of the term see *lex* in *Encyclopedic Dictionary*, p. 544. Ed.

62. Adopted in order to institute someone as an heir. Ed.

63. From the French *entre-vifs*. Ed.

64. "Witnesses in a criminal trial who testified about the blameless life of the accused." *Encyclopedic Dictionary*, p. 538. Ed.

65. "As he bequeathed . . . so let it be legal." Tr.

66. See note 38. Ed.

67. "The power of life and death. Since the earliest times the head of the family had this right over persons under his paternal power (children and wife) and over his slaves. His right to punish them comprised also the death penalty." *Encyclopedic Dictionary*, p. 534. Ed.

68. Essentially the German usage of *mundium* is analogous to the Roman legal concept of *manus*, both of which designate the power the husband and father has over his wife and children, the former in subjection all her life. Ed.

69. "Originally the term indicated the power of the head of the family over all its members and the slaves. Later *manus* was only the husband's power over his wife, and that over his children was the *patria potestas*. The husband acquired *manus* through a special agreement, which accompanied the conclusion of a marriage. The wife under the power of the husband had the legal position of a daughter." *Encyclopedic Dictionary*, p. 577. Ed.

70. See pp. 254–57. Ed.

71. Durkheim is alluding to Lefebvre. Ed.

72. A child born out of wedlock, neither through a legitimate marriage nor through concubinage, i.e., the offspring of a promiscuous intercourse. Without a father, the child was raised by the mother and acknowledged to belong to her but did not have the right of testamentary inheritance. Ed.

73. By "instituted heir" Durkheim is presumably referring to the Roman law, where the "institution (i.e. naming) of the heir" played an important part in the drawing up of a testament. Such an heir inherited all the rights and obligations of the deceased. Tr.

74. "Right over a foreign thing." Tr.

75. "For a time." Tr.

76. "Total or partial loss of civil rights." Ed.

77. See pp. 124–27. Ed.

78. Confession on the deathbed. Ed.

79. The reference is to "Comment les mots changent de sens," *AS*, 9, 1906, pp. 1–38. Ed.

80. Henry Sumner Maine uses the terms "fine" and "family" interchangeably with respect to the social and political organization of Irish society. He writes that fine "is used for the Tribe in its largest extension as pretending to some degree of political independence, and for all intermediate bodies down to the Family as we understand it, even for the portion of the Family." *Lectures on the Early History of Institutions,* London: Murray, 1875, p. 90. Ed.

81. See pp. 254–57. The correct title is: *Leçons d'instruction générale à l'histoire du droit matrimonial français.* Ed.

82. See note 68. Ed.

83. See Genesis 2:24. Two in one flesh. Ed.

84. 1 Corinthians 11:3. The context refers to "Christ is the head of everyone and the man is the head of the woman. But the head of Christ is God." Ed.

85. See note 55. Ed.

86. Custom of living together inseparably. Ed.

87. The *communauté taisible* (tacit community) constituted a type of marriage contracted tacitly by the parties concerned. See Emile Littré's *Dictionniare de la langue française,* s.v. *taisible.* According to Denis Lebrun (see his *Traité de la communauté entre marié et femme, divisé en trois livres; le premier, comment la communauté se forme; le second, comment elle se régit; le troisième, comment elle finit,* Paris: Guignard, 1709) the ancient French law defined the tacit community as "the society which was formed other than by marriage and without any written contract among certain individuals. Through cohabitation and common life for a period of *a year and a day* with the exchange of profits and gains and with a specific intention to live in community." Quoted by A. Girard in *"Communauté Taisible," GE,* vol. 12, p. 104. Ed.

88. Of that individual. Ed.

89. In J. W. Thompson's *The Middle Ages* (London: Kegan Paul, Trench, Trubner and Co., 1931) the author remarks: "Mortmain was derived directly from the originally precarious nature of the peasant's tenure. In the beginning—in late Roman times—the lord could eject the *colonus* at will. But gradually by fatal evolution the tenure became one for life and then hereditary. But the serf did not own the property; he was a permanent lessee; he could not alienate it nor sell it nor devise it to his heirs. For the title was vested in the lord. Hence the lord exacted Mortmain in virtue of a customary law of servile succession. The tax exacted under right of Mortmain was called a *heriot,* and was very heavy and very abusive. Frequently, the lord stripped the peasant's cottage of all his gear and was certain to take the best ox as his due" (vol. 2, p. 731). Tr.

90. See pp. 78–84. Ed.

91. Durkheim uses the word *opuscule.* But we think simply the number of pages is not sufficient to distinguish an opus from an opuscule. If that were the case, Durkheim's *Les Règles* would also pass as a "minor work." Ed.

92. "The solemn performance before the popular assembly was a kind of adoption to have an heir in the event of the testator's death; its primary purpose was to secure his own and his ancestors' worship." *Encyclopedic Dictionary,* p. 733. Ed.

93. "Adoption that makes one heir." Ed.

94. See note 65. Ed.

95. "House and family." Ed.

96. "A solemn act by which a testator instituted one or more heirs to his property after his death. The appointment of an heir was the fundamental element of a testament; a last will in which an heir was not appointed was not valid. A testament could confirm many other dispositions. For the testament to be legally valid, some legal acts of early origin were performed with the use of copper and scales and the pronunciation of prescribed solemn formulae. The acts thus performed required the presence of five Roman citizens as witnesses and of a man who held the scales. These acts went out of use in the later law." *Encyclopedic Dictionary*, s.v. *testamentum* and *per des et libram*. Ed.

97. See note 35. Ed.

98. See pp. 163–68. Ed.

99. "Legitimate marriage." Ed.

100. For its definition see note 32. Apparently, the father had the legal right of possession over the daughter and the right had to be transferred to the husband at the time of the wedding. Ed.

101. See note 33.

102. "Marriage is not by sexual intercourse but by mutual consent." Ed.

103. Opposed to the *patria potestas*. An individual who is legally independent and is not under the paternal power of another. Ed.

104. Near relatives or the neighbors.

105. The word has several different meanings: (1) tent companion, a dwelling together in a tent; (2) the sexual intercourse of a young man and the general he accompanies and serves during war, and in attendance; (3) the marriage of slaves; and (4) a dwelling together of animals. Here the third meaning applies. Ed.

106. "A sum of money, a commercial or industrial business, or a small separate property granted by a father to his son or by a master to his slave, for the son's (or slave's) use, free disposal, and fructification through commercial or other transactions." *Encyclopedic Dictionary*, p. 624. Obviously, here it means husband's private property. Ed.

107. "Donation before the marriage." Ed.

108. See note 75. Ed.

109. Codes of law. Ed.

110. Literal translation from the French. In fact this refers to the Araucanian Indians, who come from South America and occupy most of south-central Chile. Ed.

111. "In the presence of the Church." Ed.

112. The Circassians, whose Russian name is Cherkess and whose indigenous name is Adyge, are Muslims. With the new political organization of the USSR, they are now officially classified as three peoples: the Kabardins, in the Kabardino-Balkar Autonomous Soviet Socialist Republic; the Circassians, or Cherkess, of the Karachay-Cherkess Autonomous Oblast; and the Adyge, in the Adyge Autonomous Oblast. Ed.

113. Needless to say, the exchange rate is very old. Ed.

114. "Marriage banns." Ed.

115. "In the presence of the church." This could mean that public celebrations were recognized as legal only when observed either in front of the church or in a church building or both. Ed.

116. The witness of a person with an honorific title of a higher official in the later Empire was binding and valid for the marriage contract. Ed.

117. See pp. 234–37. Ed.

118. Tacitus' most famous work is *De origine et situ Germanorum* (Concerning the Origin and Location of the Germans), popularly called *Germania* (Germany). The work throws light on the Germanic tribes and gives an early description of Julius Caesar. Ed.

119. See note 69. Ed.

120. Also known as Livland and named after the Livs, a Finnish tribe, it was a former Russian province, comprising present-day Estonia and parts of Latvia. In 1918 it was divided between Estonia and Latvia, which have been constituent republics of the USSR since 1940. Ed.

121. Constituting the oldest comprehensive book of German law, completed about 1220 by Eike von Repgow, it came to be regarded as normative in all north Germany and as far east as Russia. It provided for the basis of the Magdeburg Law. *Sachsenspiegel* was the most widely used German municipal law of the Middle Ages. It was used not only in Germany but also in the cities of the Slavic areas to the east. Ed.

122. See note 89. Ed.

123. "Dowry." Ed.

124. In Biblical times the *mohar*, whereby the groom bought his wife from her father (Gen. 24:53; Ex. 22:15–16; Hos. 3:2), was an accepted practice. Ed.

125. Marriage ceremony. Ed.

126. Used in the Roman sense, referring to the "strangers who immigrated to Rome, where they submitted themselves to patrician families in order to obtain their protection. Men from vanquished countries also looked for a similar relation." *Encyclopedic Dictionary*, p. 391. Ed.

127. "All the *comites* forming the retinue of the emperor. In the later Empire, *comes* was the title of high military and civil officials." Ibid., p. 397. Ed.

128. Whereby the husband through a fictitious sale acquired *manus* over the wife. Consequently, the power was transferred to him by virtue of the fictitious sale by her father. Ed.

129. Marriage whereby the husband acquires power over the wife and the children and, in the second sense, without the acquisition of that power. Ed.

130. The wife under the power of her husband had the legal position of a daughter. See also note 69. Ed.

131. "A respectful behavior of a freed man toward his patron. A transgression of this duty (use of violence) exposed the freed man to the charge of ingratitude." *Reverentia* was "considered violated if the freed man sued the patron in court without permission of the competent magistrate." *Encyclopedic Dictionary*, p. 605. Ed.

132. That is, they were obliged to feed and shelter their father if he was needy. Cf. p. 847. Tr.

133. The Cynosarges was a gymnasium at Athens destined for bastards. Tr.

134. Sic. Durkheim has confused the years B.C. with the years A.D. Tr.

135. See C. Lefebvre's *Leçon d'introduction générale à l'histoire du droit matrimonial français.* Paris: Larose, 1900. Ed.

136. The allusion is to Durkheim's review of Lefebvre. See pp. 254–57. Ed.

137. The translation, "intensity," is literal, but we think Durkheim means "satisfaction." Ed.

138. "Donation before the marriage." Ed.

139. See Durkheim's review of Tsugaru's *Die Lehre von der Japanischen Adoption*, pp. 210–13. Ed.

140. Law codes of early Germanic tribes.

141. *Communauté* in French has been translated as "community," by which Durkheim does not mean community as opposed to society; instead, it signifies the common character of property. See the article "Communauté" in the *GE*. Ed.

142. See p. 390. Ed.

143. See pp. 254–57. Ed.

144. "Let all the money be considered jointly." Ed.

145. See note 87. Ed.

146. Once again, the idea generally restricts itself to the common property of husband and wife. See note 122. Ed.

147. See pp. 254–57. Ed.

148. Durkheim is alluding to a lengthy discussion of Howitt's *The Native Tribes of South-East Australia (AS,* 9, 1906, pp. 355–68), which has been included in a forthcoming volume. See note 43. Ed.

149. This piece by Durkheim will also be included in a forthcoming volume. Ed.

150. The reader may note the polemical tone Durkheim adopted throughout the review. Ed.

151. See note 121. Ed.

152. Durkheim has mentioned a woman's rights after her husband's death over two types of properties, namely the *Morgengabe* and *Mussteil,* but has left out the third type, *Witwenrade.* See page 111 of Behre's work. *Mussteil* (also *Musteil*), which is derived from *Sachsenspiegel,* constitutes basic necessities for life, such as food. Ed.

153. He wrote the preface to the book by Rol under discussion here. Ed.

154. See pp. 254–57; 218–21. Ed.

155. Berry was a former province in central France. Ed.

156. That is to say, Lefebvre. Ed.

157. See note 87. Ed.

158. In the light of Marianne Weber's illuminating works on women's status in society and her pioneer attempts in furthering the feminist movement, it behooves us to recognize her as a sociologist in her own right rather than placing her in the foot-

notes as a devoted wife and a meticulous biographer of the illustrious Max Weber. Ed.

159. See pp. 285–89. Ed.

160. "Joining of the right hands." Ed.

161. See note 68. Ed.

162. "Customs of marriage." Ed.

163. See note 128. Ed.

164. The earliest form of marriage among the Roman patricians, through the agreement of which the wife entered into the husband's family and acquired the legal position of a daughter. See *Encyclopedic Dictionary*, s.v. *confarreato*.

165. Through the legal contract of marriage whereby the husband and father as *patria potestas* acquired power over the wife and the children. Ed.

166. Five centimes. Still used in popular language, it is not officially recognized anymore as a term for money.

167. See note 87. Ed.

168. *Mainbournie,* principally in the north and east of France and in Belgium, signified "guardian," a French adaptation of the Germanic concept *mundium.* The power the guardian had over those under him (wife, children, adopted children, etc.) was known as *mainbournie.* See note 68 on *mundium.* Ed.

169. The translation is literal and the English usage is ours. The reader can well understand what Editor Durkheim mèans by the expression *cadette.* Ed.

170. See note 128. Ed.

171. See note 69. Ed.

172. See pp. 218–21. Ed.

173. "Minor clans." Ed.

174. "The status of private affairs before the time of Solon in Attica." Ed.

175. The compounding of these words is Durkheim's own. They mean "consisting of five" and "consisting of ten." Ed.

176. The nineteenth century. Tr.

177. The reference is to Wittich's *Die Grundherrschaft in Nordwestdeutschland* (Leipzig: Duncker und Humblot, 1896).

178. "The lands are occupied by everyone in turn according to the number of cultivators, who then divide them among themselves on the basis of rank." Ed.

179. According to Olympiodorus, "the term *bucellarius* was in the days of Honorius applied not only to Roman soldiers but to some *Goths* too, and similarly the term federates was applied to a mixed and various horde. This may mean that the word federate was used not only for tribal contingents serving under a treaty, but for mixed bands of barbarians who collected around a notable warrior like *Sarus,* and were by him put at the disposal of the government. It also seems to be implied that such bands were also called *bucellarii.*" Cited by A. H. M. Jones, *The Later Roman Empire 284-602: A Social, Economic, and Administrative Survey,* vol. 1, Oxford: Blackwell, 1973, p. 665.

180. "In the later Roman Empire, from the fourth century on, the term *scholae* is applied to larger groups of persons in military service or officials organized in military

fashion under the command of a *tribunus*. In particular, officials of the imperial palace or attached to the person of the emperor as the bodyguards and the *agentes* were united in *scholae*." *Encyclopedic Dictionary*, p. 691. Ed.

181. "Boys" and "vassals." Ed.

182. Voluntary followers of the old Frankish princes in the period of the national migrations. Ed.

183. See note 127. Ed.

184. *Bellator* signifies a warrior, a soldier capable of fighting, while *miles* signifies a soldier by profession. Ed.

185. Soldiers by profession. Ed.

186. Peasant or villain. Ed.

187. Dubbing someone a knight. Ed.

188. "Association of the inhabitants of a town." Ed.

189. "Faith, assistance, and counsel." Ed.

190. "Peace"; "the institution of peace." Ed.

191. "Charter of peace." Ed.

192. See note 36. Ed.

193. See note 126.

194. See note 213. Ed.

195. Berger, in his *Encyclopedic Dictionary*, gives a slightly different meaning. According to him, *pagus* was in the most ancient times "an ethnic or tribal group comprising several settlements, an arrangement found in the primitive organization of peoples in Italy" (p. 616). Obviously the fundamental character of the *pagus* is not providing military aid but functioning as an administrative unit, according to Berger's definition. Ed.

196. Family members, near relatives, and neighbors. Ed.

197. See note 126. Ed.

198. From medieval Latin; the word literally means "courtyard" and "hamlet." But in our context, it may be defined as a collection of the inhabitants of a hamlet or town. Ed.

199. Both islands are in the Pacific. Ed.

200. The book has two parts. The first part, which is called *Les Comtes de Bourgogne et leur villes domaniales*, has 102 pages; and the second part, containing 219 pages, deals with the charter of the city of Arbois, and is entitled *Cartulaire de la ville d'Arbois*. Hence two different paginations, though wrongly cited by Durkheim.

201. Sic. The paginations cited by Durkheim are in error. He means p. 101 from *Les Comtes de Bourgogne*, or the first part.

202. B. Vladimirtsov defines *Ulus* as a Mongolian tribe consisting of "many blood-related clans who together formed a tribe, a *Ulus*." *Gengis-Khan*, Paris, 1948, p. 7. Ed.

203. See Durkheim's review of Gorst, pp. 341–43. Ed.

204. πόλεις (poleis) is the plural of the Greek word πόλις (polis), which in English is usually translated as "city-state." Tr.

205. "Sympolitic" and "perioecisme" are not French words, but are neologisms from the Greek, apparently coined by Francotte, which I have simply Anglicized. Their meanings will become apparent in what follows. Tr.

206. A member of the Russian artistocratic order holding land. Ed.

207. See note 127. Ed.

208. See note 69. Ed.

209. "Regarded as a statutory law." Ed.

210. "It is statuted." Ed.

211. What Durkheim seems to be saying is that he will explain the concept later, which he does not. Ed.

212. The original meaning of *vicini* was "neighbor"; here it refers to the complex of ties which bound together the *vicini*. However, as Durkheim goes on to say, the word has taken on a different meaning in Cannobio. See p. 154 of the original work by Lattes. Ed.

213. *Commarcani* were the members of a village association, *marea* (originally a German term). Cf. G. Savioli, *Manuale di storia del diritto italiano,* Turin, 1892, pp. 383–386; Hermann Conrad, *Deutsche Rechtsgeschichte,* vol. 1, Karlsruhe, 1954, pp. 118–19. Ed.

214. "Without the knowledge of relatives." Ed.

215. "Confederation of friendly states." Ed.

216. Before the introduction of consulship, a *praetor* was the highest public official. The *praetor peregrinus* was vested with the jurisdictional power to settle disputes and clarify civil matters between foreigners and Romans. Ed.

217. In general the *Année* collaborators reviewed books which appeared during the year starting July 1 and ending June 30. The year 1896–1897 alludes to these dates when the books actually appeared during the interval, and 1898 refers to the year of publication. Since Gunther's book dates back to 1895, Durkheim seems to be apologetic for including a book published in the preceding years. Whether Gunther published the volumes in sequence or not, there is no followup in the *Année* anyway. Ed.

218. I think Durkheim is stretching the argument too far by exaggerating the repressive measures society takes in such cases. Ed.

219. Steinmetz's *Ethonologische Studien zur ersten Entwicklung der strafe* has not been reviewed. However, Durkheim reviewed Mauss's article "La Religion et les origines du droit pénal," which is essentially based on Steinmetz's illuminating work on the subject.

220. Perhaps Durkheim means "consolidation." Ed.

221. "Infantryman" or "cavalryman." Ed.

222. Common man. Ed.

223. See pp. 364–67. Ed.

224. The entire work contains six parts. Ed.

225. The word *devotio* is compounded from the word *vovere:* "to make a solemn promise, to vow." *Devotio* could be used in the sense of "a curse." Tr.

226. A "leonine" agreement is one in which one of the parties receives all the benefits.

Cf. the expression "the lion's share" and the *Oxford English Dictionary*, s.v. *leonine*. Tr.

227. Upon the application of strict law, a person's legal rights are impaired, resulting in the loss of his freedom, citizenship, or family membership. Ed.

228. Glotz's work has been reviewed by Durkheim and frequently referred to in *L'Année*. For review see pp. 369–79. Ed.

229. The loss of *caput*, or civil status, in Roman society and according to Roman law. An individual is deprived of civil status because of the loss either of freedom or of Roman citizenship, or of membership in a Roman family. This loss impairs an individual's ability to enter into legal transactions and claim the rights recognized by the law. See *Encyclopedic Dictionary*, s.v. *capitis deminutio*. Ed.

230. Compounded probably by the author himself and then adopted by Durkheim in French, the word is of Greek origin, from *epikleros*, and has a certain juridical meaning. It indicates that in ancient Greece when an individual died without leaving any other children except a daughter, the latter inherited the property. See *GE*, s.v. *épiclère*. Ed.

231. The reference is to Samuel Pufendorf's *Elementorum jurisprudentiae universalis*, libri duo. The Hague: Adrian Vlacq, 1660. Since then the original version of the book in Latin has appeared in many countries, including an edition in the United States. Ed.

232. On checking the *Catalog*, it seems that the further volumes of the work referred to here were never published. Ed.

233. From the French *insuffisamment incompétent* (insufficiently incompetent), which makes little sense and remains out of context. By rendering it as "insufficiently competent," we think we have corrected Durkheim. Ed.

234. "Civilians." Ed.

235. See note 185. Ed.

236. Here the term means "explorers" or "early settlers." Ed.

237. Owned as an alodium. Ed.

238. "Law of inheritance." Ed.

239. The author means the medieval codifications of German laws. Tr.

240. See note 87. Ed.

241. In contemporary popular language it means "picket." Ed.

Section Four: Criminal Sociology and Statistics on Morals

1. See *AS*, 1, 1898, pp. 397–406. Ed.

2. See *AS*, 1, 1898, pp. 392–94; 2, 1899, pp. 402–403. Ed.

3. See *AS*, 1, 1898, p. 392. Ed.

4. From this introduction in volume four, 1901, Durkheim's domination of the section is quite visible.

5. Several years before this introduction, Durkheim had already cautioned Bouglé not to be impatient and not to be hasty in adopting a final scheme of classification for the *Année*. He wrote: "In what concerns the special branches of sociology, we would not be complete; it is not even possible for us to accomplish too much too soon. Some margin for improvement in the future must be left." *Textes*, vol. 2, p. 397. Ed.

6. Cf. Mauss, "Divisions et proportions des divisions de la sociologie," *AS* (new series), 2, 1927, pp. 98–176 (reproduced in *Oeuvres*, vol. 3, pp. 178–245): Mauss was faced with the same problem of classification, which, he felt, was beyond his theorizing ability; it was beyond his courage to initiate and institute innovations for which he was not fully prepared.

7. However, it must be admitted that Durkheim invented almost stable divisions of sociology for the *Année,* those which were adopted throughout from the beginning to the end, in the original series of the periodical. However, the section on social morphology was improvised and included in the second volume, from then on with its permanent form.

8. After a few years, the title was changed to "Sociologie juridique et morale." Ed.

9. Durkheim means each subsection or rubric of the section on juridic and moral sociology. Ed.

10. One can see how unsuccessful Durkheim was in formulating rubrics for criminal sociology as a counterpart to juridic sociology. Or else, it was a false claim by Durkheim.

11. Which it never did in the original series, and the new series; the successor to the *Année,* the *Annales sociologiques* and the *Année* (third series) completely abolished this section, and the discussion on criminology was relegated to the section on juridic and moral sociology. Ed.

12. This review by Durkheim appeared in the miscellaneous section of the *Année.* We have transferred it to the section on criminal sociology.

13. A good part of Durkheim's entire work is dedicated to this concern for repairing the moral fabric of society.

14. In French educational terminology, even the secondary school teachers have the honor to be known and addressed as *professeurs* and *maîtres.* Ed.

15. The book is reviewed by Paul Fauconnet.

16. Such as embezzlement, fraud, breach of trust, and trickery. Ed.

17. This is the fourth article in the series. Ed.

18. These conclusions conform with Durkheim's own interpretation of suicide. See his *Suicide,* pp. 259–76. Ed.

19. The translation is literal, but Durkheim obviously is referring to families without children.

20. See pp. 197–99. Ed.

21. Cisleithania was a part of Austro-Hungarian monarchy (Hapsburg Empire) which was formed in 1867 and collapsed after World War I, in 1918. The Hapsburg Empire was divided into two states: Cisleithania and Transleithania. Cisleithania, which in Latin means "the land on this side of the Leitha River," comprised

Austria proper, Bohemia, Moravia, Austrian Silesia, Slovenia, and Austrian Poland. Ed.

22. See pp. 414–16. Ed.

23. The work by Griveau was honored with a reward in the competition of 1901, whereas that by Depinay was honored with a mention only, without any monetary reward. Ed.

24. A department in Normandy. Ed.

25. Formerly what was the department Basses-Alpes is now Alpes-de-Hautes-Provence. Ed.

26. Legal owner of the dowry. Dominus is opposed to the possessor and usufruct, who have no ownership but hold a thing. See under *dominus* and *dos* in the *Encyclopedic Dictionary*. Ed.

27. Even though the translation of the French phrase *moins de frais* is literal, we believe that it does not quite fit the context. To be consistent with what follows, it should read: "one is not content at less cost." Ed.

28. The French reads *matière sociale,* and, I hope, I come close to Durkheim's meaning of the expression. Ed.

29. Durkheim's expression *suicidogène,* an element of his overall theory of suicide, is untranslatable into English. Some translators have neologized "suicidogenic" for the French neologism *suicidogène.* Ed.

30. The reference is to Krose's *Die Ursachen der Selbstmordhäufigkeit* (Freiburg: Herder, 1906)—published, however, the same year as *Der Selbstmord.*

31. See pp. 391–92. Ed.

32. This translation is from French. But the German title would be "Suicide for Erotic Motives Among the Primitives." In *L'Année* the Durkheimians often gave inadequate renditions of titles from English and German into French. For a detailed discussion on this aspect of the *Année* see *L'École durkheimienne et son opus,* pp. 166–173. Ed.

Section Five: Economic Sociology

1. See G. Aimard, *Durkheim et la science économique: l'apport de sa sociologie à la théorie économique moderne.* Paris: PUF, 1962. Ed.

Section Seven: Miscellaneous

1. Durkheim in 1897—during the preparation of the publication of the first volume of the *Année*—wrote to Bouglé about the inadequacy of some of the areas in sociology. He stated: "We do not have a special arrangement for aesthetic sociology. Open anything relevant to aesthetics and it turns out to be a novel. When something of this type comes along, we will review it; and all those works in

a rubric which by reason of their small number need not be arranged in a separate section will be deposited in the miscellaneous section." *Textes,* vol. 2, pp. 401–402. Ed.

2. The book was reviewed at length by Bouglé in *L'Année,* 1, 1898, pp. 116–27; and Durkheim's conception of the division of labor was placed in the right perspective, refuting Barth's criticism of Durkheim. Ed.

List of Durkheim's Contributions Included

Here we are including only those references to works that Durkheim actually reviewed, or to works about which he made brief critical remarks designated as "notes" or "notices." In other words, we have not given the bibliographic references that Durkheim added to subsections and rubrics.

The first vertical column shows the type of reference. The R's are reviews, having consumed twenty-five printed lines or more. The N's are notices or notes, the former having used five to twenty-four lines and the latter four or less. The I's refer to introductions or prefaces to sections, subsections, or rubrics. This categorization of the *Analyses* part of *L'Année* corresponds to our utilization of this classification in our first two publications: *L'Ecole durkheimienne et son opus, 1975,* and *The Durkheimian School, 1977.*

The second column offers information on the *Année* volume, the year of publication, and the pagination of the particular citation. The third column refers to the section and the subsection of *L'Année* from which the particular citation has been extracted. Needless to say, the system of classification adopted in *L'Année* characterizes our edition of Durkheim's *Contributions* as well. For information on sections, the reader may consult the Contents. Arabic numerals in this column denote the subsections, which can be easily identified by counting the subsections in the Contents. For instance, third subsection in section three refers to Domestic Organization. In the fourth column we have indicated the reviewed author only, without citing the full reference. The fifth column refers to the pages in the present volume.

Type	V./Yr., pp.	Section & Subsec.	Author Reviewed	Pages
I	1/1898, I–VII	Preface	Preface	47–51
R	1/1898,333–338	three/3	B.W. Leist	163–168
N	1/1898,338	three/3	A. Moret	232
R	1/1898,339	three/3	I. von Ačimovic	168–169
N	1/1898,339–340	three/3	E. Miller	232–233
R	1/1898,340–343	three/3	E. Meynial	234–237
R	1/1898,343–344	three/3	K. Friederichs	237–238
R	1/1898,345	three/3	C.A. Garufi	238
R	1/1898,346–347	three/3	E. Schulenburg	239–240
R	1/1898,347–351	three/4	L. Gunther	362–364
R	1/1898,351–353	three/4	J. Kohler	364–366
I	2/1899,I–VI	Preface	Preface	52–55
N	2/1899,185	one/2	A. Schaeffle	99–100
R	2/1899,306–309	three/4	A. Hagelstange	306–308
N	2/1899,310	three/6	L. Warner	361
R	2/1899,310–313	three/3	W. Rudeck	299–301
N	2/1899,313–314	three/3	K. H. Schaible	303–304
N	2/1899,314	three/3	A. Reibmayr	304
N	2/1899,315	three/3	K. Weinhold	304
N	2/1899,315	three/3	P. von Gizicki	304
N	2/1899,315	three/3	J. Müller	304
R	2/1899,315–318	three/3	H. Cunow	169–171
R	2/1899,318–320	three/3	M. Kovalevski	171–172
R	2/1899,320–321	three/3	J. Smirnov P. Boyer	172–173
R	2/1899,321–323	three/3	S. Ciszewski	173–175
R	2/1899,324–325	three/3	W. Marcais	175–176
R	2/1899,325–327	three/3	A. Lefas	176–177
R	2/1899,327–328	three/3	G. Cornil	177–179
R	2/1899,328–329	three/3	W.I. Thomas	179
R	2/1899,331–334	three/3	H. N. Hutchinson	240–242
R	2/1899,334–336	three/3	D.T. Loebel	242–244
R	2/1899,336–338	three/3	D.W. Amram	244–246
R	2/1899,339–341	three/3	J. Schnitzer	246–248
R	2/1899,341–342	three/3	E. Meynial	248–249
N	2/1899,343	three/3	A. Zocco-Rosa	295
*N	2/1899,349	three/8	F. Oppenhiemer	388
R	2/1899,365–366	three/7	J. Kohler	366–367
R	2/1899,399–400	three/9	S.R. Steinmetz	391–392
R	2/1899,563–564	four/1	L. von Bortkewitsch	406
N	3/1900,160	one/1	S.M. Lindsay	90
*N	3/1900,160–161	one/1	A. Chiappelli	90
N	3/1900,161	one/1	G. Villa	90–91
N	3/1900,163	one/1	V. Pareto	91
R	3/1900,182–183	one/1	F. Giner	64–65
R	3/1900,183–184	one/1	A. Ellwood	65–66
R	3/1900,324–325	three/1	E. Neukamp	119–120
N	3/1900,330	three/1	A. Asturaro	161

* Asterisk indicates an unsigned reference, attributed to Durkheim.

Type	V./Yr., pp.	Section & Subsec.	Author Reviewed	Pages
R	3/1900,352–354	three/4	M. Wilbrandt	308–310
R	3/1900,354–356	three/4	M. Courant	310–311
R	3/1900, 365–370	three/3	C. Starcke	179–183
R	3/1900,380–381	three/3	M. Courant	183–184
N	3/1900,382	three/3	N. Tamassia	233
R	3/1900,386–388	three/3	H. Gürgens	249–251
R	3/1900,388–389	three/3	N. Klugmann	251–252
N	3/1900,389–390	three/3	V. Marx	295–296
N	3/1900,390–391	three/3	A. Lampérière	296
N	3/1900,391	three/3	A. Posada	252–253
R	3/1900,393–395	three/8	G. des Marez	379–381
R	3/1900,396–398	three/8	G. Cohn	381–382
N	3/1900,398	three/8	L. Brentano	388–389
N	3/1900,398–399	three/8	T. Veblen	389
N	3/1900,399	three/8	H. Sée	389
N	3/1900,403–404	three/9	D. Castelli	396
N	3/1900,448–449	three/4	A. de Marchi	339
R	3/1900,480–481	four/5	R. Lasch	443–444
N	3/1900,481	four/5	R. Lasch	441–442
N	4/1901,136	one/3	G. Tarde	105
N	4/1901,137	one/3	G. Palante	105–106
R	4/1901,308–309	three/1	E. Ross	120–121
R	4/1900,323–325	three/5	H. E. Gorst	341–343
R	4/1901,327–328	three/5	H. Singer	343
R	4/1901,330–332	three/5	F. de Rocca	343–345
N	4/1901,333	three/5	J. Commons	358
N	4/1901,334	three/5	Schupe	358
R	4/1901,337–338	three/5	W. Liebenam	345–346
R	4/1901,338–339	three/5	L. Stouff	346–347
*R	4/1901,339–340	three/5	C. Bellange	347–348
R	4/1901,340–342	three/3	S.R. Steinmetz	184–185
R	4/1901,342–345	three/3	A. Cahuzac	185–188
R	4/1901,345–347	three/3	A. Escher	188–189
R	4/1901,348–352	three/3	H. Auffroy	189–193
R	4/1901,357–358	three/3	F. Roeder	253–254
R	4/1901,358–362	three/3	C. Lefebvre	254–257
N	4/1901,362–363	three/3	A. Winter	297
N	4/1901,364	three/3	J. Lourbet	304
N	4/1901,365	three/3	L. Fuld	297
R	4/1901,366–367	three/8	H. Schurtz	382–383
R	4/1901,367–369	three/8	E. Dultzug	383–385
N	4/1901,373–374	three/8	K. von Rakowski	389–390
N	4/1901,374	three/9	E. Glasson	390
*R	4/1901,376–377	three/9	A. Chausse	392
R	4/1901,418–419	three/6	A. Lattes	359–360
I	4/1901,433–436	four/1	Introduction	403–406
R	4/1901,436–438	four/2	P. Kollmann	411–413
R	4/1901,438–440	four/2	F. Prinzing	413–414
N	4/1901,440	four/2	E. Fahlbeck	432
N	4/1901,440	four/2	C. Juglar	432

Type	V./Yr., pp.	Section & Subsec.	Author Reviewed	Pages
R	4/1901,441–443	four/2	F. Lindner	414–416
R	4/1901,443–445	four/1	A. Fouillée	406–408
R	4/1901,451–452	four/4	W. Rein	446
N	4/1901,452	four/4	F. Kellor	441
*N	4/1901,452	four/1	R.M. Barrett	410
N	4/1901,452	four/1	A. Marro	410
R	4/1901,460–461	four/6	E. Tarnowski	444–445
R	4/1901,462–463	four/5	R. Lasch	442–443
N	4/1901,463	four/5	R. Lasch	444
N	4/1901,475–476	four/1	G. Duprat	410
N	4/1901,476	four/1	E. F. di Verce	411
R	5/1902, 123–127	one/1	C. Seignobos	66–69
R	5/1902,127–129	one/2	J. Novicow	
			A. Espinas	93–94
R	5/1902,133–134	one/1	A. Small	69–70
N	5/1902,137	one/1	L. Ward	91
R	5/1902,140–145	one/2	G. Simmel	94–98
N	5/1902,155–156	one/2	C. Ellwood	100
N	5/1902,156	one/2	O. Ammon	100
N	5/1902,167	one/3	G. Palante	106
N	5/1902,167	one/3	L. Gumplowicz	106
R	5/1902,320–322	three/1	A. Dumont	121–122
N	5/1902,326–327	three/1	E. Westermarck	161–162
N	5/1902,334–335	three/4	J. Rhys	
			D. Brynmor-Jones	339–340
R	5/1902,336–339	three/4	H. Doniol	311–313
R	5/1902,339–342	three/4	H. Sée	313–316
R	5/1902,342–347	three/4	T. Fukuda	316–319
R	5/1902,358–359	three/5	P. Milioukov	348–349
N	5/1902,362–363	three/5	A.H. el-Maverdi	358
R	5/1902,373–376	three/3	E. Lambert	193–194
R	5/1902,376–379	three/3	J. du Plessis de Grenédan	195–197
R	5/1902,379–381	three/3	F. Dupré la Tour	197–199
R	5/1902,383–387	three/3	O. Müller	257–260
R	5/1902,387–389	three/3	E. Marcou	260–261
N	5/1902,392	three/3	R. de la Grasserie	297
N	5/1902,392	three/3	H. Ellis	305
R	5/1902,393–394	three/8	K. Beyerle	385–386
N	5/1902,395	three/8	L. Beauchet	390
N	5/1902,395–396	three/8	H. F. von Friesen	390
R	5/1902,397–399	three/9	G. des Marez	392–394
N	5/1902,399–400	three/9	W. Hopkins	396
N	5/1902,400	three/9	G. Cornil	397
R	5/1902,435–436	four/2	J. Bertillon	416–417
R	5/1902,436–437	four/2	F. Prinzing	417–418
N	5/1902,438	four/2	A. Dumont	432
N	5/1902,438	four/2	R. Kuczynski	433
N	5/1902,449–450	four/6	M.N. Work	445–446

Type	V./Yr., pp.	Section & Subsec.	Author Reviewed	Pages
N	5/1902,514	five/1	R. Lasch	447–448
N	5/1902,592	seven/1	U. Mazzola	450
N	5/1902,592	seven/1	G. Sorel	450–451
R	6/1903,123–125	one/1	G. Salvemini	
			B. Croce	
			G. Sorel	70–71
R	6/1903,146–147	one/2	S.R. Steinmetz	98
N	6/1903,147	one/2	L. Wallis	100–101
N	6/1903,147	one/2	L. Gumplowicz	101
N	6/1903,147–148	one/2	G. Sergi	101
R	6/1903,151–152	one/3	R.R. de Robertis	
			P. Romano	102–103
R	6/1903,302–303	three/1	L.von Savigny	
			R. Saleilles	122–123
R	6/1903,304–305	three/1	P. Bonfaute	123–124
I	6/1903,316	three/4	Introduction	305–306
R	6/1903,324–327	three/4	E. Szanto	
			L. Holzapfel	319–321
R	6/1903,331–333	three/4	W. Wittich	321–323
R	6/1903,333–337	three/4	P. Guilhiermoz	323–326
R	6/1903,337–341	three/4	P. Viollet	326–329
N	6/1903,341–342	three/4	E. Loncao	340
N	6/1903,342	three/4	E. Jenks	340
R	6/1903,343–345	three/3	S. Rundstein	199–200
N	6/1903,345	three/3	L. Marchand	233
R	6/1903,345–350	three/3	R. Caillemer	200–204
N	6/1903,351	three/3	H.A. Rose	233
N	6/1903,351	three/3	E. Cartier	233–234
R	6/1903,359–361	three/3	A. Esmein	261–263
R	6/1903,365–366	three/3	C. Lefebvre	263
R	6/1903,366–367	three/3	W. Rullkoeter	264
R	6/1903,373–376	three/5	H. Francotte	349–352
R	6/1903,383–385	three/8	M. P. Iovanovic	386–388
R	6/1903,388–390	three/7	P. Huvelin	367–368
R	6/1903,413–414	three/6	E. Loncao	360–361
R	6/1903,414	three/6	G. del Vecchio	361
R	6/1903,415–418	four/2	A. Pouzol	418–420
R	6/1903,418–420	four/2	J. Depinay	
			J. Griveau	420–422
R	6/1903,420–422	four/2	F. Boumberger	422–423
R	6/1903,422–423	four/2	F. Prinzing	423–424
N	6/1903,423	four/2	F. Prinzing	433
N	6/1903,423–424	four/2	R. Böckh	433
N	7/1904,158–159	one/1	E.A. Ross	92
*N	7/1904,185	one/2	A.W. Small	101–102
N	7/1904,185	one/2	A. Allin	102
R	7/1904,374–379	three/1	E. Lambert	124–127
R	7/1904,380–384	three/1	L. Lévy-Bruhl	127–130
R	7/1904,412–413	three/4	G. Oberziner	329–330

Type	V./Yr., pp.	Section & Subsec.	Author Reviewed	Pages
R	7/1904,425–427	three/3	M. Markovic	204–205
R	7/1904,427–428	three/3	H. Stockar	205–206
R	7/1904,428–433	three/3	E. Glasson	207–210
N	7/1904,433	three/3	F. Carli	234
R	7/1904,436–438	three/3	P. A. Pidoux	264–266
R	7/1904,438–440	three/3	M. Bauer	301–302
R	7/1904,440–441	three/3	K. Khamm	302–303
R	7/1904,447–450	three/5	V. Budanov	352–355
R	7/1904,453–454	three/5	H. Pirenne	355
R	7/1904,512–513	three/1	G.L. Duprat	130–131
R	7/1904,520–521	four/2	F. Prinzing	424–425
N	7/1904,521	four/2	C. Juglar	433
R	7/1904,523	four/1	A. Löwenstimm	408–409
R	7/1904,683–686	seven/2	E. Durkheim P. Barth	451–453
*R	8/1905,378–381	three/1	A. Bonucci	131–134
R	8/1905,381–382	three/1	M. Pellisson	134
N	8/1905,382	three/1	M. Mauxion	162
R	8/1905,403–404	three/5	F. Lot	356–357
R	8/1905,409–413	three/3	F. Tsugaru	210–213
R	8/1905,413–414	three/3	J. Englemann	213
N	8/1905,414	three/3	O. Clerici	234
R	8/1905,415–418	three/3	J. Neitzold	266–268
R	8/1905,418–419	three/3	R. de Ruggiero	268–269
R	8/1905,419–421	three/3	M. Mielziner	269–271
R	8/1905,421–425	three/3	S. Sakamoto K. Twasaky	271–274
R	8/1905,425–427	three/3	R. Bartsch	274–275
R	8/1905,427–429	three/3	A. Typaldo-Bassia	275–277
R	8/1905,429–431	three/3	E. Saguez	277–279
N	8/1905,431	three/3	H. d'Alméras	297
N	8/1905,432	three/3	A. Ebeling	297–298
N	8/1905,432	three/3	R. Schmidt	305
*R	8/1905,464	three/7	P. Usteri	368–369
*R	8/1905,465–472	three/7	G. Glotz	369–379
R	8/1905,474–475	three/7	R. Dareste	375–376
*R	8/1905,477–479	three/7	R. Löning	376–378
R	8/1905,487–488	four/2	F. Prinzing	425
R	8/1905,499–500	four/3	I. Stchoukine	434
R	8/1905,502	four/3	H. Rost	434–435
R	9/1906,133–135	one/1	G. Tarde	72–73
R	9/1906,139–140	one/1	A. Xenopol	73–74
*N	9/1906,141–142	one/1	A. Andreotti U. Matteucci	92
R	9/1906,142–143	one/1	G. Toniolo	74–75
R	9/1906,143–144	one/2	P. Carini	99
R	9/1906,156–158	one/3	R. Ribot	103–104
R	9/1906,159–160	one/3	R.R. de Robertis	104–105
R	9/1906,323–324	three/1	H. Höffding	134–135

Type	V./Yr., pp.	Section & Subsec.	Author Reviewed	Pages
R	9/1906,323–326	three/1	A. Bayet	135–137
R	9/1906,340–342	three/3	R. Dareste	162–163
R	9/1906,345–346	three/4	H. Chadwick	330–331
N	9/1906,346	three/4	J. Calmette	340
N	9/1906,348–349	three/4	J. Celakovski	341
R	9/1906,353–355	three/5	J. Hitier	357
N	9/1906,372–373	three/3	L. Lévy	234
R	9/1906,378–380	three/3	J. Kohler	279–280
R	9/1906,380	three/3	E. Westermarck	280–281
R	9/1906,381–383	three/3	E. Hermann	281–282
R	9/1906,383–384	three/3	E. Behre	282–283
N	9/1906,392	three/3	J. Vogt	298
N	9/1906,393	three/3	H. Detmer	298
R	9/1906,418–420	three/9	G. Dereux	394–396
R	9/1906,424–426	three/7	T. Mommsen	378–379
R	9/1906,435–438	four/2	O. Spann	425–427
R	9/1906,438–443	four/2	A. Valensi	427–432
R	9/1906,448–449	four/1	P. Frauenstädt	409
R	10/1907,171–175	one/1	S. Jankelevitch	75–78
R	10/1907,176	one/1	A. Naville	78
R	10/1907,352–369	three/1	A. Fouillée	
			G. Belot	
			A. Landry	137–149
R	10/1907,382–383	three/1	G. Richard	149–150
R	10/1907,383–395	three/1	E. Westermarck	150–159
R	10/1907,424–427	three/3	H. d'Arbois de Jou- bainville	214–216
R	10/1907,427–429	three/3	T. Engert	216–218
R	10/1907,429–433	three/3	C. Lefebvre	218–221
R	10/1907,433–434	three/3	A. de Dainville	221
R	10/1907,435–436	three/3	H. Guigon	222–223
N	10/1907,436–437	three/3	J. Bryce	298
R	10/1907,437–438	three/3	A. Rol	283–284
R	10/1907,438–439	three/3	H. Mallard	284–285
R	10/1907,494–495	four/2	B. Blau	440–441
R	10/1907,499–500	four/3	H.A. Krose	435–436
I	11/1910,I–II	Preface	Preface	55–57
R	11/1910,5–13	one/1	E. Meyer	78–84
*I	11/1910,41–42	one/4	Introduction	106–107
R	11/1910,42–45	one/4	W. Jerusalem	107–110
R	11/1910,343–347	three/3	A. Stanischitsch	223–226
R	11/1910,347–348	three/3	C.W.L. Launspach	226–227
R	11/1910,352–355	three/3	A. Obrist	227–229
R	11/1910,355–357	three/3	R. Roberts	229–230
R	11/1910,363–369	three/3	M. Weber	285–289
R	11/1910,369–371	three/3	G. Richard	289–290
N	11/1910,374	three/3	C. Lefebvre	298
R	11/1910,387–395	three/4	J. Cramer	
			C. von Schwerin	331–338

Type	V./Yr., pp.	Section & Subsec.	Author Reviewed	Pages
R	11/1910,511–515	four/3	H. Krose	436–440
R	12/1913,1–3	one/1	G. Richard	84–86
N	12/1913,14	one/1	R.P.A. Belliot	92–93
*R	12/1913,23–26	one/1	Diverse Authors	86–89
R	12/1913,26–27	one/1	H. Berr	89–90
R	12/1913,326–328	three/1	S. Deploige	159–161
R	12/1913,424–426	three/3	R. Gebhard	230–232
R	12/1913,433	three/3	O. Opet	290–291
R	12/1913,434	three/3	F. Neubecker	291–292
R	12/1913,434–437	three/3	G. Aubéry	292–294
R	12/1913,437–438	three/3	L. Laborde	294–295
N	12/1913,440	three/3	L. Freund	298
R	12/1913,441–443	three/4	G. Bloch	338–339

Appendix A

History of the Durkheimian School as Revealed Through Publications of Periodicals (in Chronological Order)*

1. *L'Année Sociologique*[a]

	Volume			
	I	(1896–1897)[b]	1898[c]
	II	(1897–1898)	1899
	III	(1898–1899)	1900
	IV	(1899–1900)	1901
	V	(1900–1901)	1902
	VI	(1901–1902)	1903
	VII	(1902–1903)	1904
	VIII	(1903–1904)	1905
	IX	(1904–1905)	1906
	X	(1905–1906)	1907
	XI	(1906–1909)	1910
	XII	(1909–1912)	1913

2. *L'Année Sociologique* (new series)[d]

	Volume		
	I	(1923–1924)	1925
	II	(1924–1925)	1927

3. *Bulletin de l'Institut Français de Sociologie*[e]

(1930–1933)
(Published irregularly in small fascicles.)

* Adopted from Nandan, *The Durkheimian School*, 1977.

[a] Conforms to the first period of formation, growth, and consolidation of the Durkheimian school.

[b] From 1 July 1896 to 30 June 1897. Each volume contains books which appeared during the year starting from 1 July and ending 30 June.

[c] Year of publication.

[d] Conforms to the second period of the Durkheimian school.

[e] Conforms to the third period of the Durkheimian school.

4. *Annales Sociologiques*

    A. Series A, four fascicles in all, published from 1934 to 1941.
    B. Series B, four fascicles in all, published from 1939 to 1940.
    C. Series C, three fascicles in all, published from 1935 to 1938.
    D. Series D, four fascicles in all, published from 1934 to 1940.
    E. Series E, four fascicles in all, published from 1935 to 1942.

Appendix B

Members of the Durkheimian School and Their Contributions to *L'Année*, 1898–1913*

L'ANNEE VOLUMES AND SECTIONS [†]

	I	II	III	IV	V	VI	VII	VIII	IX	X	XI	XII
A. Aubin	x	x	x	1	1	1	1	1	1	1	1	1
				3						3		3
H. Beuchat	x	x	x	x	x	x	x	6	2	2	x	1
								7	7			
A. Bianconi	x	x	x	x	x	x	x	7	x	1	2	1
										2	3	2
										3		
C. Bouglé	1	1	1	1	1	1	1	1	1	1	1	1
				3	3		3	3		3	3	3
							4	7				
G. Bourgin	x	x	x	x	x	x	x	3	x	5	5	5
								5				
H. Bourgin	x	x	x	5	5	5	5	5	5	5	5	5
R. Chaillié	x	x	x	x	x	2	x	x	2	1	x	x
									7			
M. David	x	x	x	x	x	x	x	x	x	x	3	1
												2
G. Davy	x	x	x	x	x	x	x	x	x	x	1	2
											2	3
											3	
											4	

* Adopted from Nandan, *The Durkheimian School*, 1977.

[†] Roman numerals denote volume and arabic numerals denote section of *L'Année*.

L'ANNÉE VOLUMES AND SECTIONS

	I	II	III	IV	V	VI	VII	VIII	IX	X	XI	XII
A. Demangeon	x	x	x	x	x	x	x	x	x	x	x	6
E. Doutté	x	x	x	x	x	x	x	x	x	x	x	1
												2
												3
E. Durkheim	3	2	1	3	1	1	1	1	1	1	1	1
		3	3	4	3	3	3	3	3	3	2	2
		6	6	6	4	4	4	4	4	4	3	3
		7			6	6	6	6			4	6
						7	7					
P. Fauconnet	7	3	3	1	1	1	1	1	1	1	1	2
			4	3	3	3	3	3	2	3	3	3
				4	7	6		4	3	6	4	
						7						
Ph. de. Félice	x	x	x	x	x	x	x	x	2	2	2	2
C. Fossey	x	x	x	x	x	2	2	x	x	x	x	x
M. Foucault	x	7	x	x	x	x	4	x	x	x	x	x
G. Gelly	x	x	x	x	x	x	x	x	2	x	x	1
												2
L. Gernet	x	x	x	x	x	x	x	x	x	x	3	3
											5	
M. Halbwachs	x	x	x	x	x	x	x	4	3	4	4	4
								6	4	5	5	5
									5	6	6	6
R. Hertz	x	x	x	x	x	x	x	1	2	2	2	2
											3	
R. Hourticq	x	x	x	x	3	3	1	1	1	1	1	1
							3		3	3		
H. Hubert	2	2	2	1	1	1	1	1	1	2	2	2
		7	2	2	2	2	2	2	2	7	7	7
			7	7	7	7	7		6			
P. Huvelin	x	x	x	x	x	3	3	3	3	3	3	3
H. Jeanmaire	x	x	x	x	x	x	x	x	x	x	x	2
												6
J. P. Lafitte	x	x	x	x	x	x	x	x	x	x	7	x
C. Lalo	x	x	x	x	x	x	7	x	x	x	x	x
P. Lapie	3	3	3	3	3	3	1	1	1	1	1	x
		7					3	3	3	3	3	
E. Laskine	x	x	x	x	x	x	x	x	x	x	x	2
E. Lévy	3	3	3	3	x	3	3	3	3	3	3	3
I. Lévy	x	2	2	x	x	2	2	2	x	x	x	x
			3			6						
C. E. Maître	x	x	x	x	7	x	x	x	x	x	x	x
J. Marx	x	x	x	x	x	x	x	x	x	x	x	1
												2
												6
M. Mauss	2	2	2	1	2	1	2	1	1	2	1	1
	3	3		2		2	3	2	2	3	2	2
						7	6	3	3	6	3	3
							7	7			7	7

L'ANNEE VOLUMES AND SECTIONS

	I	II	III	IV	V	VI	VII	VIII	IX	X	XI	XII
A. Meillet	x	x	x	x	7	7	7	7	7	7	7	7
A. Milhaud	5	x	x	x	x	x	x	x	x	x	x	x
A. Moret	x	x	x	x	2	x	x	x	x	x	x	x
H. Muffang	6	7	7	x	x	x	x	x	x	x	x	x
D. Parodi	7	1	1	1	x	1	1	1	3	1	1	x
				7			3	3				
J. Poirot	x	x	x	x	x	x	x	x	2	2	x	x
									7	6		
										7		
J. Ray	x	x	x	x	x	x	x	x	x	x	4	4
J. Reynier	x	x	x	x	x	x	x	7	x	x	2	2
G. Richard	4	4	4	4	1	3	1	4	1	4	x	x
					3	4	4		3			
					4	6			4			
P. Roussel	x	x	x	x	x	x	x	x	x	x	x	2
												3
F. Sigel	x	x	4	x	x	x	x	x	x	x	x	x
F. Simiand	5	1	5	5	5	5	5	5	5	5	5	5
		5									6	
J. T. Stickney	x	x	2	x	7	2	x	x	x	x	x	x
			3									
A. Vacher	x	x	x	x	x	x	x	6	6	x	x	x

Appendix C

Classification of the Members
of the Durkheimian School*

I. Original Members: Period One, *L'Année,* 1898–1913
  A. Pleiad: C. Bouglé, G. Davy, P. Fauconnet, M. Halbwachs, H. Hubert, M. Mauss, G. Richard, F. Simiand.
  B. Secondary Pleiad: G. Bourgin, H. Bourgin, P. Huvelin, P. Lapie, Em. Lévy, A. Meillet, D. Parodi.
  C. Marginal Members: A. Aubin, Ph. de Félice, C. Fossey, M. Foucault, R. Hourticq, C. Lalo, Is. Lévy, C. E. Maître, A. Milhaud, A. Moret, H. Muffang, J. Poirot, J. T. Stickney, F. Sigel, A. Vacher.
  D. Latecomers: A. Demangeon, E. Doutté, L. Gernet, H. Jeanmaire, E. Laskine, J. Marx, J. Ray, P. Roussel.
  E. The "Stifled Phalanx": H. Beuchat, A. Bianconi, R. Chaillié, M. David, G. Gelly, R. Hertz, J. P. Lafitte, J. Reynier.
  F. A Durkheimian in Limbo: L. Lévy-Bruhl.

II. Original Members, Intellectual Heirs, and Posterity: Period Two, *L'Année* (new series), 1925–1927
  A. Continuing Original Members: Bouglé, G. Bourgin, H. Bourgin, Ph. de Félice, Demangeon, Doutté, Fauconnet, Gernet, Halbwachs, H. Hubert, Jeanmaire, Lalo, Em. Lévy, Is. Lévy, L. Lévy-Bruhl, Marx, Mauss, Moret, Parodi, Ray, Simiand.
  B. Intellectual Heirs and New Members: Max Bonnafous, Bayet, Cohen, Czarnowski, Déat, Essertier, Granet, Fr. Henry, A. Laouist, R. Laubier, H. Lévy-Bruhl, Lenoir, Maunier, Piganiol, Radcliffe-Brown, Sion.

III. Original Members, Intellectual Heirs, and Posterity: Period Three, L'Institut Français de Sociologie, 1930–1933
  A. Continuing Original Members: Aubin, Bouglé, Davy, Ph. de Félice, Fauconnet, Gernet, Halbwachs, Jeanmaire, Em. Lévy, L. Lévy-Bruhl, J. Marx, Mauss, Meillet, Parodi, Simiand.

* Adopted from Nandan, *The Durkheimian School,* 1977.

504

B. Intellectual Heirs and New Members: Bayet, Marc Bloch, C. Blondel, Marcel Cohen, S. Czarnowski, J. Escara, G. Espinas, Ferdinand-Dreyfus, M. Granet, J. Hackin, René Hubert, Max Lazard, R. Lenoir, H. Lévy-Bruhl, p. Noailles, A. Philip, A. Piganiol, R. Polin, J. Soustelle, J. Stoetzel, P. Przyluski, E. Rabaud, P. Ramadier, P. Rivet, J. Sion.

IV. Original Members, Intellectual Heirs, and New Members: Period Four, *Annales sociologiques,* 1934–1942
   A. Original Members: Bouglé, G. Bourgin, Demangeon, Fauconnet, Halbwachs, Jeanmaire, Em. Lévy, Lalo, Mauss, Ray, Roussel, Simiand.
   B. Intellectual Heirs and New Members: R. Aron, A. Bayet, S. Czarnowski, P. Depoid, D. Essertier, V. Feldman, G. Gurvitch, M. Granet, A. Grazberg-Minkowski, R. Hubert, I. Inoué, A. Kaan, R. Klee, H. Laufenberger, H. Lévy-Bruhl, A. Levitzki, P. Leiris, G. Le Bras, C. Lutfalla, R. Maunier, E. Mestre, P. Montet, H. Mougin, R. Marjolin, R. Montagne, p. Noailles, A. Philip, A. Piganiol, R. Polin, J. Soustelle, J. Stoetzel, P. Schwob, J. Sion, L. Tesnière, M. Vulcanesco, P. Vignaux.

Name Index

Abou'l-Hassan el-Maverdi, 358
Ačimovic, Ivon, 168–169
Alcan, Félix, 40–42
Allin, Arthur, 102
Almeras, Henri d', 297
Ammon, Otto, 100
Amram, David Werner, 244–246
Andler, Charles, 26
Andreotti, A., 92
Arbois de Jubainville, Henri d', 116, 214–216
Aristotle, 3, 80, 132, 308, 373, 376–377
Asturaro, Alfonso, 161
Aubéry, Gaetan, 117, 292–294
Auffroy, Henri, 116, 189–193
Bachofen, Johann, 179, 184, 249
Baldwin, James, 62
Balzer, 199–200
Barrett, Rosa M., 410
Barth, Paul, 61, 450–453
Bartsch, Robert, 117, 274–275
Bastian, Adolf, 184
Bauer, Max, 301–302
Bayet, Albert, 112, 115, 135–137, 139n.
Beauchet, L., 276, 390
Beaumanoir, Philippe, 124
Behre, Ernst, 282–283
Belliot, R.P.A., 60, 92–93
Belot, Gustave, 112, 115, 137, 144–148
Bernès, Marcel, 31
Bernhöft, 338
Berr, Henri, 13, 61, 89–90
Bertillon, J., 402, 416–417, 418, 437
Beuchat, Antoine, 107
Beuchat, Henri, 29, 61, 89–90
Beyerle, Konrad, 385–386
Bianconi, Antoine, 20, 28, 29
Binder, 338
Blau, Bruno, 440–441

Bloch, G., 114, 118, 338–339
Blum, Léon, 25, 33
Boas, Franz, xvii
Bochard, A., 40
Böckh, Richard, 433
Bogišić, 168
Boissonnade, Prosper, 271
Bonfaure, P., 123–124
Bonucci, Alessandro, 115, 131–134
Bortkewitsch, L. von, 406
Bouché-Leclerq, Louis, 104
Bouglé, Célestin, vii, 11, 25–28, 29, 35, 37, 39, 41, 43, 59, 61, 63, 93, 111, 114
Bourgin, Georges, 28, 34, 447
Bourgin, Hubert, 10–11, 28, 32–34, 39, 41, 447
Boutroux, Emile, 13, 29, 30–31
Boyer, Paul, 172–173
Brentano, Lujo, 388–389
Briand, Aristide, 25
Brunetière, Ferdinand, 13, 30, 32, 74
Brunner, Constantin, 322, 335
Bryce, James, 298
Brynmor-Jones, D., 339–340
Bücher, Karl, 450
Budanov, V., 352–355
Buisson, Ferdinand, 12, 25
Buomberger, F., 402, 422–423
Cahuzac, Albert, 185–188
Caillemer, R., 200–204
Calmette, Joseph, 340
Carini, P., 99
Carli, F., 234
Cartier, Ernest, 233–234
Castelli, D., 396
Celakovsky, Jaromir, 341
Chadwick, H. Munro, 330–331
Chaillée, R., 34
Chausse, A., 392
Chiappelli, Alessandro, 90, 91
Ciszewski, Stanislas, 173–175
Cleisthenes, 259, 351, 374
Clemenceau, Georges, 25

Clerici, Ottorino, 234
Cohn, Georg, 381–382
Commons, John R., 358
Comte, Auguste, 9, 13, 14, 16, 19, 68, 73, 77, 91, 92, 160
Cornil, George, 116, 177–179, 397
Coste, 61
Courant, Maurice, 116, 183–184, 310–311
Cramer, Julius, 331–333, 335–338
Cresson, A., 27
Croce, B., 61, 70–71
Cunow, Heinrich, 115, 169–171
Curr, E.M., 169
Cuvillier, A., 13
Czarnowski, S., 41
Dainville, Albert de, 221
Dareste, R., 114, 162–163, 375–376
David, Maxime, 24, 28
Davy, Georges, 11, 24, 28, 29, 39, 41, 42, 114
Déat, Marcel, 39
Demangeon, Albert, 28
Demolins, 61
Denis, Ernest, 12
Depinay, J., 402, 420–422
Deploige, Simon, 11, 13, 112, 159–161
Dereux, George, 394–396
Descartes, René, 134
Detmer, Heinrich, 298
Didon, R., 26
Digeon, C., 26
Doniol, Henri, 118, 311–313
Douglas, Jack D., 403
Draco, 257, 259
Duguit, Léon, 13, 22, 114, 123
Dultzig, Eugen V., 383–385
Dumas, Georges, 41
Dumont, Arsène, 121–122, 432

Duprat, Guillaume L., 61, 75, 130–131, 402, 410
Dupré la Tour, Félix, 197–199, 402, 418
Dupuy, 25
Durkheim, André, 12
Durkheim, Emile: *see* Subject Index: Durkheim, Emile
Duvignaud, Jean, 42
Ebeling, August, 297–298
Ellis, Havelock, 305
Ellwood, Charles A., 60, 65–66, 100
Engelmann, Jean, 116, 213
Engels, Friedrich, 286
Engert, Thad, 116, 216–218
Epicurus, 3
Escher, Arnold, 188–189
Esmein, A., 261–263
Espinas, Alfred, 7–8, 31, 62, 64, 88, 93–94
Essertier, D., 41
Fahlbeck, E., 432
Fauconnet, Paul, 8, 29, 33, 34, 37, 41, 85, 114, 118
Félice, Philippe de, 29
Ferneuil, 6, 9
Ferrero, Guglielmo, 400
Ferri, Enrico, 400
Ferry, Jules, 25
Florian, 400
Fossey, Charles, 23, 28, 29
Foucault, Jean, 41
Fouillée, Alfred, 6, 112, 115, 137, 139–144, 401, 406–408
Francotte, Henri, 114, 349–352
Frauenstädt, Paul, 401, 409
Frazer, xvii, 104
Freund, L., 298
Friederichs, Karl, 237–238
Friesen, Heinrich Freiherr von, 390–391
Fukuda, Tokuzo, 316–319
Fuld, Ludwig, 297
Funck-Brentano, Théodore, 75
Fustel de Coulanges, Numa Denis, 29, 30, 48, 49, 223, 246, 314, 323, 338, 370
Galileo, 128
Garufi, C.A., 117, 238–239
Gebhard, Richard, 116, 230–232
Gelly, G., 28
Geny, F., 114, 123, 125
George, Henry, 101
Gernet, L., 28, 34, 114
Gillen, F., xvii, xviii

Giner, F., 64–65
Giraud–Teulon, 249
Gizicki, Paul von, 304
Glasson, Ernest D., 116, 207–210, 390
Glotz, Gustave, xvii, 114, 119, 368, 369–375
Goblot, Edmond, vii, 40
Gorst, Harold E., 341–343
Gothein, 88
Granet, M., 41
Grasserie, Raoul de la, 297
Griveau, Paul, 402, 420–422
Groppali, 61
Grosse, Ernst, 286
Grüneisen, 217
Guigon, Henri, 222–223
Guilhiermoz, P., 118, 323–326, 340
Gumplowicz, L., 6, 101, 106
Gunther, L., 118, 362–364
Gurgens, Heinrich, 249–251
Guyau, Marie Jean, 8
Hagelstange, Abel, 306–308
Halbwachs, Maurice, 11, 28, 41, 447
Hamelin, Octave, 27
Hammurabi, 214
Harriot, 25
Hartland, xvii
Hauriou, 114
Heck, 322
Hermann, E., 116, 281–282
Herr, Lucien, xv–xvi, 26, 28, 32–34
Hertz, R., 24, 28, 34, 41
Hesiod, 132
Hildebrandt, 204, 205
Hinojosa, E. de, 295
Hippias, 258
Hitier, Joseph, 357
Hobhouse, L. T., 112
Hoffding, Harald, xvii, 115, 134–135
Holzapfel, L., 118, 319–321
Homer, 131
Hopkins, Washburn, 396
Huber, Max, 382*n.*
Hubert, H., 11, 16, 21, 28, 29, 34, 38, 41, 107, 111, 449
Hutchinson, H. N., 240–242
Huvelin, P., 114, 119, 367–368
Iovanovic, Milan Paul, 386–388
Izoulet, Jean, 13, 31
Jankelevitch, S., 60, 75–78

Janet, Pierre, 41
Janet, Paul, 10, 13
Jannet, Claudio, 75
Jaurès, Jean, 25, 33
Jeanmaire, H., 28
Jenks, Edward, 340
Jerusalem, Wilhelm, 64, 107–110
Jhelnik, 114
John of Leyden, 298
Juglar, Clément, 432, 433
Kant, Immanuel, 27, 157
Kantorowicz, Hermann, 87
Karady, Victor, 42, 43
Kellor, Frances A., 441
Kham, Karl, 302–303
Klugmann, N., 117, 251–252
Kohler, Josef, xvii, 118, 279–280, 364–367
Kollmann, Paul, 411–413
Kovalevski, Maksim, 171–172
Krose, H.A., 435–440
Kubali, H.N., 13
Kuczynski, Robert, 433
Kuhn, Adalbert, 2
Kühne, Rear Admiral, 442
La Rochefoucauld, François de, 134
Laberthonière, Lucien, 13
Laborde, Laurent, 294–295
Lachelier, Jules, 27
Lacombe, 61
Lalande, André, 13
Lalo, C., 8, 41
Lamarck, Jean Baptiste, 91
Lambert, Edouard, 114, 116, 124–127, 193–194, 207
Lampérière, Anna, 296
Lamprecht, Karl, 61
Landry, Adolphe, 112, 115, 137, 138
Lang, Andrew, xvii
Lapie, Paul, 24, 25, 28, 41, 111, 114
Lasch, Richard, 403, 441–444, 447–448
Laskine, 28
Lattes, Alessandro, 359–360
Launspach, C.W., 116, 226–227
Laveleye, Émile de, 204
Lavisse, Ernest, 12, 25, 26
Lazarus, Moritz, 37
Lefas, Alexandre, 116, 176–177
Lefebvre, Charles, 116, 117, 196, 218–221, 254–257,

260, 263, 276, 278, 284, 298
Leist, B.W., 116, 163–168, 234, 245
Lenoir, R., 41
Letourneau, 74, 184
Lévy, Emmanuel, 33, 34, 114
Lévy, Isidore, 23, 29
Lévy, Louis Germain, 234
Lévy-Bruhl, Lucien, vii, 19–20, 22, 41, 112, 115, 127–130, 136, 139, 149, 160
Lexis, W., 406
Liard, Louis, 7, 25
Liebenam, W., 345–346
Lindner, Friedrich, 402, 414–416
Lindsay, S.M., 90
Loebel, D. Theophil, 116, 242–244
Lombroso, Cesare, 400
Loncao, Enrico, 340, 360–361
Löning, R., 376–378
Lot, Ferdinand, 356–357
Lourbet, Jacques, 304–305
Löwenstimm, August, 408
Maine, Henry Sumner, 223, 382
Maître, C.E., 28, 34
Mallard, Henri, 117, 284–285
Mannhardt, Wilhelm, 308
Marcais, W., 116, 175–176
Marchand, Lucien, 233
Marchi, Attilio, 339
Marcou, Edmond, 117, 260–261
Marez, Guillaume des, 379–381, 392–394
Marholm, Laura, 253
Markovic, Milan, 116, 204–205
Marro, Antonio, 410
Martel, Charles, 324
Marx, Karl, 3
Marx, Victor, 295–296
Matteucci, U., 92
Maurer, Georg Ludwig von, 335
Mauss, Marcel, 8, 12, 16–17, 20, 21, 27, 28–30, 33, 34, 38, 39, 41, 63, 111, 112, 449
Mauxion, M., 162
Mazzola, Ugo, 450
Meillet, A., 12, 17, 24, 215
Meyer, Eduard, 61, 78–84, 226, 306, 307*n*., 339
Meyerson, I., 13

Meynial, E., 116, 117, 234, 248–249
Mielziner, M., 269–271
Milioukov, P., 348–349
Miller, Ernest, 232–233
Mommsen, Theodor, 321, 378–379, 392
Monod, Gabriel, 41
Montesquieu, Baron de La Brède et de, 357
Moret, Alexandre, 23, 29, 232
Muffang, H., 449
Muhlfeld, Lucien, 5
Müller, Joseph, 304
Müller, Max, 17
Müller, Otto, 257–260
Naville, Adrien, 60, 78
Neubecker, F.K., 291–292
Neukamp, Ernst, 114, 119–120
Nietzold, Johannes, 116–117, 266–268, 269
Novicow, Jacques, 62, 93
Oberziner, Giovanni, 118, 329–330, 338
Obrist, Alfred, 227–229
Opet, Otto, 290–291
Oppenheimer, Franz, 388
Owen, D.R.G., 15
Palante, Georges, 105–106
Pareto, Vilfredo, 61, 91
Parodi, Dominique, 13, 27, 28, 41
Parsons, Talcott, xviii
Pasteur, Louis, 29
Pearson, Karl, 3
Pechuel-Loesche, 107
Peisker, 204, 205, 223–225
Pellison, Maurice, 134
Pericles, 258
Perrot, Georges, 29
Philo Judaeus, 133
Pidoux, Pierre-André, 117, 264–266
Pillon, Ferdinand, 41
Pirenne, H., 114, 355
Plato, 3, 132
Plessis de Grenédan, J., 195–197
Plotz, A., 87
Poincaré, Raymond, 25
Poirot, J., 23, 28
Posada, A., 117, 252–253
Post, Albert H., 28, 152, 184
Pouzol, Abel, 87, 402, 418–420
Prinzing, Friedrich, 402, 413–414, 417–418, 423–425, 433, 438

Procope, 225
Pufendorf, Samuel, 376
Quatrefages de Breau, Jean de, 98
Quételet, Lambert, 406
Rabelais, François, 134
Rakowski, Kasimir von, 389–390
Ratzel, Friedrich, xvii, xviii, 22, 38, 81
Ray, J., 28, 41
Reibmayr, Albert, 304
Rein, W., 446
Reinach, Salomon, 13
Reynier, J., 28
Rhys, J., 339–340
Ribot, A., 75
Ribot, Théodule, xvii, 41, 63–64, 103–104
Richard, Gaston, 11, 28, 59–60, 61, 84–86, 111, 117, 149–150, 289–290, 399–401
Robertis, R. Resta de, 102–105
Roberts, Robert, 116, 229–230
Rocca, Félix de, 343–345
Roeder, Fritz, 116, 253–254
Rol, Auguste, 117, 283–284
Romano, P., 102
Rose, H.A., 233
Ross, Edward Alsworth, 60, 61, 92, 120–121
Rost, Hans, 434–435, 438
Rousseau, Jean-Jacques, 134, 135
Roussel, P., 34
Rudeck, Wilhelm, 299–301
Ruggiero, Roberto de, 268–269
Rullkoeter, William, 264
Rundstein, S., 199–200
Saguez, Eugène, 117, 277–279
Saint-Simon, Comte de, 68
Sakamoto, Saburo, 271, 273–274
Saleilles, R., 114, 123
Salvemini, G., 61, 70
Savigny, L. von, 114, 122–123
Schaeffle, Albert, 6, 28, 61, 99–100
Schaible, K. Heinrich, 303–304
Schmidt, R., 305
Schmoller, Gustav, 28, 160
Schnitzer, J., 246–248
Schrader, Otto, 281
Schulenburg, Emil, 116, 239–240
Schultze, 100

Schupe, 358
Schurtz, Heinrich, 382–383
Schwerin, Claudius von, 331, 333–338
Secrétan, Charles, 27
Sée, Henri, 114, 118, 313–316, 389
Seignobos, Charles, 26, 61, 66–69
Sergi, G., 101
Sigel, F., 23
Sighele, 400
Simiand, François, 14–15, 16, 27, 28, 29, 33, 34, 38, 41, 111
Simmel, Georg, 22, 38, 62, 88–89, 94–98, 139n.
Singer, H., 343
Sismondi, Jean de, 447
Small, Albion W., 60, 61, 69–70, 101–102
Smirnov, Jean, 172–173
Socrates, 3, 132, 260
Solon, 258, 309–310, 373
Sombart, Werner, 87–88
Sorel, Georges, 13, 51, 70, 450–451
Spann, Othmar, 402, 425–427
Spencer, G., xvii, xviii
Spencer, Herbert, 64, 68, 91, 92
Spinoza, Baruch, 134
Stade, 217
Stammler, Rudolf, 123
Stanischitsch, Alexa, 116, 223–226

Starcke, Carl N., 115, 179–183
Stchoukine, Ivan, 434
Steinmetz, S.R., 22, 38, 61, 98–99, 115, 184–185, 365, 391–392, 441
Stendhal, H., 37
Stickney, Trumbull, 23, 33–34
Stockar, Hans, 116, 205–206
Strabo, 295, 333
Sumner, W.G., 112, 113
Sutherland, 100
Szanto, Emil, 118, 319–321
Tacitus, 248, 254, 264, 322, 323, 325, 332, 334
Tamassia, N., 233
Tarde, G., xvii, 11, 31, 36, 60, 62, 72–73, 75, 78, 105
Tarnowski, E., 444–445
Thiers, Louis, 25
Thomas, Albert, 33
Thomas, William I., 179
Thonissen, J.J., 368
Toennies, Ferdinand, 8–9, 86
Toniolo, Giuseppe, 60, 74–75
Troeltsch, 88
Tsuguru, Fusamaro, 210–213
Twasaky, Kojiro, 271–273
Tylor, Edward, 104
Typaldo-Bassia, A., 117, 275–277
Usteri, P., 114, 368–369
Vacher, Antoine, 28, 33, 34
Valensi, Alfred, 403, 427–432
Veblen, Thorstein, 389
Vecchio, G. del, 361
Verce, E. Fornasari di, 411

Vico, Giovanni, 338
Villa, G., 90–91
Viollet, Paul, 326–329
Vogt, Josef, 298
Voigt, A., 87
Wagner, A.H.G., 28, 160
Wallis, Louis, 100–101
Ward, Lester F., 62, 91
Warner, Lee, 361
Waxweiller, 61
Webb, C.C.J., 13
Weber, J., 246
Weber, Marianne, xvii, xviii, 113, 117, 285–289
Weber, Max, xviii, 3, 89
Weinhold, Karl, 304
Wellmuth, John, 15
Westermarck, Edward, xvii, 112, 115, 117, 150–159, 161–162, 184, 280–281
Wilbrandt, M., 118, 308–310
Wilcken, 184
Winter, A.C., 296–297
Wittich, Werner, 321–323
Work, Monroe N., 445–446
Worms, René, 11, 17, 31, 36, 38, 39, 40, 62
Wundt, Wilhelm, xvii, 7, 28
Xenopol, A.D., 61, 73–74
Zocco-Rosa, A., 295
Zola, Emile, 27

Subject Index

ABDUCTION, marriage by, 165, 239–240, 241, 291
Absolutism, 357
Academy, 3, 5
Administration of Cities under the Roman Empire (Liebenam), 345–346
Adoption, 113, 116, 171, 176–177, 186, 187, 210–213, 217, 227, 273
"Adoption testamentaire à Rome, L' " (Lefas), 176–177
Adrogation, 177
Adultery, 162, 249, 264
Aesthetic sociology, 450–451
Agnation, 226, 255, 256, 290
Agriculture, 169–170, 307, 322–323
Albania, 375–376
Alcoholism, 438
"Alcune osservazioni di natura economica circa l'aumento dei pazzi ricoverati in Italia" (Verce), 411
Altgermanische Hundertschaft, Die (Untersuchungen zur deutschen Staats- und Rechtsgeschichte, hgg. von Otto Gierke) (Schwerin), 331, 333–338
Altrum, 233
American Indians, 169–171, 289–290, 335
Amiens, marriage in, 277–279
"Anciennes coutumes albanaises, Les" (Dareste), 375–376
Anerbenrecht, 383–385
"Anfänge des Gewerbestandes, Die" (Lasch), 447–448
Anglo-Saxons, 253–254, 324, 330–331
"Anima delle folle, L' " (Robertis), 104–105
Année philosophique, L', 41
Année sociologique, L': aesthetic sociology, 450–451; aims and scope of, xv; *Analyses*, 40, 42–43; choice of books reviewed in, xv–xvi; classification for, xvi, 42; collaborators, 23; comparativism in, 17; criminal sociology section, 399–446
    editor's introduction, 399–403; general concepts, 403–411; juvenile crime, 410, 420, 446; moral statistics, 399–401, 411–440; social factors, 403, 440–441; suicide: *see* Suicide
economic sociology section, 14–15, 447–448; education, 451–453; formation, growth, and

consolidation of, 10–12, 37–40; general sociology section, 59–110
    editor's introduction, 59–64; general conceptions and methodological issues, 64–93; social psychology, 102–106; social theories, 93–102; sociological conditions of knowledge, 106–110
juridic and moral sociology section, 111–397
    contract and obligation, 391–397; editor's introduction, 111–119; family: *see* Family; general conceptions, theories, and methodological issues, 119–162; international and moral law, 359–361; juridic and moral systems, 162–163; marriage: *see* Marriage; penal law, 362–379; political organization, 341–358; property law, 379–391; sexual morality, 113, 115, 162–163, 299–305; social organization, 114, 117, 305–341
Mémoires originaux, xvii, 40, 42, 49, 56, 138; periodicals used as sources of reviews in, xiii; preface, 1898, 47–51; preface, 1899, 52–55; preface, 1911, 55–57; publisher of, 40–41; purpose of, 38; reputation of, xvi–xvii
Anomie, 9, 14, 401, 403
Anthropology, 43, 78–84, 115
Anthroposociology, 449
Application de la loi du divorce en France, L'. Tendance générale de la jurisprudence, résultats sociaux, projets de réforme (Valensi), 427–432
Artificial kinship, 173–175
Artificial Kinship among Southern Slavs (Ciszewski), 173–175
Arunta, 279
"Associations en Chine, Les" (Courant), 183–184, 310–311
Athenian clans, 308–310
Athenian marriage, 257–260
Australia, 289–290; marriage in, 240–241
"Autorité dans la Russie ancienne, L' " (Budanov), 352–355

BABYLONIAN marriage, 295–296
"Basis of Sociality, The" (Allin), 102
Bastardy: *see* Illegitimacy
Baths, 299, 301

Bau und Leben des socialen Körpers (Schaeffle), 99–100
Bavaria, illegitimacy in, 414–416
Begging, 444–445
Beginning of Landed Property (Schurtz), 382–383
"Beginning of Ownership, The" (Veblen), 389
Belgium, political organization in, 355
Berry, France, 284
Bestiality, 162
Betrothal, 234, 235, 238, 258, 270
Bibliothèque internationale de sociologie, 40
Bibliothèque de philosophie contemporaine, 41
"Biological Sociology and Caste Systems" (Bouglé), 93
Birthrate, 402, 417, 432, 433
Blacks, crime and, 445–446
Blood covenant, 174
Boyars, 353, 354
Brauttradition und Consensgespräch in mittelalterischen Trauungsritualen. Ein Beitrag zur Geschichte des deutschen Eheschliessungsrechts (Opet), 290–291
Burgundy, 346–347, 355

CANON *Law Concerning Marriage, with Comparison of Present Laws in Effect in the German Empire, Austria, Switzerland, and Countries with a Civil Code* (Schnitzer), 246–248
Canton, 347–348
"Capitalization of Social Development, The" (Wallis), 100–101
Caroline Islands, The (Singer), 343
Cartesianism, 134
Castes, 187–188, 317n.
"Castes et la sociologie biologique, Les" (Novicow), 93
Causes sociales de la folie, Les (Duprat), 130, 410
Célibat à Rome, Le (Cartier), 233–234
Celts: family, 214–216; social organization of, 331, 333–335
Charity in Ancient Rome (Marchi), 339
Children: relationships with parents, 196; sale of, 178
China: family in, 183–184, 342; political organization in, 341–343, 349; social organization in, 310–311
China (Gorst), 341–343
Chivalry, 325–326
Cities, 345–347, 349–352, 359–360
Citizen of India, The (Warner), 361
City-states, 112, 164, 319–321
Civil law, 163–167
Clans, 112, 171–172, 286–287, 308–310, 311

Class structure, 117–118
Classes rurales et le régime domanial en France au Moyen Age, Les (Sée), 313–316
Cohabitation, 235
Collection des Travaus de l'Année Sociologique, 56
Collective conscience, 6, 9, 14, 16, 38, 133
Collective consciousness, 108–110
Collective kinship, 172–173
Collective marriage, 185, 237, 238
Collective personality, 64–65
Collective psychology, 63, 72, 104–105
Collective representations, 14, 16, 21
Collective responsibility, 374
Comitatus, 324–326, 340
" 'Comitatus' germanique et la vassalité, à propos d'une théorie récente, Le" (Calmette), 340
Common law, 131–134
Communauté de biens conjugale, La. Origines et évolution du régime légal. Som amélioration (Etude d'histoire et de droit comparé) (Aubéry), 292–294
Communauté de biens conjugale dans l'ancien droit français, La. Etude de droit coutumier (Typaldo-Bassia), 275–277
"Communautés taisibles et communautés coutumières depuis la rédaction des coutumes" (Glasson), 390
Communes, 306, 307, 310–311, 326–329, 340, 352–353
Communes françaises au moyen âge, Les (Viollet), 326–329
Comparative Application of Slavic Law to History, A (Rundstein), 199–200
Comparative law, 114, 124–127, 331, 336
Comparative Studies on the Condition of Women in Antiquity: Women in the Talmud (Klugmann), 251–252
Comparativism, 14, 15, 16–17
Composition of the Population in the German Empire (Kollmann), 411–413
"Concepts of Race and Society and Several Problems Connected with Them" (Plotz), 87
Concubinage, 235, 236, 258–260, 268
Condition des féaux en Egypte, dans la famille, dans la société, dans la vie d'outre-tombe (Moret), 232
Condition of the Woman in Babylon (Marx), 295–296
Conditions of Property in Real Estate and the Right of Citizenship in Medieval Constance. The Right of the Salmann (Beyerle), 385–386
Conflit de la morale et de la sociologie, Le (Deploige), 159–161
Constance, property law in, 385–386

Constraints in the Law Considered in Their Historical Development (Neukamp), 119–120

Contract, 391–397

Contract law, 114

"Contribution à l'étude de la *patria potestas*" (Cornil), 177–179

"Contributto allo studio demografico delle famiglie e delle generazioni umane" (Fahlbeck), 432

Contubernium, 236

Corporations, 310

Cosmopolitanism, 132

Council of Trent, 208, 247, 265

Cours de doctorat sur l'histoire matrimoniale française (Lefebvre), 218–221

"Coutumes primitives dans les écrits des mythologues grecs et romains, Les" (Esmein), 261–263

Credit, 391–394, 396

Creditors and Debtors in Ancient Hebraic Society (Castelli), 396

"Crime among the Negroes of Chicago" (Work), 445–446

Criminal anthropology, 401

Criminal sociology section, 399–446; editor's introduction, 399–403; general concepts, 403–411; juvenile crime, 410, 420, 446; moral statistics, 399–401, 411–440; social factors, 403, 440–441; suicide: *see* Suicide

Crossbreeding, 304

Custom, 161–162

Customary law, 125–126

Customary Law in Lombard Cities (Lattes), 359–360

Cynosarges, 5, 258

DAGHESTAN, 171–172

De l'Autorisation maritale au XIIIe siècle comparée à celle du code civil (Marcou), 260–261

De la Forme dite inòkosna de la famille rurale chez les Serbes et les Croates (Bogišić), 168

"De l'Infécondité chez certaines populations industrielles" (Dumont), 432

De l'interprétation des actes juridiques privés (Dereux), 394–396

De Jaurès à Léon Blum (Bourgin), 11

"De la propriété dans l'ancien droit suédois" (Beauchet), 390

De la Recherche de la paternité en droit comparé et principalement en Suisse, en Angleterre et en Allemagne (Dupré la Tour), 197–199

Death penalty, 364

Debts, 391–394, 396

Demography, 449

Des Pactes successoraux dans l'ancien droit français (Dainville), 221

Des Parents et des alliés successibles en droit musulman (Marcais), 175–176

"Des Rapports que la statistique peut établir entre les mariages et les naissances d'un pays et sa situation économique" (Juglar), 432

"Des Régimes matrimoniaux chez les peuples germaniques et les peuples slaves" (Grasserie), 297

Descendant in the Swiss Inheritance Law (Escher), 188–189

Determinism, 16

Divine right, 357

Division of Labor in Society, The (Durkheim), 9, 10, 31, 37, 137–138, 139*n.*, 154, 402

Divorce, 115–117, 283–284, 402–403; French, 403, 427–432; German, 423–424; Japanese, 273–274; Jewish, 230, 244–246, 251; Roman, 244–245, 255; suicide and, 429, 431; Swiss, 422–423

Divorce in Berlin and Elsewhere (Prinzing), 423–424

Divorce in Japan (Sakamoto), 271, 273–274

Doctrinal schools, systematic theory of, 1–5

Doctrine de l'absolutisme, La (Hitier), 357

Domanial regime, 313–316

Domestic Community of the Serbs, The (Markovic), 204–205

Domestic Community of the Southern Slavs (Miller), 232–233

Domestic organization: *see* Family; Marriage; Sexual morality

Dot dans les fors et coutumes du Béarn, La (Laborde), 294–295

Dower, 278–279

Dowry, 115, 116, 221, 236–237, 243, 251, 255, 266–269, 282, 284, 291–292, 294–295, 402, 420–422

Dress, 300

Dreyfus Affair, 25

"Droits d'usage et les biens communaux en France au Moyen Age, Les" (Sée), 389

Dualism, 8–9

Durkheim, Emile. *See also L'Année sociologique:* chronological perspective on life and work, 6–12; comparativism and, 14, 16–17; criticism of doctrines, 11, 13, 19: death of, 12; disciples, followers, and collaborators, 11–12, 21–24; *The Division of Labor in Society,* 9, 10, 31, 37, 137–138, 139*n.*, 154, 402; on dualism, 8–9; at Ecole Normale Supérieure, 10–11, 28–31; *The Elementary Forms of Religious Life,* xviii, 8, 10, 12, 37; essence of doctrines, 13–21; on French revolution, 9; on German social sciences, 6–7, 28; influences on, 6, 7, 10, 28, 30; international fame of, 36–37; Lévy-Bruhl and,

Durkheim, Emile (*continued*)
19, 22–23; positivism and, 10, 13–14; psychology, position toward, 60, 62–63; rational art of morals and, 18–20; Richard and, 59–60, 399; *The Rules of Sociological Method,* 10, 16, 37; as scholarch, 5–13; scientism and, 10, 15–16; social epistemology, 20–21; societism and, 10, 16, 17–18; on space and time, 21; *Suicide: A Study in Sociology,* 10, 37, 60, 98, 399, 401, 402, 403, 437; Tarde and, 60; at University of Bordeaux, 7–8, 35; at University of Paris, 10, 35
Duty, 136, 156–157, 162
Dynamic Sociology and Outlines of Sociology (Ward), 62

"ECOLE historique et droit naturel, d'après quelques ouvrages récents" (Saleilles), 123
Ecole Normale Supérieure, 10–11, 28–32, 35
Ecole Polytechnique, 31
Ecole Pratique des Hautes Etudes, 29, 35
Economic Bases of Matriarchy (Cunow), 169–171
Economic sociology, 14–15, 447–448
"Economy and Law" (Voigt), 87
Education, 102–103, 407, 450, 451–453
Education of Boys Under the Ancient Irish Law, The (Tamassia), 233
Education and Sociology (Durkheim), 11
Egalitarianism, 132, 355
Egyptian marriage, 266–268
Ehe und Familienrecht der Hebräer (Engert), 216–218
Ehefrau und Mutter in der Rechtsentwicklung. Eine Einführung (Marianne Weber), 113, 285–289
Ehescheidung, Eheschliessung und kirchliche Trauung, nach der Schrift und der Gesetzgebung (Ebeling), 297–298
Eigentumsverhältmisse im ehelichen Güterrecht des Sachsenspiegels und magdeburger Rechts (Behre), 282–283
Elementary Forms of Religious Life, The: A Study in Religious Sociology (Durkheim), xviii, 8, 10, 12, 37
"Elemente der Anthropologie" (Meyer), 78–84
"Elemento morale nelle consuetudini e nelle leggi, L' " (Westermarck), 161–162
Eléments sociologiques de la morale, Les (Mauxion), 162
Eléments sociologiques de la morale, Les (Fouillée), 139–144
Elopement, 243
"En Quête d'une morale positive" (Belot), 137, 144–148
Endogamy, 317n.

England: juvenile crime in, 420, 446; property law in, 388–389
Epicureanism, 3
"Erbliche Rassen- und Volkscharakter, Der" (Steinmetz), 98–99
"Esprit de corps, L' " (Palante), 105–106
"Esprit de groupe, L' " (Tarde), 105
Essai sur le gouvernement local en Angleterre (Jenks), 340
Essai sur les institutions et le droit malgache (Cahuzac), 185–188
Essai sur l'origine de la noblesse en France (Guilhiermoz), 323–326
Essai sur les origines du testament romain (Obrist), 227–229
Essais sur l'histoire de la civilisation russe (Milioukov), 348–349
Ethics, 120–122, 134–135, 137–149
Ethnopsychology, 63
" 'Etre ou ne pas être' ou du postulat de la sociologie" (Espinas), 93–94
Etude sur le droit des gens mariés dans les coutumes d'Amiens (Saguez), 277–279
Etude sur le droit des gens mariés d'après les coutumes de Berry (Mallard), 284–285
Etude sur la propriété foncière dans les villes du Moyen Age (Marez), 379–381
Etude sommaire de la répresentation du temps dans la religion et dans la magie (Hubert), 107
"Evolution, historique de la vente consensuelle, L' " (Cornil), 397
Evolution du divorce, L'. Jurisprudence et sociologie (Rol), 283–284
Evolution of English Inheritance Law Concerning Landed Property (Brentano), 388–389
Evolution du testament en France (Auffroy), 189–193
"Evoluzione in biologia e nell'uomo, L' " (Sergi), 101
"Evoluzione dell'ospitalità, L' " (Vecchio), 361
Exchange, marriage by, 170
Exile, 368–369
Existentialism, 2
Exogamy, 185, 290, 317n.

FAMILIEN-*Anwartschaften in ihrer geschichtlichen Entwicklung und volkswirtschaftlichen Bedeutung, Die* (Friesen), 390–391
Familien-Sklaven-und Erbrecht im Qorân (Roberts), 229–230
Famille dans l'antiquité israélite, La (Lévy), 234
Famille Celtique, La. Etude de droit comparé (Arbois de Jubainville), 214–216
Famille dans les différentes sociétés, La (Starcke), 179–183

Family, 79–80, 94, 101, 113, 115–116, 163–234; *see also* Marriage: adoption, 113, 116, 171, 176–177, 186, 187, 210–213, 217, 227, 273; *altrum,* 233; Celtic, 214–216; Chinese, 183–184, 342; clans, 112, 171–172, 286–287, 308–310, 311; German, 384; Greek, 369–374; illegitimacy, 115, 197–199, 222–223, 402, 414–416, 418–419, 425–427, 433; inheritance, 113, 168, 175–176, 182, 188–189, 222, 231–232, 383–385; Jewish, 216–218, 234; joint, 382; in Malagasy, 185–187; matriarchal, 169–171, 176, 185, 286, 289, 316; number of children, 416–417; partnership, 381–382; paternal authority, 116, 166, 177–179, 185–187, 195–196, 205–210, 217, 218, 232, 235–237, 255, 369–370; patriarchal, 170, 286–290; Roman, 116, 166, 177–179, 183–184, 186, 205–206, 217, 219, 226–227, 288, 342; Serbian, 204–205; Slavic, 199–200, 204, 223–225, 232–233, 237, 290, 293, 316; vendettas, 158, 366, 370, 372, 375–376; wills, 163, 176–177, 189–194, 200–204, 213, 217, 222, 227–229, 231–232, 234
Family among the Anglo-Saxons, The. Part I, Husband and Wife (Roeder), 253–254
Federal system, 101
Feminism, 117, 252–253, 296
Feminism (Posada), 252–253
Femme dans l'histoire, La (Richard), 289–290
Festivals, 308
Feudalism, 118, 221, 311–315, 318, 319, 325, 326
Fidèles ou vassaux? Essai sur la nature juridique du lien qui unissait les grands vassaux à la royauté depuis le milieu du IXᵉ jusqu'à la fin du XIIᵉ siècle (Lot), 356–357
Fidelity, 307
Fiefs, 311–313, 356
Finland, marriage in, 296–297
First German Sociology Congress—Communications and Discussions, The, 86–89
Folkways (Sumner), 113
Fonction du droit civil comparé, La (Lambert), 124–127
Formation of the Great Landed Properties in Poland (Rakowski), 389–390
Formation of Large Landed Properties (Oppenheimer), 388
Formation des villes, des Etats, des confédérations, et des liques dans la Grèce ancienne (Francotte), 349–352
France au point de vue moral, La (Fouillée), 406–408
Franche-Comté, marriage in, 264–266
Free will, 376–377
French Philosophical Society, 11, 19, 36
French revolution, 9

French Sociological Institute, 35

"GARD'ORPHÈNES à Lille, Les" (Marchand), 233
Gemara, 244
Gemeinschaft und Gesellschaft (Toennies), 8
General sociology section, 59–110; editor's introduction, 59–64; general conceptions and methodological issues, 64–93; social psychology, 102–106; social theories, 93–102; sociological conditions of knowledge, 106–110
"Genesi sociale dei communi italiani, La" (Loncao), 340
"Genesis of Ethical Elements, The" (Ross), 120–121
German Law of Landed Property in the Past, Present, and Future, The (Dultzig), 383–385
German Women in the Middle Ages (Weinhold), 304
Germania (Tacitus), 248
Germany: birthrate in, 417–418, 433; composition of population, 411–413; crime in, 409; divorce in, 423–424; family in, 384; illegitimacy in, 425–427, 433; law in, 219–220, 231; marriage in, 248–249, 255–257, 264, 266, 274–275, 292–293, 297, 419, 424–425; peasants in, 306–308; penal law in, 365; property law in, 383–385; sexual morality in, 299–302; social organization in, 321–323, 325, 331–333, 335–338; social sciences in, 6–7, 25, 26–28; suicide in, 434–435
Greece: city-states in, 112, 164, 319–321; family in, 369–374; marriage in, 164–165, 166; penal law in, 368–375; philosophy of law, 131–134; political organization in, 349–352; tribes, 319–321
Greek Tribes, The (Szanto), 319–321
Group marriage, 279–280
Groups, 105–106; *see also* Clans
"Grundzüge und Kosten eines Gesetzes über die Fursorge für die Witwen und Waisen der Arbeiter" (Prinzing), 413–414

HANDBUCH *des katholischen Eherechts* (Vogt), 298
Hebrews: *see* Jews
"Heiratshäufigkeit und Heiratsalter nach Stand und Beruf" (Prinzing), 425
Heredity, 98
Histoire d l'autorité paternelle et de la société familiale en France avant 1789 (Plessis de Grenédan), 195–197
Histoire de la Belgique (Pirenne), 355
Histoire du droit et des institutions de la France (Glasson), 207–210

Histoire du droit matrimonial français. Le Droit des gens mariés (Lefebvre), 298
Histoire du mariage et du droit des gens mariés en Franche-Comté (Pidoux), 264–266
Historical sociology, 61
History of Education in the Light of Sociology, The (Barth), 451, 452–453
History of Public Morality in Germany (Rudeck), 299–301
History of the Theory of Penal Imputation (Löning), 376–378
Homicide, 158, 372–374
Hospitality, 361
Human sacrifices, 158
Human societies, classification of, 99
Hundred, 332, 335–338

IDEA *of Reprisal in the History and Philosophy of Penal Law, The. Contribution to the General History of the Development of This Law* (Gunther), 362–364
Idealism, 27
Ideas of Chastity in Their Historical Development and in Their Practical Sense, The (Müller), 304
Iliad (Homer), 372
Illegitimacy, 115, 197–199, 222–223, 258–259, 300, 402, 414–416, 418–419, 425–427, 433
Illegitimate Birth as a Social Phenomenon (Lindner), 414–416
Illegitimate Birthrate in Germany, The (Prinzing), 433
Imitation, 100
Imputability, 376
Incest, 162, 173, 262–263, 267, 290, 304
Incest and Crossbreeding in the Human Race (Reibmayr), 304
India, sexual morality in, 305
Individual psychology, 63, 104
Individualism, 18, 28, 180, 373–375, 385, 391
"Induzione sociologica nello studio del diritto penale, L' " (Andreotti), 92
Infidelity, 181
"Influence of the Puberal Development upon the Moral Character" (Marro), 410
Inheritance, 113, 168, 175–176, 182, 188–189, 221, 222, 231–232, 383–385
Insanity, 402, 410–411
"Insegnamento della sociologia, L' " (Matteucci), 92
Institute of Ethnology, 35
International Institute of Sociology, 36
International and moral law, 114, 359–361
"Interpsychologie, L' " (Tarde), 72–73
Interpsychology, 60, 72–73
Interreligious marriage, 115

"Intorno al reconoscimento della sociologia come scienza autonoma" (Matteucci), 92
Investigation of Paternity in Comparative Law, The (Dupré la Tour), 418
Inviolabilità del domicilio nell'antico diritto germanico, L' (Loncao), 360–361
Irréligion de l'avenir, L' (Guyau), 8
Islam, 358, 402
Islamic law, 229–230
Italy, penal law in, 364–367

JAPAN: divorce in, 273–274; marriage in, 271–273; social and economic organization in, 316–319
Japanese Matrimonial Law (Twasaky), 271–273
Jewish Law of Divorce According to Bible and Talmud (Amram), 244–246
Jewish Law of Marriage and Divorce in Ancient and Modern Times, The (Mielziner), 269–271
Jews: crime and, 403, 409, 440–441; divorce, 230, 244–246, 251; family and, 216–218, 234; marriage, 217–218, 229–230, 234, 251–252, 269–271; suicide and, 438; women, status of, 251–252
Joint family, 382
Joint property holdings, 212–220, 231, 250–251, 261, 275–278, 282–283, 292–294
Journal de psychologie, 41
Journal sociologique, 42
Juridic and moral sociology section, 111–397; contract and obligation, 391–397; editor's introduction, 111–119; family: *see* Family; general conceptions, theories, and methodological issues, 119–162; international and moral law, 359–361; juridic and moral systems, 162–163; marriage: *see* Marriage; penal law, 362–379; political organization, 341–358; property law, 379–391; sexual morality, 113, 115, 162–163, 299–305; social organization, 114, 117, 305–341
Juridic Situation of the Woman as Wife and Mother (Bartsch), 274–275
Juvenile crime, 407, 410, 420, 446
Juvenile Crime and How to Control It (Rein), 446

KINDNESS, 153
Kinship: *see* Family
Knighthood, 325–326
Knowledge, sociological conditions of, 64, 106–110
Koran, 229–230
Kriminalität der deutschen Juden, Die (Blau), 440–441
Kulturgeschichte, 54

LABOR, division of, 102, 448
Law, 119–120; civil, 163–167; common, 131–134; comparative, 114, 124–127, 331, 336; contract, 114; customary, 125–126; in Germany, 219–220, 231; international, 114, 359–361; Islamic, 358, 402; natural, 123, 132; penal, 114, 118, 163, 362–379; property, 114, 379–391; Roman, 117, 118–119, 123–124, 164, 168, 231; Slavic, 199–200
Law of Small Numbers, The (Bortkewitsch), 406
"Law and Sociology" (Kantorowicz), 87
League, 351, 352
Leçons d'instruction générale à l'histoire du droit matrimonial français (Lefebvre), 254–257
Legal Protection of Woman among the Ancient Germans, The (Rullkoeter), 264
Legge commune nel pensiero greco, La (Bonucci), 131–134
"Legge sociologica della storia, Una" (Gumplowicz), 101
Legislation on Landed Property in the Turkish Empire (Iovanovic), 386–388
Legitimate Birthrate in Germany, The (Prinzing), 417–418
Lettre de foire à Ypres au XIIIᵉ siècle, La. Contribution à l'étude des papiers de crédit (Marez), 392–394
Librairie Félix Alcan, 41–42
Liebe und Ehe im alten und modernen Indien (Schmidt), 305
Life of the Peasants in Southern Germany in the Middle Ages (Hagelstange), 306–308
Liege homage, 356
Linguistics, 450
Livonian marriage, 249–251
Logic, 143
Logique des sentiments, La (Ribot), 103–104
"Loi des Homérites, La" (Dareste), 162–163
"Lois de la solidarité morale, Les" (Richard), 149–150
Lombardy, 359–360
Lyceum, 5
Lying, 130–131

MADAGASCAR, family in, 185–187
Magdeburg Law, 282
Magic Tablets and the Roman Law, The (Huvelin), 367–368
Malagasy, family in, 185–187
"Manner in Which the Body of a Suicide Is Treated, The" (Lasch), 442–443
Manuel de sociologie catholique. Histoire, théorie, pratique (Belliot), 92–93
"Mariage après les invasions, Le" (Meynial), 234, 248–249

Mariage chez tous les peuples, Le (Almeras), 297
"Mariage civil n'es-il qu'un contrat? Le" (Lefebvre), 263
Market letter, 392–394
Marriage, 113, 115, 116–117, 158, 181–182, 234–298; by abduction, 165, 239–240, 241, 291; in Amiens, 277–279; Anglo-Saxon, 253–254; Athenian, 257–260; Australian tribes, 240–241; Babylonian, 295–296; betrothal, 234, 235, 238, 258, 270; Celtic, 216; Chinese, 184; Church and, 196–197, 208–209, 246–248, 291; collective, 185, 237, 238; concubinage, 235, 236, 258–260, 268; divorce: *see* Divorce; dower, 278–279; dowry, 115, 116, 221, 236–237, 243, 251, 255, 266–269, 282, 284, 291–292, 294–295, 402, 420–422; Egyptian, 266–268; elopement, 243; by exchange, 170; Finnish, 296–297; in Franche-Comté, 264–266; German, 248–249, 255–257, 264, 266, 274–275, 292–293, 297, 419, 424–425; Greek, 164–165, 166; group, 279–280; incest, 162, 173, 262–263, 267, 290, 304; interreligious, 115; Japanese, 271–273; Jewish, 217–218, 229–230, 234, 251–252, 269–271; joint property holdings, 218–220, 231, 250–251, 261, 275–278, 282–283, 292–294; Livonian, 249–251; in Malagasy, 187; by purchase, 165, 184, 239, 257, 281–282, 291, 295; rate, 402, 419, 424–425; Roman, 117, 164–165, 234–237, 255–256, 261, 274–275, 292–293, 295; Russian, 230–232; Sicilian, 238–239; Slavic, 237; Swiss, 422–423; terms of, 235–236; Tibetan, 237; trial, 117, 267; Turkish, 242–244; widowhood, 411–414, 445
Marriage Customs in Many Lands (Hutchinson), 240–242
Marriage Customs in Turkey (Loebel), 242–244
Marriage and Divorce (Bryce), 298
Marriage in Egypt in the Roman Period during the Ptolemaic Era (Nietzold), 266–268
Marriage of Peasants in Karelian Russia (Winter), 296–297
Marxism, 2
Matriarchal family, 169–171, 176, 185, 286, 289, 316
"Means and the End of Sociology, The" (Toennies), 86
"Mechanique sociale, La" (Ward), 91
Mémoires originaux (Durkheim), xvii, 40, 42, 49, 56, 138
Mendicancy, 444–445
"Mendicancy in Russia" (Tarnowski), 444–445
Mensonge, Le. Etude de psycho-sociologie pathologique et normale (Duprat), 130–131
"Mensonge de groupe, Le: Etude sociologique" (Palante), 106

Méthode historique appliquée aux sciences sociales, La (Seignobos), 61, 66–69

Mitgift in rechtsvergleichender Darstellung, Die (Neubecker), 291–292

Modesty, 305

"Momento economico nell'arte, Il" (Mazzola), 450

Money, philosophy of, 94–98

Monogamy, 181, 237

"Moot Points in Sociology, I: The Scope and Task of Sociology" (Ross), 92

Moral sociology: *see* Juridic and moral sociology

Moral statistics, 399–401, 411–440

Morale basée sur la démographie, La (Dumont), 121–122

Morale de Kant, La (Cresson), 27

Morale et la science des moeurs, La (Lévy-Bruhl), 112, 127–130, 139

Morale scientifique, La. Essai sur les applications morales des sciences sociologiques (Bayet), 135–137

Morals in Evolution (Hobhouse), 112

Mordvinians, 173

Mortality rate, 419

NATURAL law, 123, 132

Natural selection, 100

Nature et société: Essai d'une application du point de vue finaliste aux phénomènes sociaux (Jankelevitch), 75–78

"Naturrechtsproblem und die Methode seiner Lösung, Das" (Savigny), 122–123

Negligence, 377

Neo-criticism, 27, 160

Neo-positivism, 14–15

Neo-spiritualism, 27, 28

Newborn infants, exposure of, 177–178

Newtonian physics, 2

Nobility, 323–326

"Nombre d'enfants par famille" (Bertillon), 416–417

Norway, suicide in, 435

OBLIGATION, 391–397

Obscenity, 300

Odierno problema sociologico, L' (Toniolo), 74–75

Odyssey (Homer), 372

On the Domestic Community (Cohn), 381–382

"On the Hindu Custom of Dying to Redress a Grievance" (Hopkins), 396

On the Method of the Social Sciences (Chiappelli), 90

"On the Relation Between Sociology and Ethics" (Höffding), 134–135

Organicism, 62, 93–94

Organization of the Clan of Daghestan, The (Kovalevski), 171–172

Origin and Development of the Moral Ideas, The (Westermarck), 150–159

Origine della plebe romana (Oberziner), 329–330

"Origines de la constitution municipale de Prague, Les" (Celakovsky), 341

Origines et développement de l'exécution testamentaire (Caillemer), 200–204

Orphans, 233

PACTS of succession, 221

Pagus, 332–333, 338

Pan-Germanism, 352, 355

Pan-Hellenism, 355

Pan-Latinism, 352

Pan-Slavism, 352, 354–355

Partnership, 381–382

Paternal authority, 116, 142, 163, 166, 177–179, 185–187, 195–196, 205–210, 217, 218, 232, 235–237, 255, 369–370

Paternity, 197–198, 402, 418–420

Patriarchal family, 170, 286–290

Patriarchy, 170

Peasants, 306–308, 315, 321–323

"Pedagogia nelle sue relazioni con la sociologia, La" (Romano), 102

"Pédagogie et sociologie" (Durkheim), 450, 451–452

Penal law, 114, 118, 163, 362–379

Penal Law According to the Italian Statutes from the Twelfth to Sixteenth Century, The (Kohler), 364–367

Pentateuch, 244

Perioecism, 351–352

Peripatetic school, 3

Philosophie der Geschichte als Soziologie, Die (Barth), 450

Philosophie sociale du XVIIIe siècle et la révolution (1898), La (Espinas), 88

Philosophy of Money (Simmel), 62, 94–98

"Places of Rest Attributed to the Souls of Suicides" (Lasch), 442–443

Plebs, The: Studies on the History of Roman Law (Binder), 338

Poland, property law in, 389–390

Political organization, 113–114, 118, 341–358

Political and Social Significance of Attic Clans before Solon (Wilbrandt), 308–310

Polyandry, 216

Polygamy, 249, 298

Populations finnoises des bassins de la Volga et de la Kama, Les (Smirnov and Boyer), 172–173

"Position of Women in Early Civilization, The" (Westermarck), 280–281

Positive science, 152

Positivism, 2, 10, 13–14, 30, 60, 122, 401
Practical morality, 127–130
Primitive Civil Law Among the Aryan Societies (Leist), 163–168
Primitive Classification (Durkheim), 64, 103, 107
Primitive Means of Coercion Against Debtors (Steinmetz), 391–392
Primogeniture, 221, 388, 389
Principes de 1789 et la science sociale, Les (Ferneuil), 6, 9
Principles de morale rationnelle (Landry), 137, 138
Private property, 199–200
Problème des sexes, Le (Lourbet), 304–305
Problems of Sociology, The (Pareto), 91
"Progressiva diversificazione del diritto publico e privato, La" (Bonfaure), 123–124
"Prolegomena to Social Psychology" (Ellwood), 65–66
Promiscuity, 262–263, 299, 301, 302
Property law, 114, 379–391
Propriété sociale et la démocracie, La (Fouillée), 6
Proscription, 368–369
Proscription and Banishment in Greek Law (Usteri), 368–369
Prostitution, 162, 299–300, 302, 441
"Psicologia collettiva della scuola, La" (Robertis), 102–103
"Psychological and Environmental Study of Women Criminals" (Kellor), 441
Psychologie des sentiments (Ribot), 103
Psychology, 60, 61, 62–63, 103–104
Psychology and the Moral Sciences (Villa), 90–91
Punishment, 153–154, 163; *see also* Penal law
Purchase, marriage by, 165, 184, 239, 257, 281–282, 291, 295
Purification, 241

QUESTIONS *of Free Peasants, The. Research on the Social Organization of the German People in Germanic and Carolingian Times* (Wittich), 321–323

RATIONAL art of morals, 18–20
Rationalism, 2, 134
Recent Researchers on the History of the Family (Steinmetz), 184–185
Recherche de la paternité, La. Etude critique de sociologie et de législation comparée (Pouzol), 418–420
"Recherches sur les premiers, seconds, troisièmes mariages considérés au moment de leur dissolution" (Böckh), 433
Recividism, 409

Régime dotal, Le: Etude historique, critique et pratique (Depinay), 420–422
Régime dotal en France, Le. Ses avantages et ses inconvénients (Griveau), 420–422
"Relation of Sex to Primitive Social Control, The" (Thomas), 179
Religion, 115; marriage and, 196–197, 208–209, 246–248, 291
"Religione naturale e la famiglia, La" (Carli), 234
Religious sociology, xvi
"Religious Sociology and the Theory of Knowledge" (Durkheim), 21
"Religious Suicide: Its Relation to Human Sacrifice" (Lasch), 443–444
Renaissance, 134
Reprisal, 362–364
Researches on Nuptial Usages in Sicily during the Middle Ages, with Unpublished Documents (Garufi), 238–239
Responsibility, 376–377
Retaliation, 362, 364
Retributive emotions, 154–156
Revenge, 370–371, 441–442, 443
Revue historique, 41
Revue philosophique, 41
Rights, 156, 157
Ritual deflowering, 290
Rôle social de la femme, Le. Devoirs, droits, éducation (Lampérière), 296
Roman Plebs, The: Essay on Some Recent Theories (Bloch), 338–339
Rome: adoption in, 212–213; charity in, 339; cities, 345–346; divorce in, 244–245, 255; family in, 116, 166, 177–179, 183–184, 186, 205–206, 217, 219, 226–227, 288, 342; law, 117, 118–119, 123–124, 164, 168, 231; marriage in, 117, 164–165, 234–237, 255–256, 261, 274–275, 292–293, 295; penal law, 365, 367–368, 378–379; political organization, 345–346; sale contract, 392; social organization, 112, 118, 323–324, 329–330, 338–339; tribes, 319–321; wills, 192–194, 202, 212, 227–229
Rules of Sociological Method, The (Durkheim), 10, 16, 37
Russia: marriage in, 230–232; mendicancy in, 444–445; political organization in, 348–349, 352–355; social organization in, 348, 352–353
Russisches Familien-und Erbrecht (Gebhard), 230–232

SACHSENSPIEGEL, 249, 282
Sacrifices, 158, 241
"Saggio di una classificazione delle società" (Carini), 99
Sale contract, 392

Salmann, 385–386
Sanctions, theory of, 155, 157*n*.
Scholarch: defined, 2–3; Durkheim as, 5–13; heir to, 4
Science of morals and customs, 14, 18, 114, 127–130, 135–137
Science of Morals and General Sociology, The (Asturaro), 161
Scientism, 10, 15–16, 60
"Scope of Sociology, VI, The" (Small), 69–70
"Scope of Sociology, VIII, The" (Small), 101–102
"Sécularisation de la morale au XVIIIᵉ siècle, La" (Pellisson), 134
Selbstmord im 19 Jahrhundert nach seiner verteilung auf Staaten und Verwaltungsbezirke, mit einer Karte, Der (Krose), 435–436
Serbia, family in, 204–205
Serfdom, 311–315
Serfs et villains au Moyen Age (Doniol), 311–313
Sex roles, 115
Sexual Life in Ancient Germany (Bauer), 301–302
Sexual morality, 113, 115, 162–163, 299–305
Sexual Relations Among the Slavs (Khamm), 302–303
Sharecroppers, 314, 316
Sicilian marriage, 238–239
"Singularités de la vente romaine, Les" (Chausse), 392
Slavery, 118, 303, 313–315
Slavs, 316; family, 199–200, 204, 223–225, 232–233, 237, 290, 293, 316; law, 199–200; marriage, 237; sexual morality, 302–303
Sobors, 343–345
Social Condition of the Widow in Germany, The (Prinzing), 413–414
Social consensus, 14
Social constraint, 14, 16
Social and Economic Evolution of Japan (Fukuda), 316–319
Social and Ethical Interpretation in Mental Development (Baldwin), 62
Social Meaning of Suicide, The (Douglas), 403
Social morphology, xvi, xviii, 55, 63, 401, 449
Social organization, 112, 113–114, 117, 118, 166–167, 305–341
Social person, 64–65
Social philosophy, 61–62
Social physiology, xvi
Social psychology, 63, 65–66, 102–106
Social solidarity, 14
Social theories, 62, 93–102
Socialism, 32–34

Société Française de Philosophie, 11, 19, 36
Société Nouvelle de Librairie et d'Edition, 33
Societism, 10, 16, 17–18
Society as reality sui generis, 14, 16
Sociogeography, 449
"Sociologia e storia" (Xenopol), 73–74
Sociological conditions of knowledge, 64, 106–110
Sociological epistemology, 20–21
Sociological Society of Paris, 36
"Sociological View of Sovereignty, A" (Commons), 358
"Sociologie, La" (Durkheim), 12
"Sociologie abstraite et ses divisions, La" (Naville), 78
Sociologie générale et les lois sociologiques, La (Richard), 59, 84–86
"Sociologie et sciences sociales" (Durkheim), 85
Sociologism, 10, 34
Sociology: aesthetic, 450–451; criminal: *see* Criminal sociology section; economic, 4–15, 447–448; general: *see* General sociology section; juridic and moral: *see* Juridic and moral sociology section
"Sociology of Panic" (Gothein), 88
Sociology and Philosophy (Durkheim), 11
"Sociology of Sociability" (Simmel), 88–89
Sodomy, 162
Solidarité de la famille dans le droit criminel en Grèce, La (Glotz), 368, 369–375
Solidarity, 105–106
Sovereignty, 358
Sozialwissenschaften, 9
"Soziologie des Erkennens" (Jerusalem), 64, 107–110
"Spiritualism and Kantism in France" (Bouglé), 27
Stade expérimental, 43
State, the, 65, 80, 167
State and Family in Early Rome (Launspach), 226–227
"Stiefvaterfamilie unehelichen Ursprungs. Zugleigh eine Studie zur Methodologie der Unehelichkeits-Statistik, Die" (Spann), 425–427
Stoa, 5
"Stoic-Christian Natural Law and the Secular Natural Law of the Modern Age" (Troeltsch), 88
Stoicism, 3, 132
"Storia considerata come scienza, La" (Croce), 70–71
"Storia considerata come scienza, La" (Salvemini), 70
"Storia e scienze sociali" (Sorel), 70
Studi papirologici sul matrimonio e sul divorzio nell'egitto greco-romano (Ruggiero), 268–269

Studies on Anglo-Saxon Institutions (Chadwick), 330–331
Studies on the History of the Athenian Right of Citizenship and Matrimonial Law (Müller), 257–260
Studies in the Psychology of Sex (Ellis), 305
Studies on the Social Person (Giner), 64–65
Succession: see Inheritance
Succession des bâtards dans l'ancienne Bourgogne, La (Guigon), 222–223
"Suggestione sociale, La" (Gumplowicz), 106
Suicide, 138, 391, 396, 406, 434–440; divorce and, 429, 431; Jews and, 438; for love, 444; religious, 443–444; as vengeance, 441–442, 443
Suicide: A Study in Sociology (Durkheim), 10, 37, 60, 98, 399, 401, 402, 403, 437
"Suicide in the Cities" (Rost), 434–435
Suicide collectif dans le Raskol russe, Le (Stchoukine), 434
"Suicide for Love among the Primitives" (Lasch), 444
"Suicide as Vengeance" (Lasch), 441–442
Sul diritto successorio dell XII tavole. Ingagini storiche di diritto Romano (Clerici), 234
"Sul valore sociale dei pazzi" (Verce), 411
"Sulle cerimonie nuziali dei Lusitani" (Zocco-Rosa), 295
Summary of the Serb Inheritance Law as Reflected by the Introduction of a Reform (Ačimovic), 168–169
Superstition, 158, 408
Superstition and Crime (Löwenstimm), 408
Suppression of Paternal Power in Roman Law, The (Stockar), 205–206
Surrealism, 2
Sweden, suicide in, 437
Swiss Legislation on Marriage in the Light of Statistics (Buomberger), 422–423
Switzerland: marriage and divorce in, 422–423; partnership in, 381–382
Sympolity, 351
Synoecism, 349–351
Synthèse en histoire, La. Essai critique et théorique (Berr), 89–90

TABOO, 150
Taiho Code, 271, 273
Talmud, 251–252
Technology, 450
"Technology and Culture" (Sombart), 87–88
Testamentary adoption, 176–177
Testamentary law, 113, 116
Testaments: see Wills
Testaments coutumiers au XVe siècle, Les (Engelmann), 213
Theoretical morality, 127–130
Theory of Adoption in Japan, The (Tsugaru), 210–213

Theory of Common Ownership Among Spouses Under the Law of the Cities of Livonia, The (Gurgens), 249–251
"Theory of Imitation in Social Psychology, The" (Ellwood), 100
Third Republic, 24–25
Three Oldest Roman Tribes, The (Holzapfel), 319–321
Tibetan marriage, 237
Totemism, 112, 169, 170, 179, 267, 290
Traces of Marriage by Abduction, of Marriage by Purchase, and of Analogous Practices in the French Epics of the Middle Ages (Schulenburg), 239–240
Tradition romaine sur la succession des formes du testament devant l'histoire, La (Lambert), 193–194
Traité de droit public musulman (Abou'l-Hassan el-Maverdi), 358
Travaux de l'Année, 40, 41
"Treatment of Juvenile Offenders, Together with Statistics of Their Numbers, The" (Barrett), 410
Trial by combat, 373
Trial marriage, 117, 267
Tribes, 167, 319–321
Turkey: marriage in, 242–244; property law in, 386–388
Types of Family and Forms of Marriage (Friederichs), 237–238

ÜBER *die Auffassung von der Ehe und die Durchführung der Vielweiberei in Münster während der Tauferherrschaft* (Detmer), 298
Über den Ursprung der Zadruga: Eine soziologische Untersuchung (Stanischitsch), 223–226
"Unehelichen Kinder in Berlin, Die" (Kuczynski), 433
Union pour la Vérité (Union for Truth), 11
"Unit of Investigation in Sociology, The" (Lindsay), 90
University of Bordeaux, 7–8, 35
University of Paris, 10, 35
"Unlucky Children" (Rose), 233
Urban title to property, 379–381
Ursachen der Selbstmordhäufigkeit, Die (Krose), 436–440
"Ursprung der sozialen Triebe, Der" (Ammon), 100
Uterine filiation: see Matriarchal family
Utilitarianism, 138

"VALEUR sociale de l'art, La" (Sorel), 450–451
"Variations in the Rate of Marriage and in the Average Age of Marriage" (Prinzing), 424–425
Vassalage, 324–326, 340, 356

Vendettas, 158, 366, 370, 372, 375–376
Vengeance, suicide as, 441–442, 443
Verfassungsgeschichte der Germanen und Kelten Ein Beitrag zur vergleichenden Altertumskunde, Die (Cramer), 331–333, 335–338
Virginity, 247, 307
Völkerkunde, 53–54
Völkerpsychologie, 7, 9, 28

WALES, 339–340
War, 450
"Was ist der Staat?" (Schupe), 358
Weberian sociology, 2
Welsh People, The: Chapters on Their Origin, History, Laws, Language, Literature, and Characteristics (Rhys and Brynmor-Jones), 339–340
Widowhood, 411–414, 445
Wills, 163, 176–177, 189–194, 200–204, 212, 213, 217, 222, 227–229, 231–232, 234
Woman, The (Gizicki), 304
Woman in Antiquity, The (Schaible), 303–304
Women. *See also* Family; Marriage: begging and, 445; crime and, 401–402, 409, 441, 446; division of labor, 448; status of, 113,
116, 117, 209, 251–252, 303–304; suicide and, 436–437
Women and the Civil Code (Fuld), 297

"Y A-T-IL des périodes pour les mariages et les naissances comme pour les crises commerciales?" (Juglar), 433
Yamato tribe, 316

ZADRUGA, 199–200, 204, 223–225, 232–233, 237, 290, 293, 316
Zeitschrift für Völkerpsychologie, 37
Zemskie Sobors, Les. Etude historique (Rocca), 343–345
Zum ältesten Strafrecht der Kulturvölker. Fragen zur Rechtsvergleichung gestellt von Theodor Mommsen, beantwortet von H. Brunner, B. Freudenthal, J. Goldziber, etc. (Mommsen), 378–379
Zur Geschichte des Brautkaufs bei den indogermanischen Völkern (Hermann) 281–282
"Zur Geschichte des Ehegüterrechts bei den Semiten" (Freund), 298
"Zur Urgeschichte der Ehe" (Kohler), 279–280
"Zwanzig Jahre Kriminalstatistik" (Frauenstädt), 409

DATE DUE